PRISON SCHOOL

Akira Hiramoto

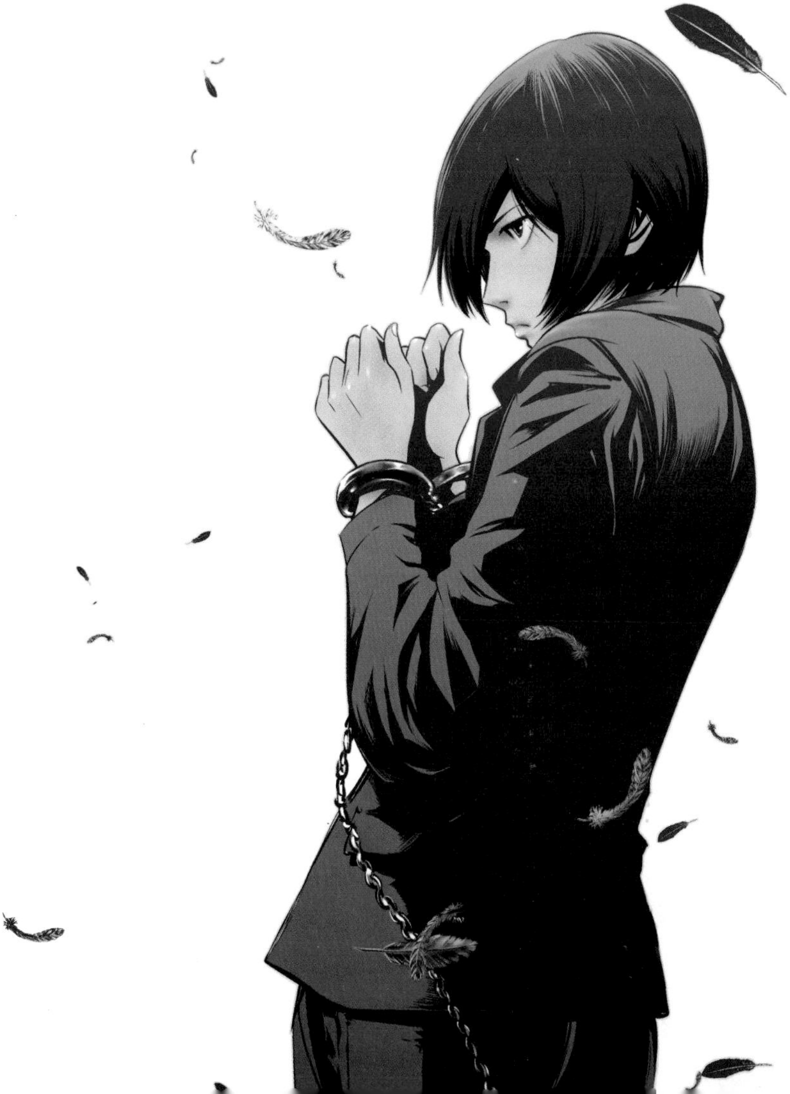

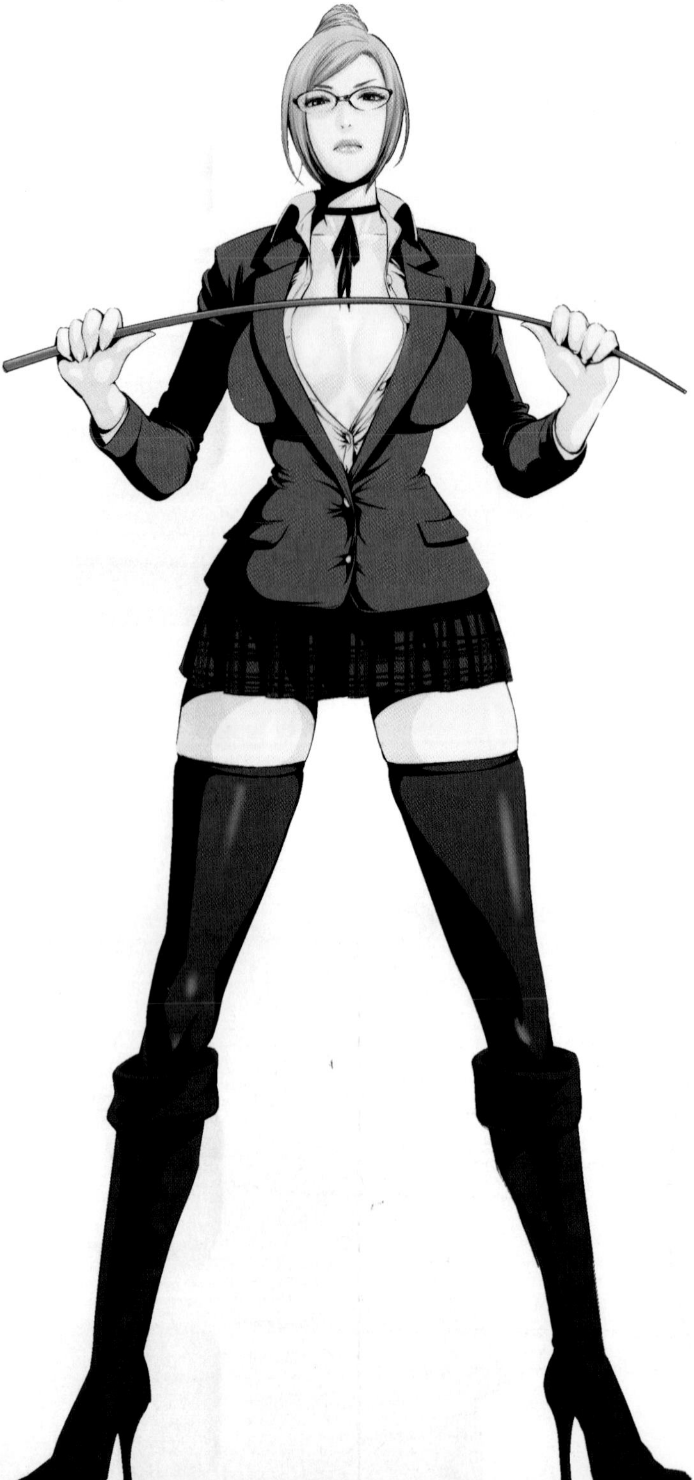

PRISON SCHOOL

1

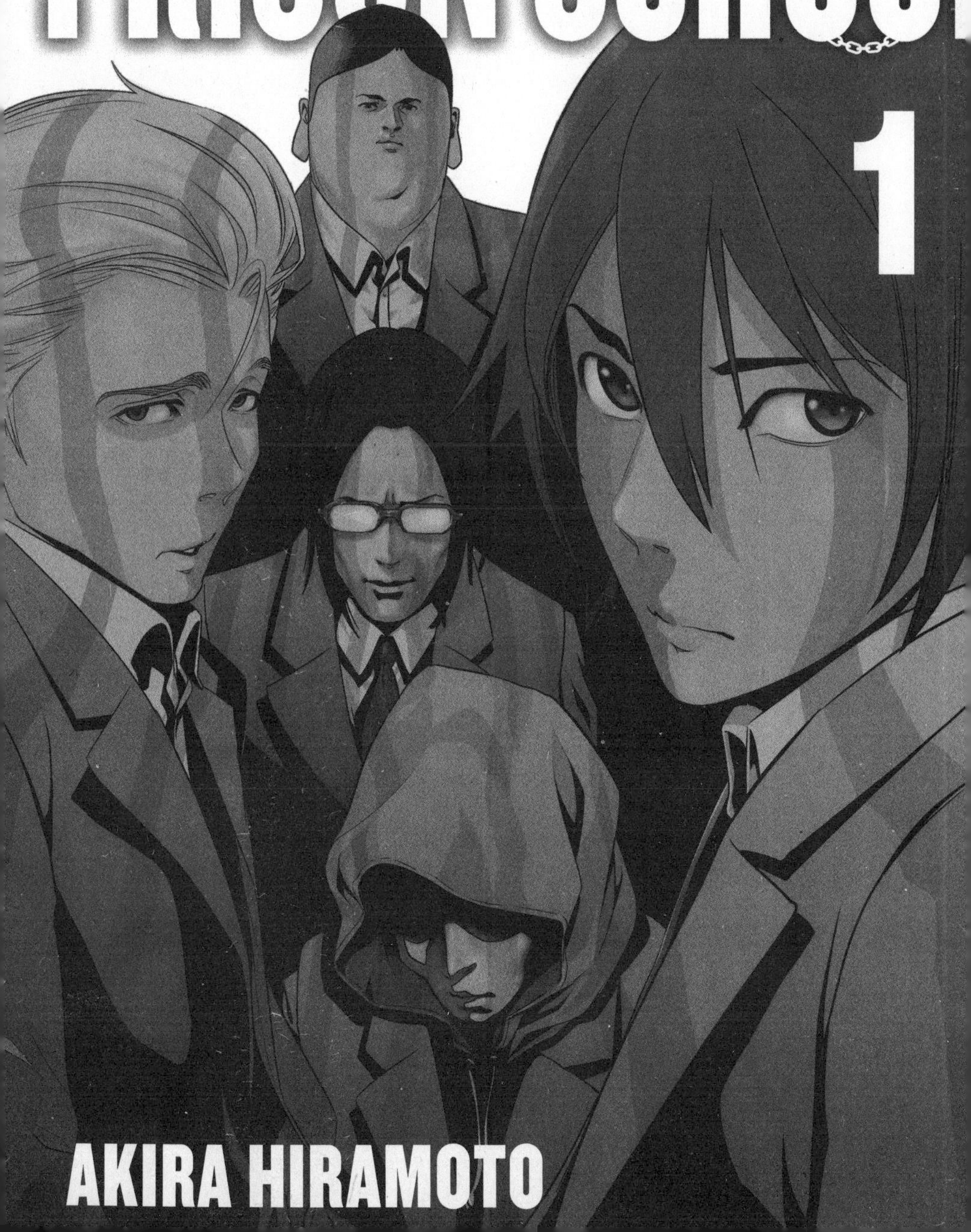

AKIRA HIRAMOTO

CONTENTS

PRISON SCHOOL

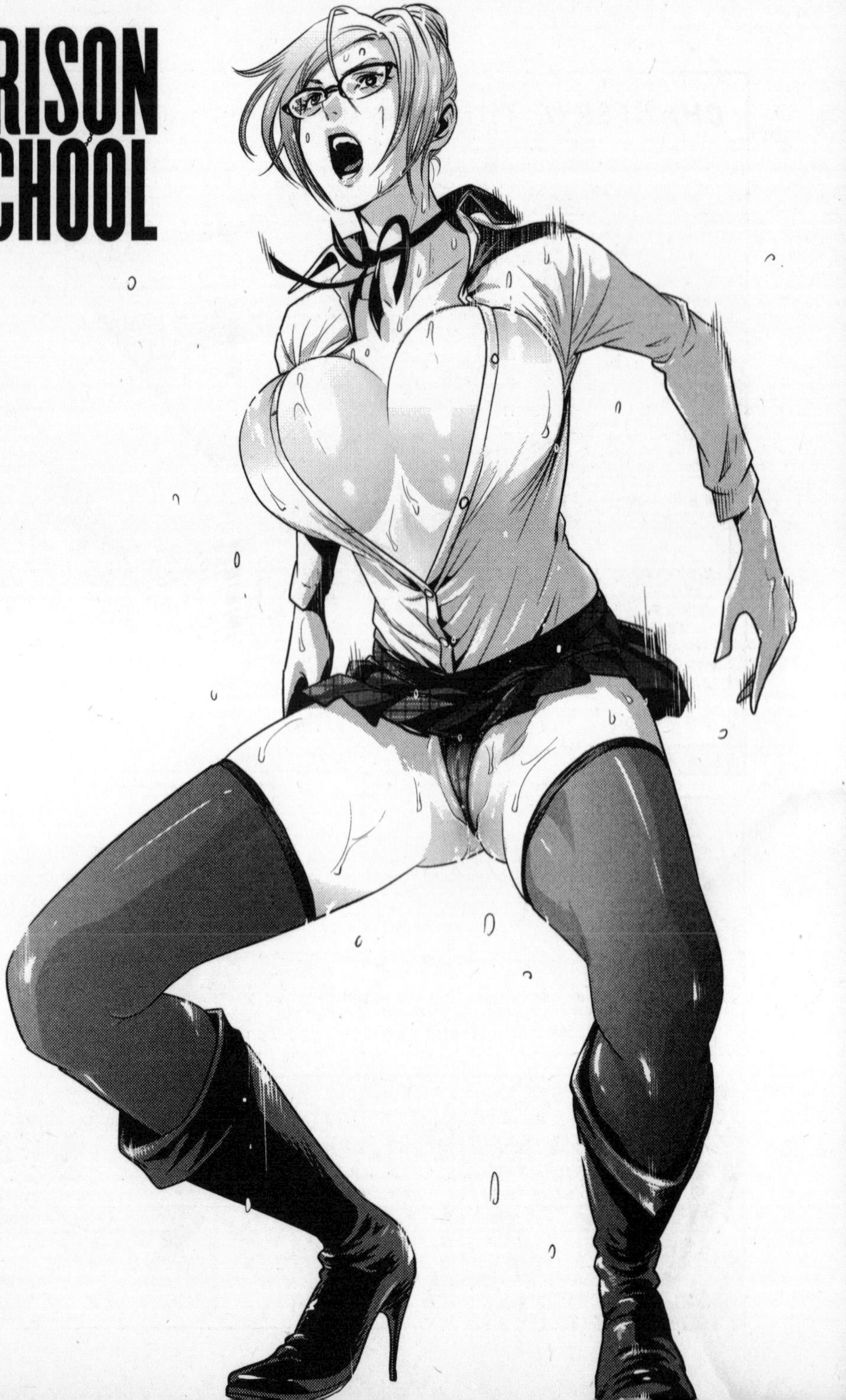

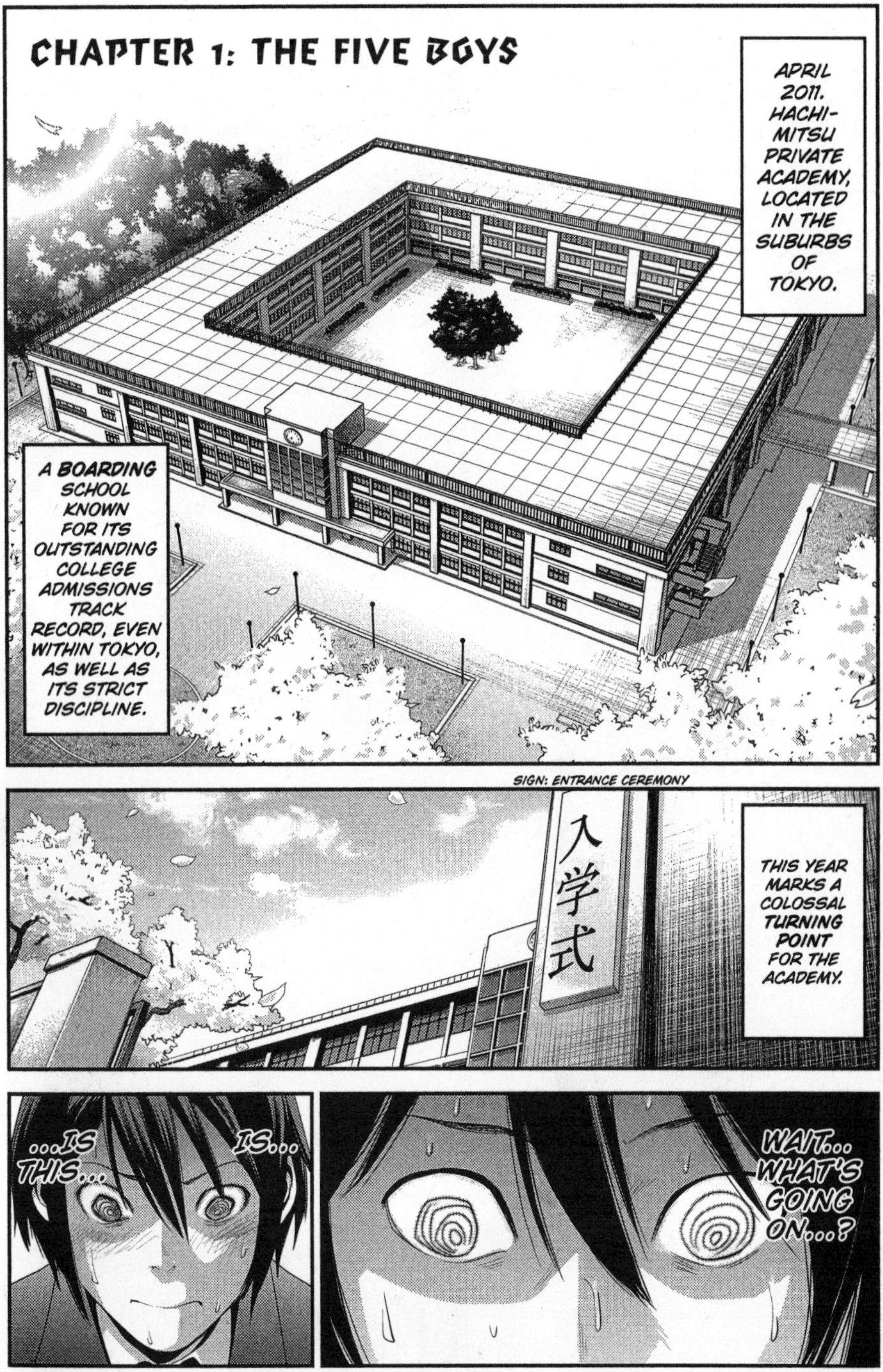
CHAPTER 1: THE FIVE BOYS
APRIL 2011. HACHI-MITSU PRIVATE ACADEMY, LOCATED IN THE SUBURBS OF TOKYO.
A BOARDING SCHOOL KNOWN FOR ITS OUTSTANDING COLLEGE ADMISSIONS TRACK RECORD, EVEN WITHIN TOKYO, AS WELL AS ITS STRICT DISCIPLINE.
SIGN: ENTRANCE CEREMONY
入学式
THIS YEAR MARKS A COLOSSAL TURNING POINT FOR THE ACADEMY.
WAIT... WHAT'S GOING ON...?
IS...
...IS THIS...

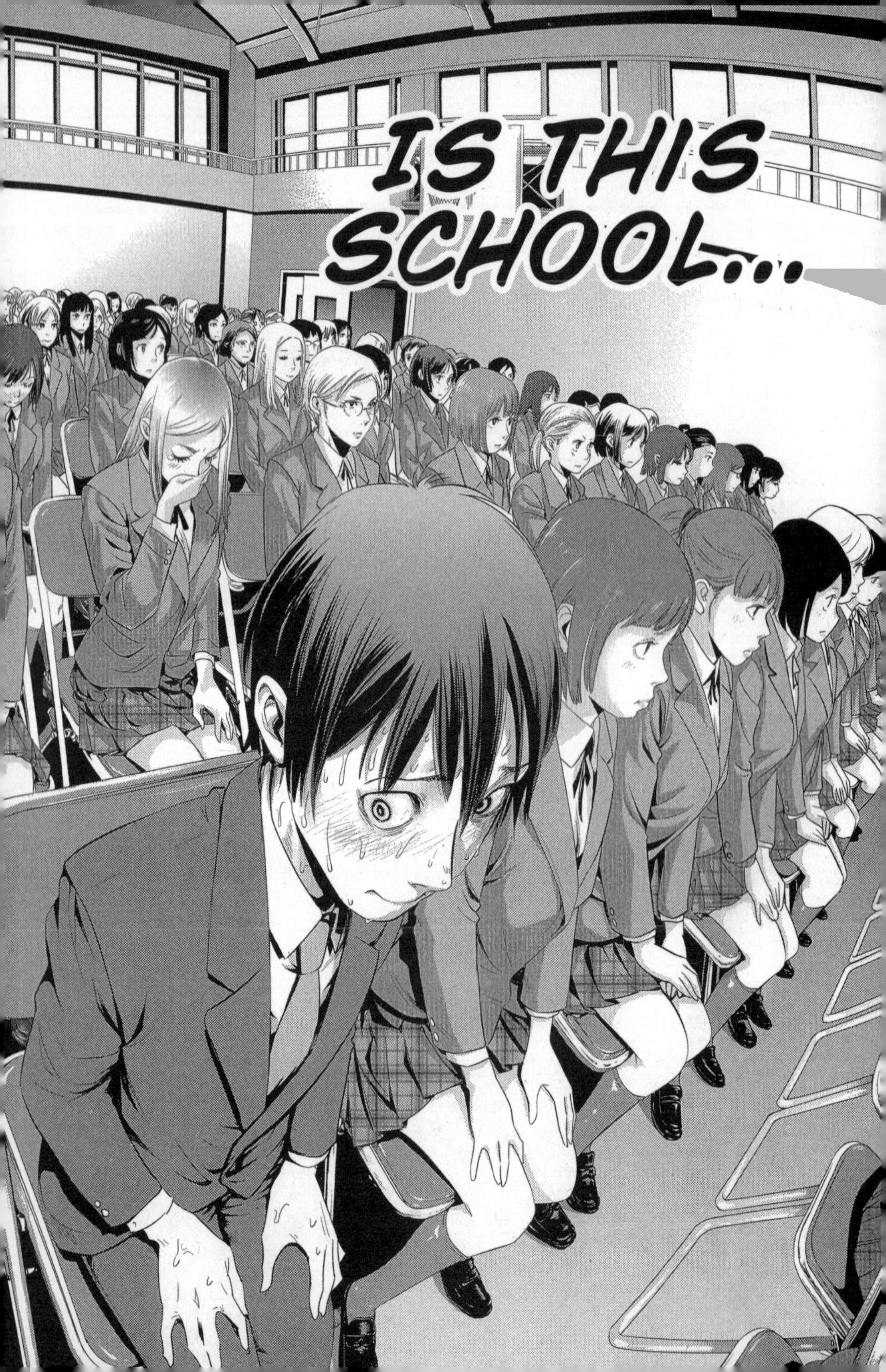
IS THIS SCHOOL...

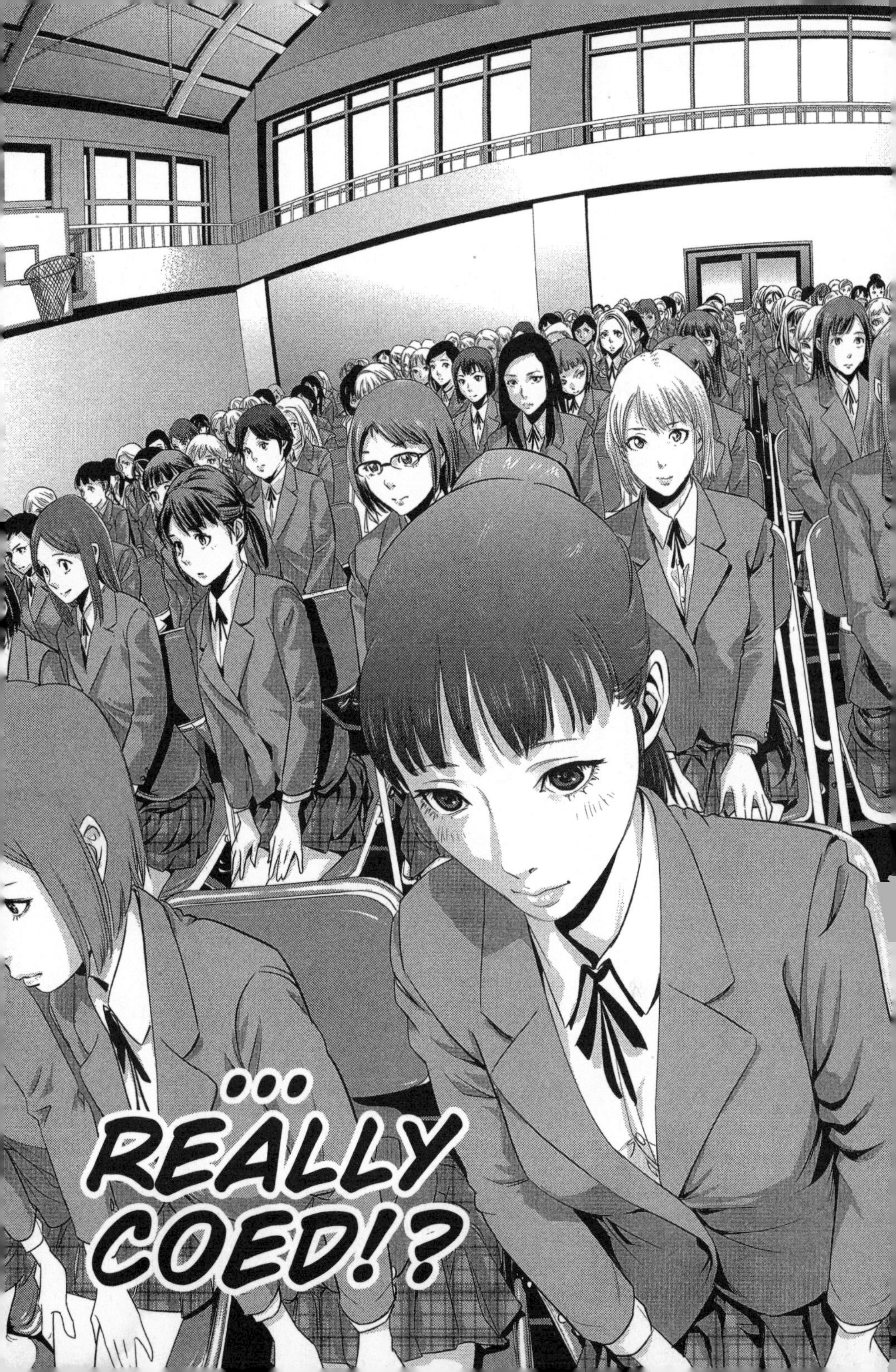
...
REALLY COED!?

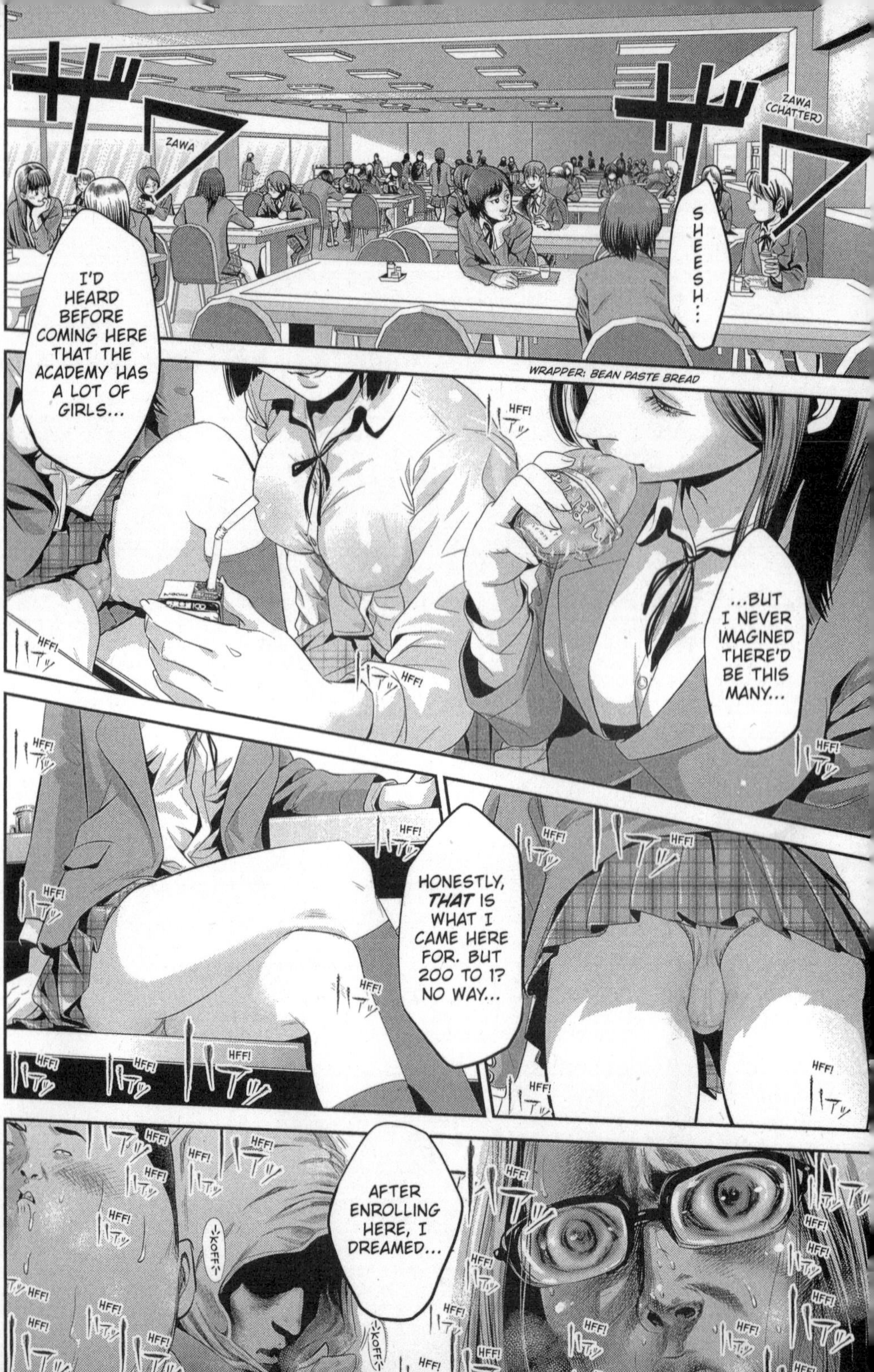

ZAWA (CHATTER)
SHEESH...
ZAWA
I'D HEARD BEFORE COMING HERE THAT THE ACADEMY HAS A LOT OF GIRLS...
WRAPPER: BEAN PASTE BREAD
HFF!
HFF!
HFF!
...BUT I NEVER IMAGINED THERE'D BE THIS MANY...
HFF!
HFF!
HFF!
HFF!
HONESTLY, *THAT* IS WHAT I CAME HERE FOR. BUT 200 TO 1? NO WAY...
HFF!
HFF!
HFF!
HFF!
HFF!
HFF!
HFF!
HFF!
HFF!
AFTER ENROLLING HERE, I DREAMED...
HFF!
HFF!
HFF!
-KOFF-
-KOFF-
HFF!
HFF!
HFF!

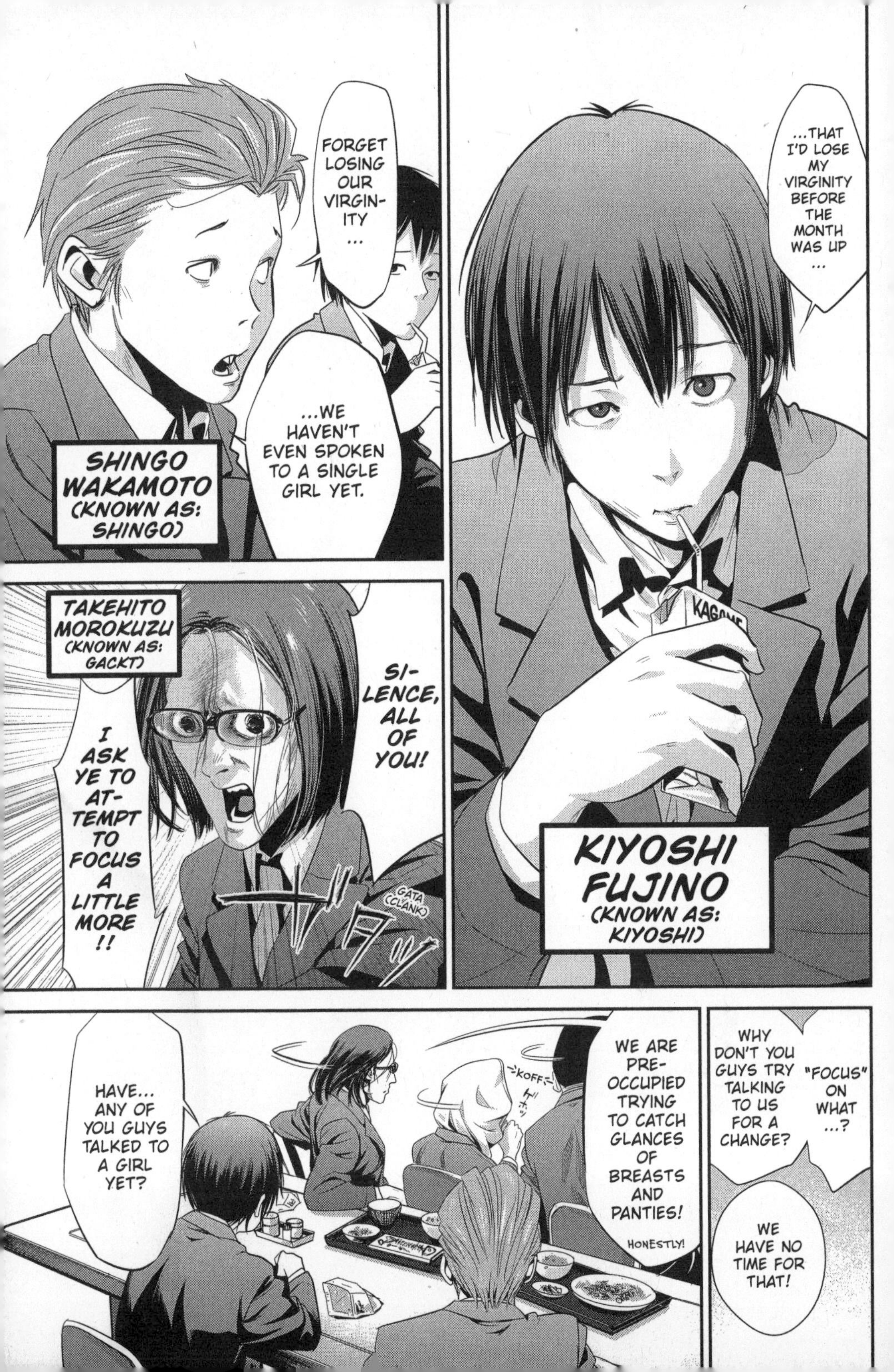
...THAT I'D LOSE MY VIRGINITY BEFORE THE MONTH WAS UP ...
KIYOSHI FUJINO (KNOWN AS: KIYOSHI)
FORGET LOSING OUR VIRGINITY ...
...WE HAVEN'T EVEN SPOKEN TO A SINGLE GIRL YET.
SHINGO WAKAMOTO (KNOWN AS: SHINGO)
TAKEHITO MOROKUZU (KNOWN AS: GACKT)
SILENCE, ALL OF YOU!
I ASK YE TO ATTEMPT TO FOCUS A LITTLE MORE !!
GATA (CLANK)
"FOCUS" ON WHAT ...?
WHY DON'T YOU GUYS TRY TALKING TO US FOR A CHANGE?
WE HAVE NO TIME FOR THAT!
WE ARE PREOCCUPIED TRYING TO CATCH GLANCES OF BREASTS AND PANTIES!
HONESTLY!
KOFF
HAVE... ANY OF YOU GUYS TALKED TO A GIRL YET?

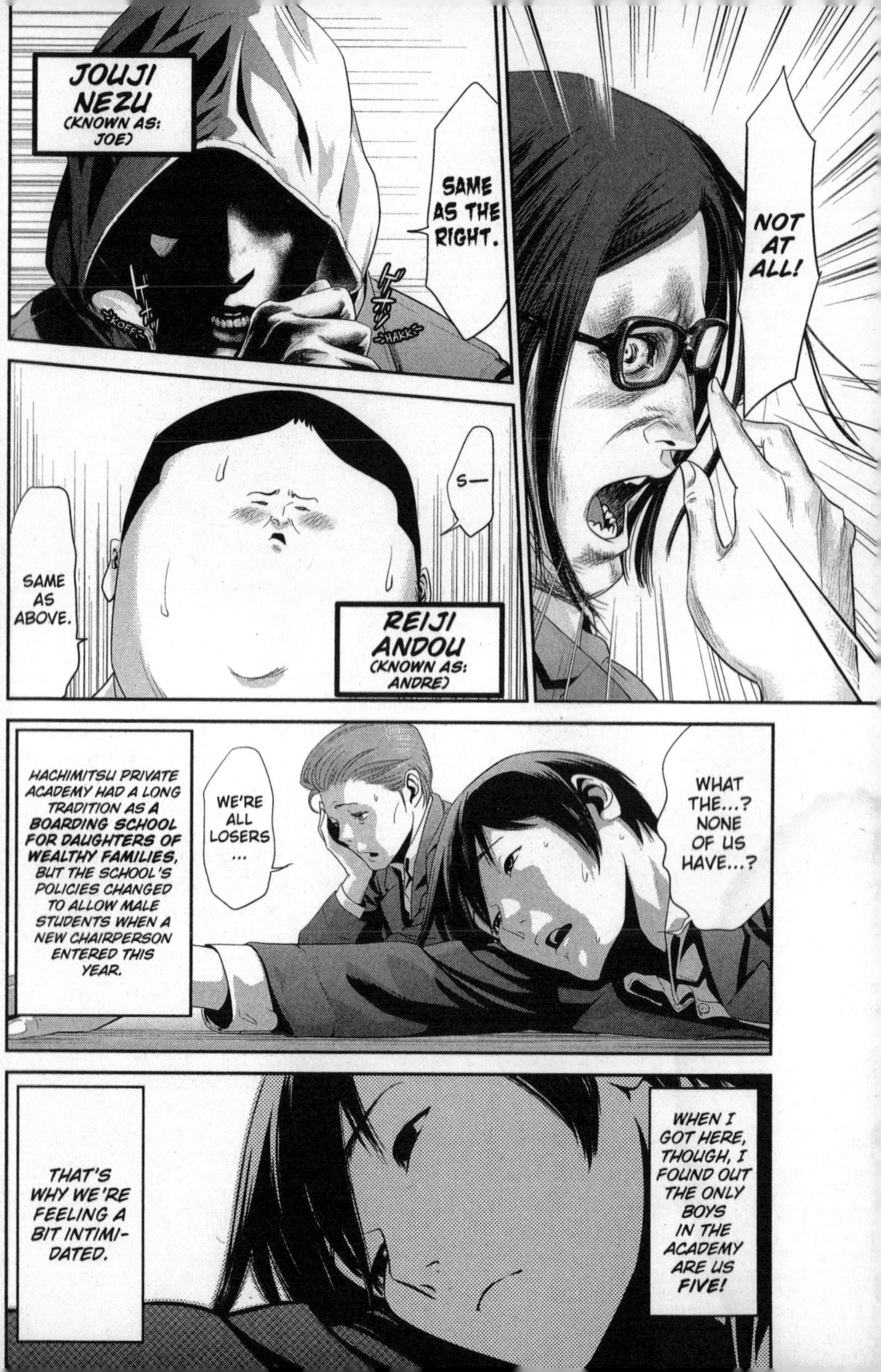

NOT AT ALL!
SAME AS THE RIGHT.
JOUJI NEZU (KNOWN AS: JOE)
HAKK
KOFF
S—
SAME AS ABOVE.
REIJI ANDOU (KNOWN AS: ANDRE)
WHAT THE...? NONE OF US HAVE...?
WE'RE ALL LOSERS...
HACHIMITSU PRIVATE ACADEMY HAD A LONG TRADITION AS A BOARDING SCHOOL FOR DAUGHTERS OF WEALTHY FAMILIES, BUT THE SCHOOL'S POLICIES CHANGED TO ALLOW MALE STUDENTS WHEN A NEW CHAIRPERSON ENTERED THIS YEAR.
WHEN I GOT HERE, THOUGH, I FOUND OUT THE ONLY BOYS IN THE ACADEMY ARE US FIVE!
THAT'S WHY WE'RE FEELING A BIT INTIMI-DATED.

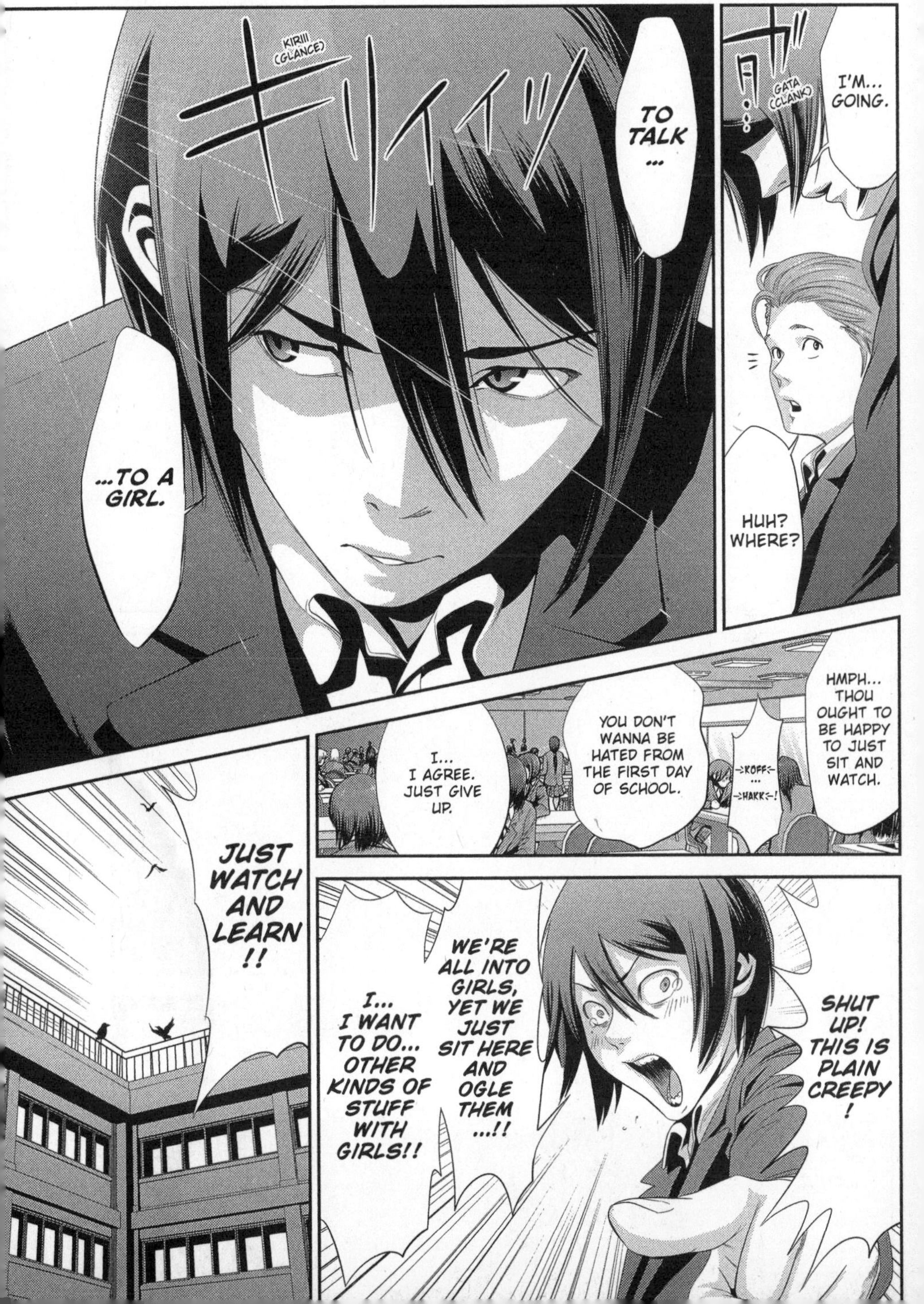
GATA (CLANK)
I'M... GOING.
HUH? WHERE?
キリイイッ
KIRIII (GLANCE)
TO TALK ...
...TO A GIRL.
HMPH... THOU OUGHT TO BE HAPPY TO JUST SIT AND WATCH.
-KOFF- ... -HAKK-!
YOU DON'T WANNA BE HATED FROM THE FIRST DAY OF SCHOOL.
I... I AGREE. JUST GIVE UP.
SHUT UP! THIS IS PLAIN CREEPY!
WE'RE ALL INTO GIRLS, YET WE JUST SIT HERE AND OGLE THEM ...!!
I... I WANT TO DO... OTHER KINDS OF STUFF WITH GIRLS!!
JUST WATCH AND LEARN!!

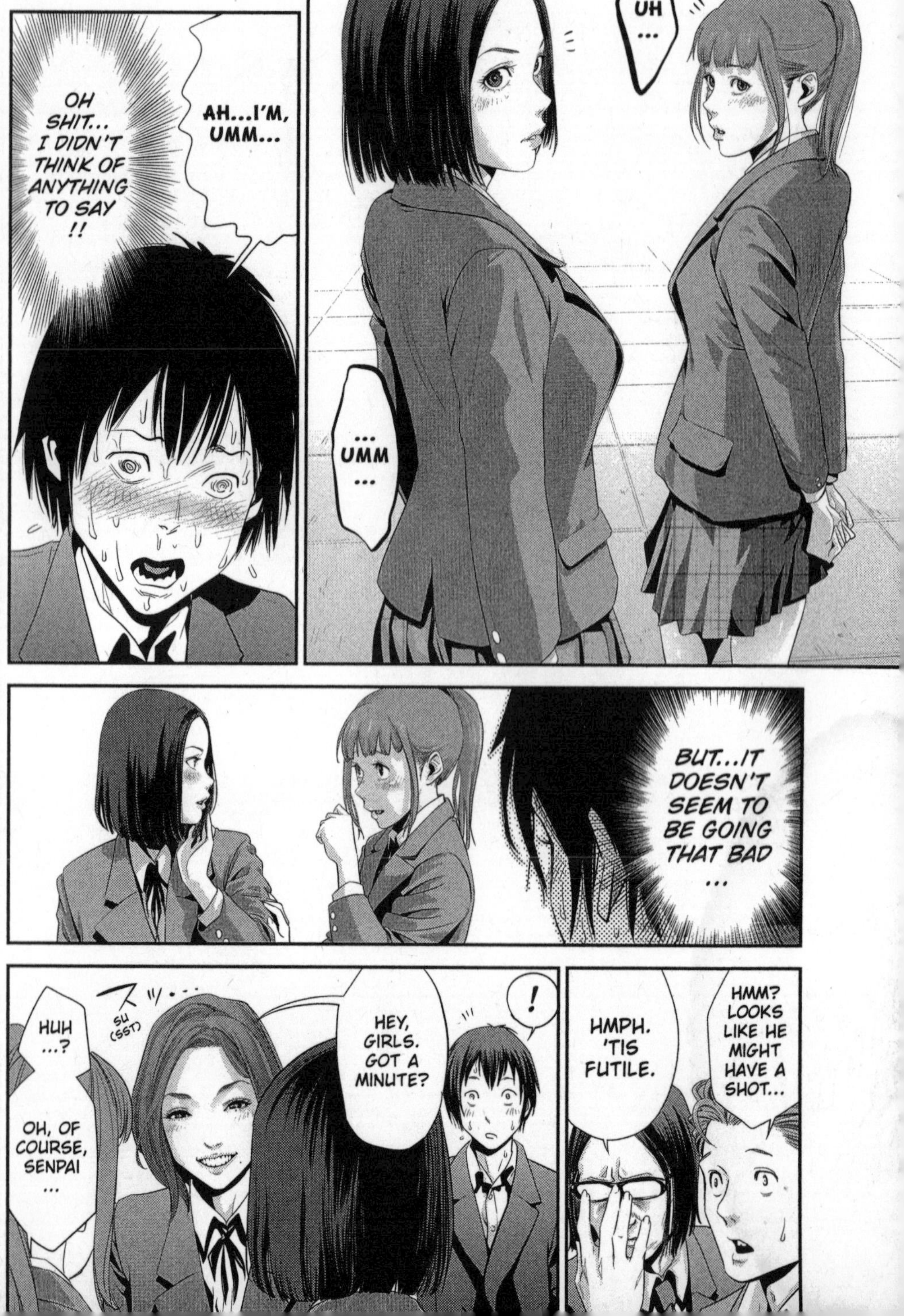
UH ...
... UMM ...
AH...I'M, UMM...
OH SHIT... I DIDN'T THINK OF ANYTHING TO SAY !!
BUT...IT DOESN'T SEEM TO BE GOING THAT BAD ...
HMM? LOOKS LIKE HE MIGHT HAVE A SHOT...
HMPH. 'TIS FUTILE.
!
HEY, GIRLS. GOT A MINUTE?
SU (SST)
HUH ...?
OH, OF COURSE, SENPAI ...

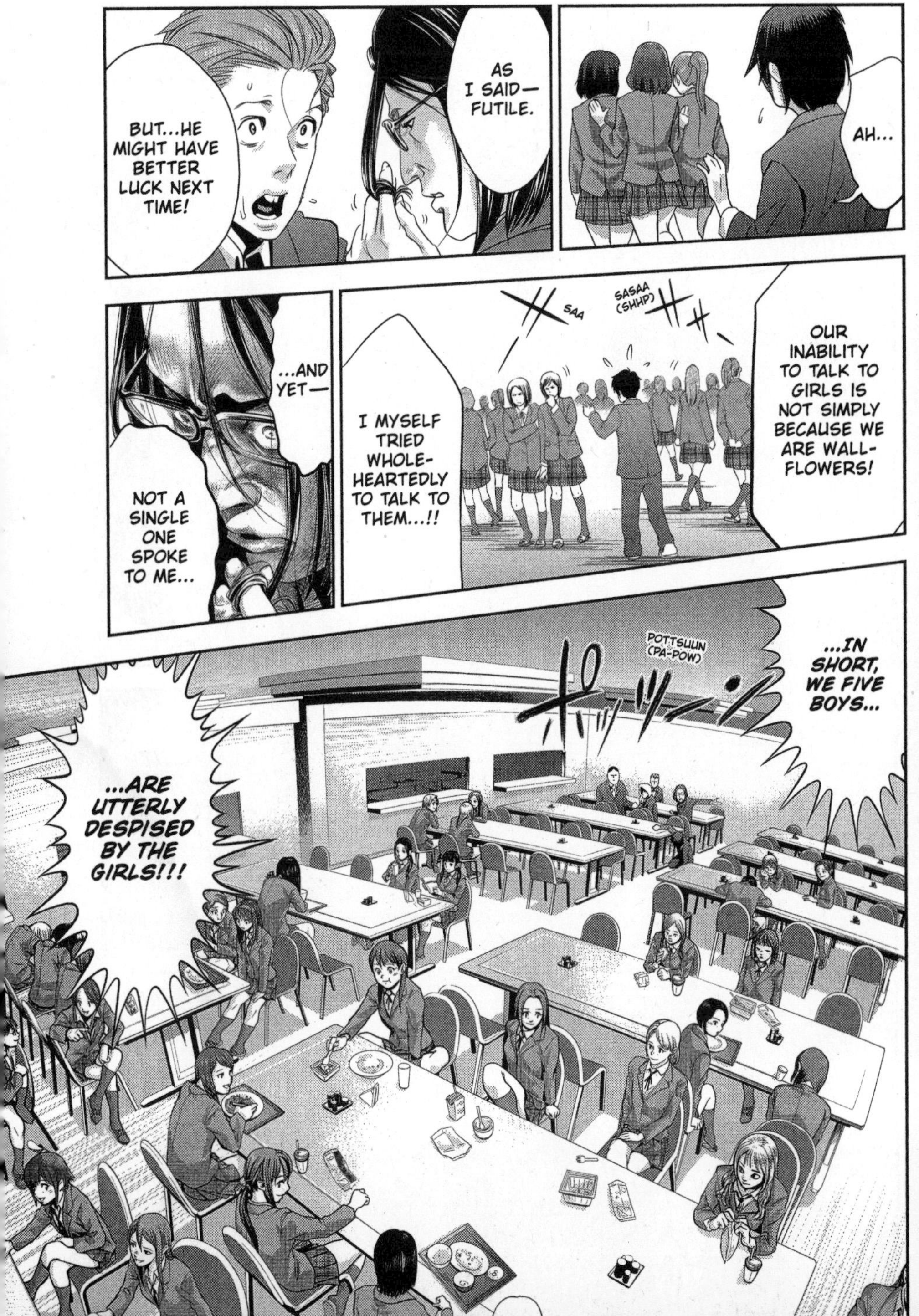
AH...
AS I SAID—FUTILE.
BUT...HE MIGHT HAVE BETTER LUCK NEXT TIME!
OUR INABILITY TO TALK TO GIRLS IS NOT SIMPLY BECAUSE WE ARE WALL-FLOWERS!
SASAA (SHHP)
SAA
I MYSELF TRIED WHOLE-HEARTEDLY TO TALK TO THEM...!!
...AND YET—
NOT A SINGLE ONE SPOKE TO ME...
...IN SHORT, WE FIVE BOYS...
POTTSUUN (PA-POW)
...ARE UTTERLY DESPISED BY THE GIRLS!!!

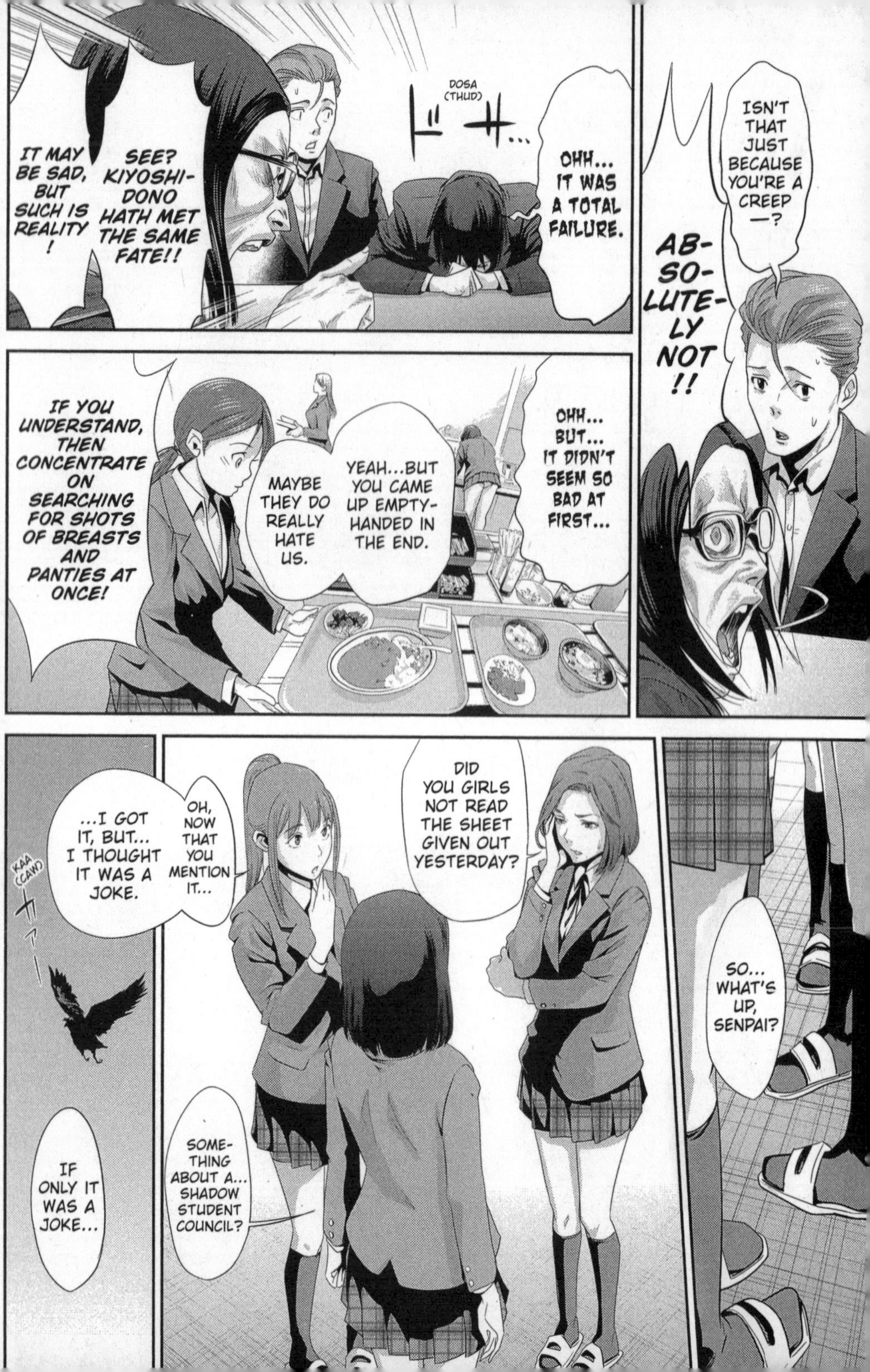
DOSA (THUD)
OHH... IT WAS A TOTAL FAILURE.
SEE? KIYOSHI-DONO HATH MET THE SAME FATE!!
IT MAY BE SAD, BUT SUCH IS REALITY!
ISN'T THAT JUST BECAUSE YOU'RE A CREEP—?
ABSOLUTELY NOT!!
OHH... BUT... IT DIDN'T SEEM SO BAD AT FIRST...
YEAH...BUT YOU CAME UP EMPTY-HANDED IN THE END.
MAYBE THEY DO REALLY HATE US.
IF YOU UNDERSTAND, THEN CONCENTRATE ON SEARCHING FOR SHOTS OF BREASTS AND PANTIES AT ONCE!
SO... WHAT'S UP, SENPAI?
DID YOU GIRLS NOT READ THE SHEET GIVEN OUT YESTERDAY?
OH, NOW THAT YOU MENTION IT...
SOMETHING ABOUT A... SHADOW STUDENT COUNCIL?
...I GOT IT, BUT... I THOUGHT IT WAS A JOKE.
KAA (CAW)
IF ONLY IT WAS A JOKE...

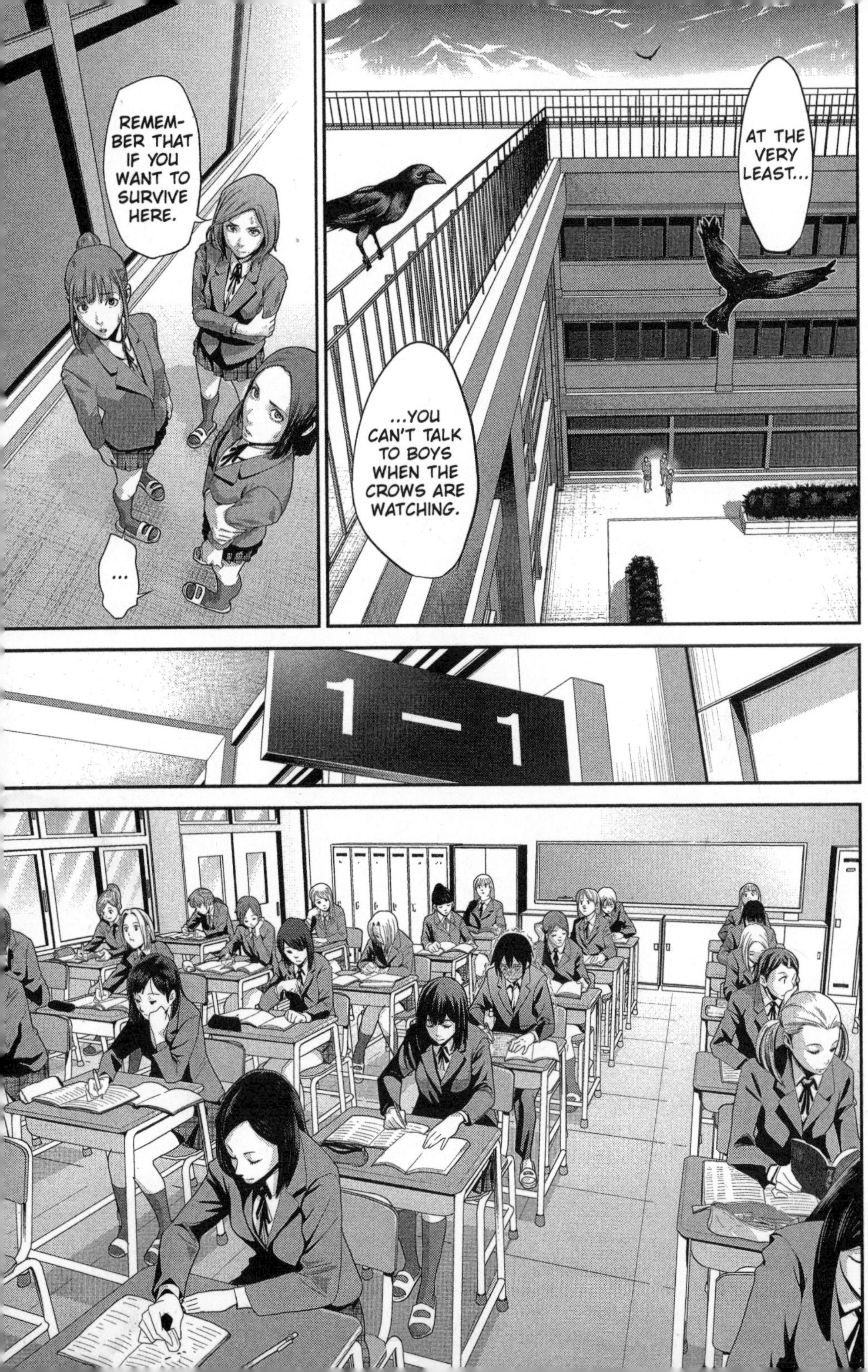
AT THE VERY LEAST...
...YOU CAN'T TALK TO BOYS WHEN THE CROWS ARE WATCHING.
REMEMBER THAT IF YOU WANT TO SURVIVE HERE.
...
1-1

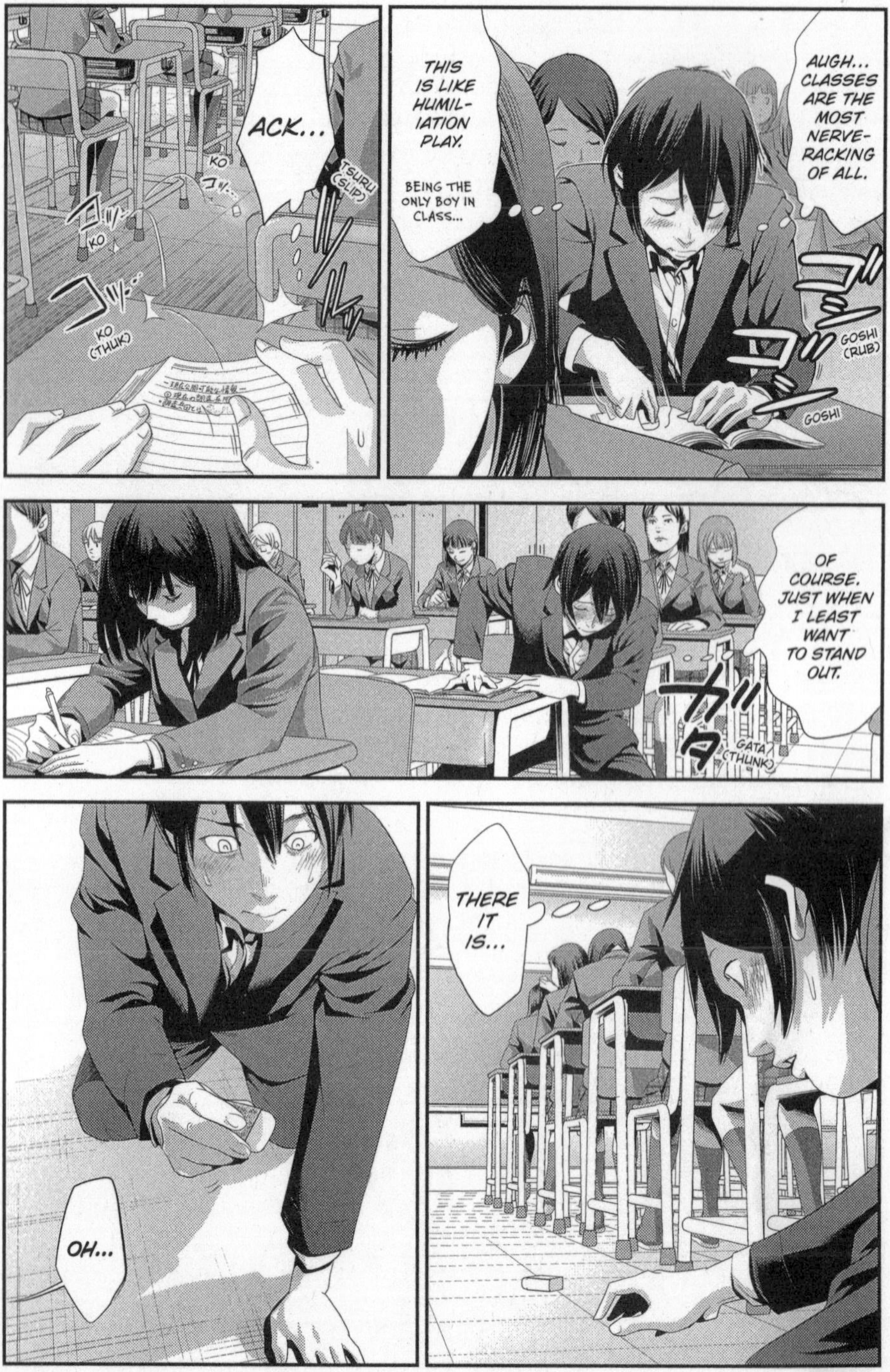
AUGH... CLASSES ARE THE MOST NERVE-RACKING OF ALL.
THIS IS LIKE HUMIL-IATION PLAY.
BEING THE ONLY BOY IN CLASS...
GOSHI (RUB)
GOSHI
TSURU (SLIP)
ACK...
KO
KO
KO (THUK)
OF COURSE. JUST WHEN I LEAST WANT TO STAND OUT.
GATA (THUNK)
THERE IT IS...
OH...

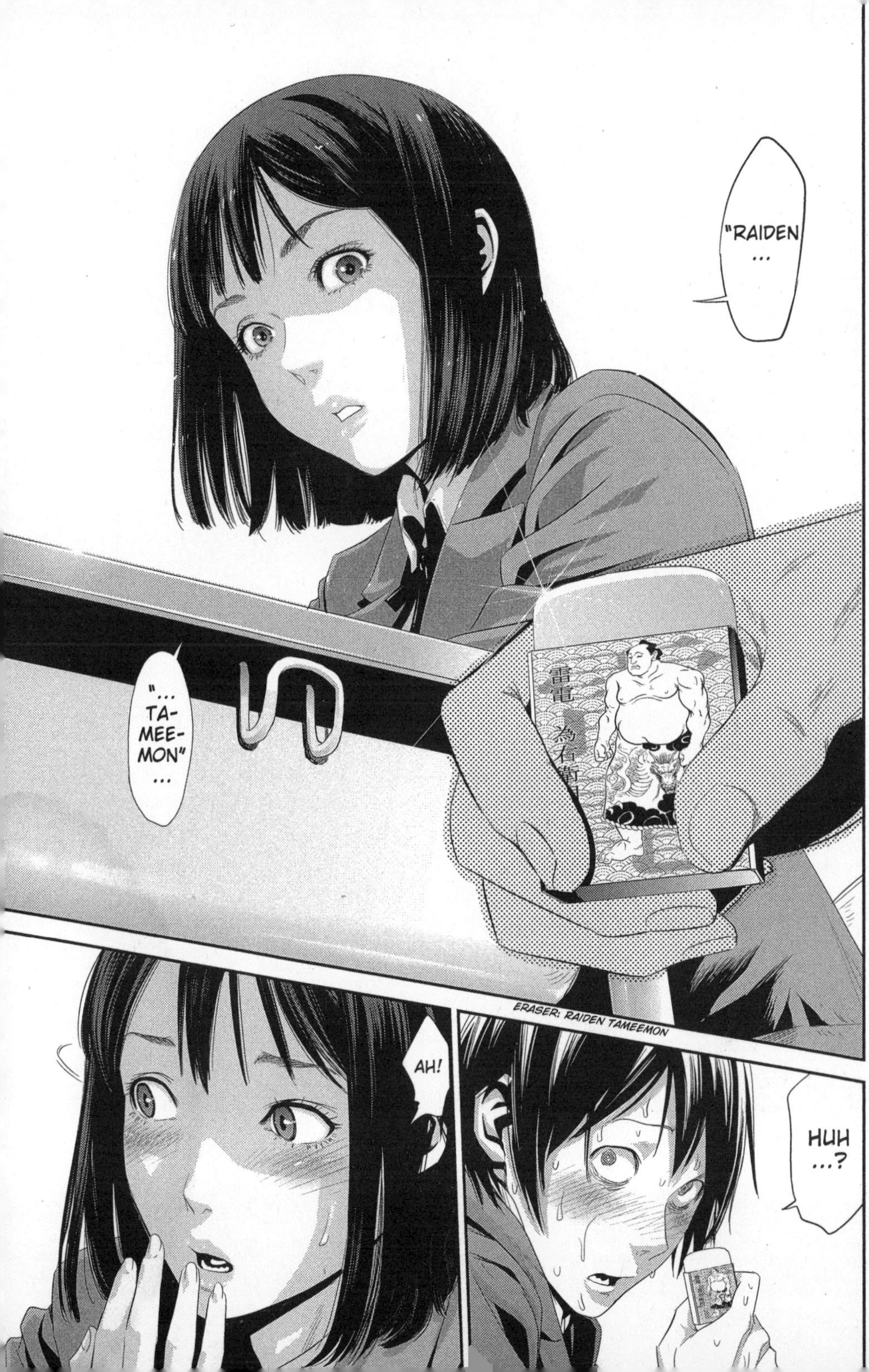
"RAIDEN
...
"... TA-MEE-MON" ...
雷電
ERASER: RAIDEN TAMEEMON
HUH ...?
AH!

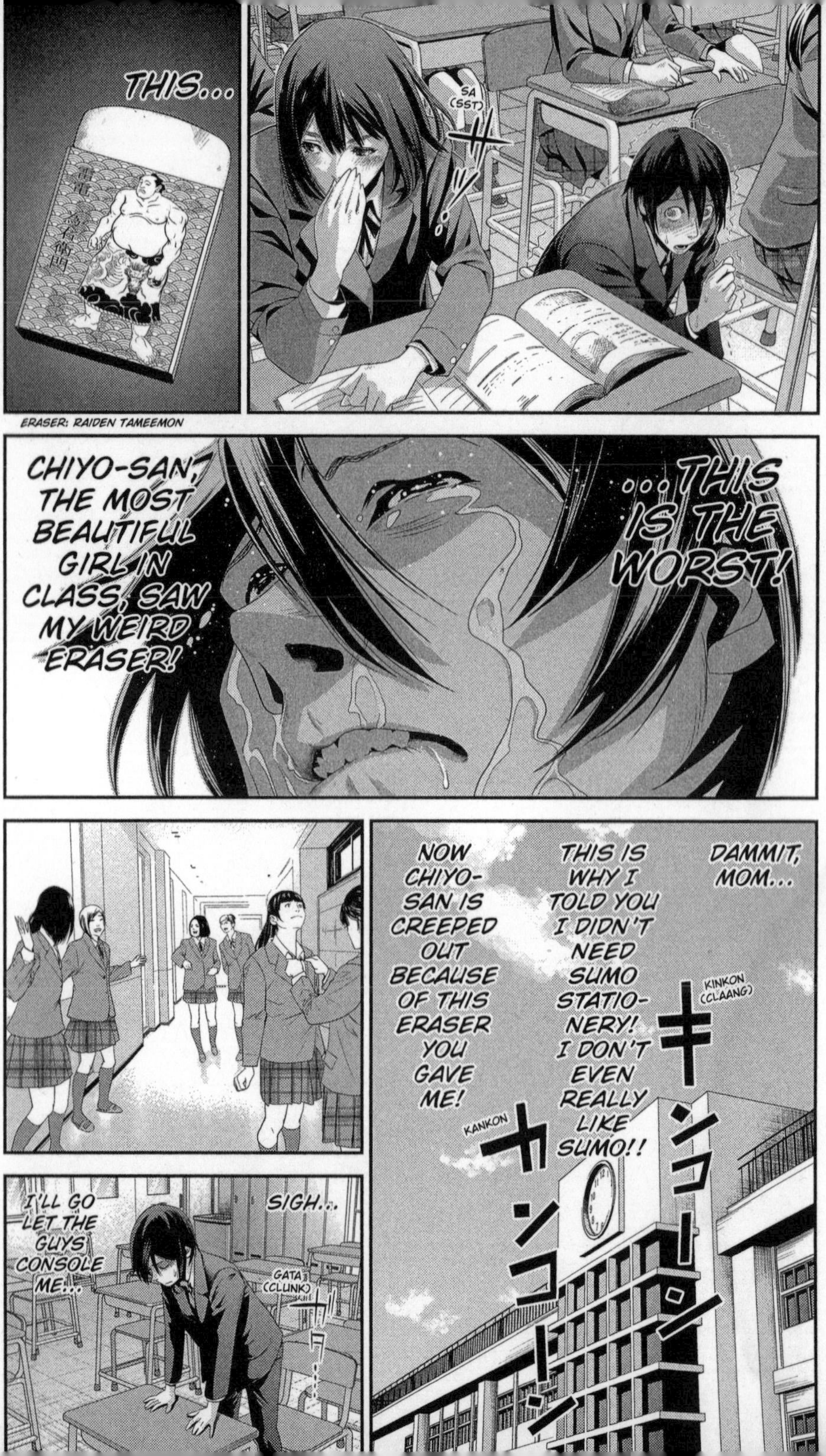
SA (SST)
THIS...
ERASER: RAIDEN TAMEEMON
...THIS IS THE WORST!
CHIYO-SAN, THE MOST BEAUTIFUL GIRL IN CLASS, SAW MY WEIRD ERASER!
DAMMIT, MOM...
THIS IS WHY I TOLD YOU I DIDN'T NEED SUMO STATIONERY! I DON'T EVEN REALLY LIKE SUMO!!
NOW CHIYO-SAN IS CREEPED OUT BECAUSE OF THIS ERASER YOU GAVE ME!
KINKON (CLAANG)
KANKON
SIGH...
I'LL GO LET THE GUYS CONSOLE ME...
GATA (CLUNK)

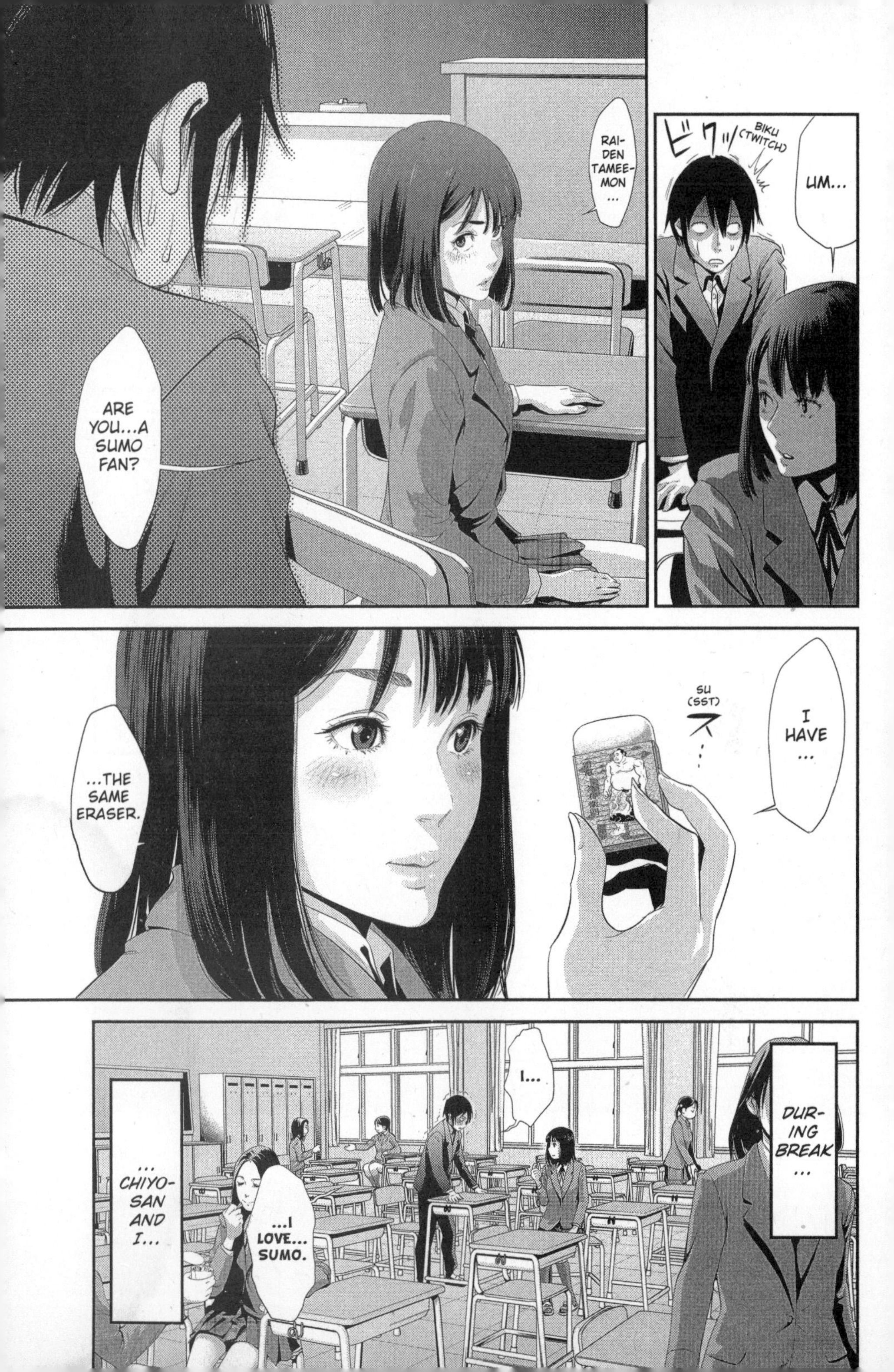
UM...
BIKU (TWITCH)
ビクッ
RAI-DEN TAMEE-MON ...
ARE YOU...A SUMO FAN?
I HAVE ...
SU (SST)
ス
...THE SAME ERASER.
DUR-ING BREAK ...
I...
... CHIYO-SAN AND I...
...I LOVE... SUMO.

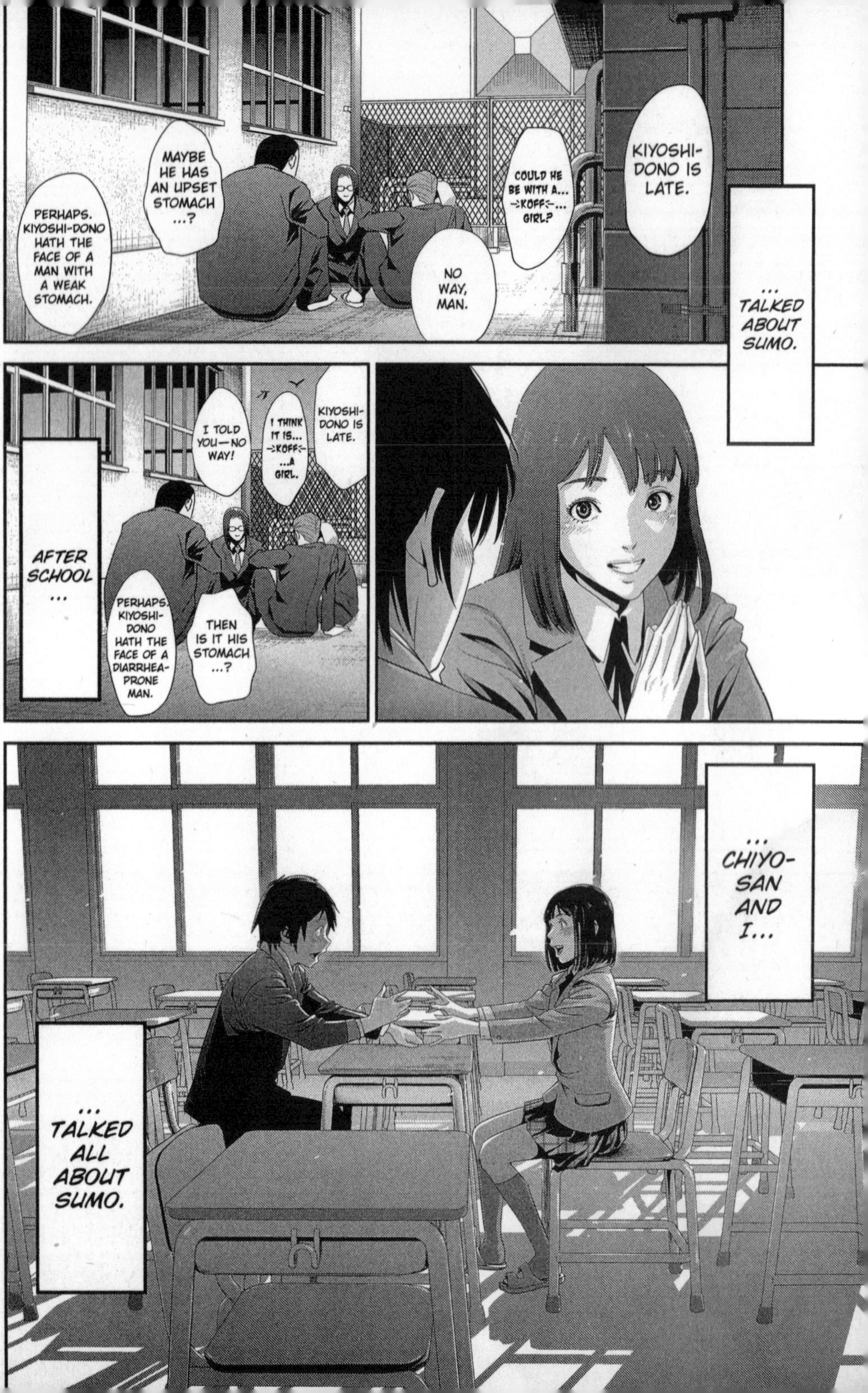
KIYOSHI-DONO IS LATE.
COULD HE BE WITH A... -KOFF-... GIRL?
NO WAY, MAN.
MAYBE HE HAS AN UPSET STOMACH...?
PERHAPS. KIYOSHI-DONO HATH THE FACE OF A MAN WITH A WEAK STOMACH.
...TALKED ABOUT SUMO.
AFTER SCHOOL...
KIYOSHI-DONO IS LATE.
I THINK IT IS... -KOFF- ...A GIRL.
I TOLD YOU—NO WAY!
THEN IS IT HIS STOMACH...?
PERHAPS. KIYOSHI-DONO HATH THE FACE OF A DIARRHEA-PRONE MAN.
...CHIYO-SAN AND I...
...TALKED ALL ABOUT SUMO.

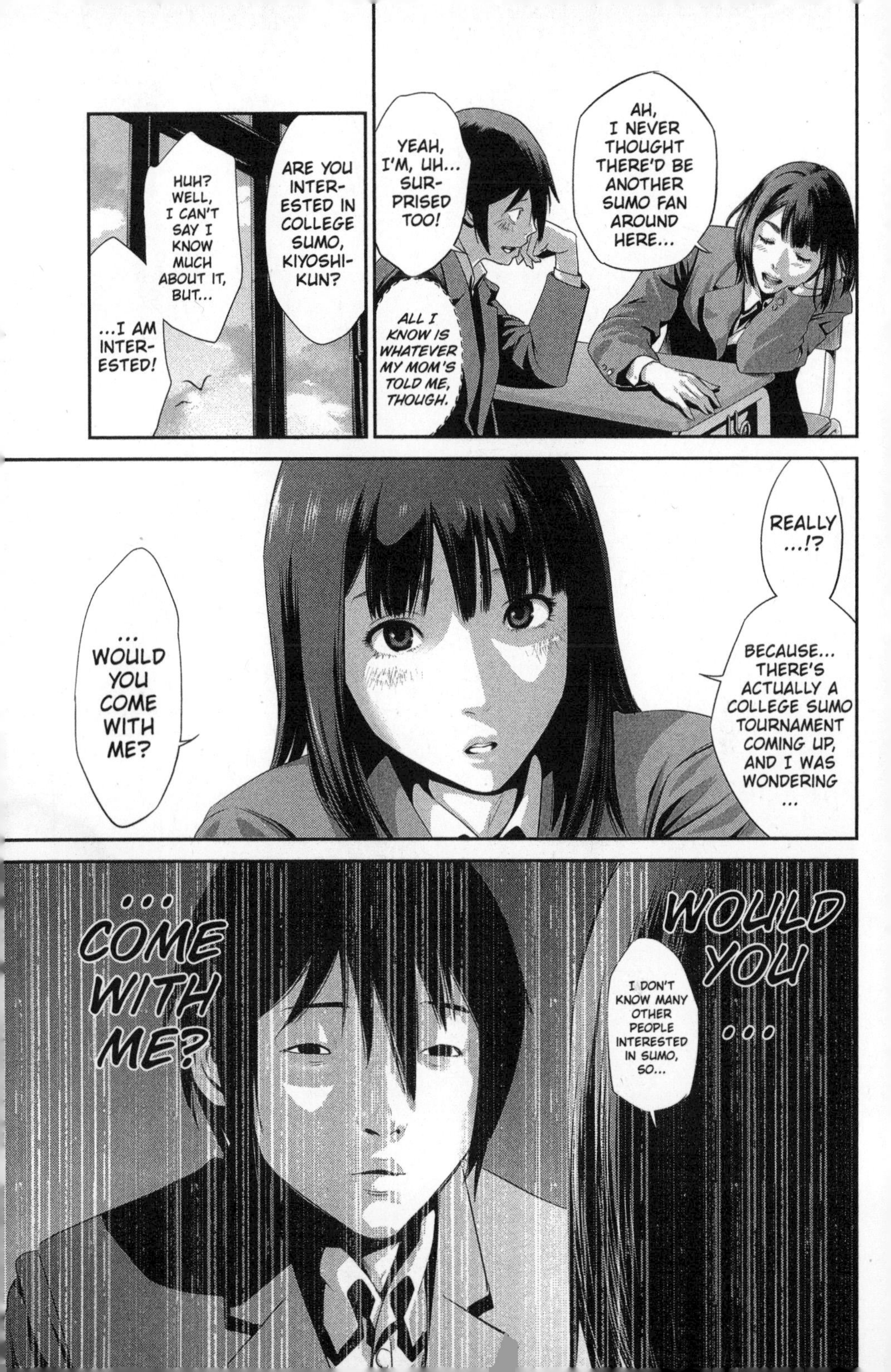
AH, I NEVER THOUGHT THERE'D BE ANOTHER SUMO FAN AROUND HERE...
YEAH, I'M, UH... SURPRISED TOO!
ALL I KNOW IS WHATEVER MY MOM'S TOLD ME, THOUGH.
ARE YOU INTERESTED IN COLLEGE SUMO, KIYOSHI-KUN?
HUH? WELL, I CAN'T SAY I KNOW MUCH ABOUT IT, BUT...
...I AM INTERESTED!
REALLY...!?
BECAUSE... THERE'S ACTUALLY A COLLEGE SUMO TOURNAMENT COMING UP, AND I WAS WONDERING...
...WOULD YOU COME WITH ME?
WOULD YOU...
I DON'T KNOW MANY OTHER PEOPLE INTERESTED IN SUMO, SO...
...COME WITH ME?

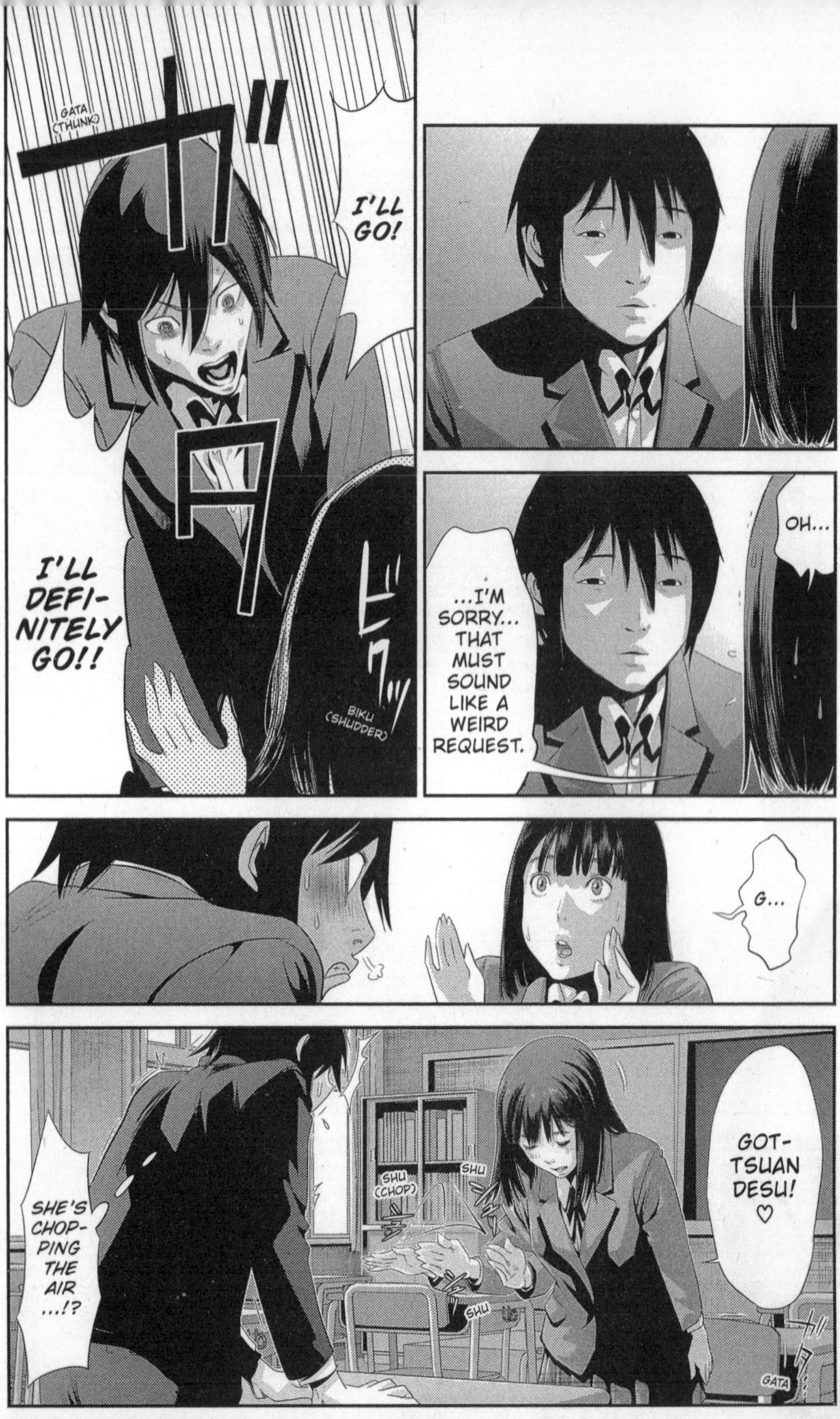
OH...
...I'M SORRY... THAT MUST SOUND LIKE A WEIRD REQUEST.
GATA (THUNK)
I'LL GO!
I'LL DEFINITELY GO!!
BIKU (SHUDDER)
G...
GOT-TSUAN DESU! ♡
GATA
SHU
SHU (CHOP)
SHU
SHE'S CHOPPING THE AIR ...!?

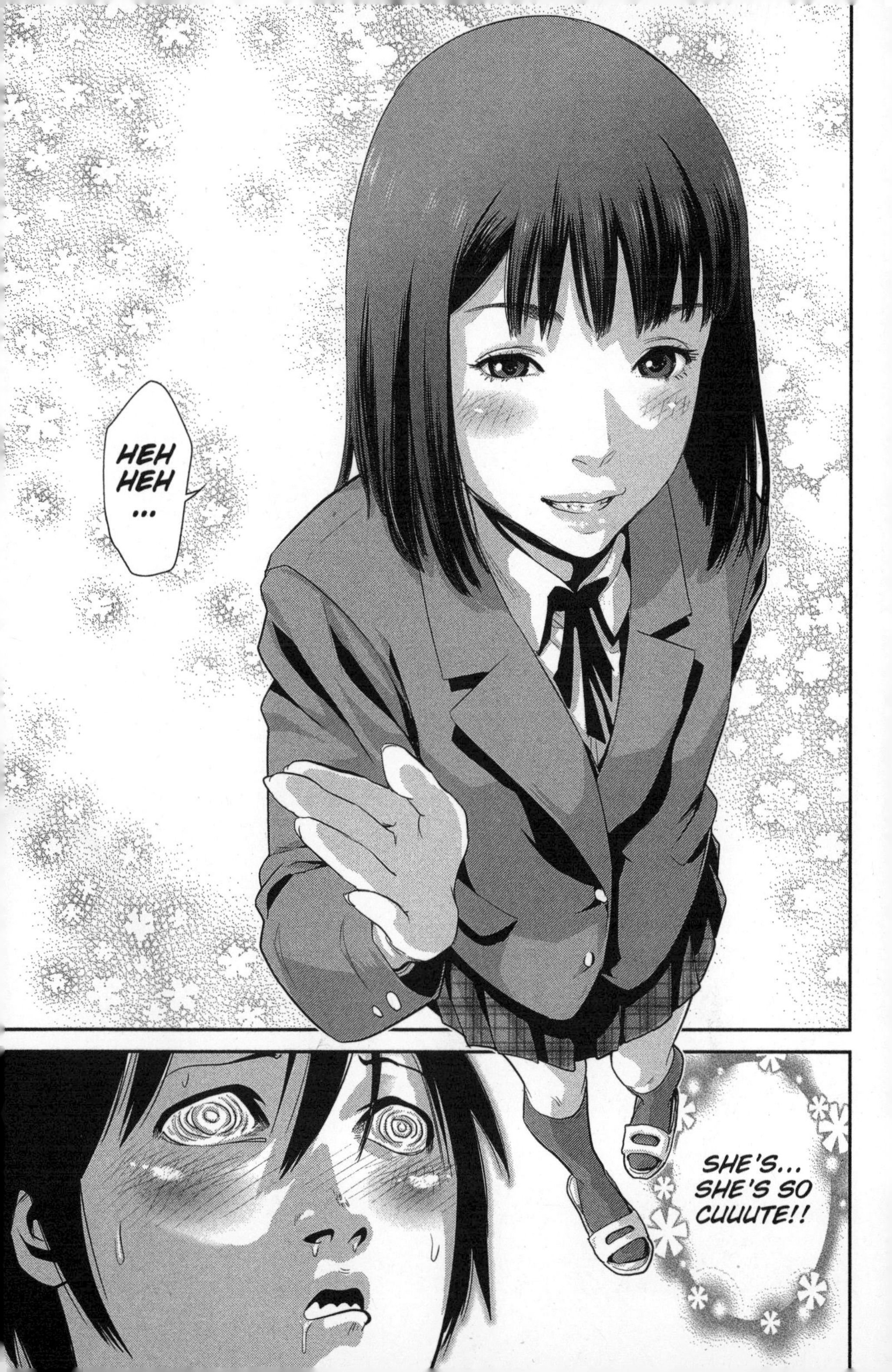
HEH HEH ...
SHE'S... SHE'S SO CUUUTE!!

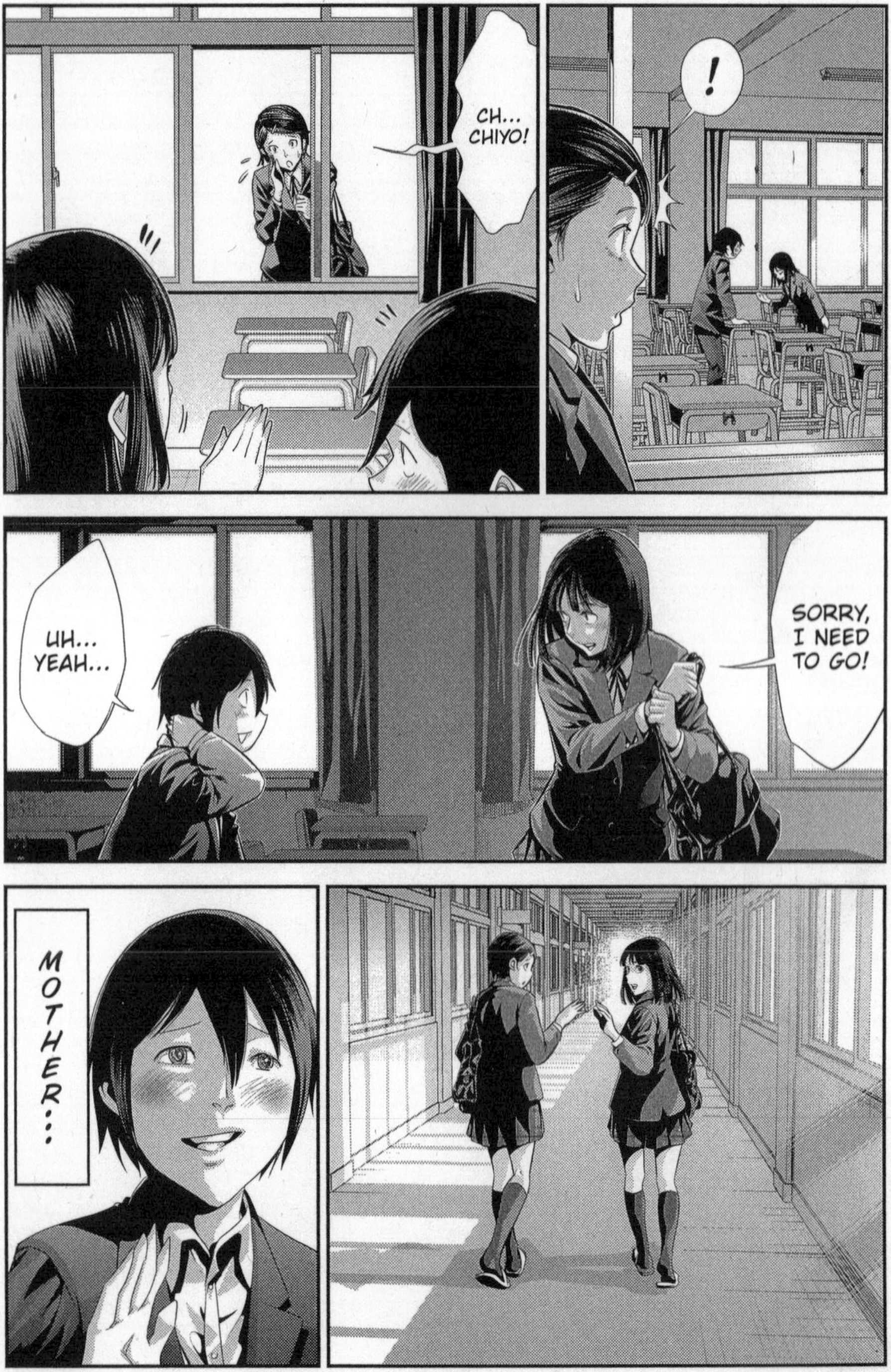
!
CH... CHIYO!
SORRY, I NEED TO GO!
UH... YEAH...
MOTHER...

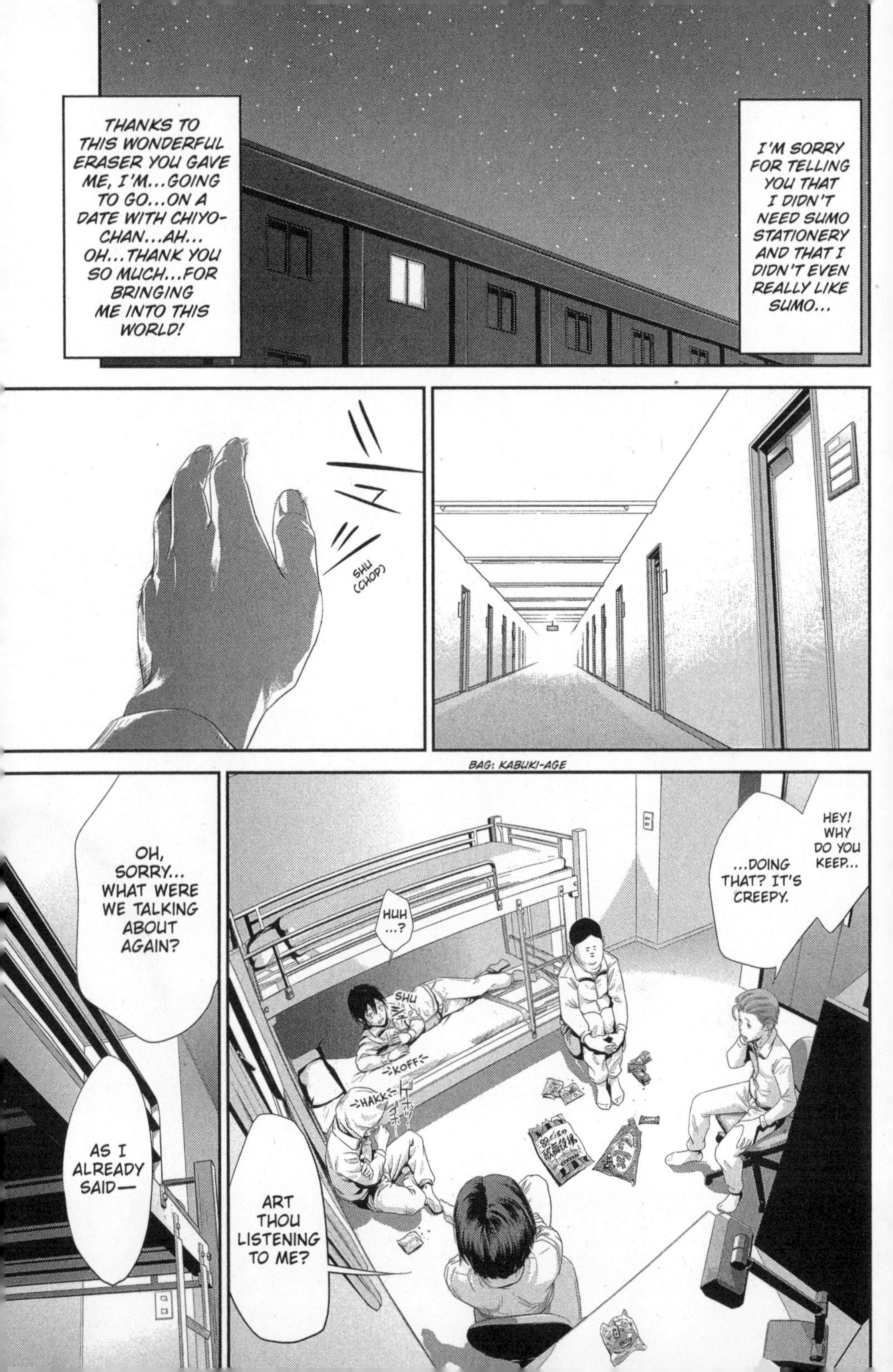
I'M SORRY FOR TELLING YOU THAT I DIDN'T NEED SUMO STATIONERY AND THAT I DIDN'T EVEN REALLY LIKE SUMO...
THANKS TO THIS WONDERFUL ERASER YOU GAVE ME, I'M...GOING TO GO...ON A DATE WITH CHIYO-CHAN...AH... OH...THANK YOU SO MUCH...FOR BRINGING ME INTO THIS WORLD!
SHU (CHOP)
BAG: KABUKI-AGE
HEY! WHY DO YOU KEEP...
...DOING THAT? IT'S CREEPY.
HUH ...?
SHU
KOFF
HAKK
OH, SORRY... WHAT WERE WE TALKING ABOUT AGAIN?
AS I ALREADY SAID—
ART THOU LISTENING TO ME?

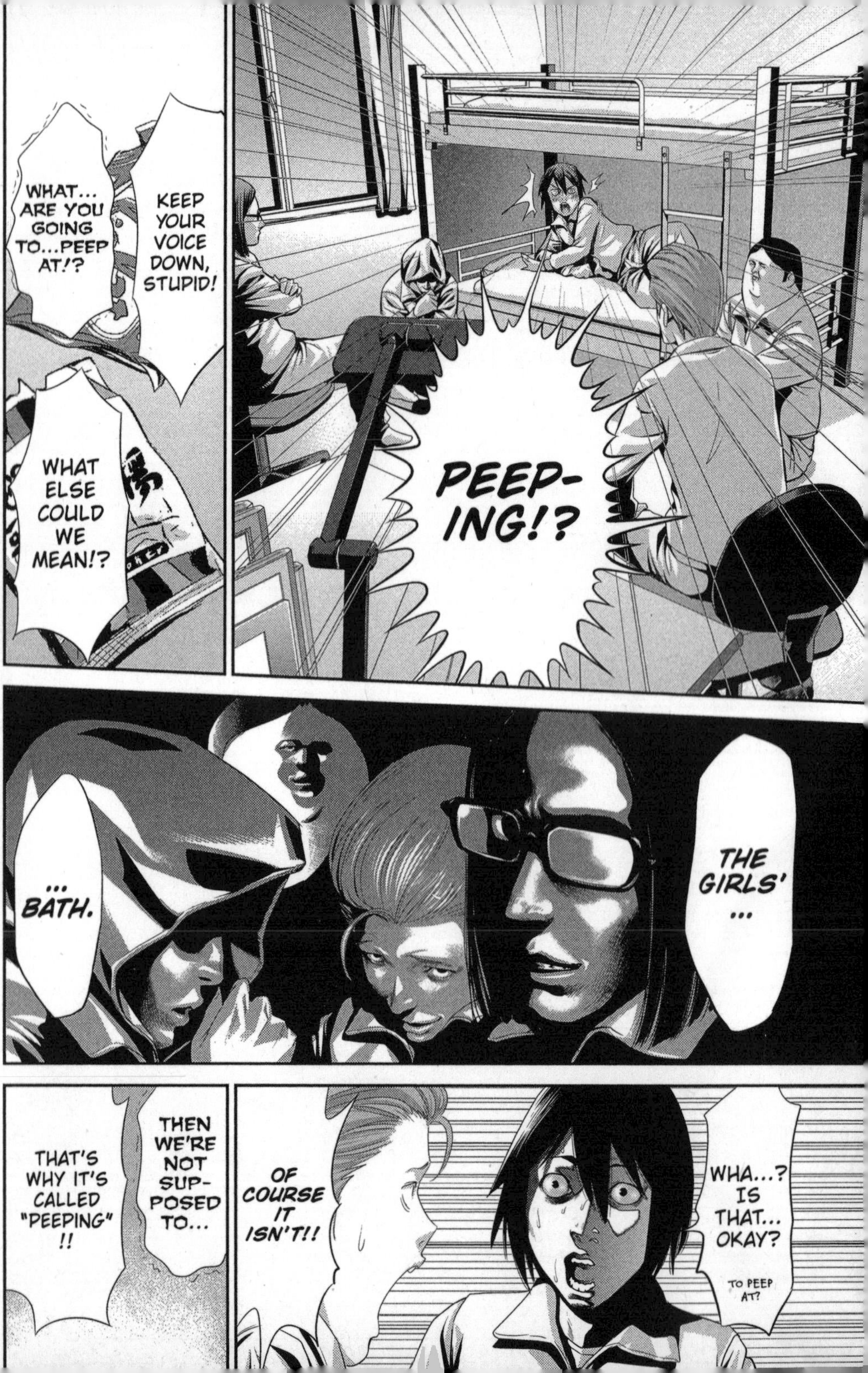
PEEP-ING!?
KEEP YOUR VOICE DOWN, STUPID!
WHAT... ARE YOU GOING TO...PEEP AT!?
WHAT ELSE COULD WE MEAN!?
THE GIRLS' ...
... BATH.
WHA...? IS THAT... OKAY?
TO PEEP AT?
OF COURSE IT ISN'T!!
THEN WE'RE NOT SUP-POSED TO...
THAT'S WHY IT'S CALLED "PEEPING" !!

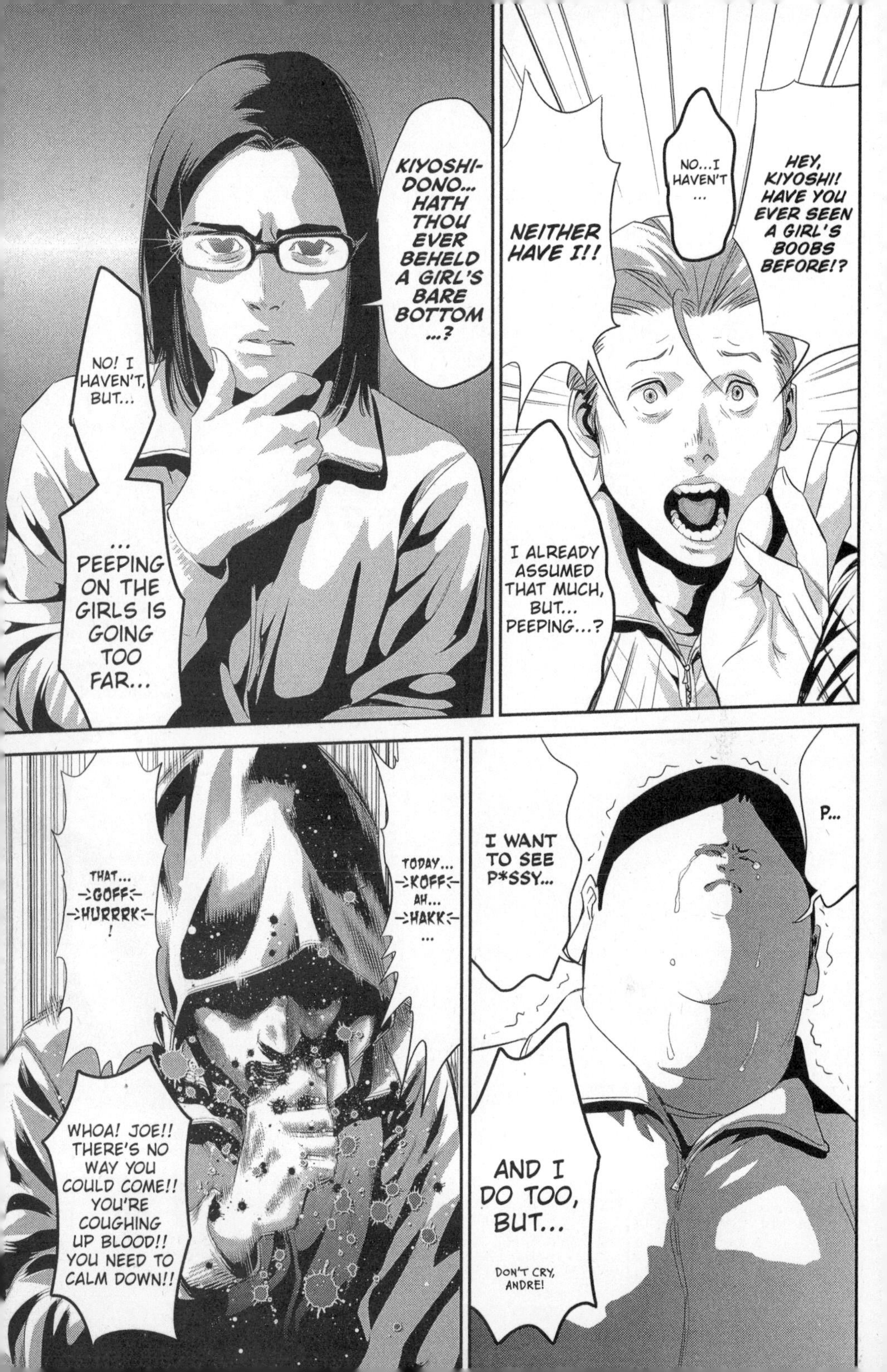
HEY, KIYOSHI! HAVE YOU EVER SEEN A GIRL'S BOOBS BEFORE!?
NO...I HAVEN'T...
NEITHER HAVE I!!
I ALREADY ASSUMED THAT MUCH, BUT... PEEPING...?
KIYOSHI-DONO... HATH THOU EVER BEHELD A GIRL'S BARE BOTTOM ...?
NO! I HAVEN'T, BUT...
... PEEPING ON THE GIRLS IS GOING TOO FAR...
P...
I WANT TO SEE P*SSY...
AND I DO TOO, BUT...
DON'T CRY, ANDRE!
TODAY... -KOFF- AH... -HAKK- ...
THAT... -GOFF- -HURRRK- !
WHOA! JOE!! THERE'S NO WAY YOU COULD COME!! YOU'RE COUGHING UP BLOOD!! YOU NEED TO CALM DOWN!!

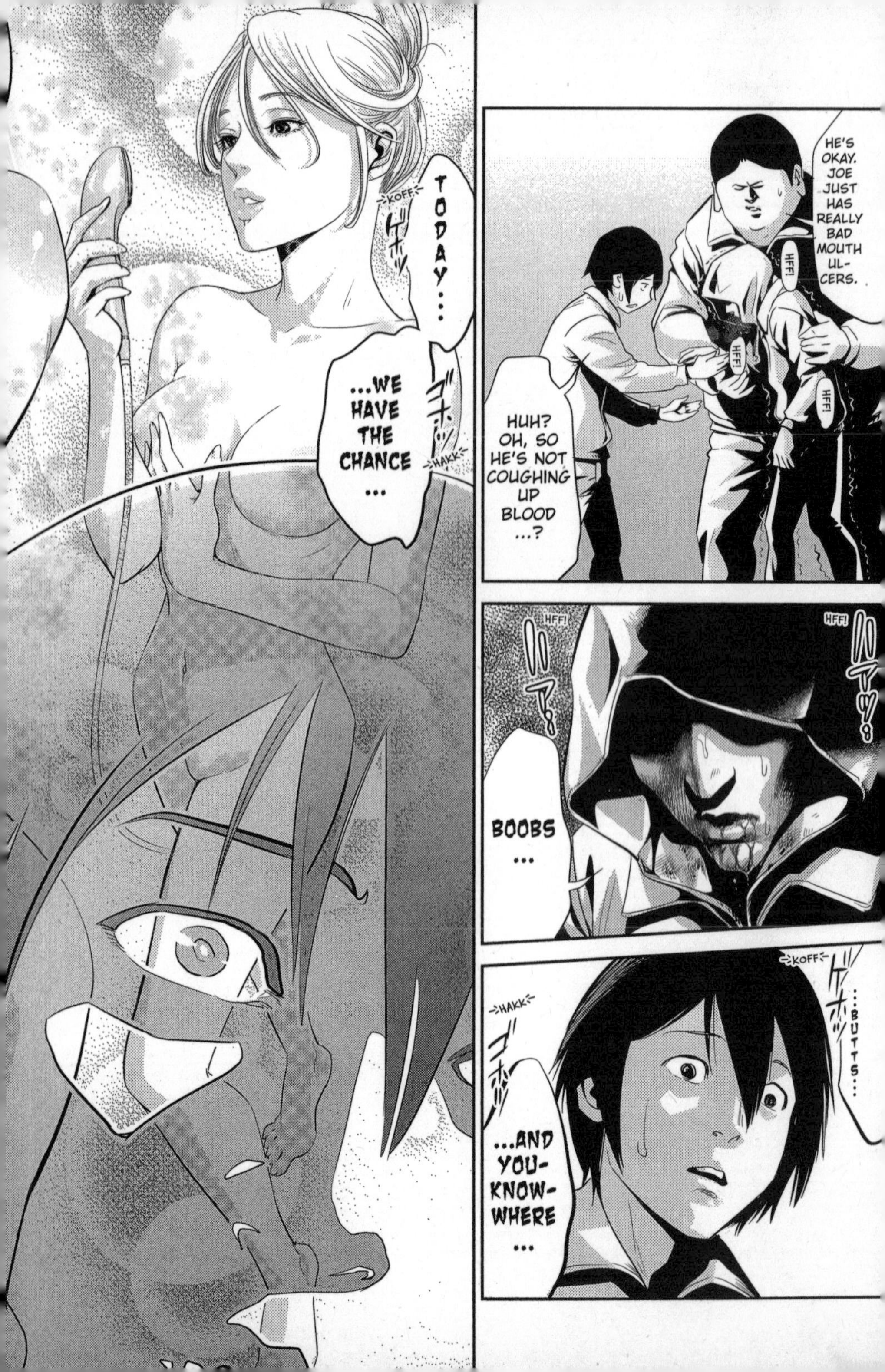
HE'S OKAY. JOE JUST HAS REALLY BAD MOUTH UL-CERS.
HFF!
HFF!
HFF!
HUH? OH, SO HE'S NOT COUGHING UP BLOOD ...?
HFF!
HFF!
BOOBS ...
KOFF
...BUTTS...
HAKK
...AND YOU-KNOW-WHERE ...
KOFF
TODAY...
HAKK
...WE HAVE THE CHANCE ...

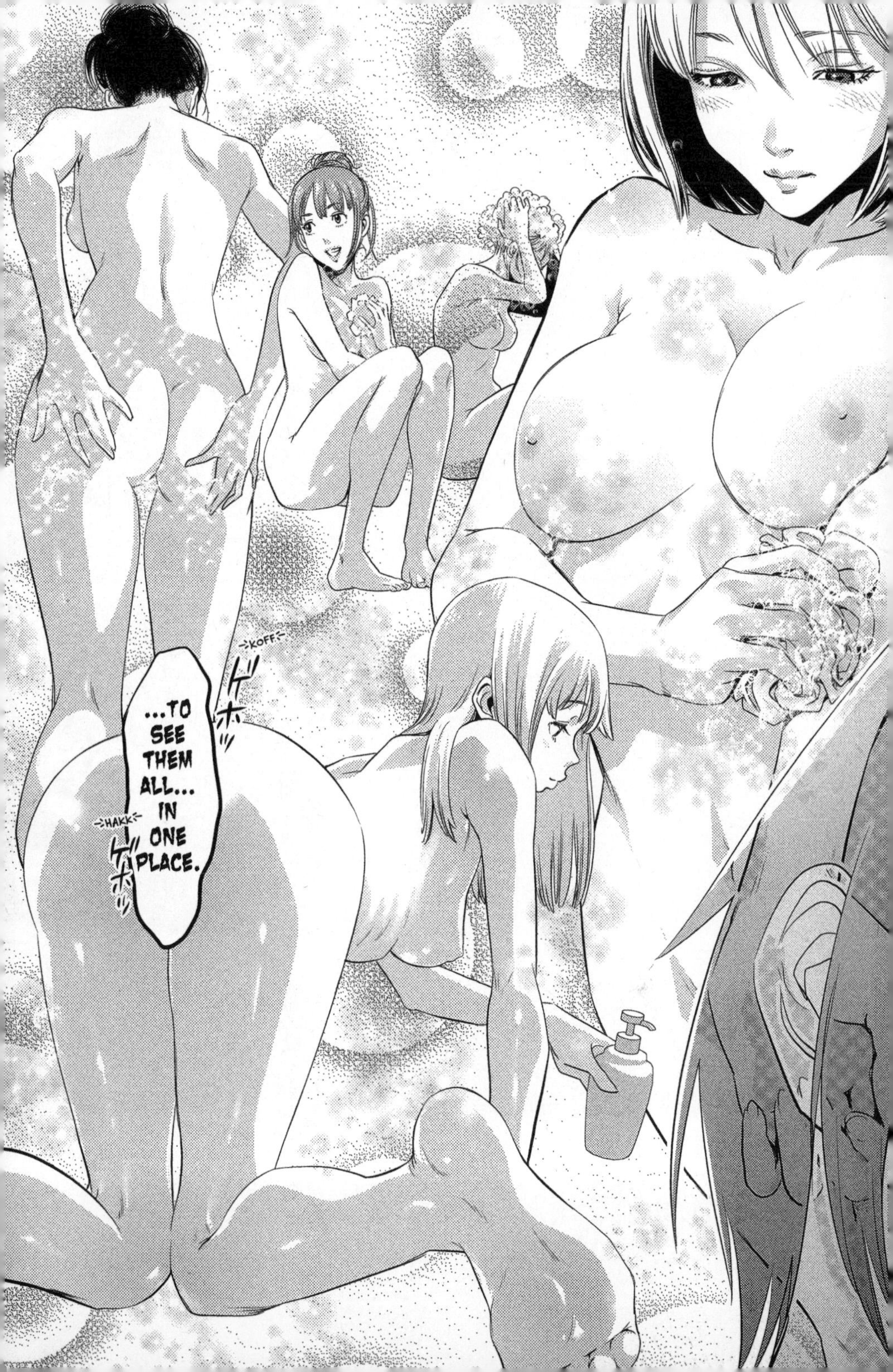
KOFF
...TO SEE THEM ALL... IN ONE PLACE.
HAKK

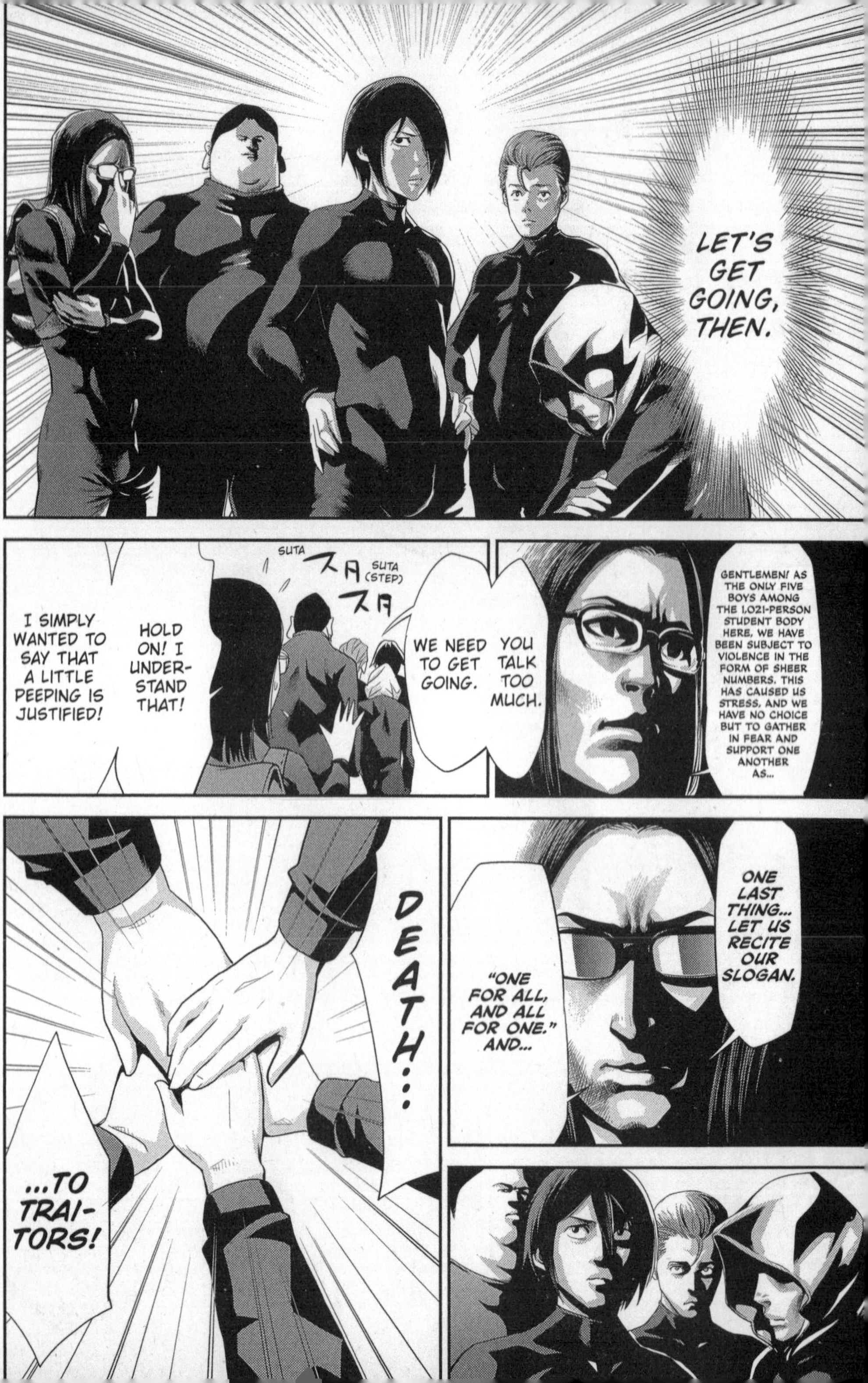
LET'S GET GOING, THEN.
GENTLEMEN! AS THE ONLY FIVE BOYS AMONG THE 1,021-PERSON STUDENT BODY HERE, WE HAVE BEEN SUBJECT TO VIOLENCE IN THE FORM OF SHEER NUMBERS. THIS HAS CAUSED US STRESS, AND WE HAVE NO CHOICE BUT TO GATHER IN FEAR AND SUPPORT ONE ANOTHER AS...
YOU TALK TOO MUCH.
WE NEED TO GET GOING.
SUTA スタ
SUTA (STEP) スタ
HOLD ON! I UNDER-STAND THAT!
I SIMPLY WANTED TO SAY THAT A LITTLE PEEPING IS JUSTIFIED!
ONE LAST THING... LET US RECITE OUR SLOGAN.
"ONE FOR ALL, AND ALL FOR ONE." AND...
DEATH...
...TO TRAI-TORS!

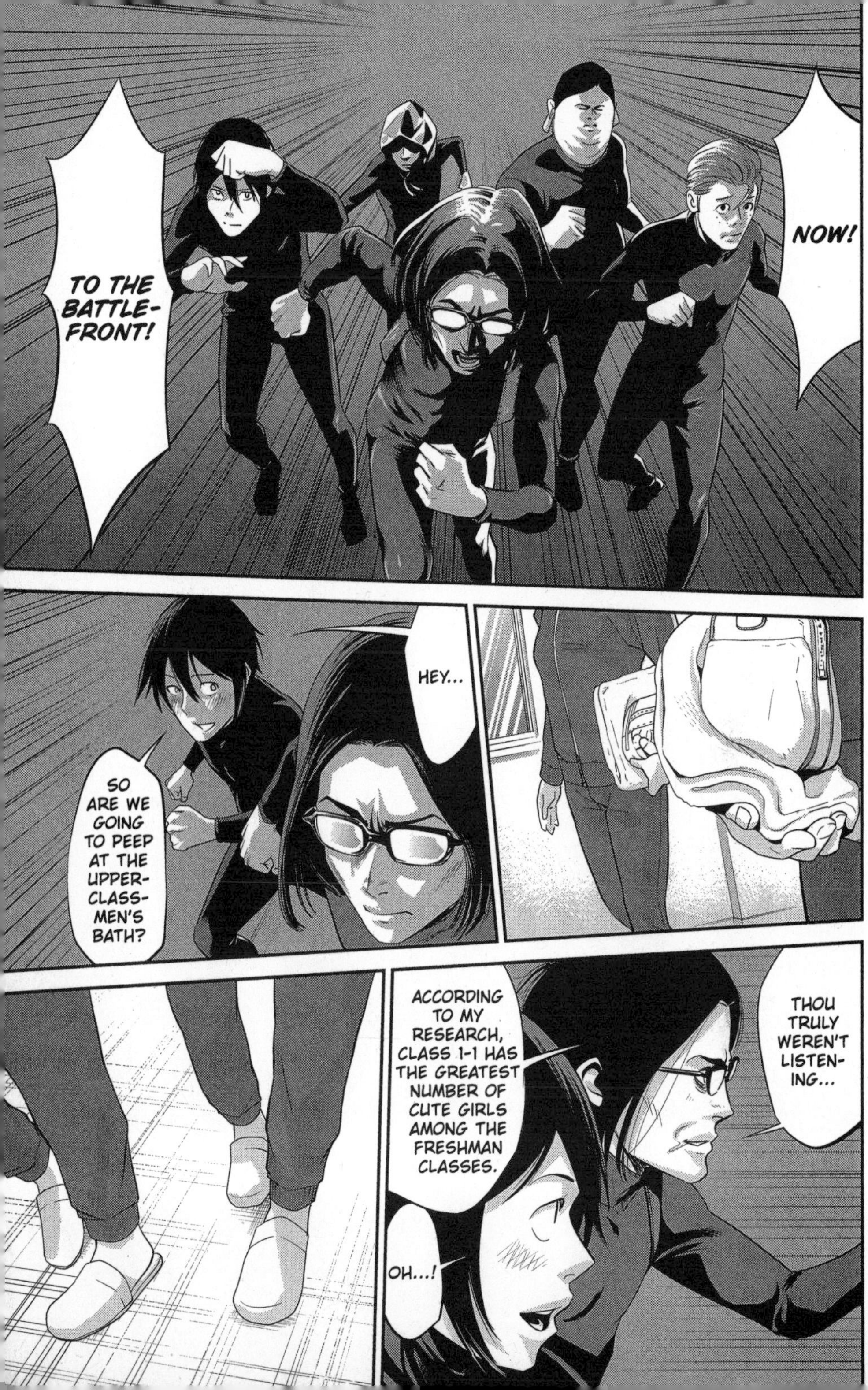
NOW!
TO THE BATTLE-FRONT!
HEY...
SO ARE WE GOING TO PEEP AT THE UPPER-CLASS-MEN'S BATH?
THOU TRULY WEREN'T LISTEN-ING...
ACCORDING TO MY RESEARCH, CLASS 1-1 HAS THE GREATEST NUMBER OF CUTE GIRLS AMONG THE FRESHMAN CLASSES.
OH...!

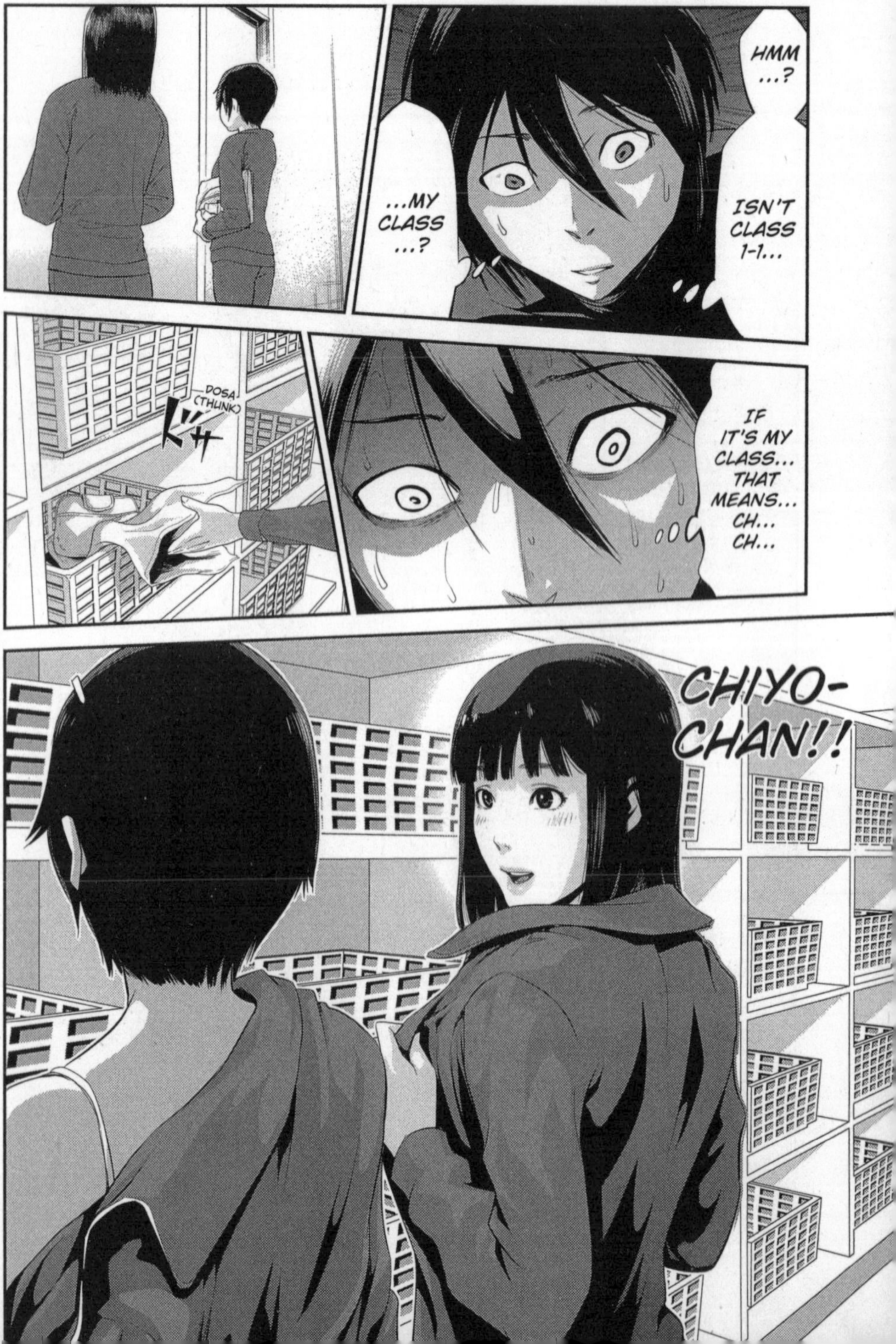
HMM ...?
ISN'T CLASS 1-1...
...MY CLASS ...?
IF IT'S MY CLASS... THAT MEANS... CH... CH...
DOSA (THUNK)
ドサ
CHIYO-CHAN!!

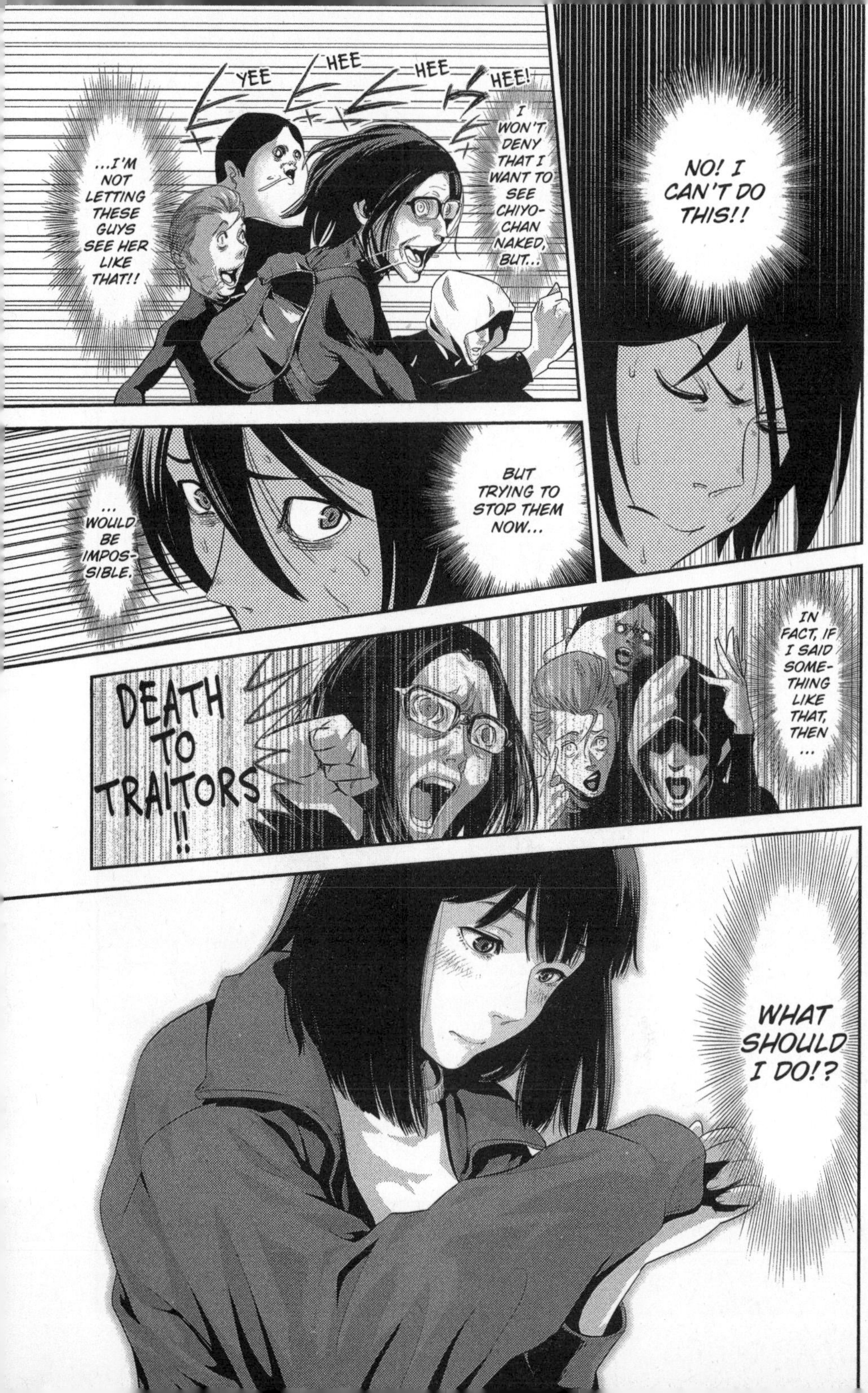
NO! I CAN'T DO THIS!!
YEE HEE HEE HEE!
I WON'T DENY THAT I WANT TO SEE CHIYO-CHAN NAKED, BUT...
...I'M NOT LETTING THESE GUYS SEE HER LIKE THAT!!
BUT TRYING TO STOP THEM NOW...
...WOULD BE IMPOSSIBLE.
IN FACT, IF I SAID SOMETHING LIKE THAT, THEN ...
DEATH TO TRAITORS!!
WHAT SHOULD I DO!?

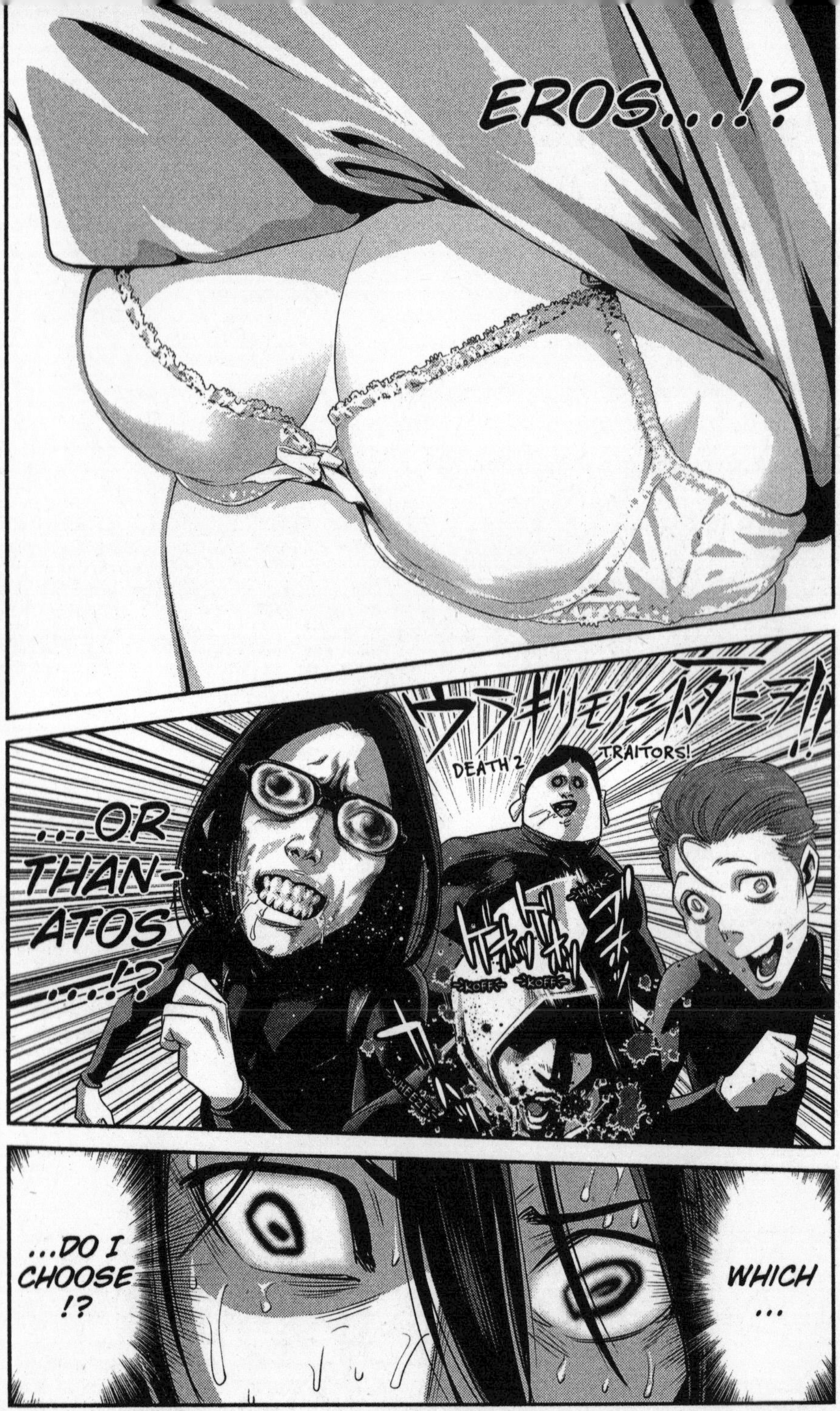
EROS...!?
DEATH 2 TRAITORS!
HAKK
KOFF
KOFF
WHEEZE
...OR THANATOS ...!?
WHICH ...
...DO I CHOOSE !?

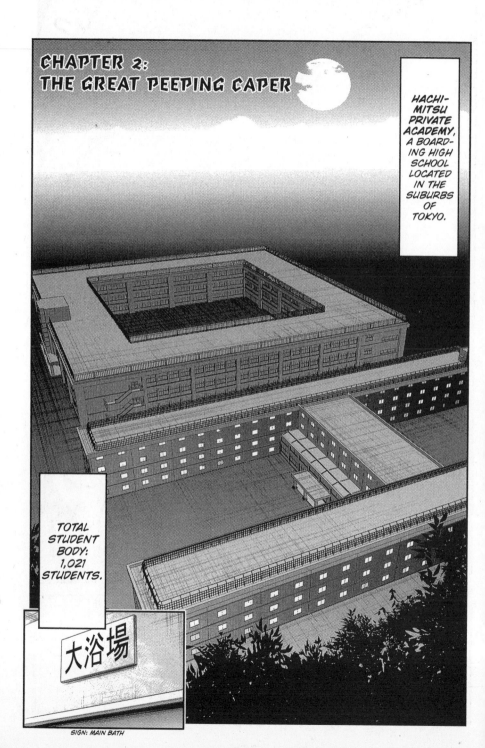

CHAPTER 2:
THE GREAT PEEPING CAPER

HACHI-MITSU PRIVATE ACADEMY, A BOARDING HIGH SCHOOL LOCATED IN THE SUBURBS OF TOKYO.

TOTAL STUDENT BODY: 1,021 STUDENTS.

SIGN: MAIN BATH

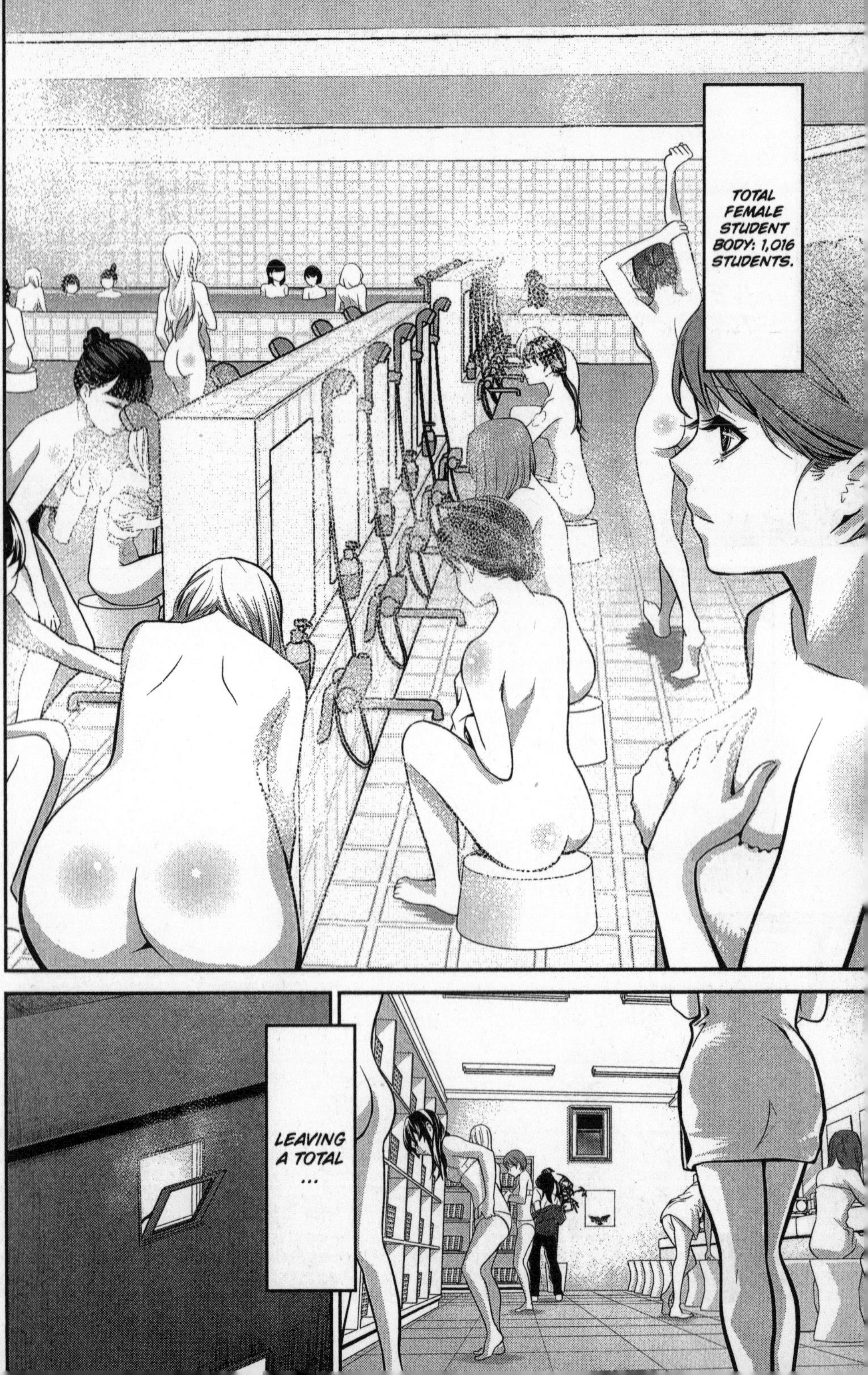
TOTAL FEMALE STUDENT BODY: 1,016 STUDENTS.
LEAVING A TOTAL ...

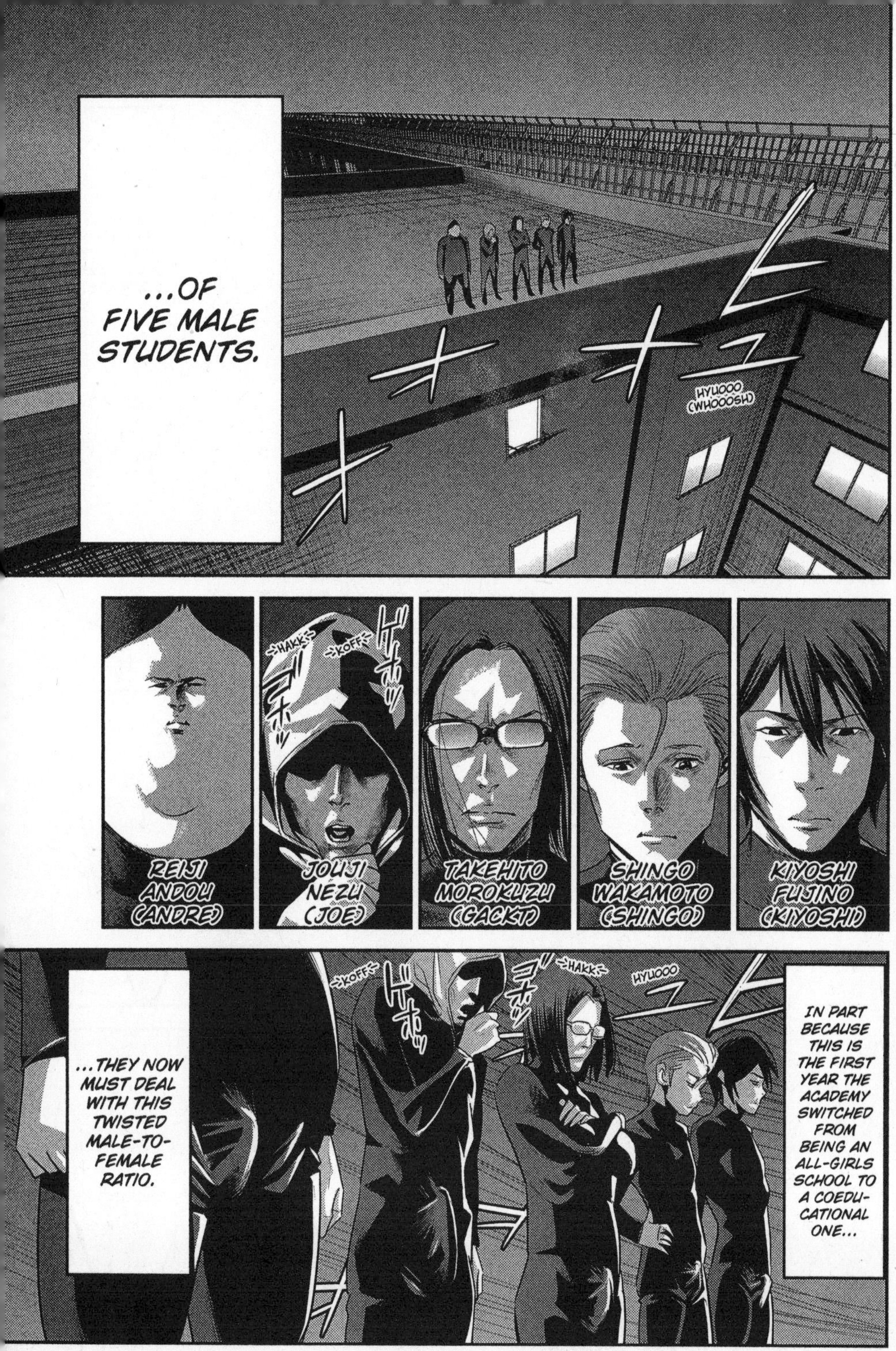
...OF FIVE MALE STUDENTS.
HYUOOO (WHOOOSH)
KIYOSHI FUJINO (KIYOSHI)
SHINGO WAKAMOTO (SHINGO)
TAKEHITO MOROKUZU (GACKT)
JOUJI NEZU (JOE)
~KOFF~
~HAKK~
REIJI ANDOU (ANDRE)
IN PART BECAUSE THIS IS THE FIRST YEAR THE ACADEMY SWITCHED FROM BEING AN ALL-GIRLS SCHOOL TO A COEDUCATIONAL ONE...
HYUOOO
~HAKK~
~KOFF~
...THEY NOW MUST DEAL WITH THIS TWISTED MALE-TO-FEMALE RATIO.

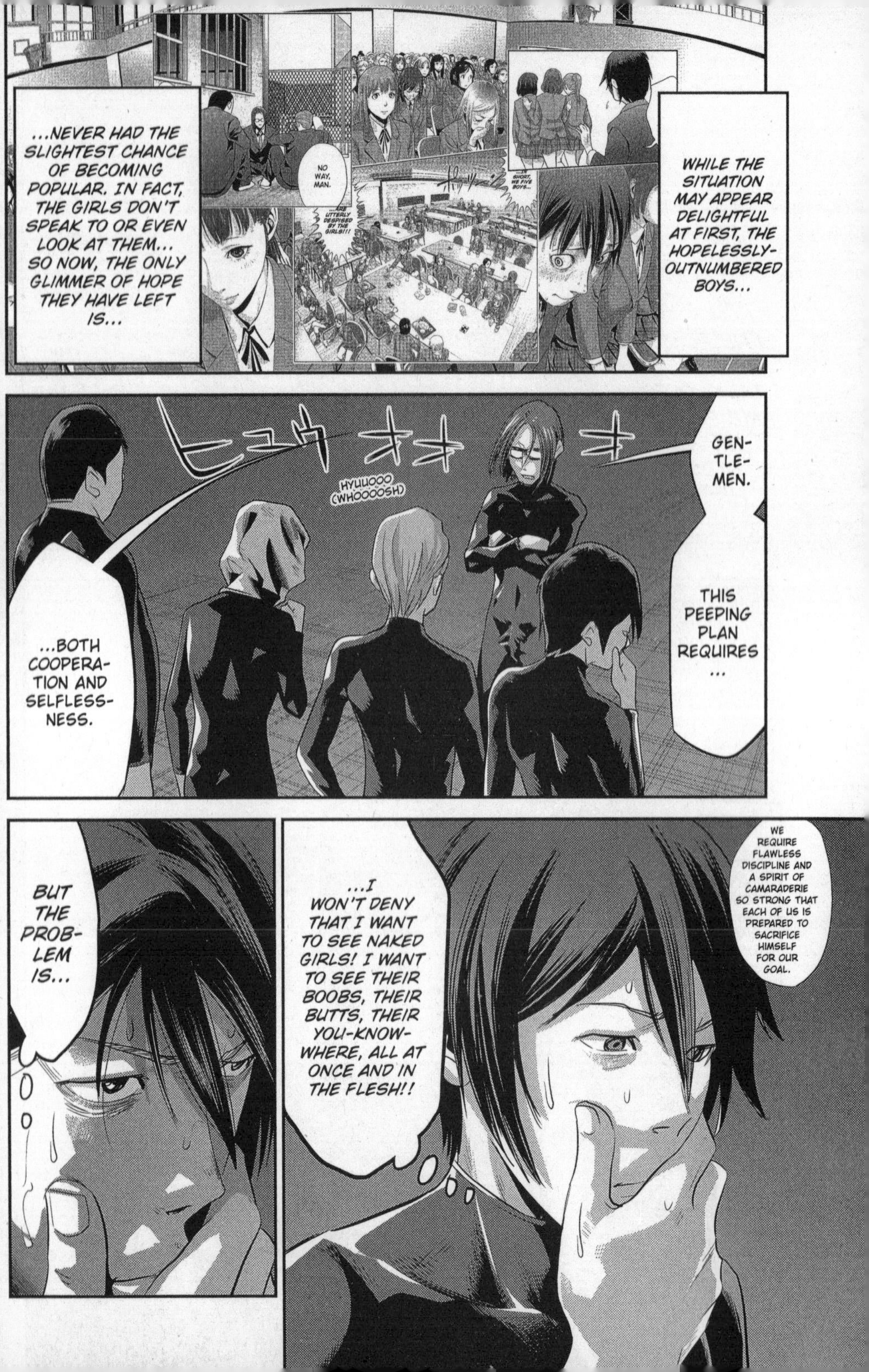
WHILE THE SITUATION MAY APPEAR DELIGHTFUL AT FIRST, THE HOPELESSLY-OUTNUMBERED BOYS...
...IN SHORT, WE FIVE BOYS...
...ARE UTTERLY DESPISED BY THE GIRLS!!!
NO WAY, MAN.
...NEVER HAD THE SLIGHTEST CHANCE OF BECOMING POPULAR. IN FACT, THE GIRLS DON'T SPEAK TO OR EVEN LOOK AT THEM... SO NOW, THE ONLY GLIMMER OF HOPE THEY HAVE LEFT IS...
HYUUOOO (WHOOOOSH)
GEN-TLE-MEN.
THIS PEEPING PLAN REQUIRES...
...BOTH COOPERA-TION AND SELFLESS-NESS.
WE REQUIRE FLAWLESS DISCIPLINE AND A SPIRIT OF CAMARADERIE SO STRONG THAT EACH OF US IS PREPARED TO SACRIFICE HIMSELF FOR OUR GOAL.
...I WON'T DENY THAT I WANT TO SEE NAKED GIRLS! I WANT TO SEE THEIR BOOBS, THEIR BUTTS, THEIR YOU-KNOW-WHERE, ALL AT ONCE AND IN THE FLESH!!
BUT THE PROB-LEM IS...

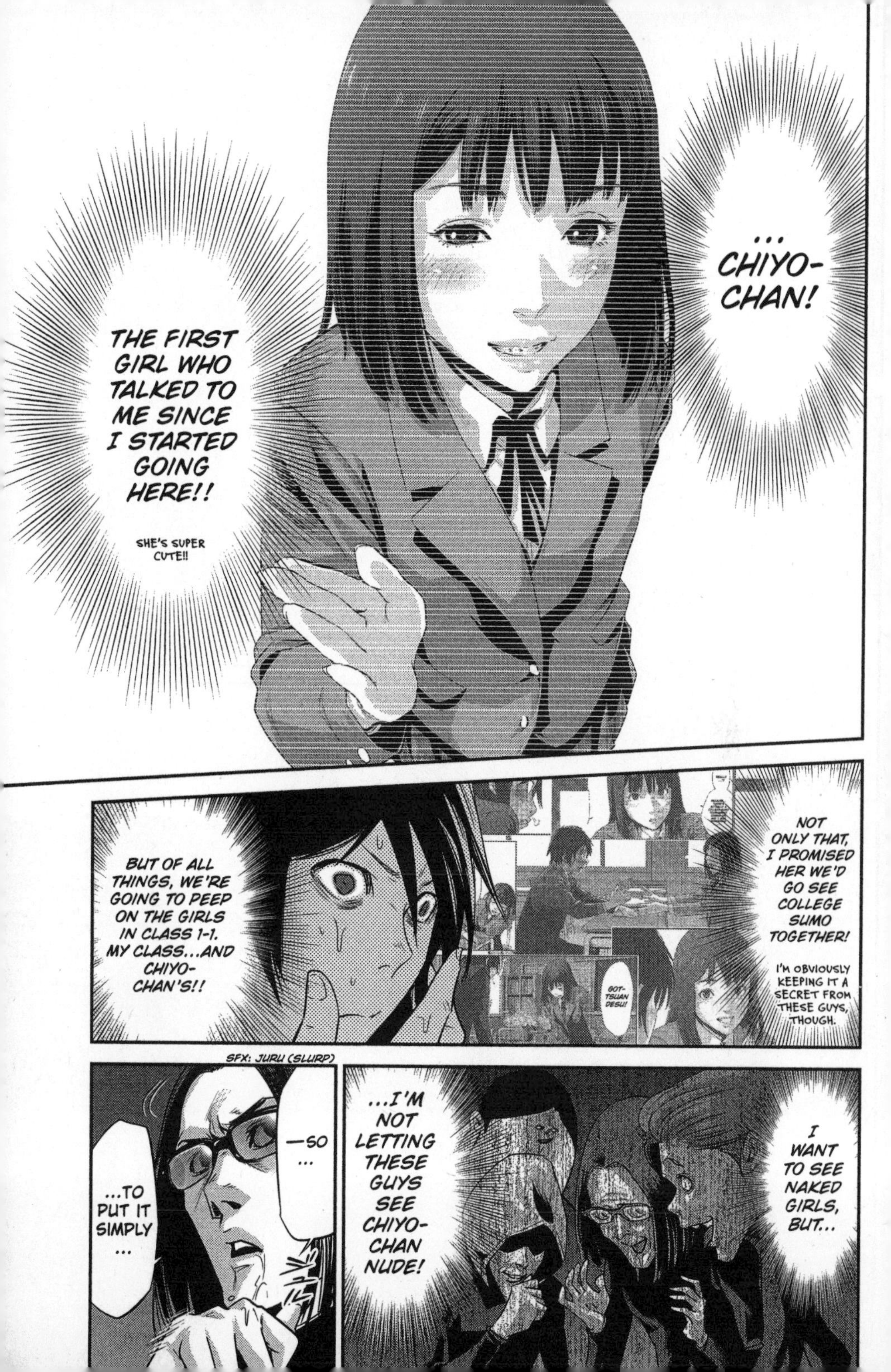
... CHIYO-CHAN!
THE FIRST GIRL WHO TALKED TO ME SINCE I STARTED GOING HERE!!
SHE'S SUPER CUTE!!
NOT ONLY THAT, I PROMISED HER WE'D GO SEE COLLEGE SUMO TOGETHER!
I'M OBVIOUSLY KEEPING IT A SECRET FROM THESE GUYS, THOUGH.
REALLY ...!?
GOT-TSUAN DESU!
BUT OF ALL THINGS, WE'RE GOING TO PEEP ON THE GIRLS IN CLASS 1-1. MY CLASS...AND CHIYO-CHAN'S!!
SFX: JURU (SLURP)
I WANT TO SEE NAKED GIRLS, BUT...
...I'M NOT LETTING THESE GUYS SEE CHIYO-CHAN NUDE!
—SO ...
...TO PUT IT SIMPLY ...

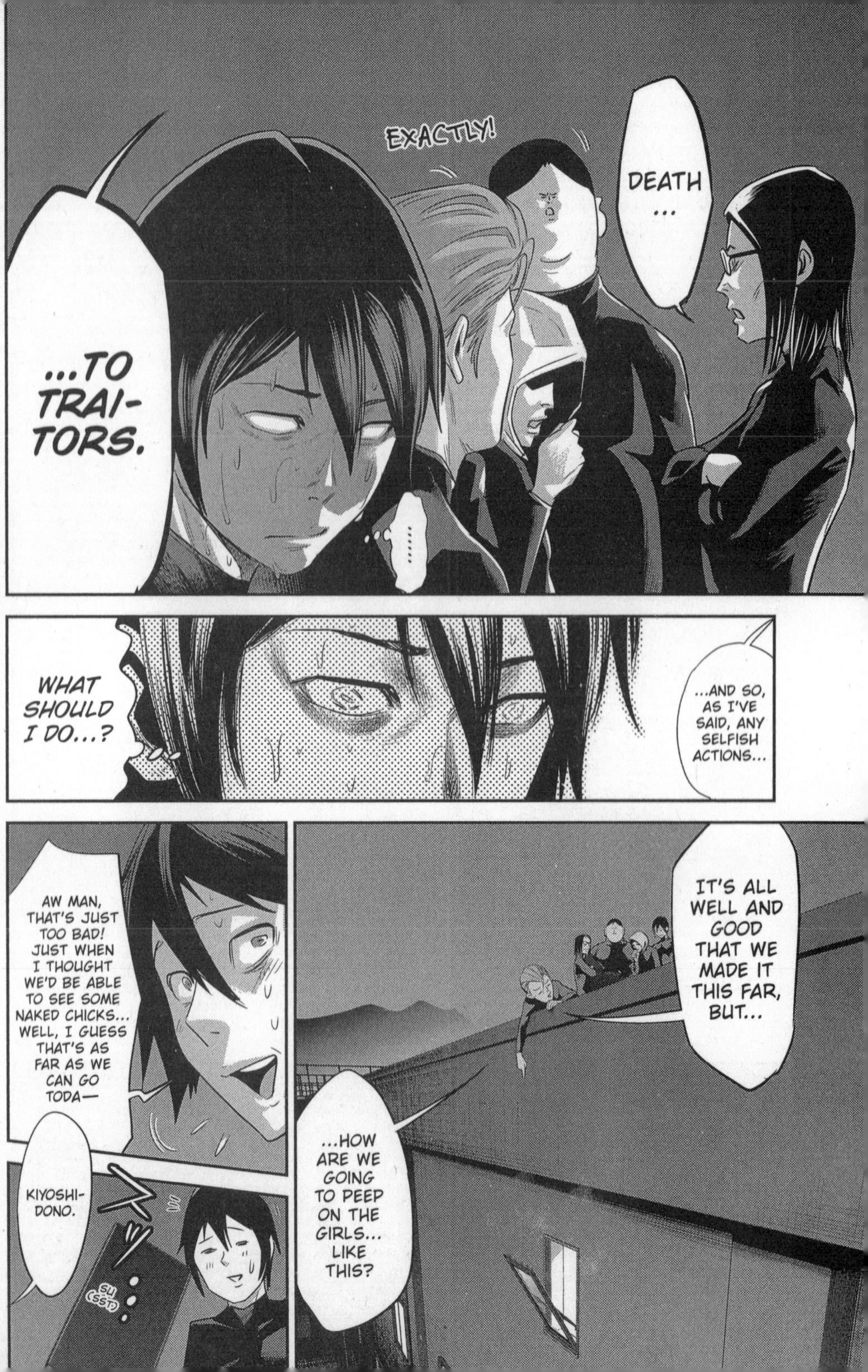
DEATH...
EXACTLY!
...
...TO TRAITORS.
...AND SO, AS I'VE SAID, ANY SELFISH ACTIONS...
WHAT SHOULD I DO...?
IT'S ALL WELL AND GOOD THAT WE MADE IT THIS FAR, BUT...
...HOW ARE WE GOING TO PEEP ON THE GIRLS... LIKE THIS?
AW MAN, THAT'S JUST TOO BAD! JUST WHEN I THOUGHT WE'D BE ABLE TO SEE SOME NAKED CHICKS... WELL, I GUESS THAT'S AS FAR AS WE CAN GO TODA—
KIYOSHI-DONO.
SU (SST)

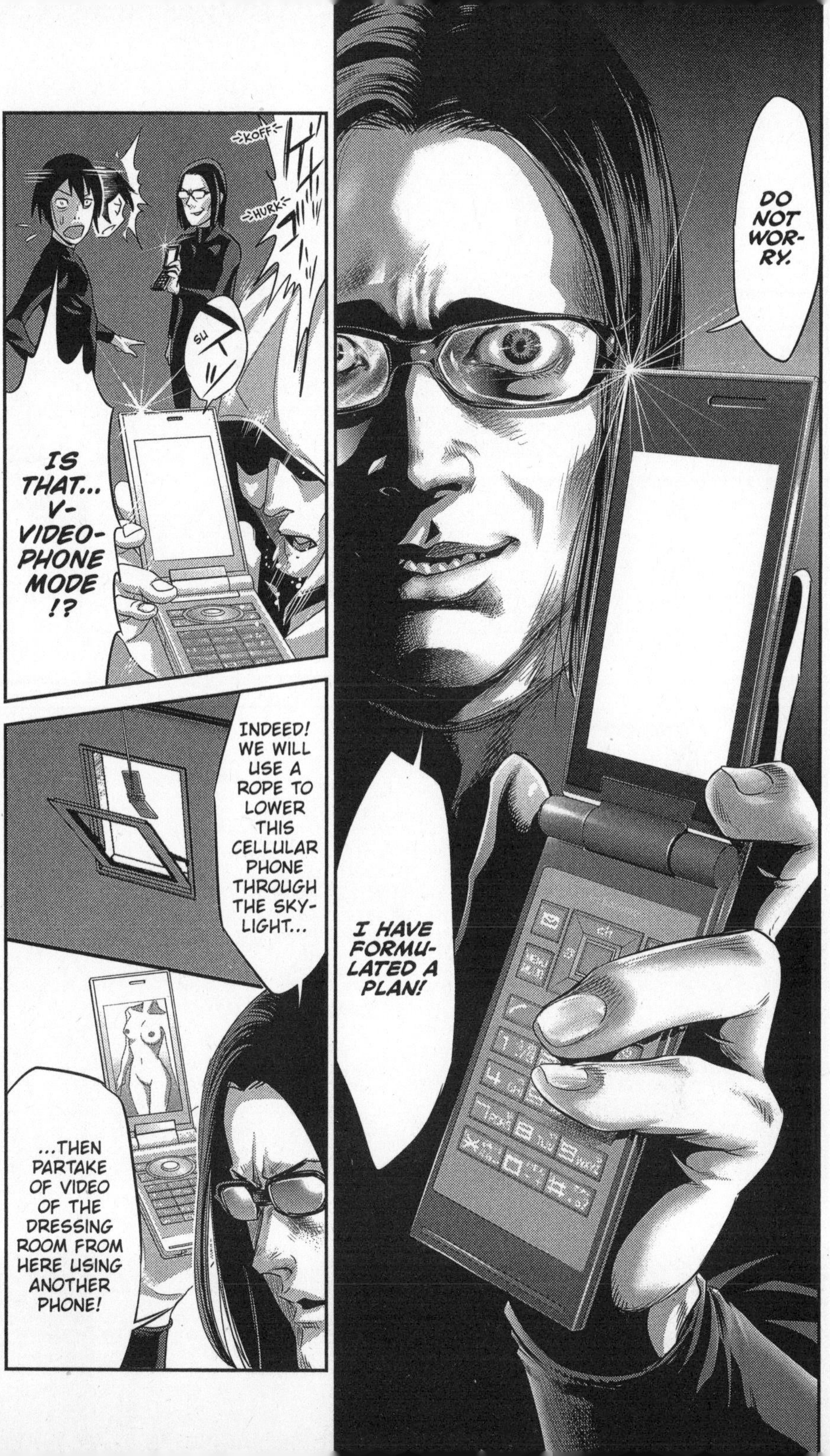
DO NOT WORRY.
I HAVE FORMULATED A PLAN!
KOFF
HURK
SU
IS THAT... V-VIDEOPHONE MODE!?
INDEED! WE WILL USE A ROPE TO LOWER THIS CELLULAR PHONE THROUGH THE SKYLIGHT...
...THEN PARTAKE OF VIDEO OF THE DRESSING ROOM FROM HERE USING ANOTHER PHONE!

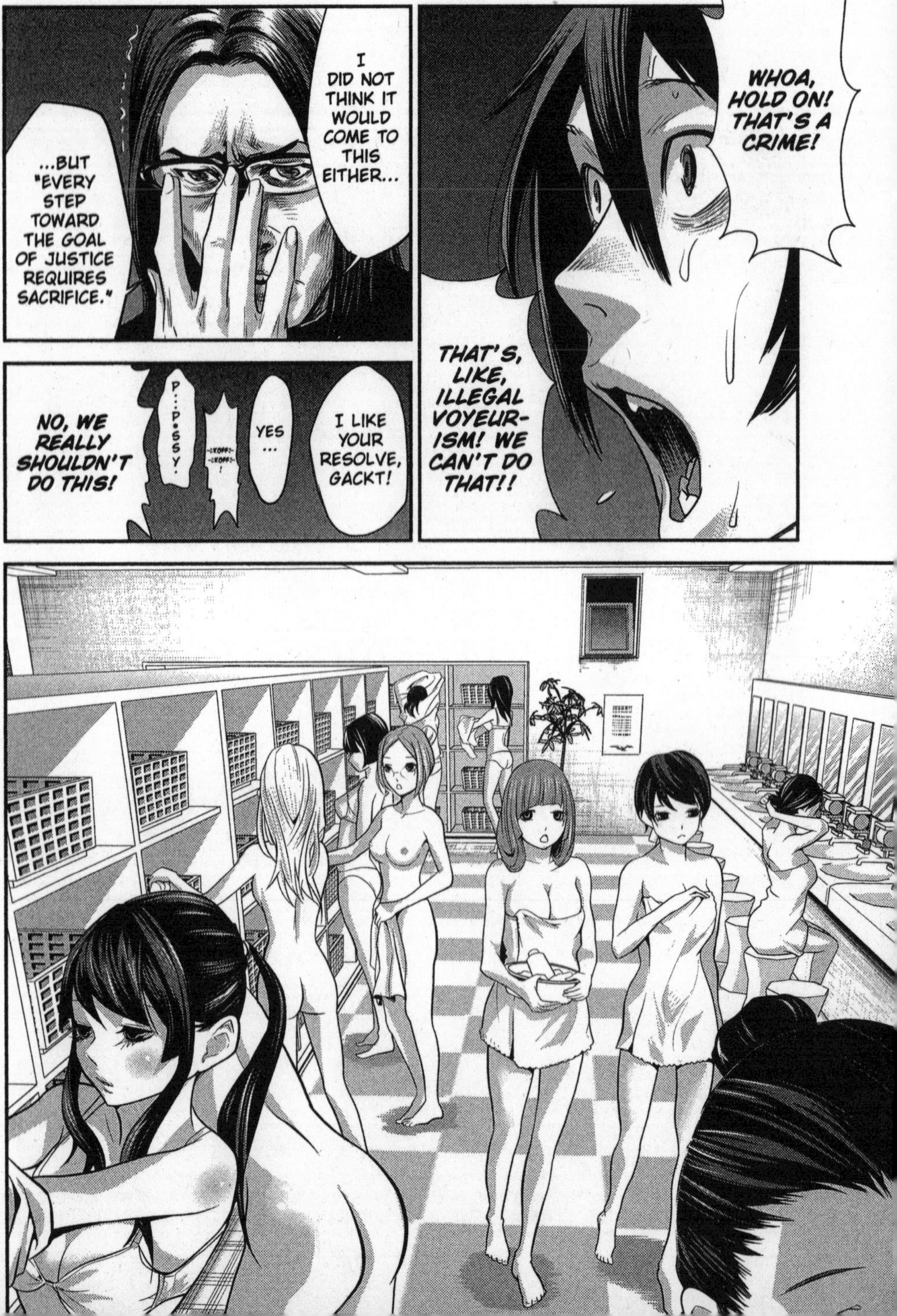
WHOA, HOLD ON! THAT'S A CRIME!
THAT'S, LIKE, ILLEGAL VOYEURISM! WE CAN'T DO THAT!!
I DID NOT THINK IT WOULD COME TO THIS EITHER...
...BUT "EVERY STEP TOWARD THE GOAL OF JUSTICE REQUIRES SACRIFICE."
I LIKE YOUR RESOLVE, GACKT!
YES...
-KOFF- -KOFF-!
P...P•SSY.
NO, WE REALLY SHOULDN'T DO THIS!

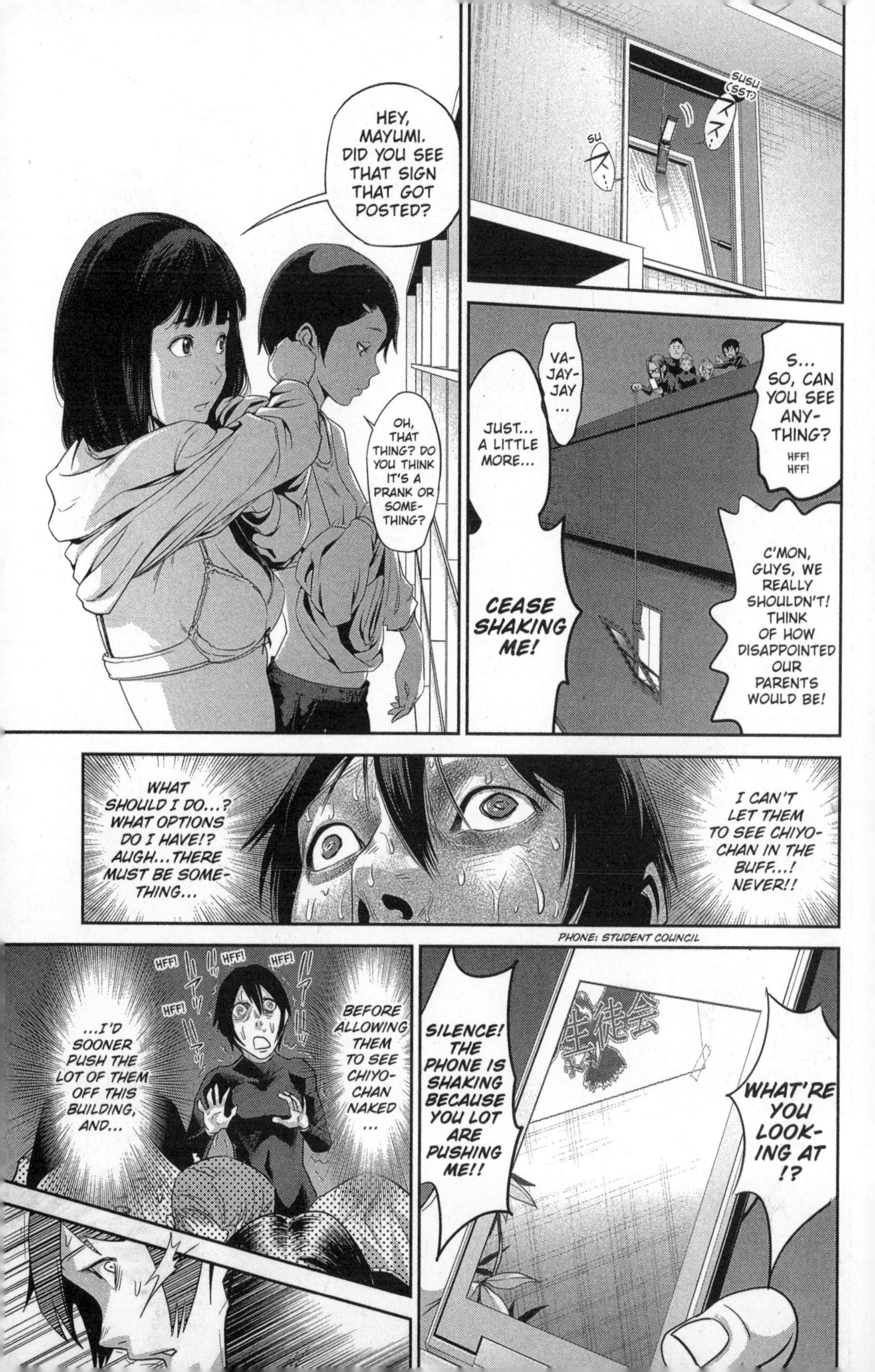
SUSU (SST)
SU
S... SO, CAN YOU SEE ANYTHING?
HFF! HFF!
VA-JAY-JAY...
JUST... A LITTLE MORE...
C'MON, GUYS, WE REALLY SHOULDN'T! THINK OF HOW DISAPPOINTED OUR PARENTS WOULD BE!
CEASE SHAKING ME!
HEY, MAYUMI. DID YOU SEE THAT SIGN THAT GOT POSTED?
OH, THAT THING? DO YOU THINK IT'S A PRANK OR SOMETHING?
I CAN'T LET THEM TO SEE CHIYO-CHAN IN THE BUFF...! NEVER!!
WHAT SHOULD I DO...? WHAT OPTIONS DO I HAVE!? AUGH...THERE MUST BE SOMETHING...
PHONE: STUDENT COUNCIL
生徒会
WHAT'RE YOU LOOKING AT!?
SILENCE! THE PHONE IS SHAKING BECAUSE YOU LOT ARE PUSHING ME!!
HFF! HFF! HFF! HFF!
BEFORE ALLOWING THEM TO SEE CHIYO-CHAN NAKED...
...I'D SOONER PUSH THE LOT OF THEM OFF THIS BUILDING, AND...

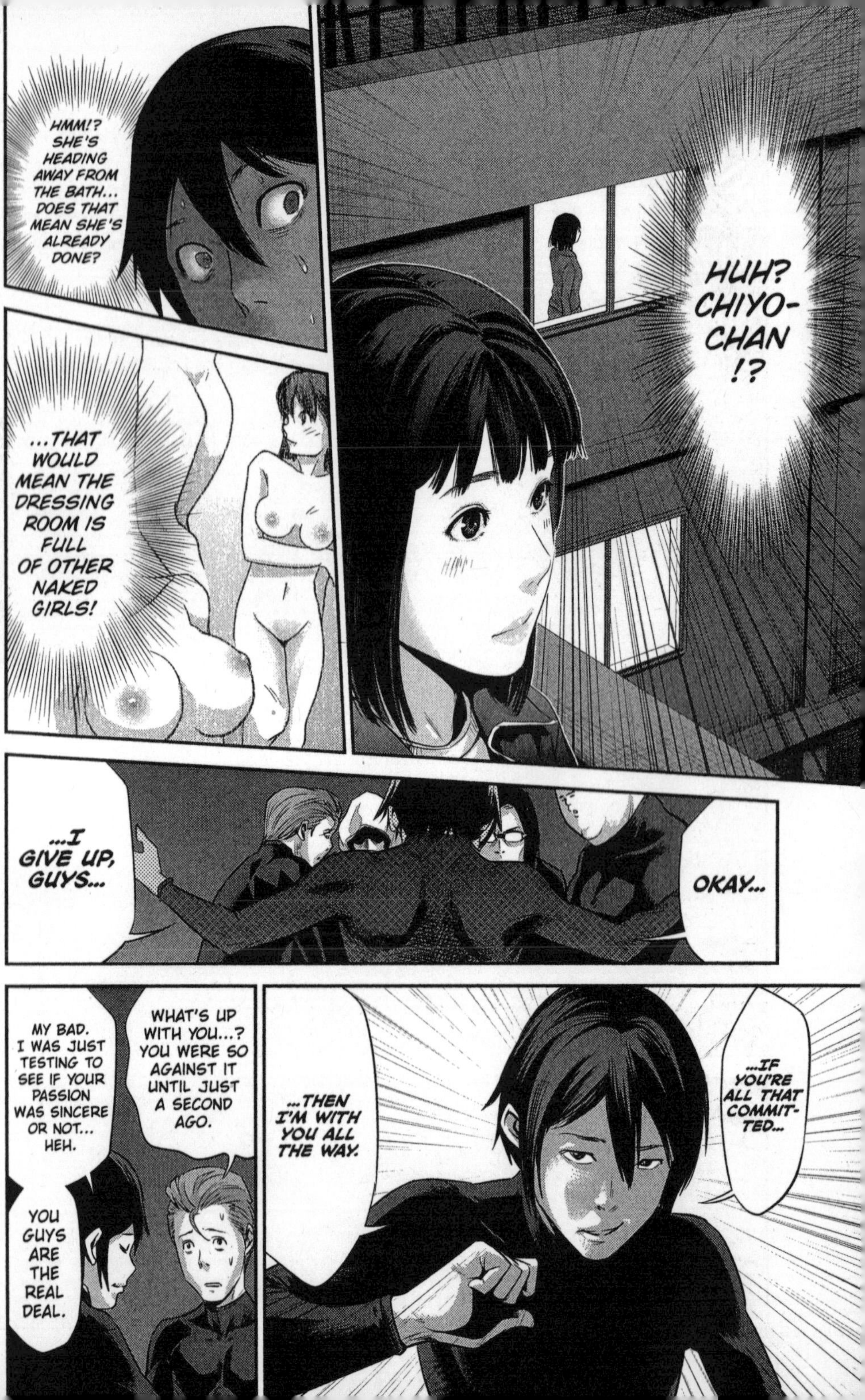
HUH? CHIYO-CHAN!?
HMM!? SHE'S HEADING AWAY FROM THE BATH... DOES THAT MEAN SHE'S ALREADY DONE?
...THAT WOULD MEAN THE DRESSING ROOM IS FULL OF OTHER NAKED GIRLS!
OKAY...
...I GIVE UP, GUYS...
...IF YOU'RE ALL THAT COMMIT-TED...
...THEN I'M WITH YOU ALL THE WAY.
WHAT'S UP WITH YOU...? YOU WERE SO AGAINST IT UNTIL JUST A SECOND AGO.
MY BAD. I WAS JUST TESTING TO SEE IF YOUR PASSION WAS SINCERE OR NOT... HEH.
YOU GUYS ARE THE REAL DEAL.

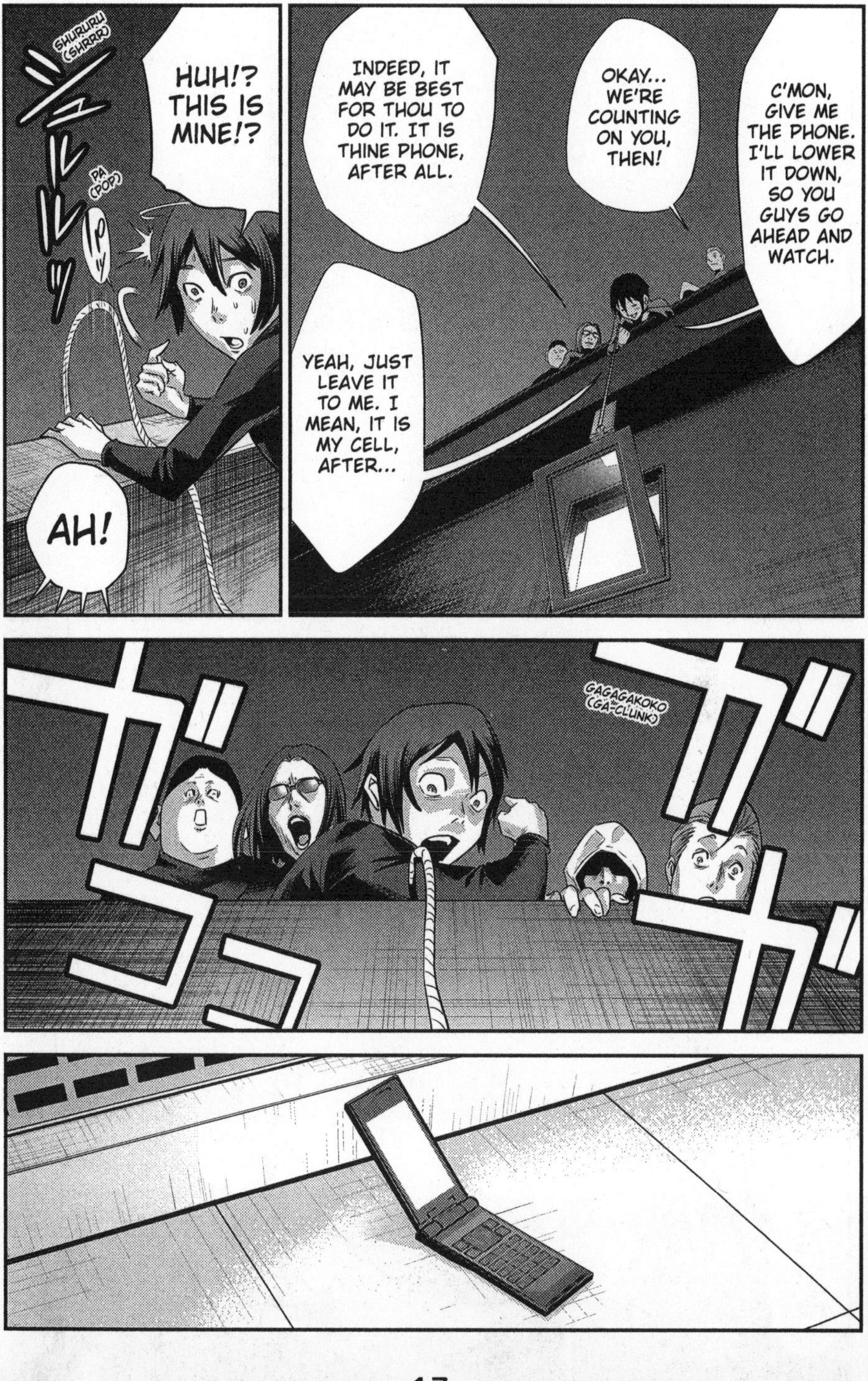
C'MON, GIVE ME THE PHONE. I'LL LOWER IT DOWN, SO YOU GUYS GO AHEAD AND WATCH.
OKAY... WE'RE COUNTING ON YOU, THEN!
INDEED, IT MAY BE BEST FOR THOU TO DO IT. IT IS THINE PHONE, AFTER ALL.
YEAH, JUST LEAVE IT TO ME. I MEAN, IT IS MY CELL, AFTER...
HUH!? THIS IS MINE!?
SHURURU (SHRRR)
PA (POP)
AH!
GAGAGAKOKO (GA-CLUNK)

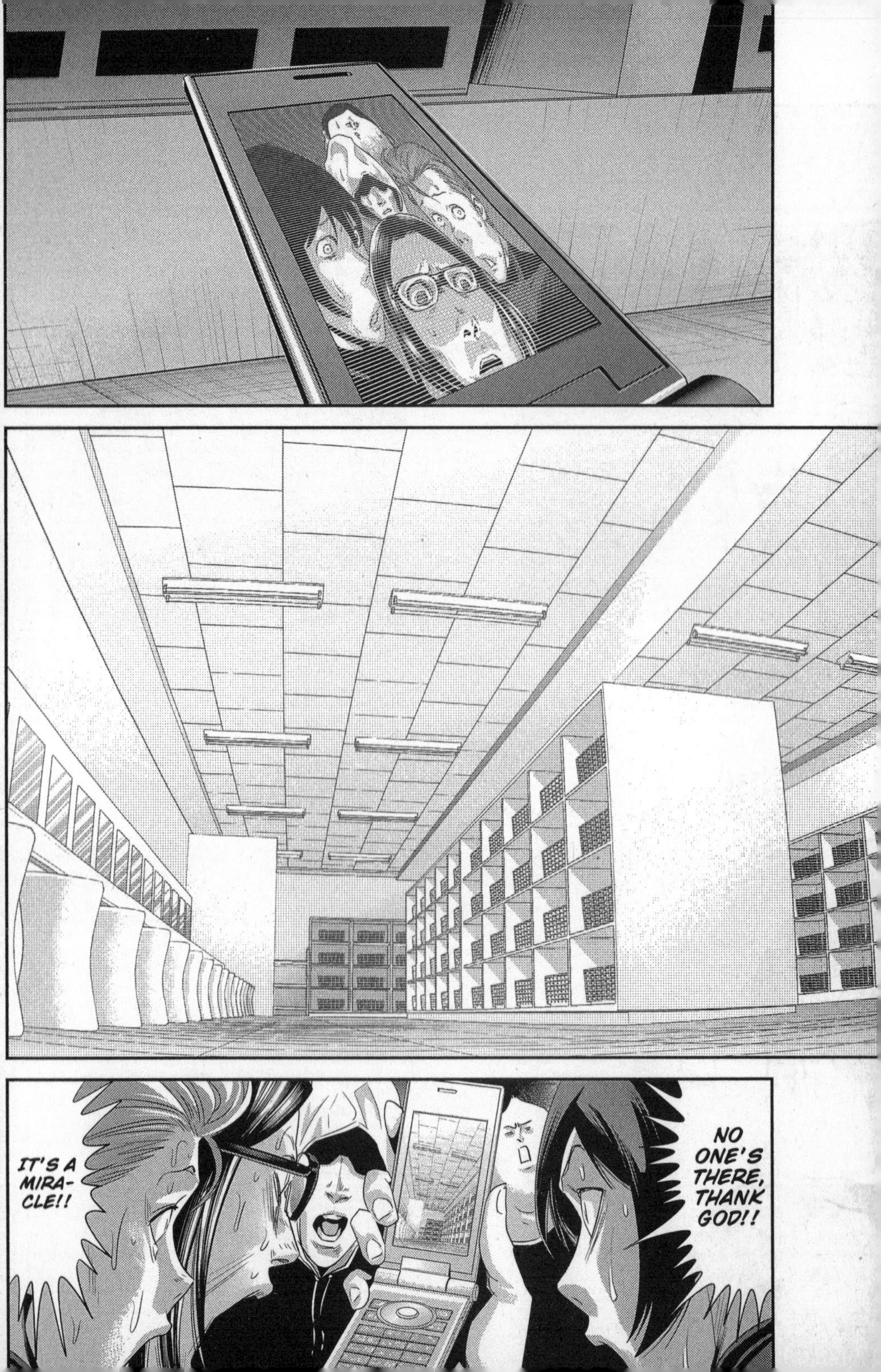
NO ONE'S THERE, THANK GOD!!
IT'S A MIRA-CLE!!

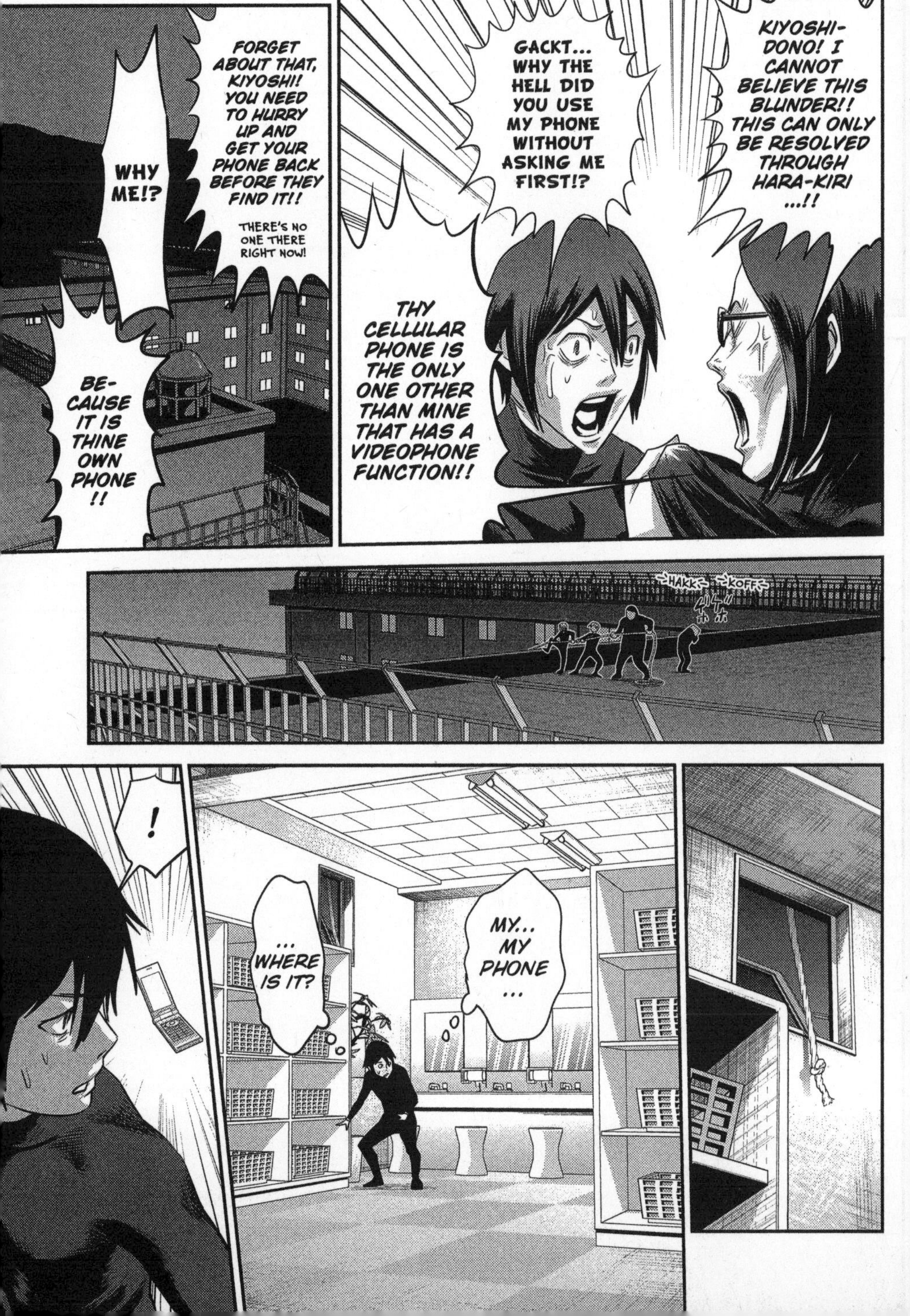
KIYOSHI-DONO! I CANNOT BELIEVE THIS BLUNDER!! THIS CAN ONLY BE RESOLVED THROUGH HARA-KIRI ...!!
GACKT... WHY THE HELL DID YOU USE MY PHONE WITHOUT ASKING ME FIRST!?
THY CELLULAR PHONE IS THE ONLY ONE OTHER THAN MINE THAT HAS A VIDEOPHONE FUNCTION!!
FORGET ABOUT THAT, KIYOSHI! YOU NEED TO HURRY UP AND GET YOUR PHONE BACK BEFORE THEY FIND IT!!
THERE'S NO ONE THERE RIGHT NOW!
WHY ME!?
BE-CAUSE IT IS THINE OWN PHONE !!
HAKK
KOFF
MY... MY PHONE ...
... WHERE IS IT?
!

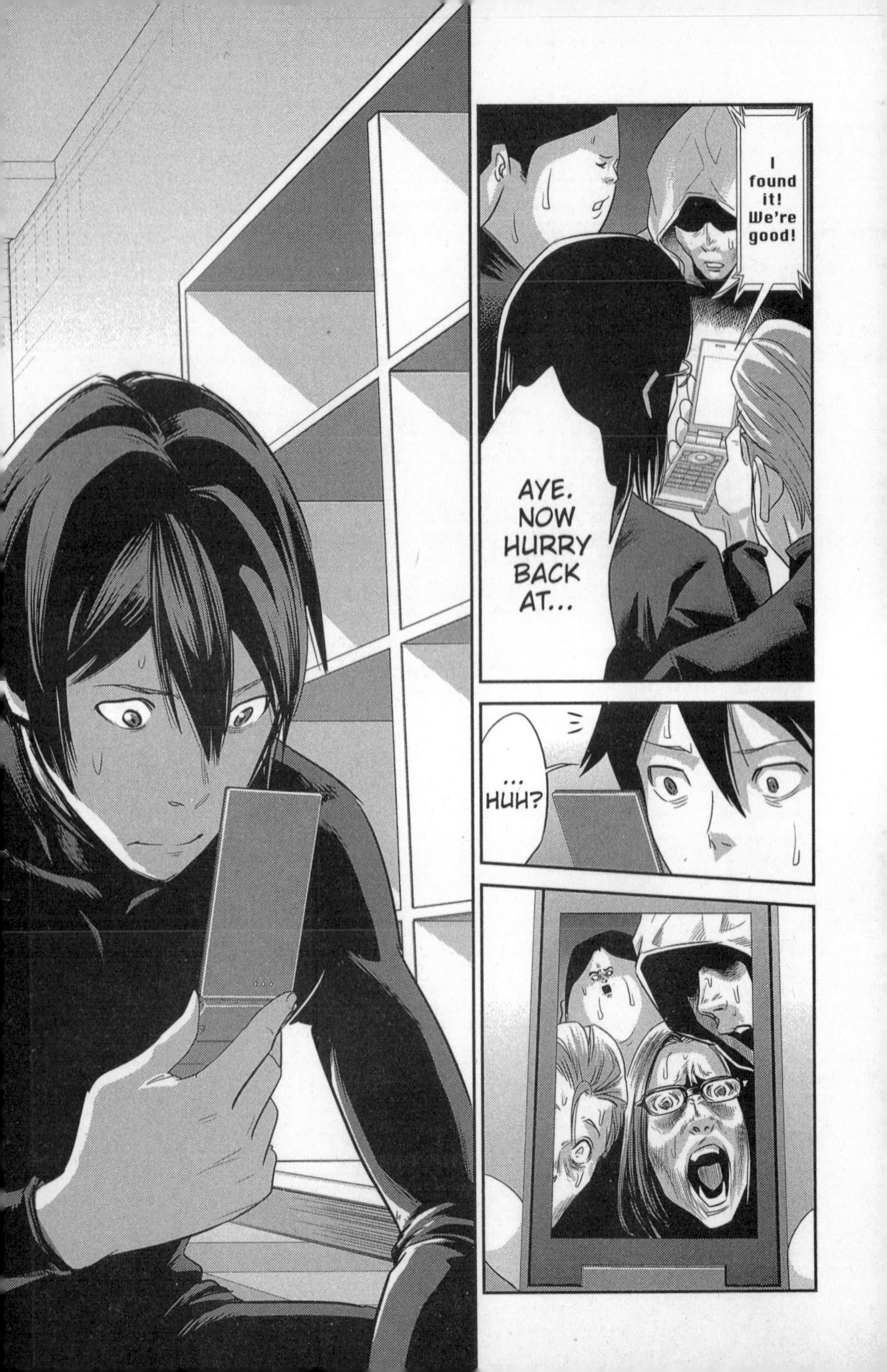
I found it! We're good!
AYE. NOW HURRY BACK AT...
... HUH?

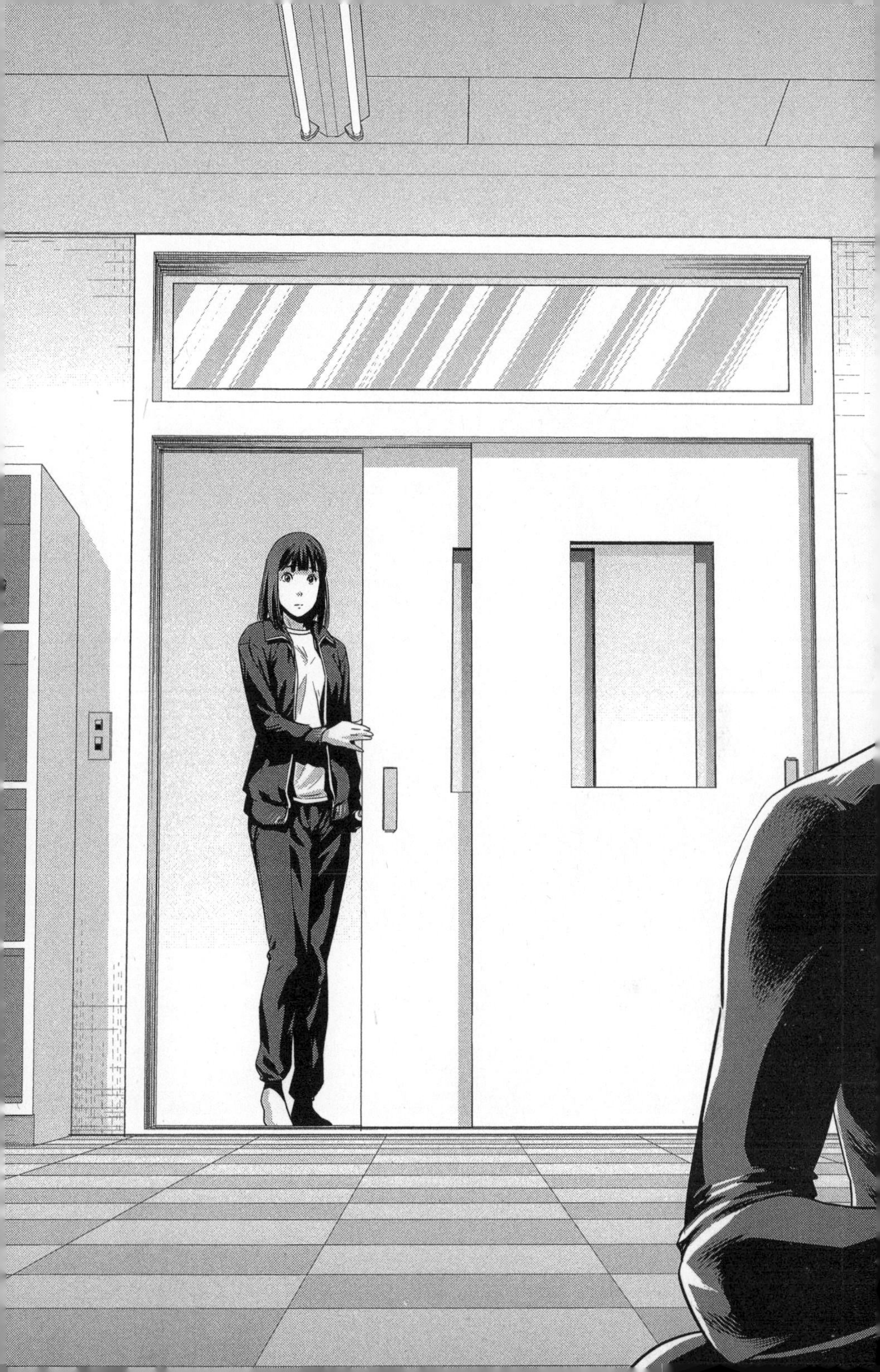

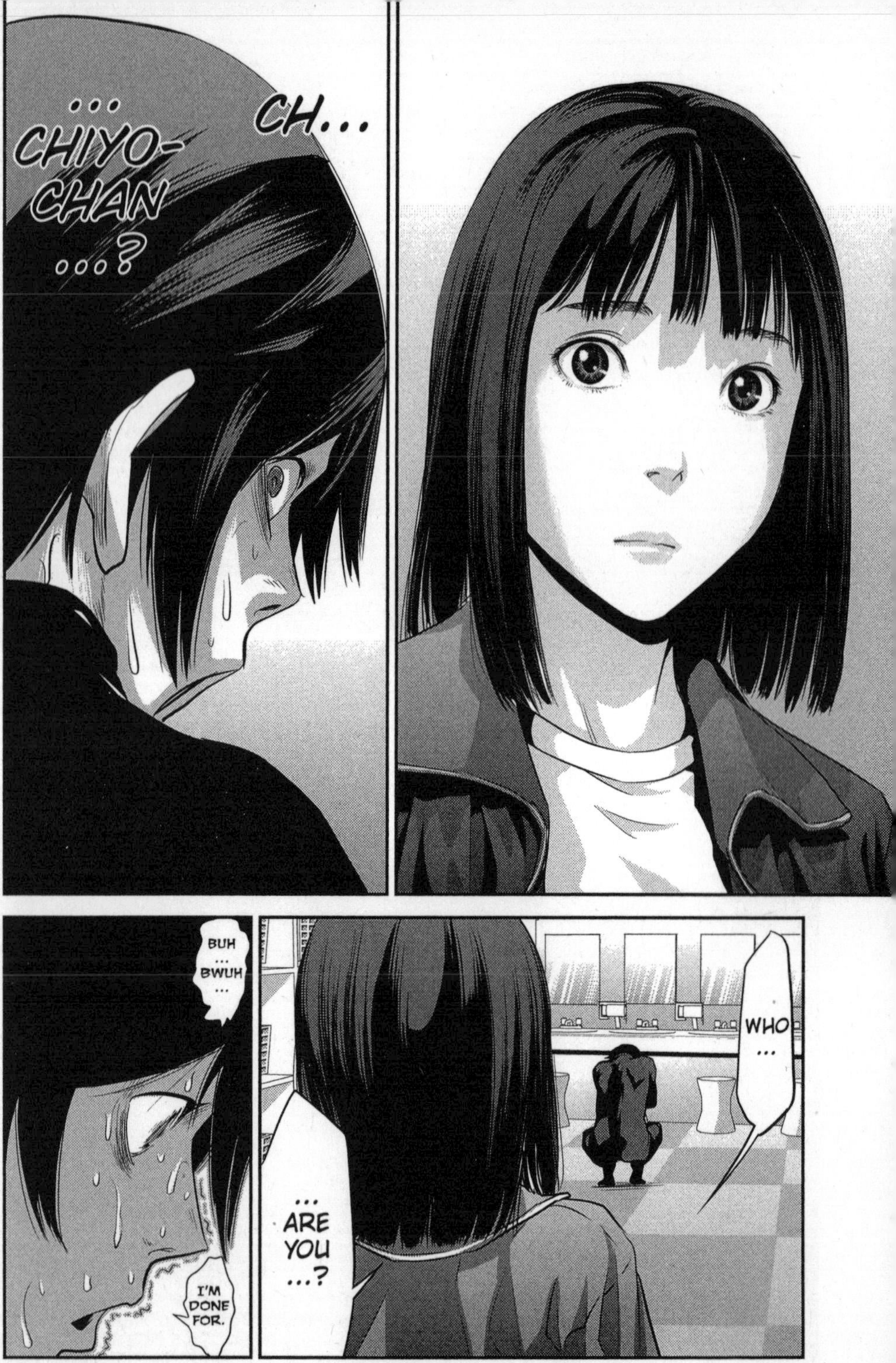
CH...
... CHIYO-CHAN ...?
WHO ...
... ARE YOU ...?
BUH ... BWUH ...
I'M DONE FOR.

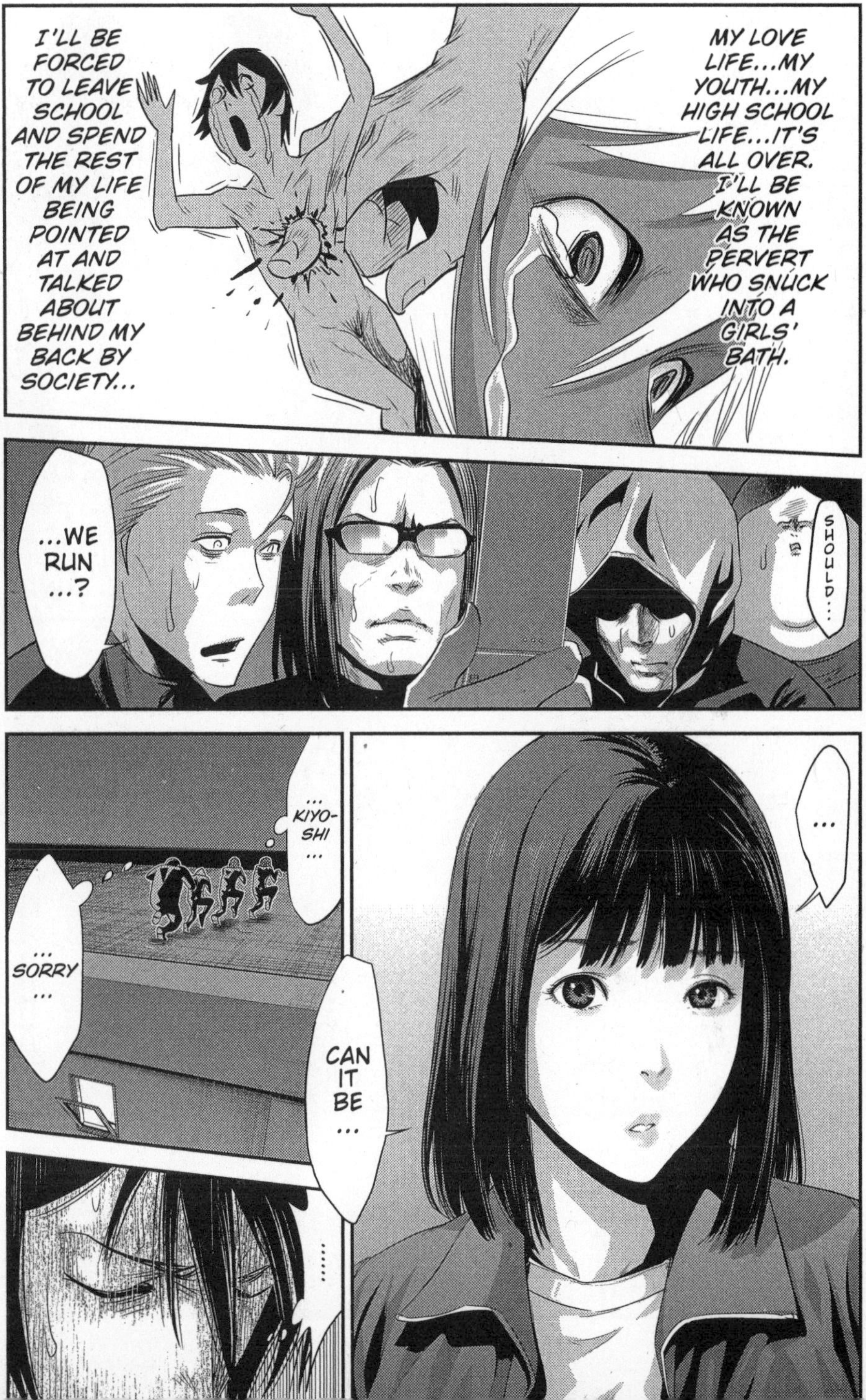
MY LOVE LIFE...MY YOUTH...MY HIGH SCHOOL LIFE...IT'S ALL OVER. I'LL BE KNOWN AS THE PERVERT WHO SNUCK INTO A GIRLS' BATH.
I'LL BE FORCED TO LEAVE SCHOOL AND SPEND THE REST OF MY LIFE BEING POINTED AT AND TALKED ABOUT BEHIND MY BACK BY SOCIETY...
SHOULD...
...WE RUN...?
...
CAN IT BE...
...KIYOSHI...
...SORRY...
......

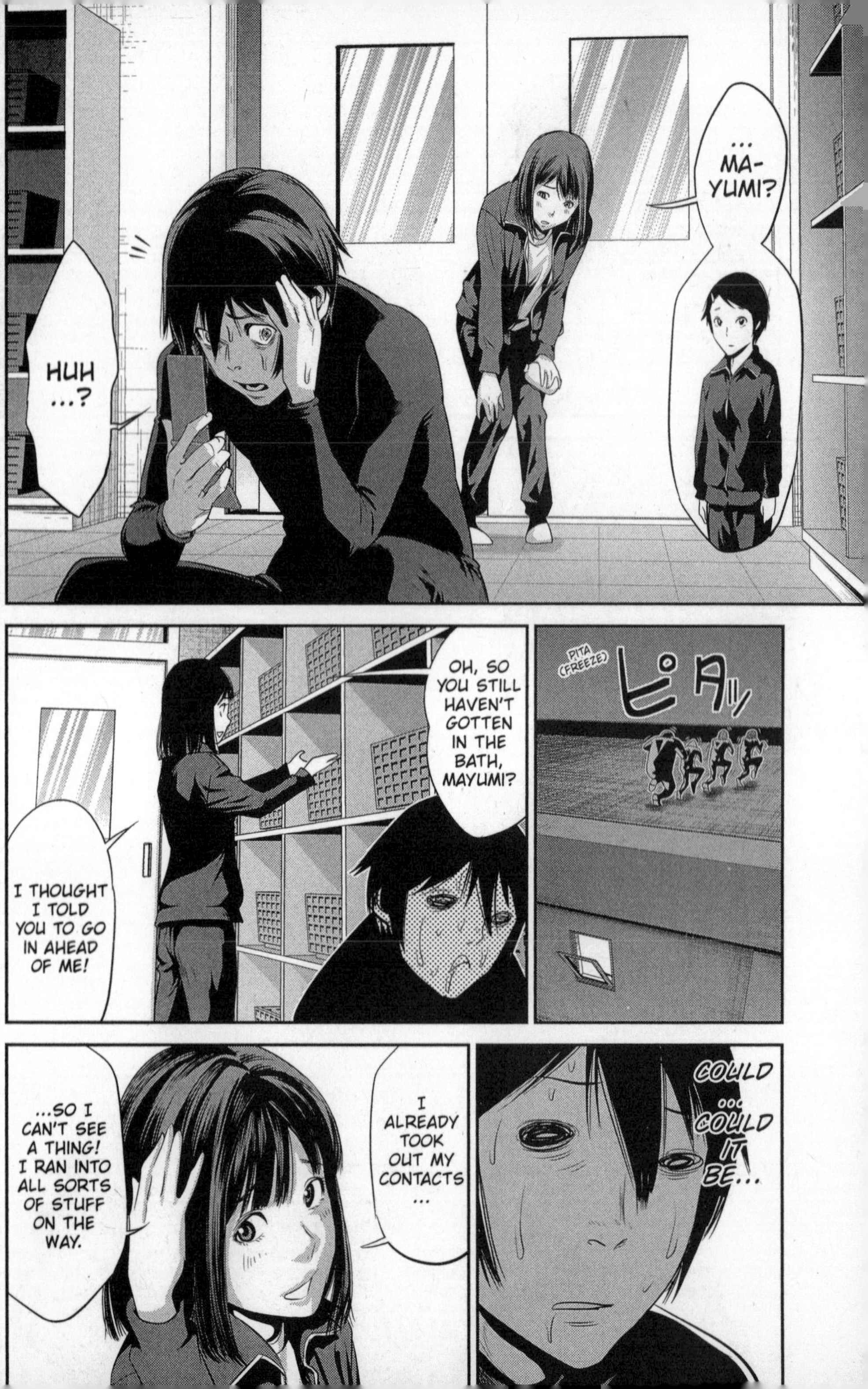
... MA-YUMI?
HUH ...?
PITA (FREEZE)
OH, SO YOU STILL HAVEN'T GOTTEN IN THE BATH, MAYUMI?
I THOUGHT I TOLD YOU TO GO IN AHEAD OF ME!
COULD ... COULD IT BE...
I ALREADY TOOK OUT MY CONTACTS ...
...SO I CAN'T SEE A THING! I RAN INTO ALL SORTS OF STUFF ON THE WAY.

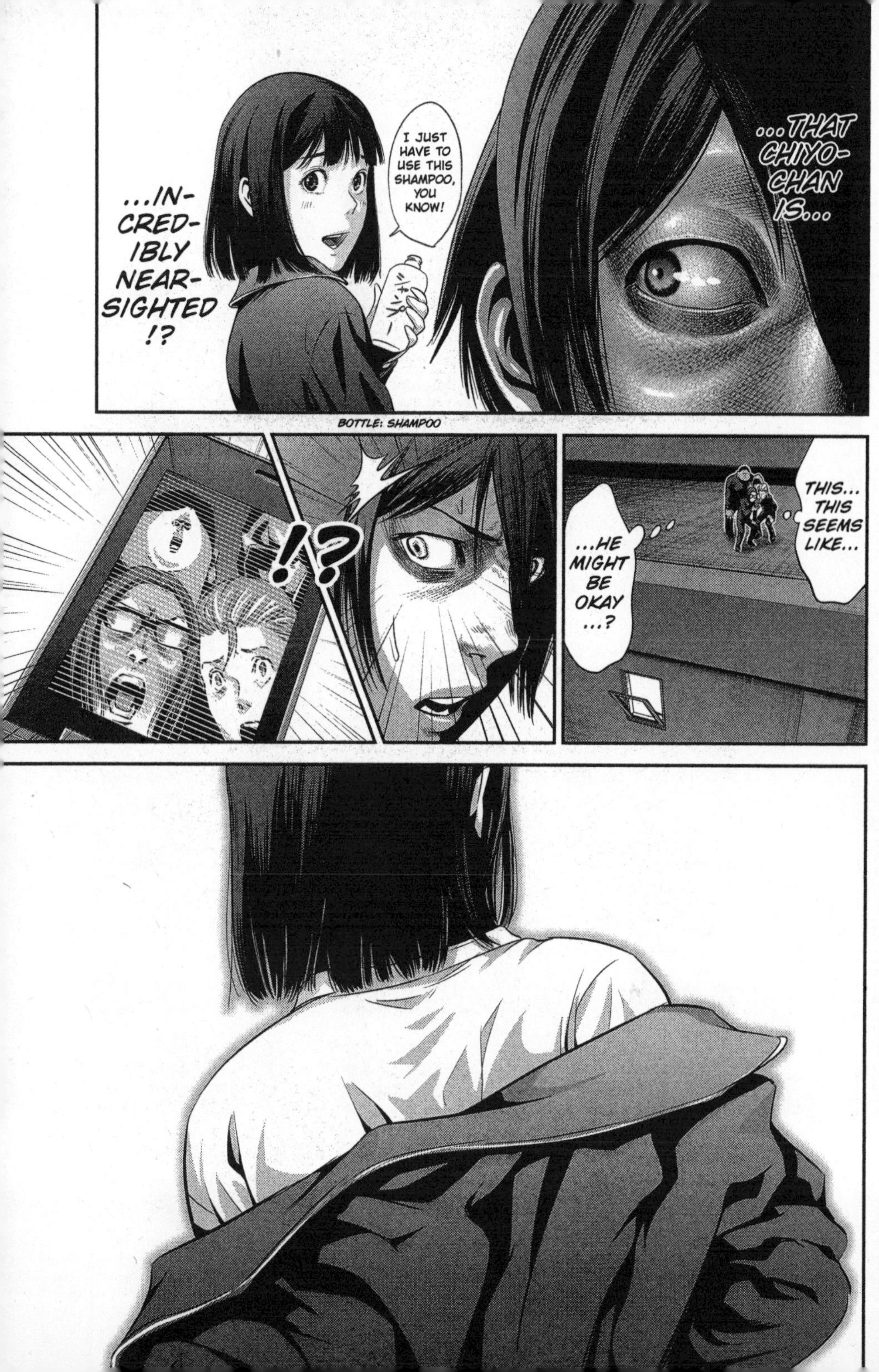
...THAT CHIYO-CHAN IS...
I JUST HAVE TO USE THIS SHAMPOO, YOU KNOW!
...IN-CRED-IBLY NEAR-SIGHTED !?
BOTTLE: SHAMPOO
THIS... THIS SEEMS LIKE...
...HE MIGHT BE OKAY ...?
!?

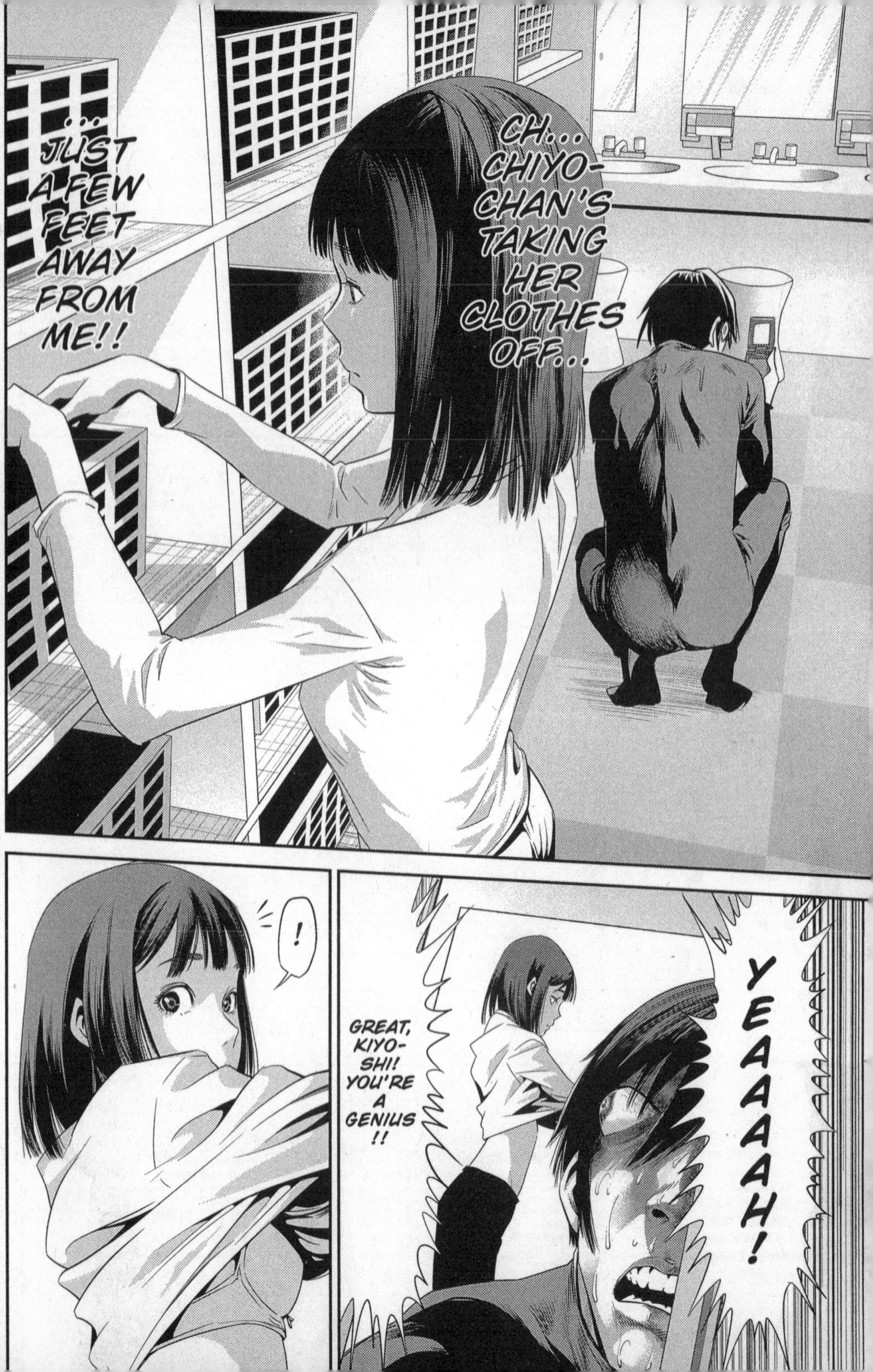
CH... CHIYO-CHAN'S TAKING HER CLOTHES OFF...
...JUST A FEW FEET AWAY FROM ME!!
YEAAAAAH!
GREAT, KIYOSHI! YOU'RE A GENIUS!!
!

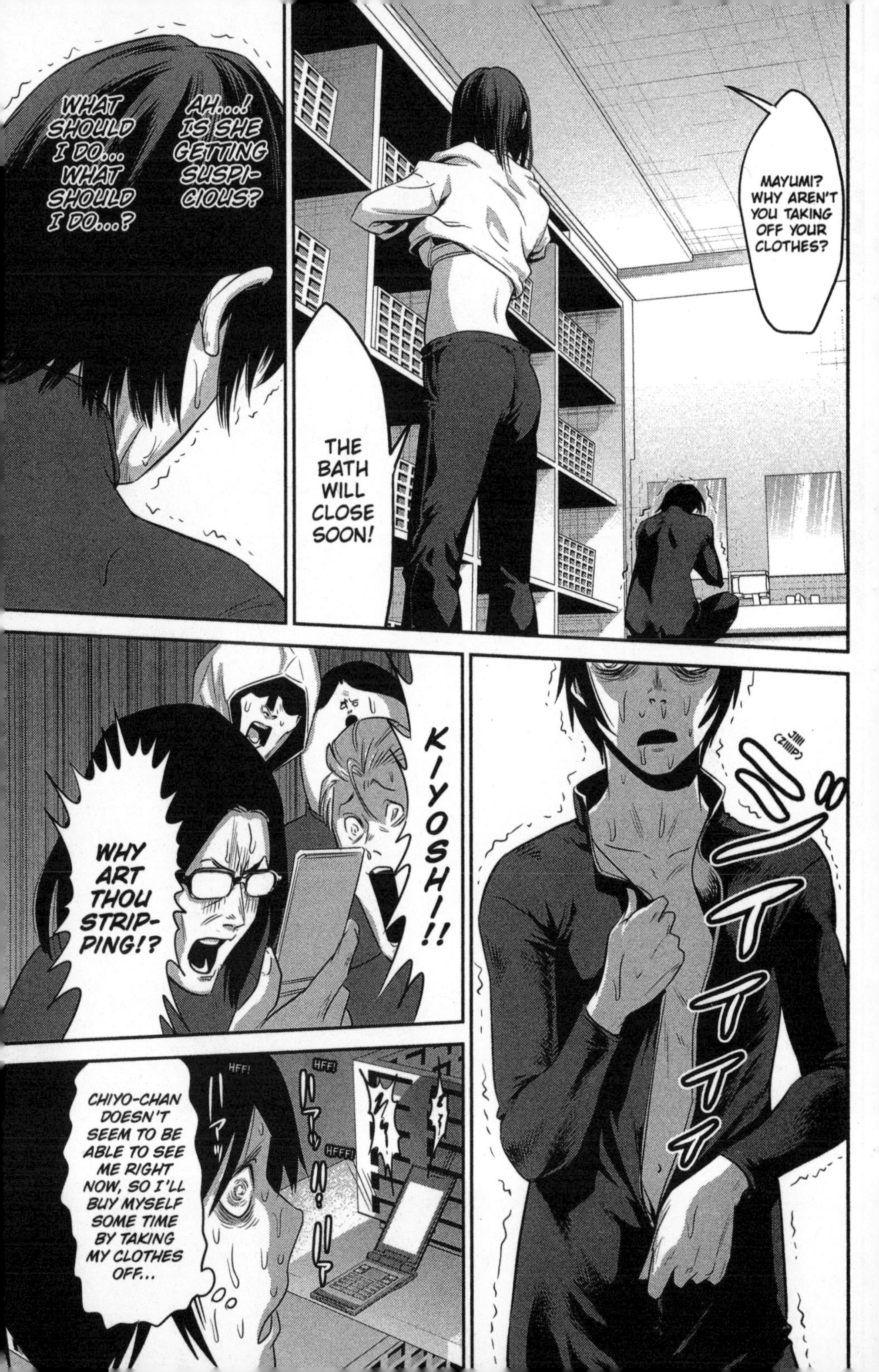
MAYUMI? WHY AREN'T YOU TAKING OFF YOUR CLOTHES?
THE BATH WILL CLOSE SOON!
AH...! IS SHE GETTING SUSPICIOUS?
WHAT SHOULD I DO... WHAT SHOULD I DO...?
JIII (ZIIIP)
KIYOSHI!!
WHY ART THOU STRIPPING!?
HFF!
HFF!
HFFF!
CHIYO-CHAN DOESN'T SEEM TO BE ABLE TO SEE ME RIGHT NOW, SO I'LL BUY MYSELF SOME TIME BY TAKING MY CLOTHES OFF...

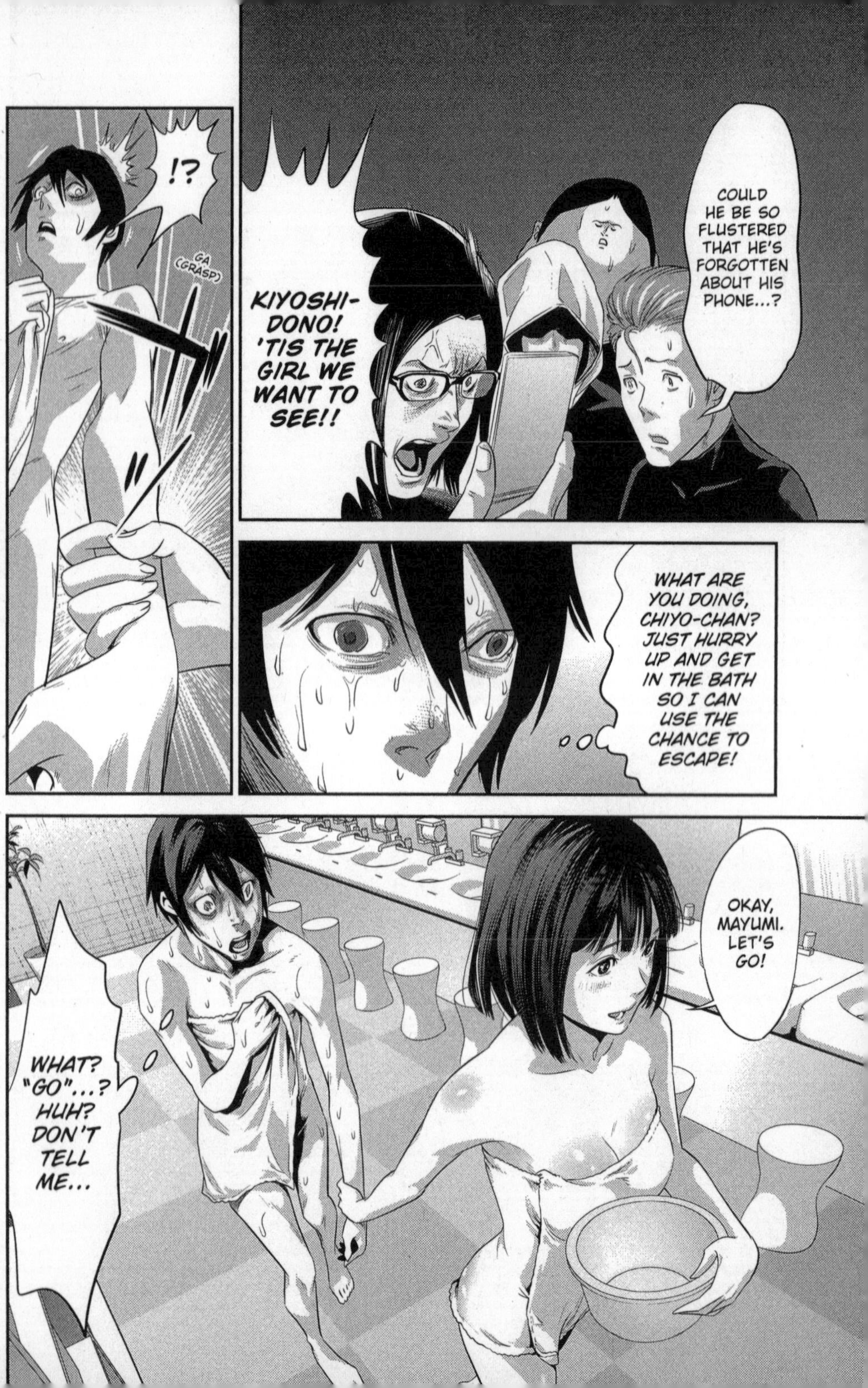
COULD HE BE SO FLUSTERED THAT HE'S FORGOTTEN ABOUT HIS PHONE...?
KIYOSHI-DONO! 'TIS THE GIRL WE WANT TO SEE!!
!?
GA (GRASP)
WHAT ARE YOU DOING, CHIYO-CHAN? JUST HURRY UP AND GET IN THE BATH SO I CAN USE THE CHANCE TO ESCAPE!
OKAY, MAYUMI. LET'S GO!
WHAT? "GO"...? HUH? DON'T TELL ME...

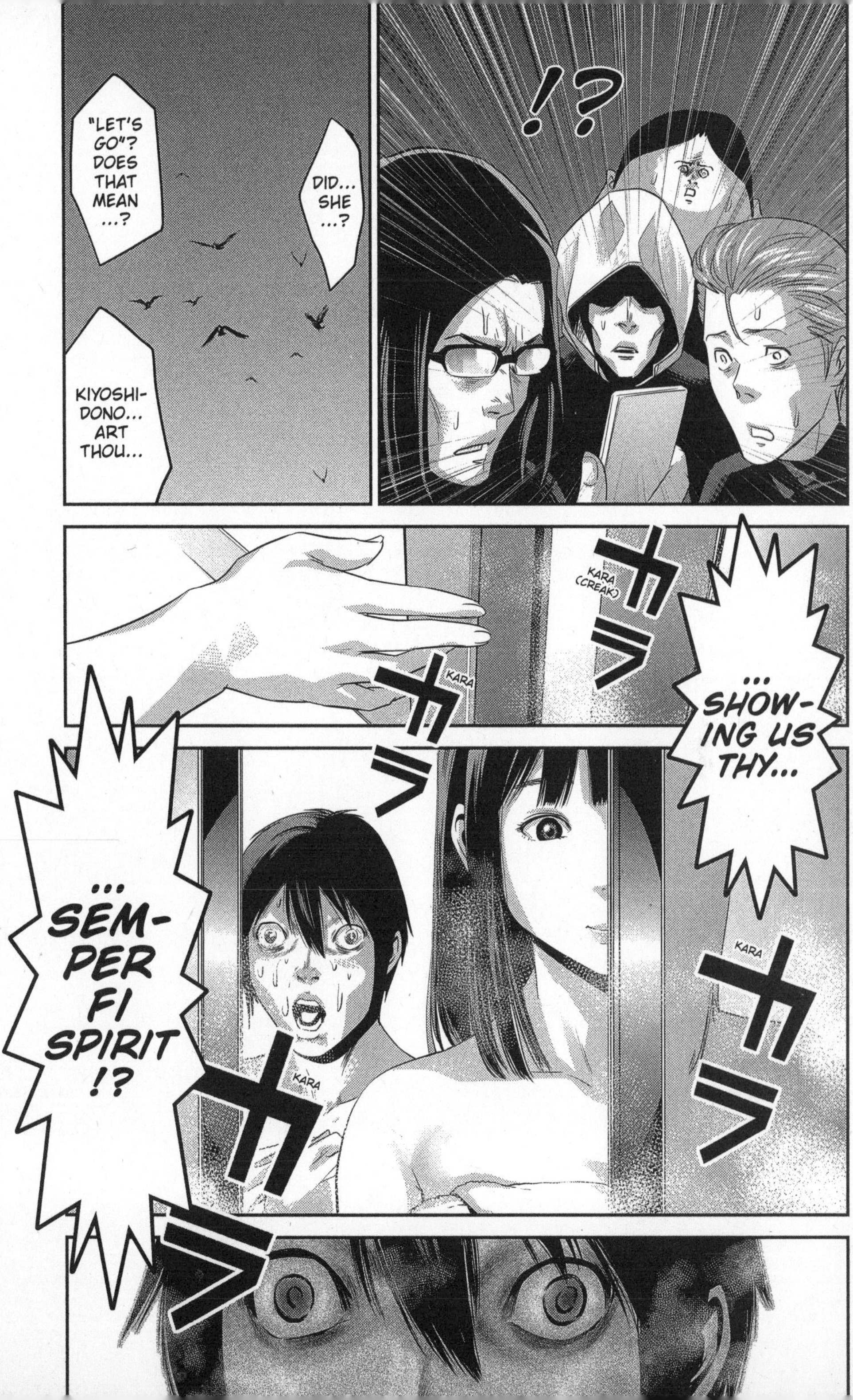
!?
DID... SHE ...?
"LET'S GO"? DOES THAT MEAN ...?
KIYOSHI-DONO... ART THOU...
KARA (CREAK)
KARA
... SHOWING US THY...
KARA
KARA
... SEMPER FI SPIRIT !?

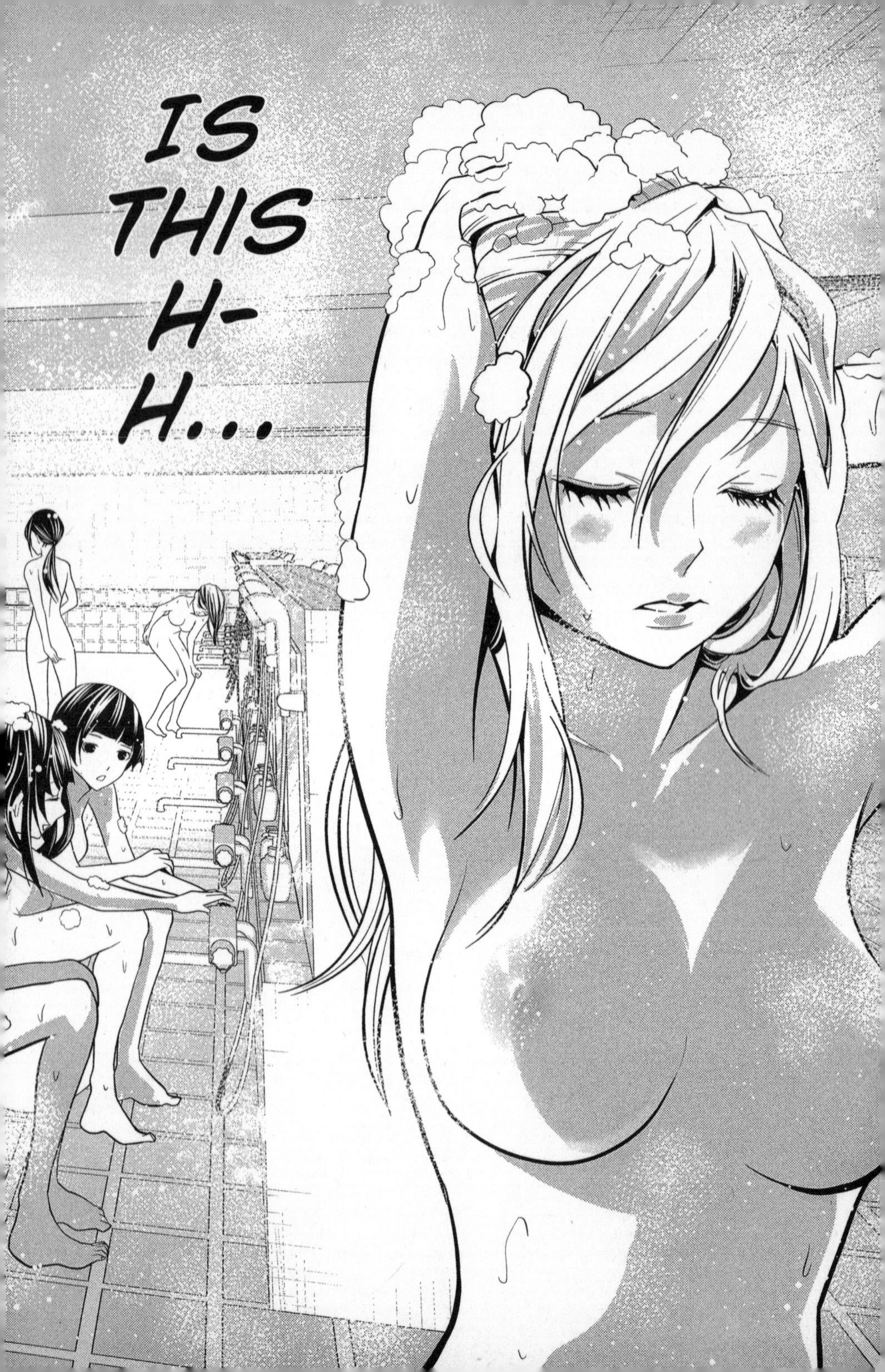
IS THIS H-H...

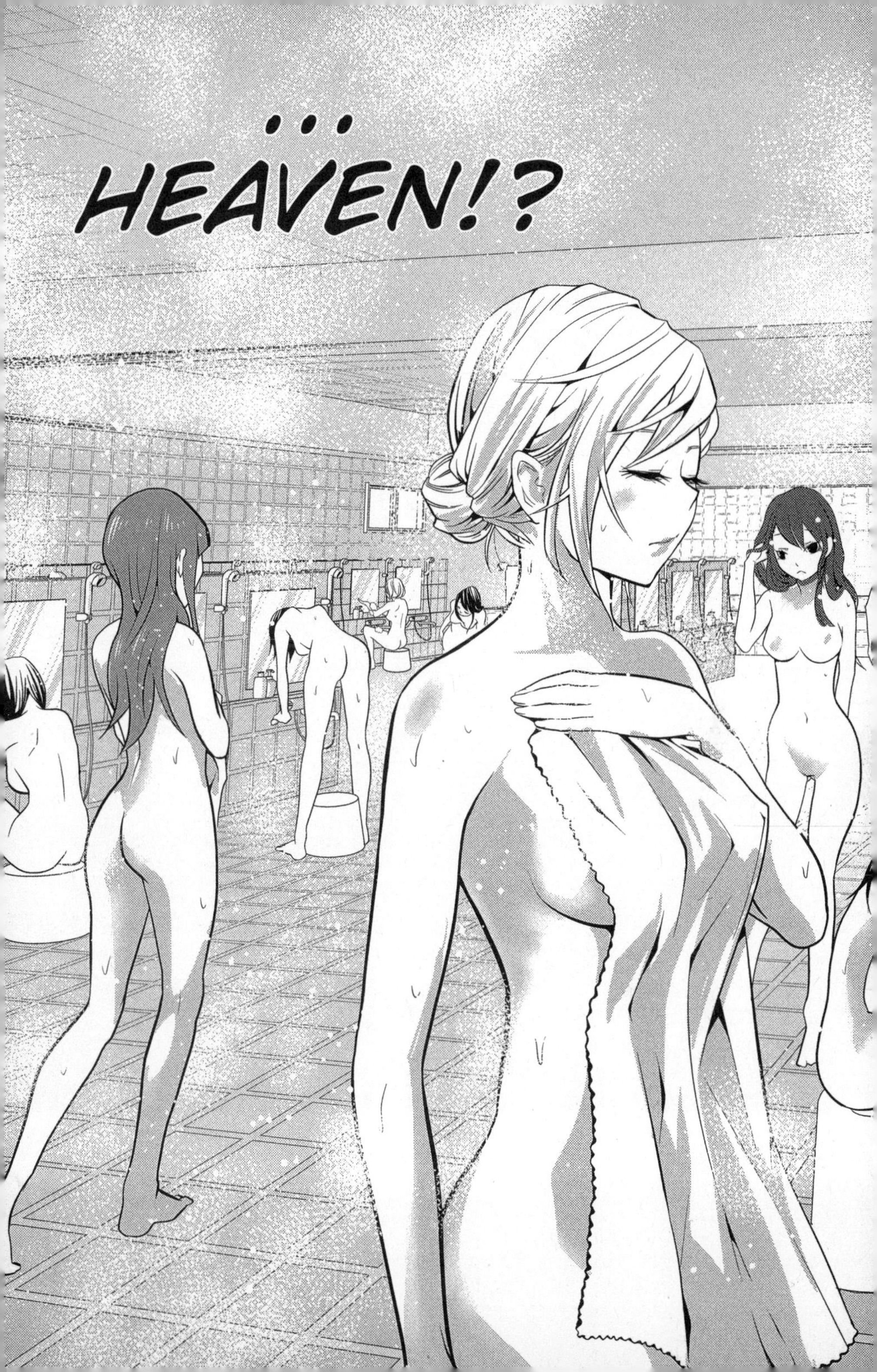
...
HEAVEN!?

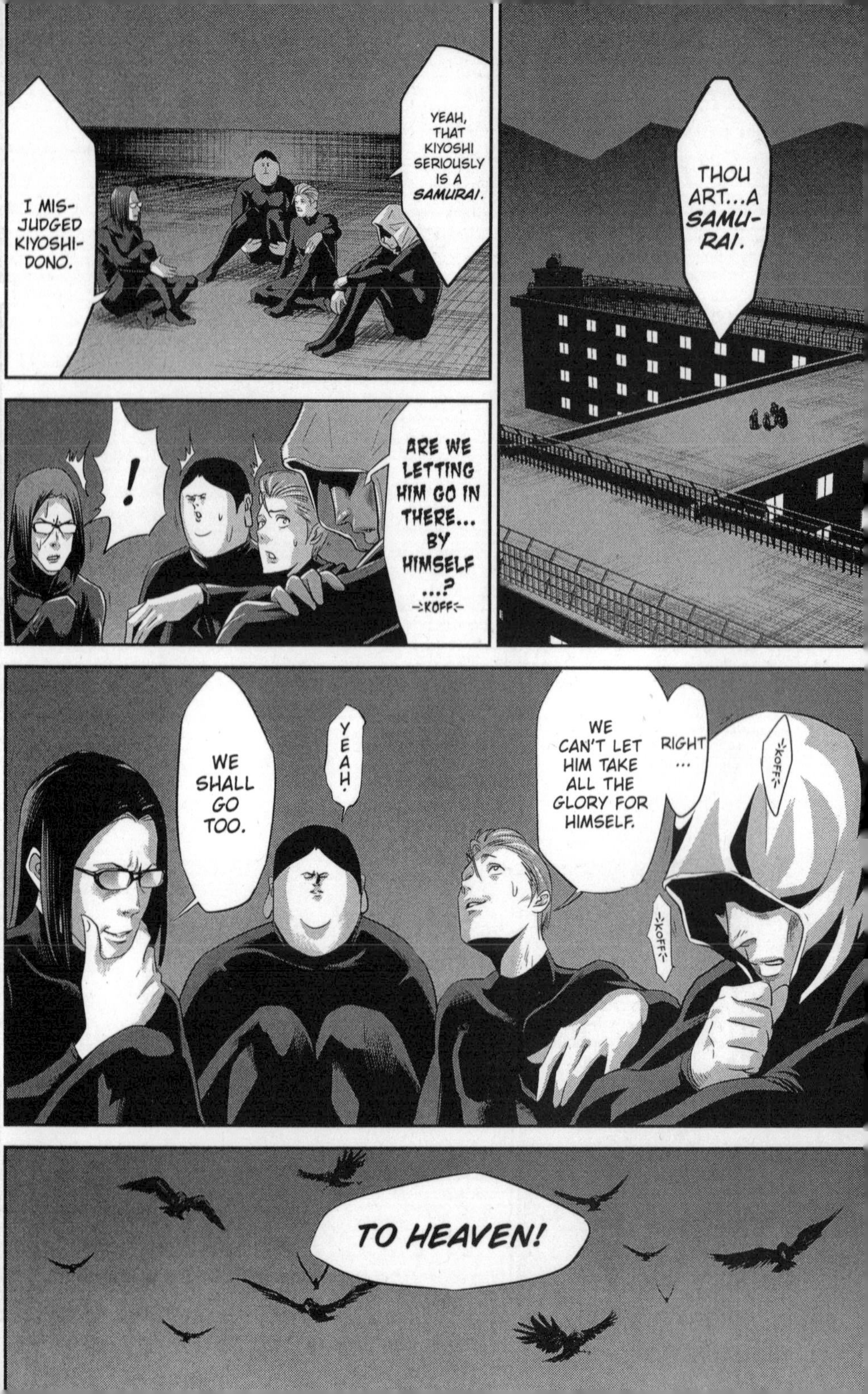
THOU ART...A SAMURAI.
YEAH, THAT KIYOSHI SERIOUSLY IS A SAMURAI.
I MISJUDGED KIYOSHI-DONO.
ARE WE LETTING HIM GO IN THERE... BY HIMSELF ...?
KOFF
!
KOFF
KOFF
RIGHT ...
WE CAN'T LET HIM TAKE ALL THE GLORY FOR HIMSELF.
YEAH.
WE SHALL GO TOO.
TO HEAVEN!

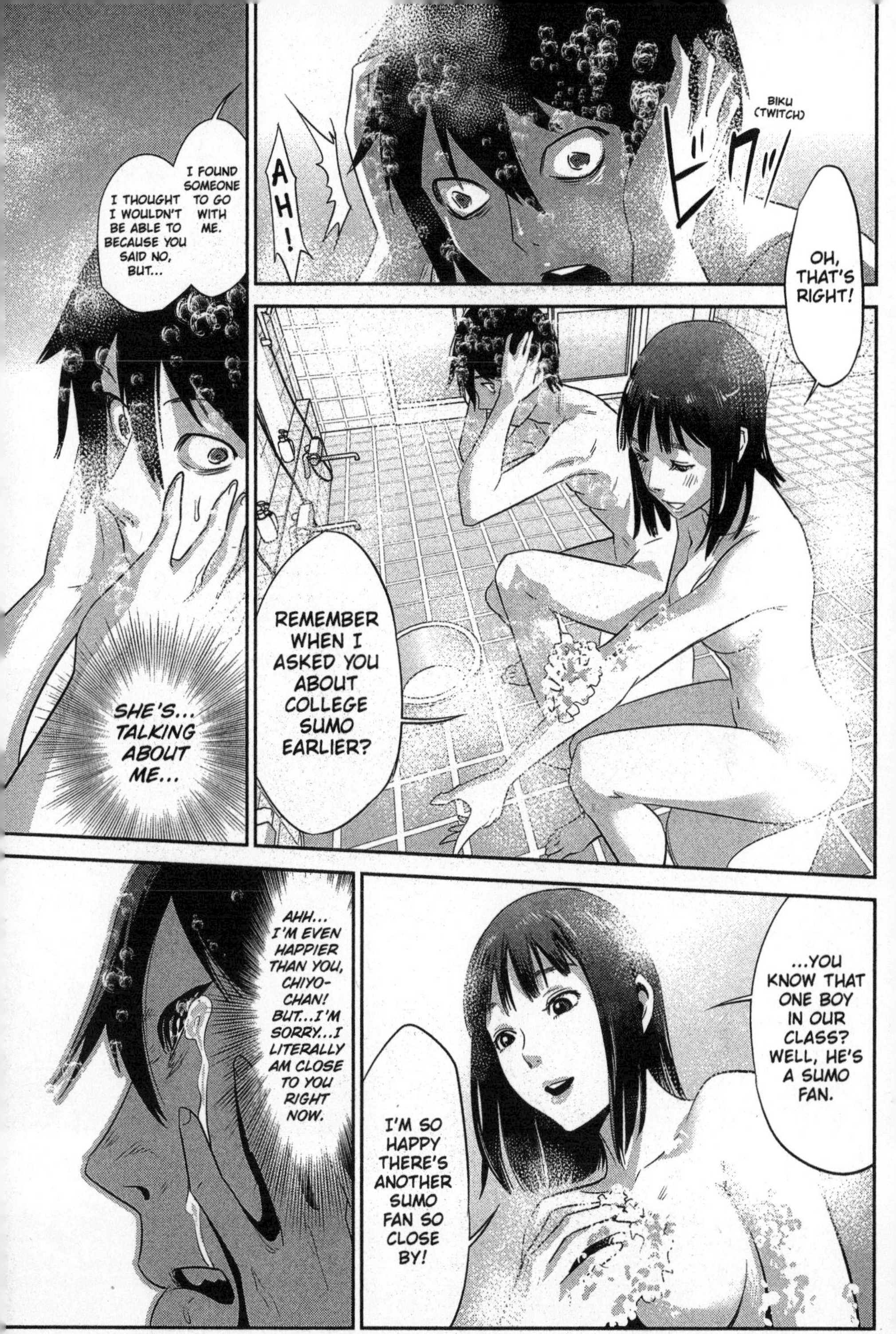
BIKU (TWITCH)
OH, THAT'S RIGHT!
AH!
I FOUND SOMEONE TO GO WITH ME.
I THOUGHT I WOULDN'T BE ABLE TO BECAUSE YOU SAID NO, BUT...
REMEMBER WHEN I ASKED YOU ABOUT COLLEGE SUMO EARLIER?
SHE'S... TALKING ABOUT ME...
...YOU KNOW THAT ONE BOY IN OUR CLASS? WELL, HE'S A SUMO FAN.
I'M SO HAPPY THERE'S ANOTHER SUMO FAN SO CLOSE BY!
AHH... I'M EVEN HAPPIER THAN YOU, CHIYO-CHAN! BUT...I'M SORRY...I LITERALLY AM CLOSE TO YOU RIGHT NOW.

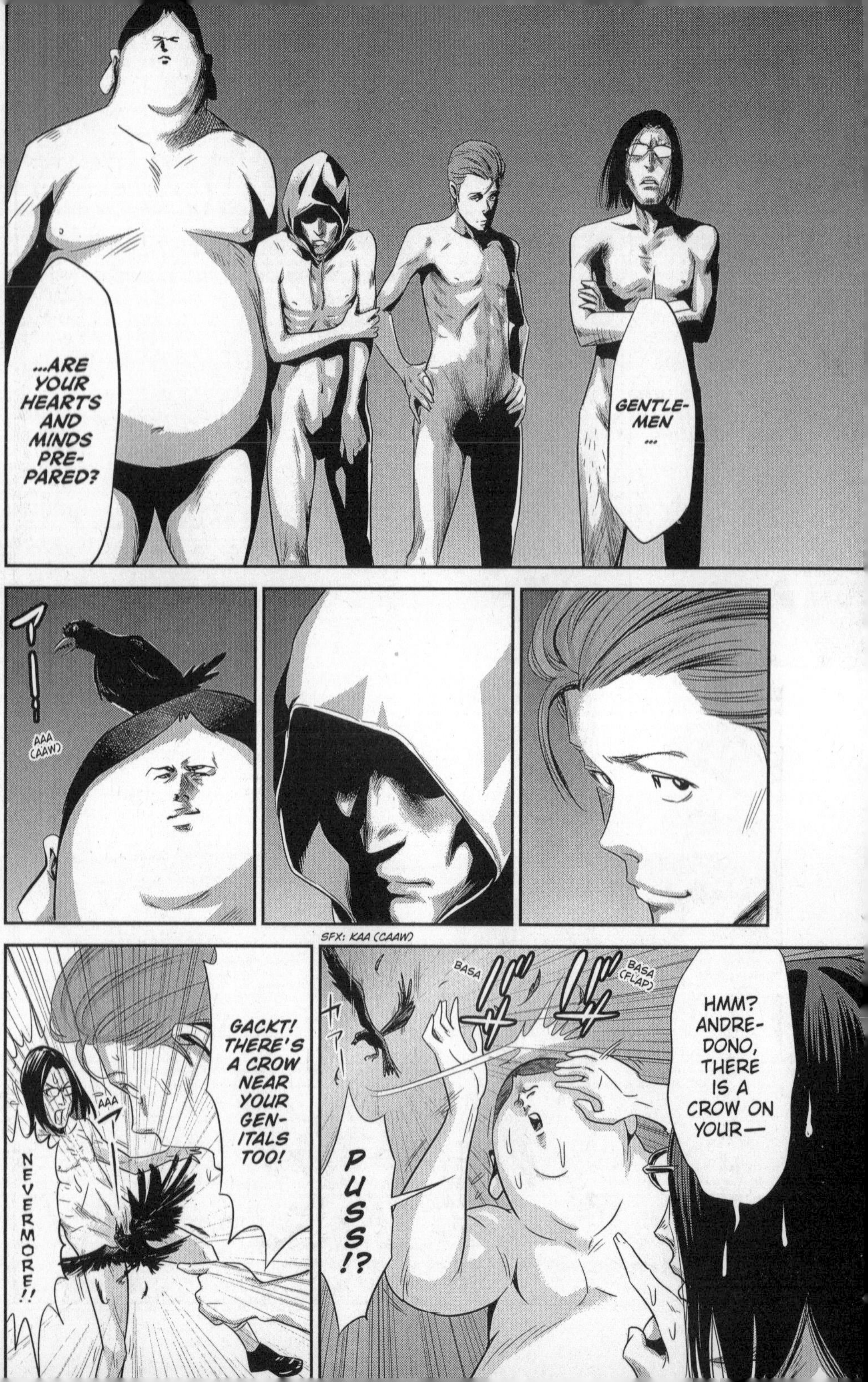
GENTLEMEN...
...ARE YOUR HEARTS AND MINDS PREPARED?
AAA (CAAW)
SFX: KAA (CAAW)
HMM? ANDRE-DONO, THERE IS A CROW ON YOUR—
BASA BASA (FLAP)
PUSS!?
GACKT! THERE'S A CROW NEAR YOUR GENITALS TOO!
AAA
NEVERMORE!!

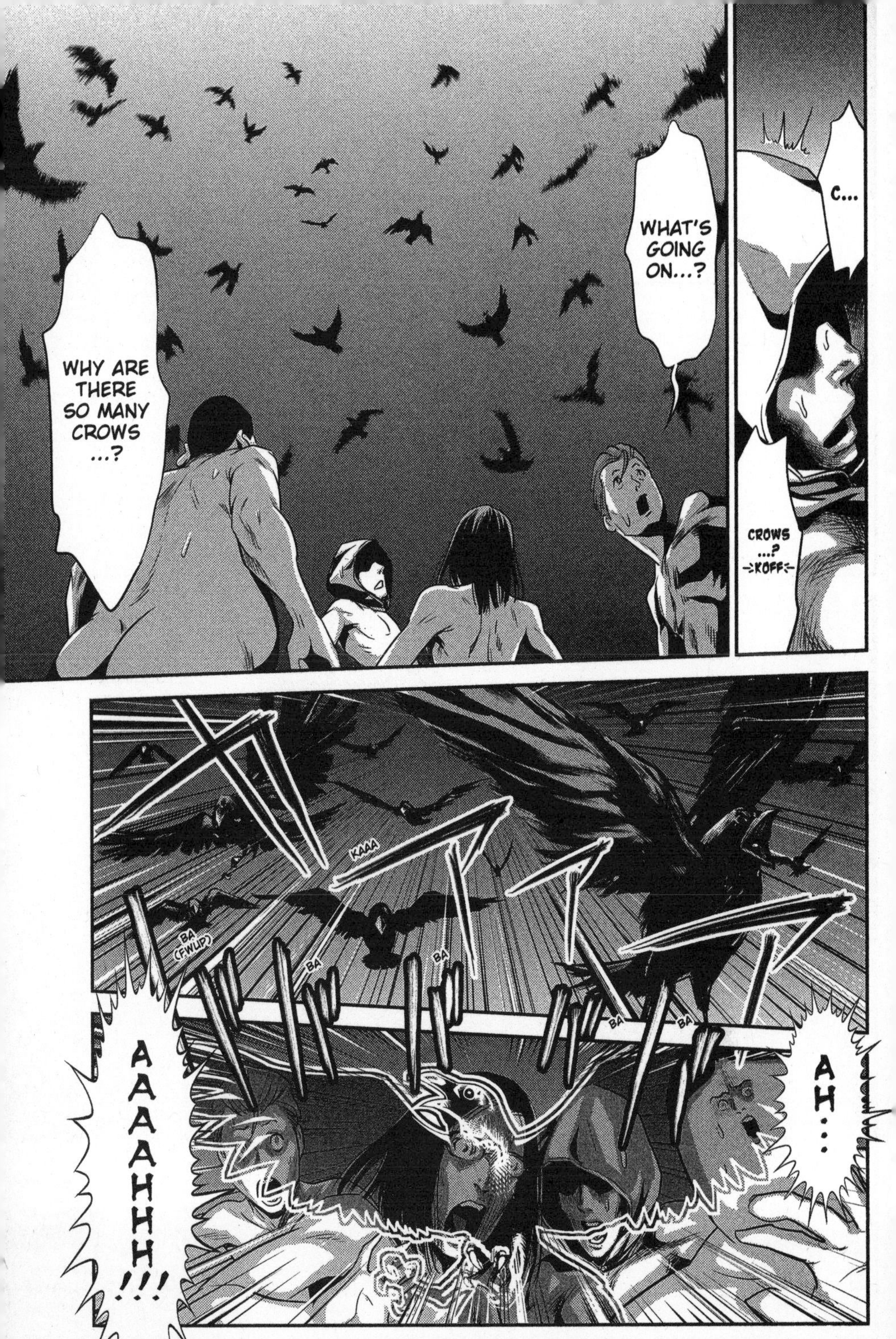
C...
CROWS ...? -KOFF-
WHAT'S GOING ON...?
WHY ARE THERE SO MANY CROWS ...?
KAAA
BA (FWUP)
BA
BA
BA
BA
AH...
AAAAHHH!!!

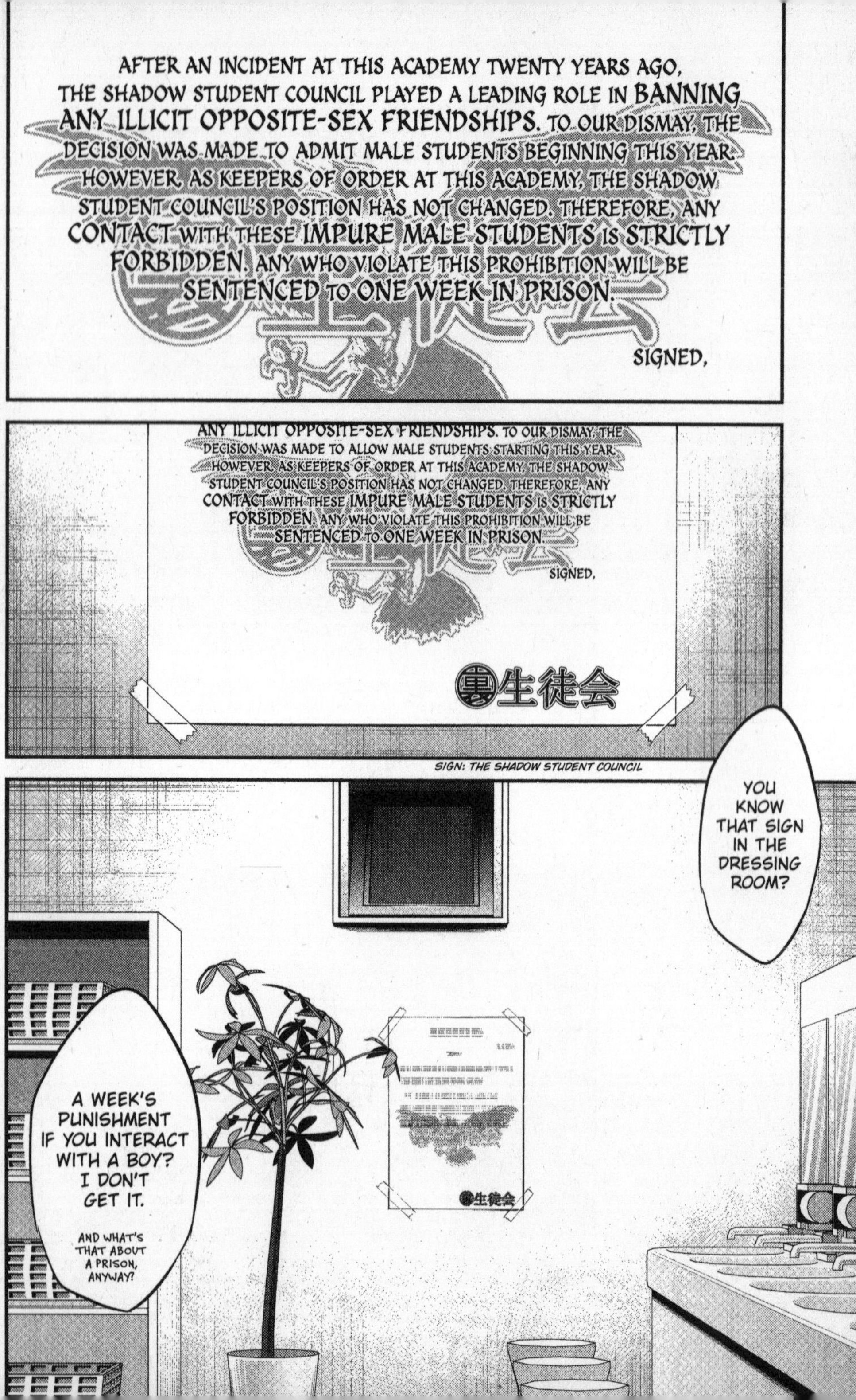
AFTER AN INCIDENT AT THIS ACADEMY TWENTY YEARS AGO, THE SHADOW STUDENT COUNCIL PLAYED A LEADING ROLE IN BANNING ANY ILLICIT OPPOSITE-SEX FRIENDSHIPS. TO OUR DISMAY, THE DECISION WAS MADE TO ADMIT MALE STUDENTS BEGINNING THIS YEAR. HOWEVER, AS KEEPERS OF ORDER AT THIS ACADEMY, THE SHADOW STUDENT COUNCIL'S POSITION HAS NOT CHANGED. THEREFORE, ANY CONTACT WITH THESE IMPURE MALE STUDENTS IS STRICTLY FORBIDDEN. ANY WHO VIOLATE THIS PROHIBITION WILL BE SENTENCED TO ONE WEEK IN PRISON.
SIGNED,
ANY ILLICIT OPPOSITE-SEX FRIENDSHIPS. TO OUR DISMAY, THE DECISION WAS MADE TO ALLOW MALE STUDENTS STARTING THIS YEAR. HOWEVER, AS KEEPERS OF ORDER AT THIS ACADEMY, THE SHADOW STUDENT COUNCIL'S POSITION HAS NOT CHANGED. THEREFORE, ANY CONTACT WITH THESE IMPURE MALE STUDENTS IS STRICTLY FORBIDDEN. ANY WHO VIOLATE THIS PROHIBITION WILL BE SENTENCED TO ONE WEEK IN PRISON.
SIGNED,
裏生徒会
SIGN: THE SHADOW STUDENT COUNCIL
YOU KNOW THAT SIGN IN THE DRESSING ROOM?
A WEEK'S PUNISHMENT IF YOU INTERACT WITH A BOY? I DON'T GET IT.
AND WHAT'S THAT ABOUT A PRISON, ANYWAY?
裏生徒会

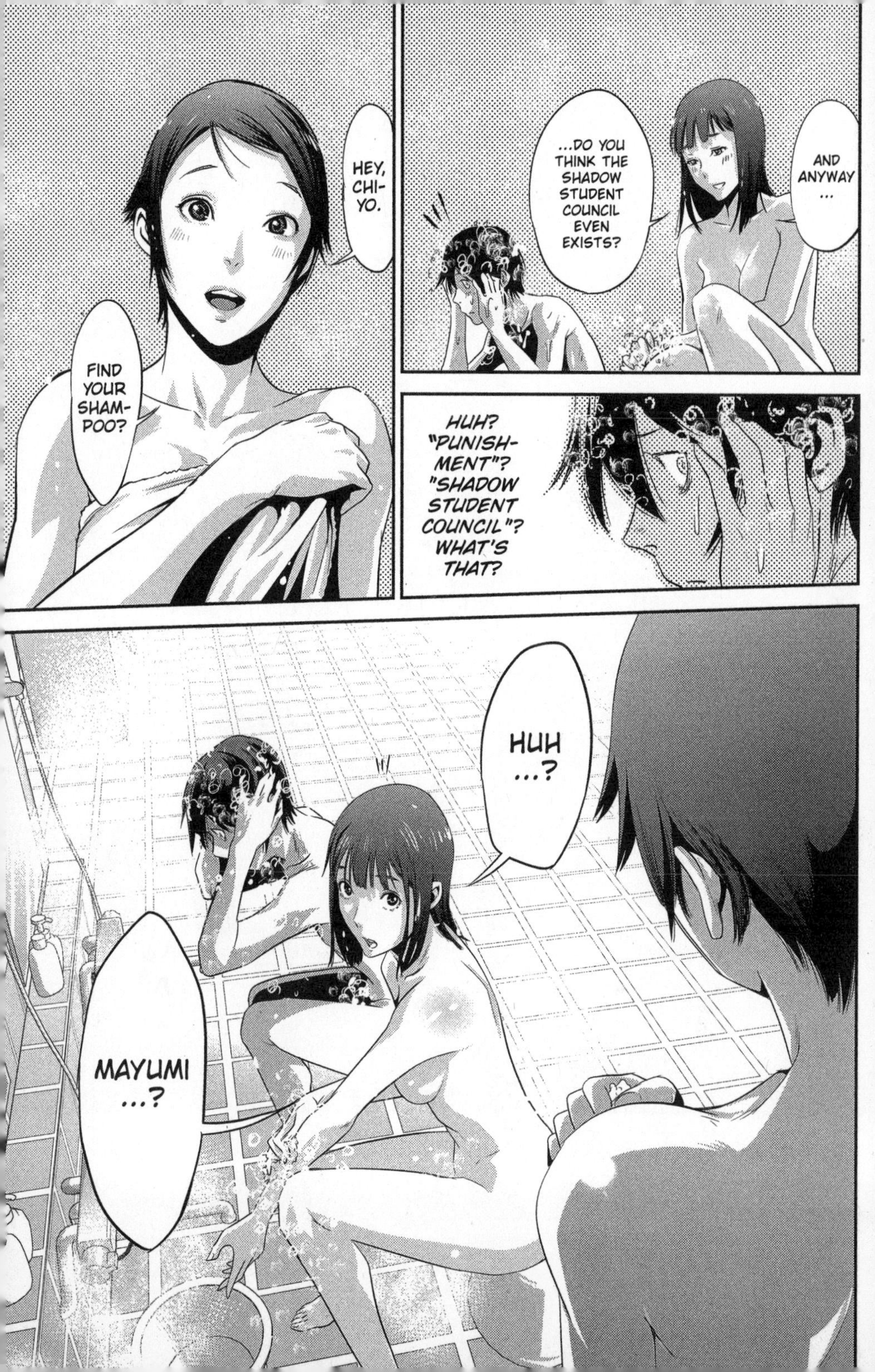
AND ANYWAY ...
...DO YOU THINK THE SHADOW STUDENT COUNCIL EVEN EXISTS?
HUH? "PUNISHMENT"? "SHADOW STUDENT COUNCIL"? WHAT'S THAT?
HEY, CHI-YO.
FIND YOUR SHAMPOO?
HUH ...?
MAYUMI ...?

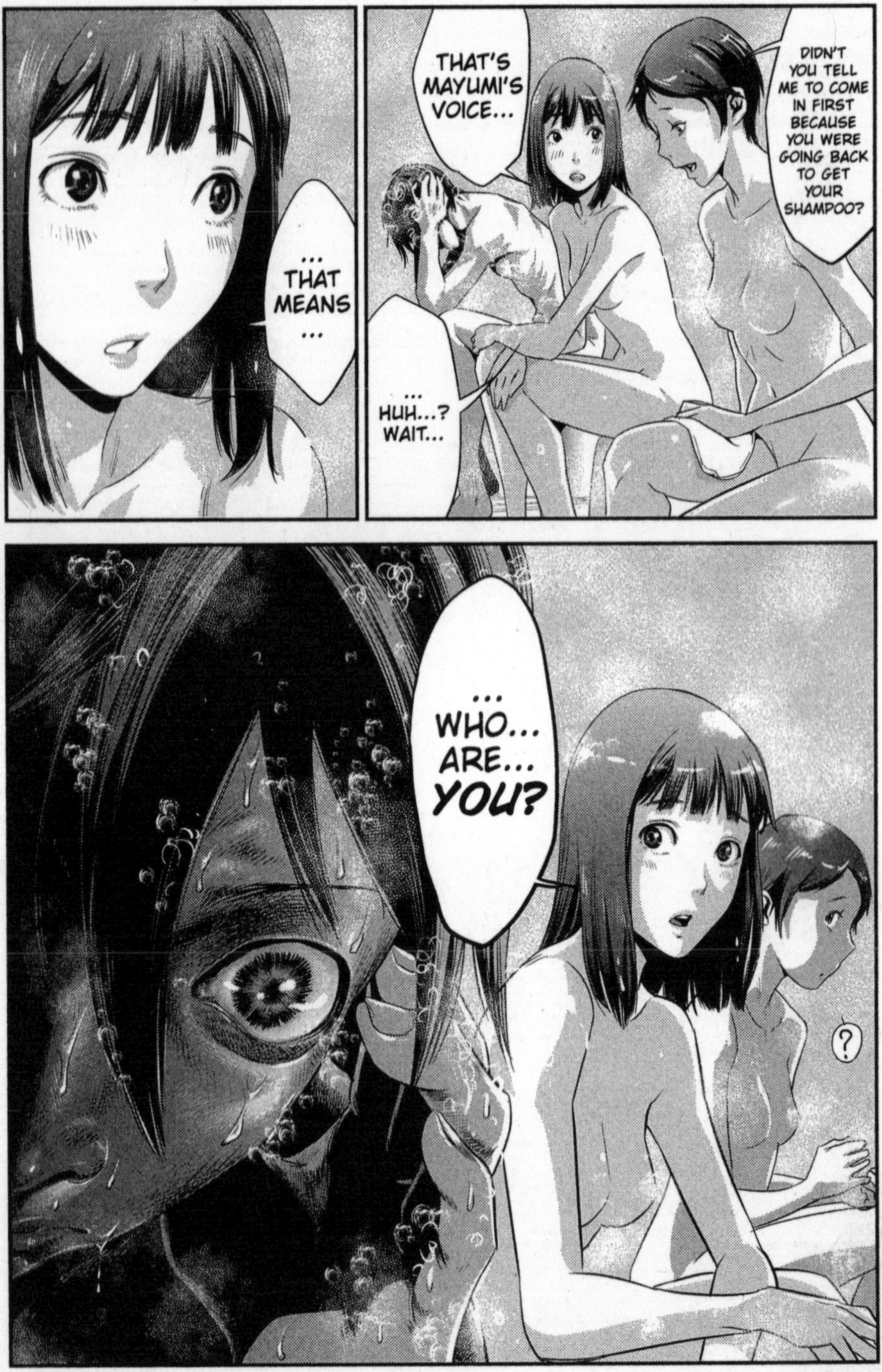
DIDN'T YOU TELL ME TO COME IN FIRST BECAUSE YOU WERE GOING BACK TO GET YOUR SHAMPOO?
THAT'S MAYUMI'S VOICE...
... HUH...? WAIT...
... THAT MEANS ...
... WHO... ARE... *YOU?*
?

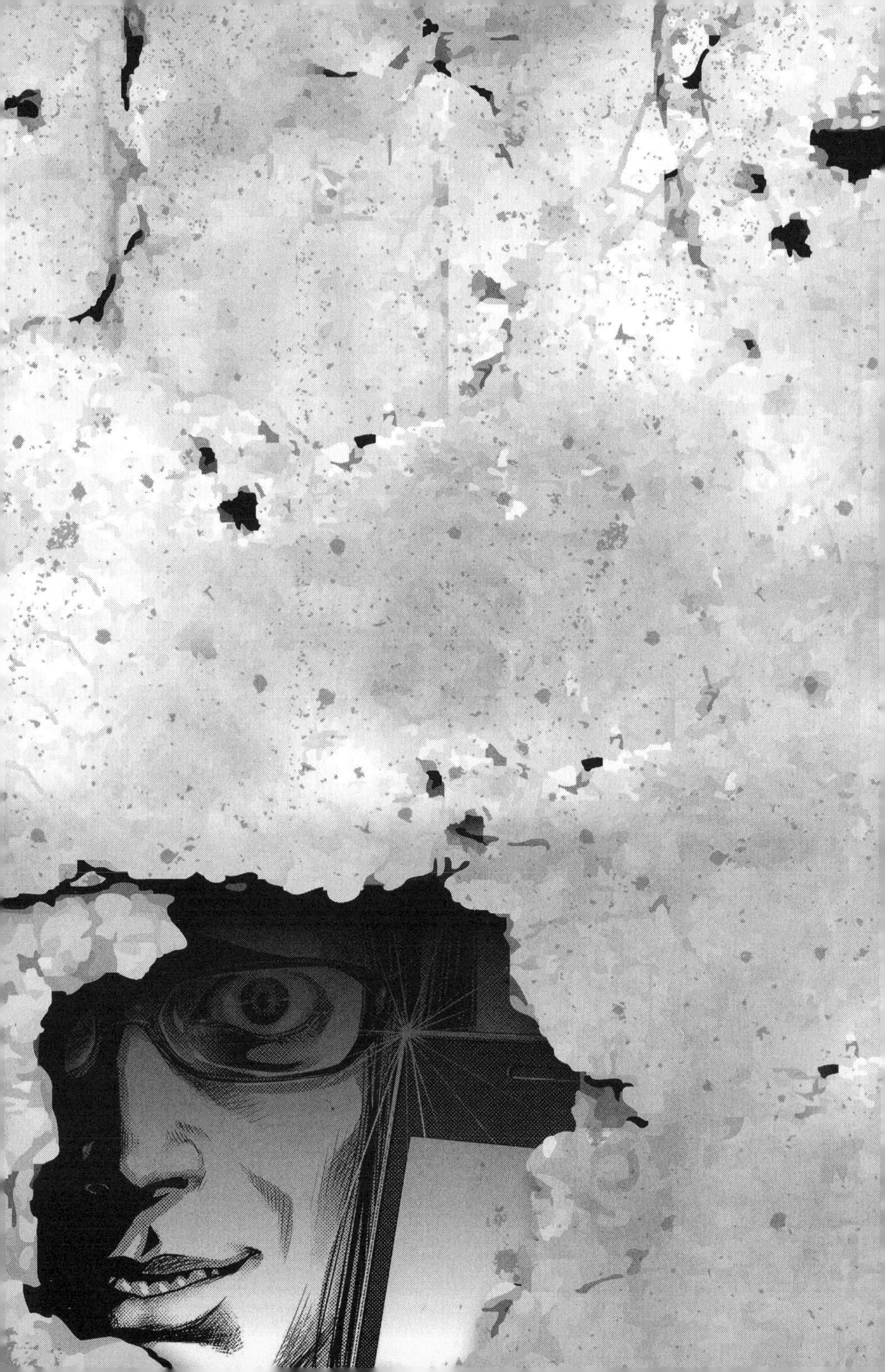

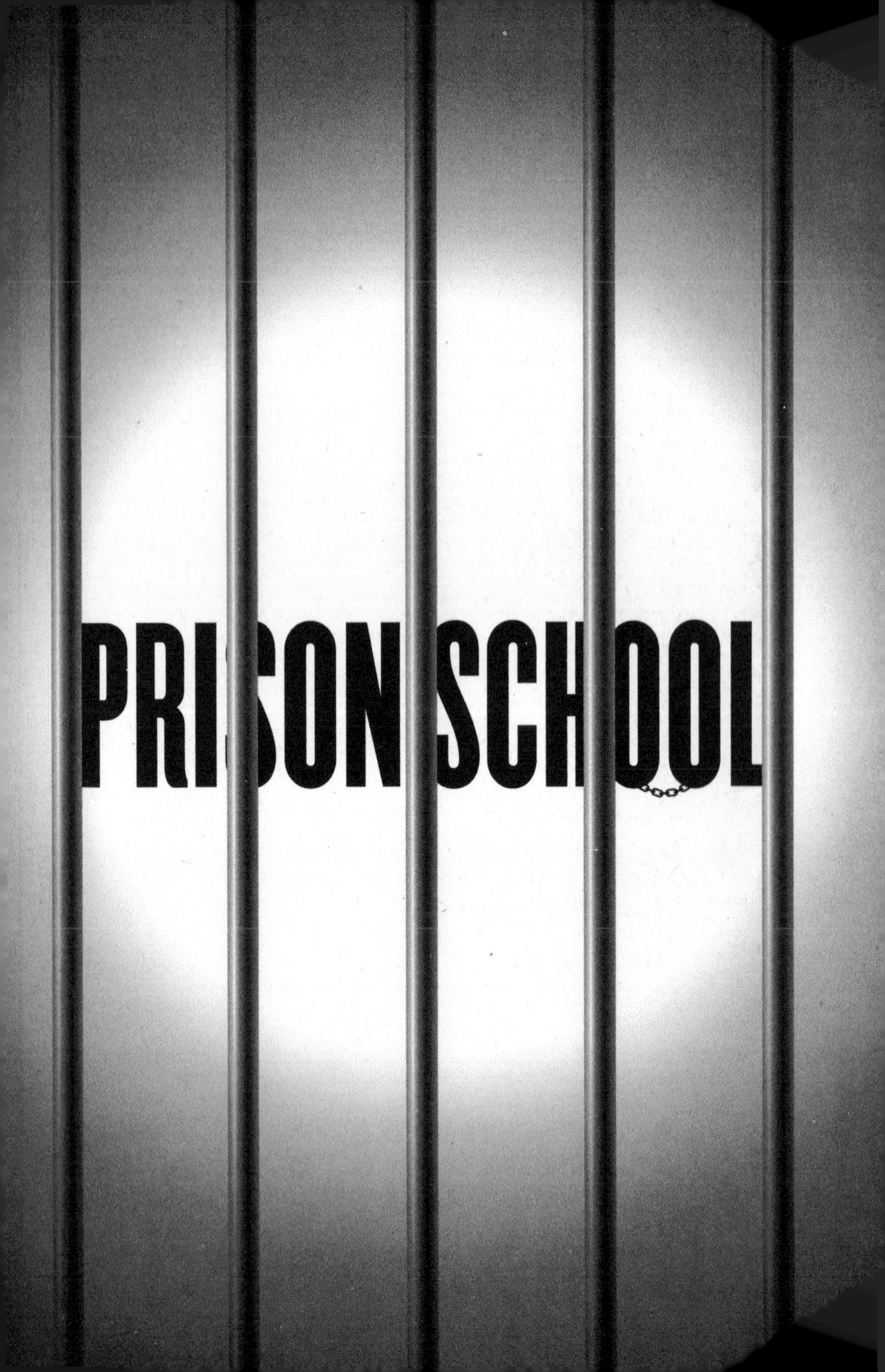
PRISON SCHOOL

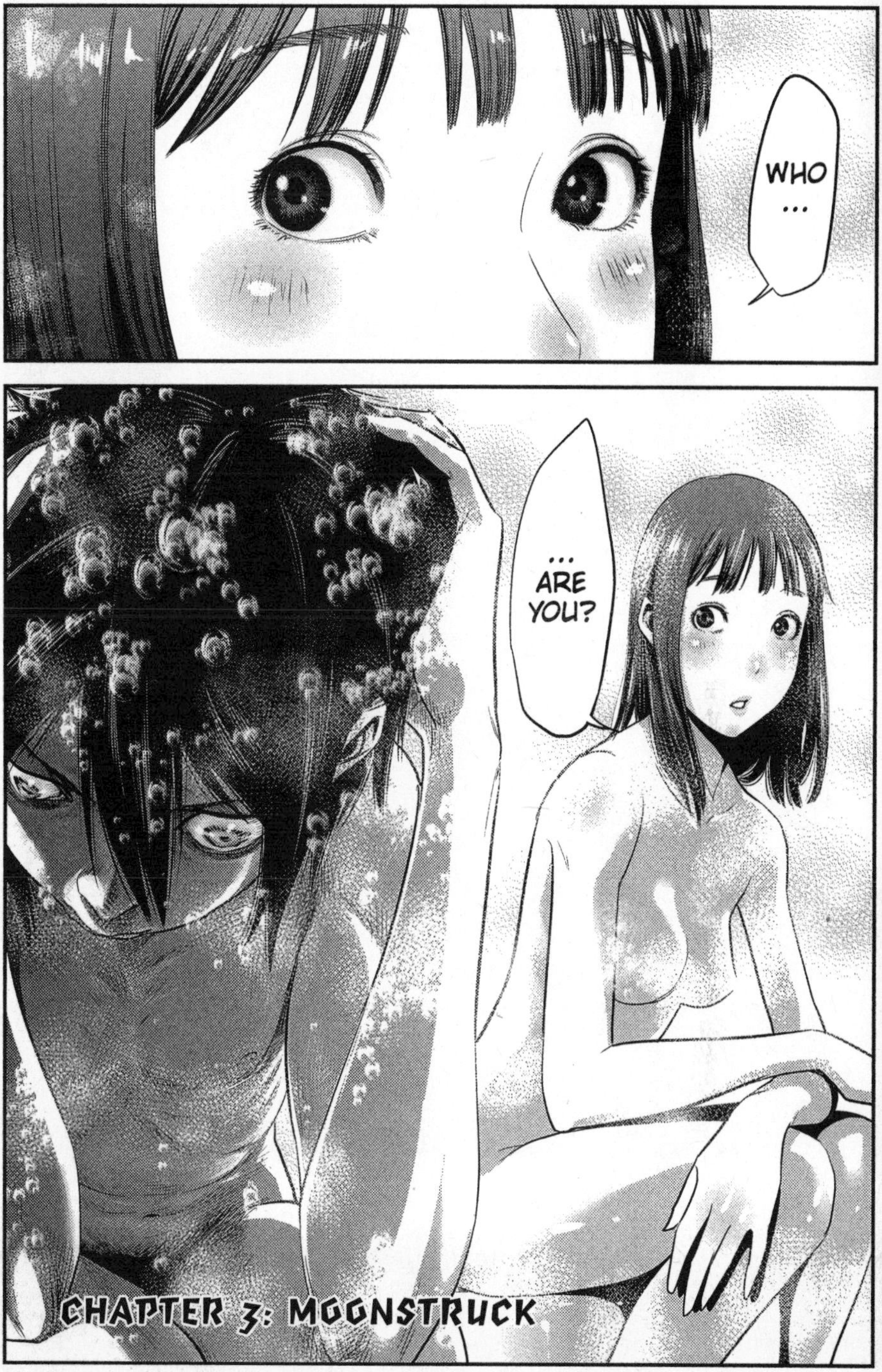
WHO ...
... ARE YOU?
CHAPTER 3: MOONSTRUCK

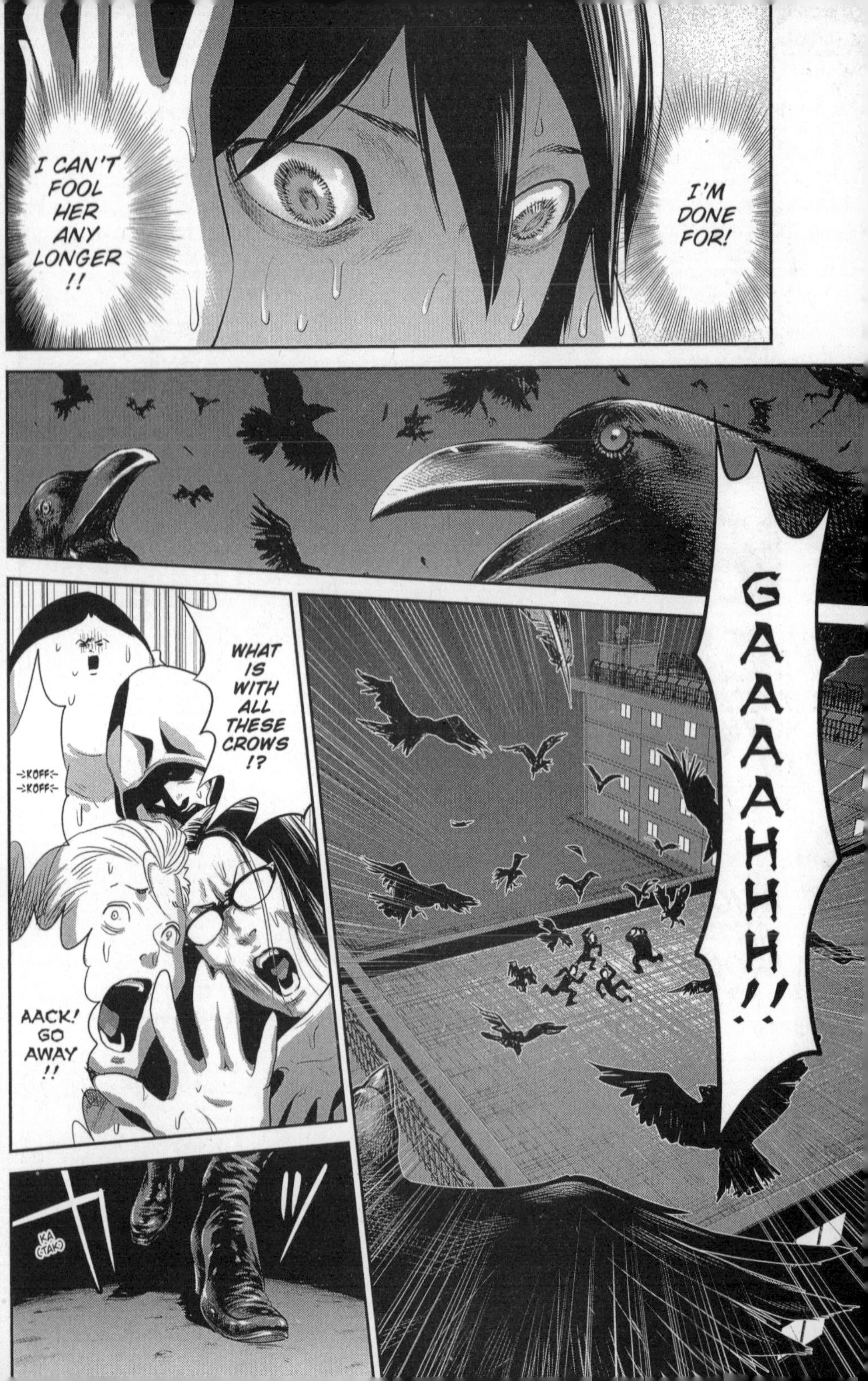
I'M DONE FOR!
I CAN'T FOOL HER ANY LONGER !!
GAAAAHHH!!
WHAT IS WITH ALL THESE CROWS !?
KOFF KOFF
AACK! GO AWAY !!
KA CHAK

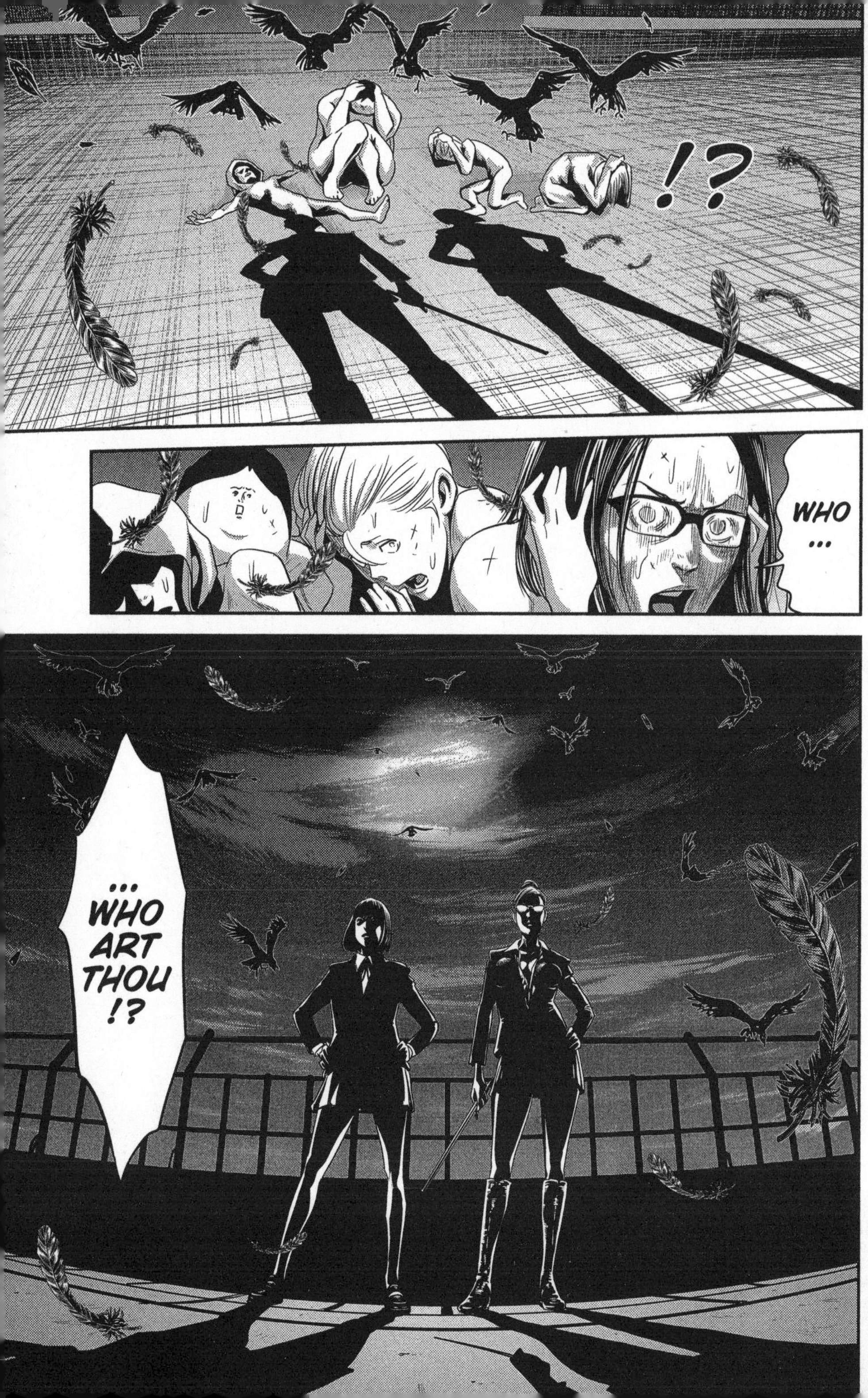
!?
WHO ...
... WHO ART THOU !?

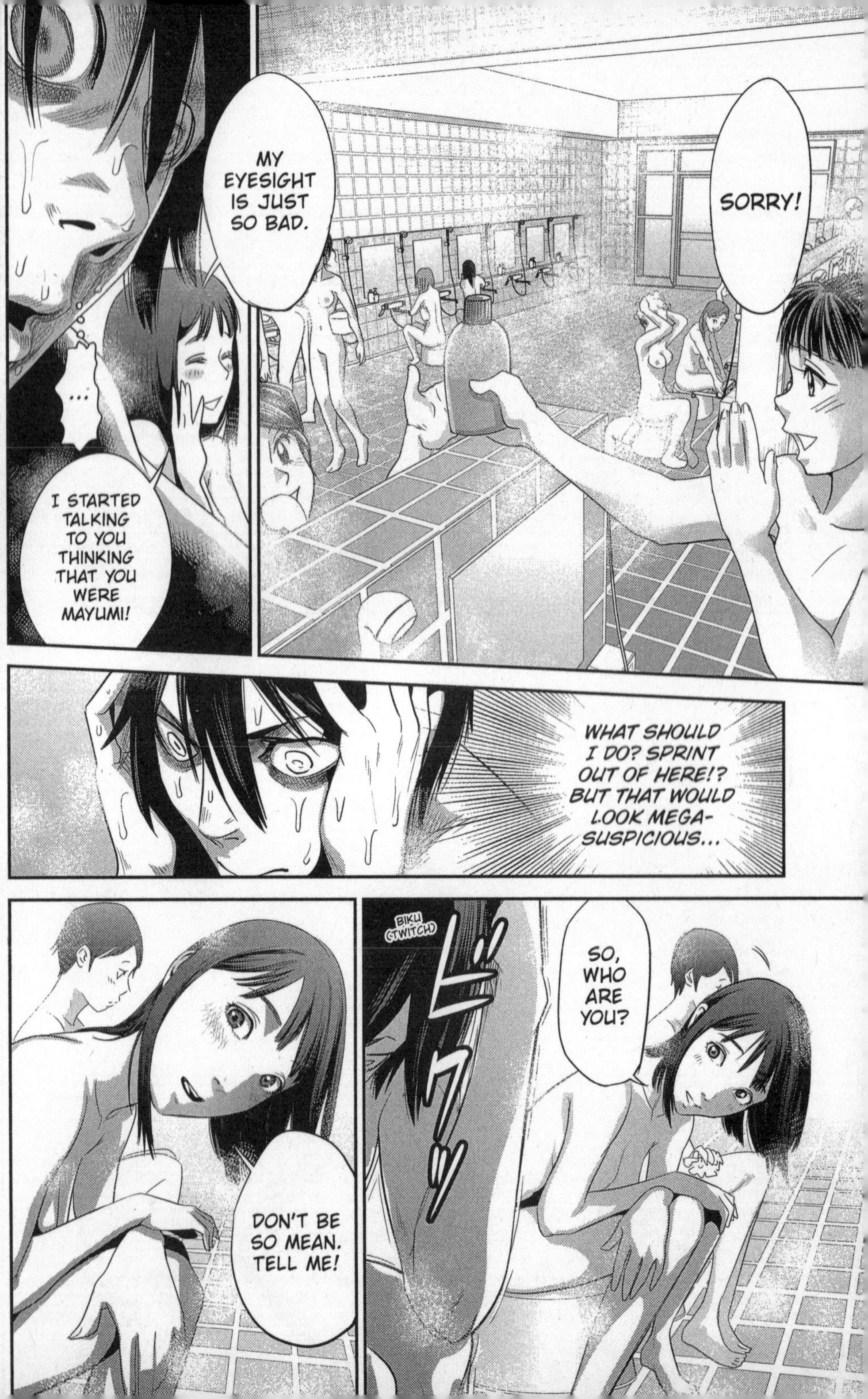
SORRY!
MY EYESIGHT IS JUST SO BAD.
...
I STARTED TALKING TO YOU THINKING THAT YOU WERE MAYUMI!
WHAT SHOULD I DO? SPRINT OUT OF HERE!? BUT THAT WOULD LOOK MEGA-SUSPICIOUS...
SO, WHO ARE YOU?
BIKU (TWITCH)
DON'T BE SO MEAN. TELL ME!

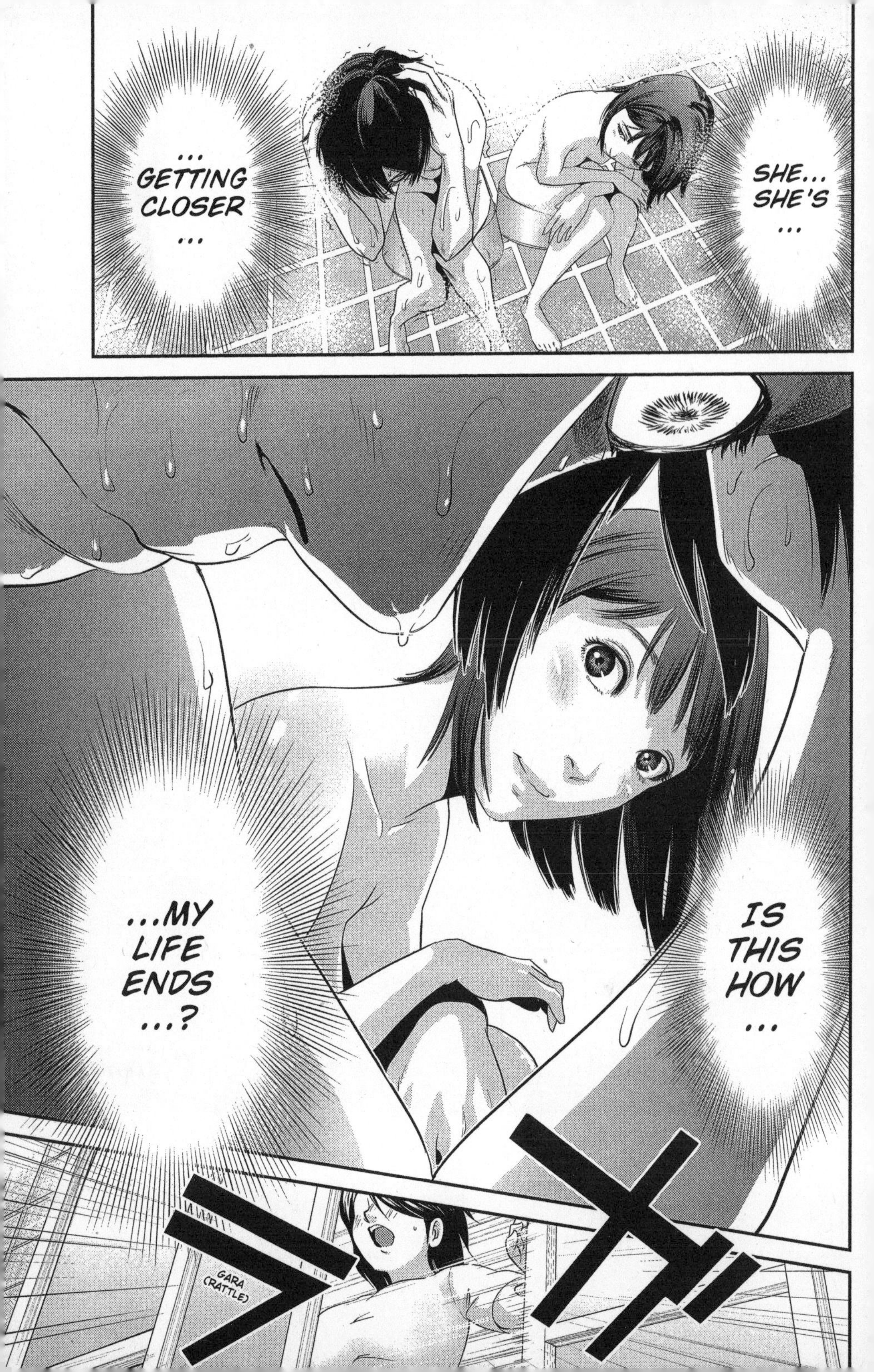
SHE... SHE'S ...
... GETTING CLOSER ...
IS THIS HOW ...
...MY LIFE ENDS ...?
GARA (RATTLE)

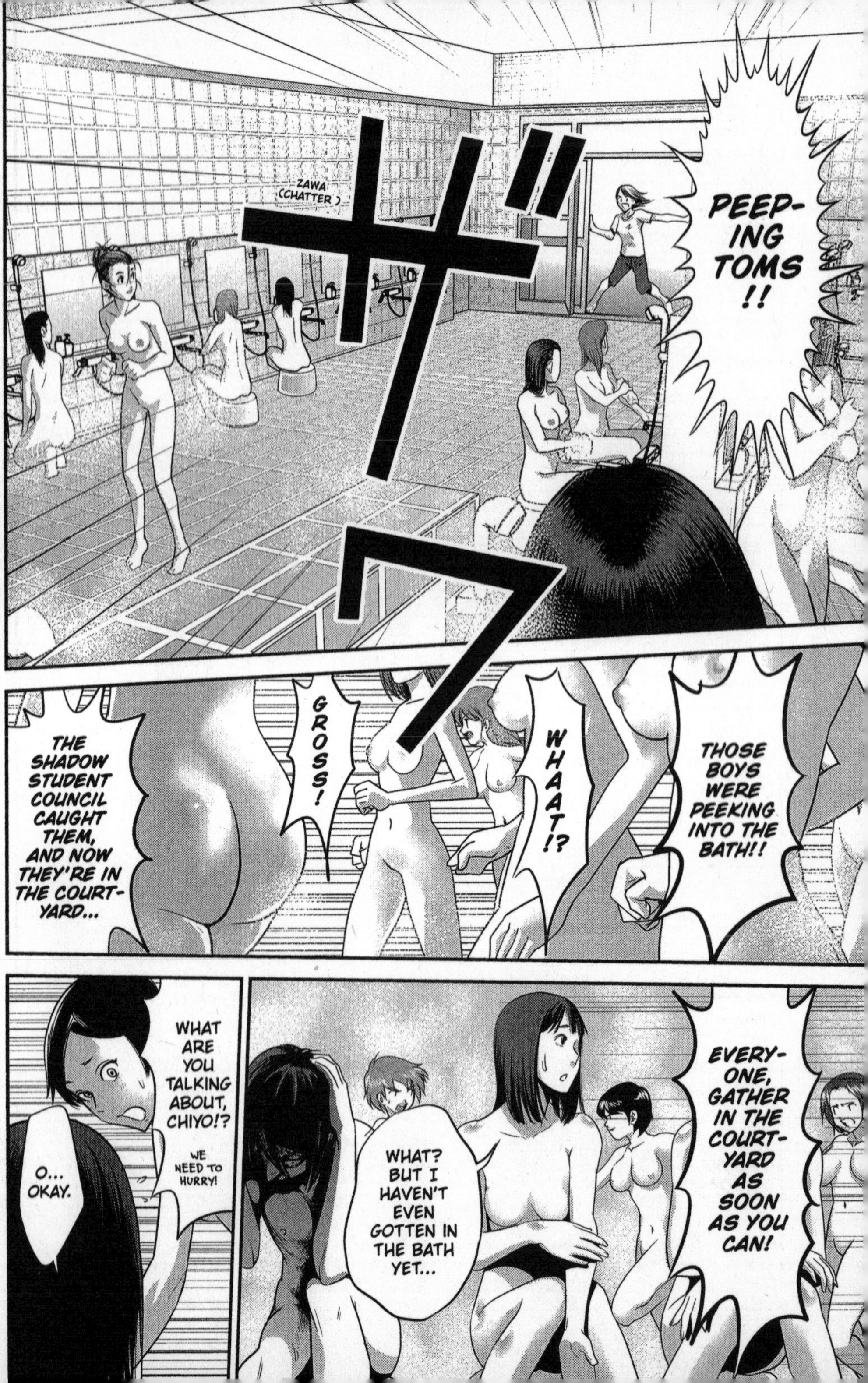

PEEP-ING TOMS!!
ZAWA (CHATTER)
ザワ
THOSE BOYS WERE PEEKING INTO THE BATH!!
WHAAT!?
GROSS!
THE SHADOW STUDENT COUNCIL CAUGHT THEM, AND NOW THEY'RE IN THE COURT-YARD...
EVERY-ONE, GATHER IN THE COURT-YARD AS SOON AS YOU CAN!
WHAT? BUT I HAVEN'T EVEN GOTTEN IN THE BATH YET...
WHAT ARE YOU TALKING ABOUT, CHIYO!?
WE NEED TO HURRY!
O... OKAY.

HEY, YOU NEED TO HURRY AND...
... HUH ...?
SHE'S ... GONE.
ドドドド
DO DO DO DO (THUD)
I'M LEAVING, CHIYO!
キャー
AHHH!
EEEK!
W-WAIT, MAYUMI!!
ド DO ド DO
ZABA (SPLOOSH)
BAAAHH!!
TH... THANK GOD!!

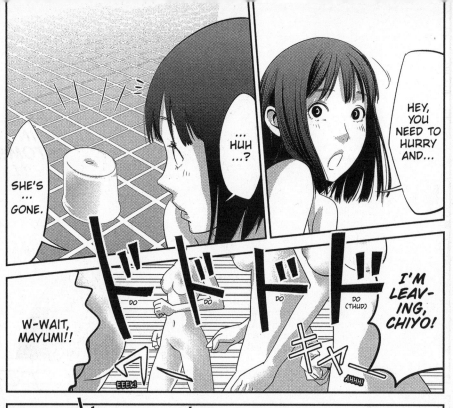

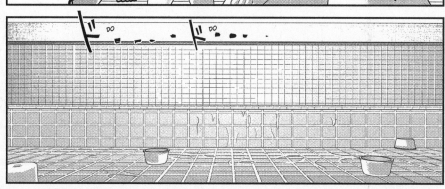

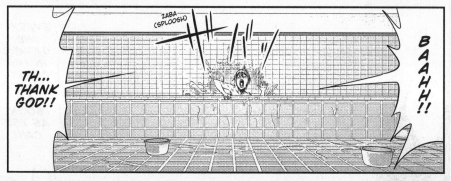

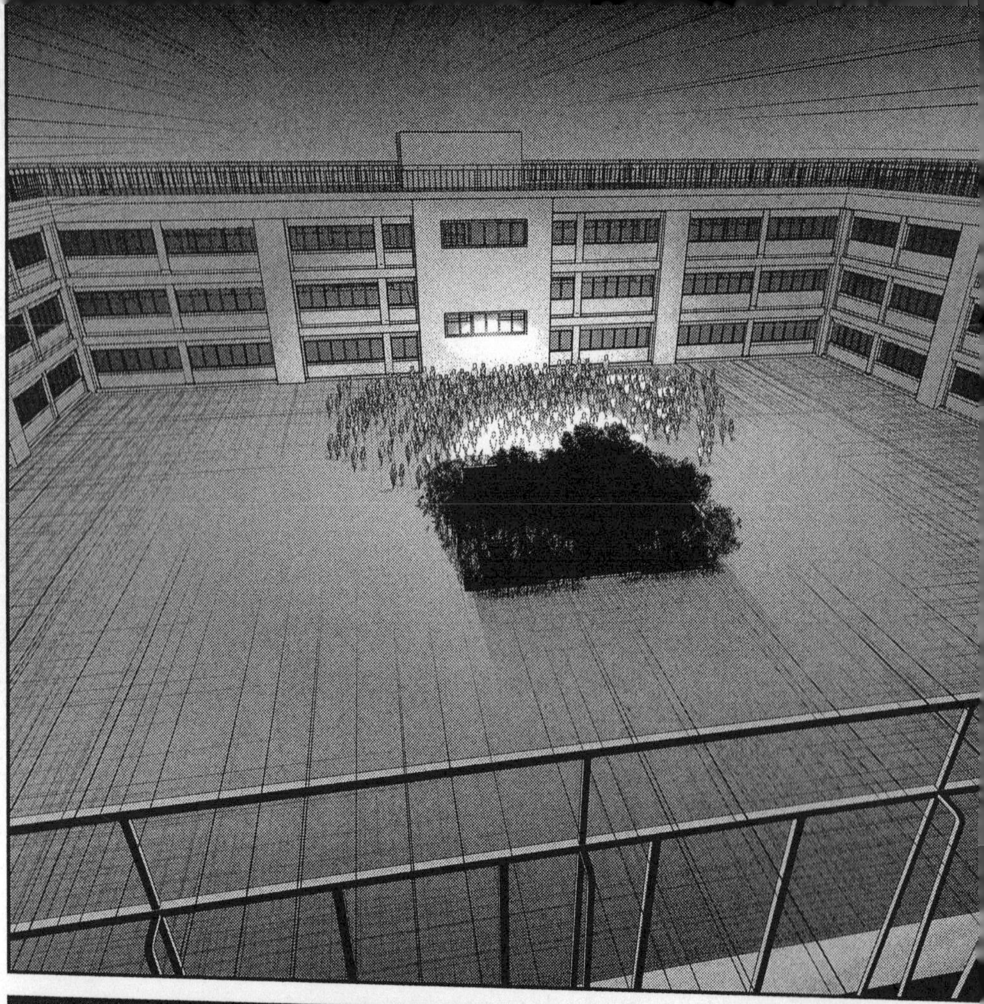

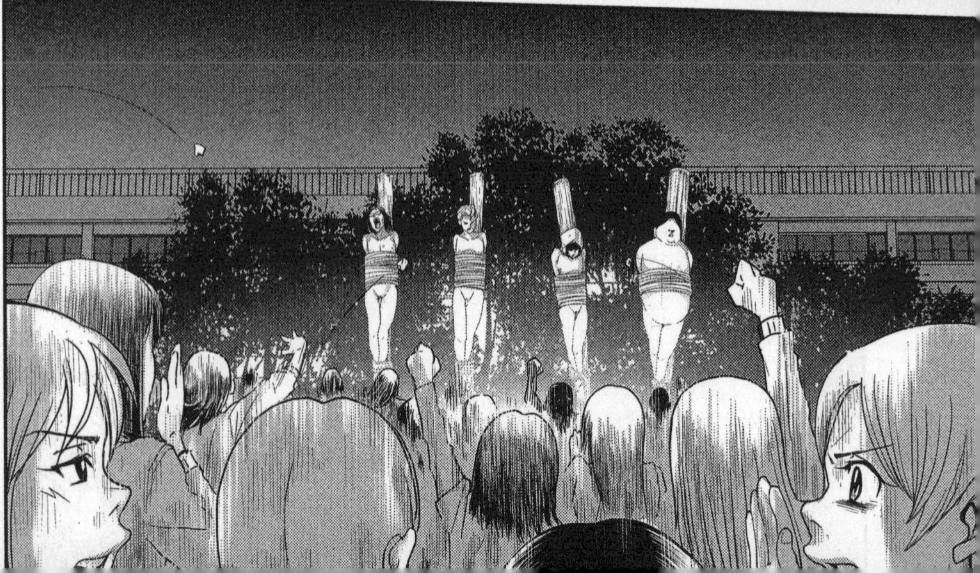

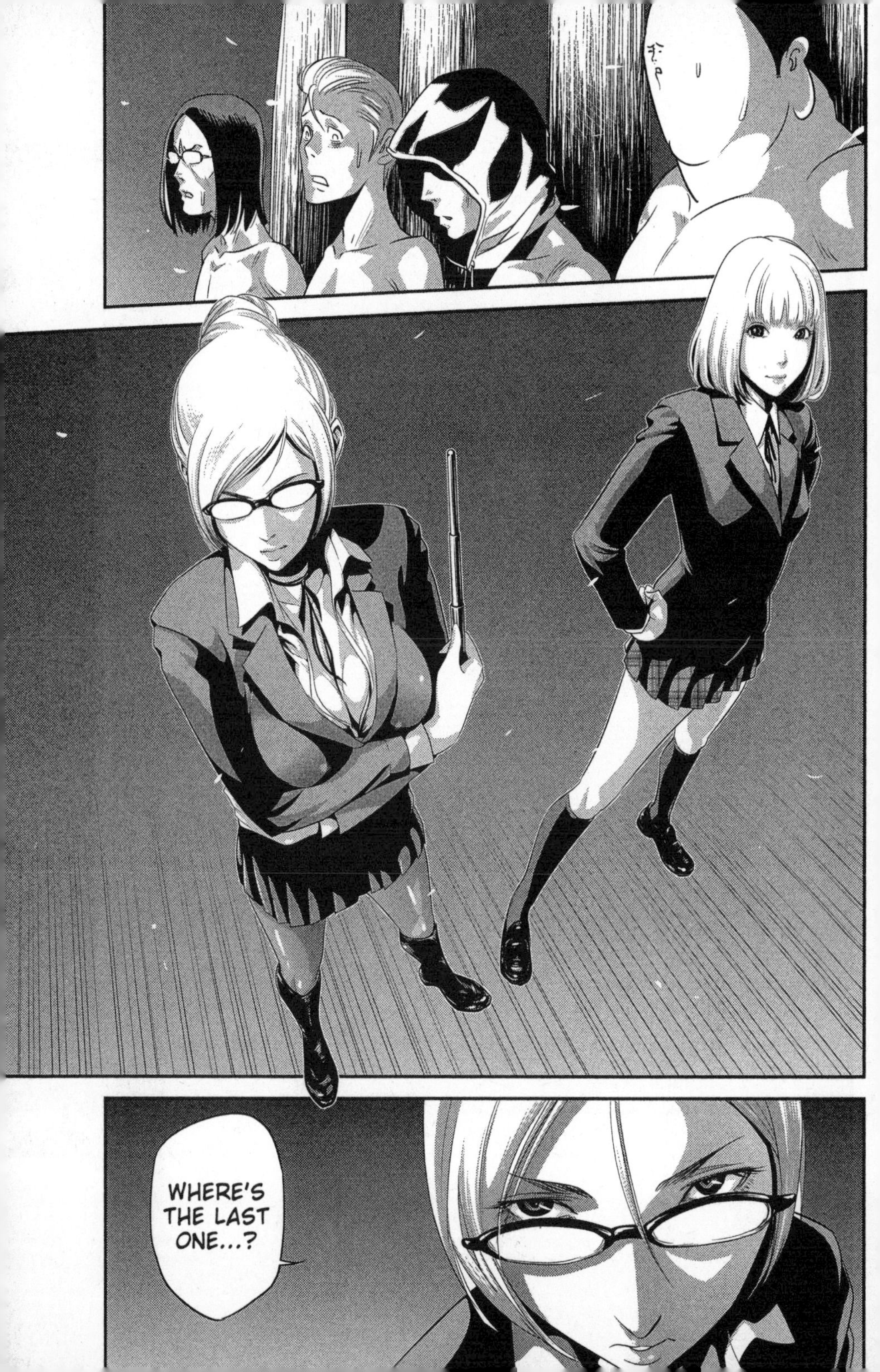
WHERE'S THE LAST ONE...?

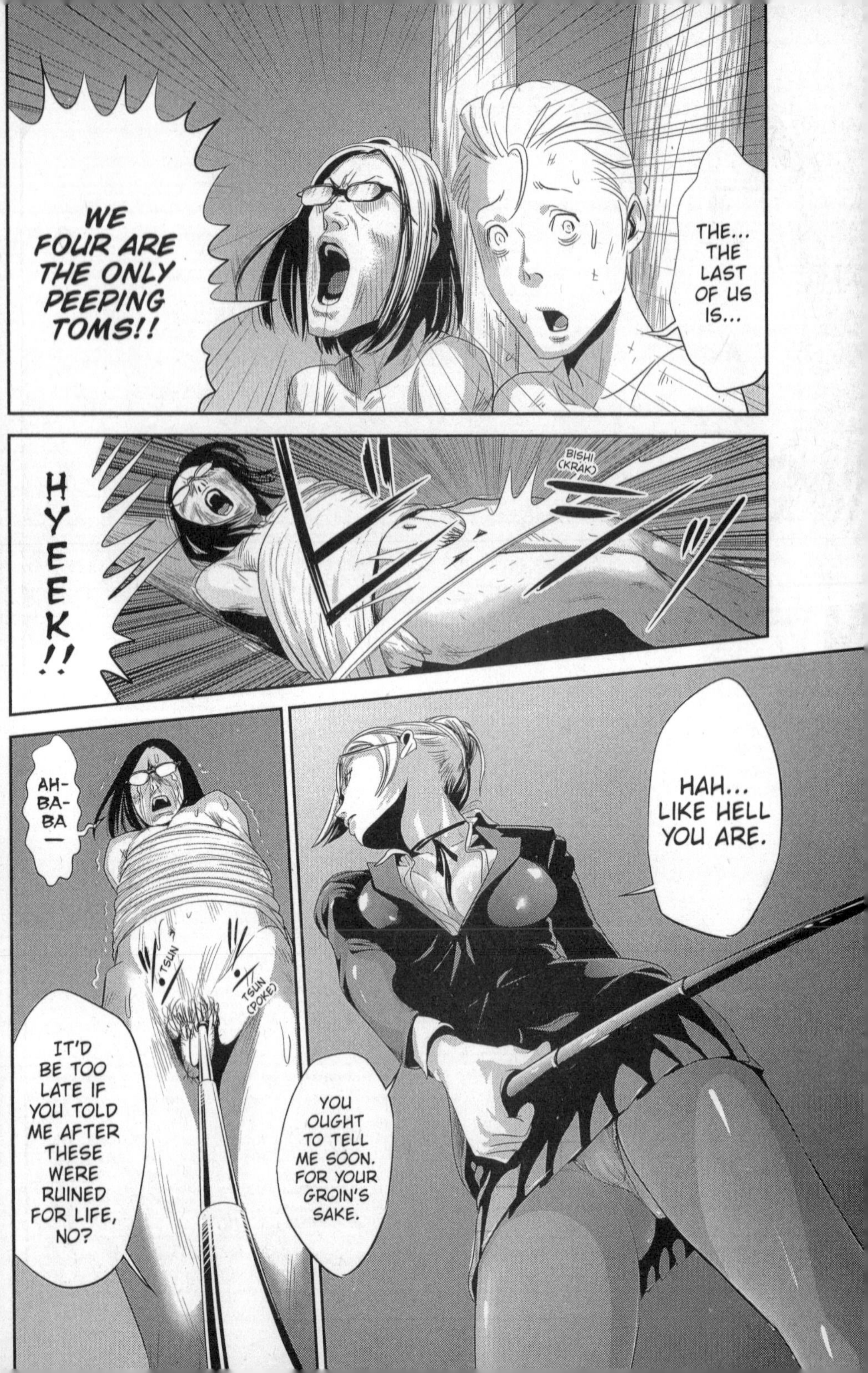
THE... THE LAST OF US IS...
WE FOUR ARE THE ONLY PEEPING TOMS!!
BISHI (KRAK)
HYEEK!!
HAH... LIKE HELL YOU ARE.
AH-BA-BA—
TSUN
TSUN (POKE)
YOU OUGHT TO TELL ME SOON. FOR YOUR GROIN'S SAKE.
IT'D BE TOO LATE IF YOU TOLD ME AFTER THESE WERE RUINED FOR LIFE, NO?

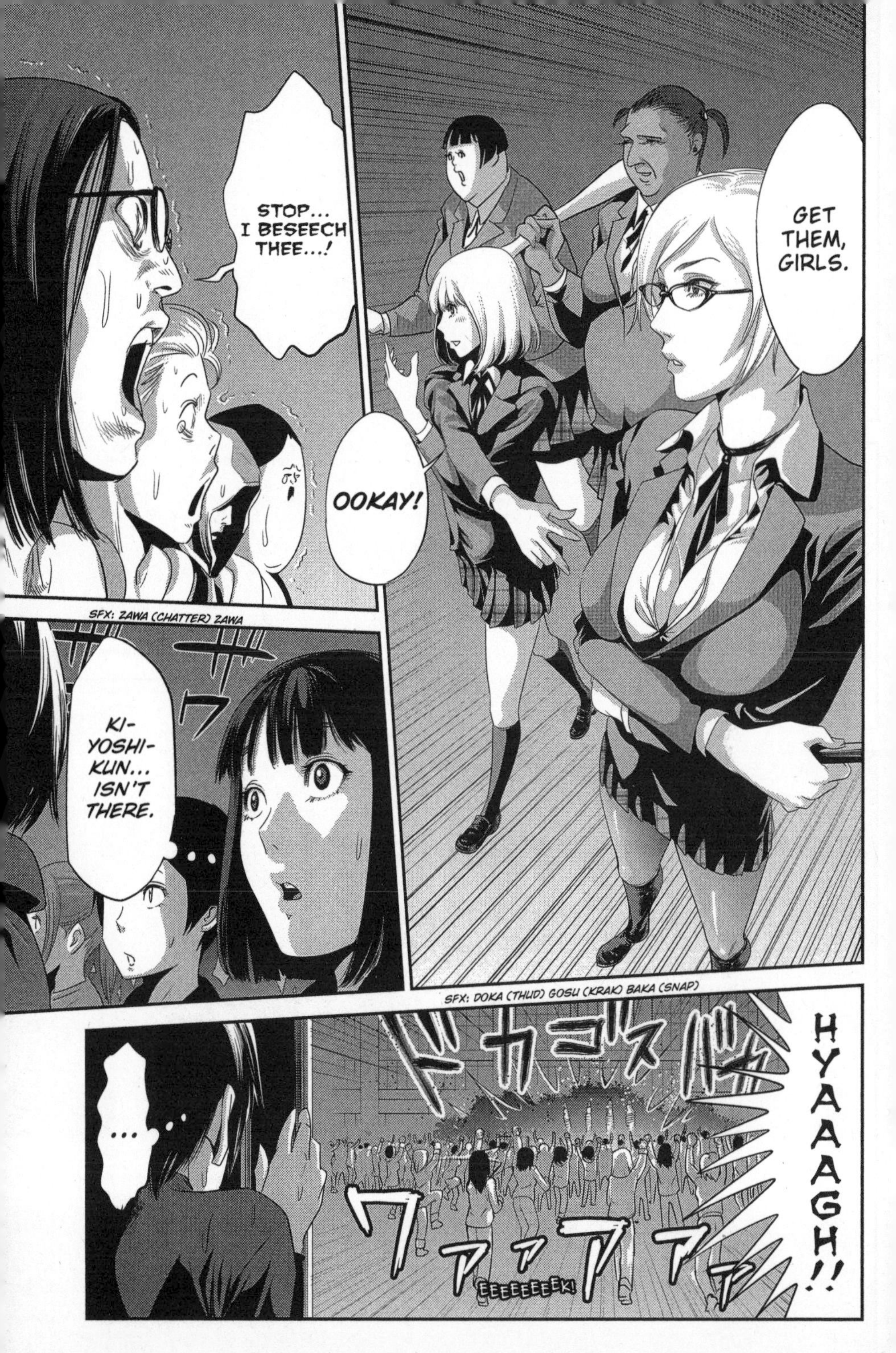
GET THEM, GIRLS.
OOKAY!
STOP... I BESEECH THEE...!
SFX: ZAWA (CHATTER) ZAWA
KI-YOSHI-KUN... ISN'T THERE.
SFX: DOKA (THUD) GOSU (KRAK) BAKA (SNAP)
HYAAAGH!!
EEEEEEEEK!
...

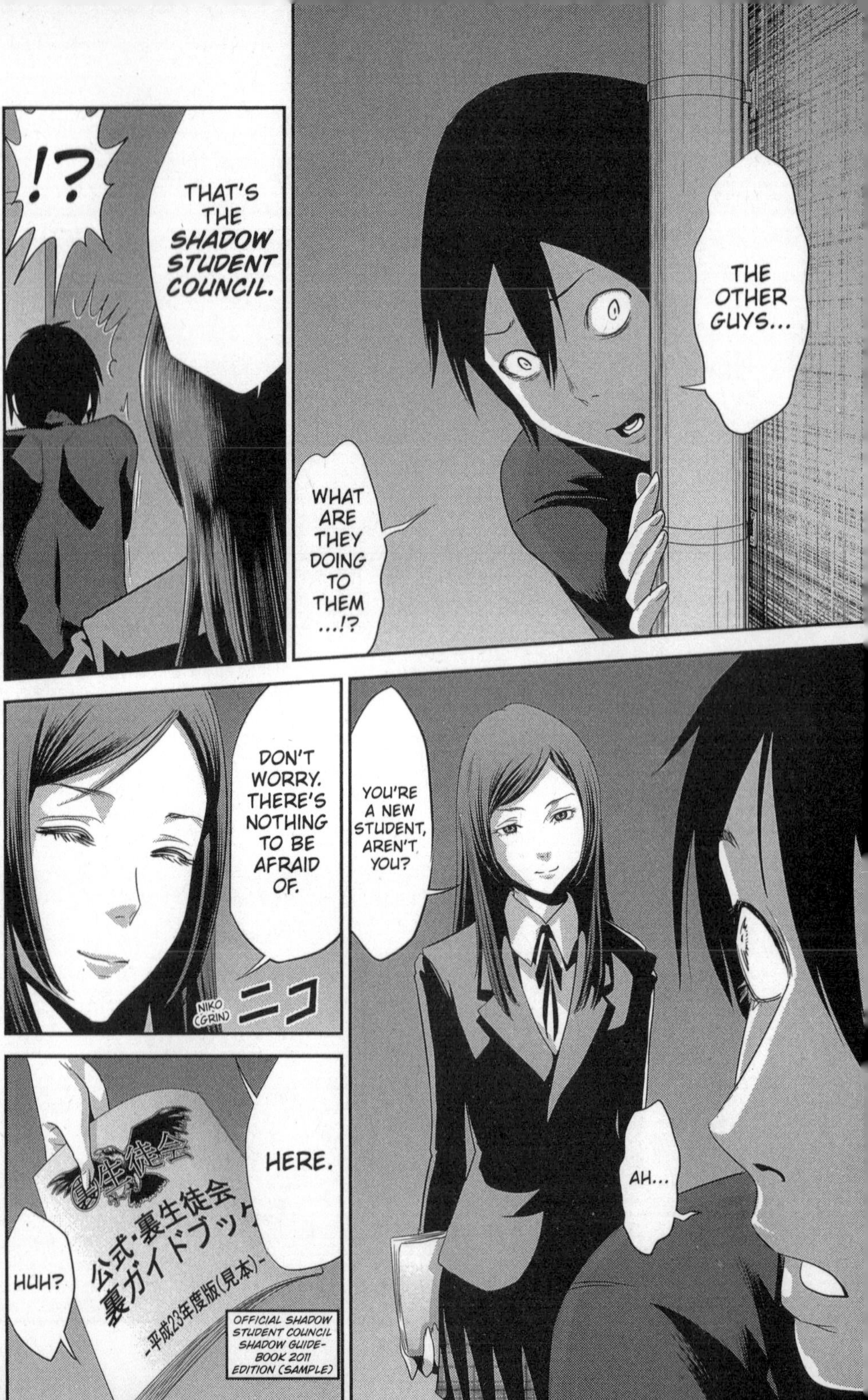
THE OTHER GUYS...
WHAT ARE THEY DOING TO THEM ...!?
THAT'S THE SHADOW STUDENT COUNCIL.
!?
YOU'RE A NEW STUDENT, AREN'T YOU?
DON'T WORRY. THERE'S NOTHING TO BE AFRAID OF.
ニコ
NIKO (GRIN)
AH...
HERE.
HUH?
公式・裏生徒会
裏ガイドブック
-平成23年度版(見本)-
OFFICIAL SHADOW STUDENT COUNCIL SHADOW GUIDE-BOOK 2011 EDITION (SAMPLE)

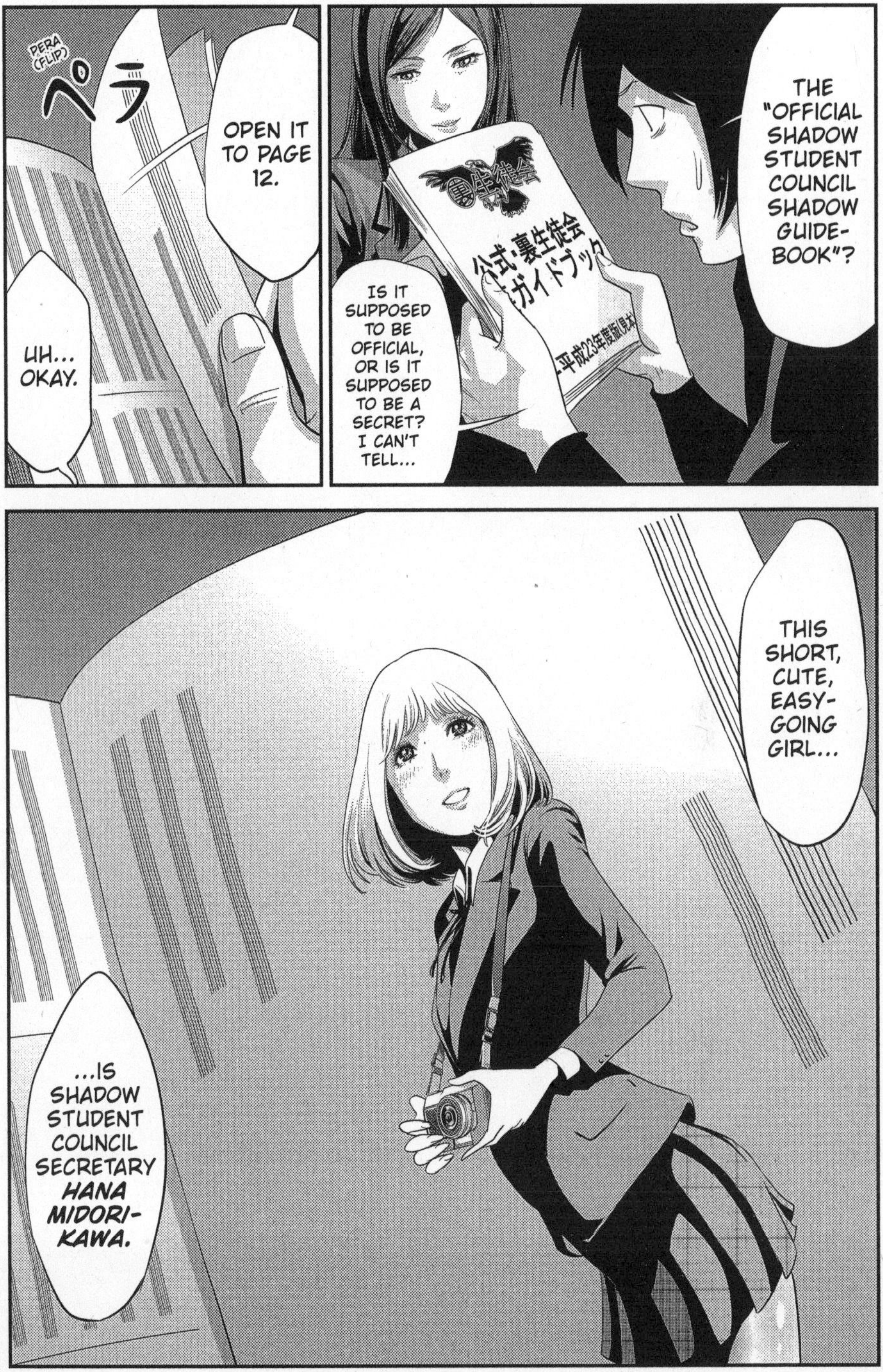
THE "OFFICIAL SHADOW STUDENT COUNCIL SHADOW GUIDE-BOOK"?
IS IT SUPPOSED TO BE OFFICIAL, OR IS IT SUPPOSED TO BE A SECRET? I CAN'T TELL...
PERA (FLIP)
ペラ
OPEN IT TO PAGE 12.
UH... OKAY.
THIS SHORT, CUTE, EASY-GOING GIRL...
...IS SHADOW STUDENT COUNCIL SECRETARY *HANA MIDORI-KAWA.*

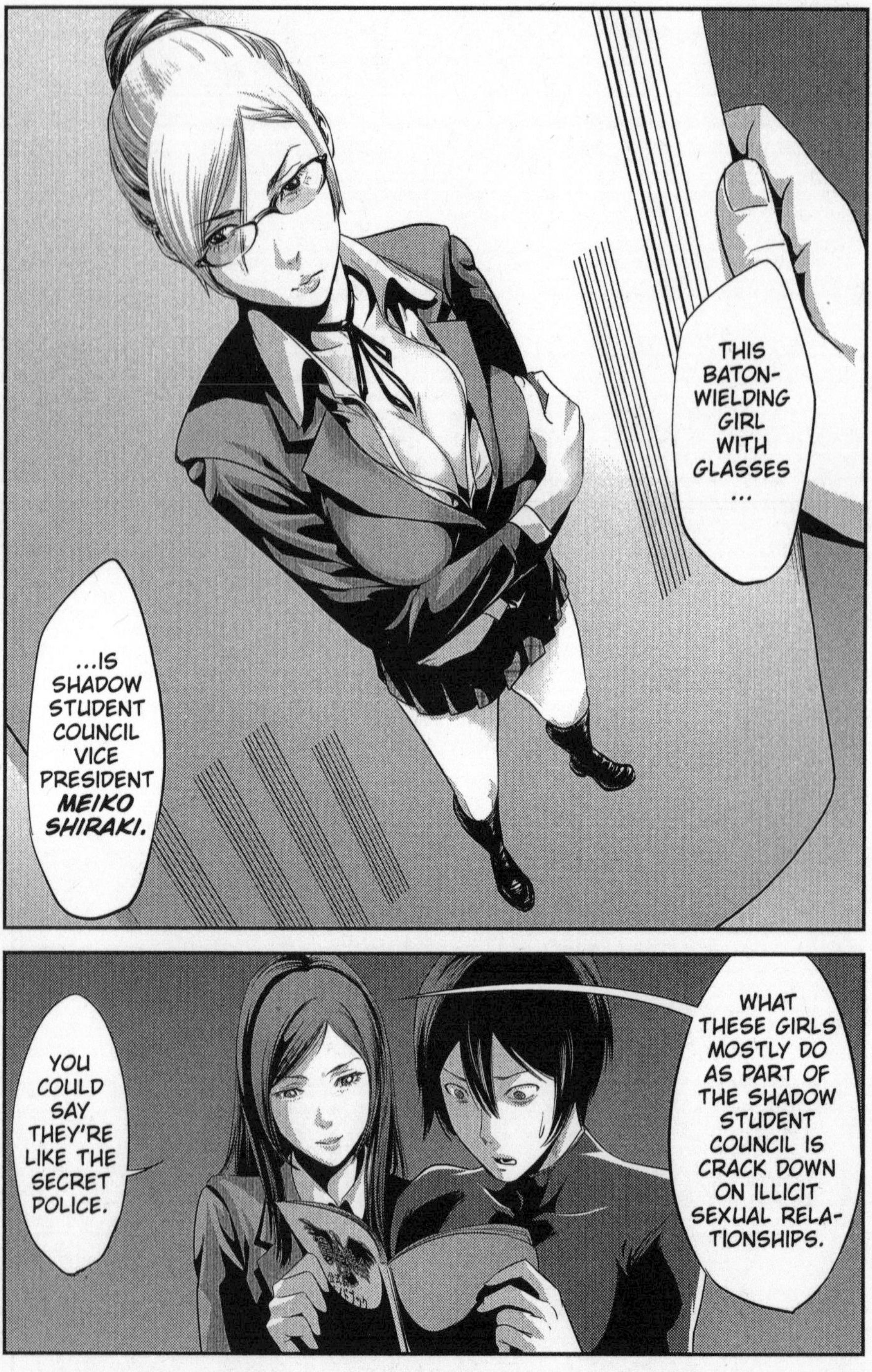
THIS BATON-WIELDING GIRL WITH GLASSES...
...IS SHADOW STUDENT COUNCIL VICE PRESIDENT MEIKO SHIRAKI.
WHAT THESE GIRLS MOSTLY DO AS PART OF THE SHADOW STUDENT COUNCIL IS CRACK DOWN ON ILLICIT SEXUAL RELA-TIONSHIPS.
YOU COULD SAY THEY'RE LIKE THE SECRET POLICE.

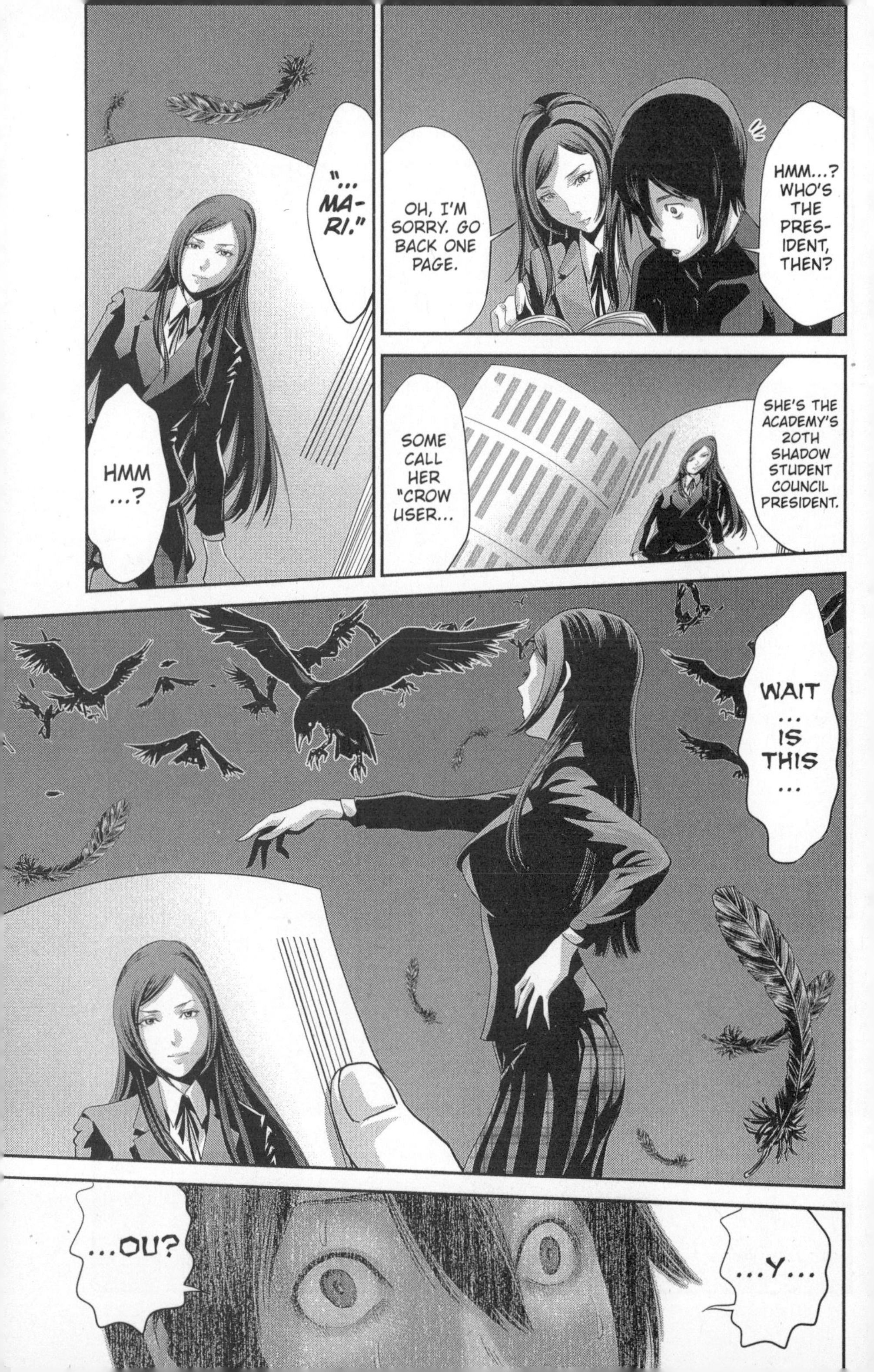
HMM...? WHO'S THE PRES-IDENT, THEN?
OH, I'M SORRY. GO BACK ONE PAGE.
SHE'S THE ACADEMY'S 20TH SHADOW STUDENT COUNCIL PRESIDENT.
SOME CALL HER "CROW USER...
"...MA-RI."
HMM ...?
WAIT ... IS THIS ...
...Y...
...OU?

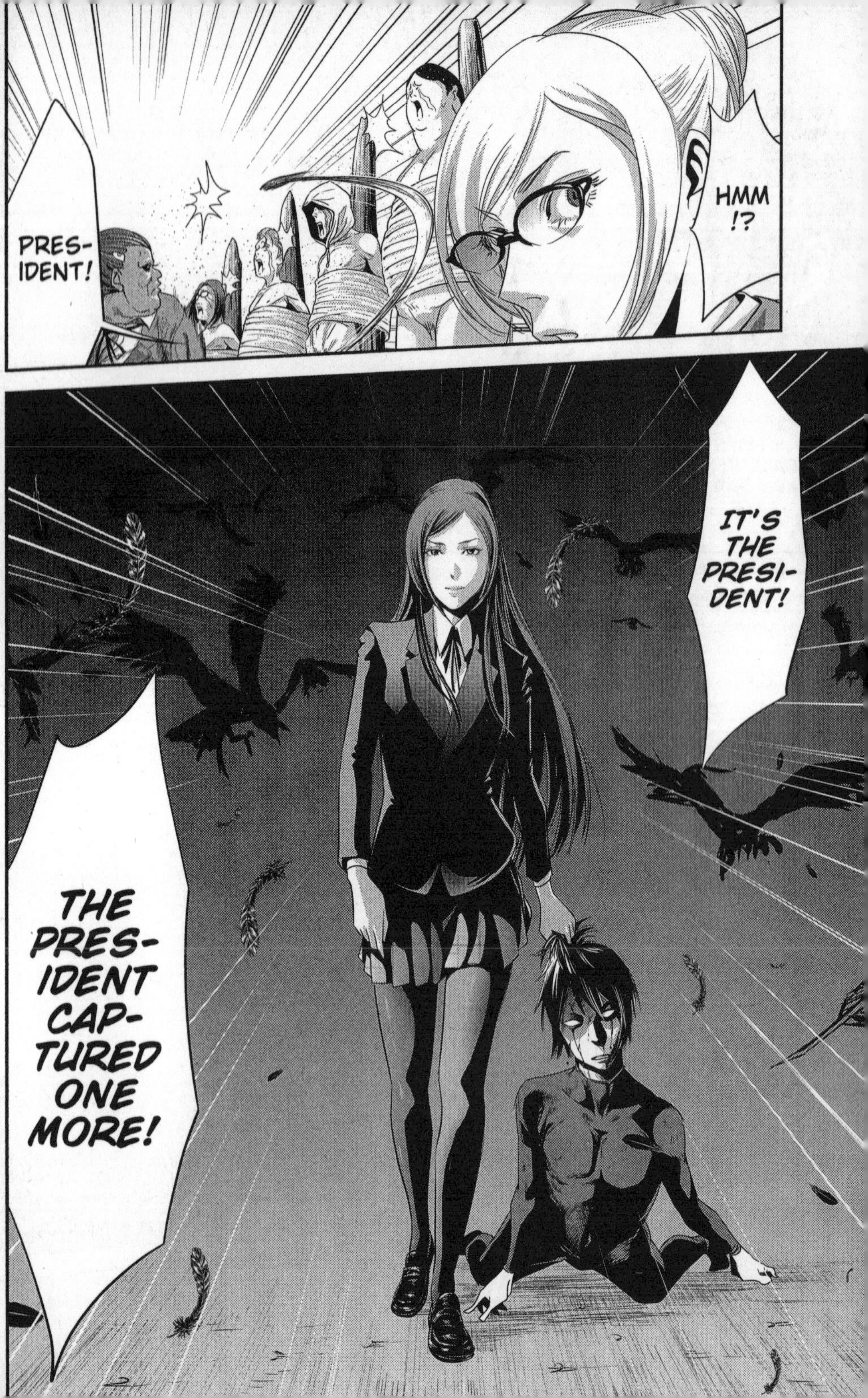
HMM !?
PRES- IDENT!
IT'S THE PRESI- DENT!
THE PRES- IDENT CAP- TURED ONE MORE!

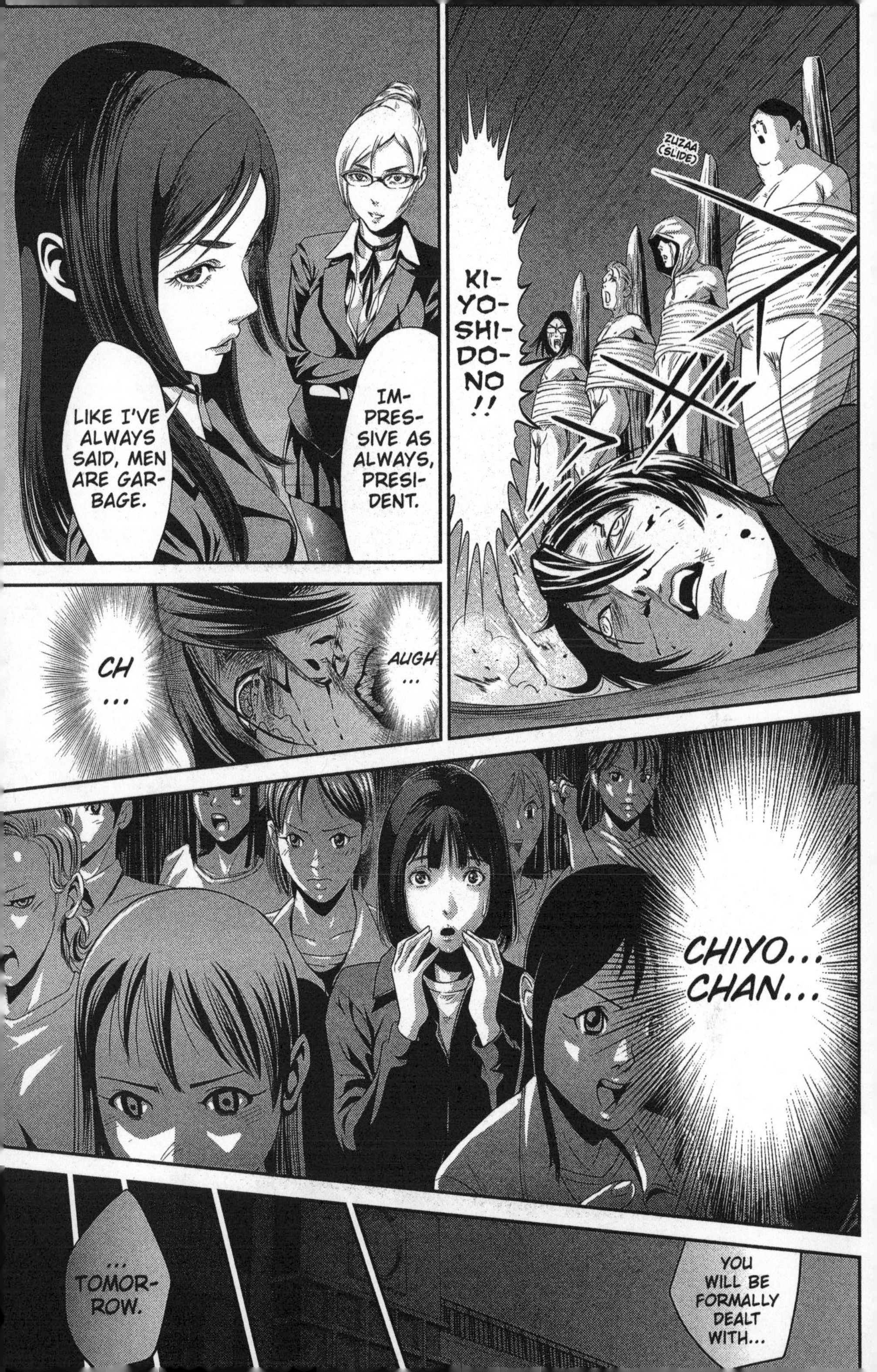

ZUZAA (SLIDE)
KI-YO-SHI-DO-NO!!
IM-PRES-SIVE AS ALWAYS, PRESI-DENT.
LIKE I'VE ALWAYS SAID, MEN ARE GAR-BAGE.
AUGH ...
CH ...
CHIYO... CHAN...
YOU WILL BE FORMALLY DEALT WITH...
... TOMOR-ROW.

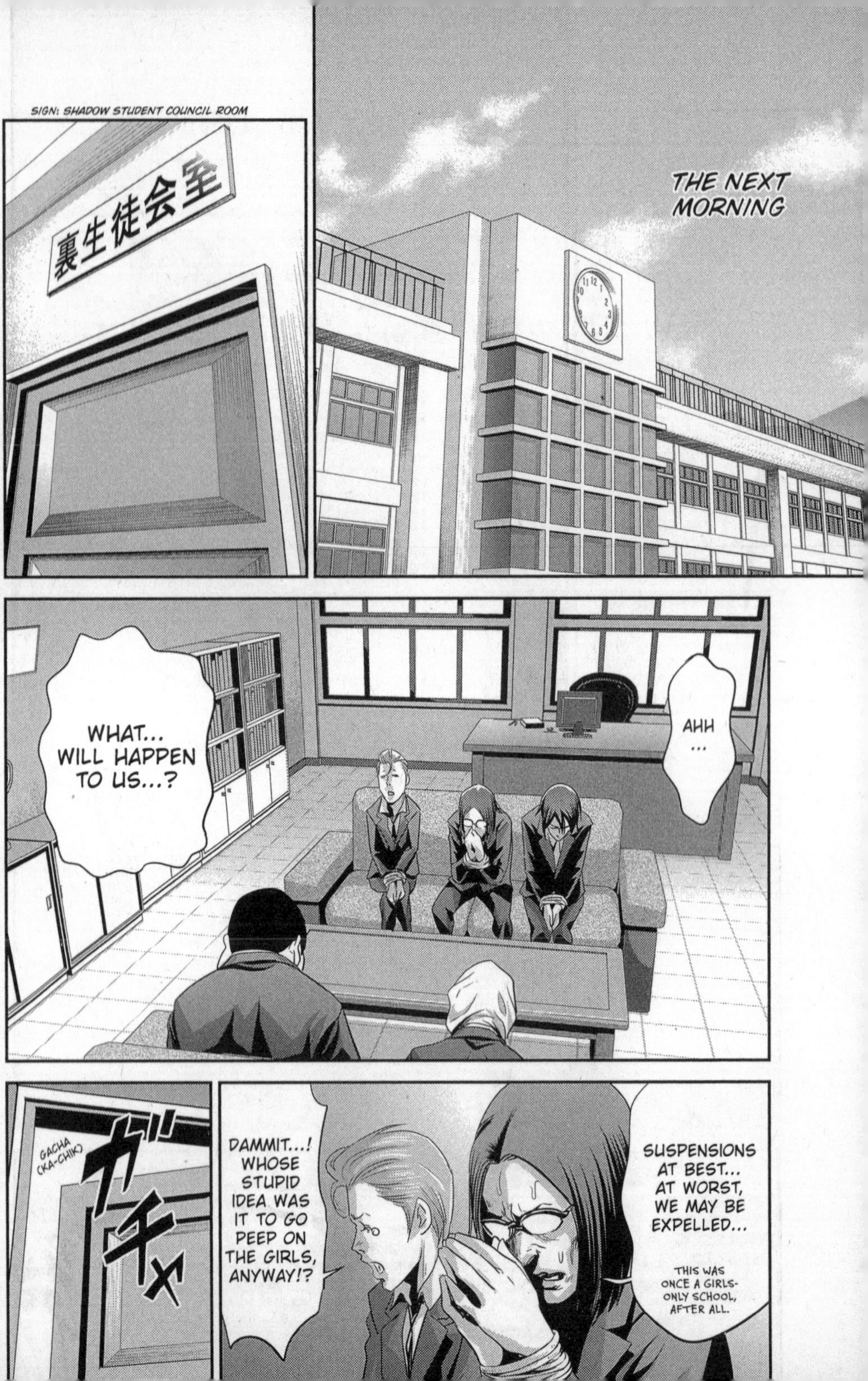
THE NEXT MORNING
裏生徒会室
SIGN: SHADOW STUDENT COUNCIL ROOM
AHH...
WHAT... WILL HAPPEN TO US...?
SUSPENSIONS AT BEST... AT WORST, WE MAY BE EXPELLED...
THIS WAS ONCE A GIRLS-ONLY SCHOOL, AFTER ALL.
DAMMIT...! WHOSE STUPID IDEA WAS IT TO GO PEEP ON THE GIRLS, ANYWAY!?
ガチャ
GACHA (KA-CHIK)

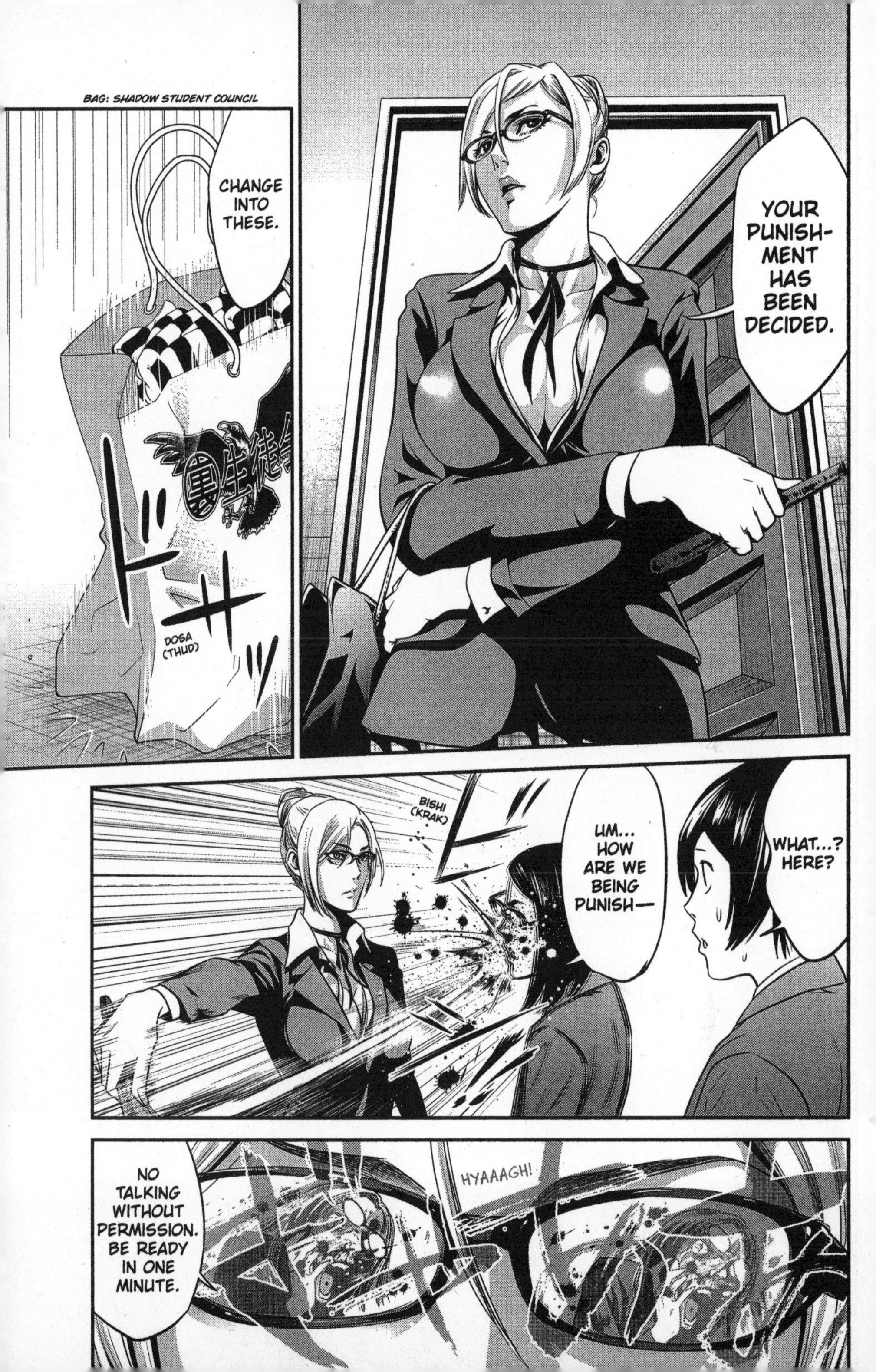
YOUR PUNISHMENT HAS BEEN DECIDED.
BAG: SHADOW STUDENT COUNCIL
CHANGE INTO THESE.
DOSA (THUD)
WHAT...? HERE?
UM... HOW ARE WE BEING PUNISH—
BISHI (KRAK)
HYAAAGH!
NO TALKING WITHOUT PERMISSION. BE READY IN ONE MINUTE.

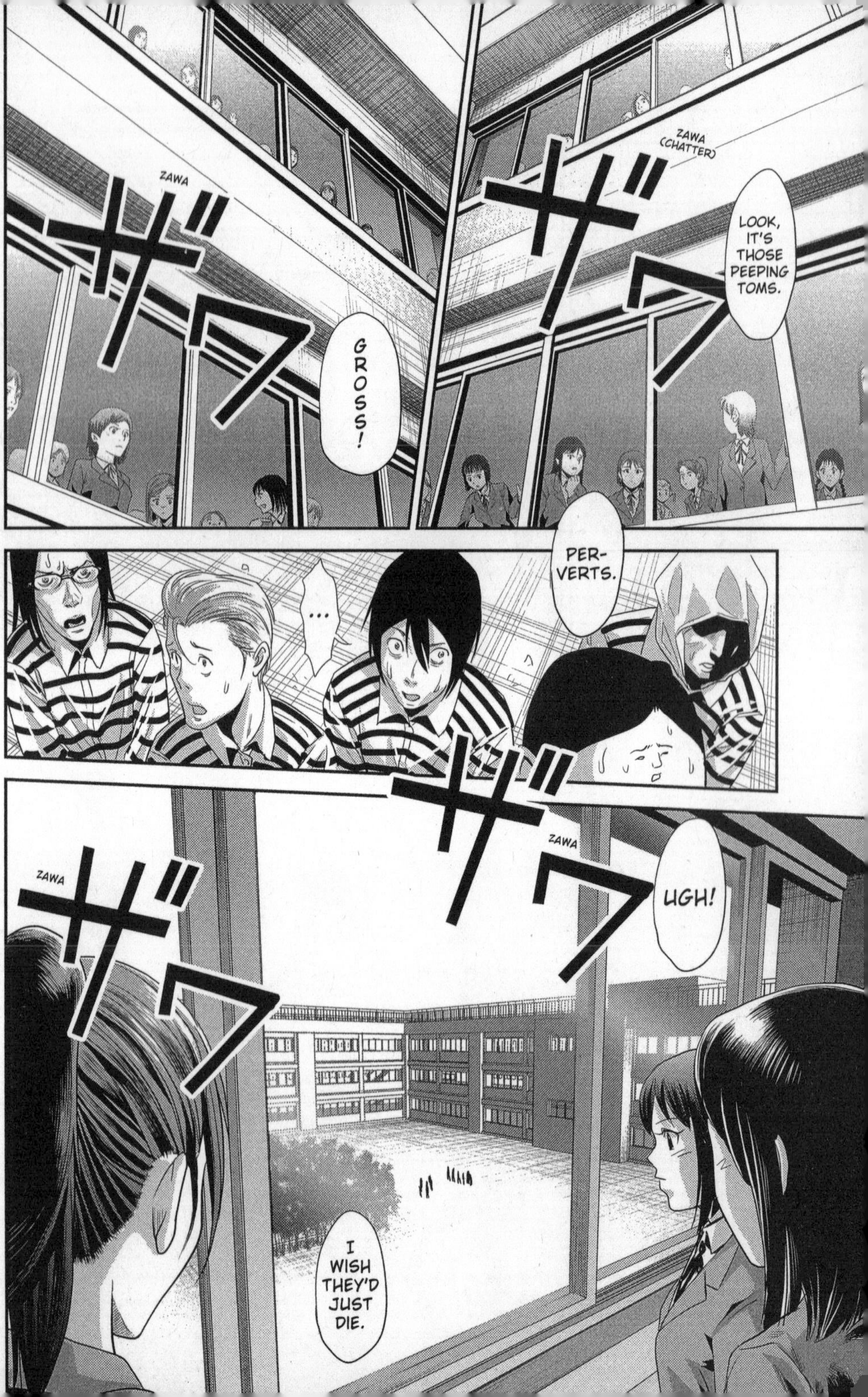

ザワ
ZAWA (CHATTER)
LOOK, IT'S THOSE PEEPING TOMS.
ザワ
ZAWA
GROSS!
PER-VERTS.
...
ザワ
ZAWA
UGH!
ザワ
ZAWA
I WISH THEY'D JUST DIE.

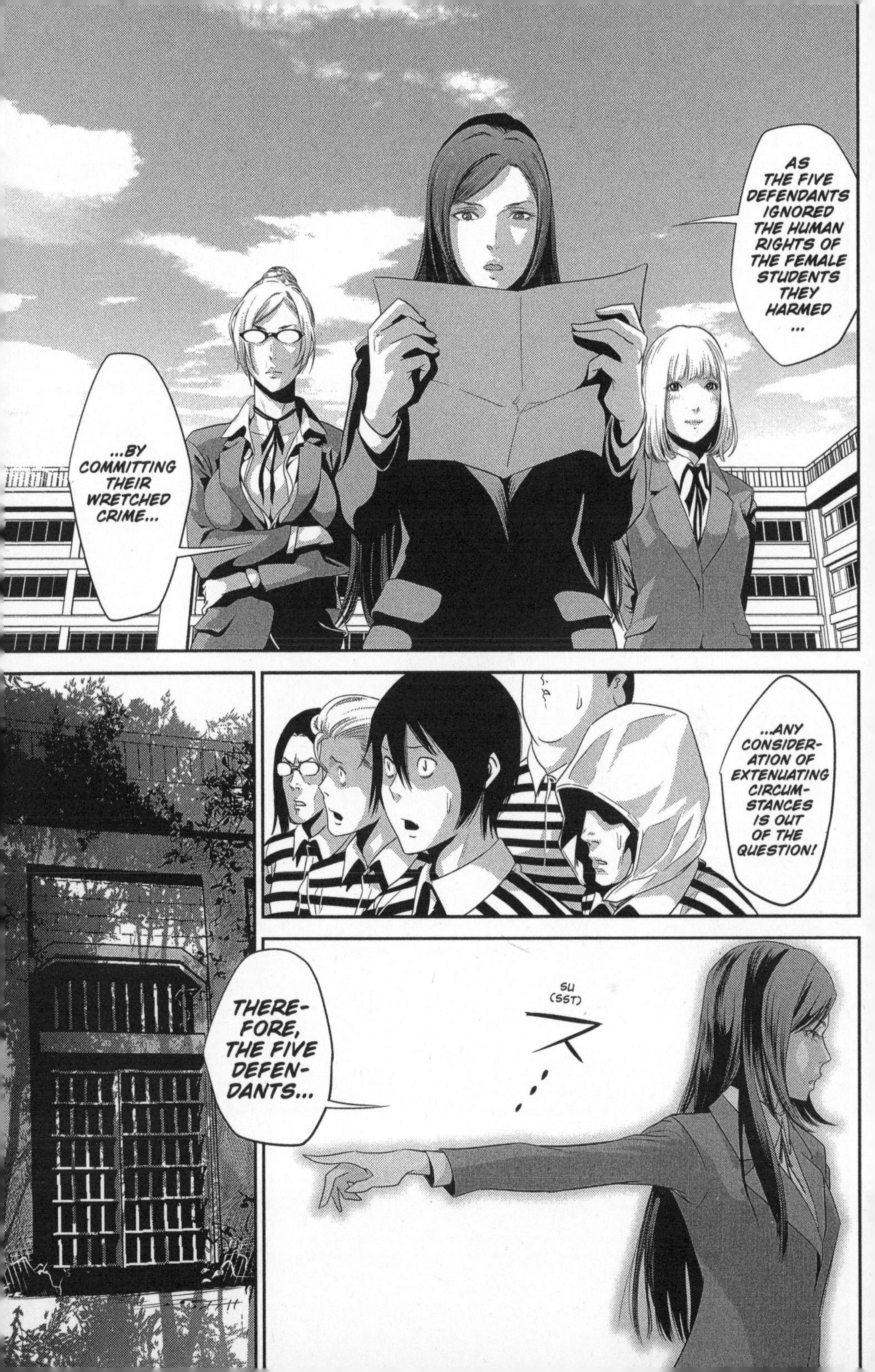
AS THE FIVE DEFENDANTS IGNORED THE HUMAN RIGHTS OF THE FEMALE STUDENTS THEY HARMED ...
...BY COMMITTING THEIR WRETCHED CRIME...
...ANY CONSIDER-ATION OF EXTENUATING CIRCUM-STANCES IS OUT OF THE QUESTION!
SU (SST)
ス
THERE-FORE, THE FIVE DEFEN-DANTS...

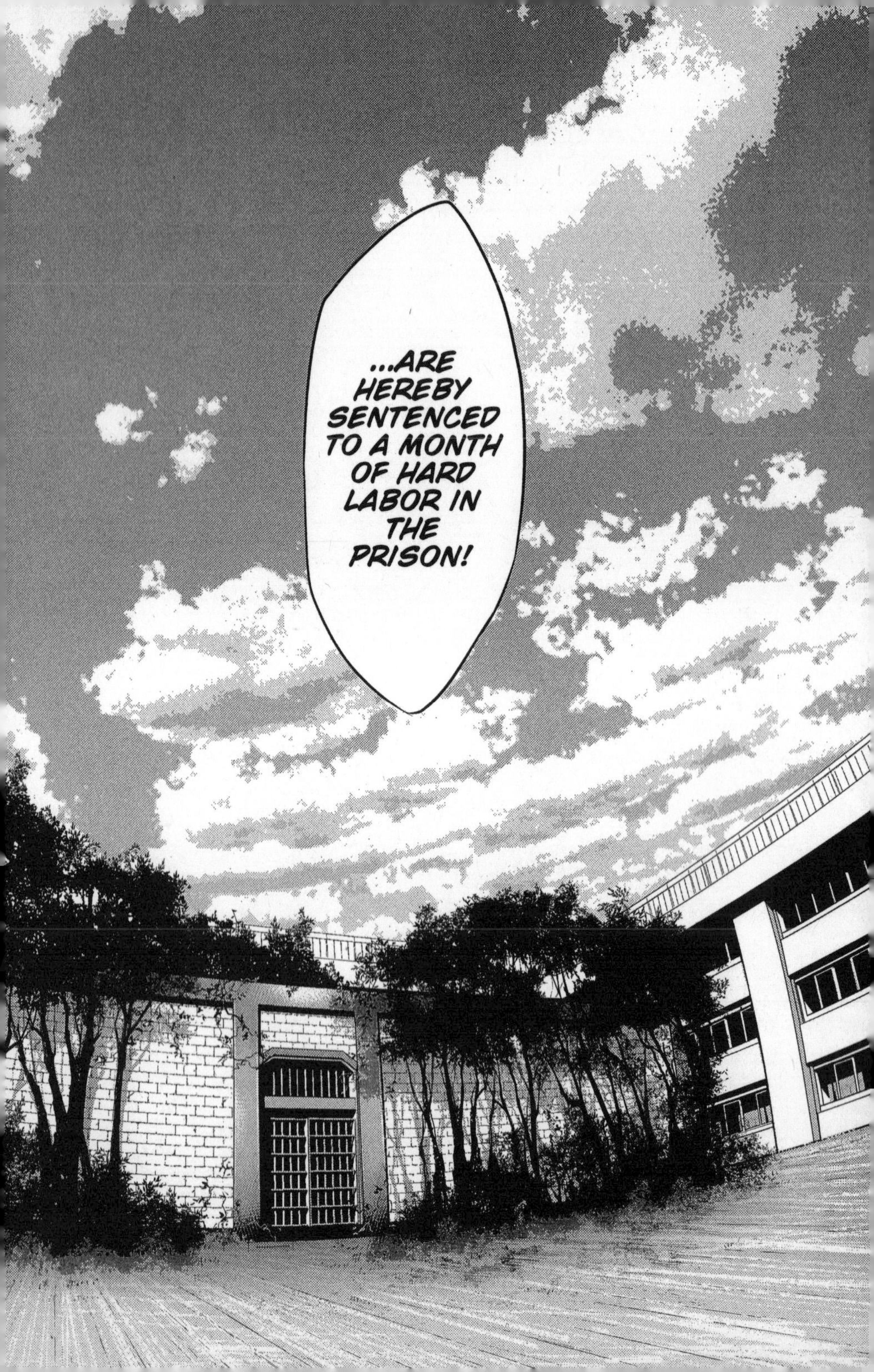
...ARE HEREBY SENTENCED TO A MONTH OF HARD LABOR IN THE PRISON!

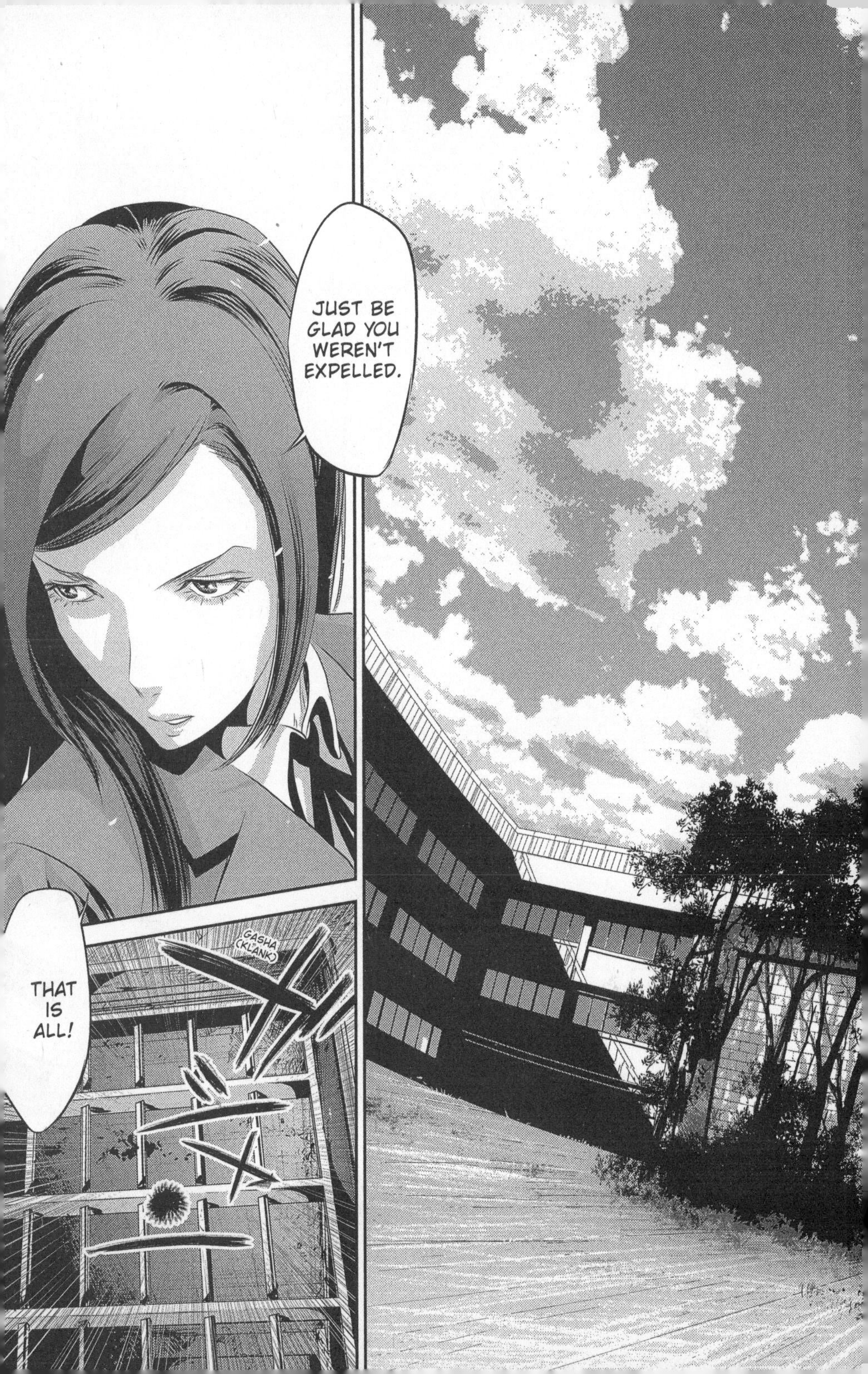
JUST BE GLAD YOU WEREN'T EXPELLED.
THAT IS ALL!
GASHA (KLANK)

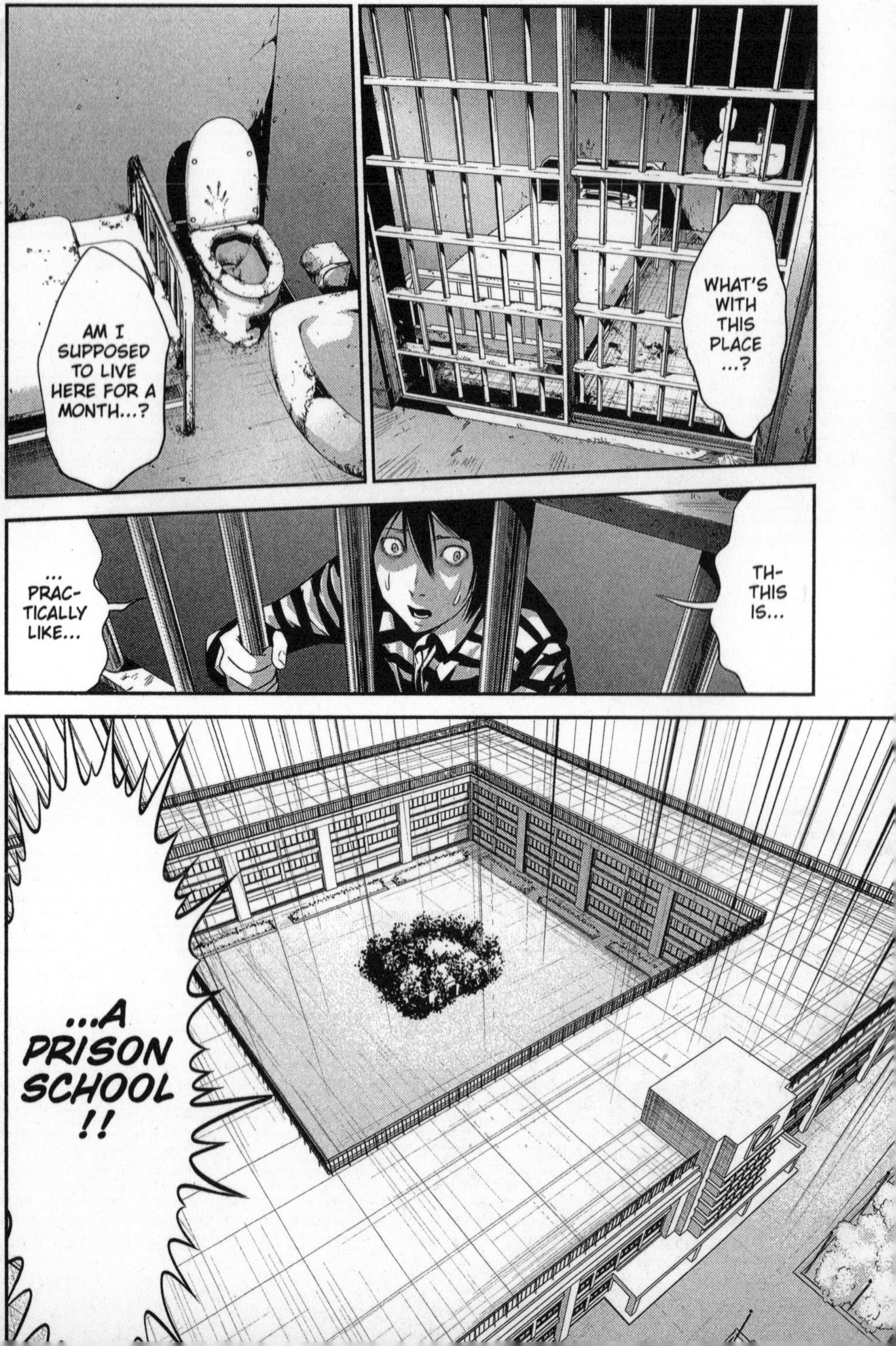
WHAT'S WITH THIS PLACE ...?
AM I SUPPOSED TO LIVE HERE FOR A MONTH...?
TH- THIS IS...
... PRAC- TICALLY LIKE...
...A PRISON SCHOOL !!

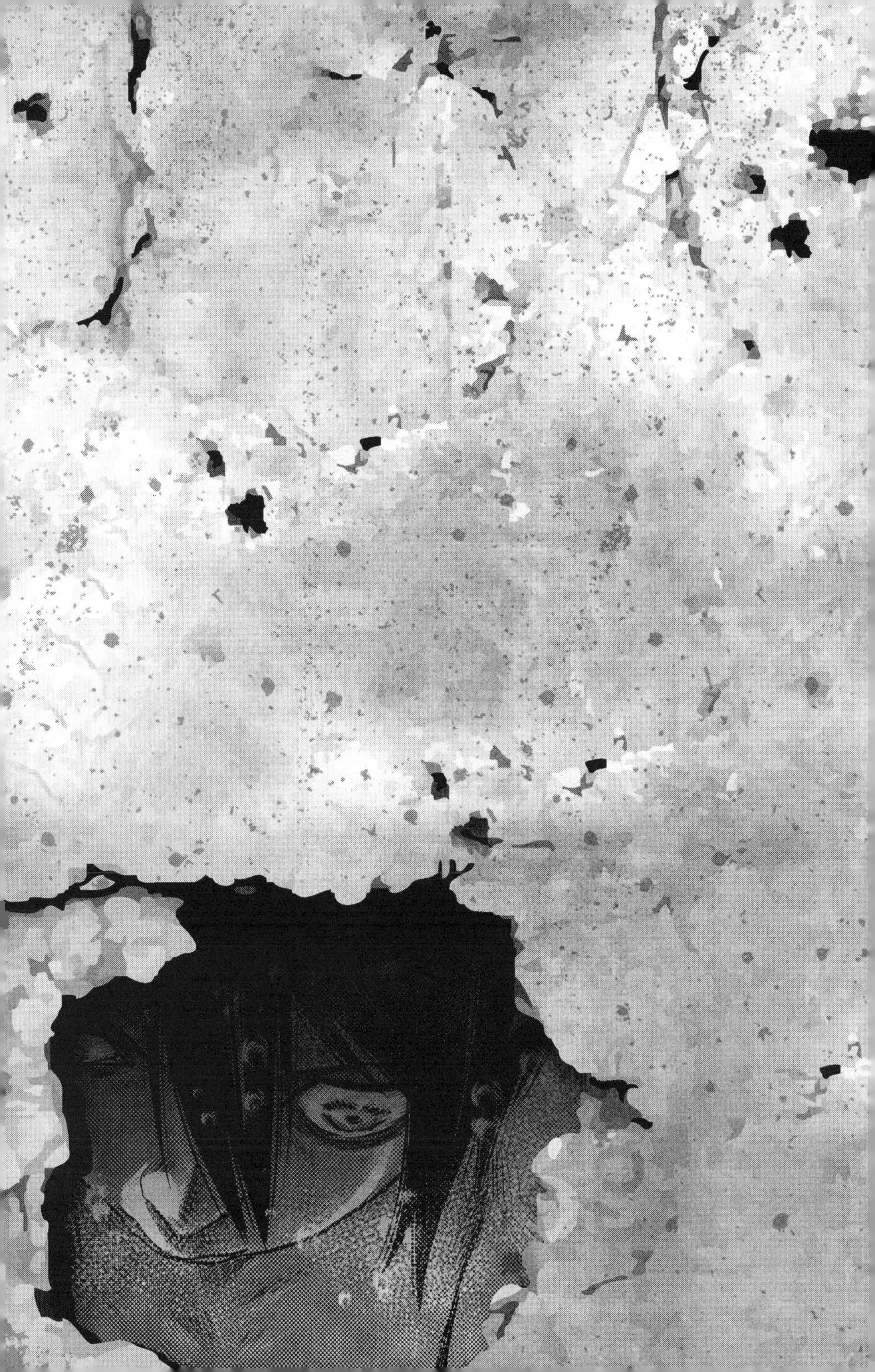

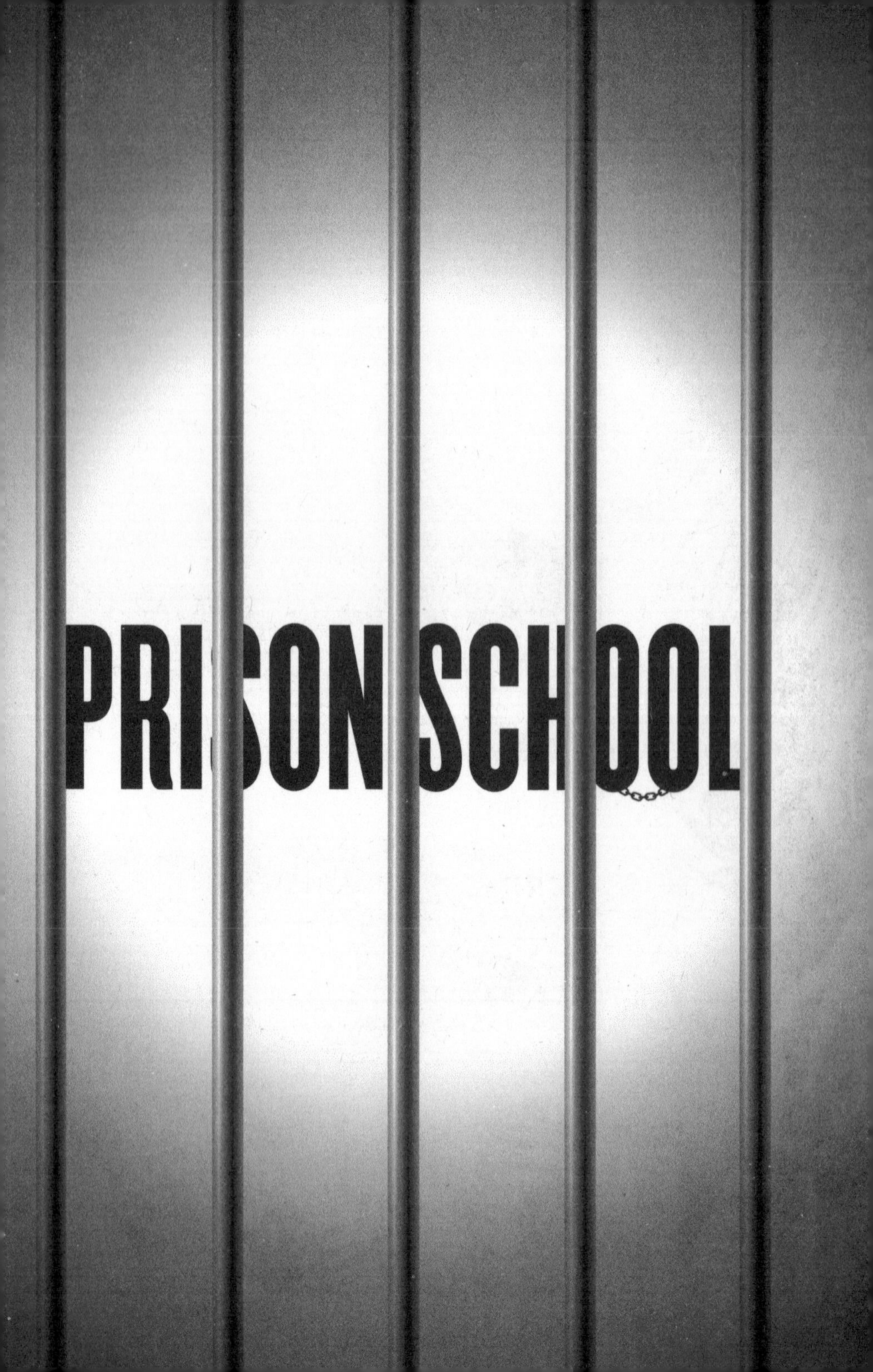
PRISON SCHOOL

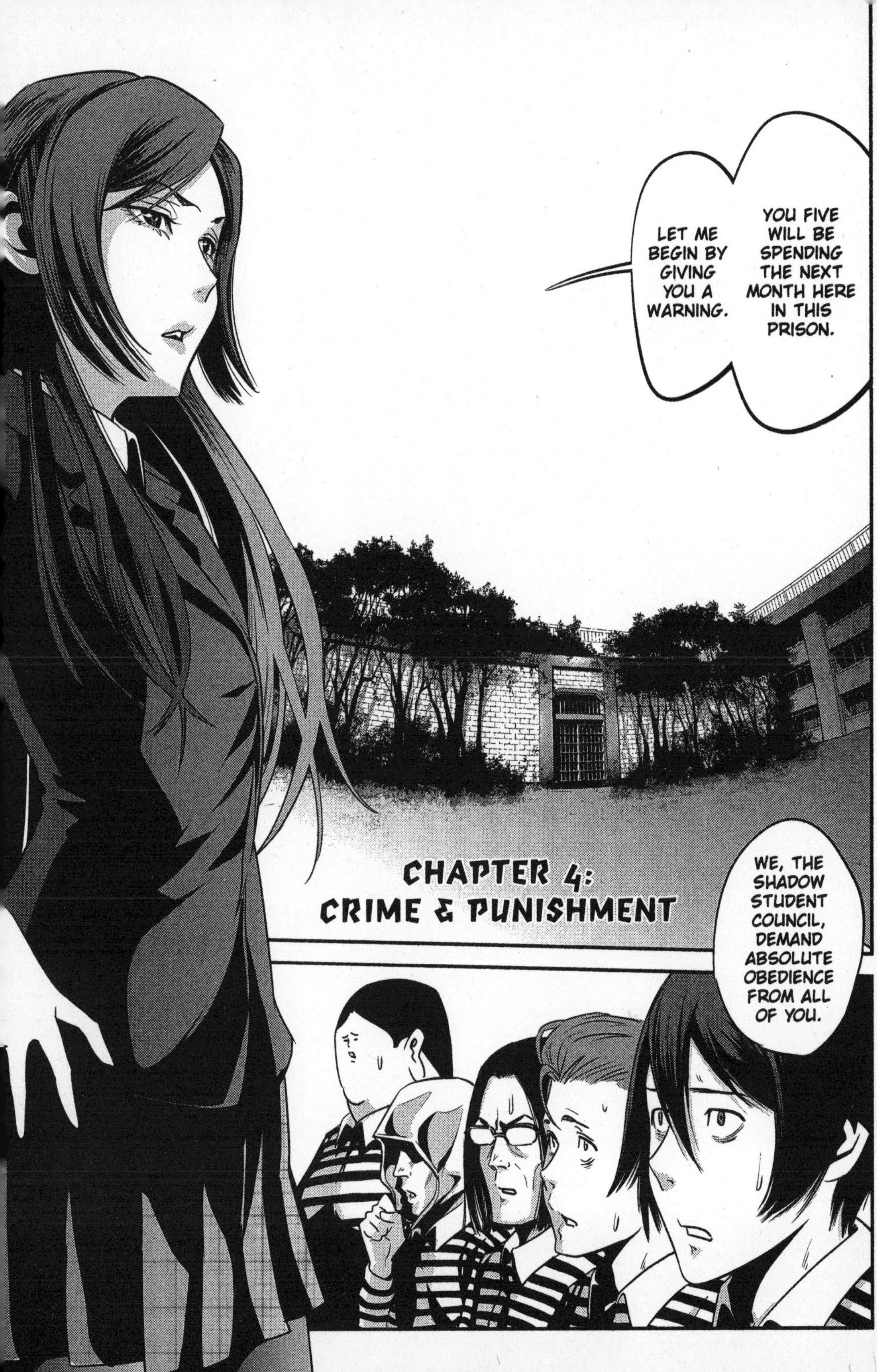
YOU FIVE WILL BE SPENDING THE NEXT MONTH HERE IN THIS PRISON.
LET ME BEGIN BY GIVING YOU A WARNING.
CHAPTER 4: CRIME & PUNISHMENT
WE, THE SHADOW STUDENT COUNCIL, DEMAND ABSOLUTE OBEDIENCE FROM ALL OF YOU.

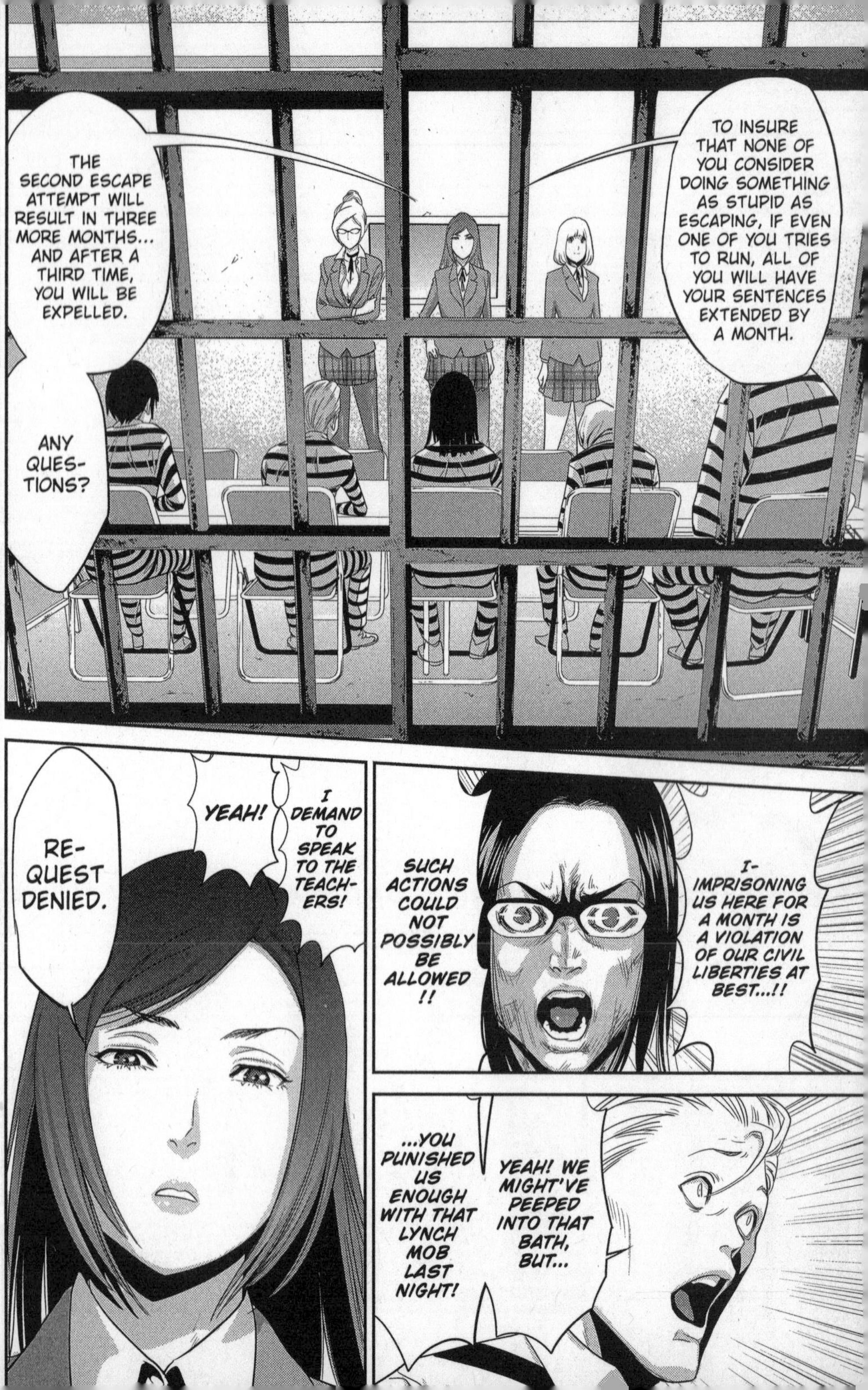

TO INSURE THAT NONE OF YOU CONSIDER DOING SOMETHING AS STUPID AS ESCAPING, IF EVEN ONE OF YOU TRIES TO RUN, ALL OF YOU WILL HAVE YOUR SENTENCES EXTENDED BY A MONTH.
THE SECOND ESCAPE ATTEMPT WILL RESULT IN THREE MORE MONTHS... AND AFTER A THIRD TIME, YOU WILL BE EXPELLED.
ANY QUESTIONS?
I- IMPRISONING US HERE FOR A MONTH IS A VIOLATION OF OUR CIVIL LIBERTIES AT BEST...!!
SUCH ACTIONS COULD NOT POSSIBLY BE ALLOWED !!
YEAH! WE MIGHT'VE PEEPED INTO THAT BATH, BUT...
...YOU PUNISHED US ENOUGH WITH THAT LYNCH MOB LAST NIGHT!
I DEMAND TO SPEAK TO THE TEACHERS!
YEAH!
REQUEST DENIED.

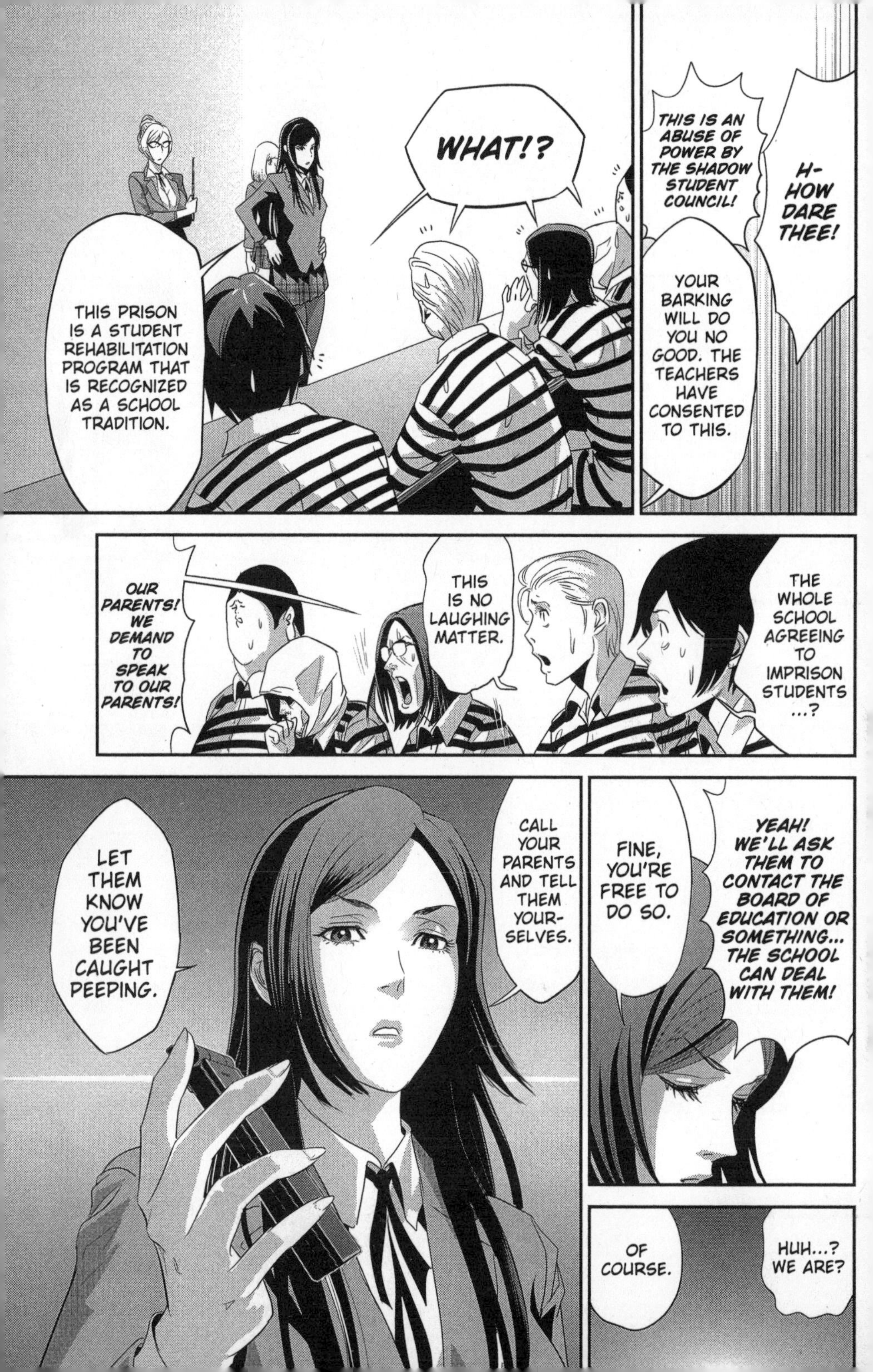
H-HOW DARE THEE!
THIS IS AN ABUSE OF POWER BY THE SHADOW STUDENT COUNCIL!
YOUR BARKING WILL DO YOU NO GOOD. THE TEACHERS HAVE CONSENTED TO THIS.
WHAT!?
THIS PRISON IS A STUDENT REHABILITATION PROGRAM THAT IS RECOGNIZED AS A SCHOOL TRADITION.
THE WHOLE SCHOOL AGREEING TO IMPRISON STUDENTS ...?
THIS IS NO LAUGHING MATTER.
OUR PARENTS! WE DEMAND TO SPEAK TO OUR PARENTS!
YEAH! WE'LL ASK THEM TO CONTACT THE BOARD OF EDUCATION OR SOMETHING... THE SCHOOL CAN DEAL WITH THEM!
FINE, YOU'RE FREE TO DO SO.
HUH...? WE ARE?
OF COURSE.
CALL YOUR PARENTS AND TELL THEM YOUR-SELVES.
LET THEM KNOW YOU'VE BEEN CAUGHT PEEPING.

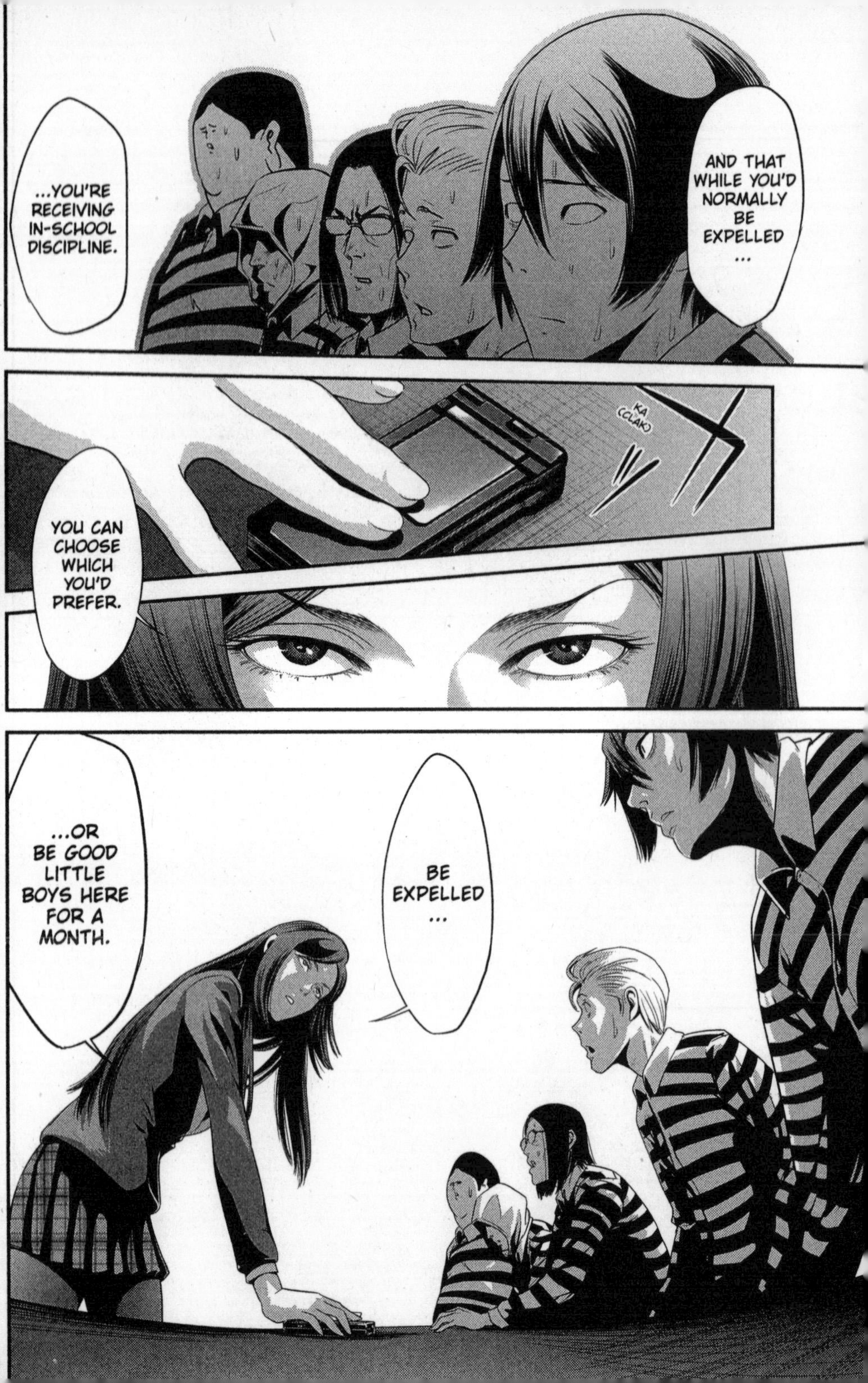
AND THAT WHILE YOU'D NORMALLY BE EXPELLED ...
...YOU'RE RECEIVING IN-SCHOOL DISCIPLINE.
KA (CLAK)
YOU CAN CHOOSE WHICH YOU'D PREFER.
BE EXPELLED ...
...OR BE GOOD LITTLE BOYS HERE FOR A MONTH.

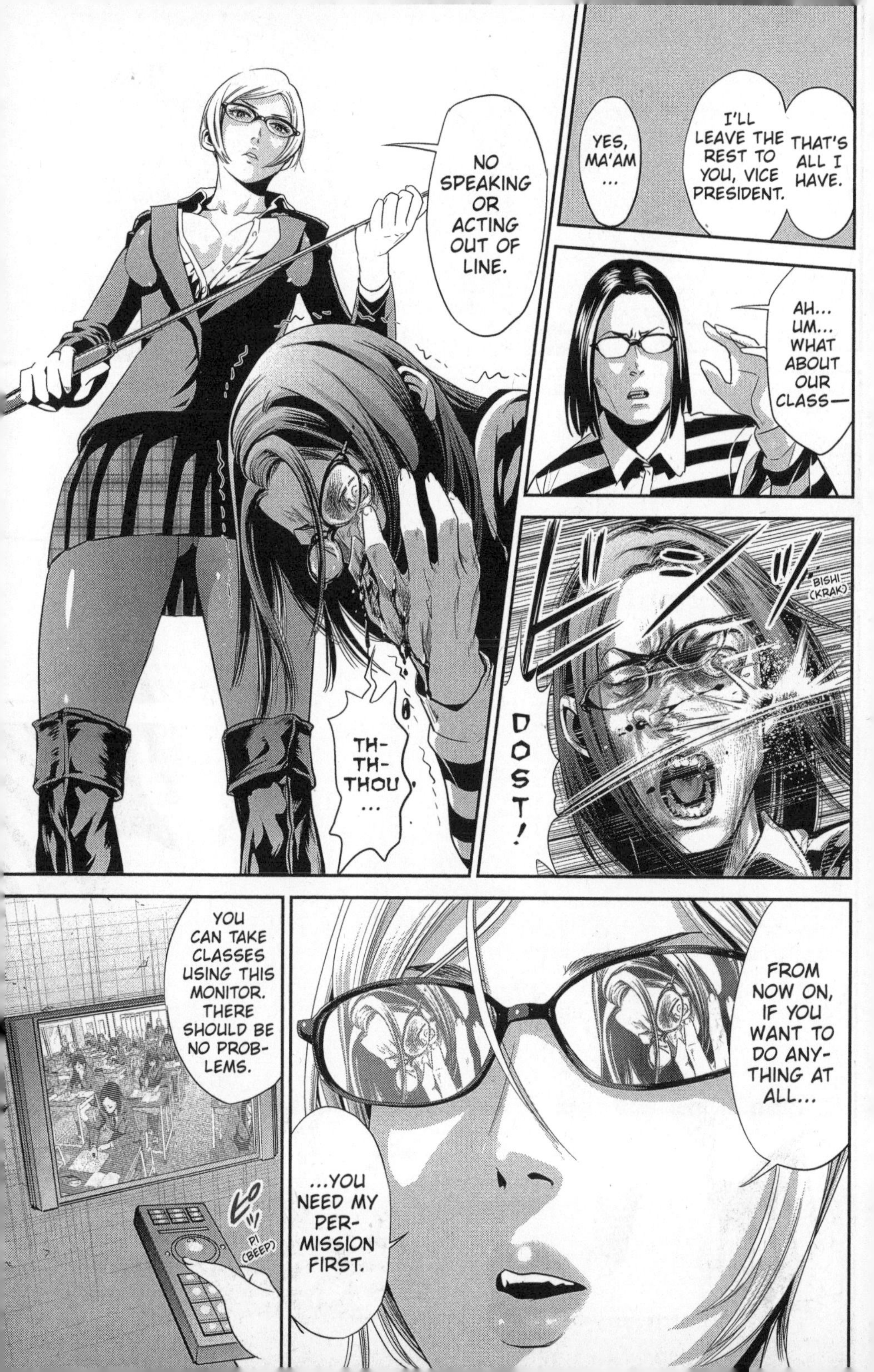

THAT'S ALL I HAVE.
I'LL LEAVE THE REST TO YOU, VICE PRESIDENT.
YES, MA'AM...
AH... UM... WHAT ABOUT OUR CLASS—
BISHI (KRAK)
DOST!
NO SPEAKING OR ACTING OUT OF LINE.
TH-TH-THOU...
FROM NOW ON, IF YOU WANT TO DO ANYTHING AT ALL...
...YOU NEED MY PERMISSION FIRST.
YOU CAN TAKE CLASSES USING THIS MONITOR. THERE SHOULD BE NO PROBLEMS.
PI (BEEP)

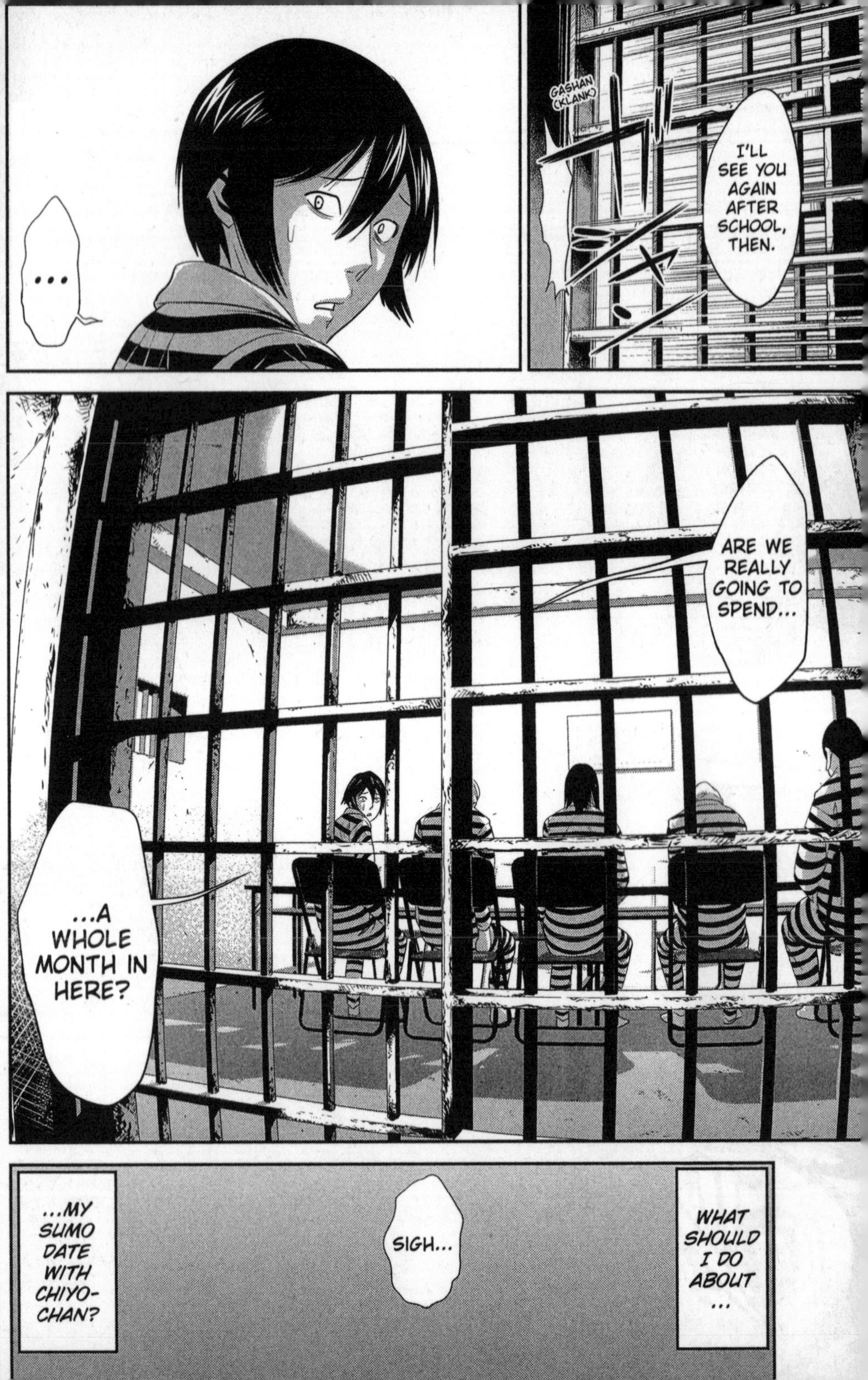
GASHAN (KLANK)
I'LL SEE YOU AGAIN AFTER SCHOOL, THEN.
...
ARE WE REALLY GOING TO SPEND...
...A WHOLE MONTH IN HERE?
WHAT SHOULD I DO ABOUT ...
SIGH...
...MY SUMO DATE WITH CHIYO-CHAN?

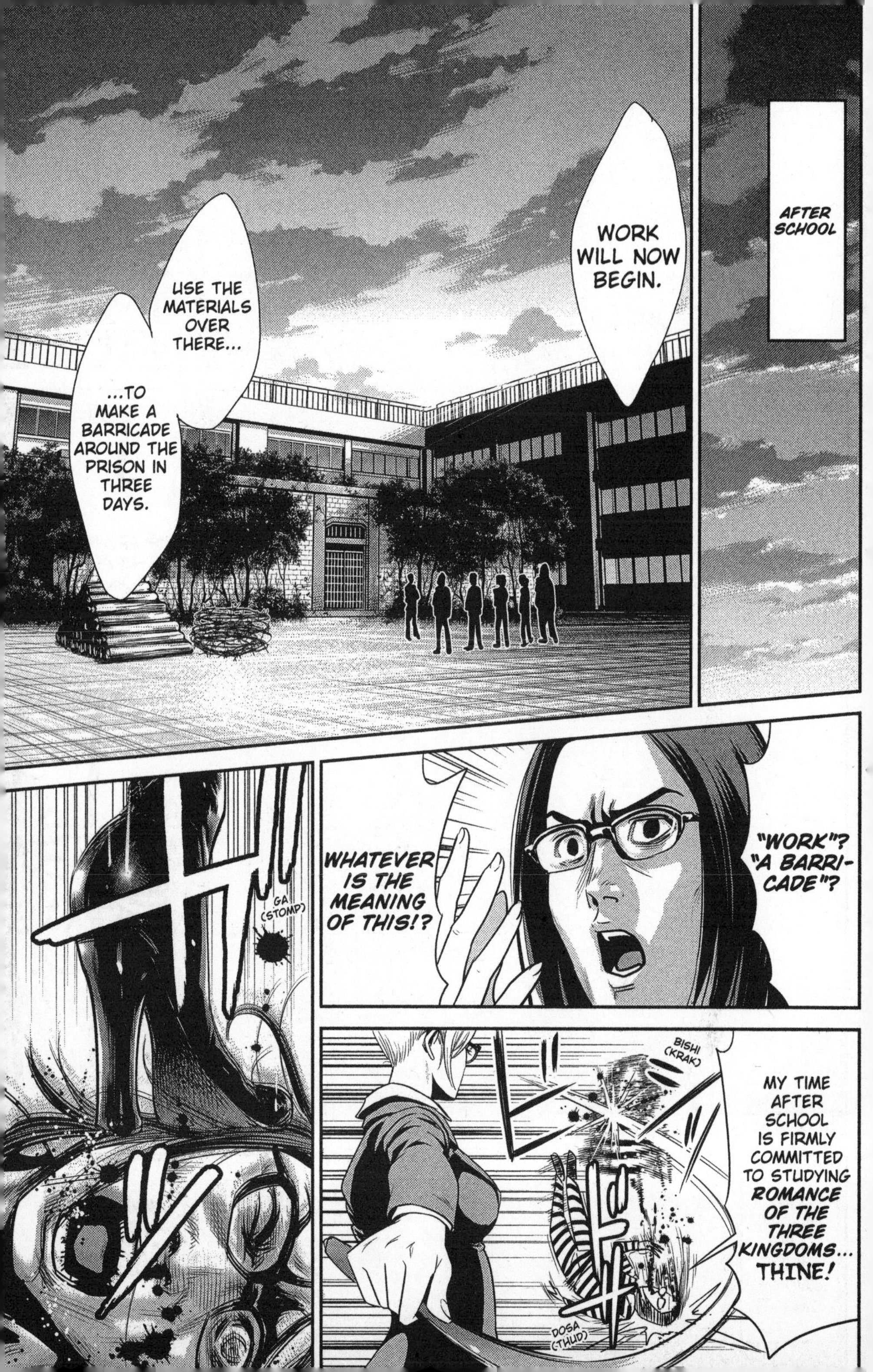

AFTER SCHOOL
WORK WILL NOW BEGIN.
USE THE MATERIALS OVER THERE...
...TO MAKE A BARRICADE AROUND THE PRISON IN THREE DAYS.
"WORK"? "A BARRI-CADE"?
WHATEVER IS THE MEANING OF THIS!?
GA (STOMP)
MY TIME AFTER SCHOOL IS FIRMLY COMMITTED TO STUDYING ROMANCE OF THE THREE KINGDOMS... THINE!
BISHI (KRAK)
DOSA (THUD)

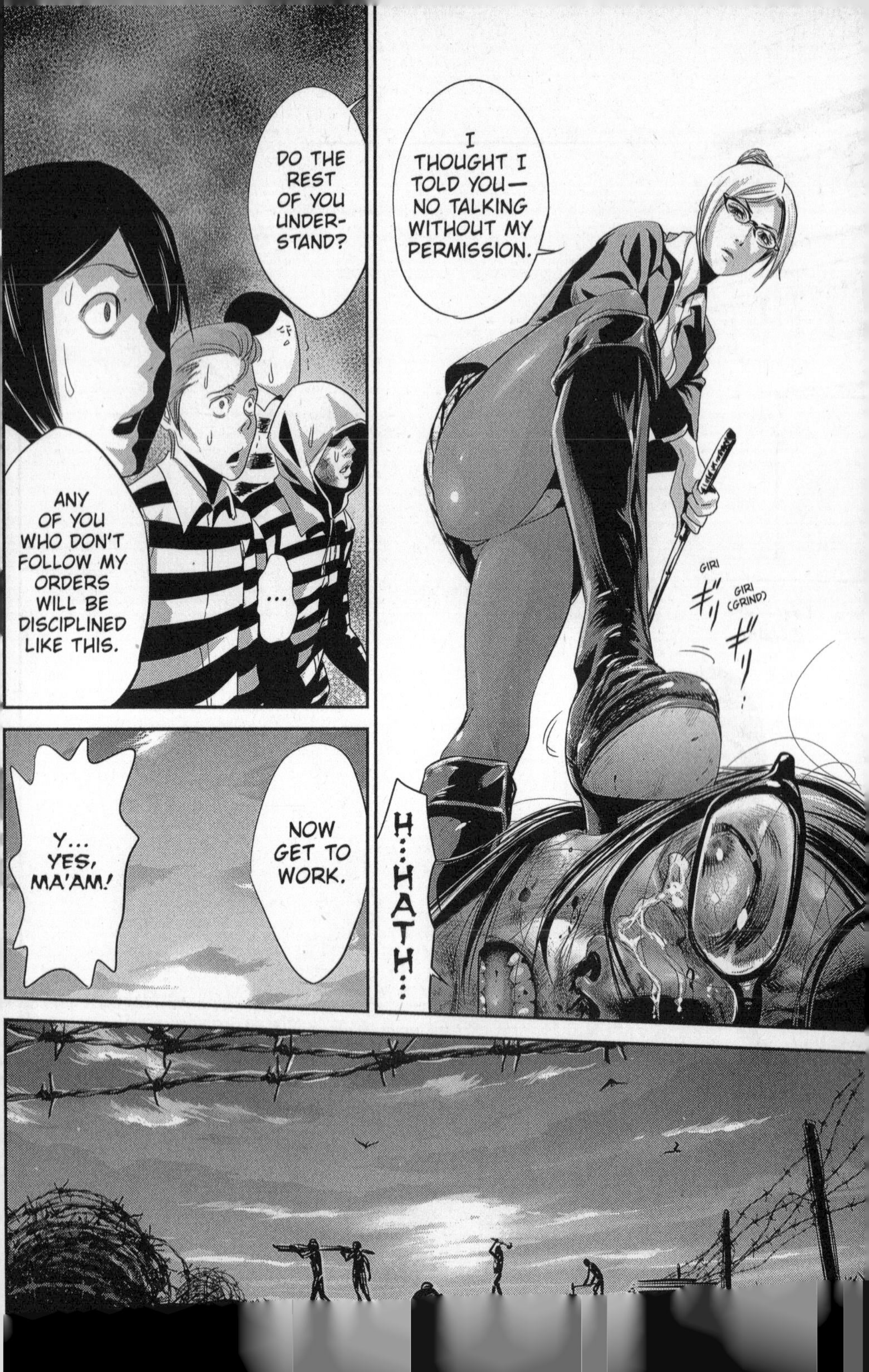

I THOUGHT I TOLD YOU— NO TALKING WITHOUT MY PERMISSION.
GIRI
GIRI (GRIND)
H...HATH...
ANY OF YOU WHO DON'T FOLLOW MY ORDERS WILL BE DISCIPLINED LIKE THIS.
DO THE REST OF YOU UNDERSTAND?
...
NOW GET TO WORK.
Y... YES, MA'AM!

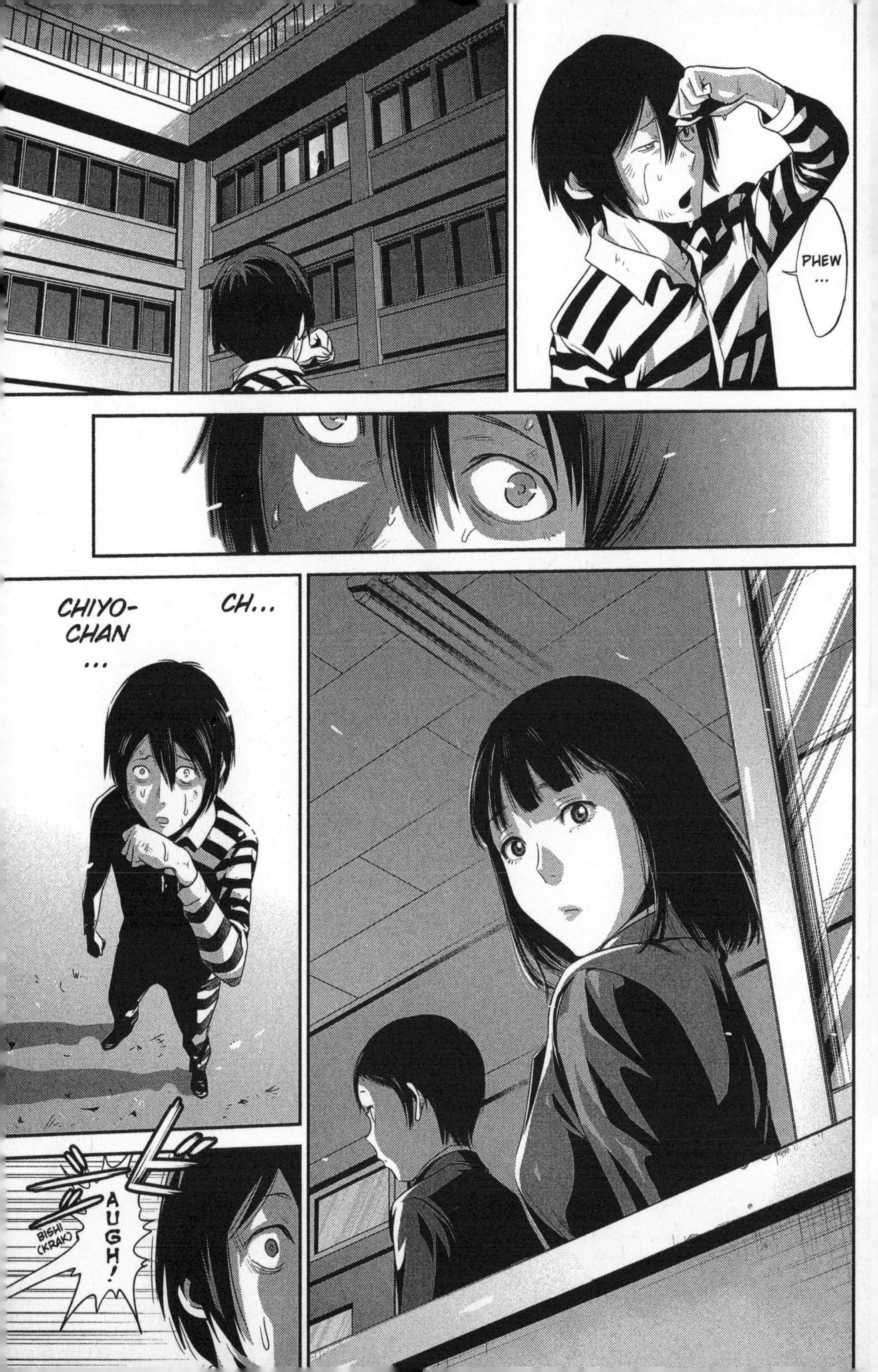
PHEW ...
CH...
CHIYO-CHAN ...
AUGH!
BISHI (KRAK)

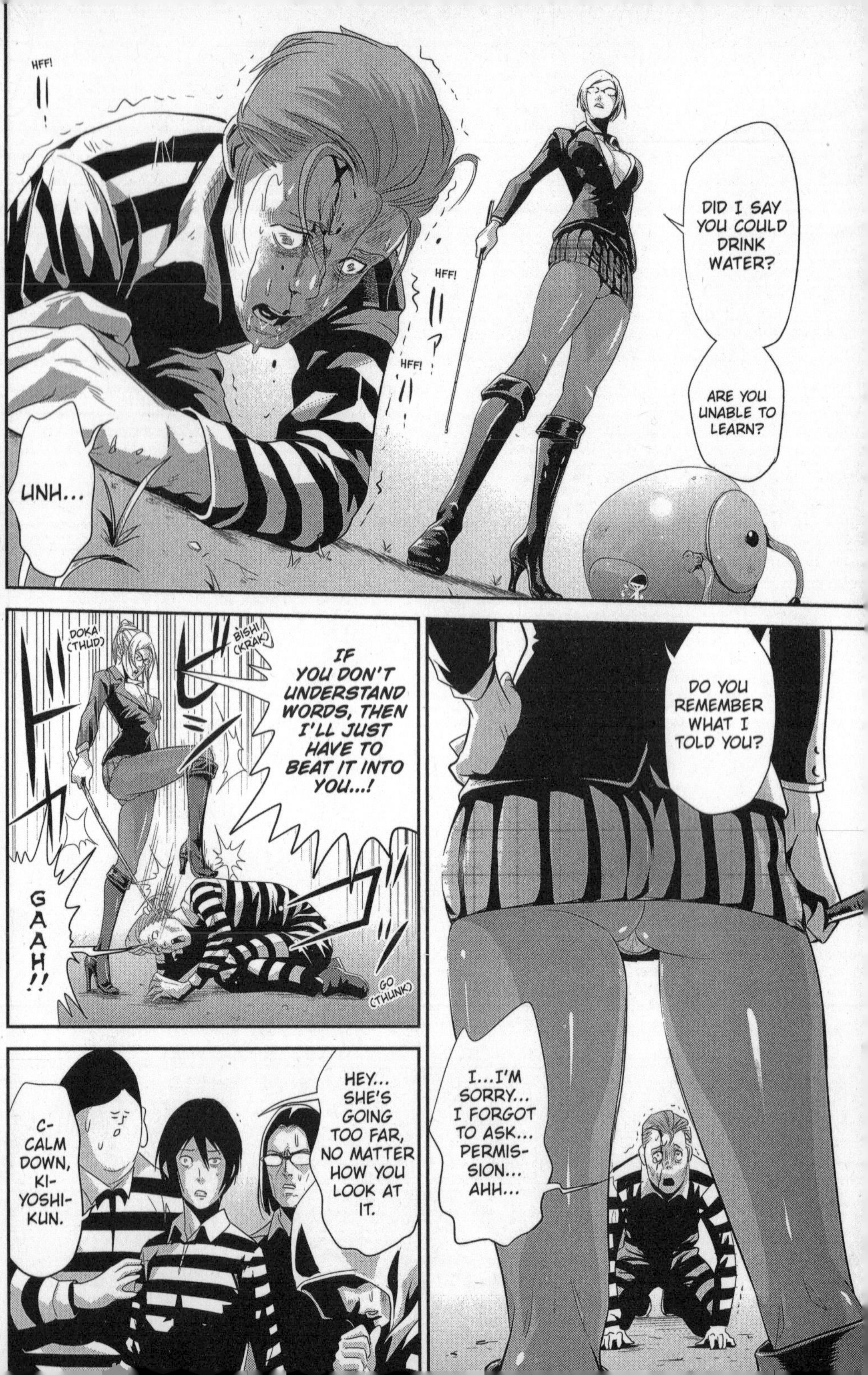
HFF!
HFF!
HFF!
DID I SAY YOU COULD DRINK WATER?
ARE YOU UNABLE TO LEARN?
UNH...
DO YOU REMEMBER WHAT I TOLD YOU?
BISHI (KRAK)
DOKA (THUD)
IF YOU DON'T UNDERSTAND WORDS, THEN I'LL JUST HAVE TO BEAT IT INTO YOU...!
GAAH!!
GO (THUNK)
I...I'M SORRY... I FORGOT TO ASK... PERMIS-SION... AHH...
HEY... SHE'S GOING TOO FAR, NO MATTER HOW YOU LOOK AT IT.
C-CALM DOWN, KI-YOSHI-KUN.

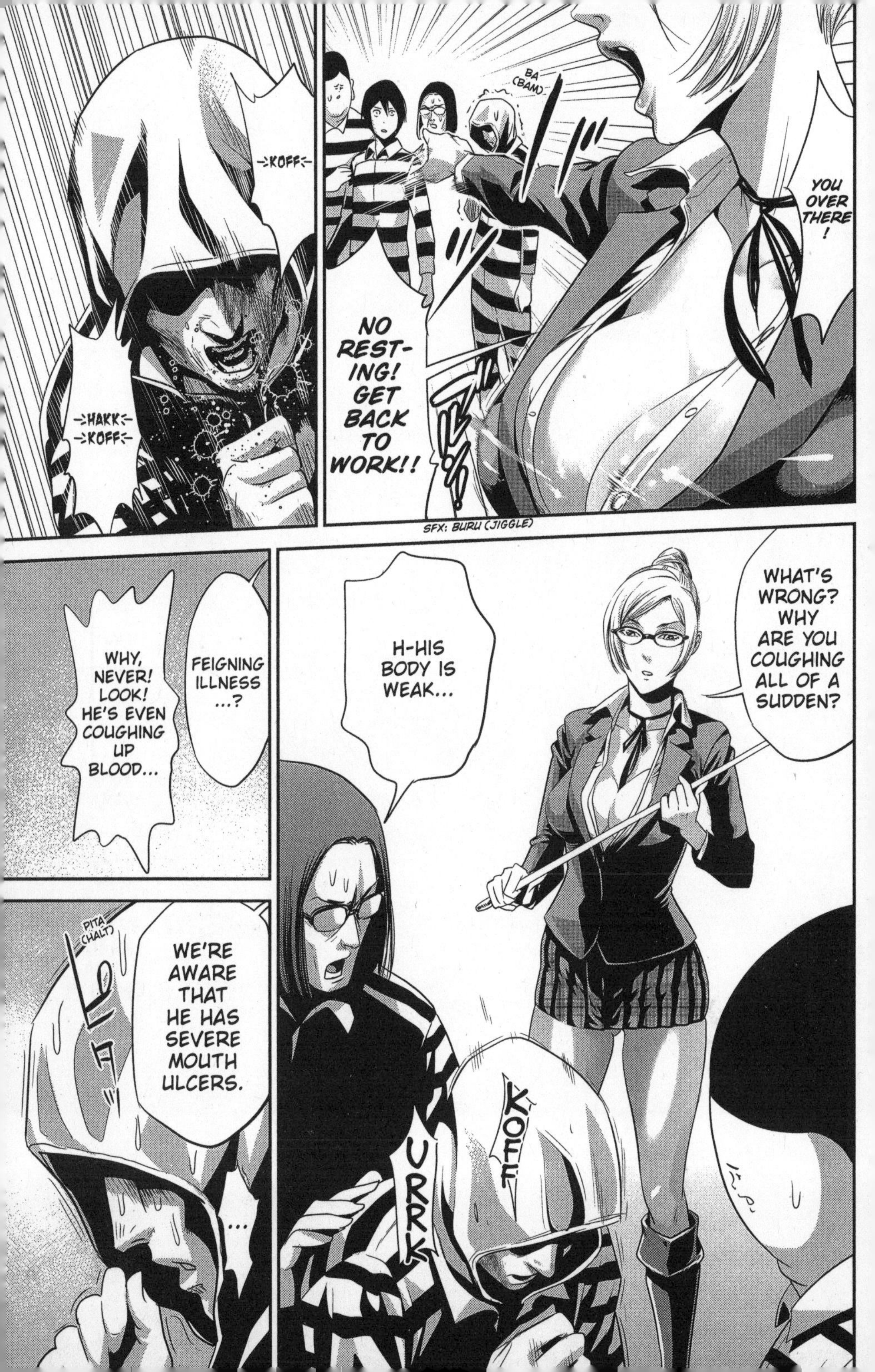

YOU OVER THERE!
BA (BAM)
NO RESTING! GET BACK TO WORK!!
SFX: BURU (JIGGLE)
-KOFF-
-HAKK- -KOFF-
WHAT'S WRONG? WHY ARE YOU COUGHING ALL OF A SUDDEN?
H-HIS BODY IS WEAK...
FEIGNING ILLNESS ...?
WHY, NEVER! LOOK! HE'S EVEN COUGHING UP BLOOD...
WE'RE AWARE THAT HE HAS SEVERE MOUTH ULCERS.
PITA (HALT)
KOFF
URRK
...

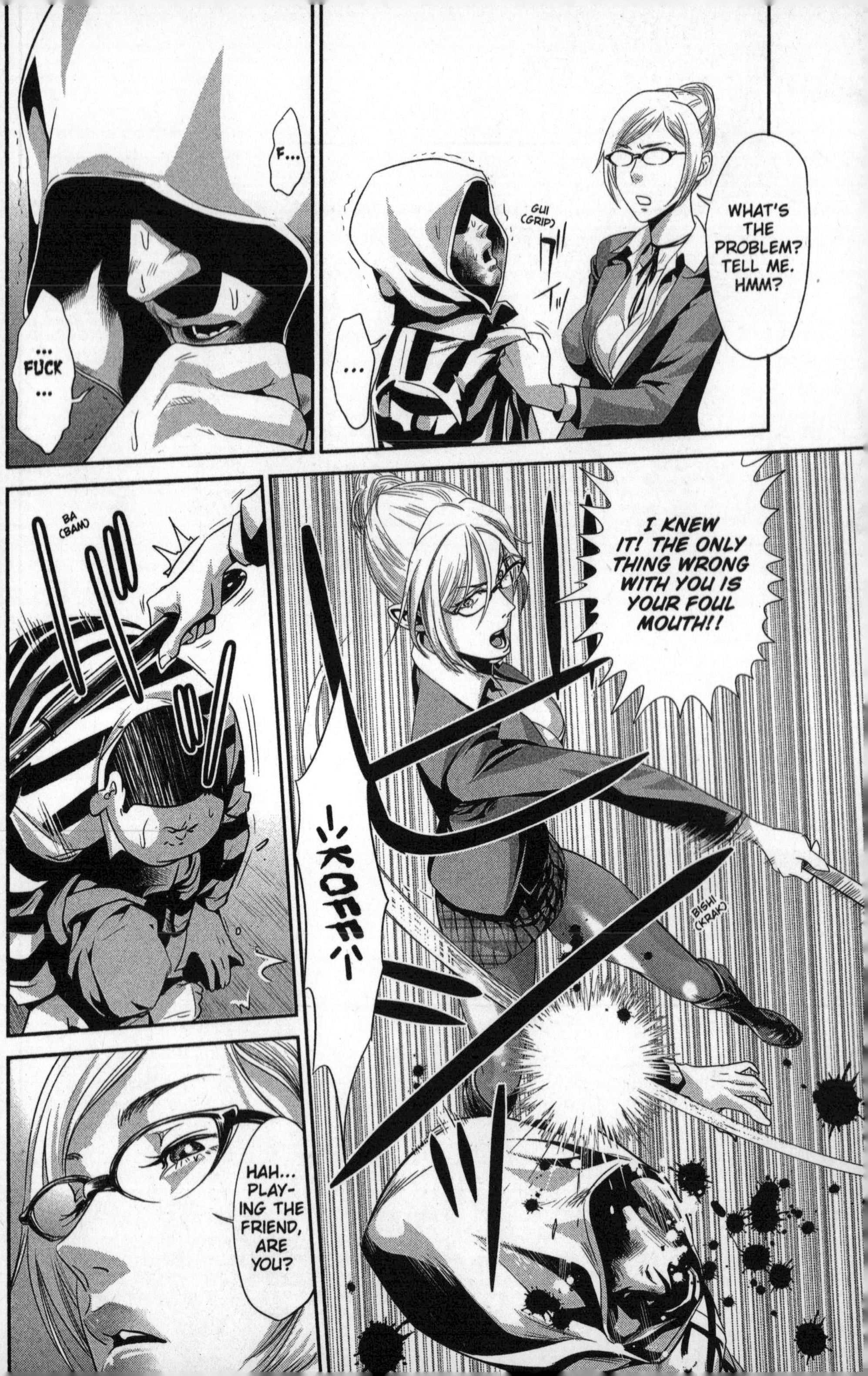
WHAT'S THE PROBLEM? TELL ME. HMM?
GUI (GRIP)
...
F...
...FUCK...
I KNEW IT! THE ONLY THING WRONG WITH YOU IS YOUR FOUL MOUTH!!
BISHI (KRAK)
KOFF
BA (BAM)
HAH... PLAY-ING THE FRIEND, ARE YOU?

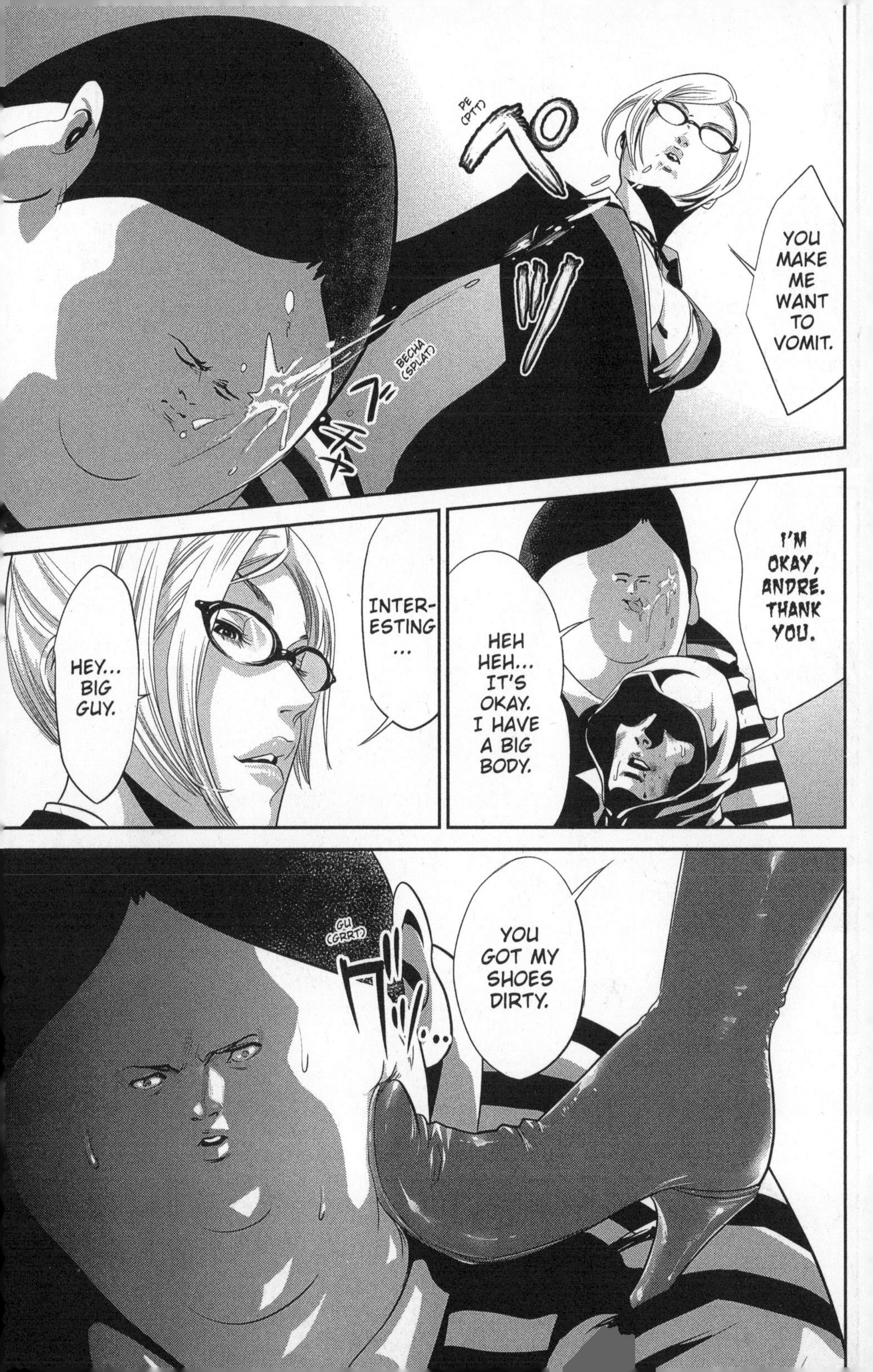
PE (PTT)
YOU MAKE ME WANT TO VOMIT.
BECHA (SPLAT)
I'M OKAY, ANDRE. THANK YOU.
HEH HEH... IT'S OKAY. I HAVE A BIG BODY.
INTER-ESTING...
HEY... BIG GUY.
GU (GRRT)
YOU GOT MY SHOES DIRTY.

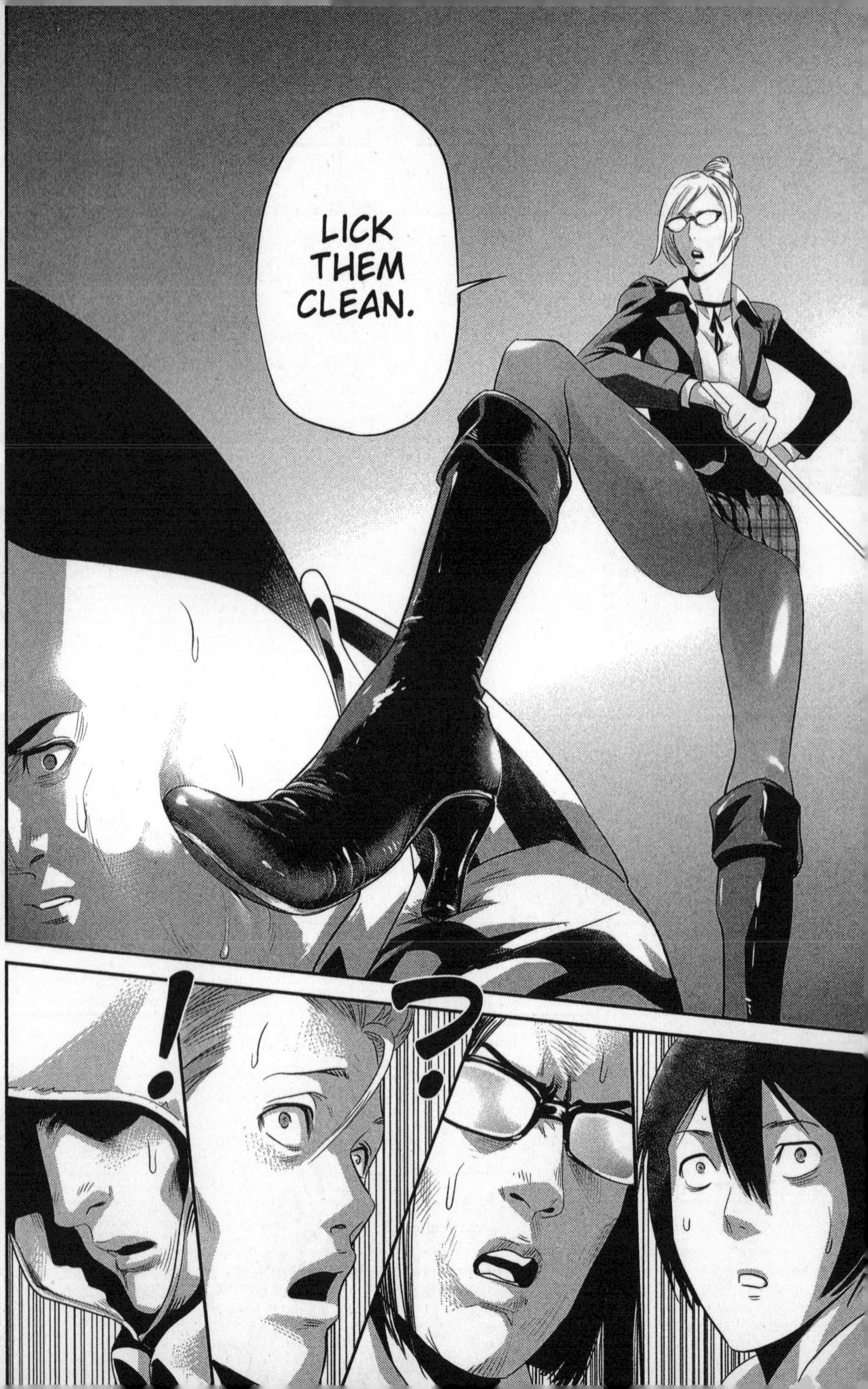
LICK THEM CLEAN.
!
?

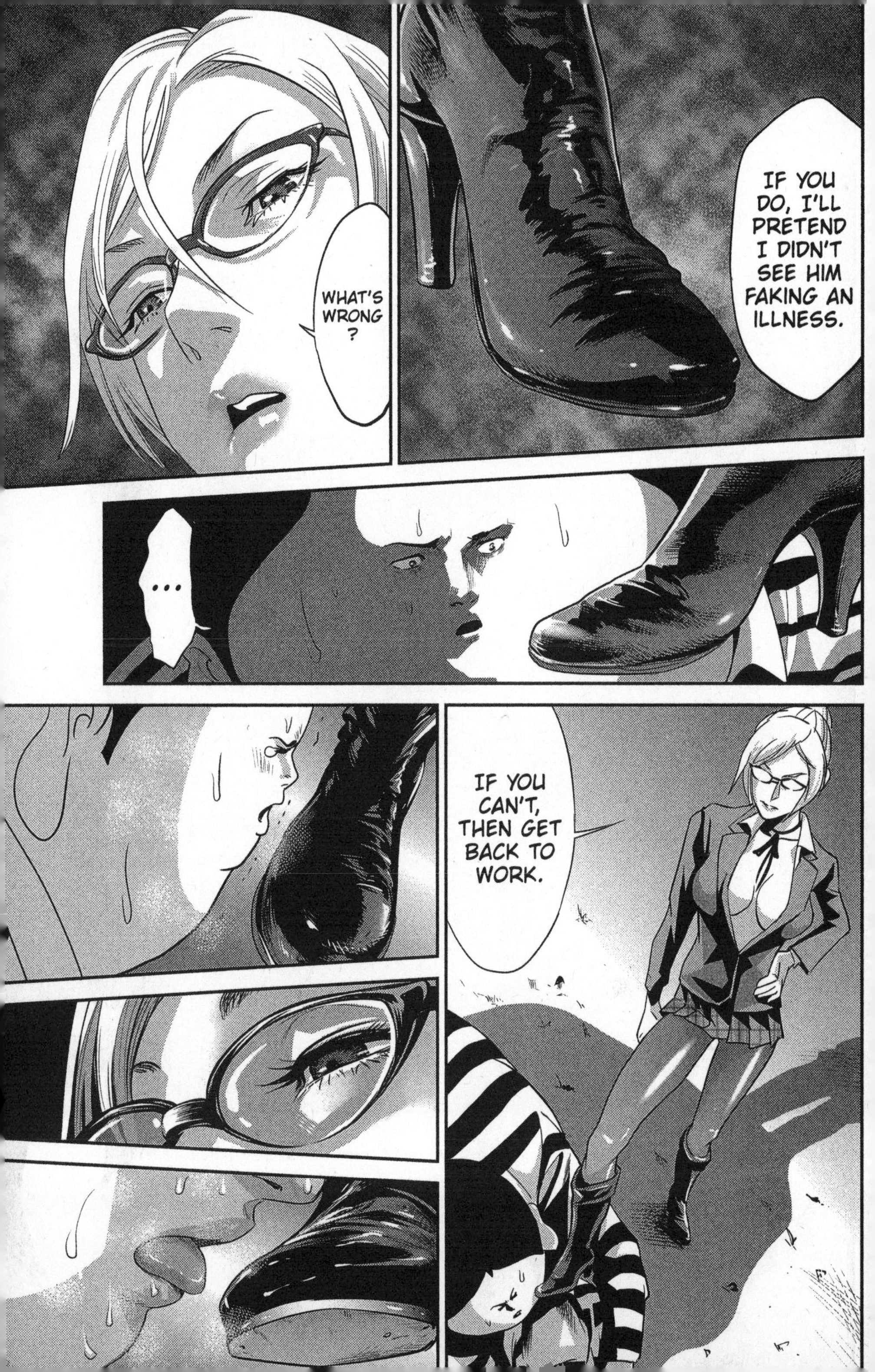
IF YOU DO, I'LL PRETEND I DIDN'T SEE HIM FAKING AN ILLNESS.
WHAT'S WRONG?
...
IF YOU CAN'T, THEN GET BACK TO WORK.

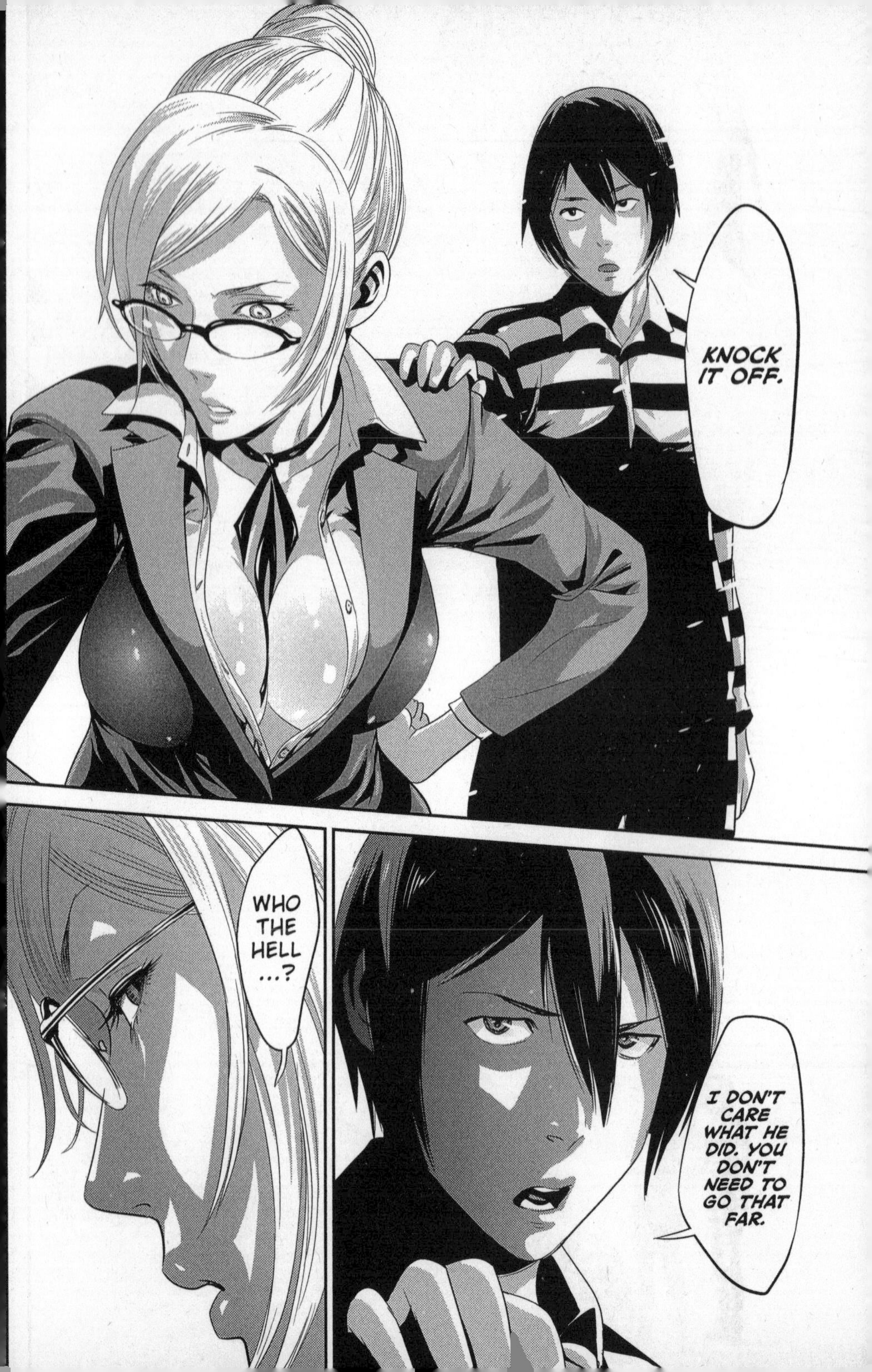
KNOCK IT OFF.
WHO THE HELL ...?
I DON'T CARE WHAT HE DID. YOU DON'T NEED TO GO THAT FAR.

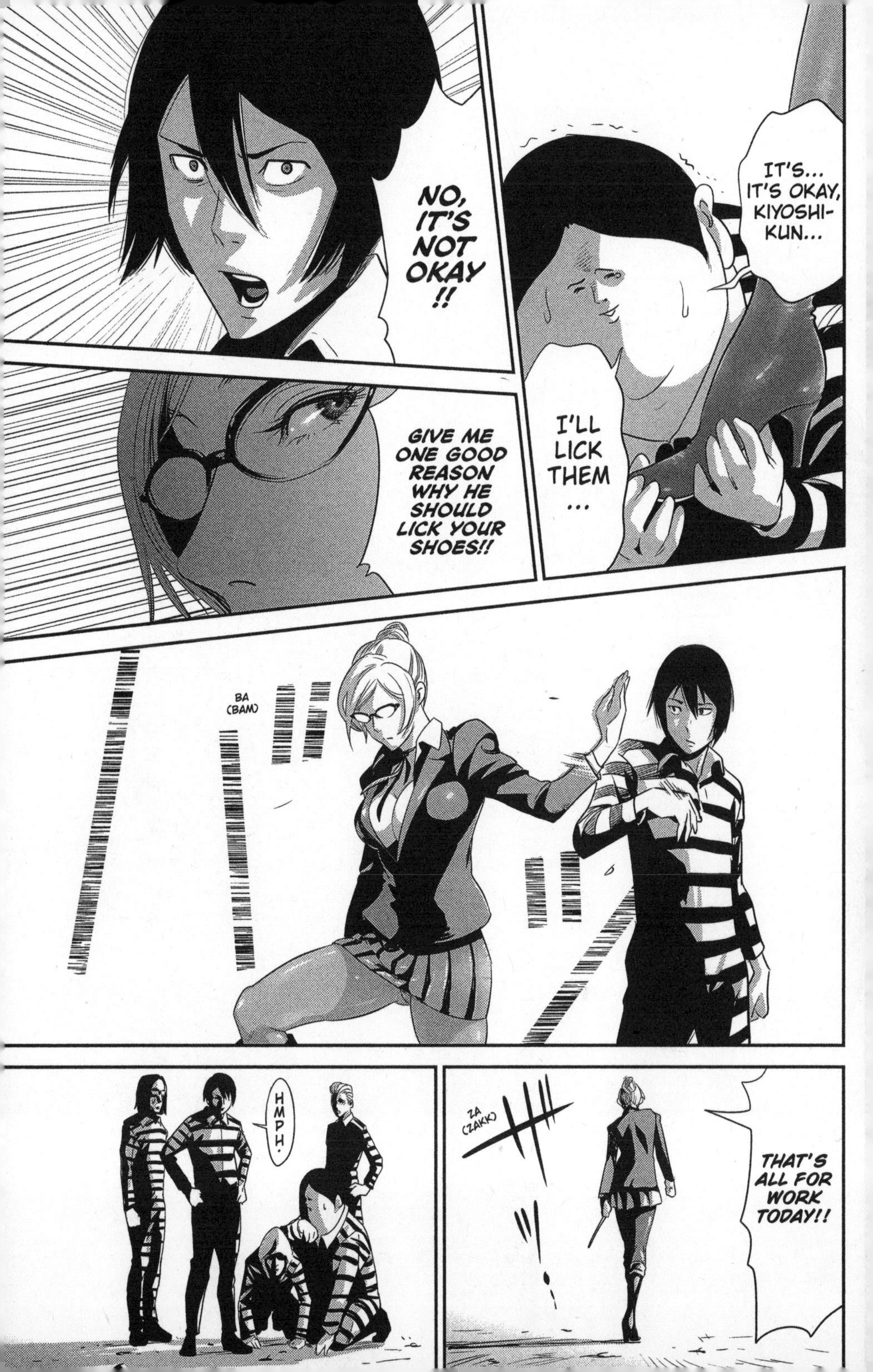
IT'S... IT'S OKAY, KIYOSHI-KUN...
NO, IT'S NOT OKAY!!
I'LL LICK THEM...
GIVE ME ONE GOOD REASON WHY HE SHOULD LICK YOUR SHOES!!
BA (BAM)
THAT'S ALL FOR WORK TODAY!!
ZA (ZAKK)
HMPH.

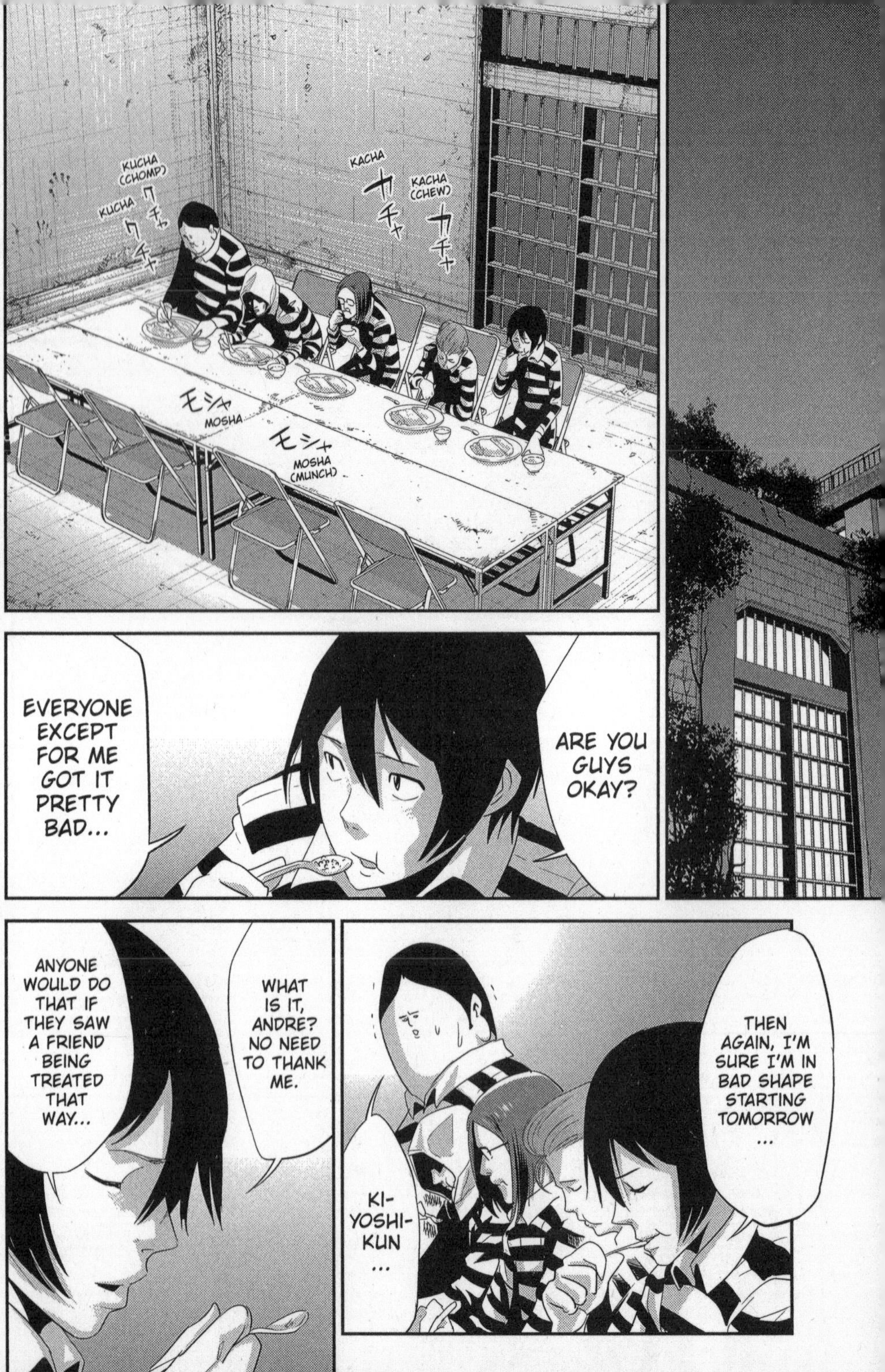
KACHA
KACHA (CHEW)
KUCHA (CHOMP)
KUCHA
MOSHA
MOSHA (MUNCH)
ARE YOU GUYS OKAY?
EVERYONE EXCEPT FOR ME GOT IT PRETTY BAD...
THEN AGAIN, I'M SURE I'M IN BAD SHAPE STARTING TOMORROW...
KI-YOSHI-KUN...
WHAT IS IT, ANDRE? NO NEED TO THANK ME.
ANYONE WOULD DO THAT IF THEY SAW A FRIEND BEING TREATED THAT WAY...

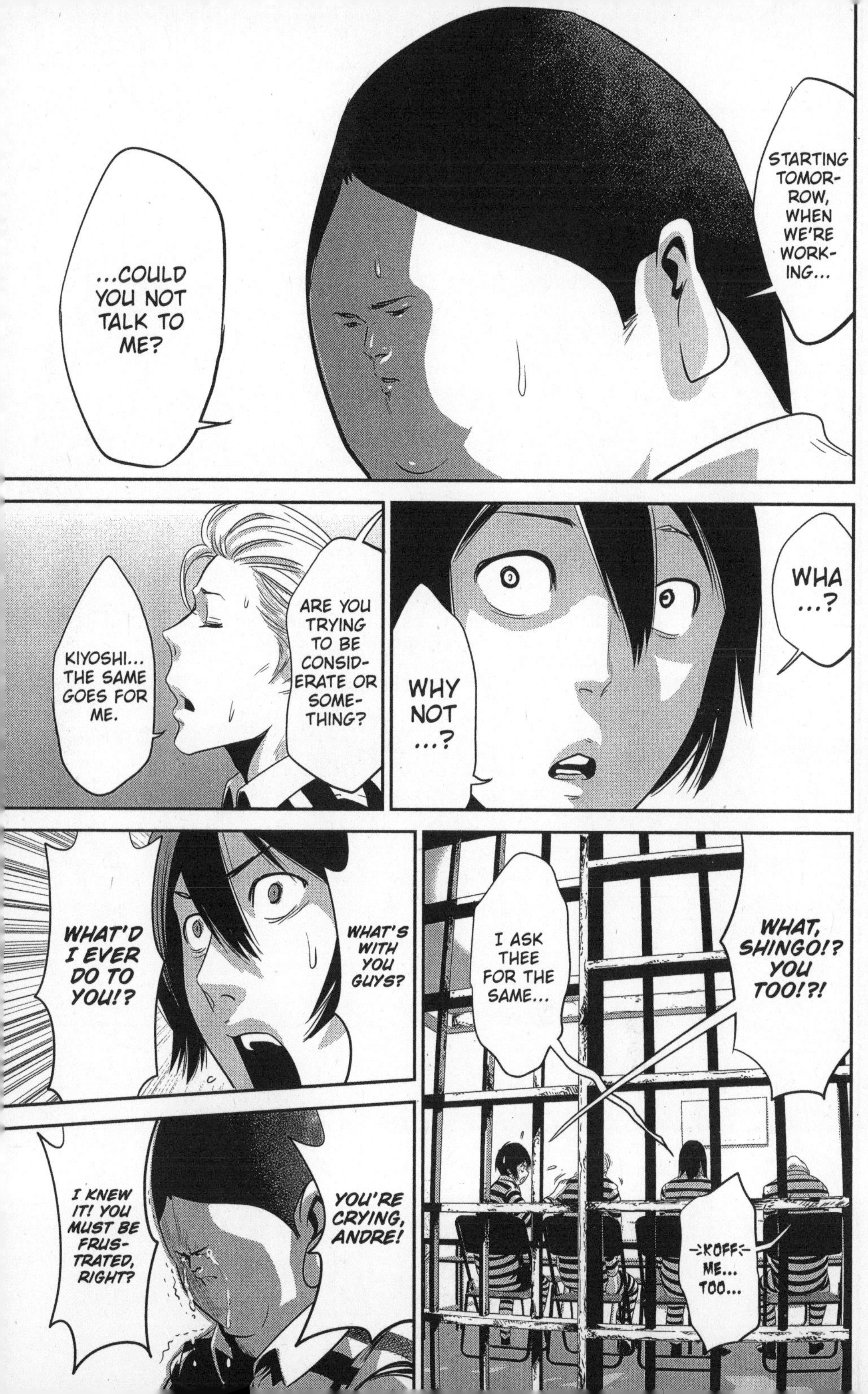
STARTING TOMORROW, WHEN WE'RE WORKING...
...COULD YOU NOT TALK TO ME?
WHA...?
WHY NOT...?
ARE YOU TRYING TO BE CONSIDERATE OR SOMETHING?
KIYOSHI... THE SAME GOES FOR ME.
WHAT, SHINGO!? YOU TOO!?!
I ASK THEE FOR THE SAME...
-KOFF- ME... TOO...
WHAT'S WITH YOU GUYS?
WHAT'D I EVER DO TO YOU!?
YOU'RE CRYING, ANDRE!
I KNEW IT! YOU MUST BE FRUSTRATED, RIGHT?

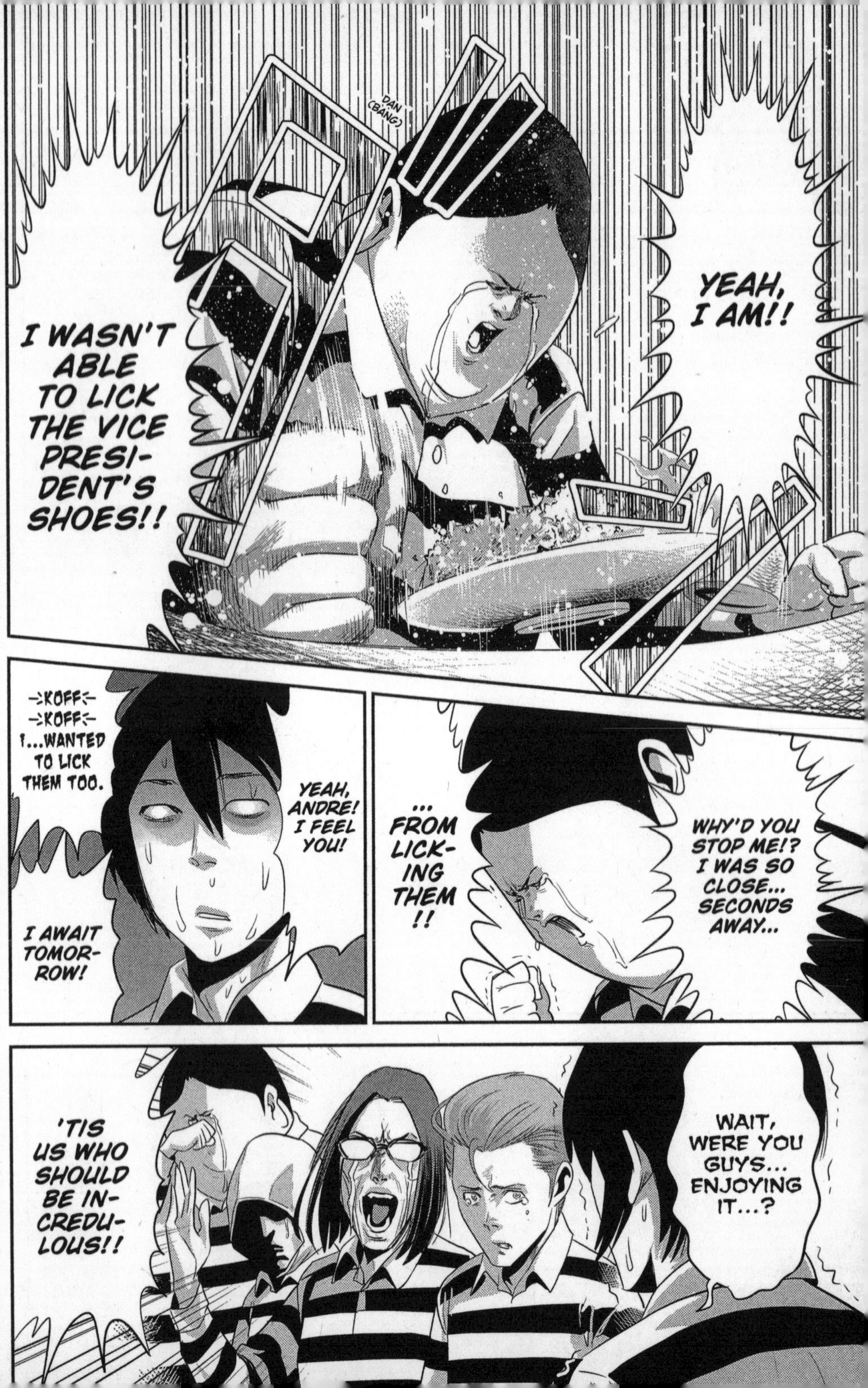
DAN (BANG)
YEAH, I AM!!
I WASN'T ABLE TO LICK THE VICE PRESI-DENT'S SHOES!!
WHY'D YOU STOP ME!? I WAS SO CLOSE... SECONDS AWAY...
...FROM LICK-ING THEM!!
YEAH, ANDRE! I FEEL YOU!
I AWAIT TOMOR-ROW!
-KOFF- -KOFF- I...WANTED TO LICK THEM TOO.
WAIT, WERE YOU GUYS... ENJOYING IT...?
'TIS US WHO SHOULD BE IN-CREDU-LOUS!!

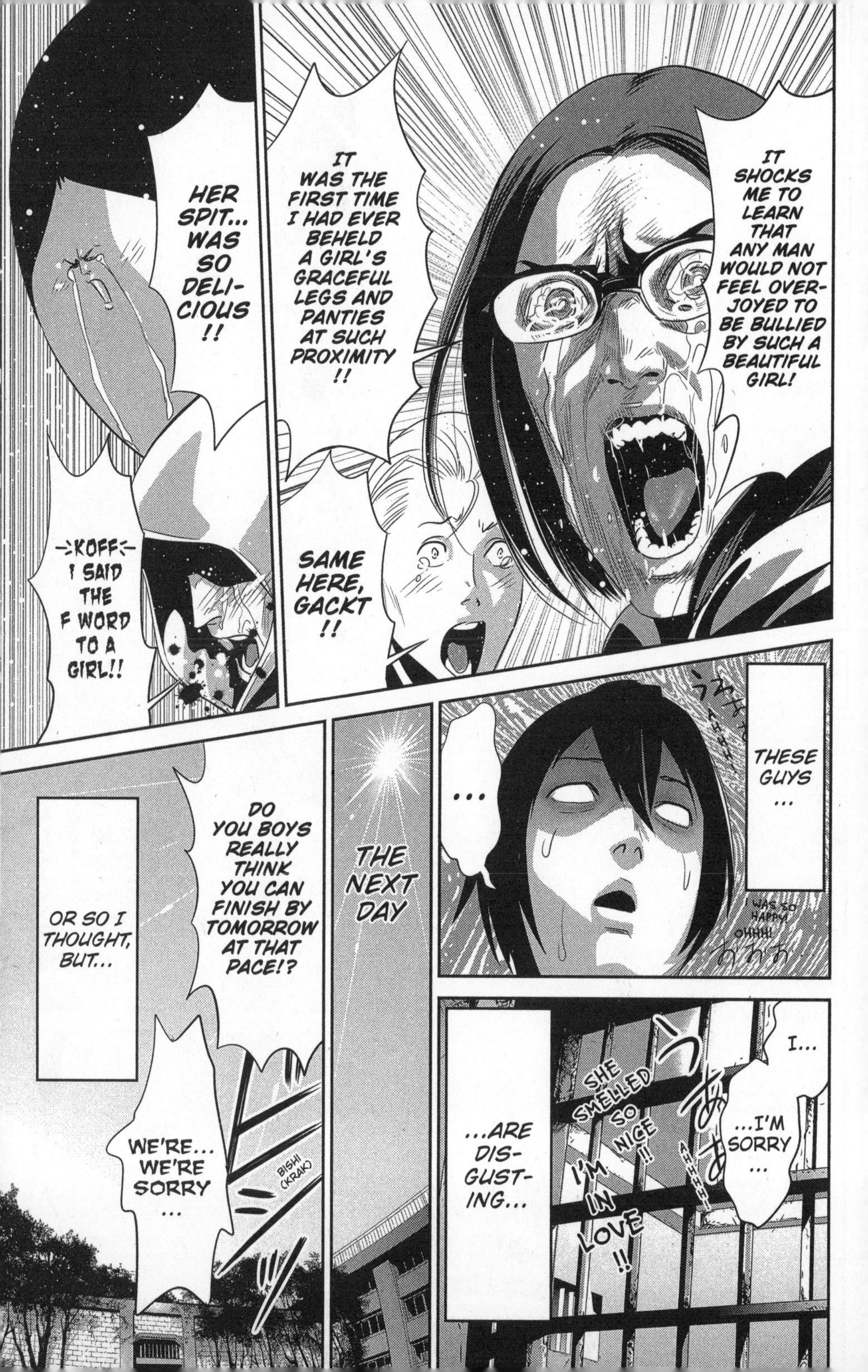
IT SHOCKS ME TO LEARN THAT ANY MAN WOULD NOT FEEL OVER-JOYED TO BE BULLIED BY SUCH A BEAUTIFUL GIRL!
IT WAS THE FIRST TIME I HAD EVER BEHELD A GIRL'S GRACEFUL LEGS AND PANTIES AT SUCH PROXIMITY !!
SAME HERE, GACKT !!
HER SPIT... WAS SO DELI-CIOUS !!
-KOFF- I SAID THE F WORD TO A GIRL!!
THESE GUYS ...
...
WAS SO HAPPY! OHHH!
THE NEXT DAY
DO YOU BOYS REALLY THINK YOU CAN FINISH BY TOMORROW AT THAT PACE!?
OR SO I THOUGHT, BUT...
I...
...I'M SORRY ...
SHE SMELLED SO NICE !!
AHHHH!!
I'M IN LOVE !!
...ARE DIS-GUST-ING...
WE'RE... WE'RE SORRY ...
BISHI (KRAK)

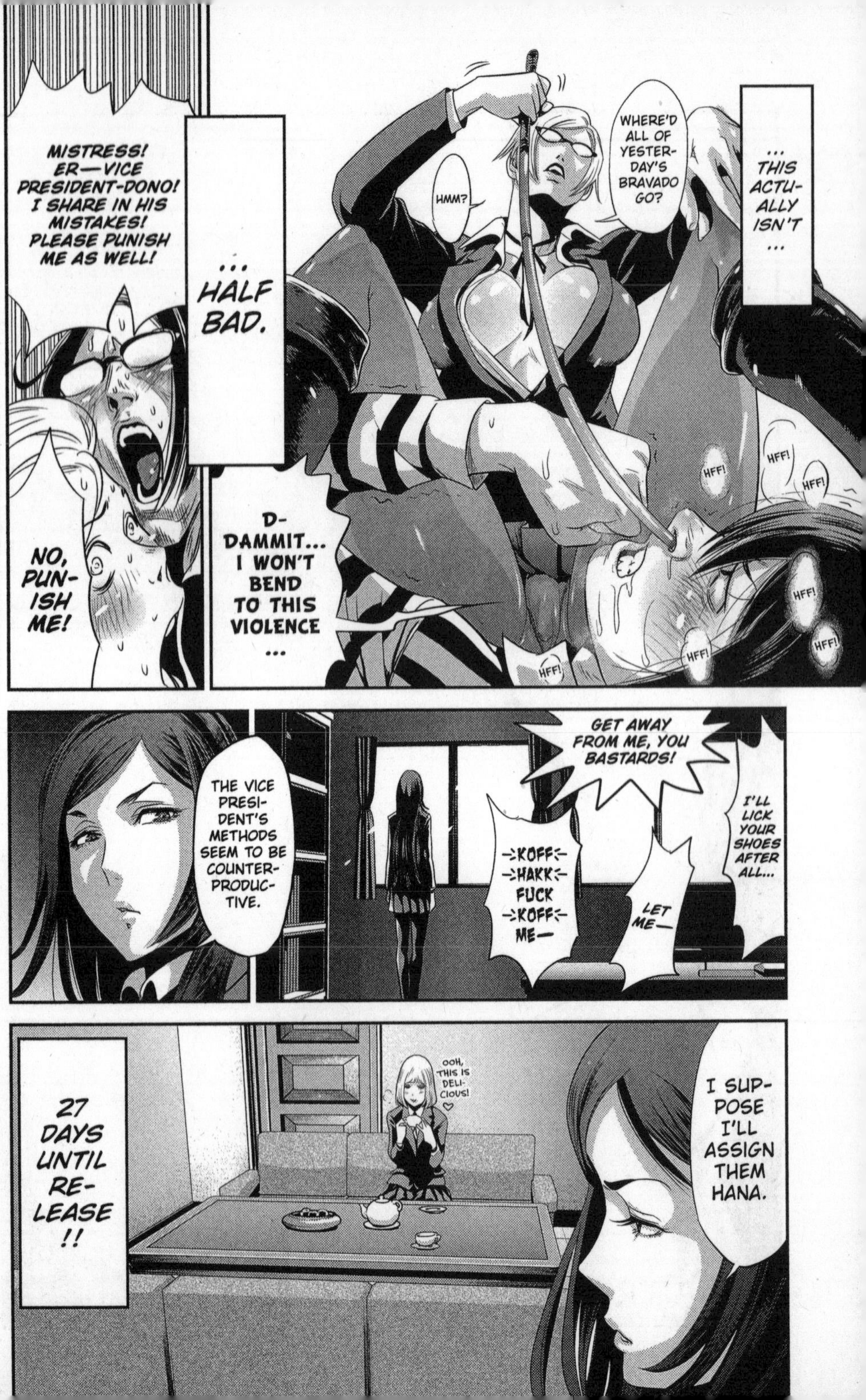
...THIS ACTUALLY ISN'T ...
WHERE'D ALL OF YESTERDAY'S BRAVADO GO?
HMM?
...HALF BAD.
MISTRESS! ER—VICE PRESIDENT-DONO! I SHARE IN HIS MISTAKES! PLEASE PUNISH ME AS WELL!
HFF! HFF! HFF! HFF! HFF! HFF! HFF!
D-DAMMIT... I WON'T BEND TO THIS VIOLENCE ...
NO, PUNISH ME!
I'LL LICK YOUR SHOES AFTER ALL...
GET AWAY FROM ME, YOU BASTARDS!
LET ME—
-KOFF- -HAKK- FUCK -KOFF- ME—
THE VICE PRESIDENT'S METHODS SEEM TO BE COUNTERPRODUCTIVE.
I SUPPOSE I'LL ASSIGN THEM HANA.
OOH, THIS IS DELICIOUS!
27 DAYS UNTIL RELEASE !!

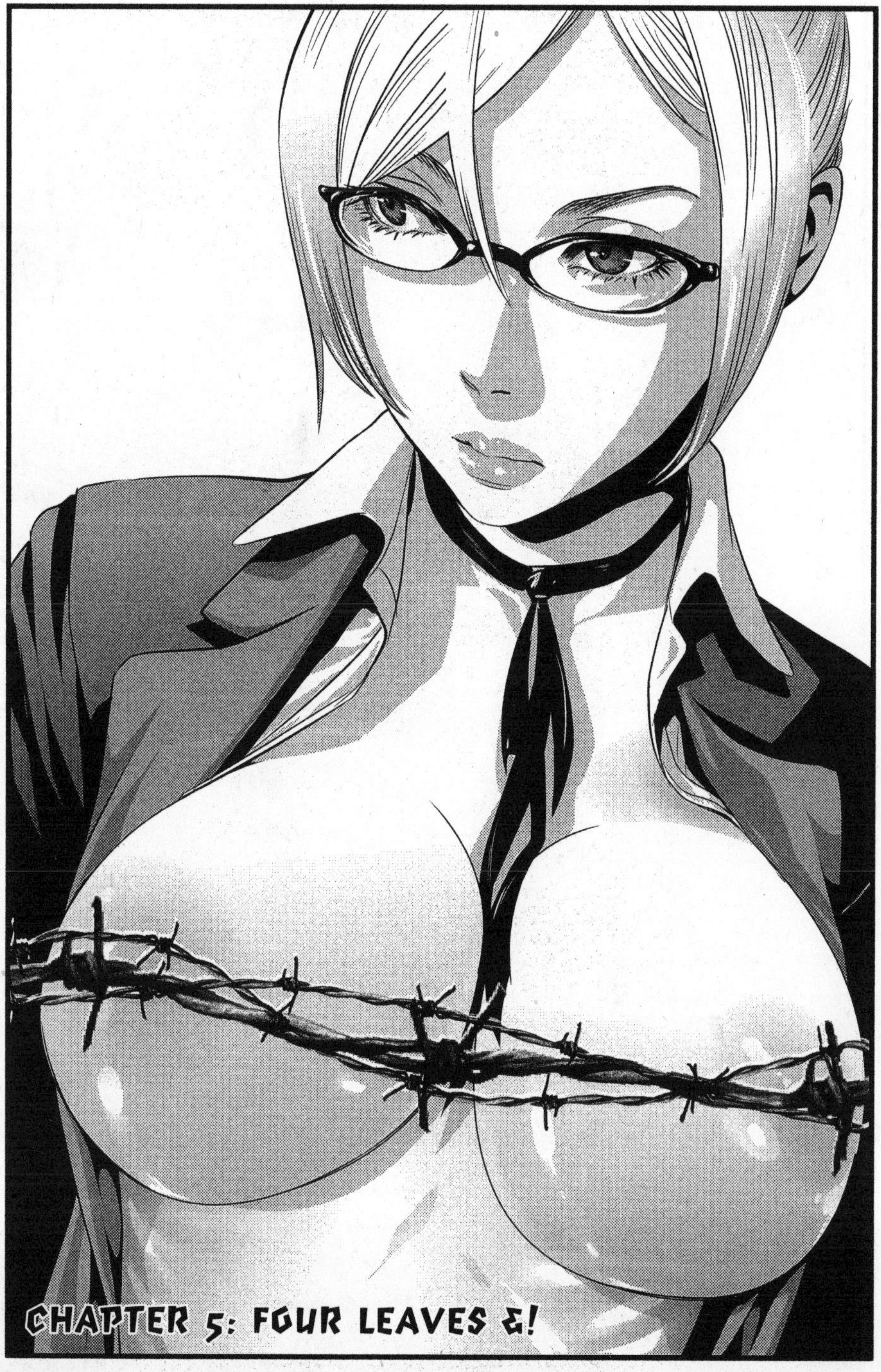
CHAPTER 5: FOUR LEAVES &!

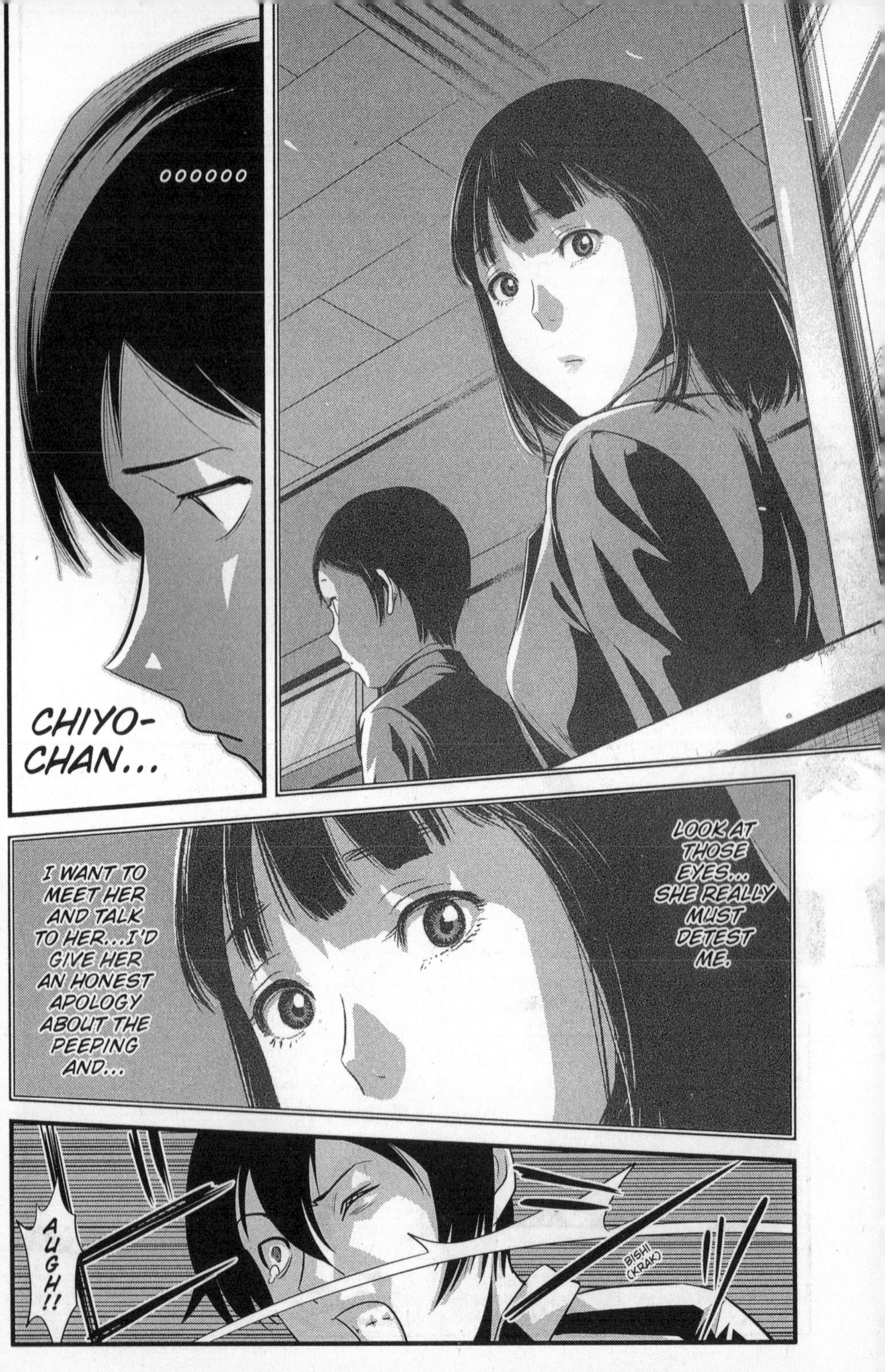
OOOOOO
CHIYO-CHAN...
LOOK AT THOSE EYES... SHE REALLY MUST DETEST ME.
I WANT TO MEET HER AND TALK TO HER...I'D GIVE HER AN HONEST APOLOGY ABOUT THE PEEPING AND...
BISHI (KRAK)
AUGH!!

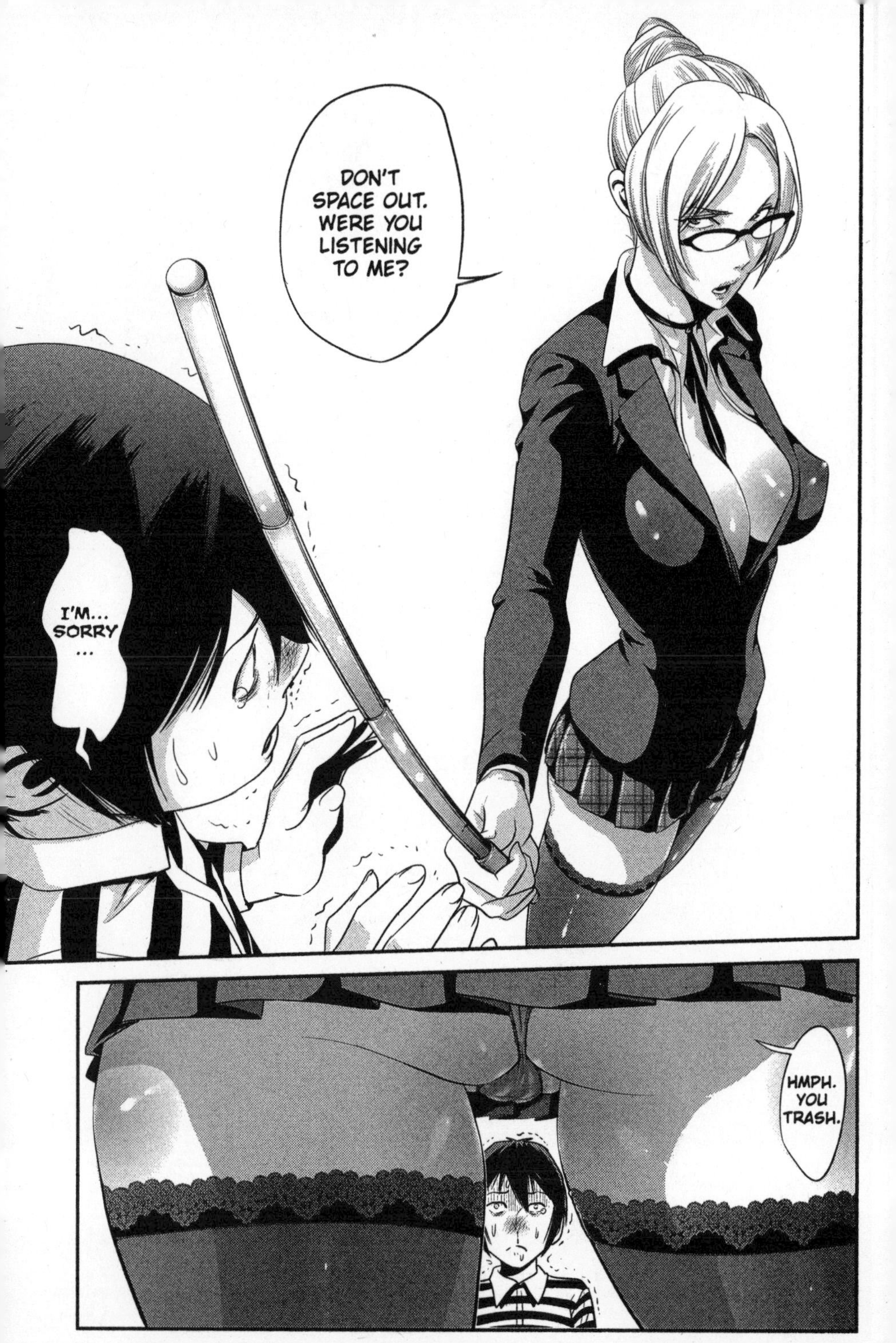
DON'T SPACE OUT. WERE YOU LISTENING TO ME?
I'M... SORRY ...
HMPH. YOU TRASH.

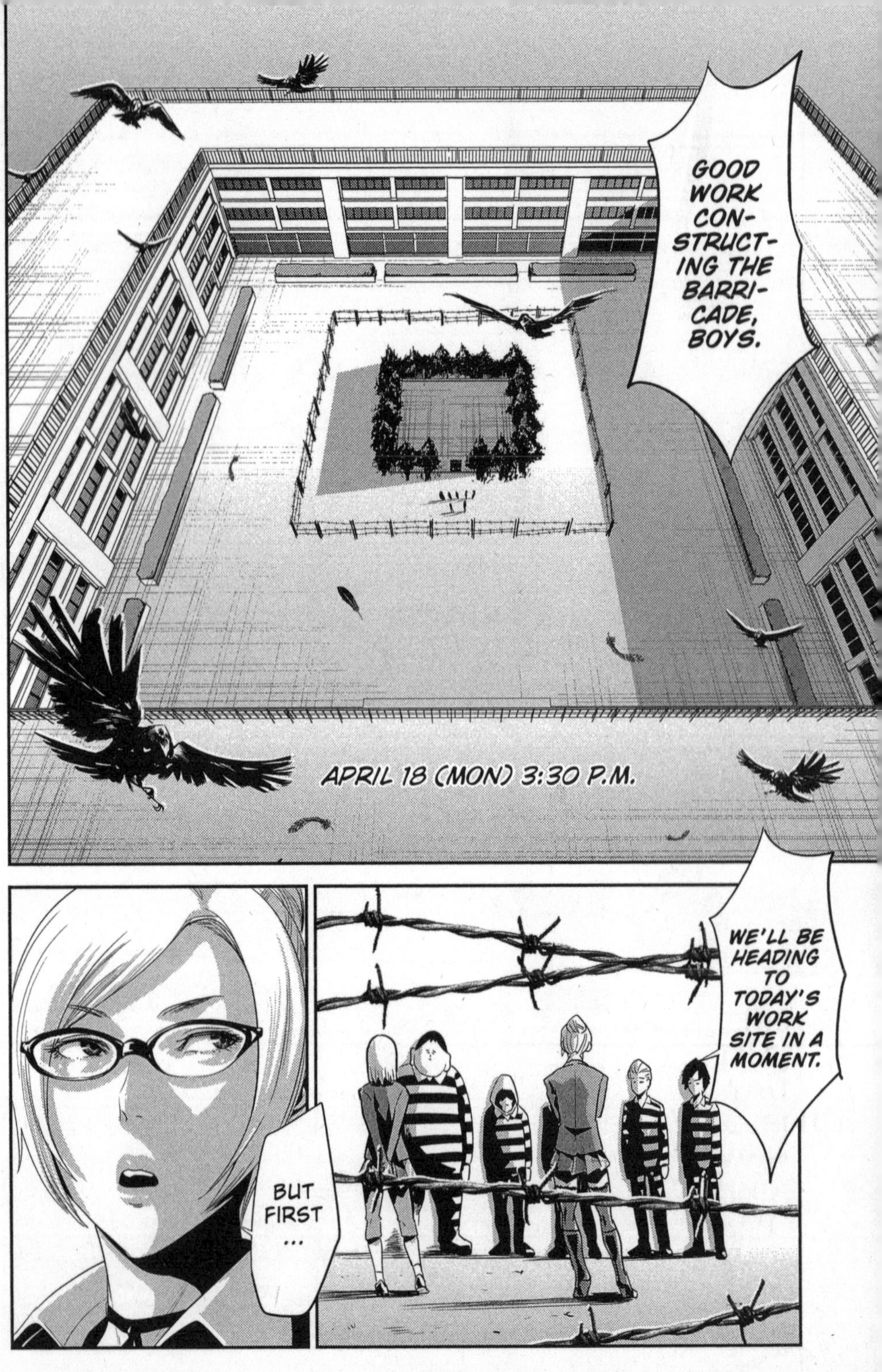
GOOD WORK CON-STRUCT-ING THE BARRI-CADE, BOYS.
APRIL 18 (MON) 3:30 P.M.
WE'LL BE HEADING TO TODAY'S WORK SITE IN A MOMENT.
BUT FIRST ...

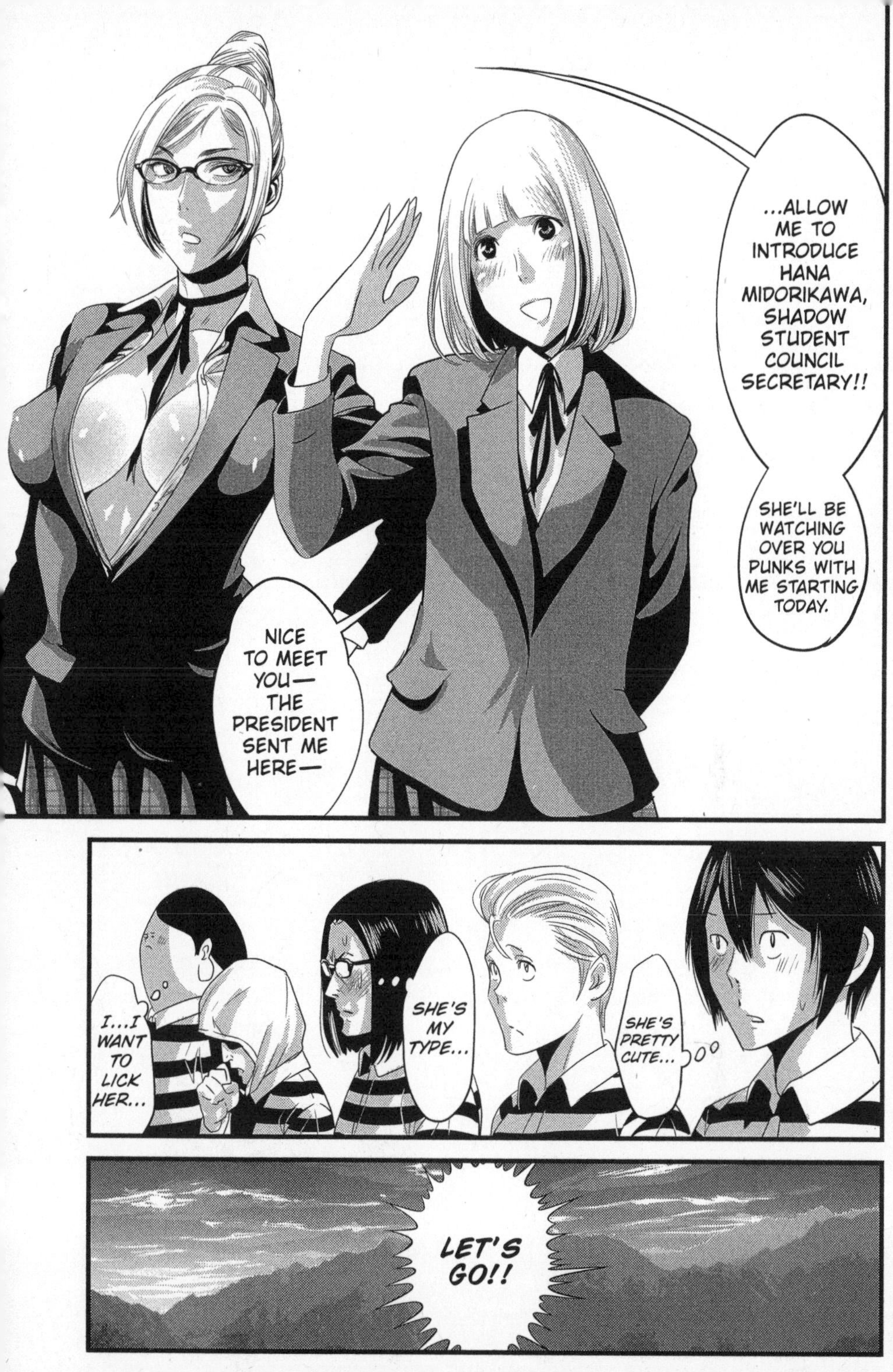
...ALLOW ME TO INTRODUCE HANA MIDORIKAWA, SHADOW STUDENT COUNCIL SECRETARY!!
SHE'LL BE WATCHING OVER YOU PUNKS WITH ME STARTING TODAY.
NICE TO MEET YOU— THE PRESIDENT SENT ME HERE—
SHE'S PRETTY CUTE...
SHE'S MY TYPE...
...
I...I WANT TO LICK HER...
LET'S GO!!

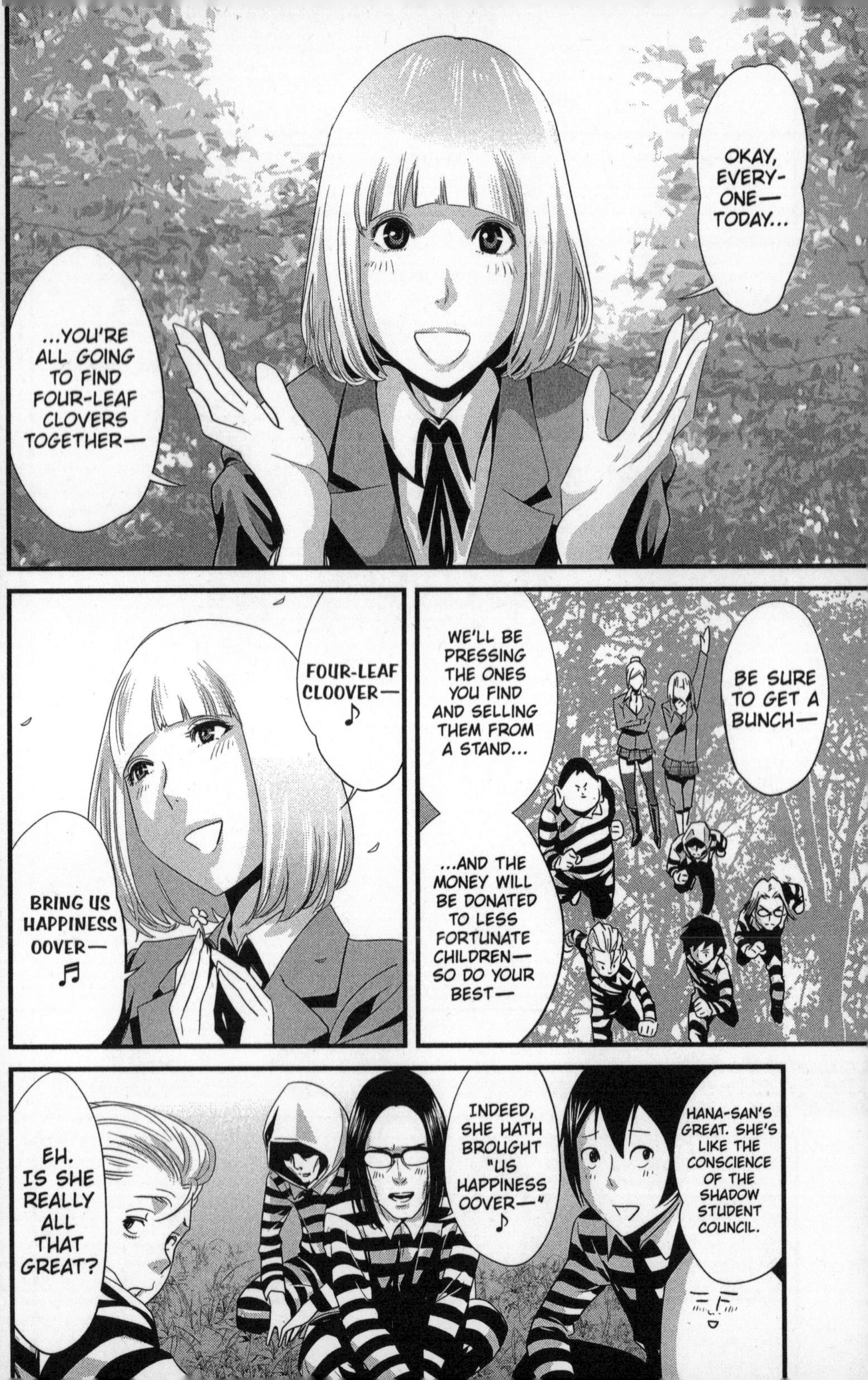
OKAY, EVERY-ONE— TODAY...
...YOU'RE ALL GOING TO FIND FOUR-LEAF CLOVERS TOGETHER—
BE SURE TO GET A BUNCH—
WE'LL BE PRESSING THE ONES YOU FIND AND SELLING THEM FROM A STAND...
...AND THE MONEY WILL BE DONATED TO LESS FORTUNATE CHILDREN— SO DO YOUR BEST—
FOUR-LEAF CLOOVER— ♪
BRING US HAPPINESS OOVER— ♬
HANA-SAN'S GREAT. SHE'S LIKE THE CONSCIENCE OF THE SHADOW STUDENT COUNCIL.
INDEED, SHE HATH BROUGHT "US HAPPINESS OOVER—" ♪
EH. IS SHE REALLY ALL THAT GREAT?

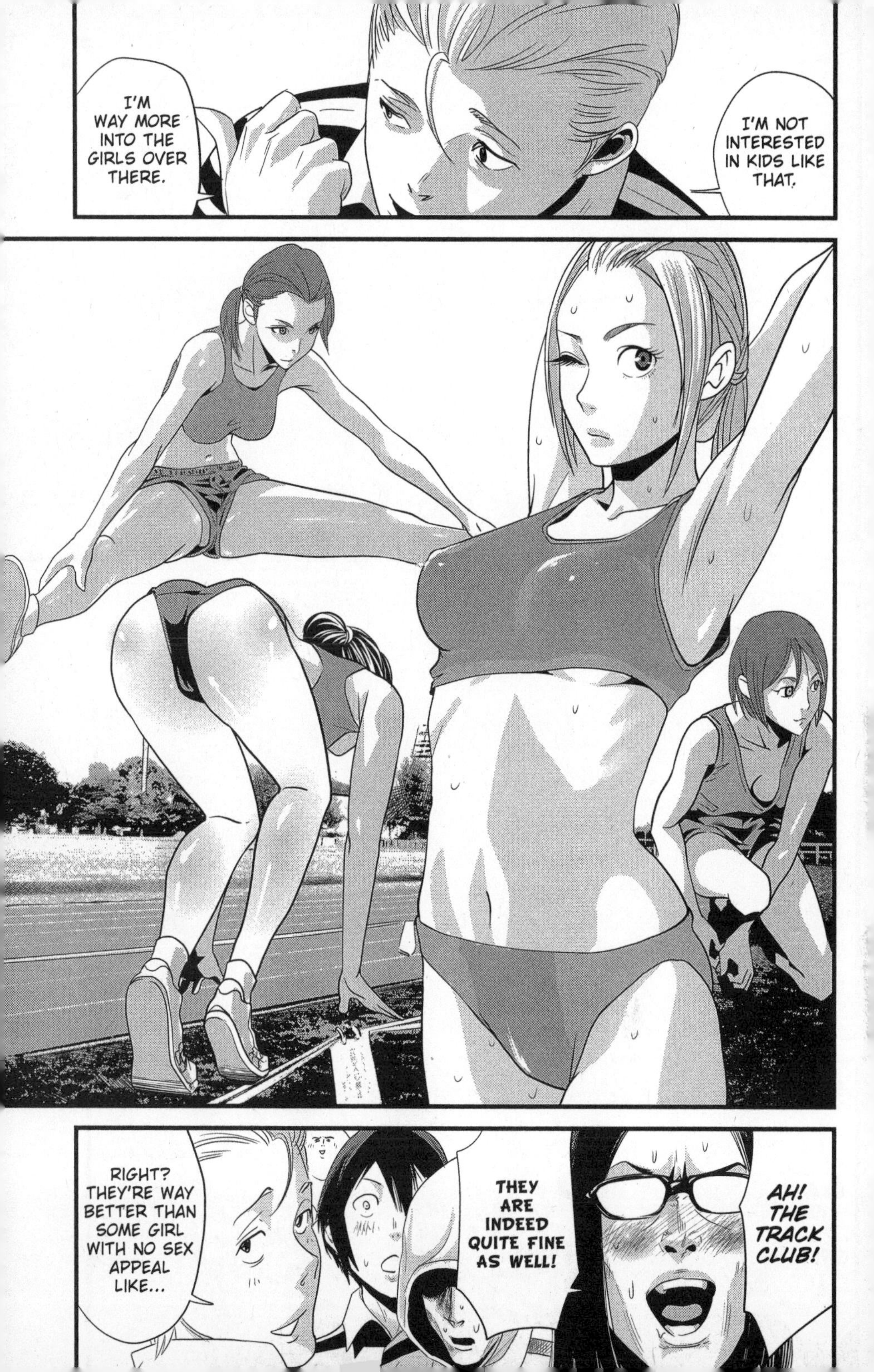
I'M NOT INTERESTED IN KIDS LIKE THAT.
I'M WAY MORE INTO THE GIRLS OVER THERE.
AH! THE TRACK CLUB!
THEY ARE INDEED QUITE FINE AS WELL!
RIGHT? THEY'RE WAY BETTER THAN SOME GIRL WITH NO SEX APPEAL LIKE...

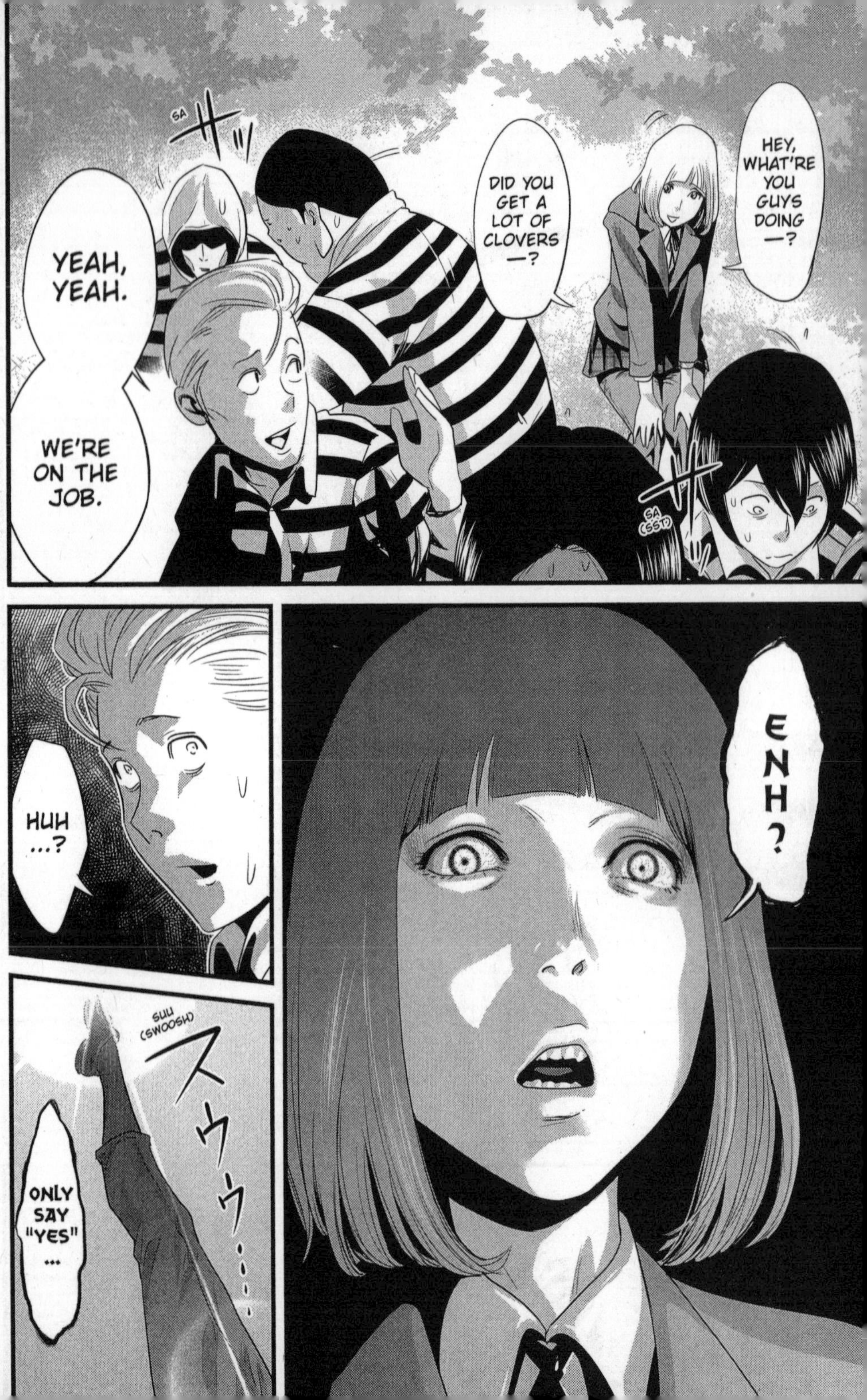
HEY, WHAT'RE YOU GUYS DOING—?
DID YOU GET A LOT OF CLOVERS—?
SA
YEAH, YEAH.
WE'RE ON THE JOB.
SA (SST)
ENH?
HUH ...?
SUU (SWOOSH)
ONLY SAY "YES" ...

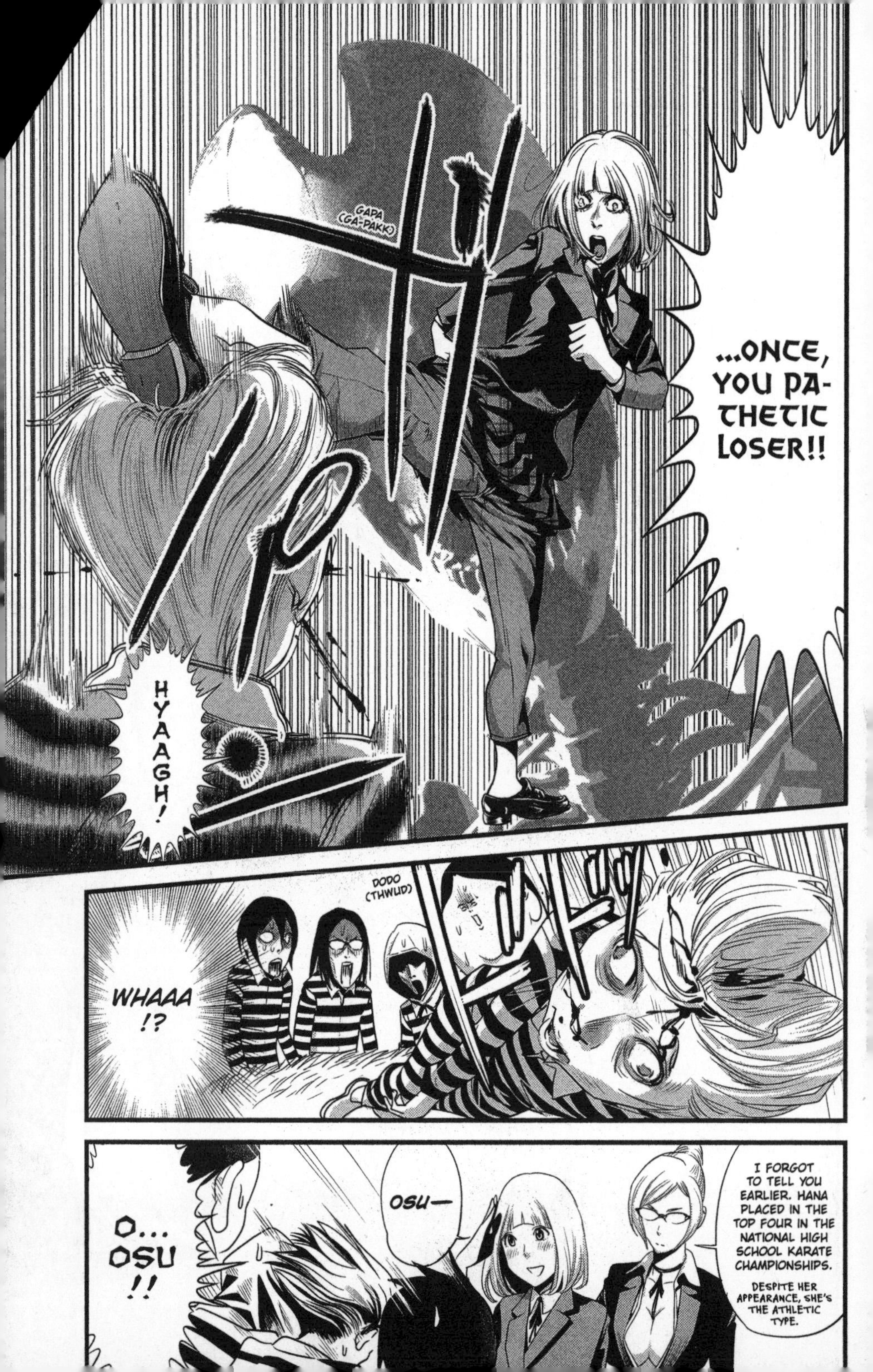
GAPA (GA-PAKK)
...ONCE, YOU PA-THETIC LOSER!!
HYAAGH!
DODO (THWUD)
WHAAA !?
I FORGOT TO TELL YOU EARLIER. HANA PLACED IN THE TOP FOUR IN THE NATIONAL HIGH SCHOOL KARATE CHAMPIONSHIPS.
DESPITE HER APPEARANCE, SHE'S THE ATHLETIC TYPE.
OSU—
O... OSU !!

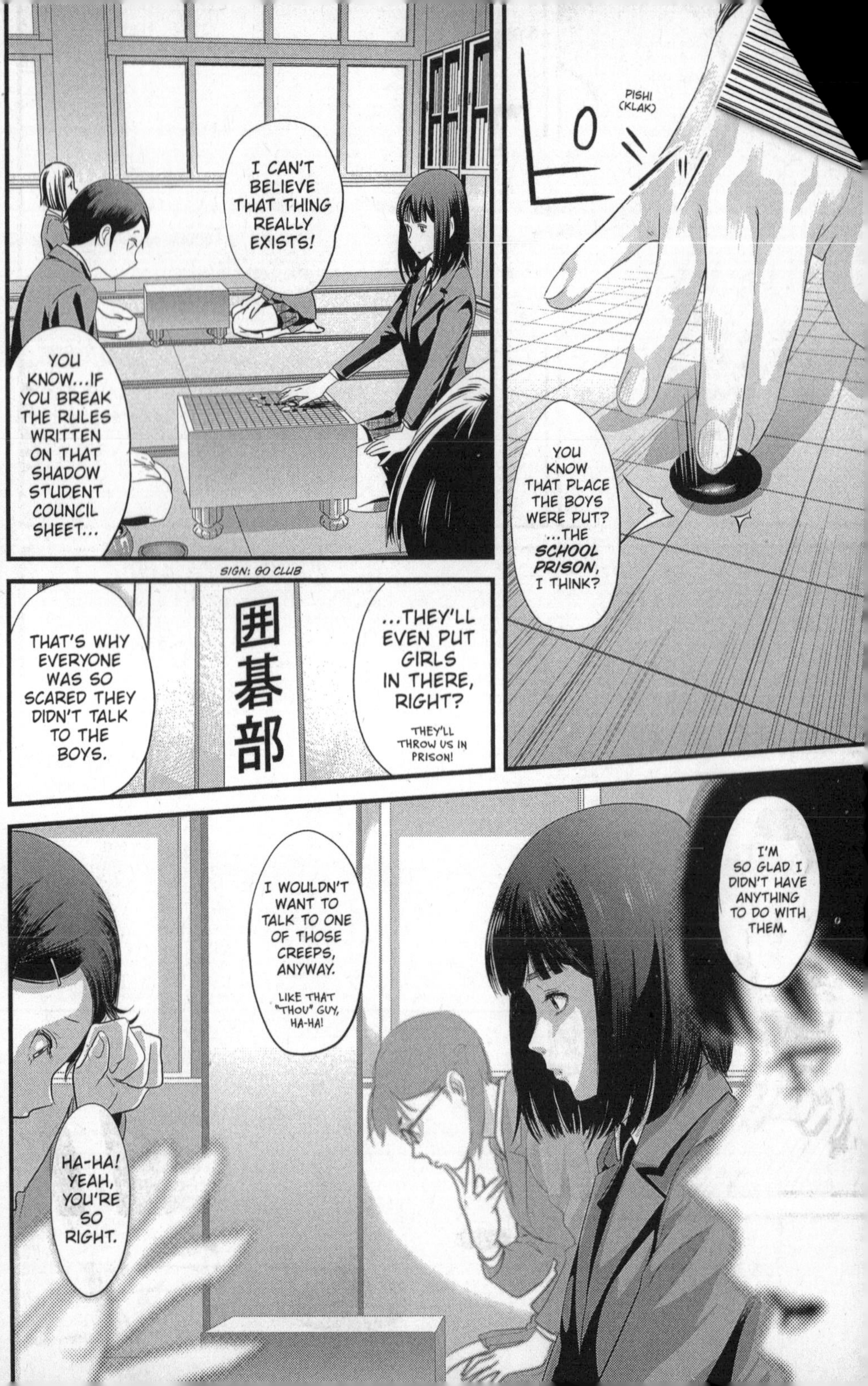
PISHI (KLAK)
YOU KNOW THAT PLACE THE BOYS WERE PUT? ...THE *SCHOOL PRISON*, I THINK?
I CAN'T BELIEVE THAT THING REALLY EXISTS!
YOU KNOW...IF YOU BREAK THE RULES WRITTEN ON THAT SHADOW STUDENT COUNCIL SHEET...
SIGN: GO CLUB
...THEY'LL EVEN PUT GIRLS IN THERE, RIGHT?
THEY'LL THROW US IN PRISON!
囲碁部
THAT'S WHY EVERYONE WAS SO SCARED THEY DIDN'T TALK TO THE BOYS.
I'M SO GLAD I DIDN'T HAVE ANYTHING TO DO WITH THEM.
I WOULDN'T WANT TO TALK TO ONE OF THOSE CREEPS, ANYWAY.
LIKE THAT "THOU" GUY, HA-HA!
HA-HA! YEAH, YOU'RE SO RIGHT.

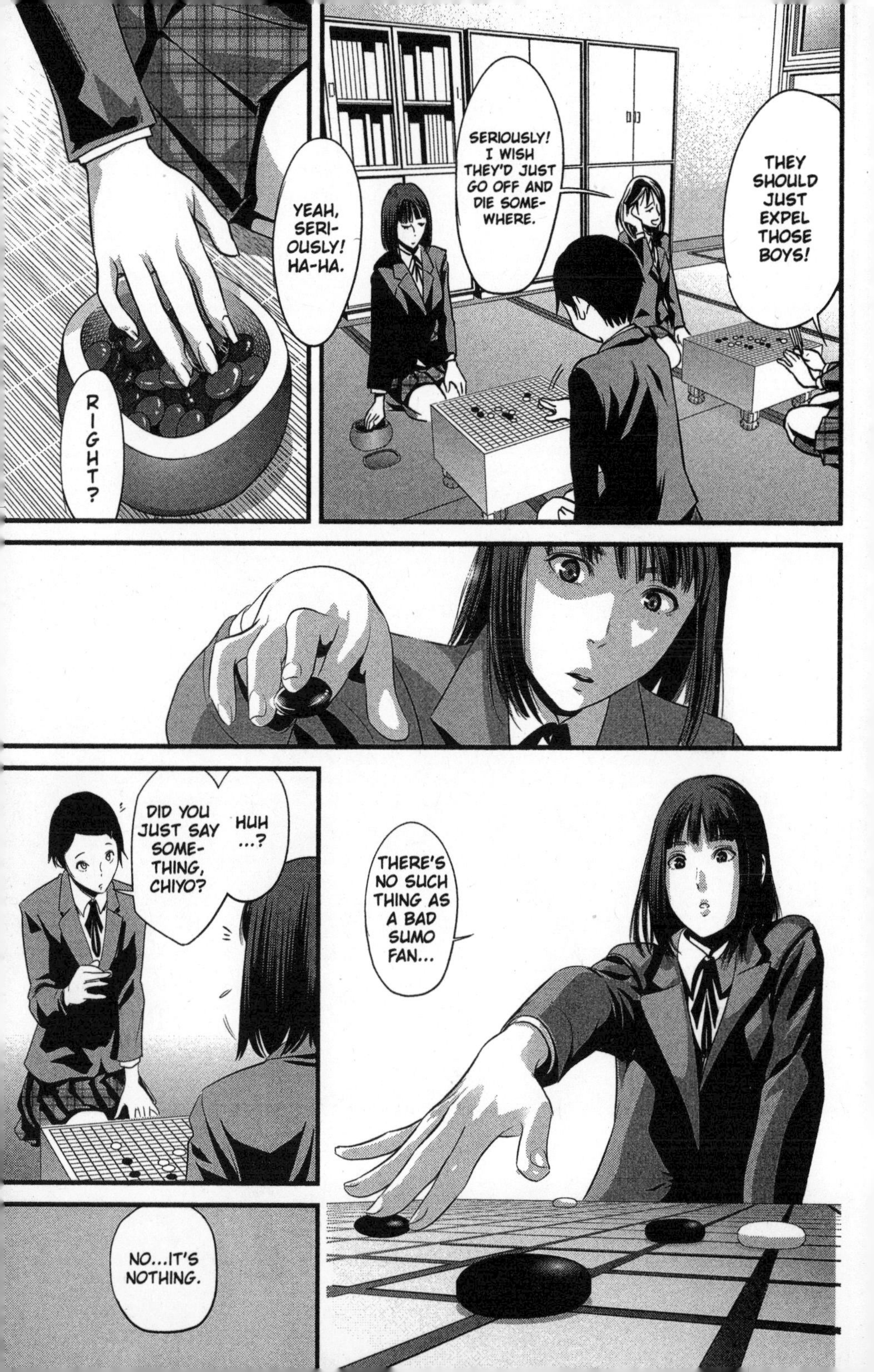
THEY SHOULD JUST EXPEL THOSE BOYS!
SERIOUSLY! I WISH THEY'D JUST GO OFF AND DIE SOME-WHERE.
YEAH, SERI-OUSLY! HA-HA.
RIGHT?
THERE'S NO SUCH THING AS A BAD SUMO FAN...
HUH ...?
DID YOU JUST SAY SOME-THING, CHIYO?
NO...IT'S NOTHING.

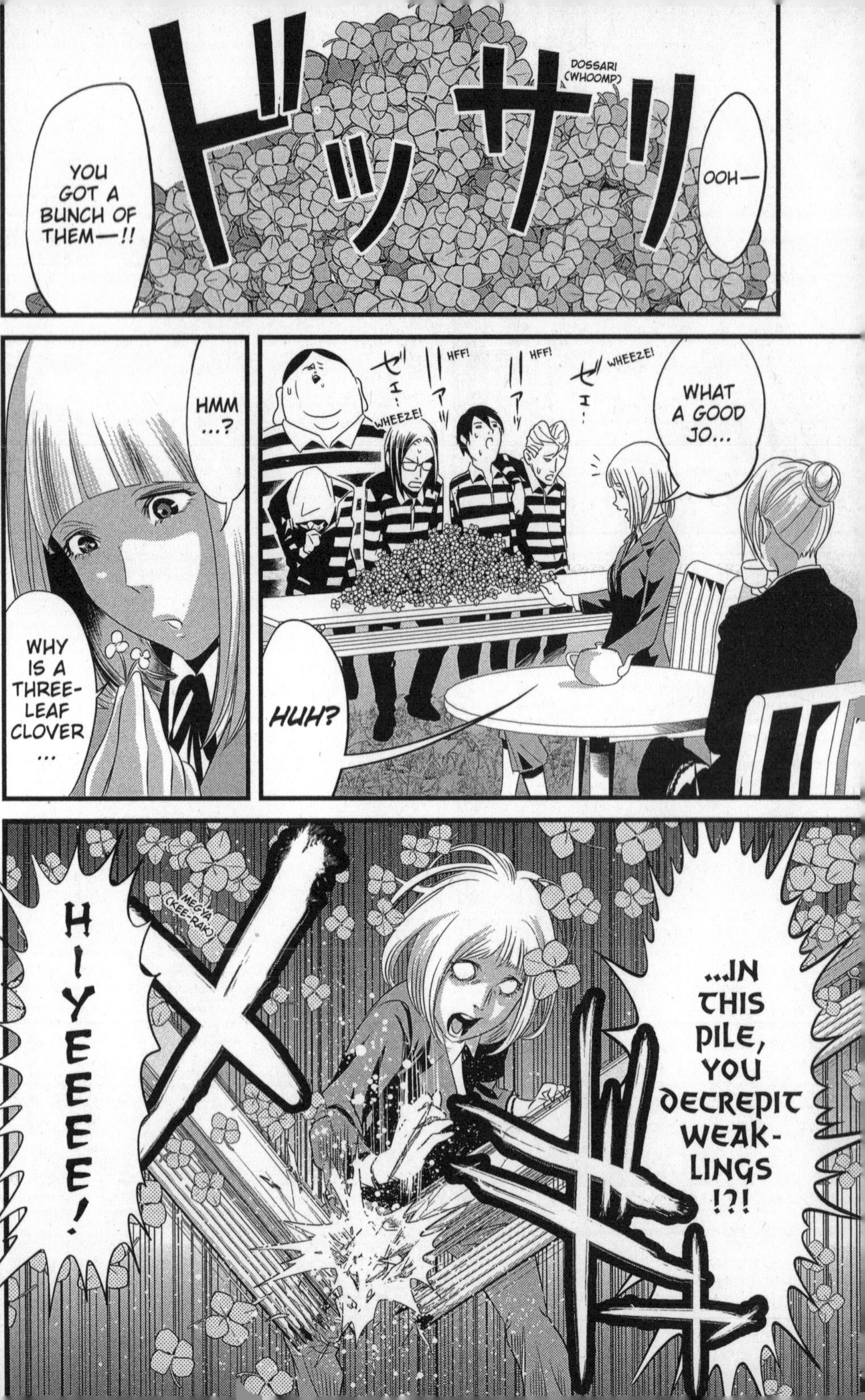
ドッサリ
DOSSARI (WHOOMP)
OOH—
YOU GOT A BUNCH OF THEM—!!
WHAT A GOOD JO...
ゼェ WHEEZE!
ハァッ HFF!
ハァッ HFF!
ゼェ WHEEZE!
HUH?
HMM ...?
WHY IS A THREE-LEAF CLOVER ...
...IN THIS PILE, YOU DECREPIT WEAK-LINGS !?!
MEGYA (KEE-RAK)
HIYEEEEE!

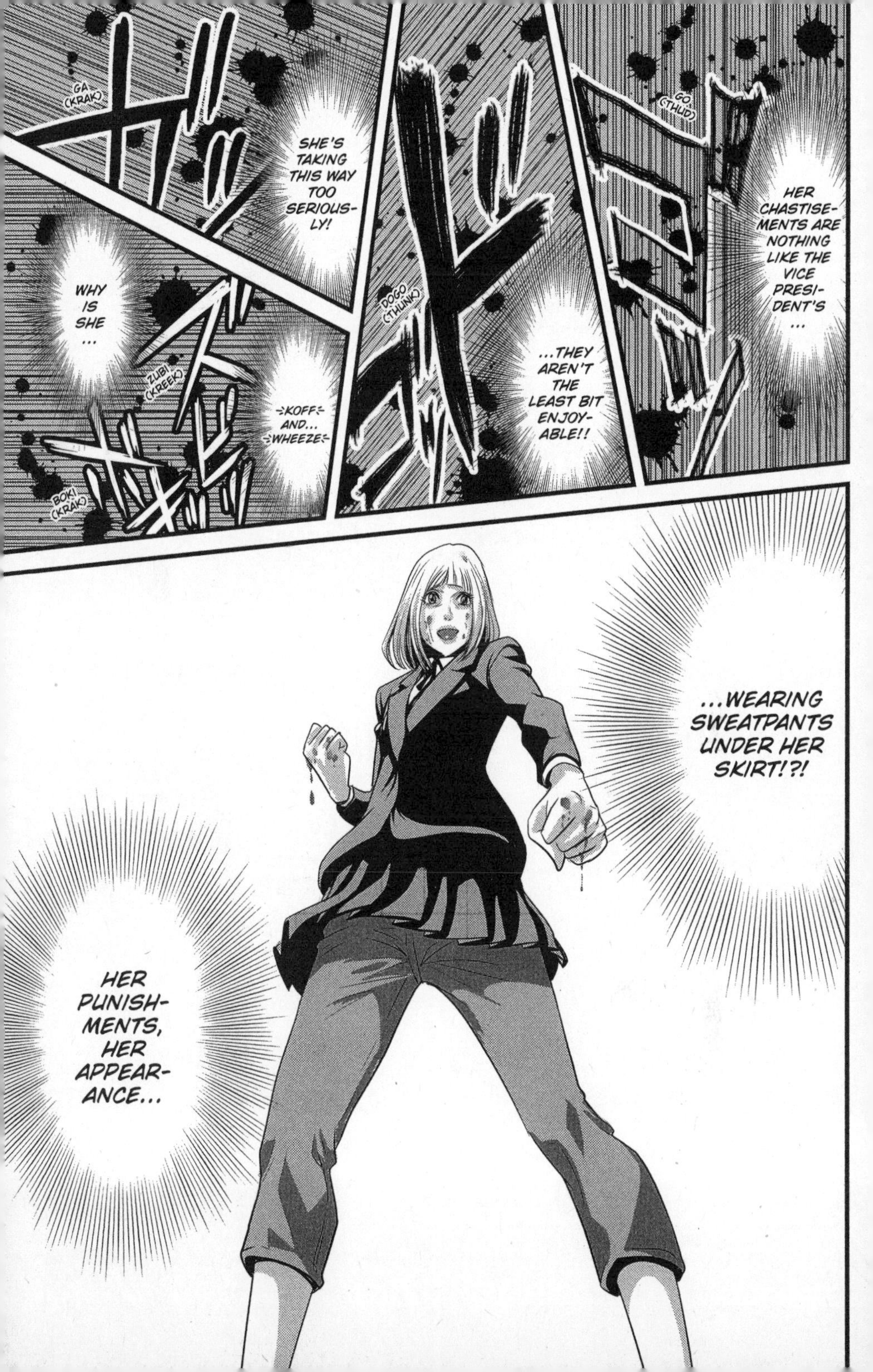
GO (THUD)
HER CHASTISEMENTS ARE NOTHING LIKE THE VICE PRESIDENT'S...
DOGO (THUNK)
...THEY AREN'T THE LEAST BIT ENJOYABLE!!
GA (KRAK)
SHE'S TAKING THIS WAY TOO SERIOUSLY!
WHY IS SHE...
ZUBI (KREEK)
-KOFF- AND... -WHEEZE-
BOKI (KRAK)
...WEARING SWEATPANTS UNDER HER SKIRT!?!
HER PUNISHMENTS, HER APPEARANCE...

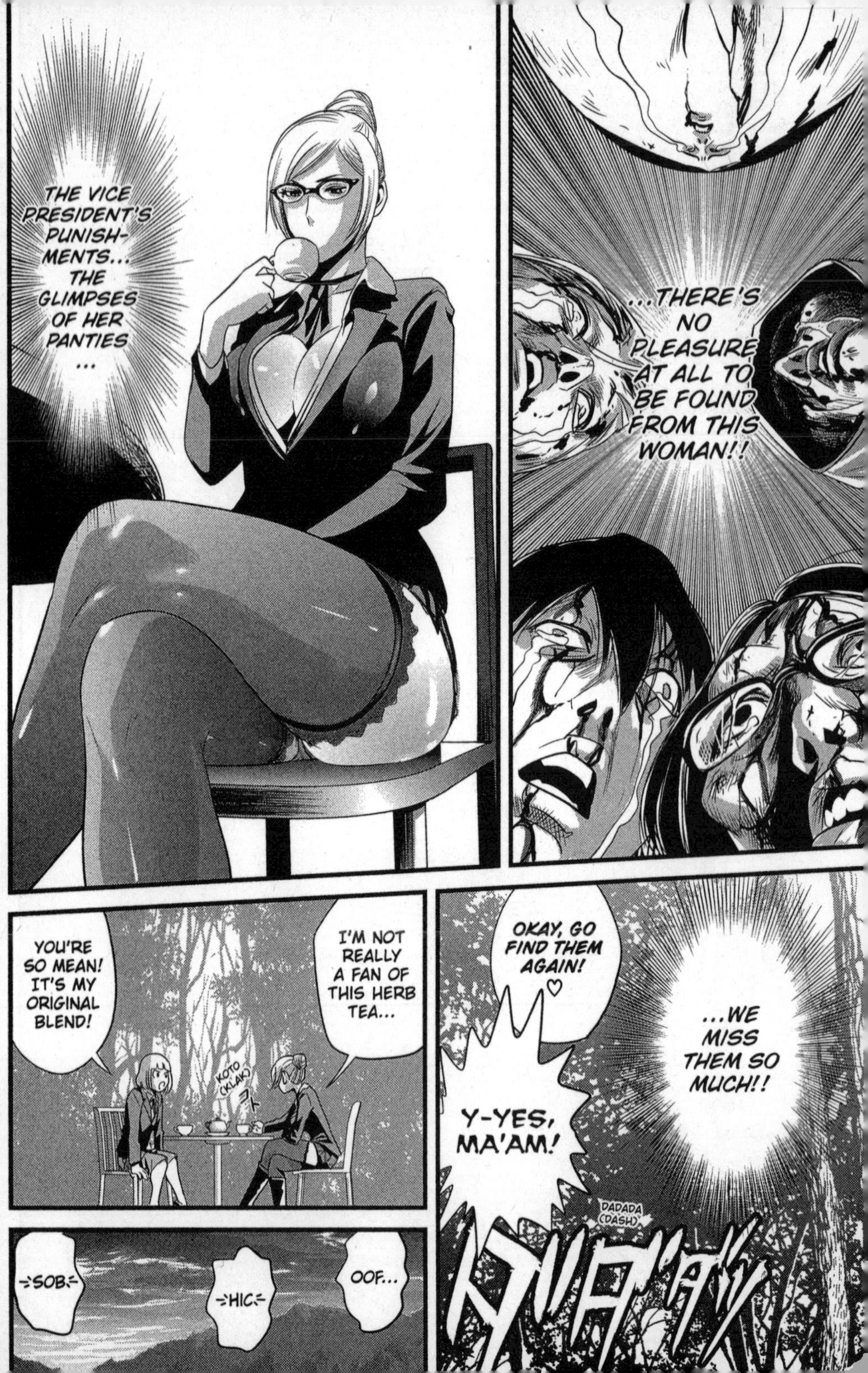
THE VICE PRESIDENT'S PUNISHMENTS... THE GLIMPSES OF HER PANTIES ...
...THERE'S NO PLEASURE AT ALL TO BE FOUND FROM THIS WOMAN!!
OKAY, GO FIND THEM AGAIN! ♡
Y-YES, MA'AM!
...WE MISS THEM SO MUCH!!
DADADA (DASH)
I'M NOT REALLY A FAN OF THIS HERB TEA...
KOTO (KLAK)
YOU'RE SO MEAN! IT'S MY ORIGINAL BLEND!
OOF...
HIC
SOB

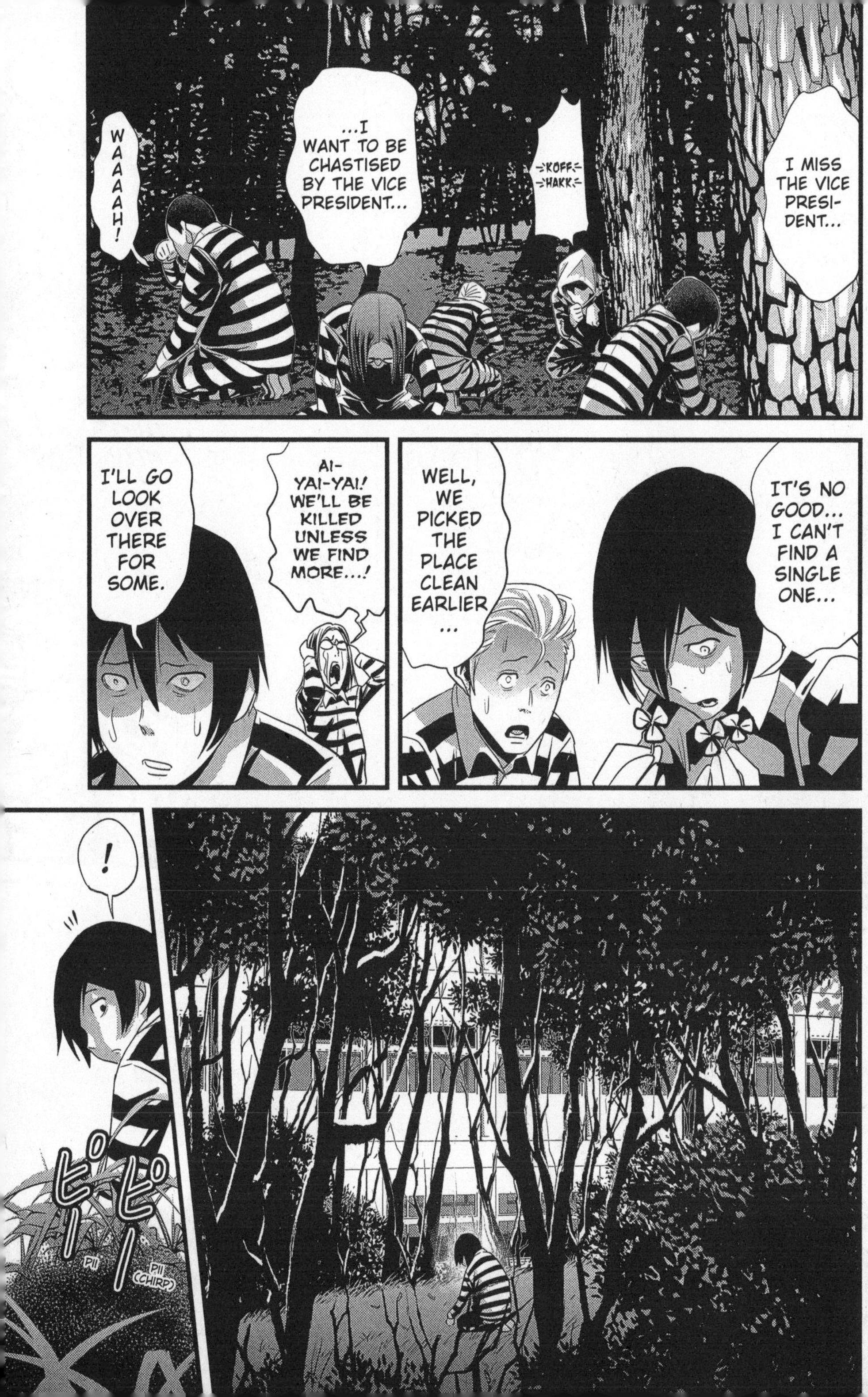
I MISS THE VICE PRESI-DENT...
KOFF HAKK
...I WANT TO BE CHASTISED BY THE VICE PRESIDENT...
WAAAAAH!
IT'S NO GOOD... I CAN'T FIND A SINGLE ONE...
WELL, WE PICKED THE PLACE CLEAN EARLIER...
AI-YAI-YAI! WE'LL BE KILLED UNLESS WE FIND MORE...!
I'LL GO LOOK OVER THERE FOR SOME.
!
ピー ピー
PII PII (CHIRP)

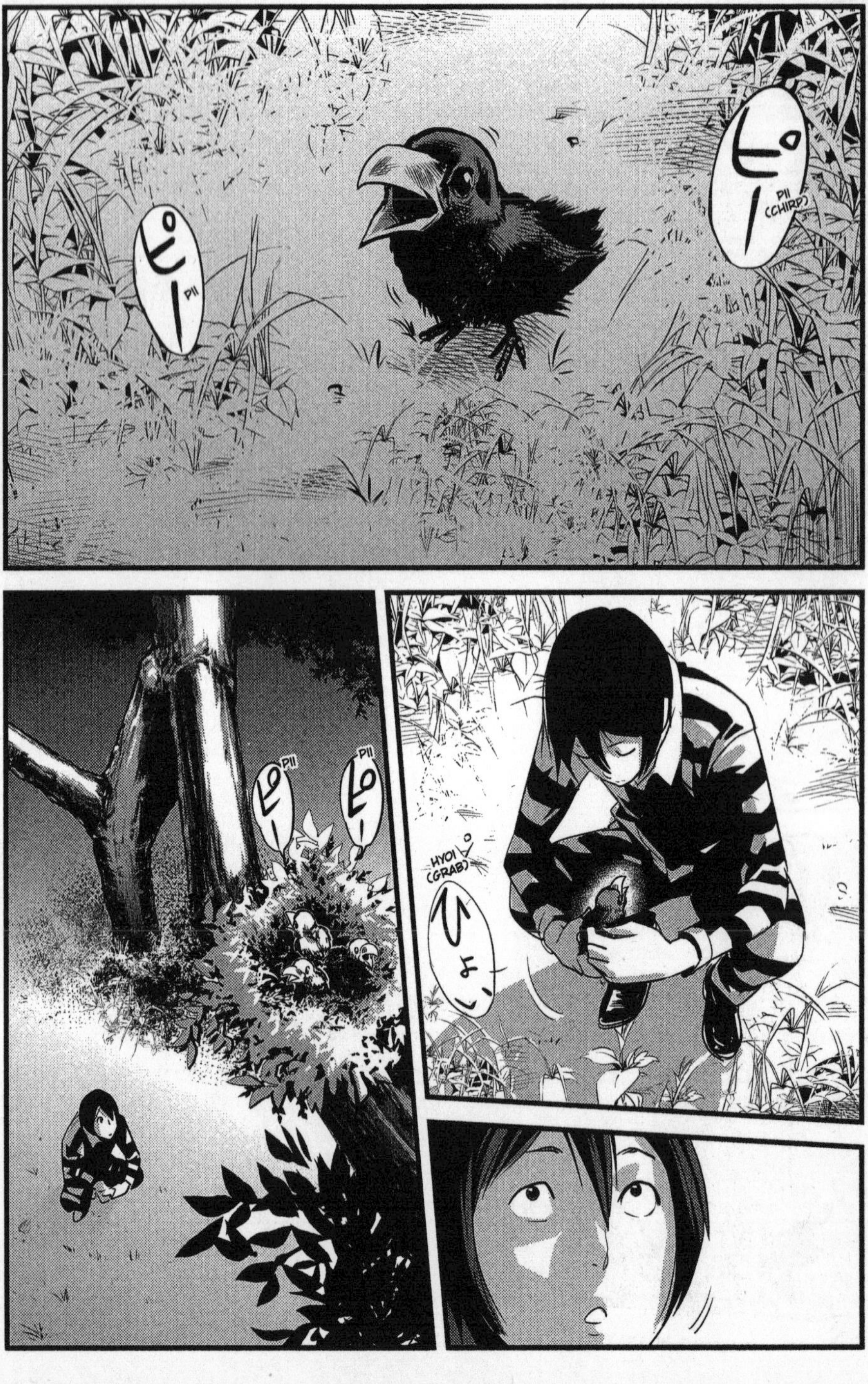
ピー
PII (CHIRP)
ピー
PII
ピー
PII
ピー
PII
ひょい
HYOI (GRAB)

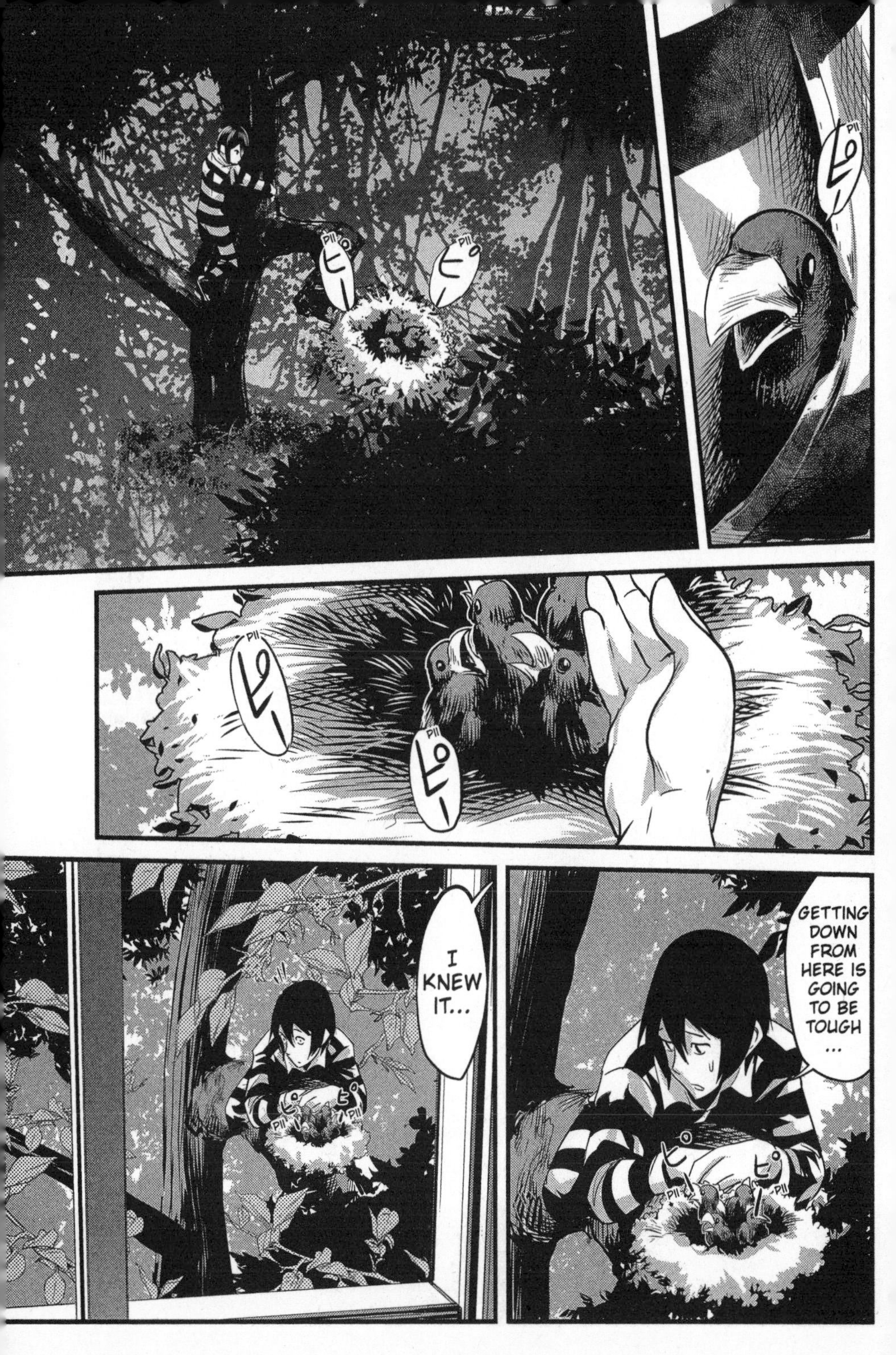
ピー
PII
ピー
PII
ピー
PII
ピー
PII
ピー
PII
GETTING DOWN FROM HERE IS GOING TO BE TOUGH ...
ピ
PII
ピ
PII
I KNEW IT...
ピ
PII
ピ
PII

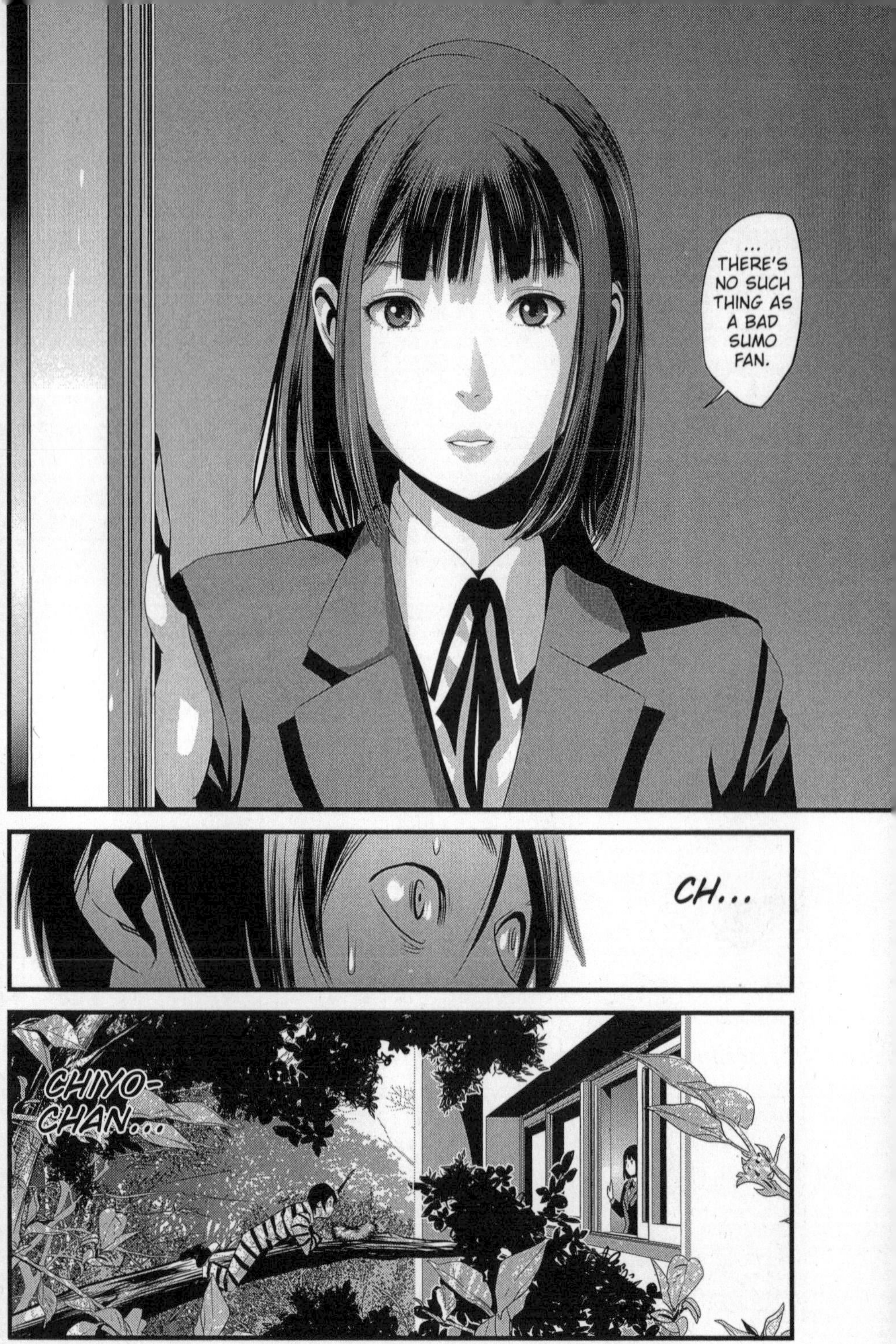
... THERE'S NO SUCH THING AS A BAD SUMO FAN.
CH...
CHIYO-CHAN...

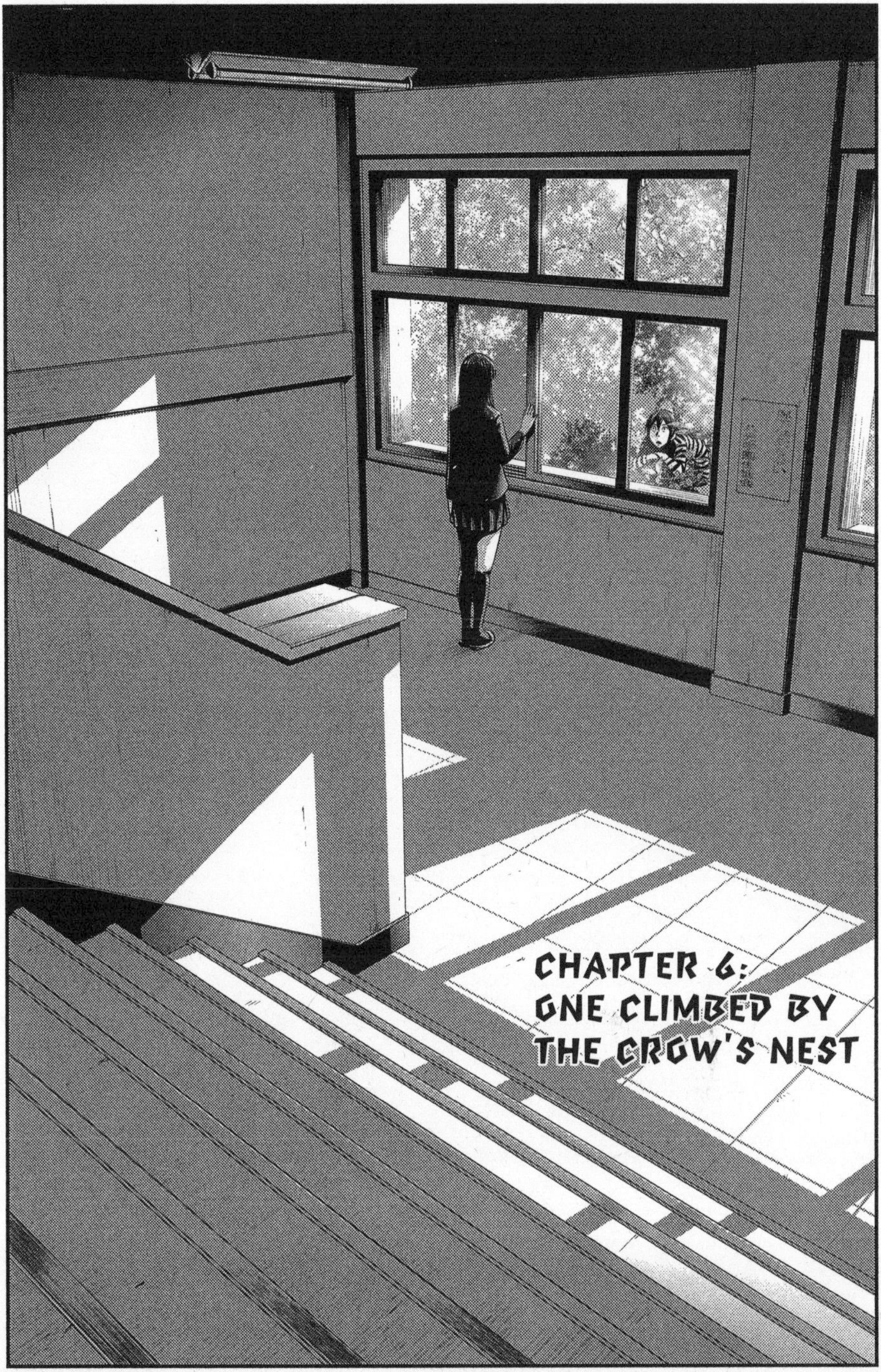
CHAPTER 6:
ONE CLIMBED BY
THE CROW'S NEST

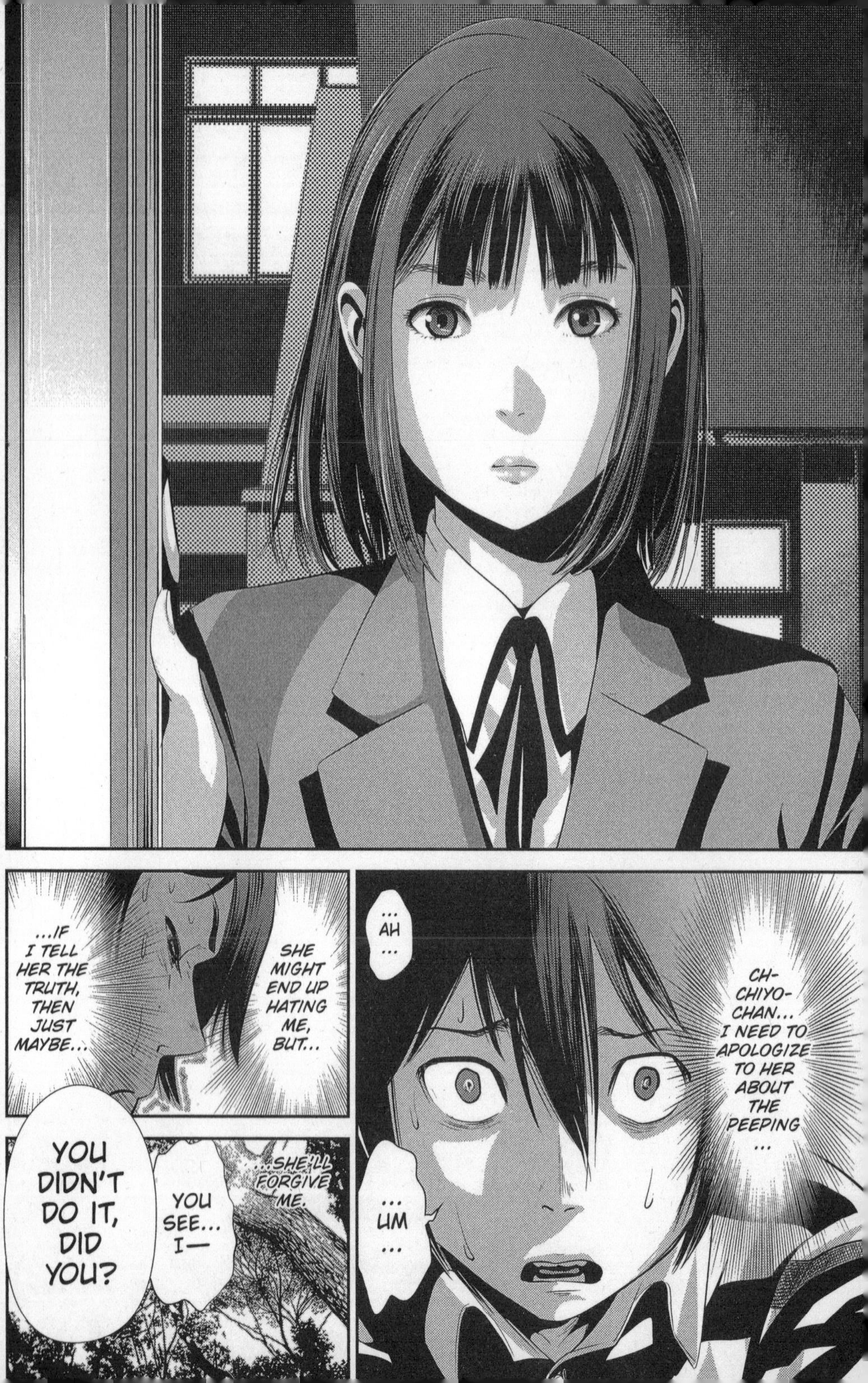
CH-CHIYO-CHAN... I NEED TO APOLOGIZE TO HER ABOUT THE PEEPING...
...AH...
SHE MIGHT END UP HATING ME, BUT...
...IF I TELL HER THE TRUTH, THEN JUST MAYBE...
...SHE'LL FORGIVE ME.
...UM...
YOU SEE... I—
YOU DIDN'T DO IT, DID YOU?

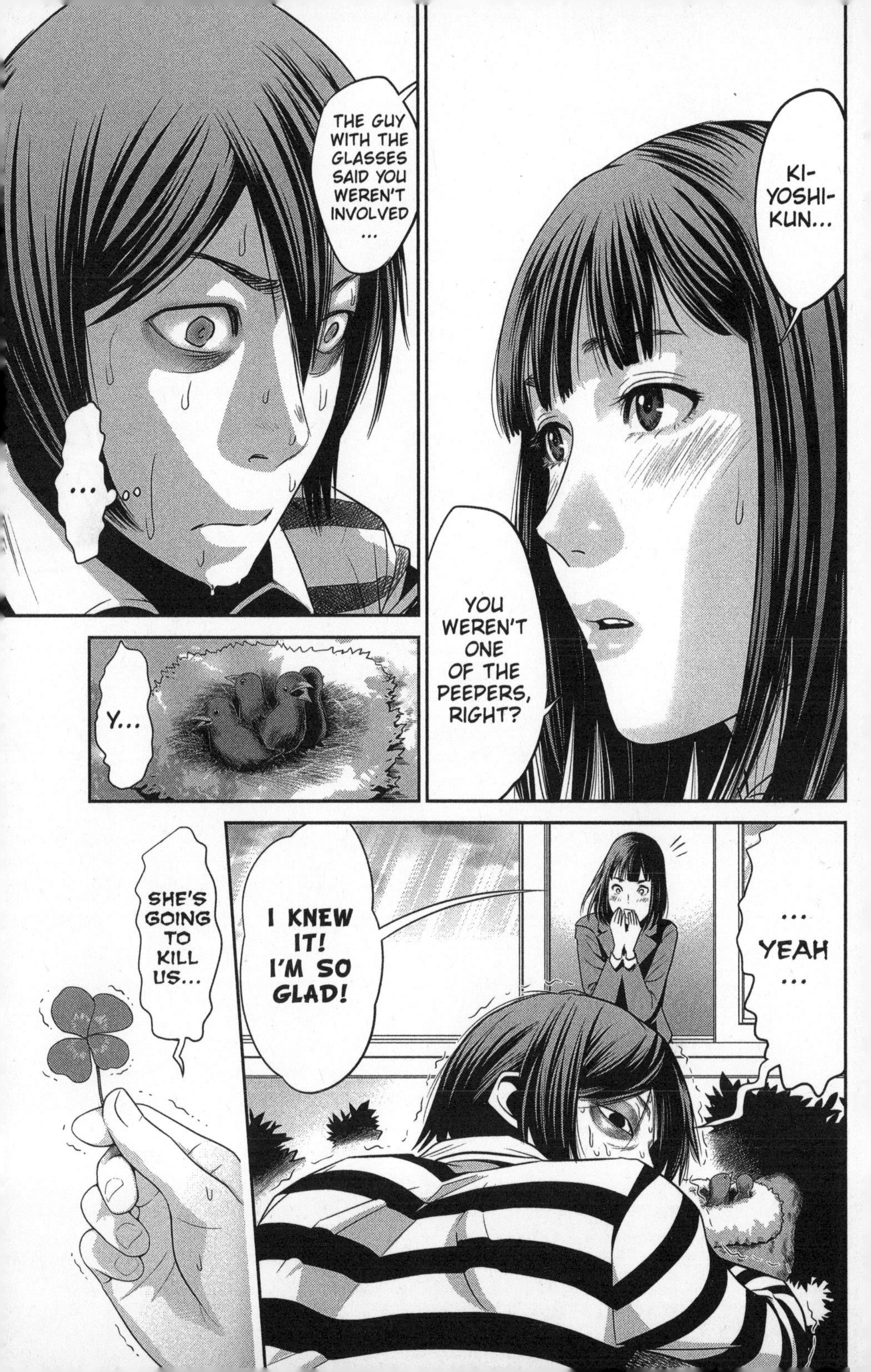
KI-YOSHI-KUN...
YOU WEREN'T ONE OF THE PEEPERS, RIGHT?
THE GUY WITH THE GLASSES SAID YOU WEREN'T INVOLVED...
...
Y...
... YEAH ...
I KNEW IT! I'M SO GLAD!
SHE'S GOING TO KILL US...

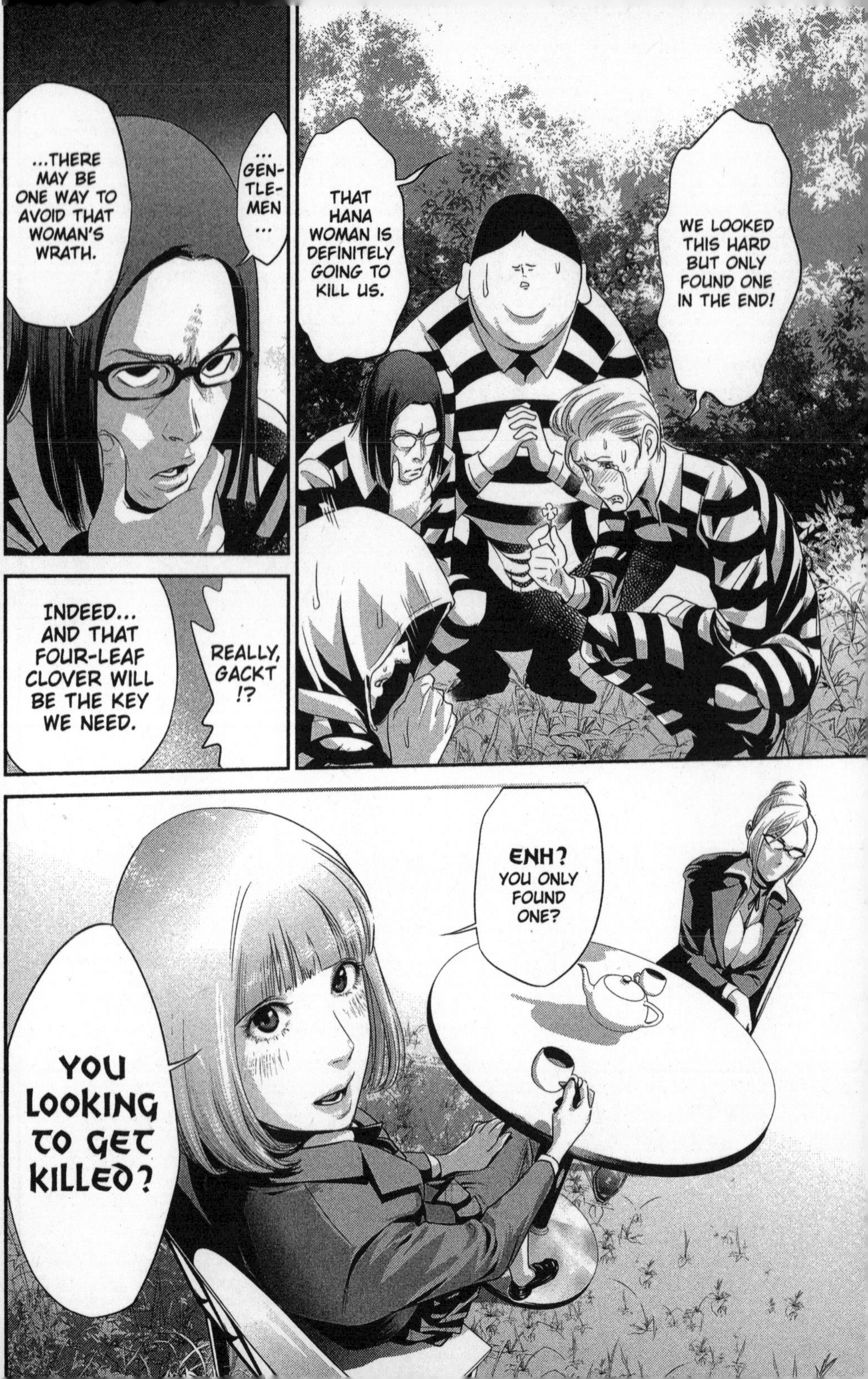
WE LOOKED THIS HARD BUT ONLY FOUND ONE IN THE END!
THAT HANA WOMAN IS DEFINITELY GOING TO KILL US.
...GENTLEMEN...
...THERE MAY BE ONE WAY TO AVOID THAT WOMAN'S WRATH.
REALLY, GACKT!?
INDEED... AND THAT FOUR-LEAF CLOVER WILL BE THE KEY WE NEED.
ENH? YOU ONLY FOUND ONE?
YOU LOOKING TO GET KILLED?

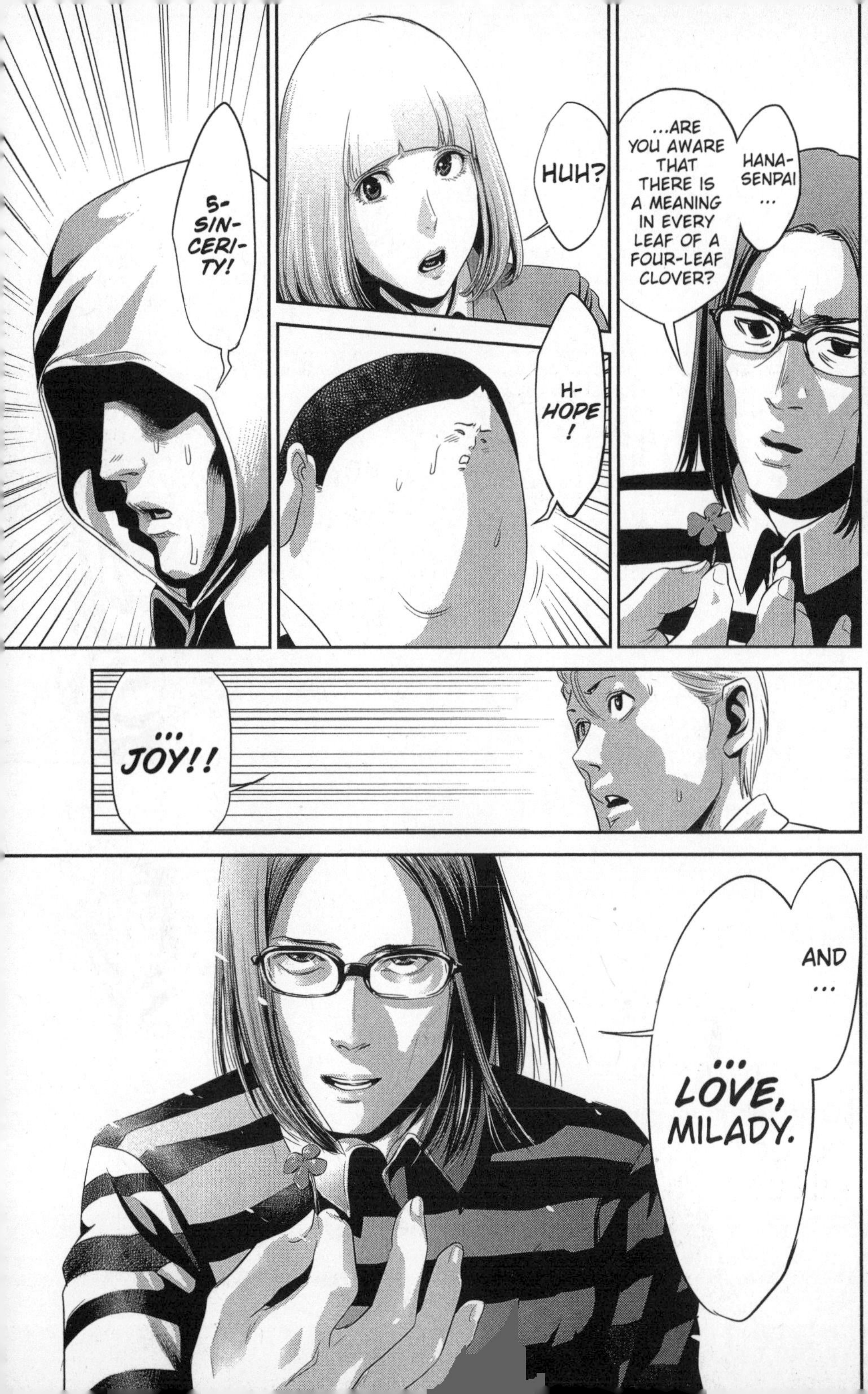
HANA-SENPAI...
...ARE YOU AWARE THAT THERE IS A MEANING IN EVERY LEAF OF A FOUR-LEAF CLOVER?
HUH?
H-HOPE!
S-SINCERITY!
...JOY!!
AND...
...LOVE, MILADY.

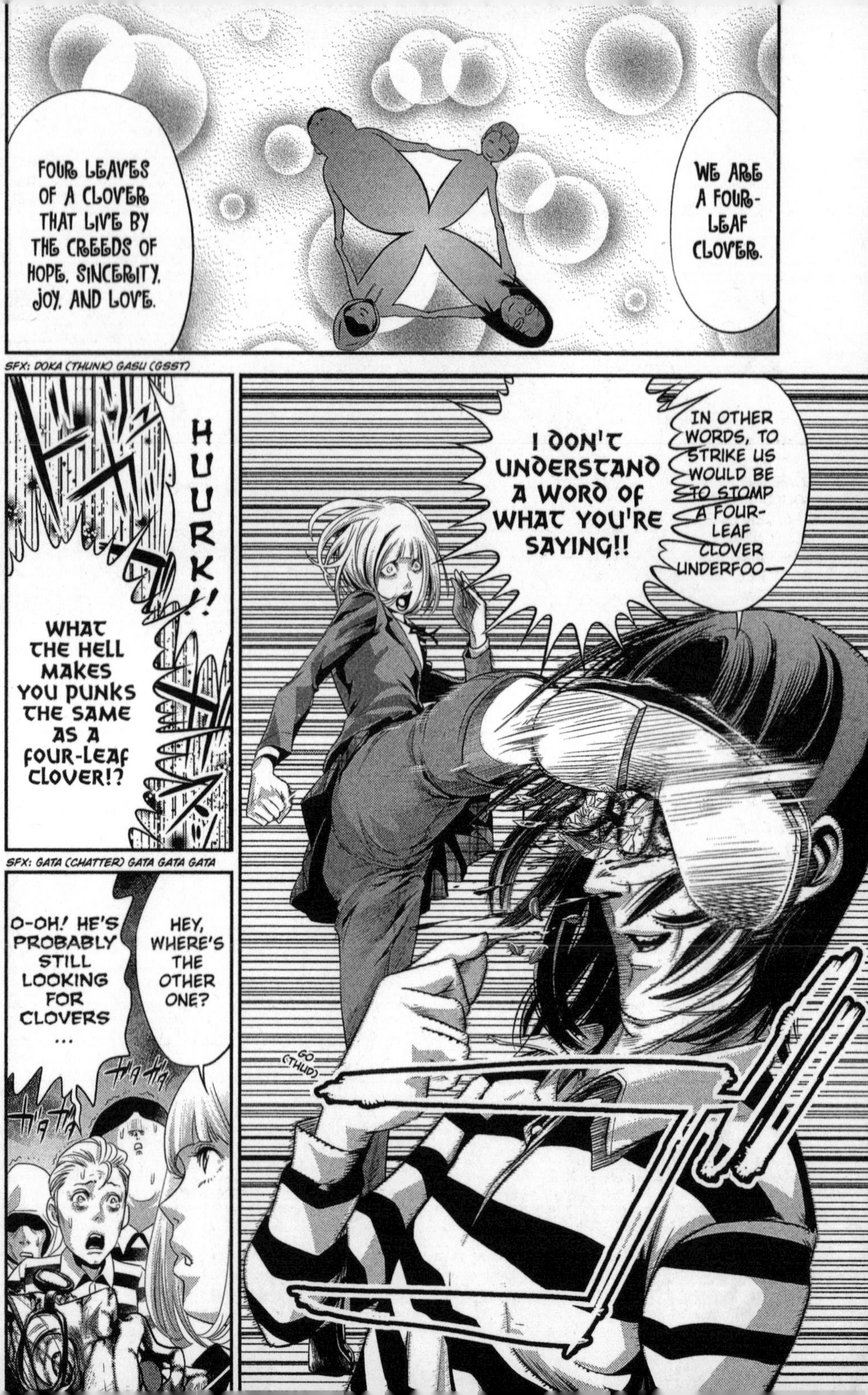
WE ARE A FOUR-LEAF CLOVER.
FOUR LEAVES OF A CLOVER THAT LIVE BY THE CREEDS OF HOPE, SINCERITY, JOY, AND LOVE.
SFX: DOKA (THUNK) GASU (GSST)
IN OTHER WORDS, TO STRIKE US WOULD BE TO STOMP A FOUR-LEAF CLOVER UNDERFOO—
I DON'T UNDERSTAND A WORD OF WHAT YOU'RE SAYING!!
GO (THUD)
HUURK!
WHAT THE HELL MAKES YOU PUNKS THE SAME AS A FOUR-LEAF CLOVER!?
SFX: GATA (CHATTER) GATA GATA GATA
HEY, WHERE'S THE OTHER ONE?
O-OH! HE'S PROBABLY STILL LOOKING FOR CLOVERS...

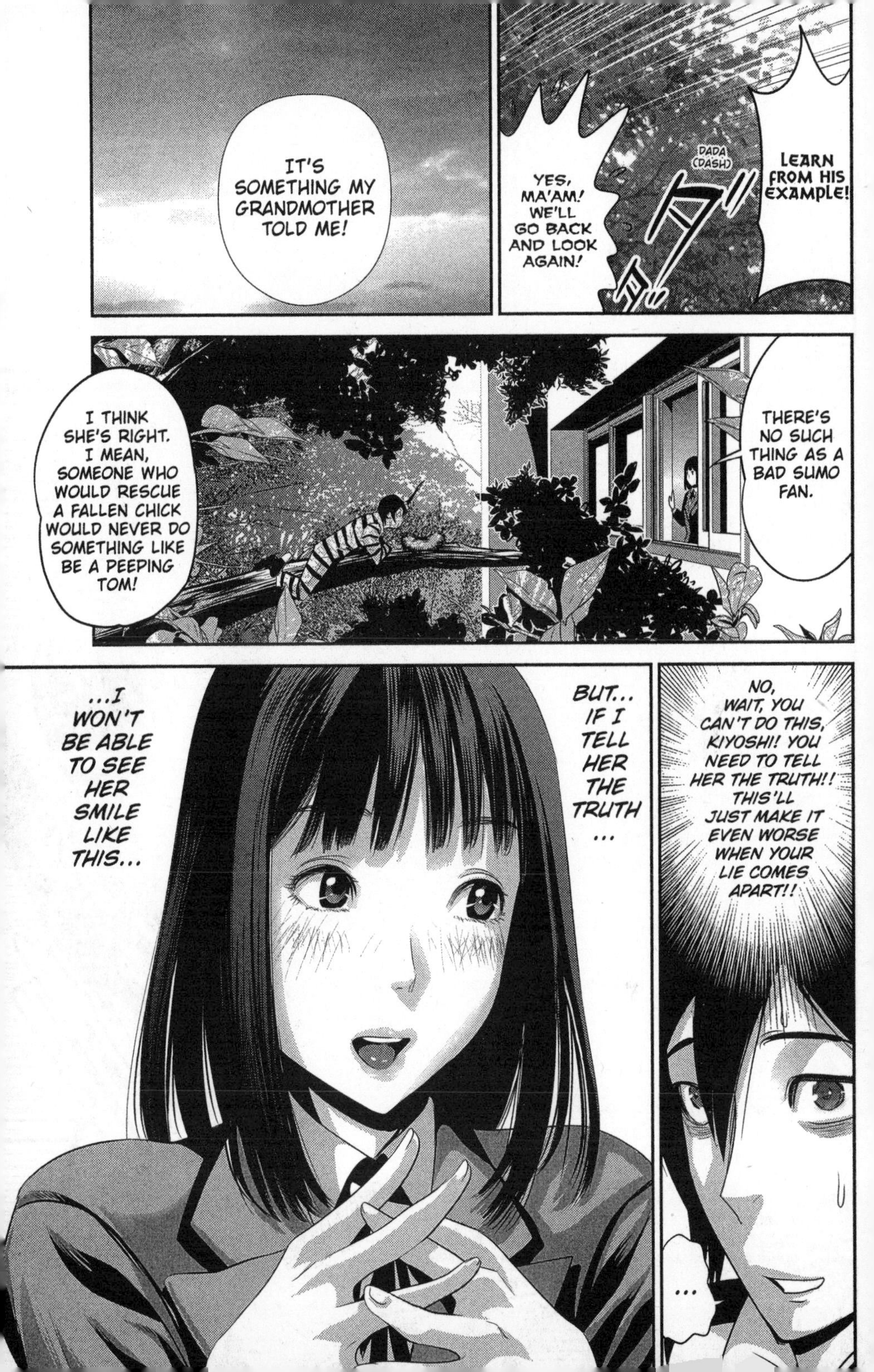
LEARN FROM HIS EXAMPLE!
YES, MA'AM! WE'LL GO BACK AND LOOK AGAIN!
DADA (DASH)
IT'S SOMETHING MY GRANDMOTHER TOLD ME!
THERE'S NO SUCH THING AS A BAD SUMO FAN.
I THINK SHE'S RIGHT. I MEAN, SOMEONE WHO WOULD RESCUE A FALLEN CHICK WOULD NEVER DO SOMETHING LIKE BE A PEEPING TOM!
NO, WAIT, YOU CAN'T DO THIS, KIYOSHI! YOU NEED TO TELL HER THE TRUTH!! THIS'LL JUST MAKE IT EVEN WORSE WHEN YOUR LIE COMES APART!!
...
BUT... IF I TELL HER THE TRUTH...
...I WON'T BE ABLE TO SEE HER SMILE LIKE THIS...

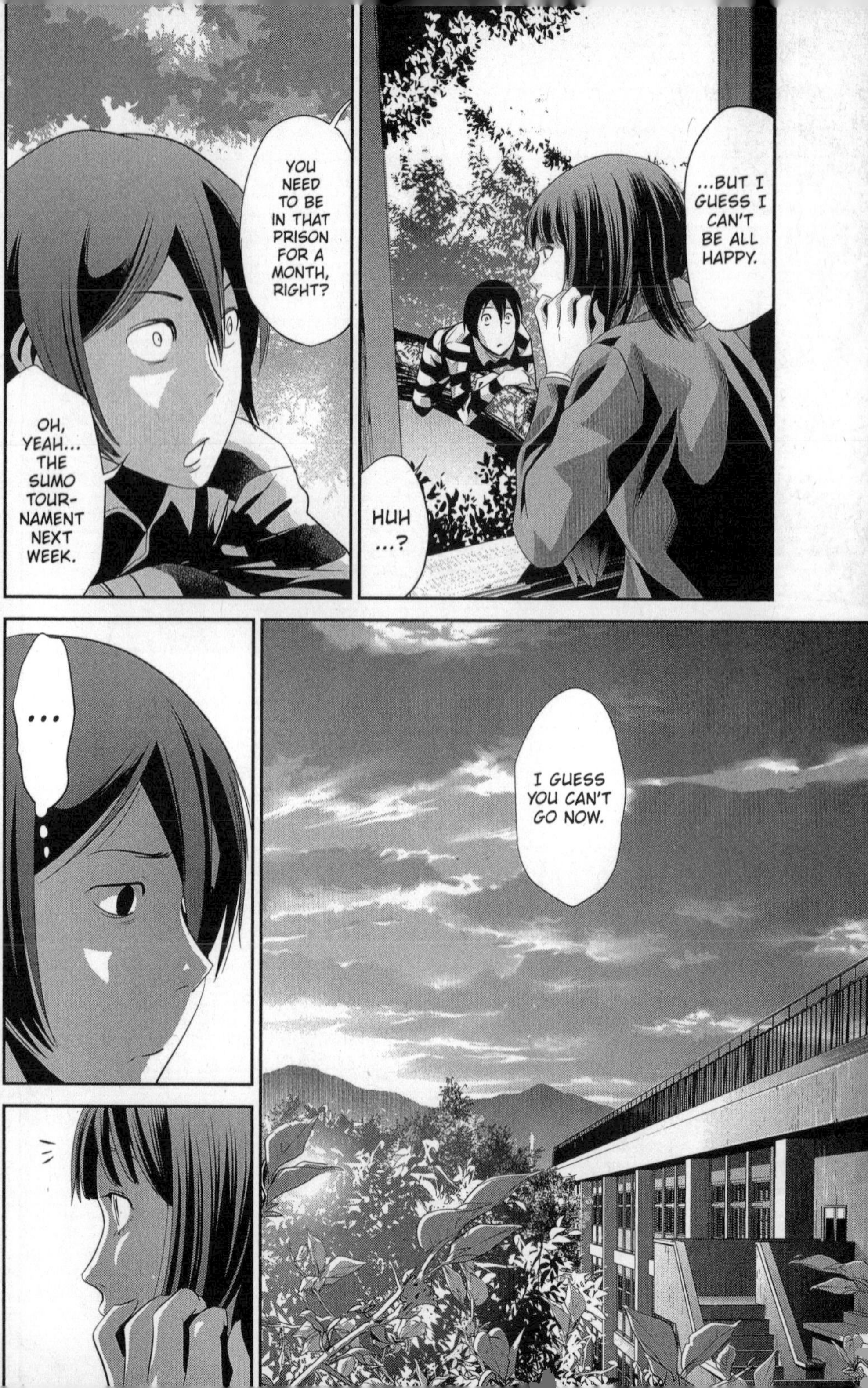
...BUT I GUESS I CAN'T BE ALL HAPPY.
HUH ...?
YOU NEED TO BE IN THAT PRISON FOR A MONTH, RIGHT?
OH, YEAH... THE SUMO TOURNAMENT NEXT WEEK.
I GUESS YOU CAN'T GO NOW.
...

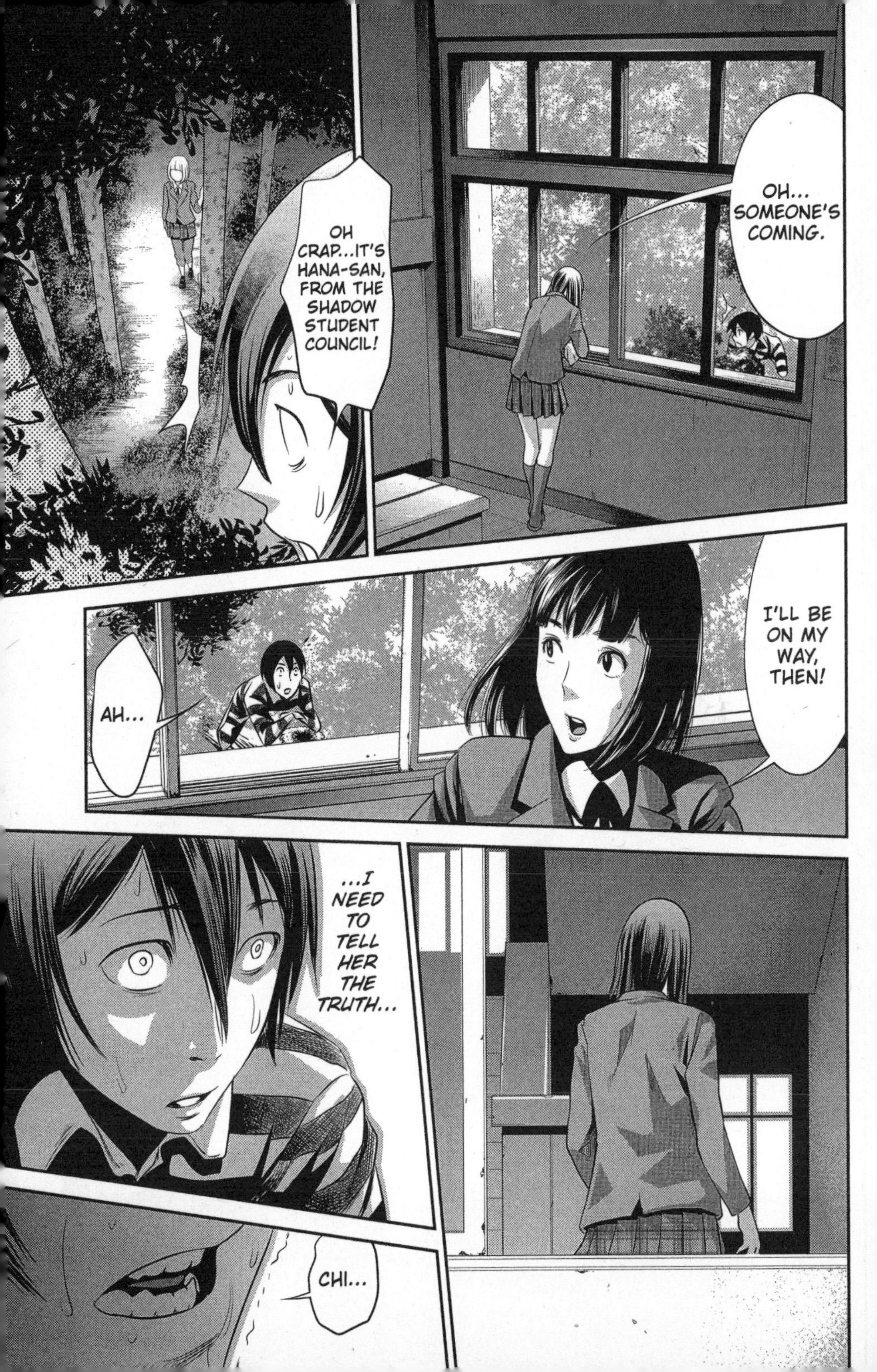
OH... SOMEONE'S COMING.
OH CRAP...IT'S HANA-SAN, FROM THE SHADOW STUDENT COUNCIL!
I'LL BE ON MY WAY, THEN!
AH...
...I NEED TO TELL HER THE TRUTH...
CHI...

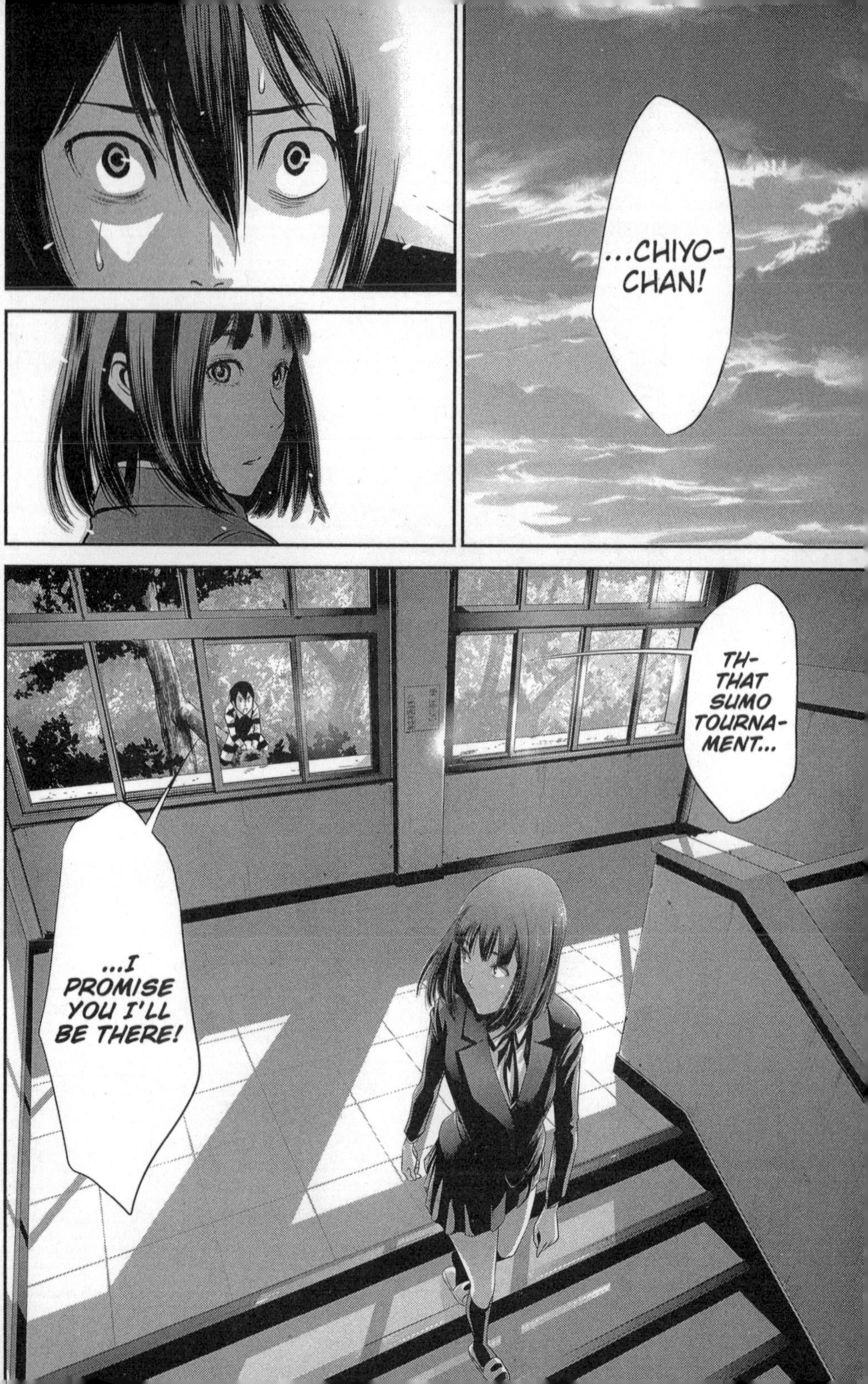
...CHIYO-CHAN!
TH-THAT SUMO TOURNAMENT...
...I PROMISE YOU I'LL BE THERE!

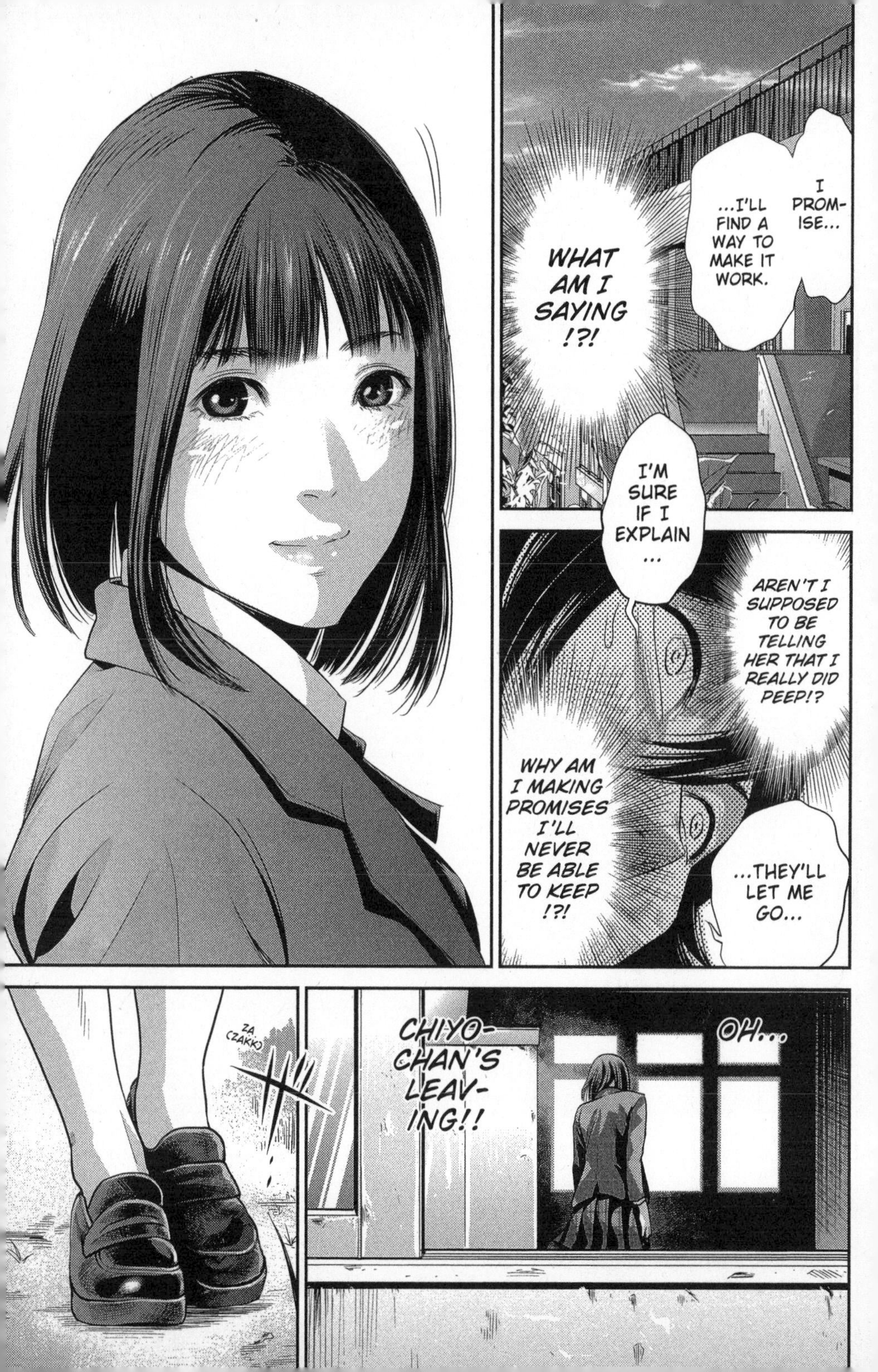

I PROMISE...
...I'LL FIND A WAY TO MAKE IT WORK.
WHAT AM I SAYING !?!
I'M SURE IF I EXPLAIN ...
AREN'T I SUPPOSED TO BE TELLING HER THAT I REALLY DID PEEP!?
...THEY'LL LET ME GO...
WHY AM I MAKING PROMISES I'LL NEVER BE ABLE TO KEEP !?!
OH...
CHIYO-CHAN'S LEAV-ING!!
ZA (ZAKK)

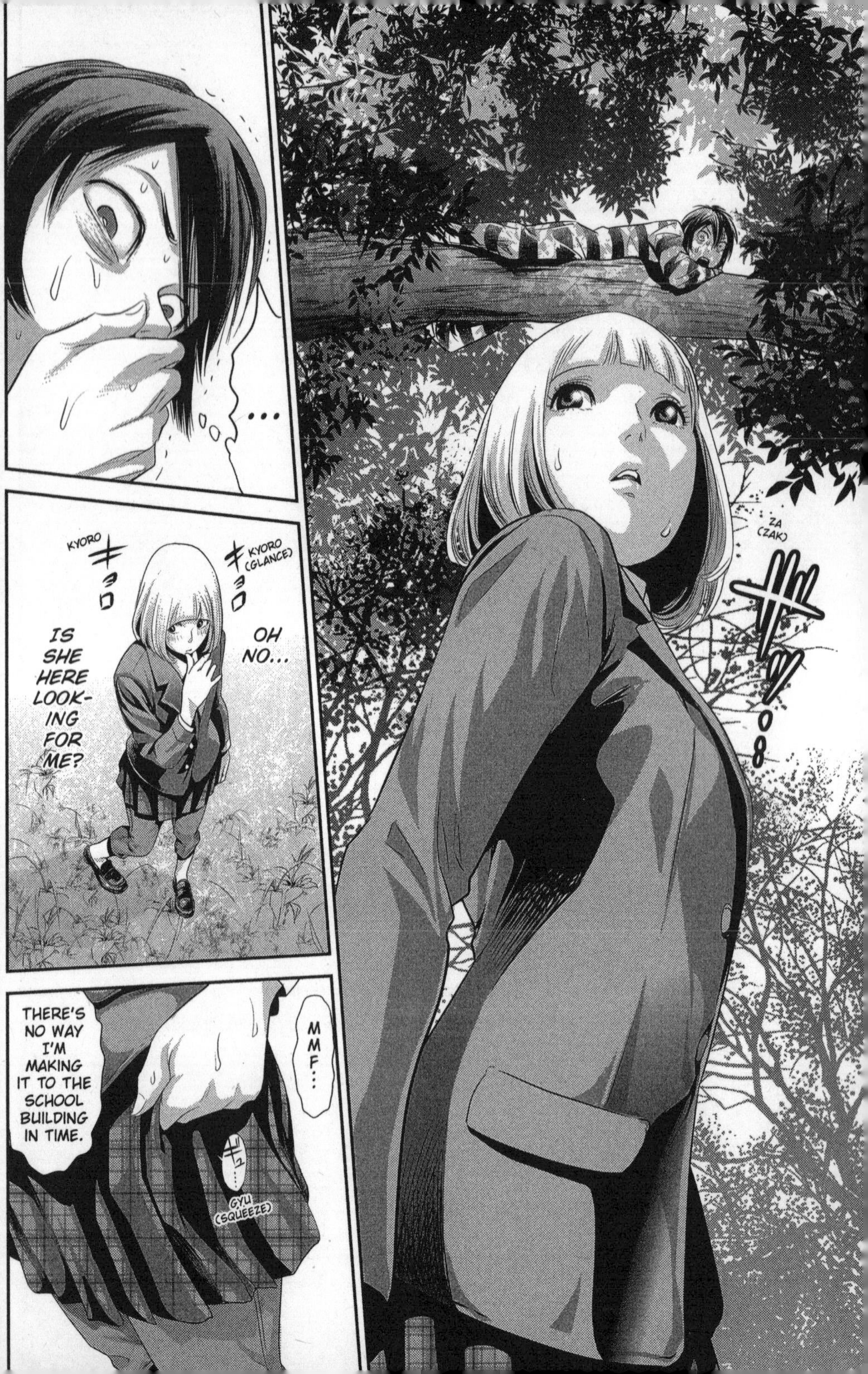
ZA (ZAK)
...
KYORO (GLANCE)
KYORO
OH NO...
IS SHE HERE LOOKING FOR ME?
MMF...
THERE'S NO WAY I'M MAKING IT TO THE SCHOOL BUILDING IN TIME.
GYU (SQUEEZE)

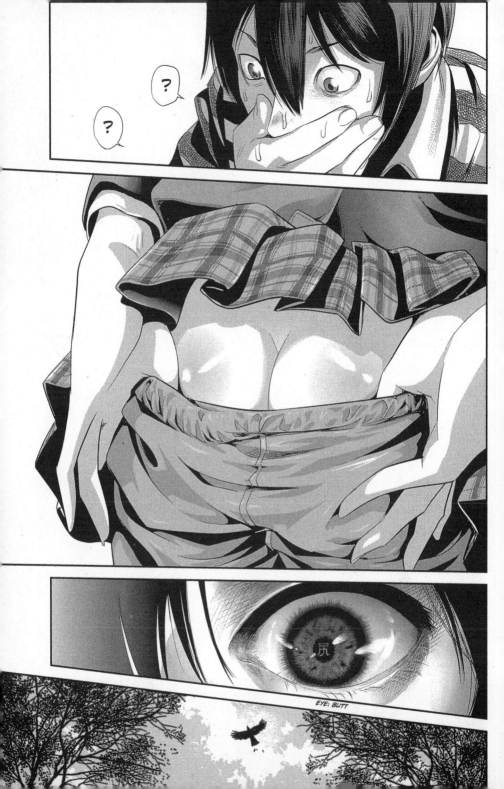

EYE: BUTT

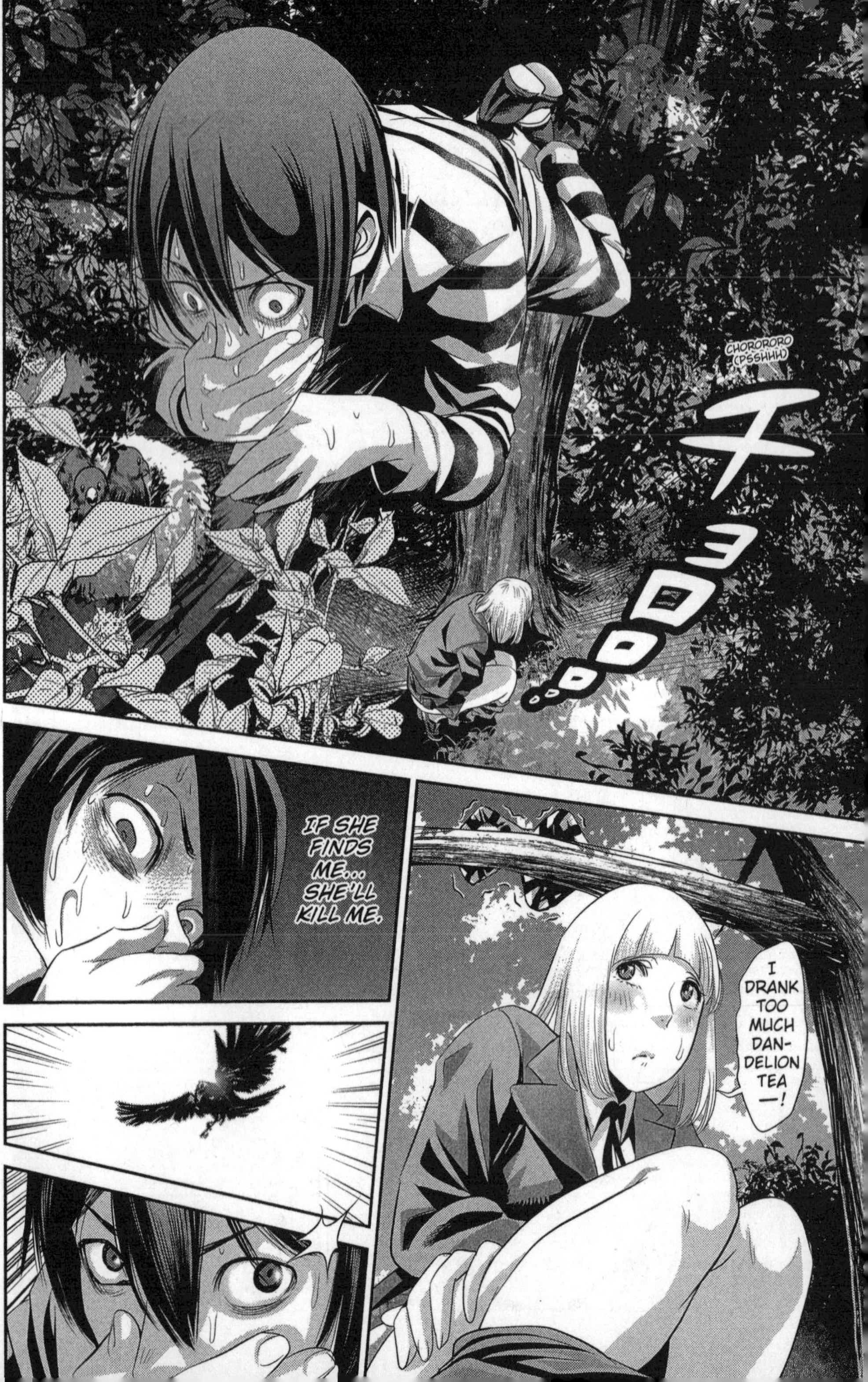
CHORORORO (PSSHHH)
チョロロロ…
IF SHE FINDS ME... SHE'LL KILL ME.
I DRANK TOO MUCH DAN-DELION TEA—!

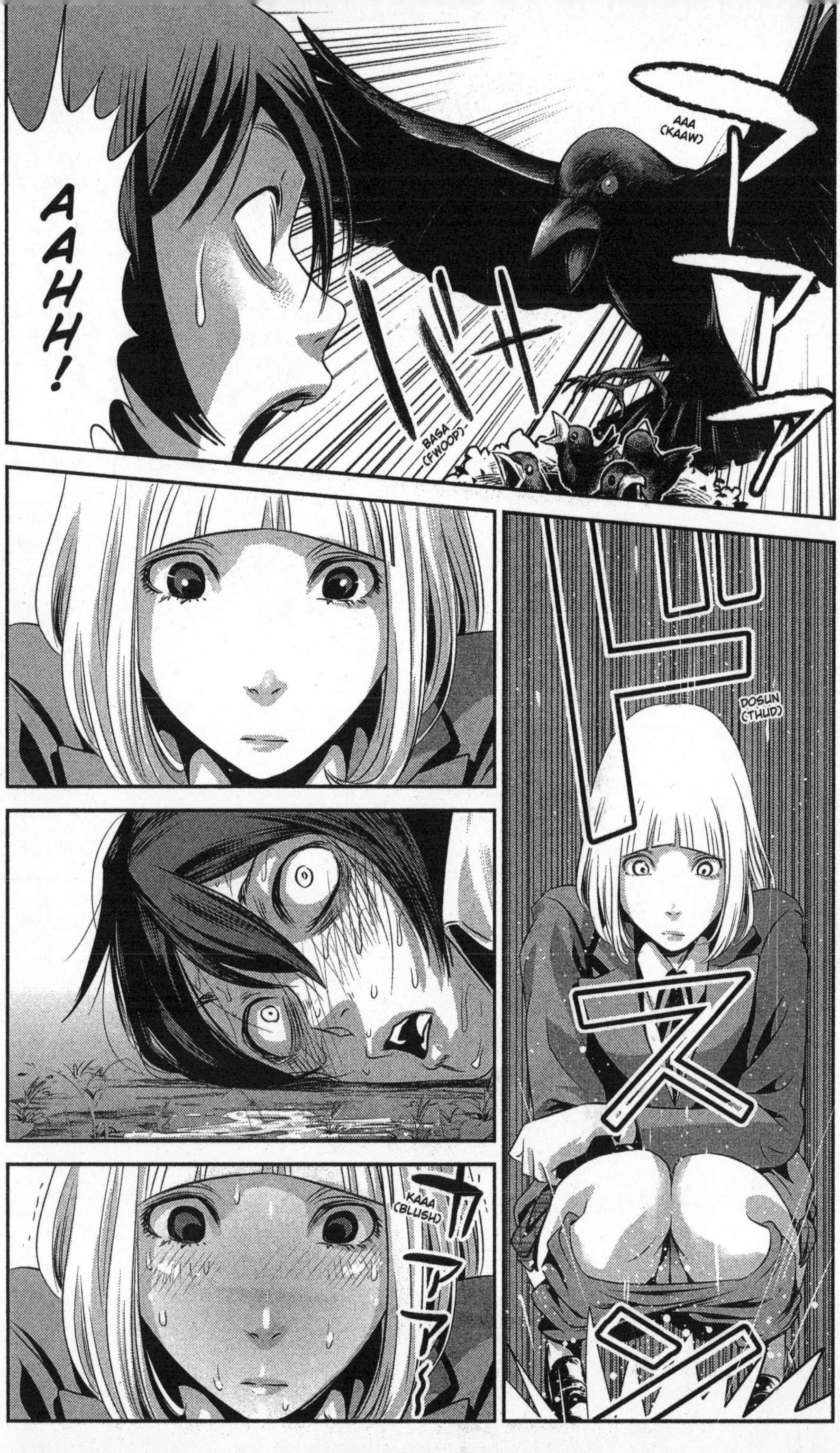
AAA (KAAW)
AAHH!
BASA (FWOOP)
DOSUN (THUD)
KAAA (BLUSH)

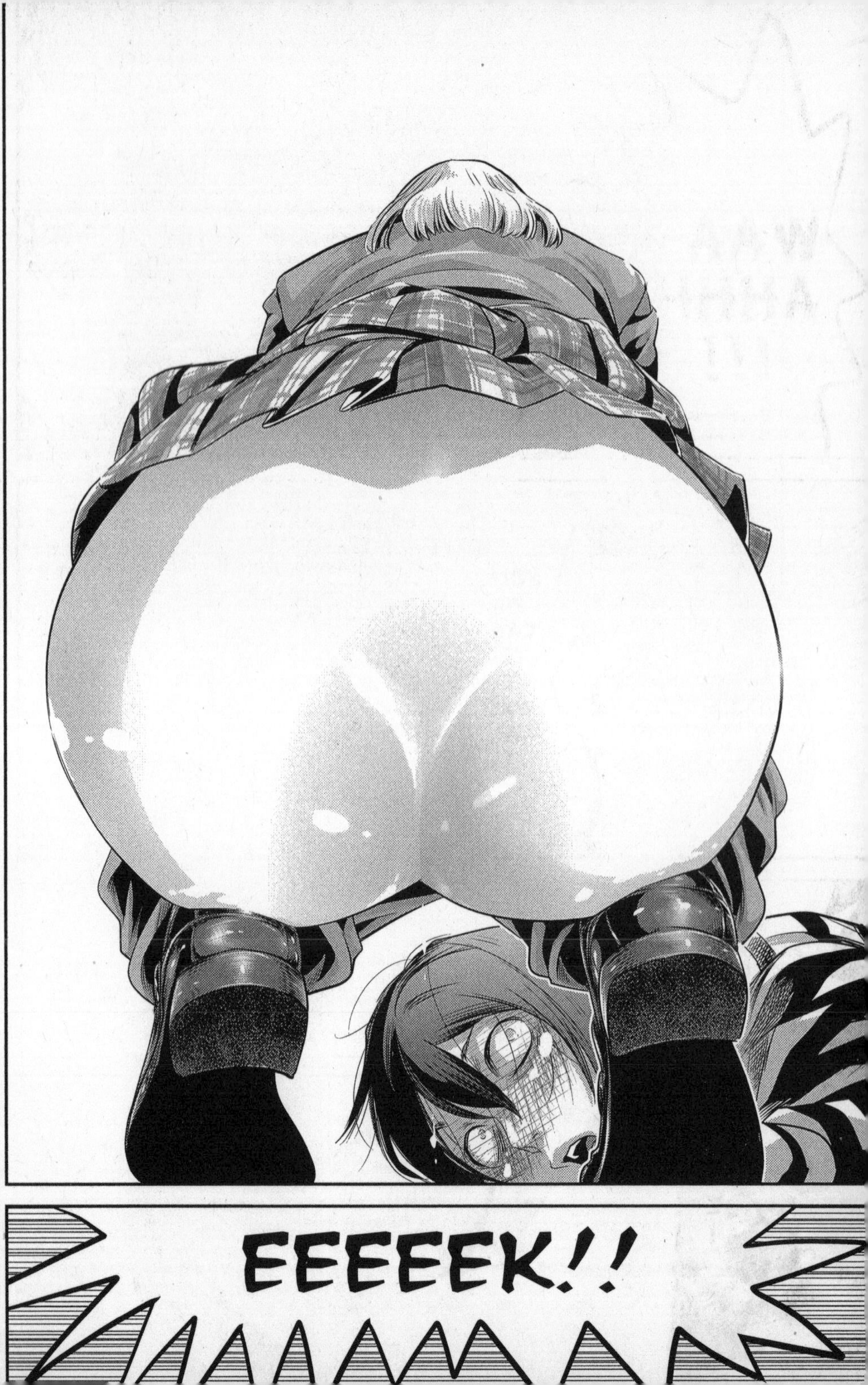
EEEEEK!!

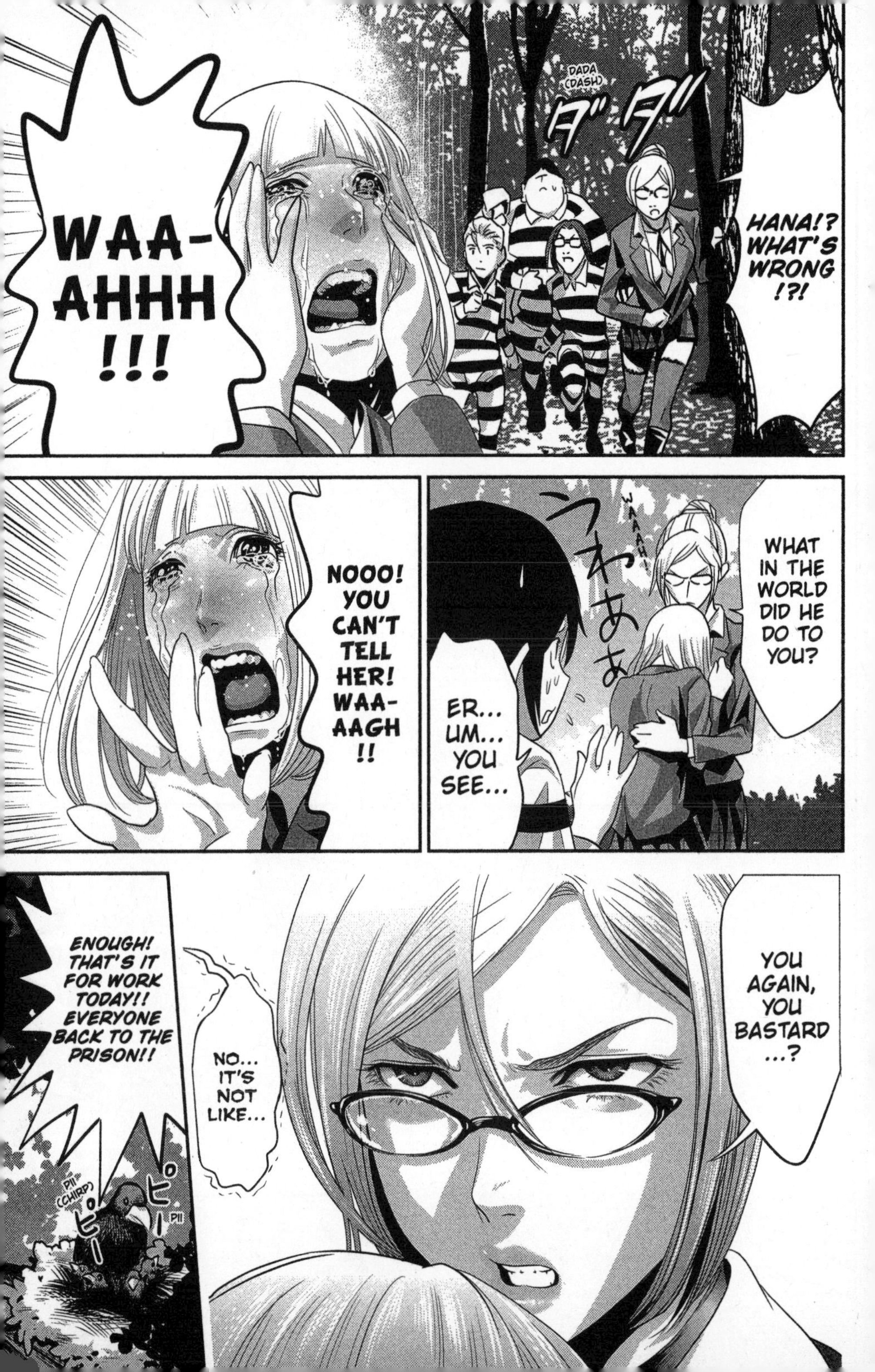
HANA!? WHAT'S WRONG !?!
DADA (DASH)
WAA-AHHH !!!
WHAT IN THE WORLD DID HE DO TO YOU?
WAAAH
ER... UM... YOU SEE...
NOOO! YOU CAN'T TELL HER! WAA-AAGH !!
YOU AGAIN, YOU BASTARD ...?
NO... IT'S NOT LIKE...
ENOUGH! THAT'S IT FOR WORK TODAY!! EVERYONE BACK TO THE PRISON!!
PII (CHIRP) PII

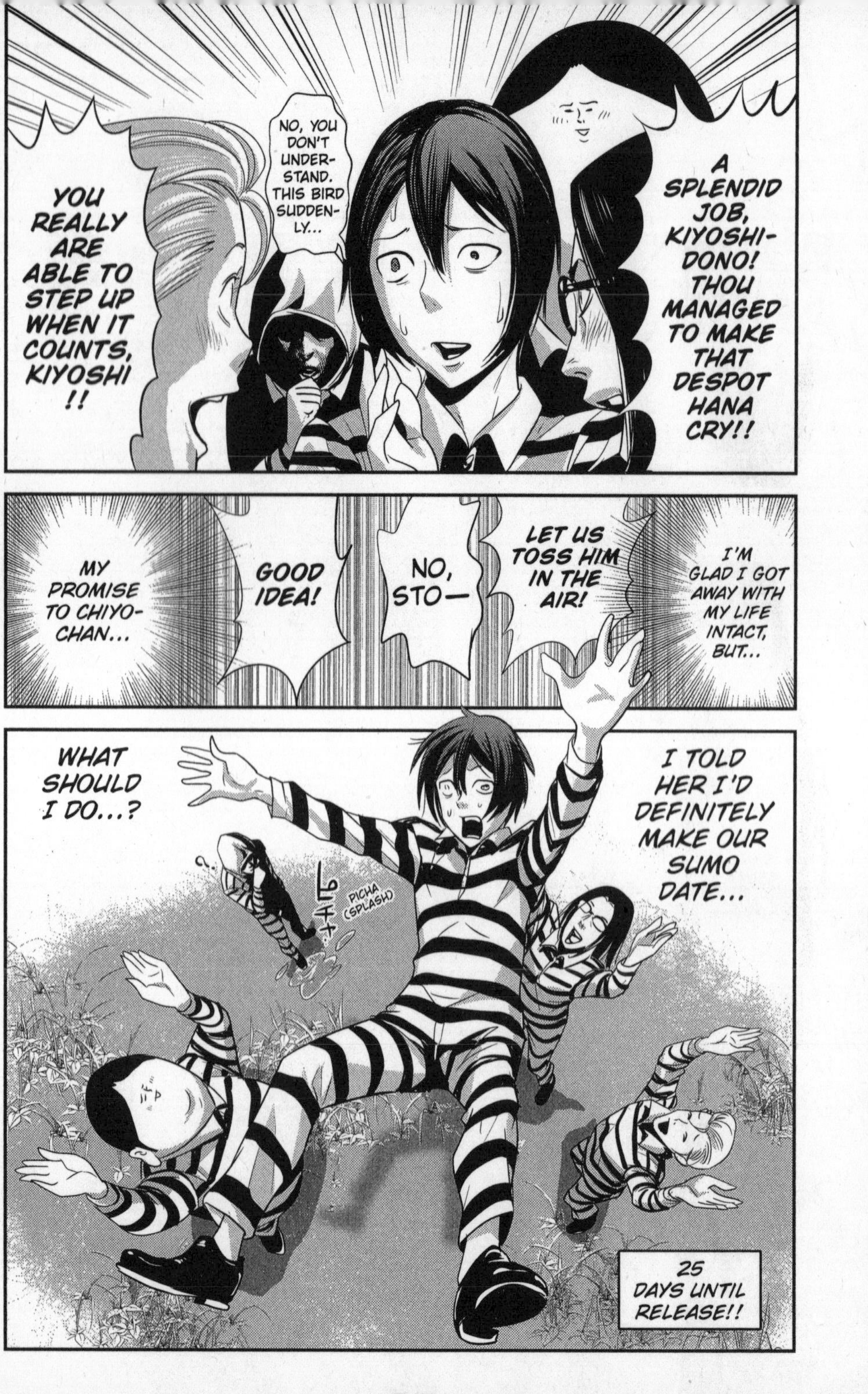
A SPLENDID JOB, KIYOSHI-DONO! THOU MANAGED TO MAKE THAT DESPOT HANA CRY!!
NO, YOU DON'T UNDER-STAND. THIS BIRD SUDDEN-LY...
YOU REALLY ARE ABLE TO STEP UP WHEN IT COUNTS, KIYOSHI!!
I'M GLAD I GOT AWAY WITH MY LIFE INTACT, BUT...
LET US TOSS HIM IN THE AIR!
NO, STO—
GOOD IDEA!
MY PROMISE TO CHIYO-CHAN...
I TOLD HER I'D DEFINITELY MAKE OUR SUMO DATE...
WHAT SHOULD I DO...?
PICHA (SPLASH)
25 DAYS UNTIL RELEASE!!

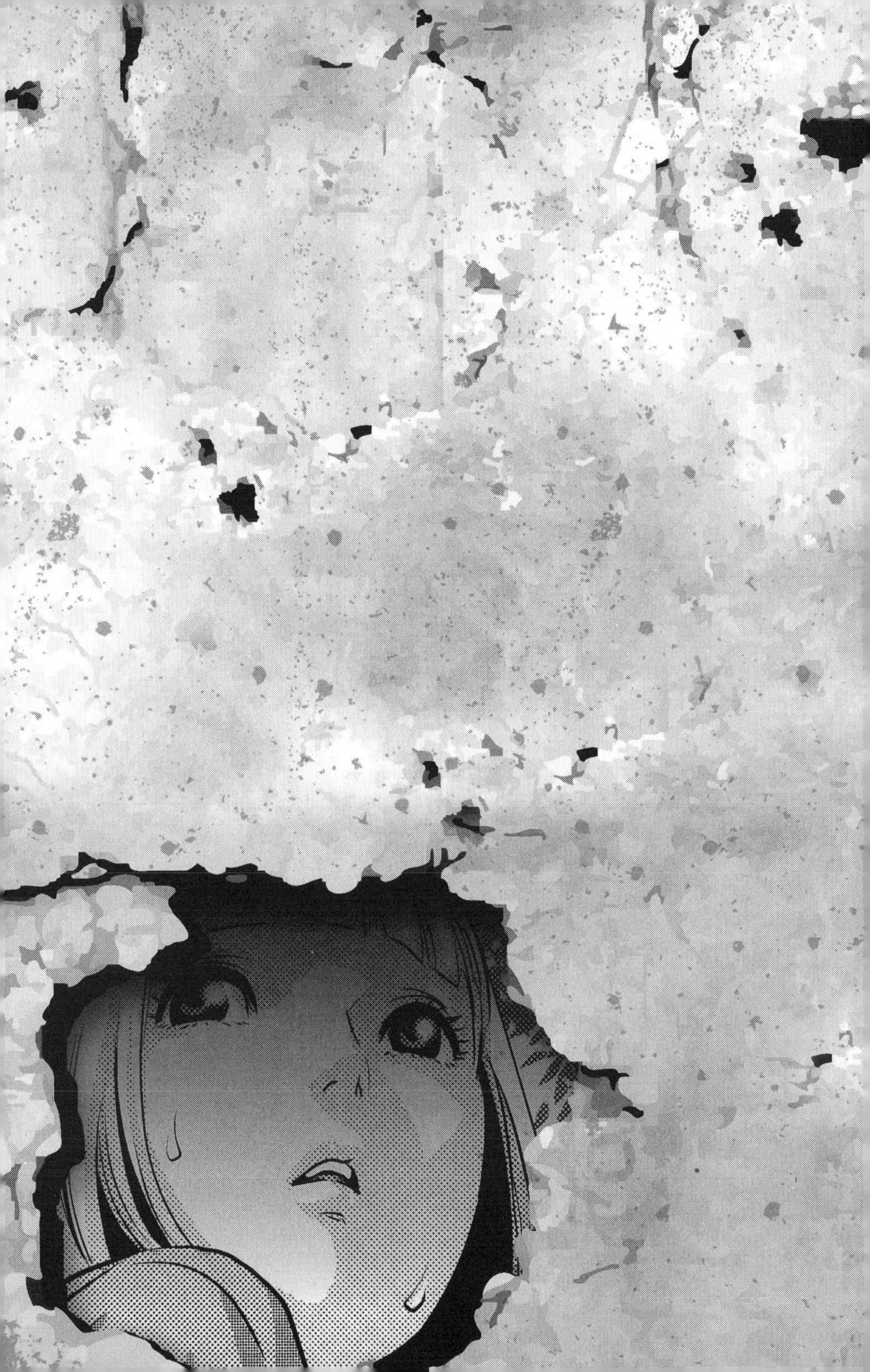

PRISON SCHOOL

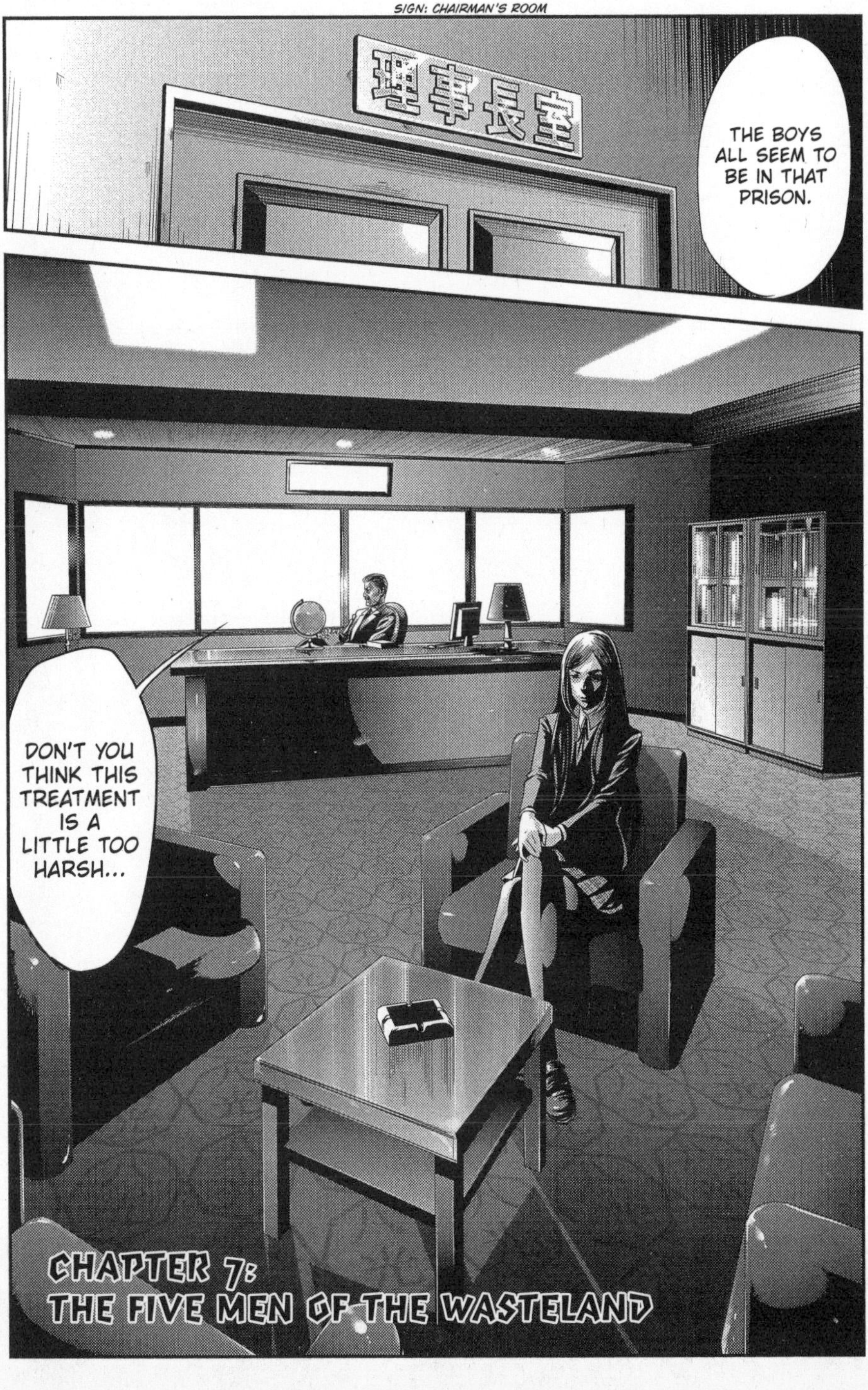
SIGN: CHAIRMAN'S ROOM
理事長室
THE BOYS ALL SEEM TO BE IN THAT PRISON.
DON'T YOU THINK THIS TREATMENT IS A LITTLE TOO HARSH...
CHAPTER 7: THE FIVE MEN OF THE WASTELAND

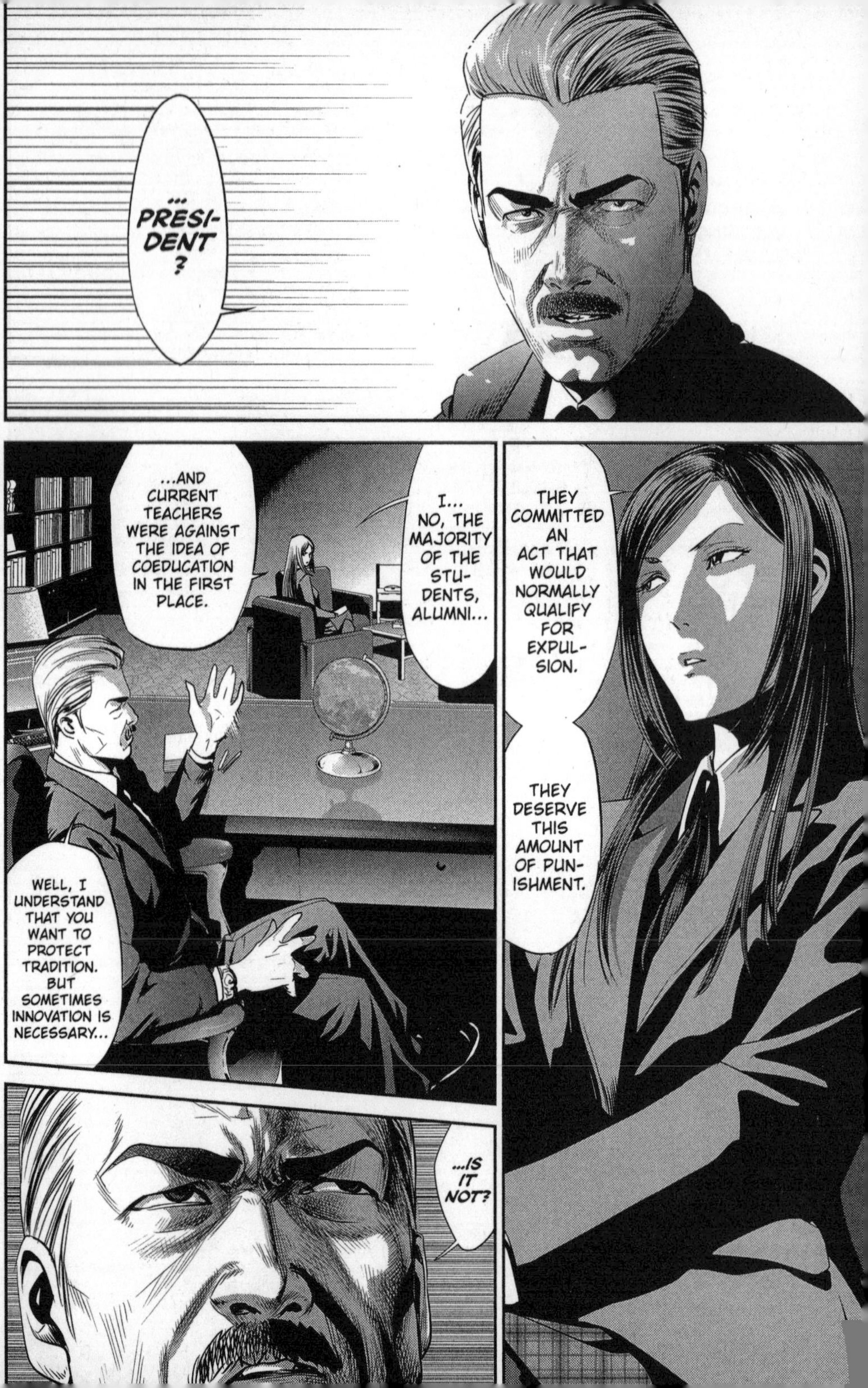
...PRESI-DENT?
THEY COMMITTED AN ACT THAT WOULD NORMALLY QUALIFY FOR EXPUL-SION.
THEY DESERVE THIS AMOUNT OF PUN-ISHMENT.
I... NO, THE MAJORITY OF THE STU-DENTS, ALUMNI...
...AND CURRENT TEACHERS WERE AGAINST THE IDEA OF COEDUCATION IN THE FIRST PLACE.
WELL, I UNDERSTAND THAT YOU WANT TO PROTECT TRADITION. BUT SOMETIMES INNOVATION IS NECESSARY...
...IS IT NOT?

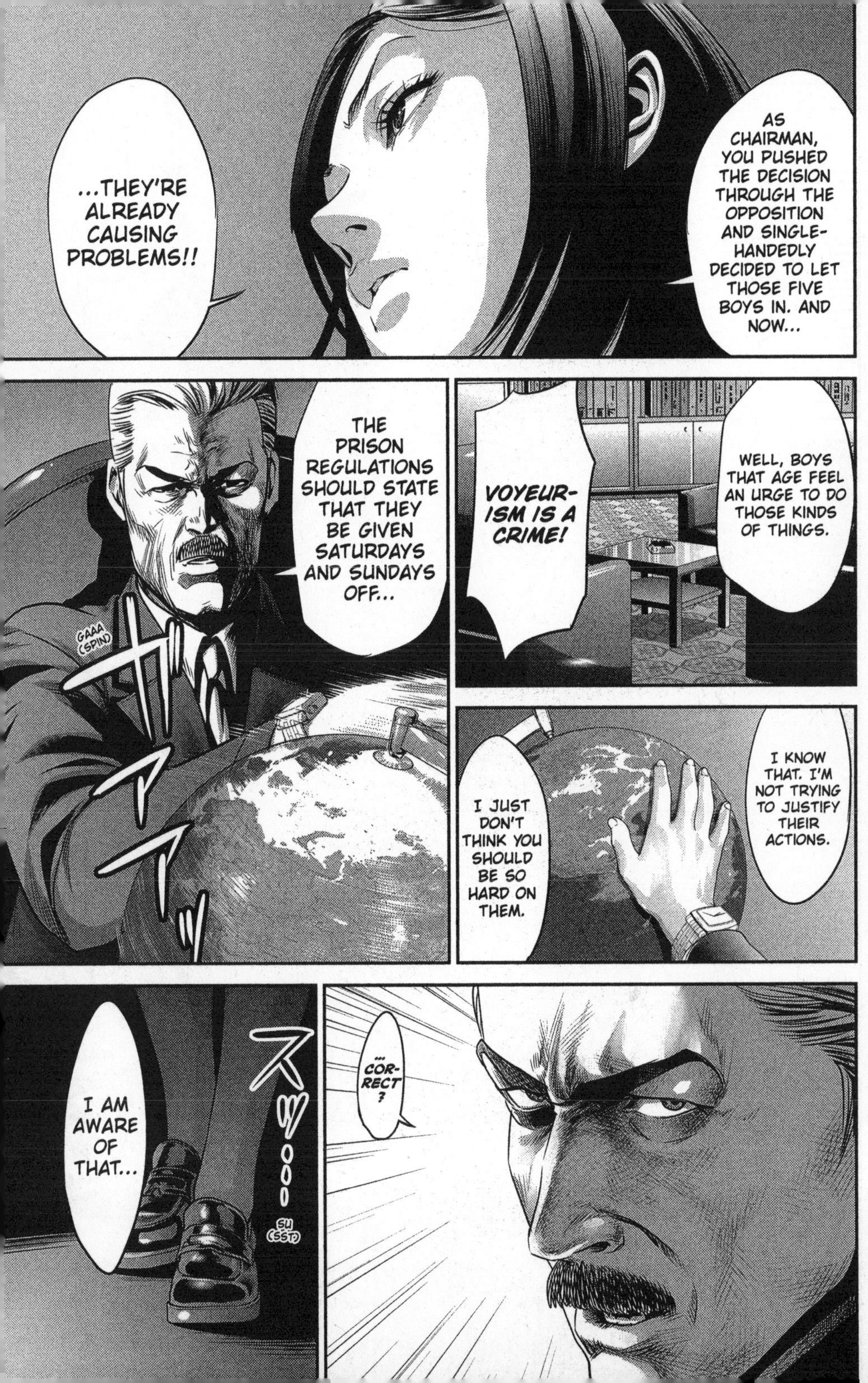
AS CHAIRMAN, YOU PUSHED THE DECISION THROUGH THE OPPOSITION AND SINGLE-HANDEDLY DECIDED TO LET THOSE FIVE BOYS IN. AND NOW...
...THEY'RE ALREADY CAUSING PROBLEMS!!
WELL, BOYS THAT AGE FEEL AN URGE TO DO THOSE KINDS OF THINGS.
VOYEUR-ISM IS A CRIME!
I KNOW THAT. I'M NOT TRYING TO JUSTIFY THEIR ACTIONS.
I JUST DON'T THINK YOU SHOULD BE SO HARD ON THEM.
THE PRISON REGULATIONS SHOULD STATE THAT THEY BE GIVEN SATURDAYS AND SUNDAYS OFF...
GAAA (SPIN)
...COR-RECT?
I AM AWARE OF THAT...
SU (SSST)

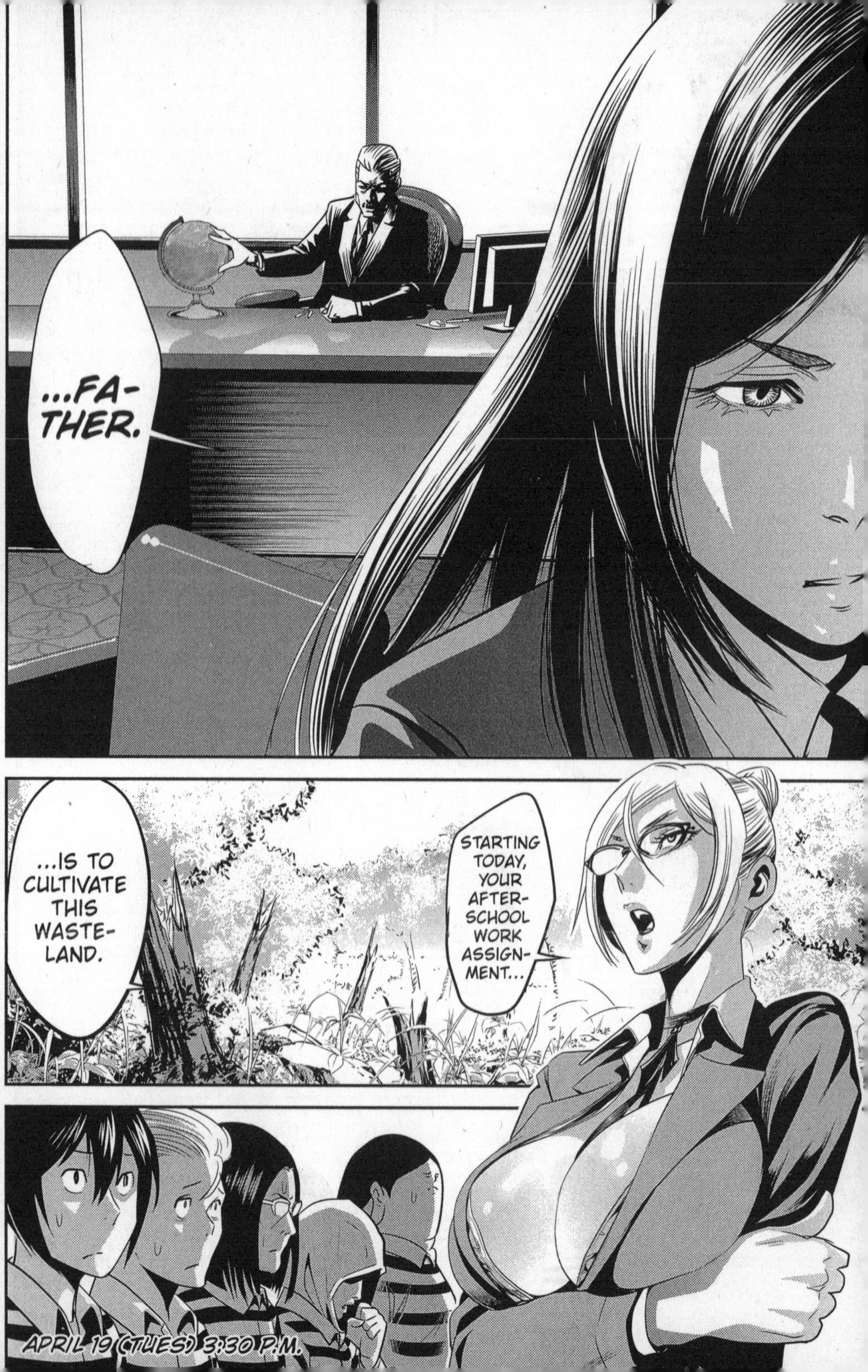
...FA-
THER.
STARTING TODAY, YOUR AFTER-SCHOOL WORK ASSIGNMENT...
...IS TO CULTIVATE THIS WASTE-LAND.
APRIL 19 (TUES) 3:30 P.M.

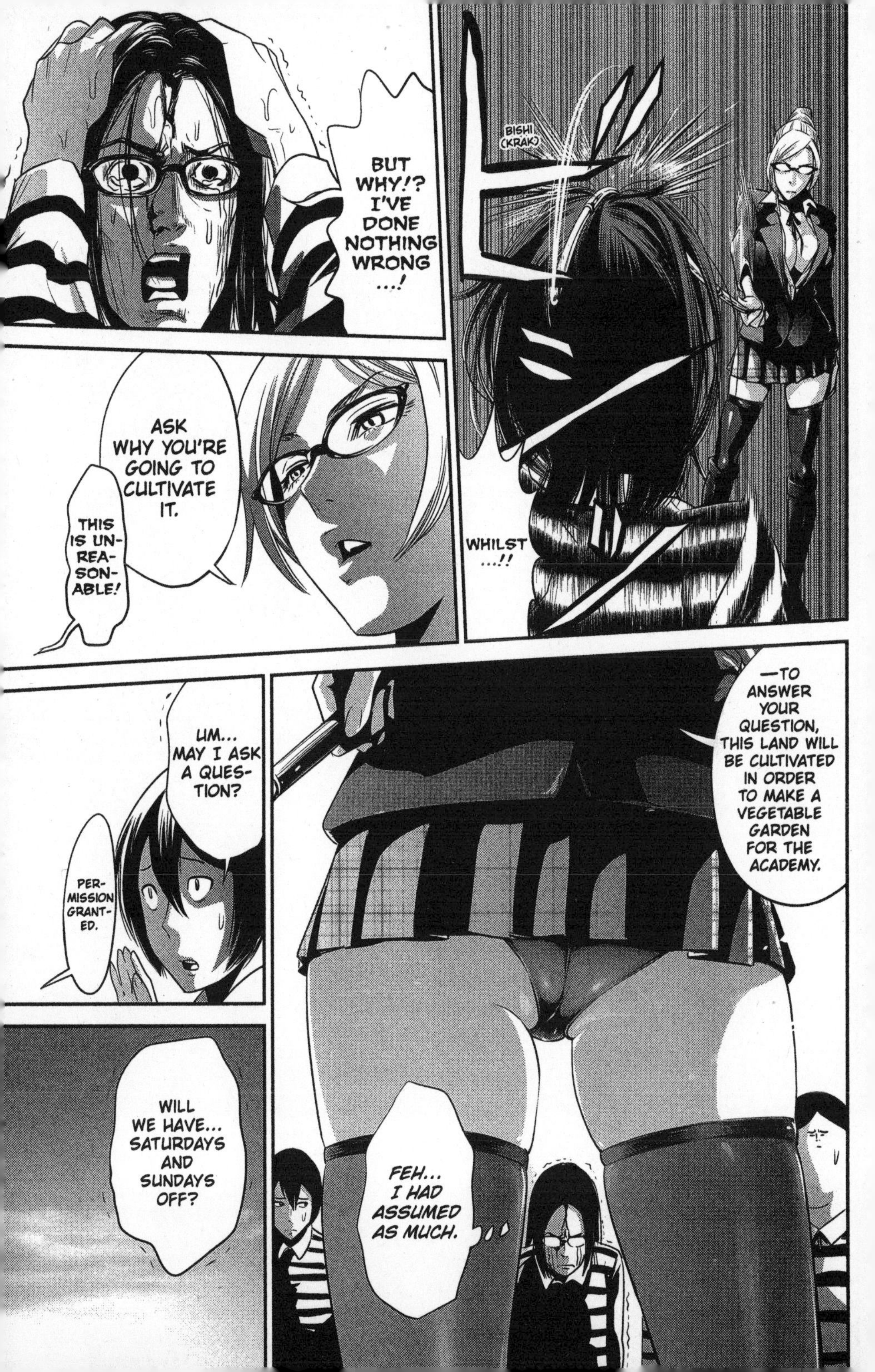

BISHI (KRAK)
WHILST ...!!
BUT WHY!? I'VE DONE NOTHING WRONG ...!
ASK WHY YOU'RE GOING TO CULTIVATE IT.
THIS IS UNREASONABLE!
UM... MAY I ASK A QUESTION?
PERMISSION GRANTED.
—TO ANSWER YOUR QUESTION, THIS LAND WILL BE CULTIVATED IN ORDER TO MAKE A VEGETABLE GARDEN FOR THE ACADEMY.
FEH... I HAD ASSUMED AS MUCH.
WILL WE HAVE... SATURDAYS AND SUNDAYS OFF?

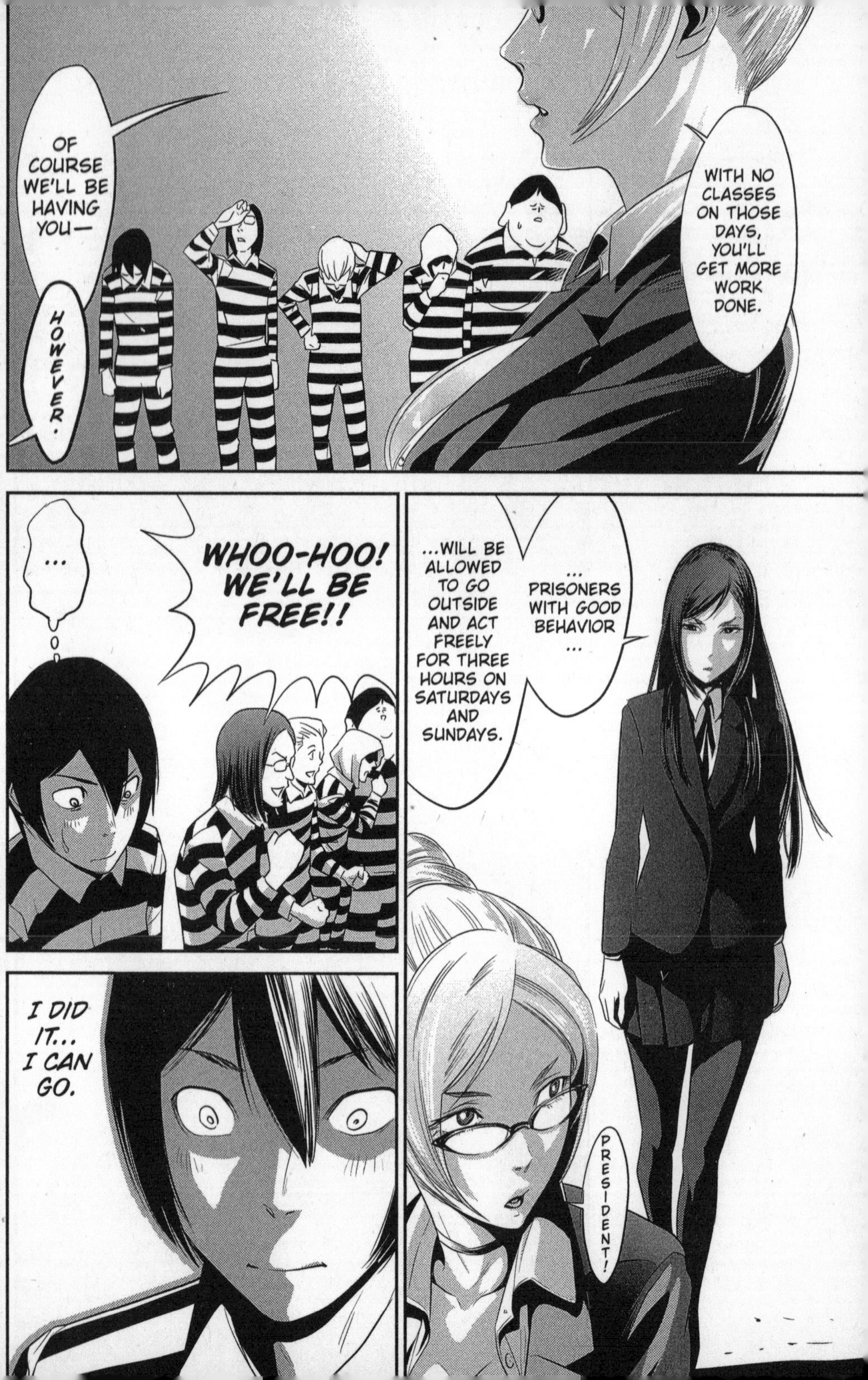
WITH NO CLASSES ON THOSE DAYS, YOU'LL GET MORE WORK DONE.
OF COURSE WE'LL BE HAVING YOU—
HOWEVER.
... PRISONERS WITH GOOD BEHAVIOR ...
...WILL BE ALLOWED TO GO OUTSIDE AND ACT FREELY FOR THREE HOURS ON SATURDAYS AND SUNDAYS.
WHOO-HOO! WE'LL BE FREE!!
...
PRESIDENT!
I DID IT... I CAN GO.

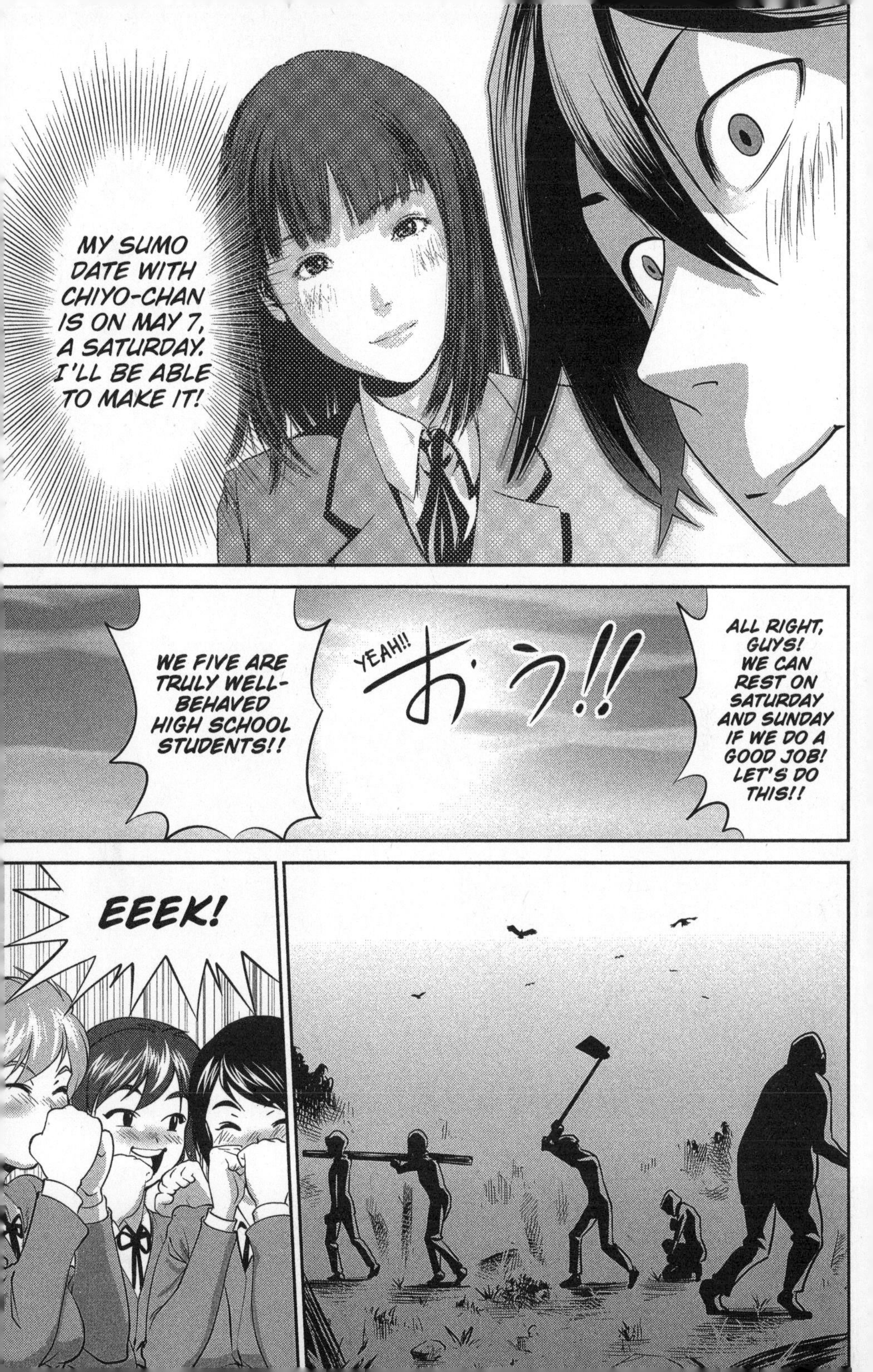
MY SUMO DATE WITH CHIYO-CHAN IS ON MAY 7, A SATURDAY. I'LL BE ABLE TO MAKE IT!
ALL RIGHT, GUYS! WE CAN REST ON SATURDAY AND SUNDAY IF WE DO A GOOD JOB! LET'S DO THIS!!
YEAH!!
おう!!
WE FIVE ARE TRULY WELL-BEHAVED HIGH SCHOOL STUDENTS!!
EEEK!

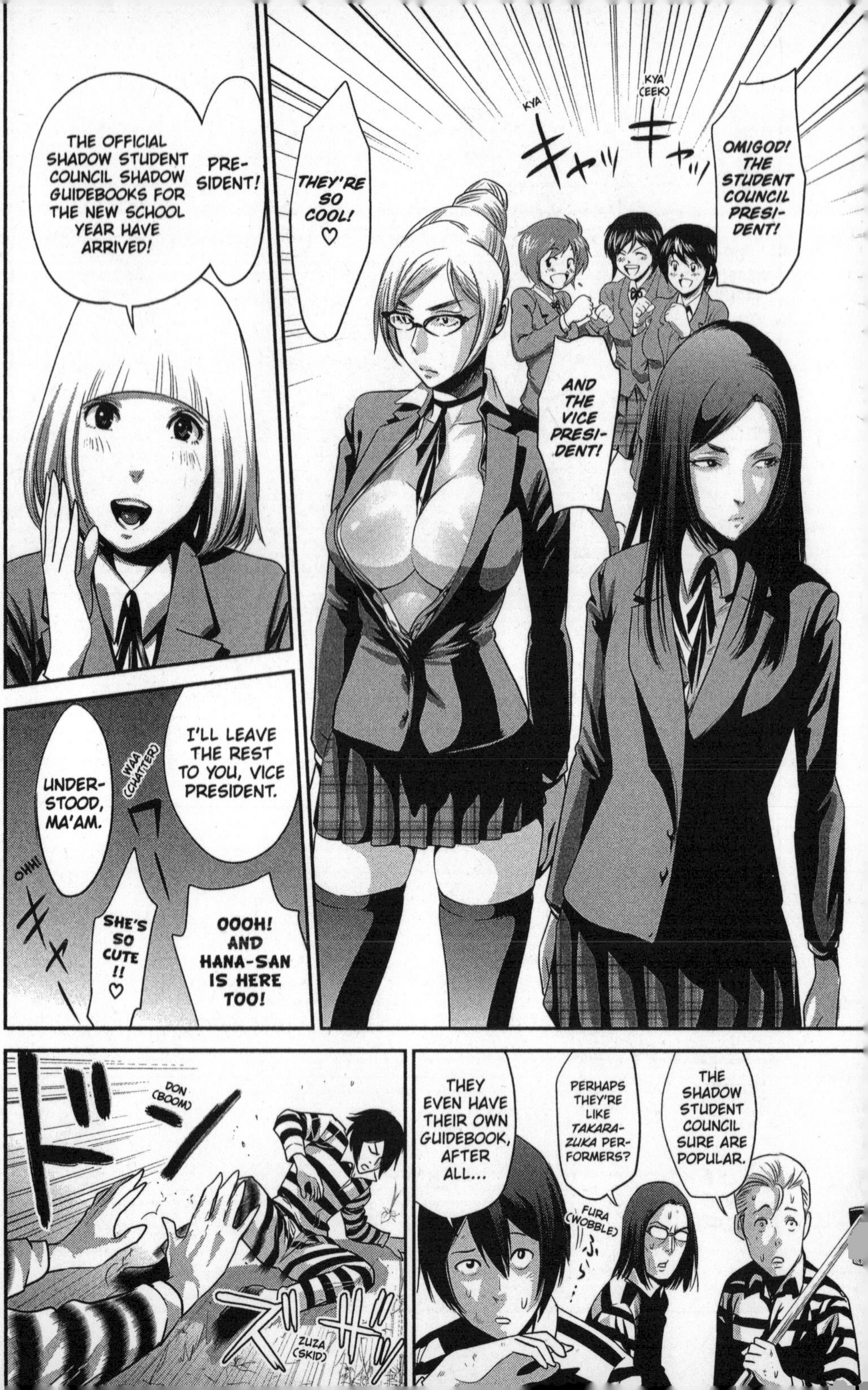

KYA (EEK)
KYA
OMIGOD! THE STUDENT COUNCIL PRESI-DENT!
AND THE VICE PRESI-DENT!
THEY'RE SO COOL! ♡
PRE-SIDENT!
THE OFFICIAL SHADOW STUDENT COUNCIL SHADOW GUIDEBOOKS FOR THE NEW SCHOOL YEAR HAVE ARRIVED!
I'LL LEAVE THE REST TO YOU, VICE PRESIDENT.
WAA (CHATTER)
UNDER-STOOD, MA'AM.
OOOH! AND HANA-SAN IS HERE TOO!
SHE'S SO CUTE !! ♡
OHH!
THE SHADOW STUDENT COUNCIL SURE ARE POPULAR.
PERHAPS THEY'RE LIKE *TAKARA-ZUKA* PER-FORMERS?
FURA (WOBBLE)
THEY EVEN HAVE THEIR OWN GUIDEBOOK, AFTER ALL...
DON (BOOM)
ZUZA (SKID)

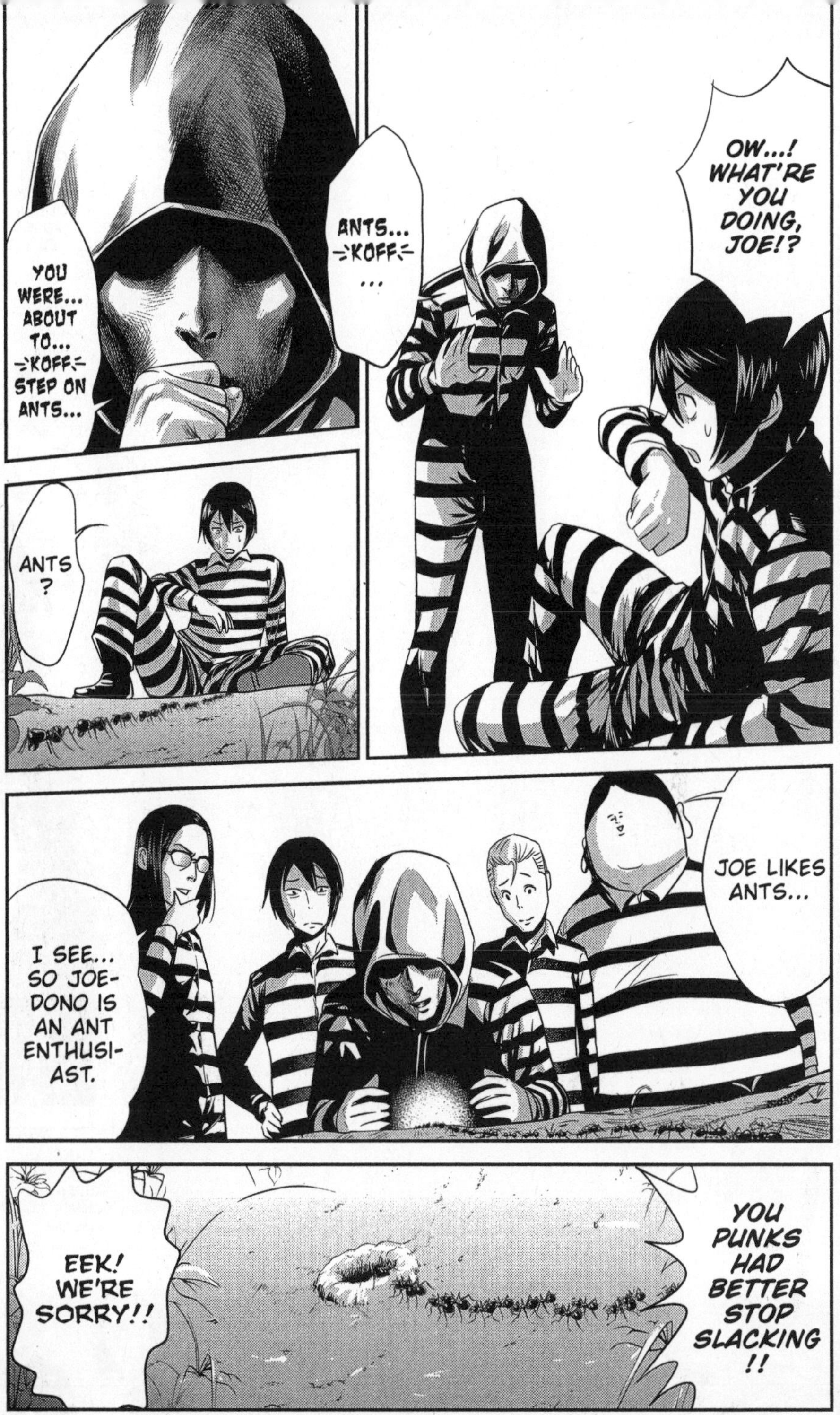
OW...! WHAT'RE YOU DOING, JOE!?
ANTS... =KOFF= ...
YOU WERE... ABOUT TO... =KOFF= STEP ON ANTS...
ANTS ?
JOE LIKES ANTS...
I SEE... SO JOE-DONO IS AN ANT ENTHUSI-AST.
YOU PUNKS HAD BETTER STOP SLACKING !!
EEK! WE'RE SORRY!!

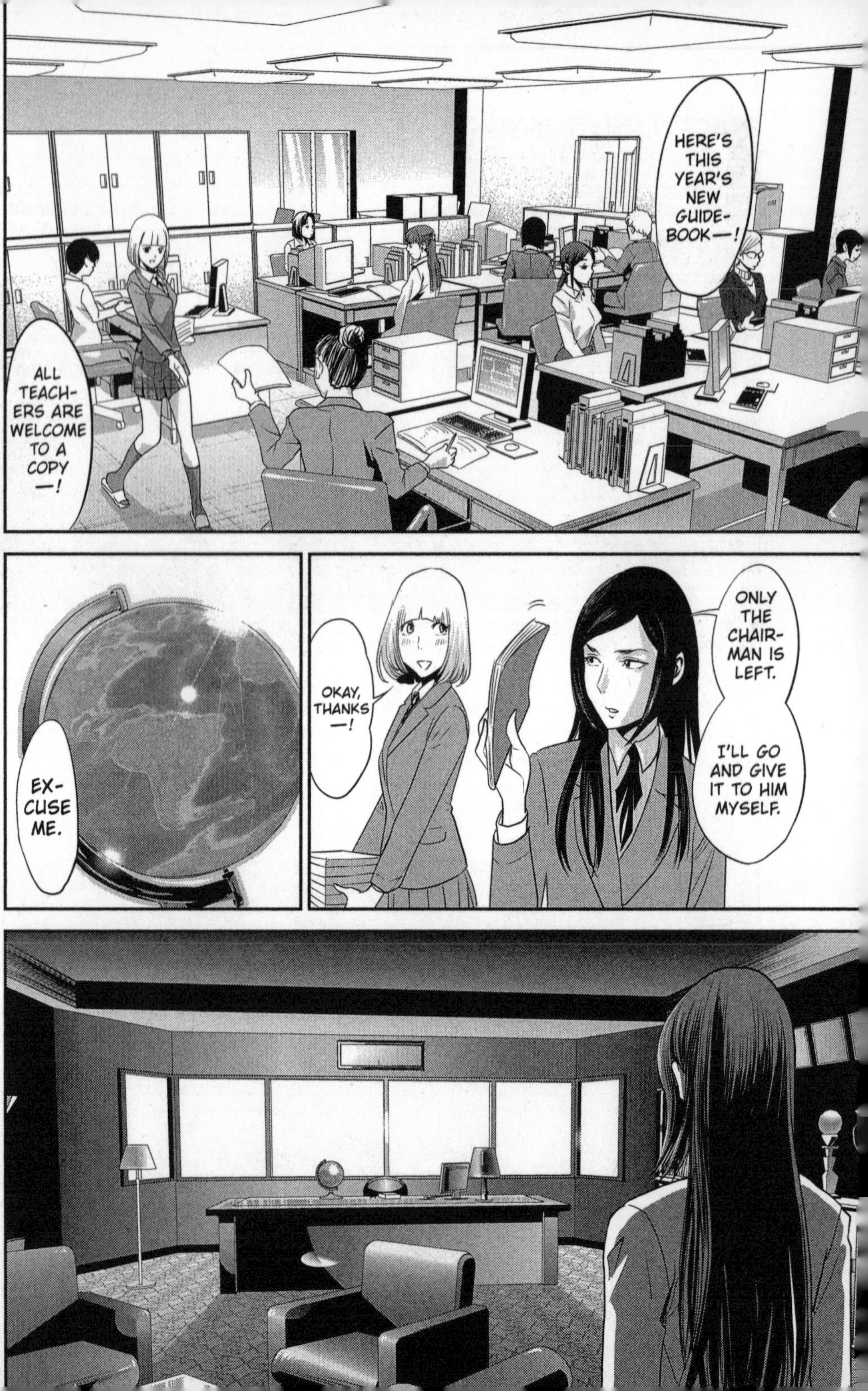
HERE'S THIS YEAR'S NEW GUIDE-BOOK—!
ALL TEACH-ERS ARE WELCOME TO A COPY—!
ONLY THE CHAIR-MAN IS LEFT.
I'LL GO AND GIVE IT TO HIM MYSELF.
OKAY, THANKS—!
EX-CUSE ME.

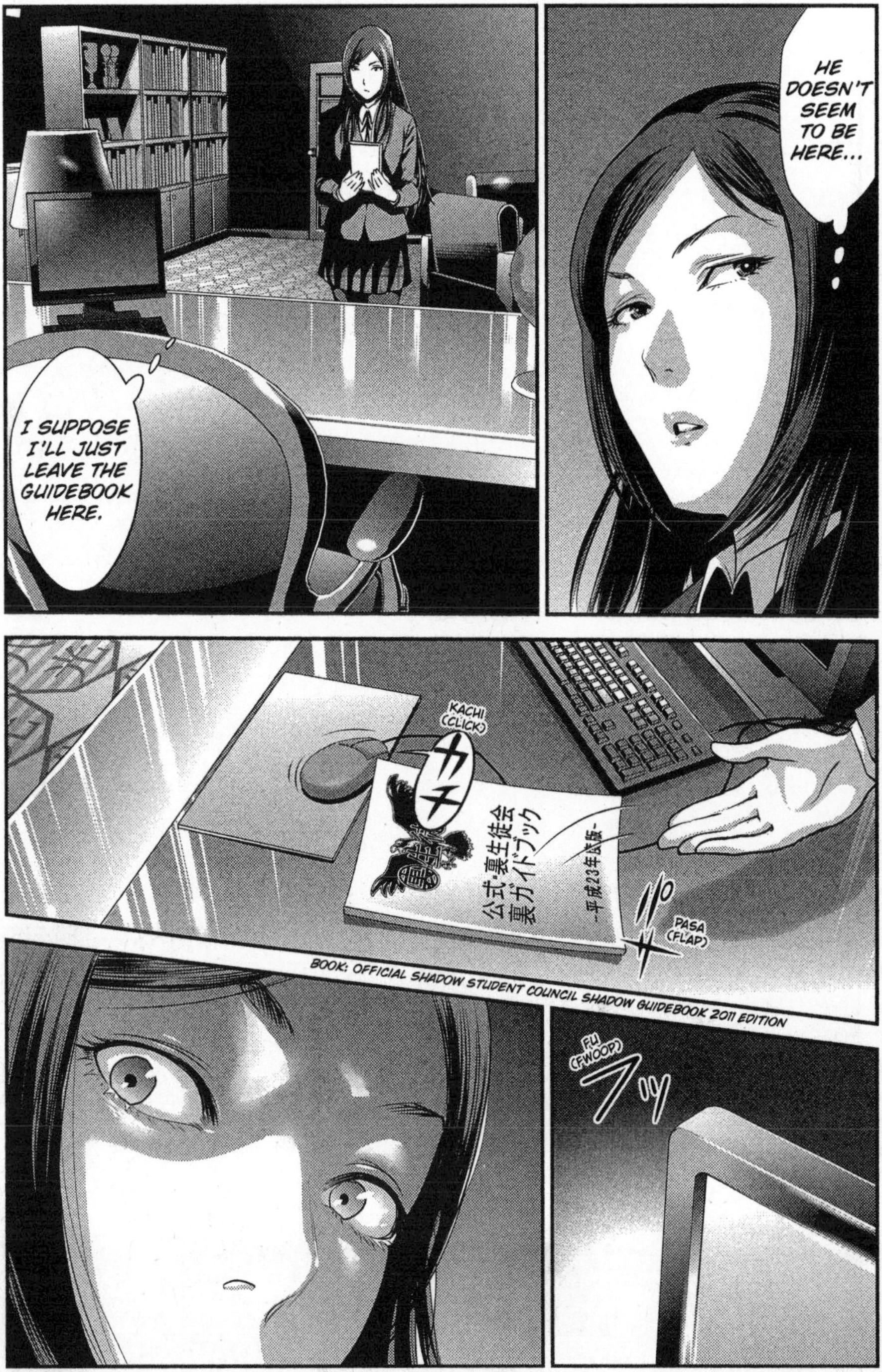
HE DOESN'T SEEM TO BE HERE...
I SUPPOSE I'LL JUST LEAVE THE GUIDEBOOK HERE.
KACHI (CLICK)
公式・裏生徒会
裏ガイドブック
-平成23年度版-
PASA (FLAP)
BOOK: OFFICIAL SHADOW STUDENT COUNCIL SHADOW GUIDEBOOK 2011 EDITION
FU (FWOOP)

ASS JOB
LOVELY LATINA ASS JOBS
ALL THE GORGEOUS LATINAS YOU WANT
SOFT OMANDO
SOFT OMANDO
ASS JOB
LOVELY LATINA ASS JOBS
125 minutes
¥2,980
BEST
ASSES!!!!
ONE THING EVERY MAN WANTS TO EXPERIENCE!
AN ASS JOB FOR THE AGES!
ASSES ASSES ASSES ASSES ASSES ASSES ASSES
4589852009653
Bookmarks
Folder
Chairman's folder
X-Hamstar (18+)
Ass job Station Guide
Buy Adult Videos Online Home Edition
Lewd Blonde Bombshells Japanese Edition...
http av shop.xxx.co...
Yohee! JAPAN naughty...
ma on co.jp
Pussy Nurse
Captain Pussy
Voyeur Girls Bath
Voyeur Girls Changing Room
Shaved Policewoman
European
ONE THING EVERY MAN WANTS TO EXPERIENCE!
AN ASS JOB FOR THE AGES!

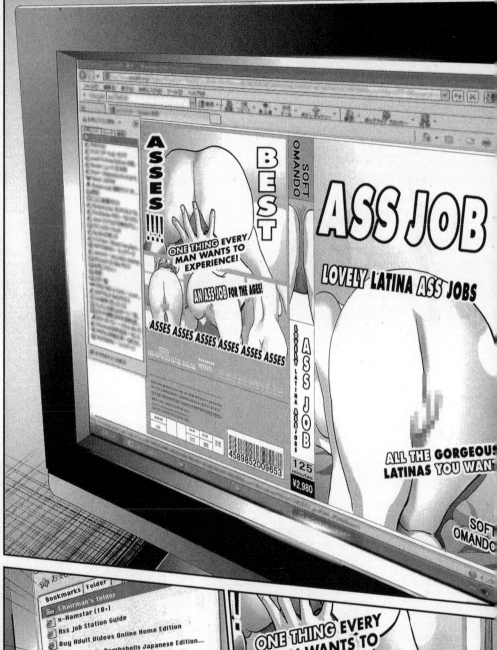

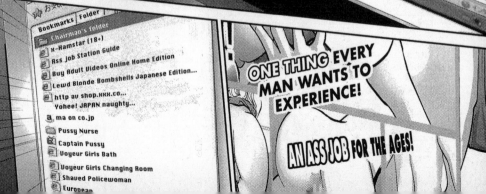

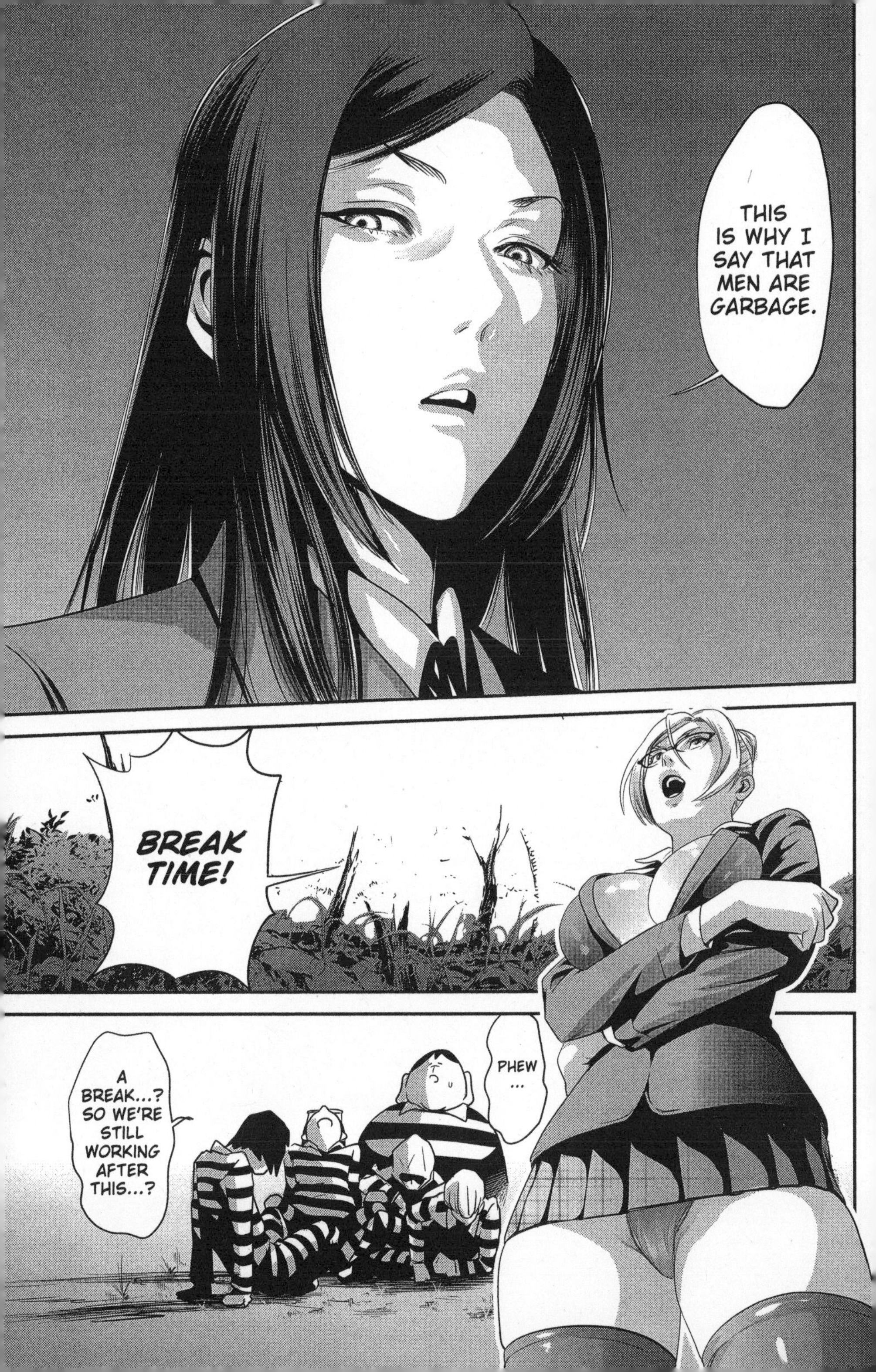
THIS IS WHY I SAY THAT MEN ARE GARBAGE.
BREAK TIME!
PHEW...
A BREAK...? SO WE'RE STILL WORKING AFTER THIS...?

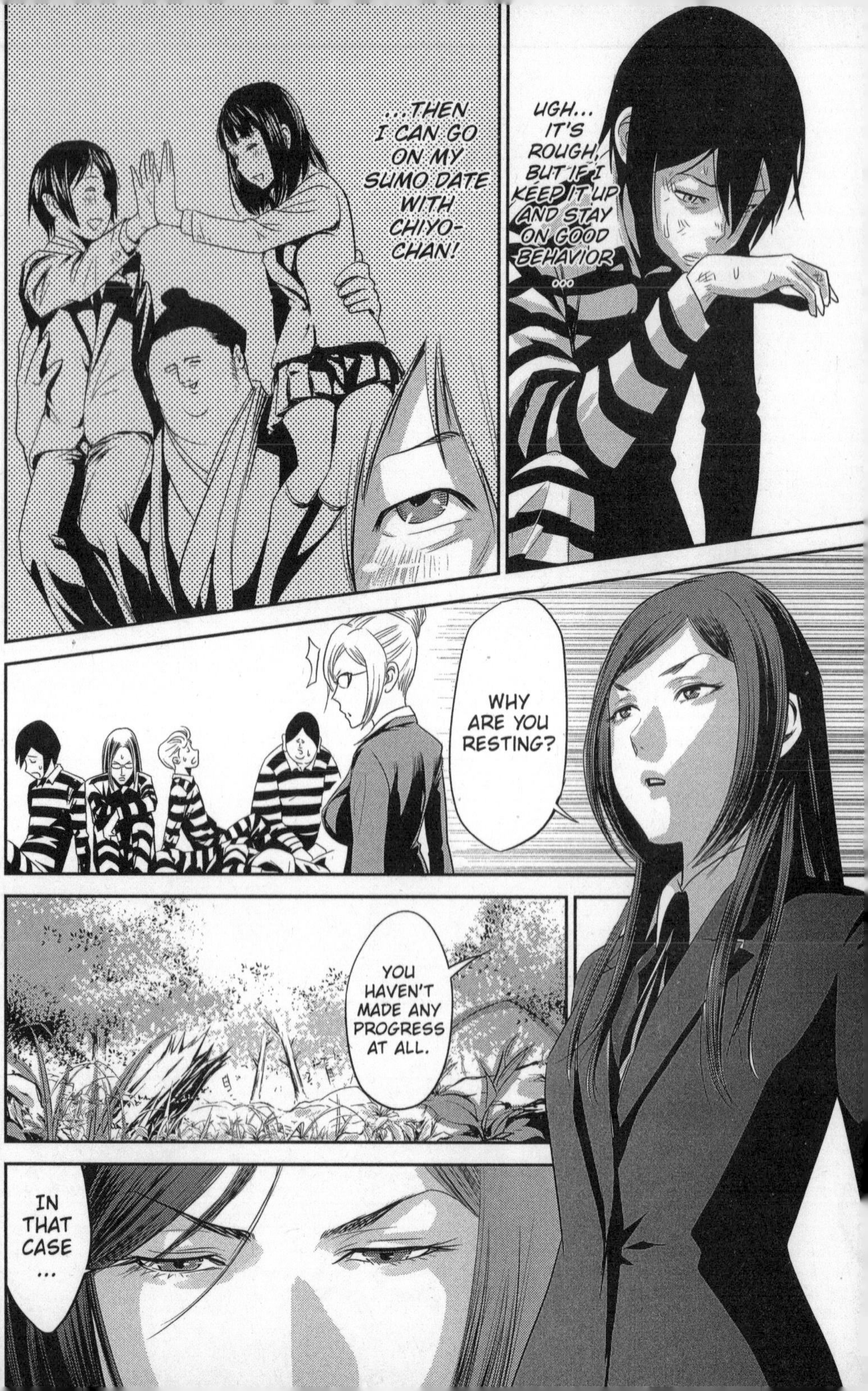
UGH... IT'S ROUGH, BUT IF I KEEP IT UP AND STAY ON GOOD BEHAVIOR...
...THEN I CAN GO ON MY SUMO DATE WITH CHIYO-CHAN!
WHY ARE YOU RESTING?
YOU HAVEN'T MADE ANY PROGRESS AT ALL.
IN THAT CASE...

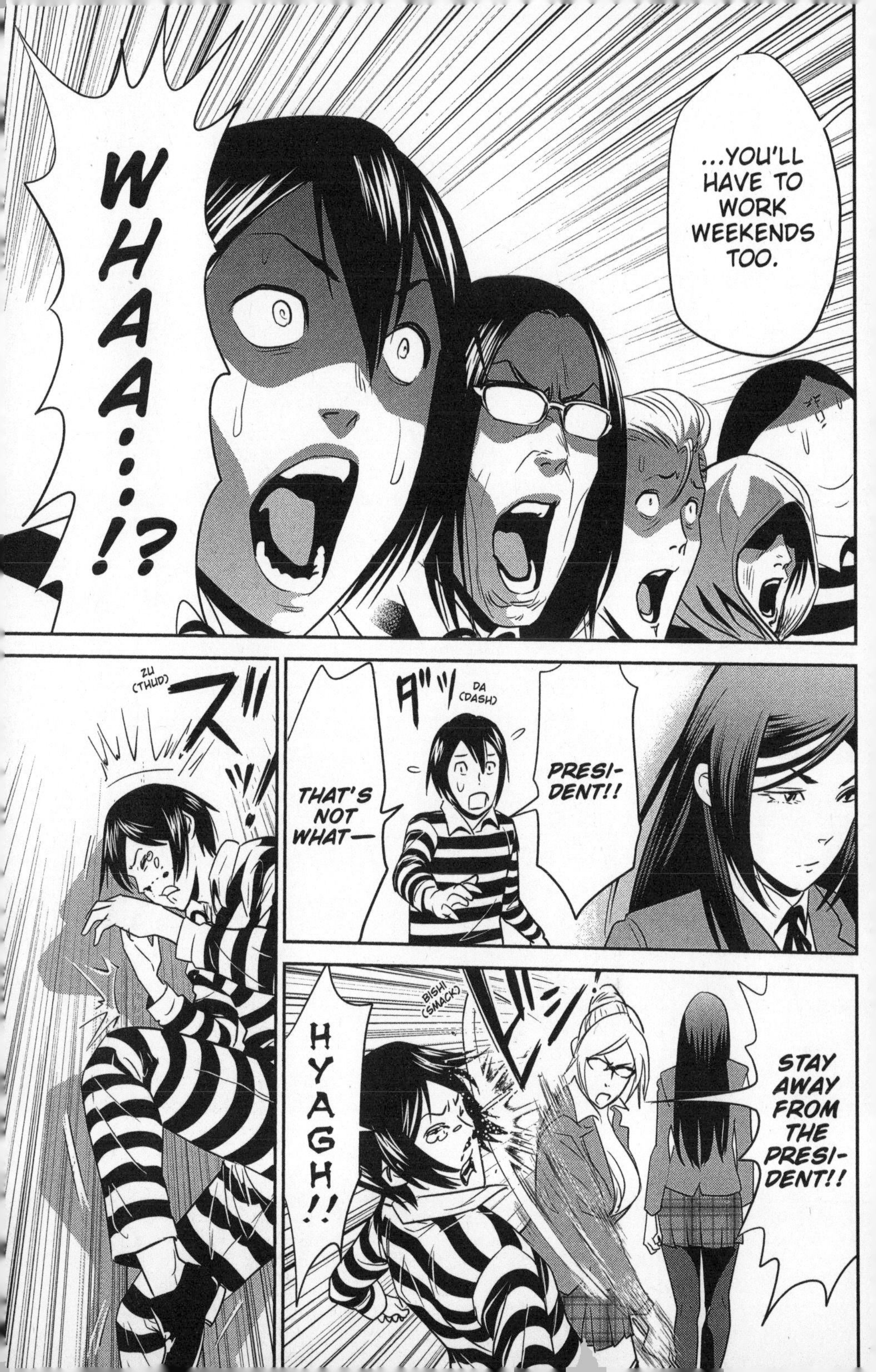

...YOU'LL HAVE TO WORK WEEKENDS TOO.
WHAA...!?
DA (DASH)
PRESI-DENT!!
THAT'S NOT WHAT—
ZU (THUD)
BISHI (SMACK)
STAY AWAY FROM THE PRESI-DENT!!
HYAGH!!

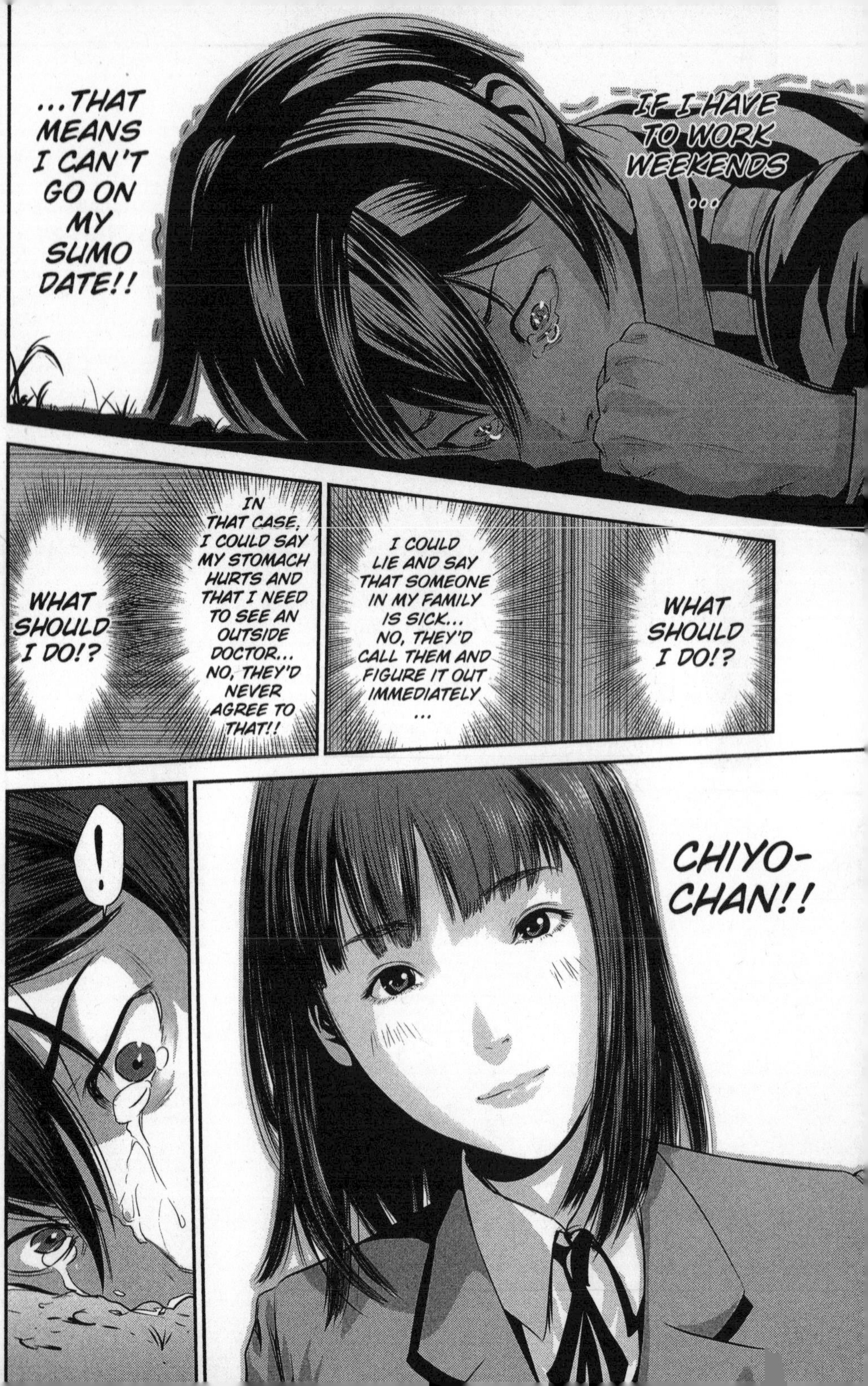
IF I HAVE TO WORK WEEKENDS ...
...THAT MEANS I CAN'T GO ON MY SUMO DATE!!
WHAT SHOULD I DO!?
I COULD LIE AND SAY THAT SOMEONE IN MY FAMILY IS SICK... NO, THEY'D CALL THEM AND FIGURE IT OUT IMMEDIATELY ...
IN THAT CASE, I COULD SAY MY STOMACH HURTS AND THAT I NEED TO SEE AN OUTSIDE DOCTOR... NO, THEY'D NEVER AGREE TO THAT!!
WHAT SHOULD I DO!?
CHIYO-CHAN!!
!

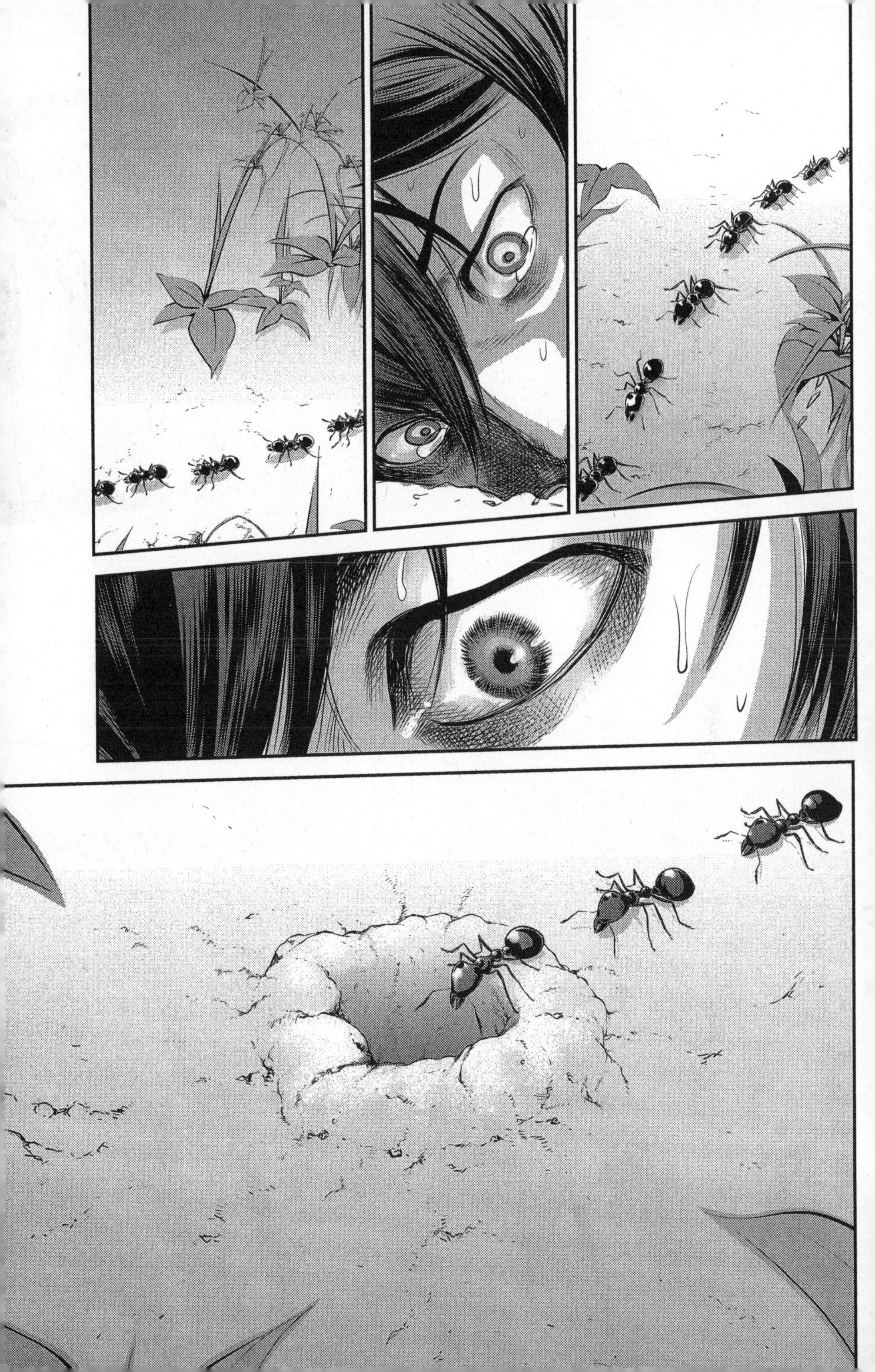

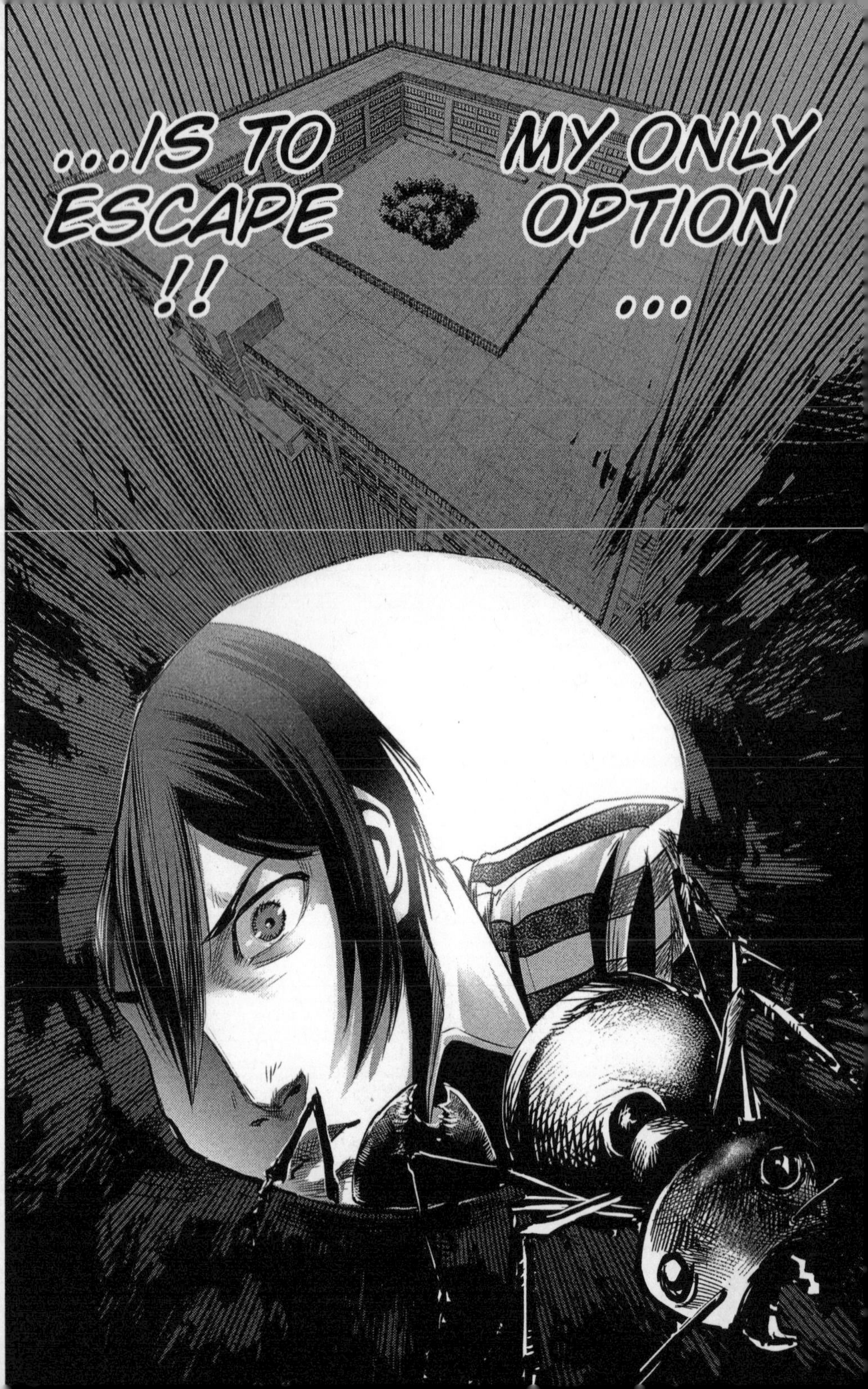
MY ONLY OPTION ...
...IS TO ESCAPE !!

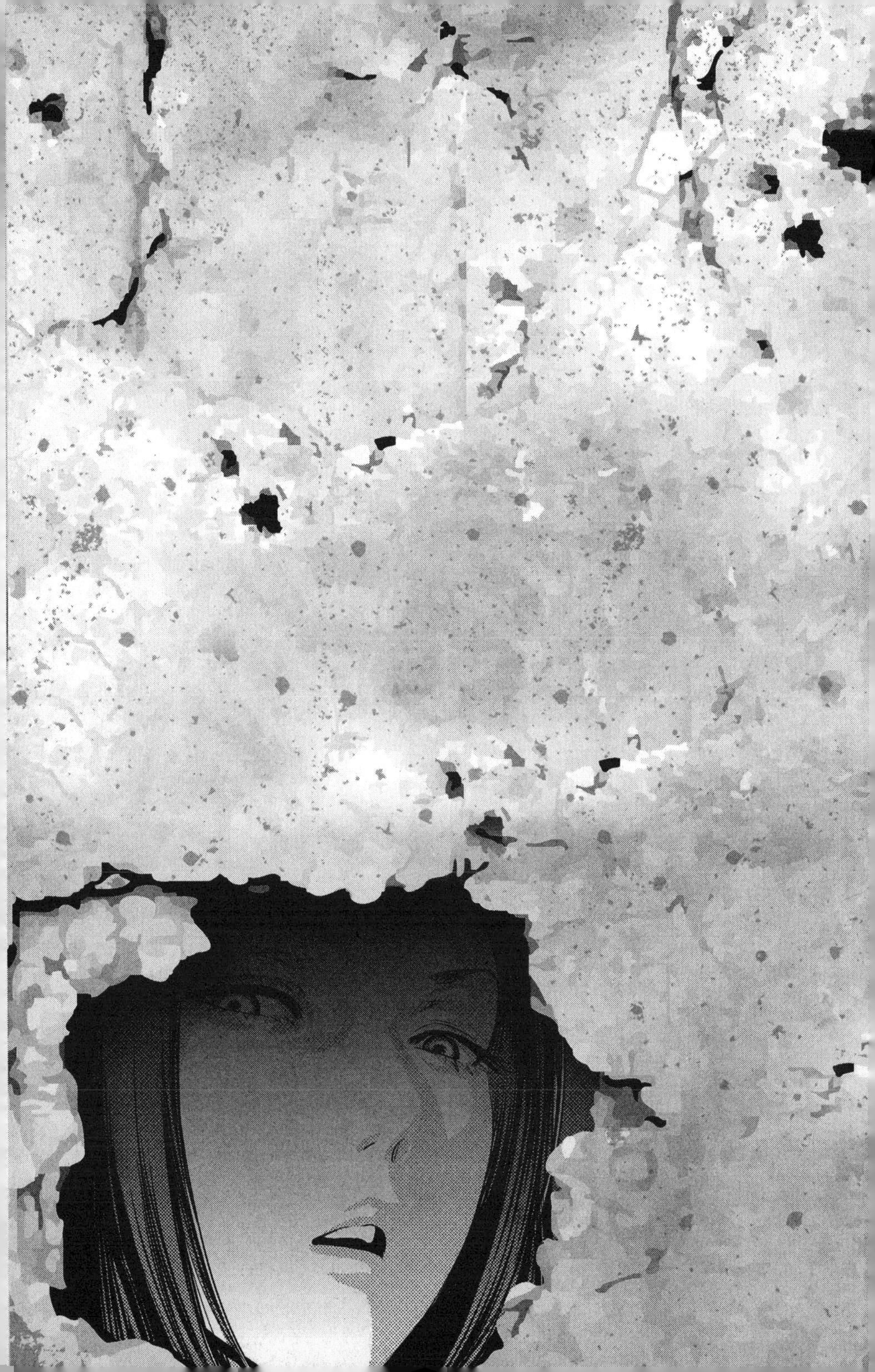

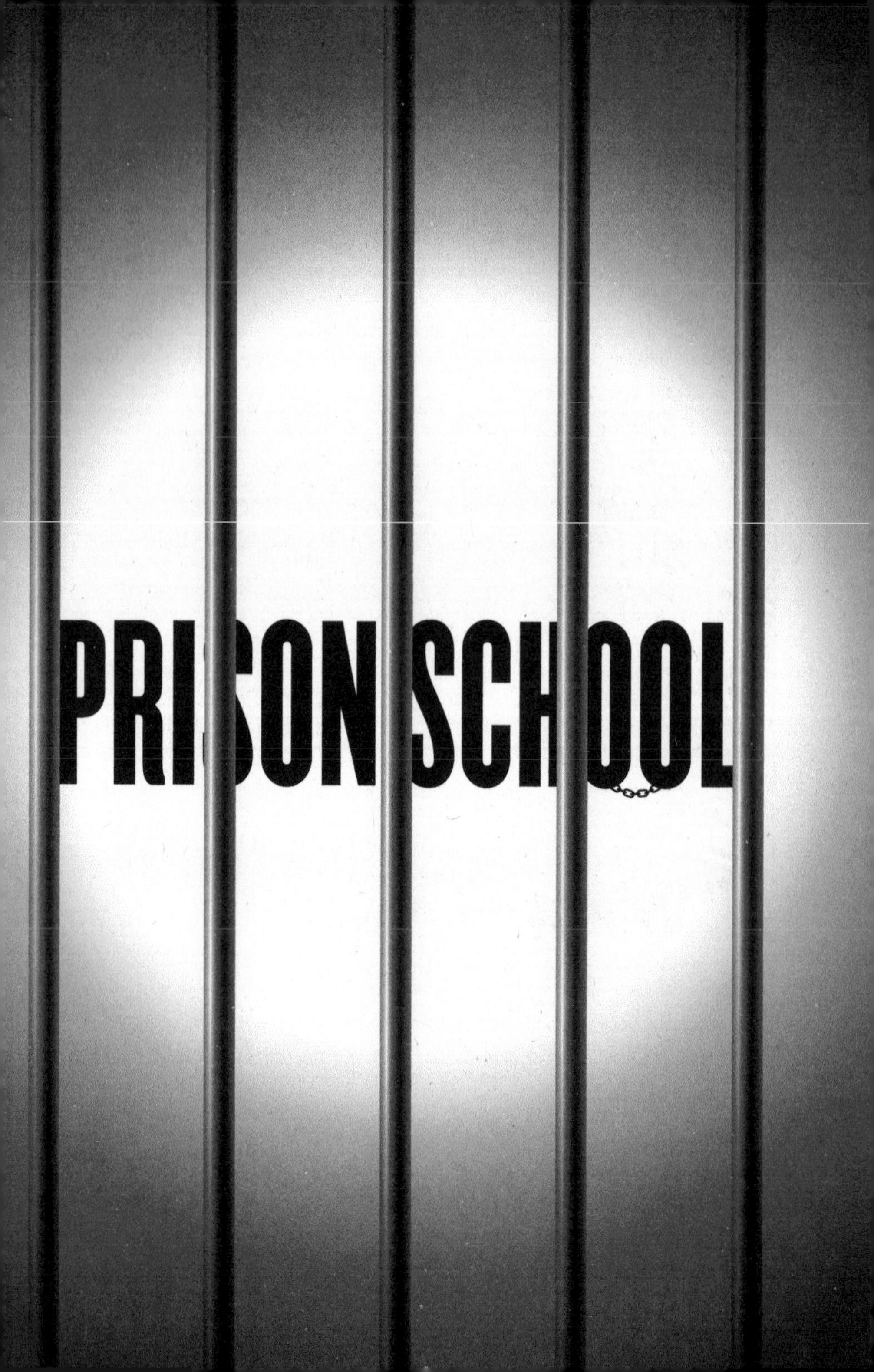
PRISON SCHOOL

CHAPTER 8: DOIN' TIME

JIRIRIRIRIN (RRRRING)
BA (BOLT)
KO
KA (TAK)
PISHI (PTTT)
GARARARA (RATTLE)
CELLS OPEN!
KA

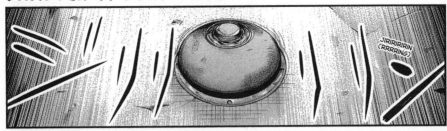

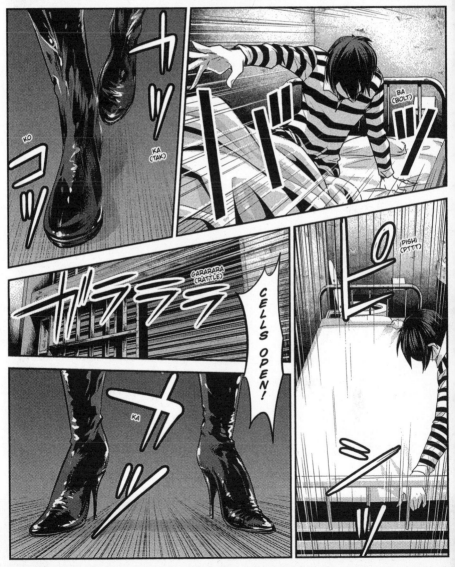

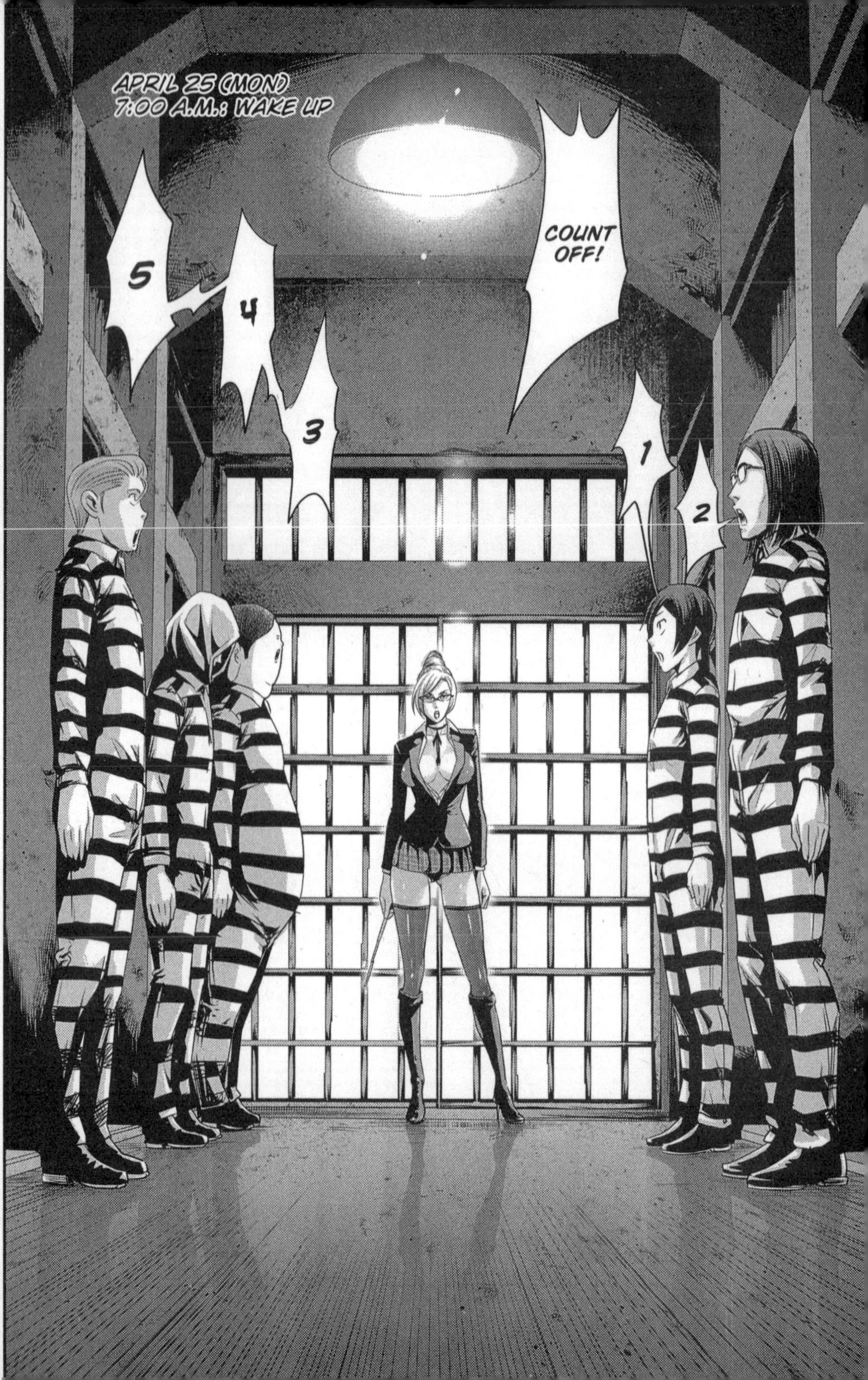
APRIL 25 (MON)
7:00 A.M.: WAKE UP
COUNT OFF!
1
2
3
4
5

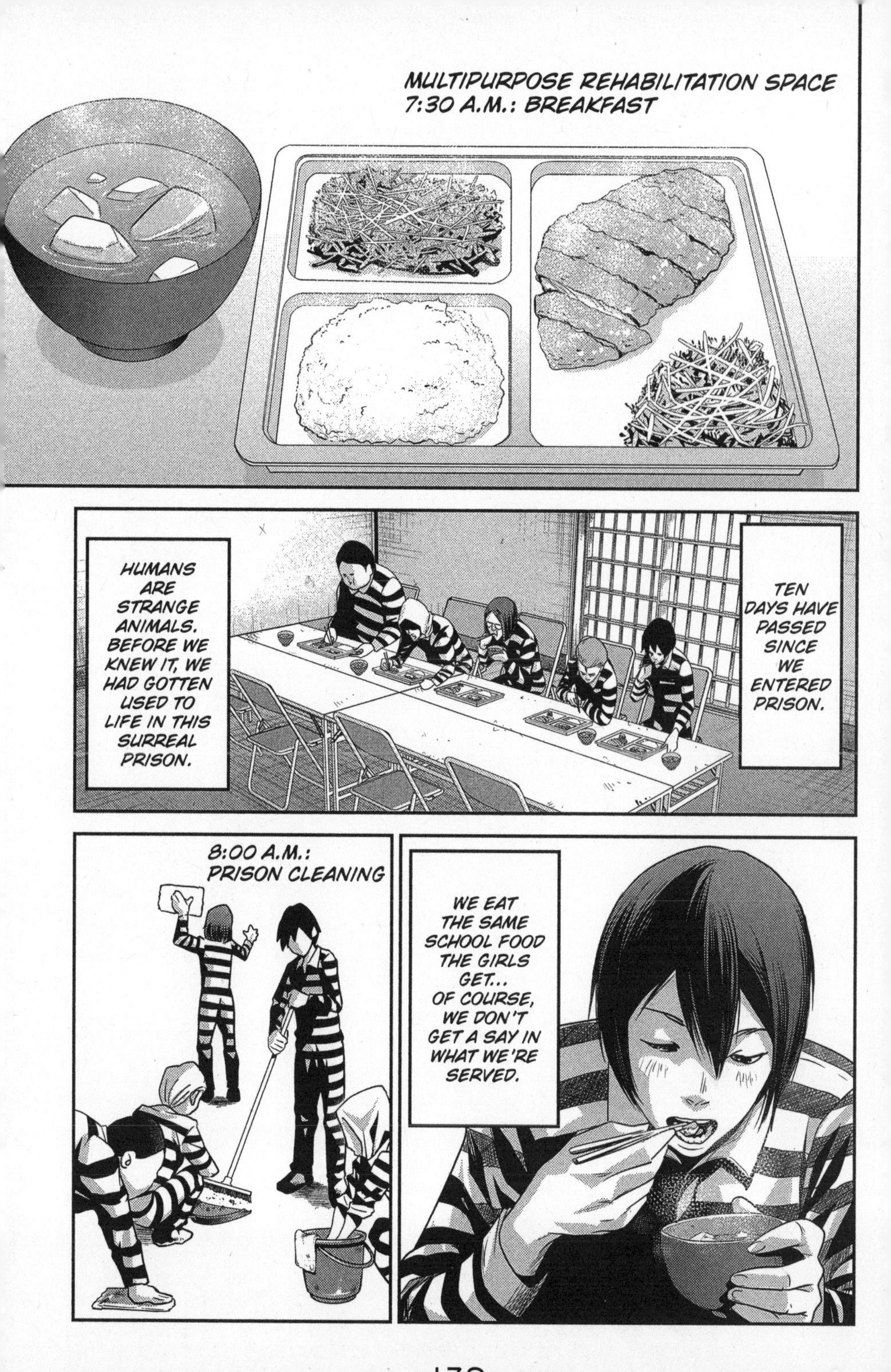
MULTIPURPOSE REHABILITATION SPACE
7:30 A.M.: BREAKFAST
TEN DAYS HAVE PASSED SINCE WE ENTERED PRISON.
HUMANS ARE STRANGE ANIMALS. BEFORE WE KNEW IT, WE HAD GOTTEN USED TO LIFE IN THIS SURREAL PRISON.
WE EAT THE SAME SCHOOL FOOD THE GIRLS GET... OF COURSE, WE DON'T GET A SAY IN WHAT WE'RE SERVED.
8:00 A.M.: PRISON CLEANING

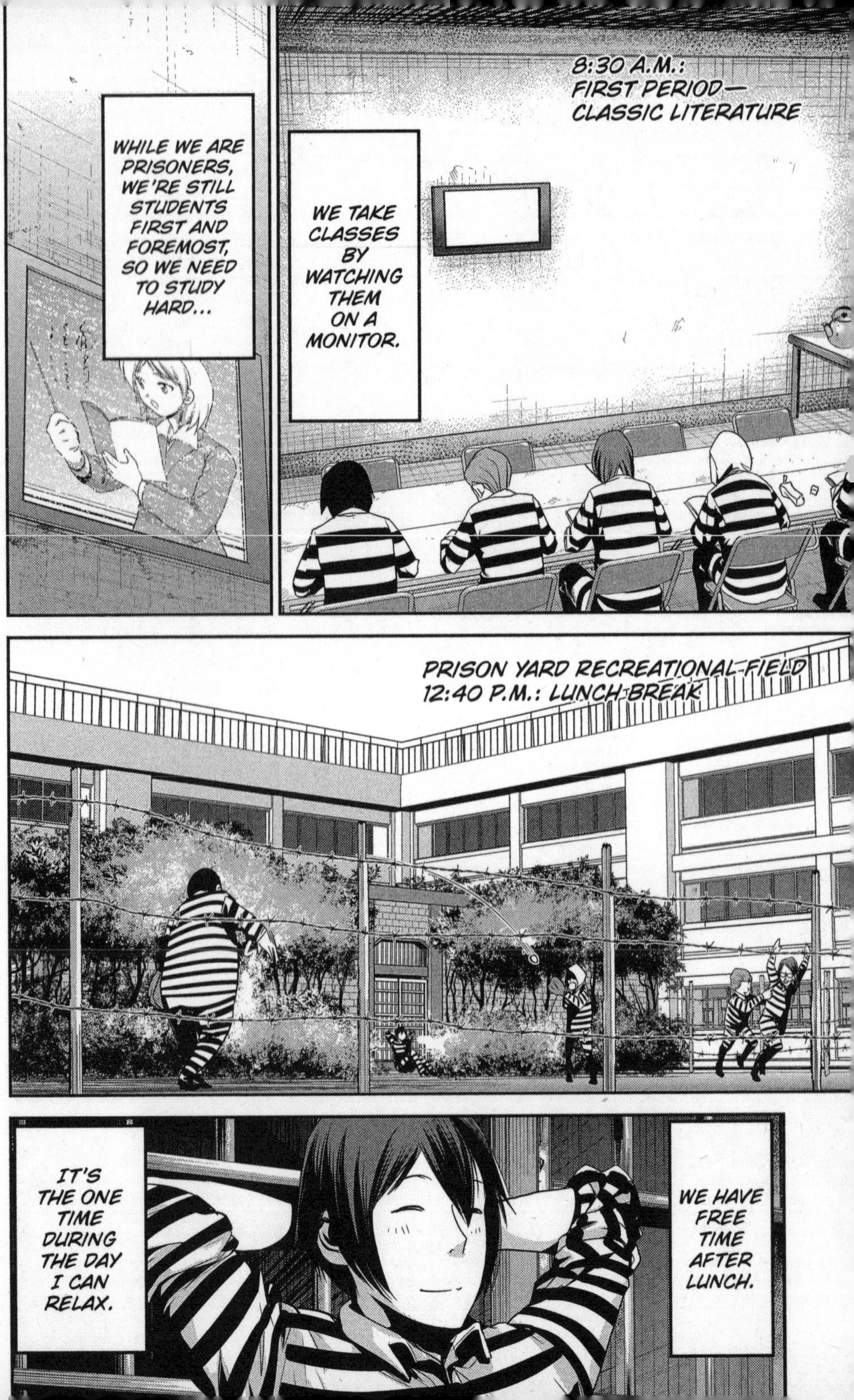
8:30 A.M.: FIRST PERIOD— CLASSIC LITERATURE
WE TAKE CLASSES BY WATCHING THEM ON A MONITOR.
WHILE WE ARE PRISONERS, WE'RE STILL STUDENTS FIRST AND FOREMOST, SO WE NEED TO STUDY HARD...
PRISON YARD RECREATIONAL FIELD
12:40 P.M.: LUNCH BREAK
WE HAVE FREE TIME AFTER LUNCH.
IT'S THE ONE TIME DURING THE DAY I CAN RELAX.

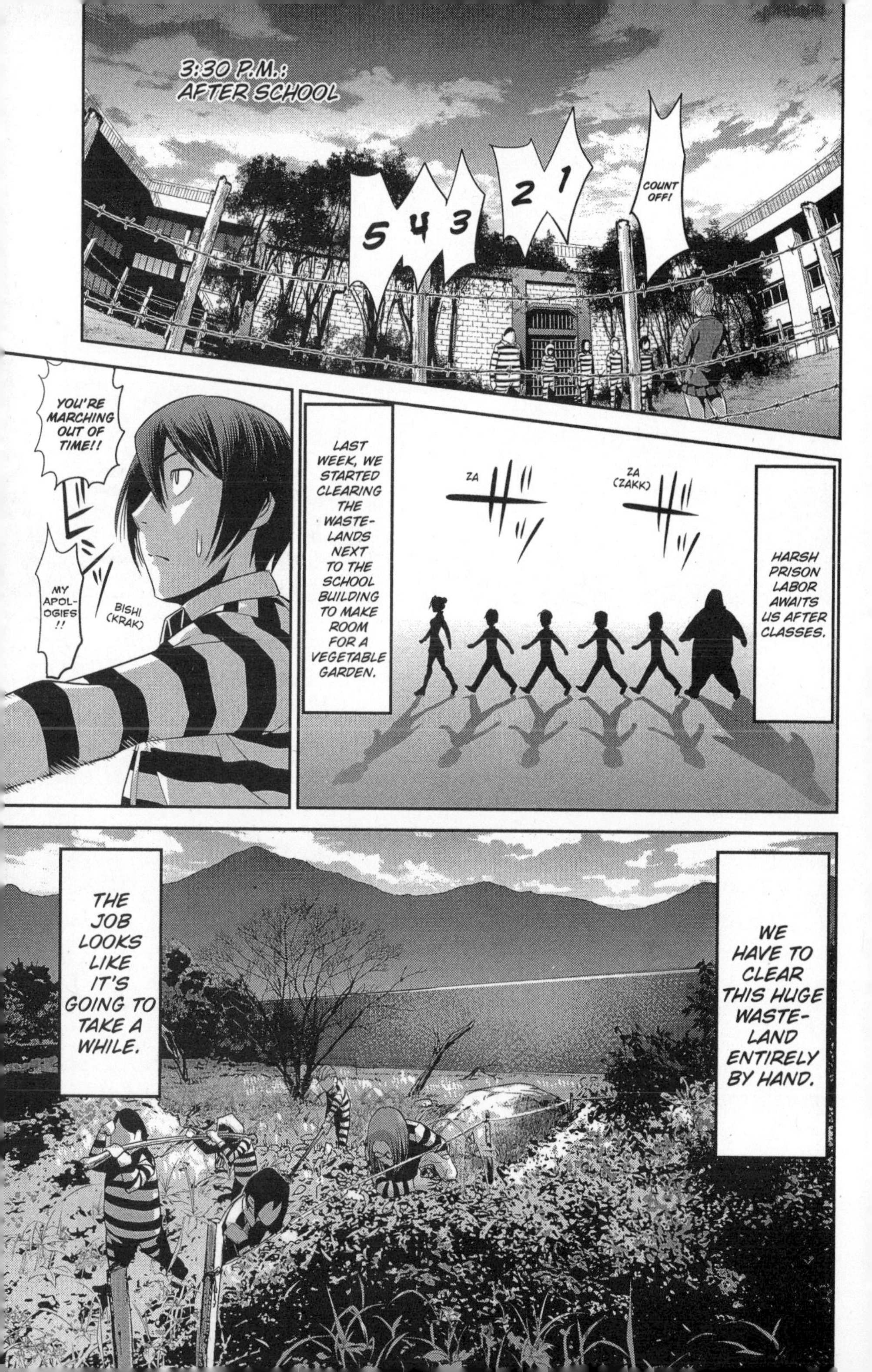
3:30 P.M.:
AFTER SCHOOL
COUNT OFF!
1
2
3
4
5
LAST WEEK, WE STARTED CLEARING THE WASTE-LANDS NEXT TO THE SCHOOL BUILDING TO MAKE ROOM FOR A VEGETABLE GARDEN.
HARSH PRISON LABOR AWAITS US AFTER CLASSES.
ZA (ZAKK)
ZA
YOU'RE MARCHING OUT OF TIME!!
BISHI (KRAK)
MY APOLO-GIES!!
WE HAVE TO CLEAR THIS HUGE WASTE-LAND ENTIRELY BY HAND.
THE JOB LOOKS LIKE IT'S GOING TO TAKE A WHILE.

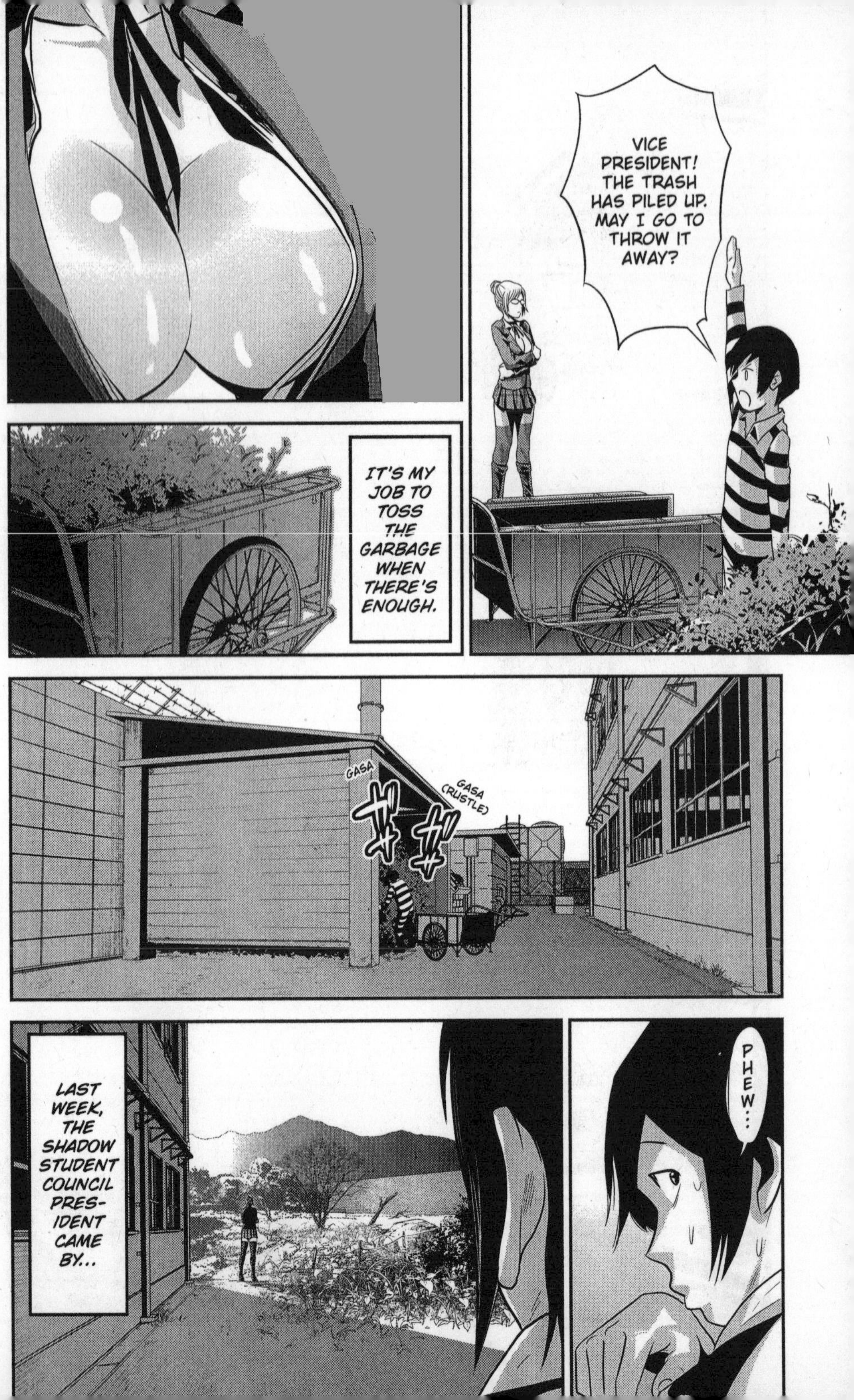
VICE PRESIDENT! THE TRASH HAS PILED UP. MAY I GO TO THROW IT AWAY?
IT'S MY JOB TO TOSS THE GARBAGE WHEN THERE'S ENOUGH.
GASA (RUSTLE)
GASA
PHEW...
LAST WEEK, THE SHADOW STUDENT COUNCIL PRES-IDENT CAME BY...

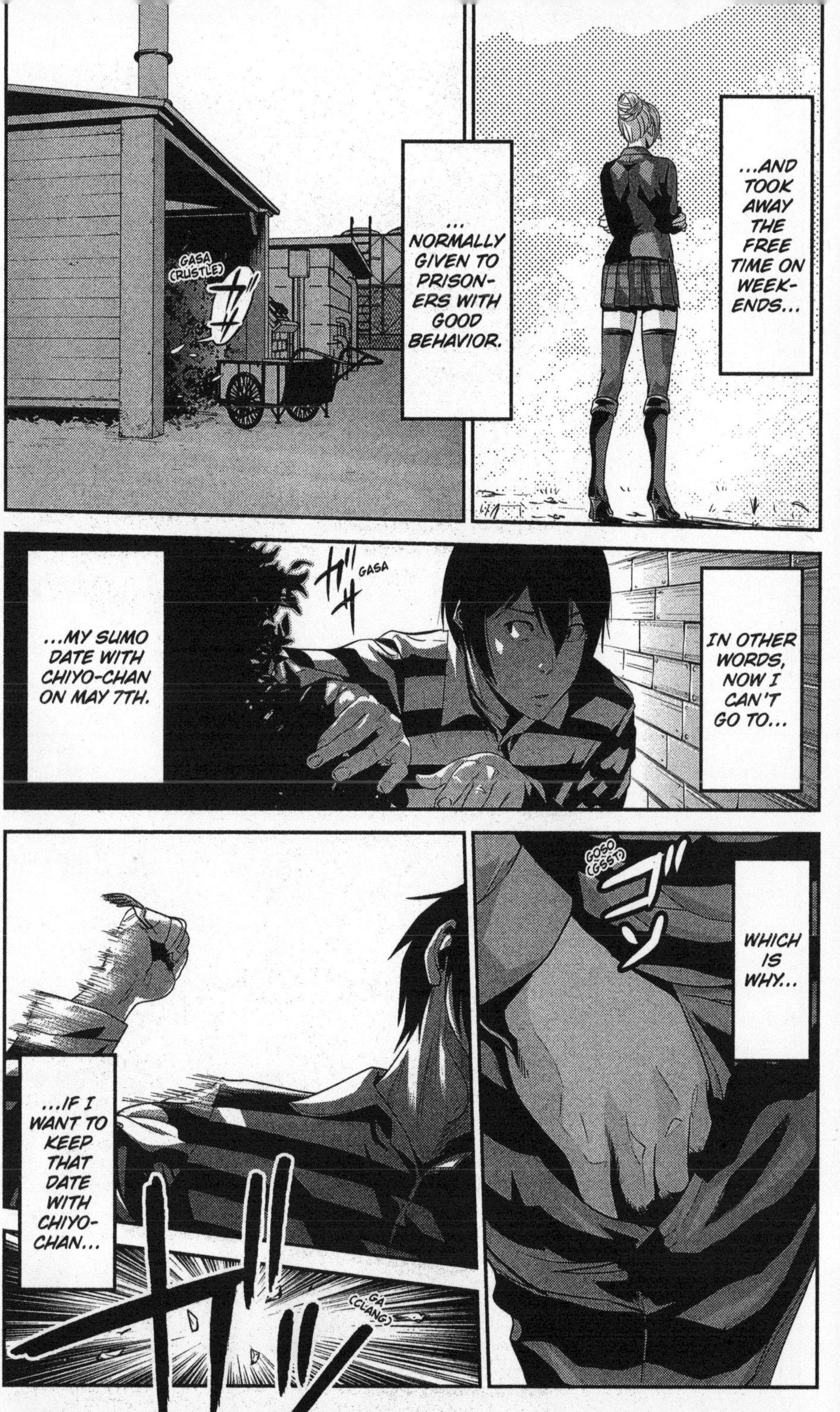
...AND TOOK AWAY THE FREE TIME ON WEEK-ENDS...
... NORMALLY GIVEN TO PRISON-ERS WITH GOOD BEHAVIOR.
GASA (RUSTLE)
IN OTHER WORDS, NOW I CAN'T GO TO...
GASA
...MY SUMO DATE WITH CHIYO-CHAN ON MAY 7TH.
GOSO (GSST)
WHICH IS WHY...
...IF I WANT TO KEEP THAT DATE WITH CHIYO-CHAN...
GA (CLANG)

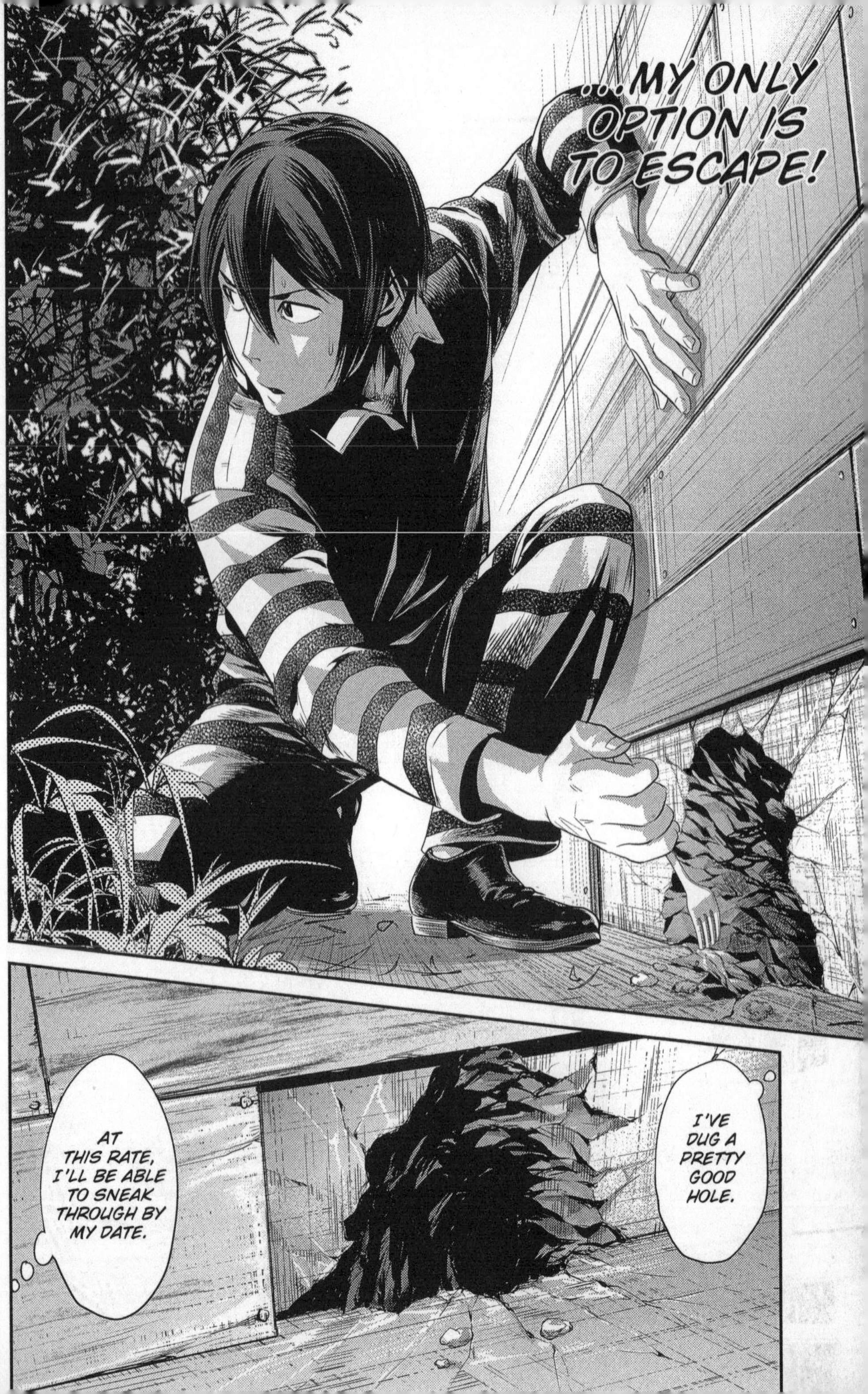
...MY ONLY OPTION IS TO ESCAPE!
I'VE DUG A PRETTY GOOD HOLE.
AT THIS RATE, I'LL BE ABLE TO SNEAK THROUGH BY MY DATE.

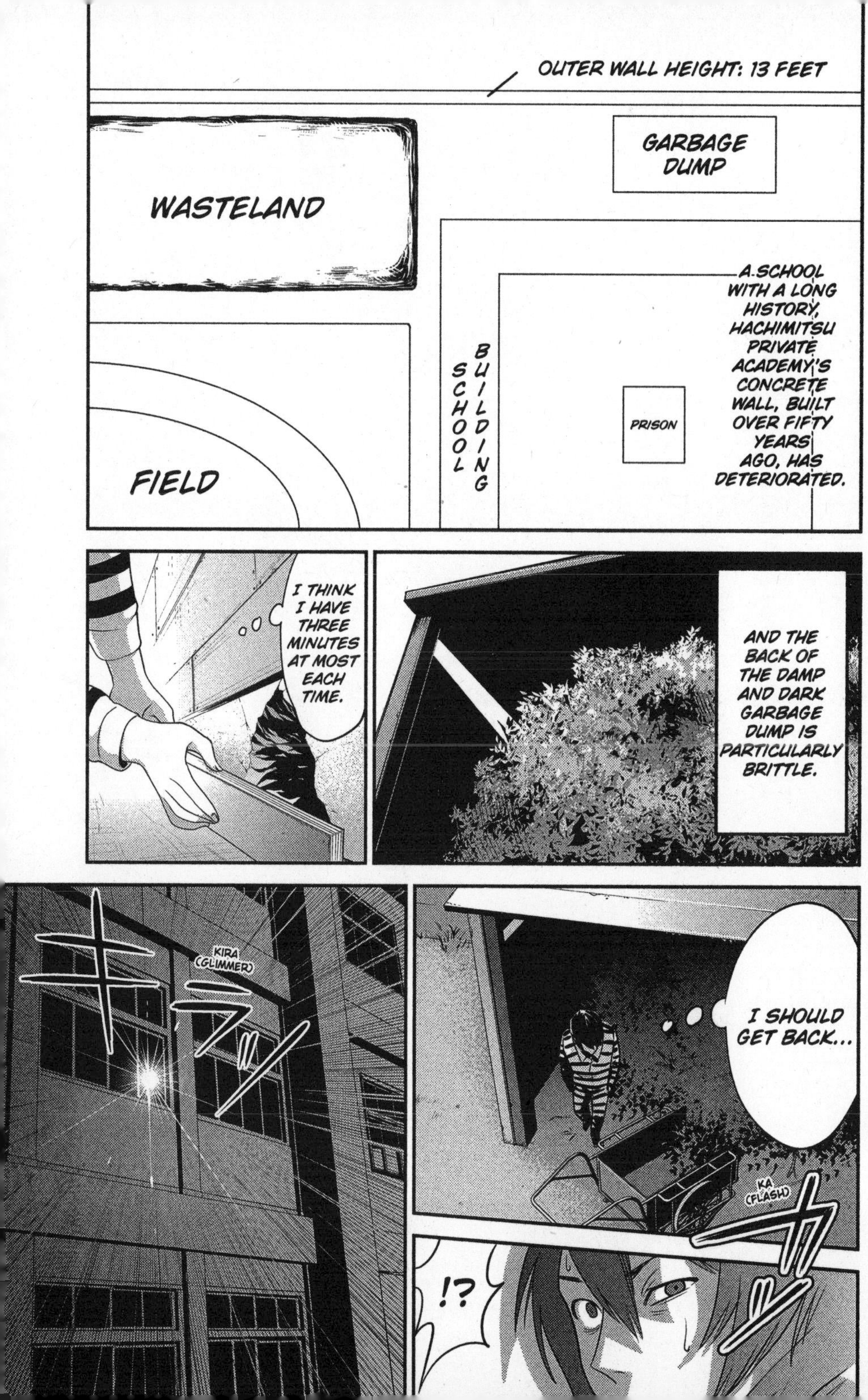
OUTER WALL HEIGHT: 13 FEET
GARBAGE DUMP
WASTELAND
A SCHOOL WITH A LONG HISTORY, HACHIMITSU PRIVATE ACADEMY'S CONCRETE WALL, BUILT OVER FIFTY YEARS AGO, HAS DETERIORATED.
PRISON
SCHOOL BUILDING
FIELD
AND THE BACK OF THE DAMP AND DARK GARBAGE DUMP IS PARTICULARLY BRITTLE.
I THINK I HAVE THREE MINUTES AT MOST EACH TIME.
I SHOULD GET BACK...
KA (FLASH)
!?
KIRA (GLIMMER)

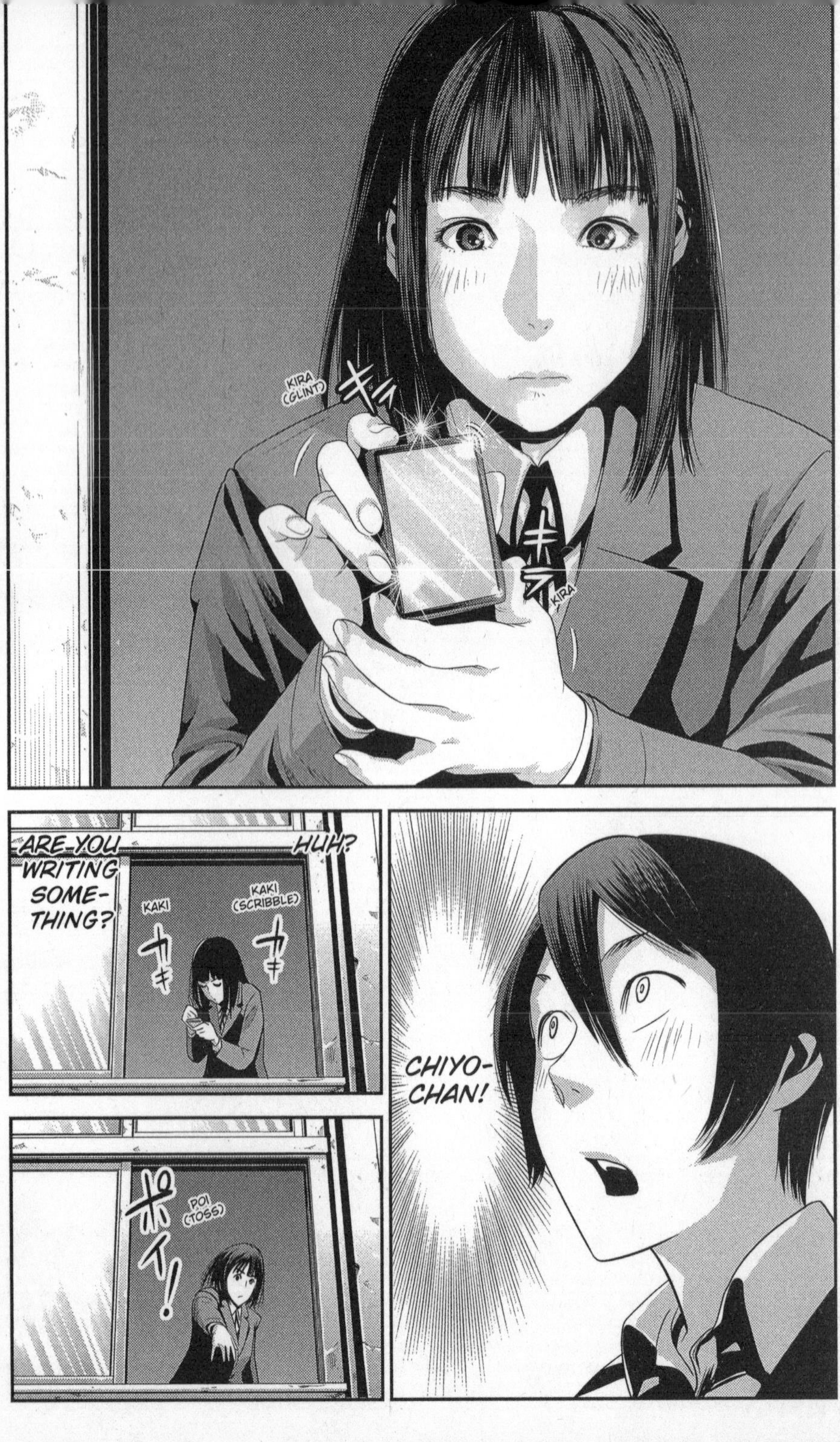
KIRA (GLINT)
KIRA
CHIYO-CHAN!
HUH?
ARE YOU WRITING SOMETHING?
KAKI (SCRIBBLE)
KAKI
POI (TOSS)

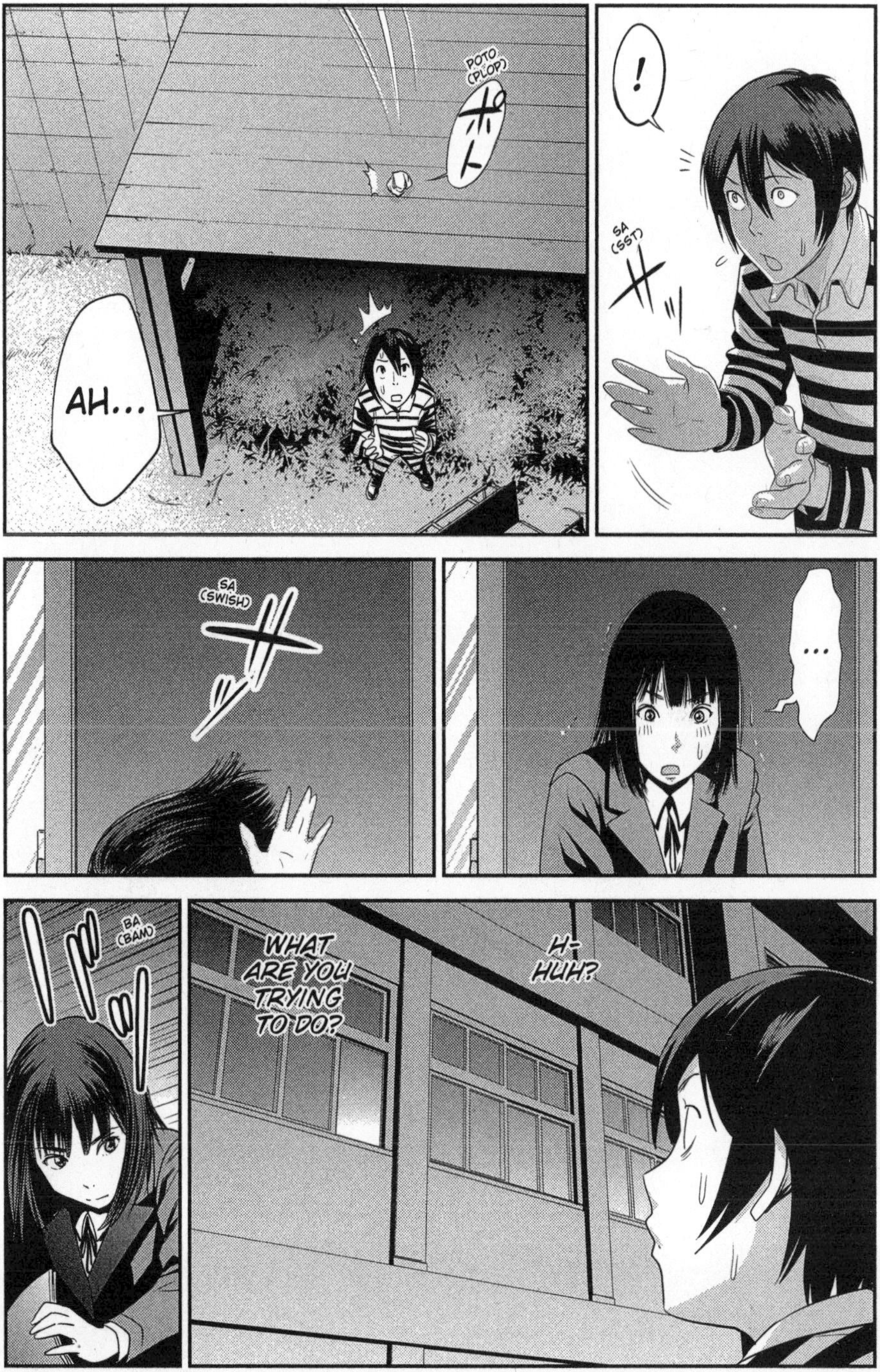
!
SA (SST)
POTO (PLOP)
ポト
AH...
...
SA (SWISH)
H-HUH?
WHAT ARE YOU TRYING TO DO?
BA (BAM)

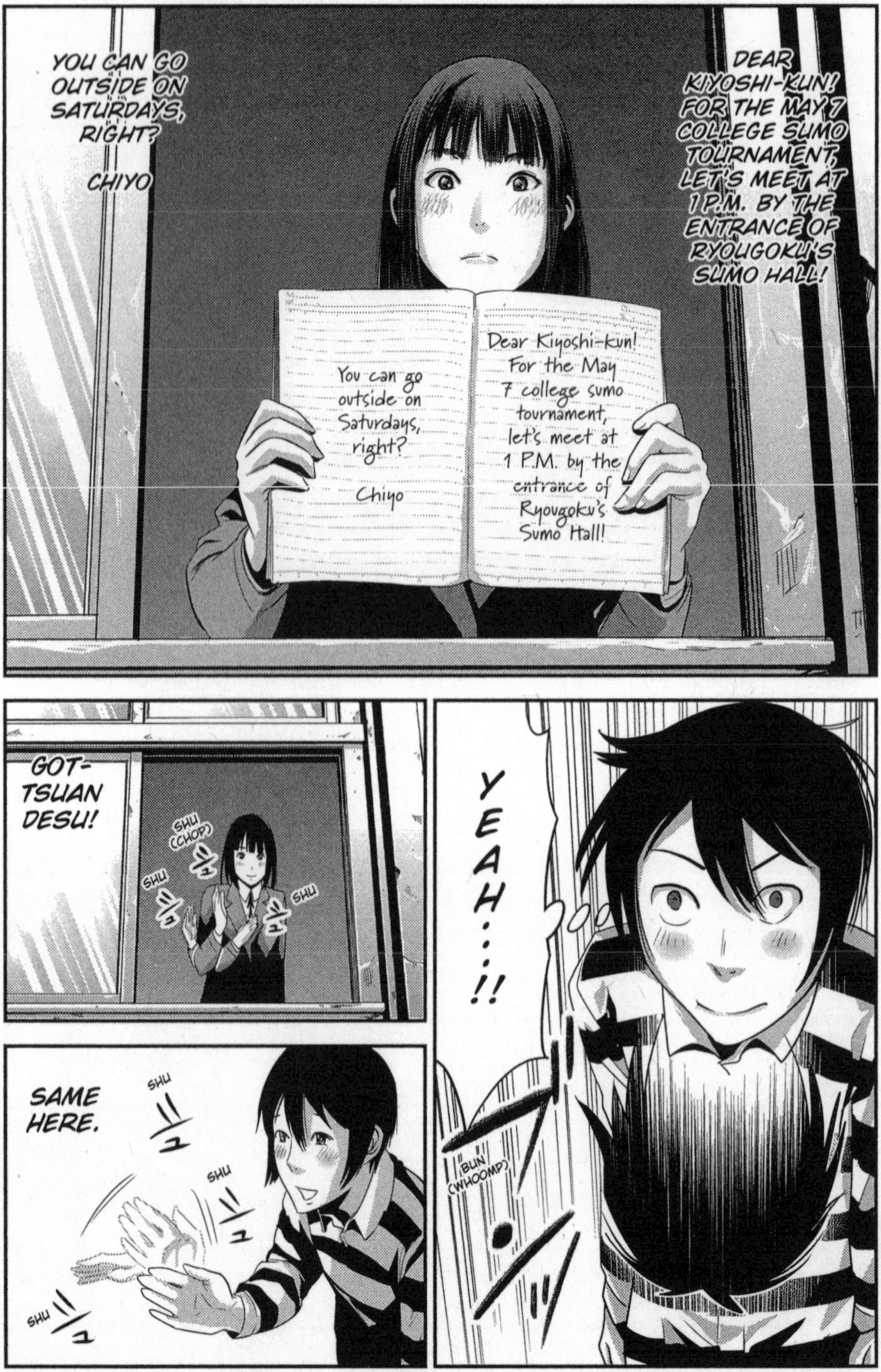
DEAR KIYOSHI-KUN! FOR THE MAY 7 COLLEGE SUMO TOURNAMENT, LET'S MEET AT 1 P.M. BY THE ENTRANCE OF RYOUGOKU'S SUMO HALL!
YOU CAN GO OUTSIDE ON SATURDAYS, RIGHT?
CHIYO
Dear Kiyoshi-kun! For the May 7 college sumo tournament, let's meet at 1 P.M. by the entrance of Ryougoku's Sumo Hall!
You can go outside on Saturdays, right?
Chiyo
YEAH...!!
BUN (WHOOMP)
GOT-TSUAN DESU!
SHU (CHOP)
SHU
SHU
SAME HERE.
SHU
SHU
SHU

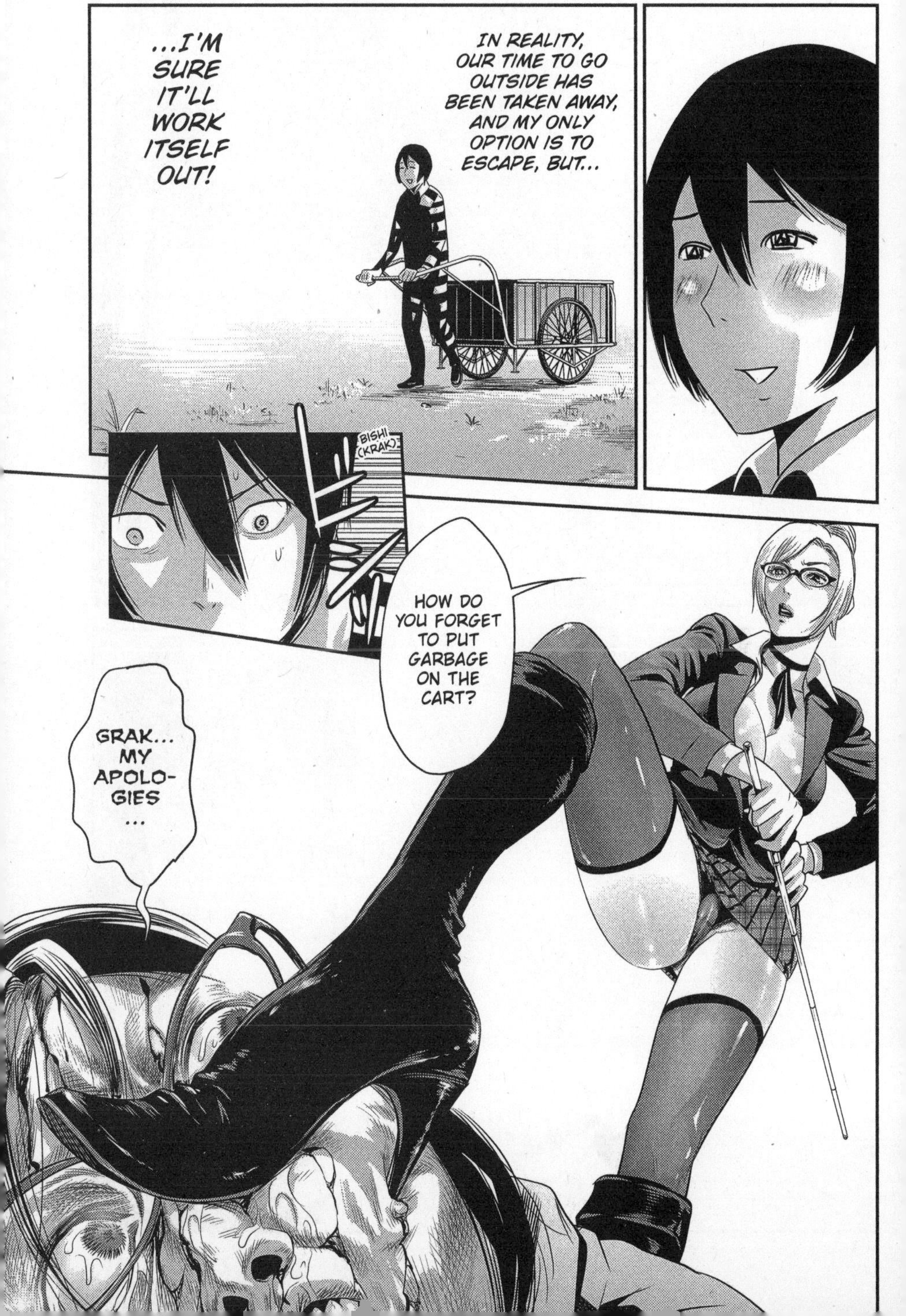
IN REALITY, OUR TIME TO GO OUTSIDE HAS BEEN TAKEN AWAY, AND MY ONLY OPTION IS TO ESCAPE, BUT...
...I'M SURE IT'LL WORK ITSELF OUT!
BISHI (KRAK)
HOW DO YOU FORGET TO PUT GARBAGE ON THE CART?
GRAK... MY APOLOGIES ...

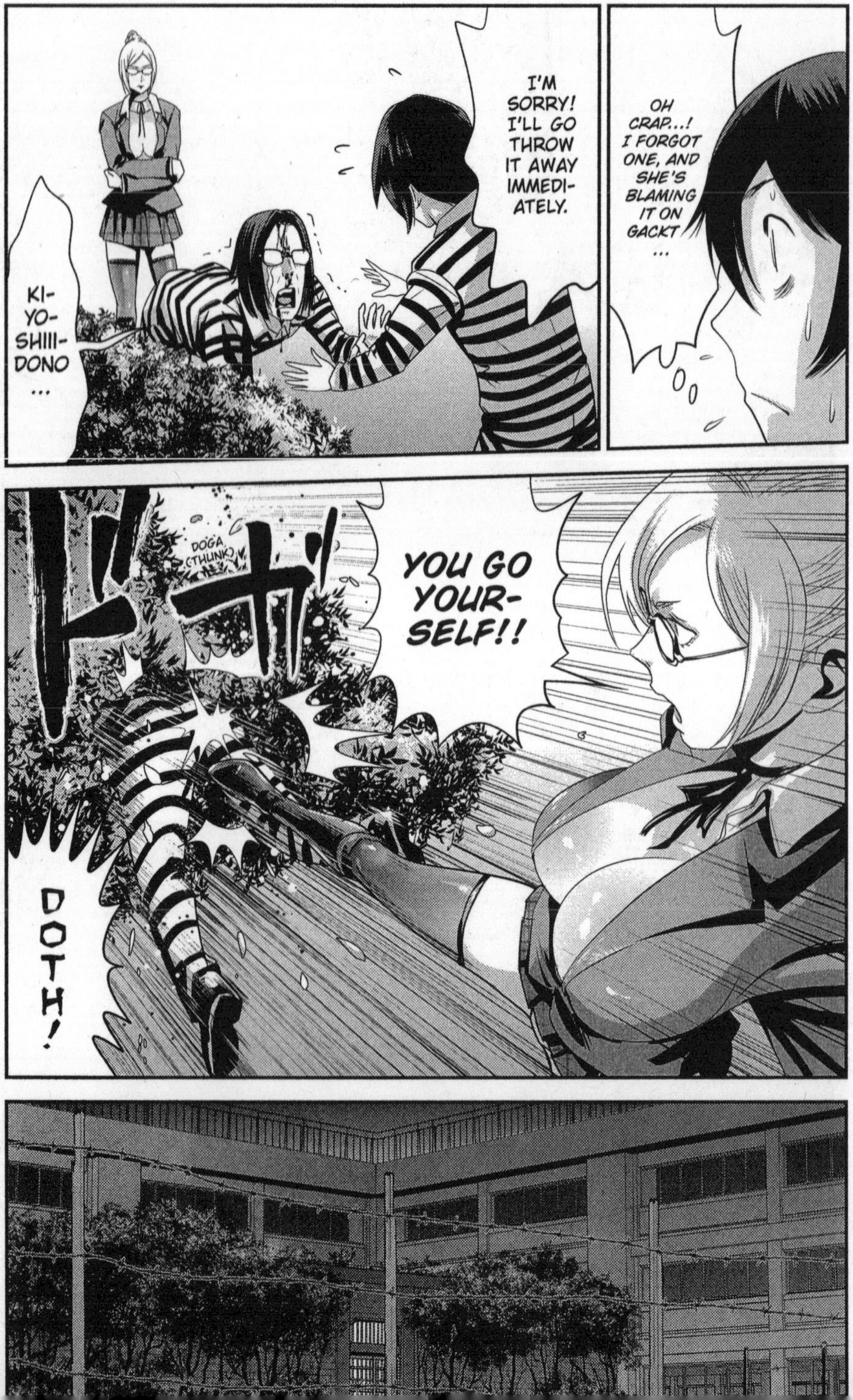
OH CRAP...! I FORGOT ONE, AND SHE'S BLAMING IT ON GACKT ...
I'M SORRY! I'LL GO THROW IT AWAY IMMEDI-ATELY.
KI-YO-SHIII-DONO ...
YOU GO YOUR-SELF!!
DOGA (THUNK)
DOTH!

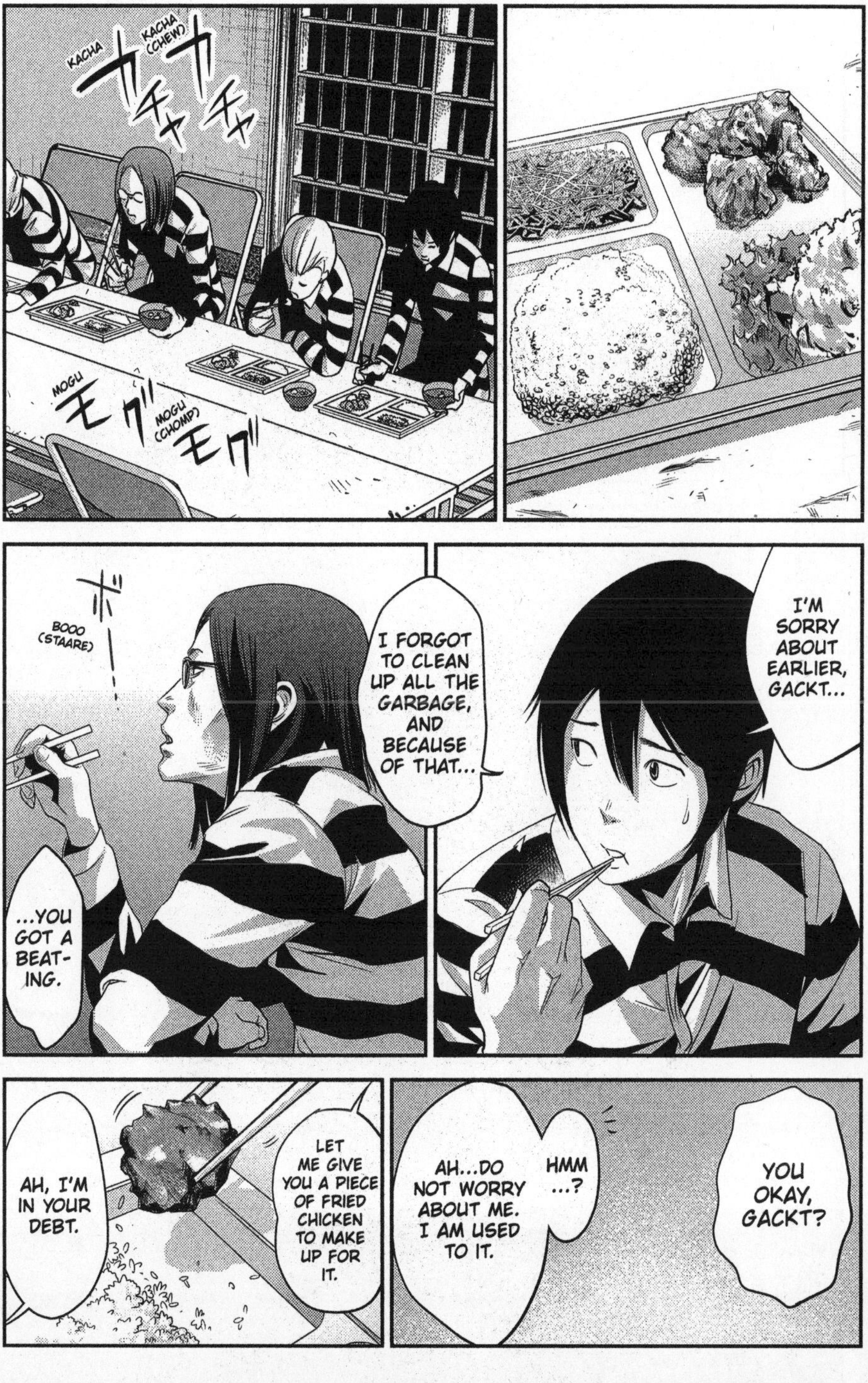
KACHA
KACHA (CHEW)
MOGU
MOGU (CHOMP)
I'M SORRY ABOUT EARLIER, GACKT...
I FORGOT TO CLEAN UP ALL THE GARBAGE, AND BECAUSE OF THAT...
BOOO (STAARE)
...YOU GOT A BEATING.
YOU OKAY, GACKT?
HMM...?
AH...DO NOT WORRY ABOUT ME. I AM USED TO IT.
LET ME GIVE YOU A PIECE OF FRIED CHICKEN TO MAKE UP FOR IT.
AH, I'M IN YOUR DEBT.

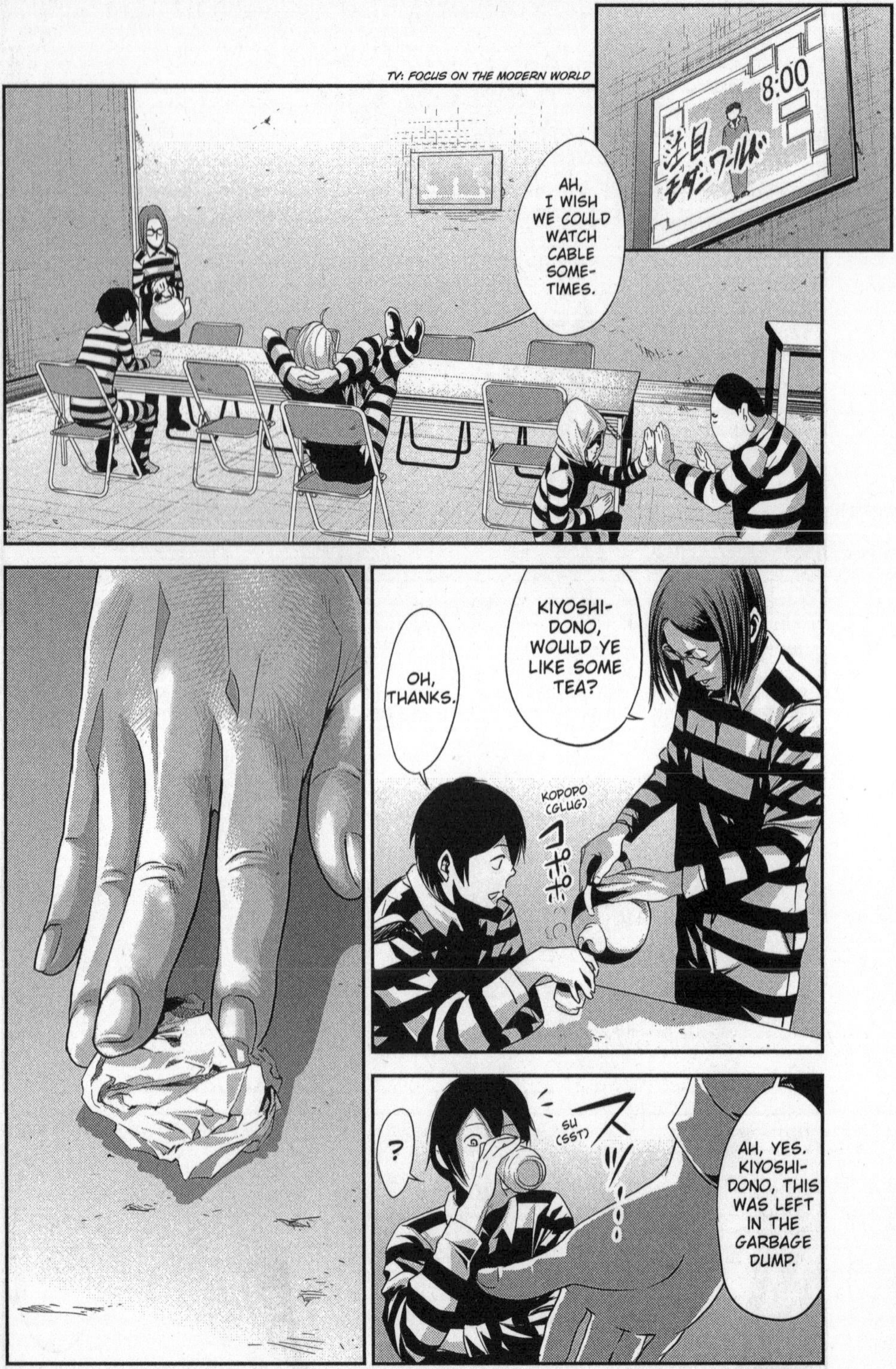
TV: FOCUS ON THE MODERN WORLD
8:00
注目
AH, I WISH WE COULD WATCH CABLE SOME-TIMES.
KIYOSHI-DONO, WOULD YE LIKE SOME TEA?
OH, THANKS.
KOPOPO (GLUG)
コポポ
AH, YES. KIYOSHI-DONO, THIS WAS LEFT IN THE GARBAGE DUMP.
SU (SST)
ス
?

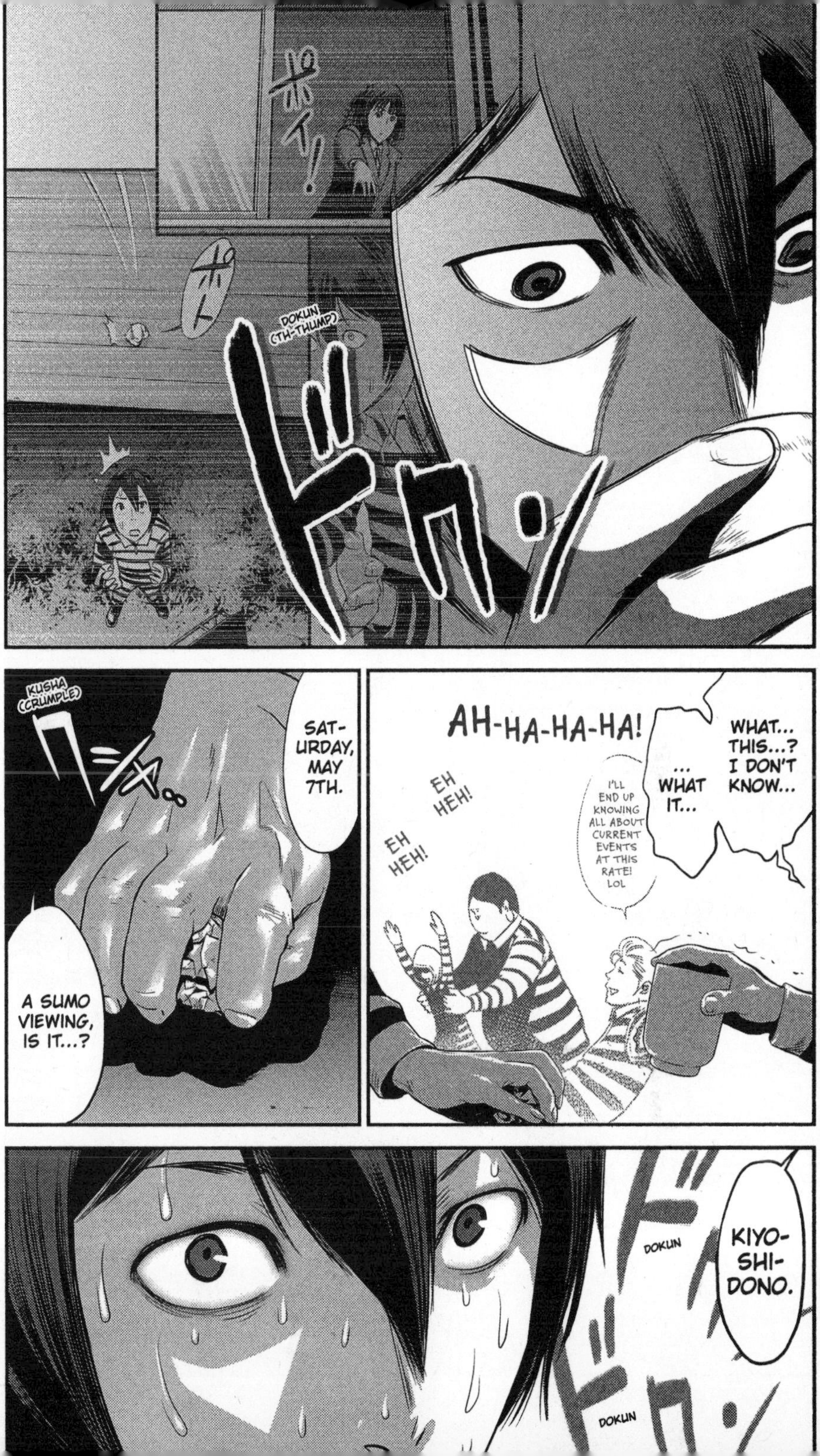
DOKUN (TH-THUMP)
WHAT... THIS...? I DON'T KNOW...
...WHAT IT...
I'LL END UP KNOWING ALL ABOUT CURRENT EVENTS AT THIS RATE! LOL
AH-HA-HA-HA!
EH HEH!
EH HEH!
SAT-URDAY, MAY 7TH.
KUSHA (CRUMPLE)
A SUMO VIEWING, IS IT...?
KIYO-SHI-DONO.
DOKUN
DOKUN

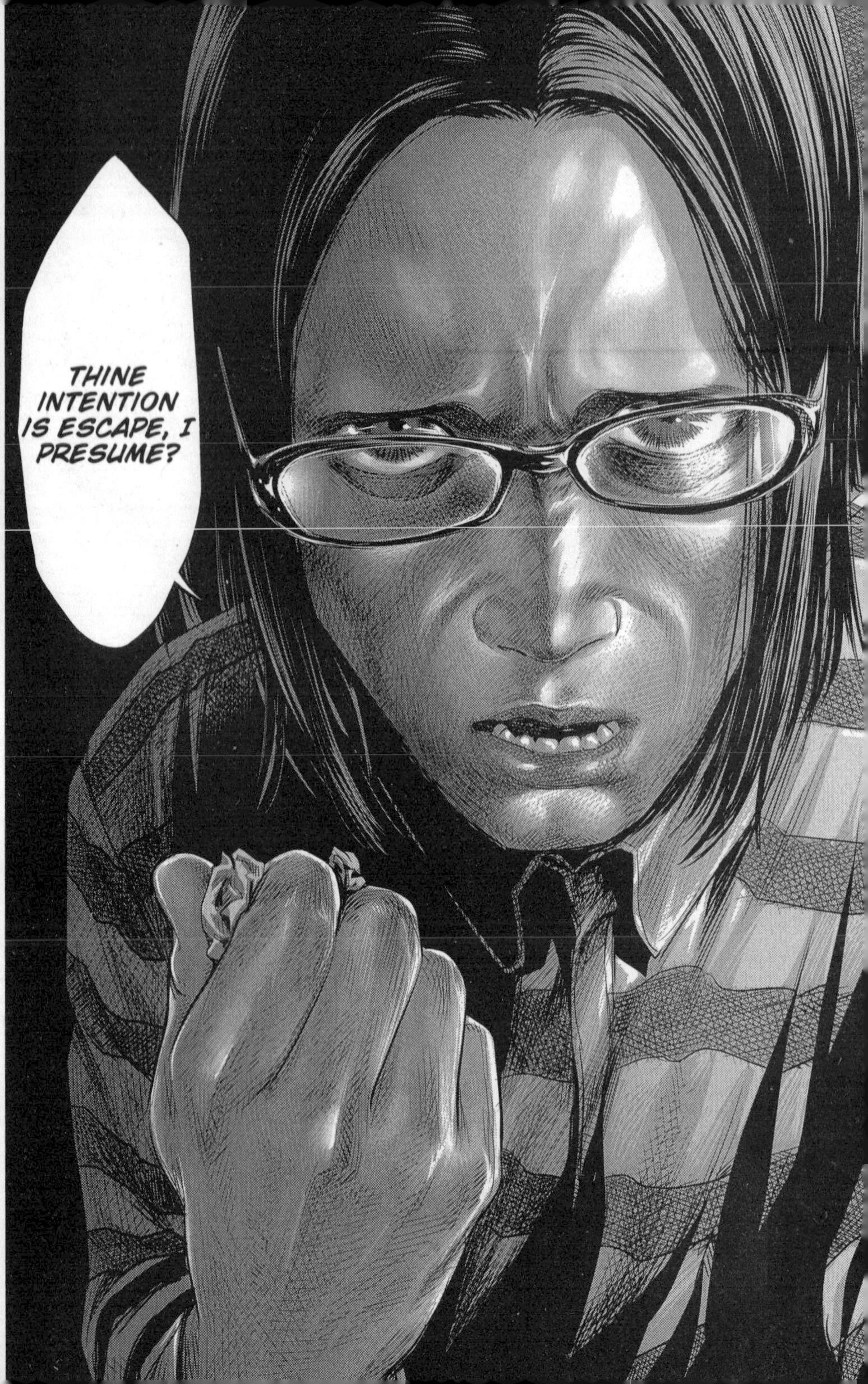
THINE INTENTION IS ESCAPE, I PRESUME?

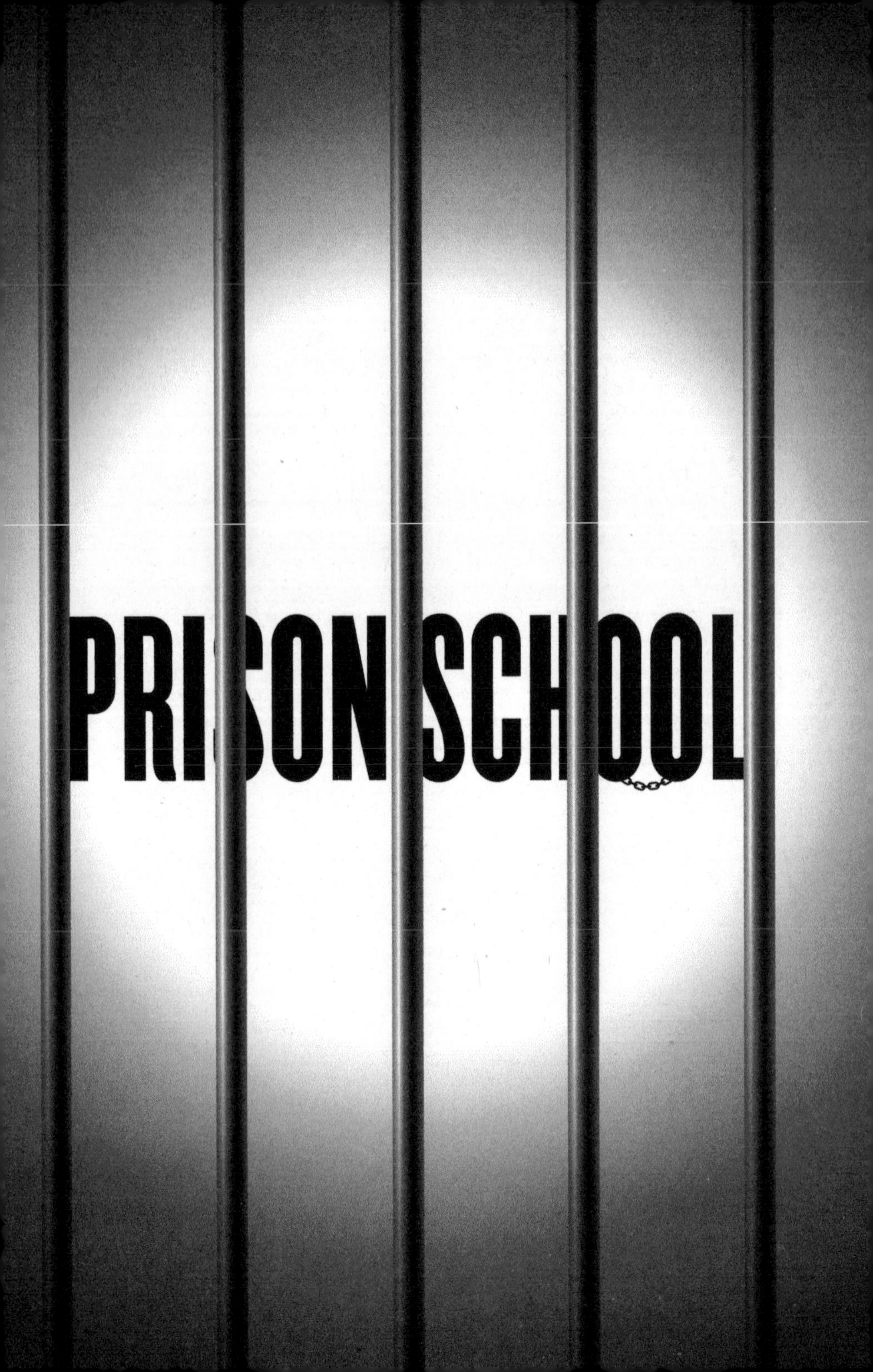
PRISON SCHOOL

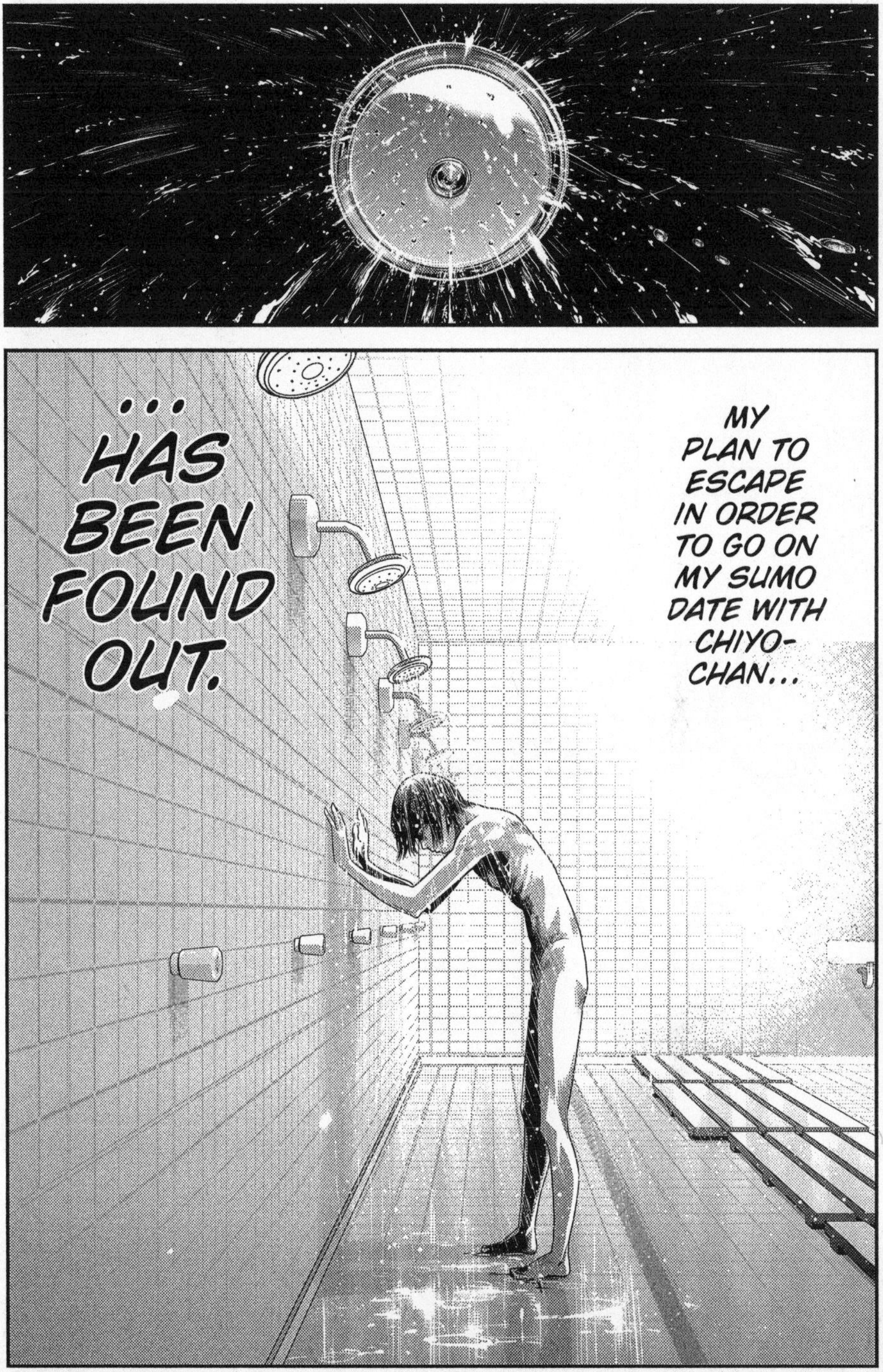
MY PLAN TO ESCAPE IN ORDER TO GO ON MY SUMO DATE WITH CHIYO-CHAN...
...HAS BEEN FOUND OUT.

CHAPTER 9: THE MAN WHO KNEW TOO MUCH

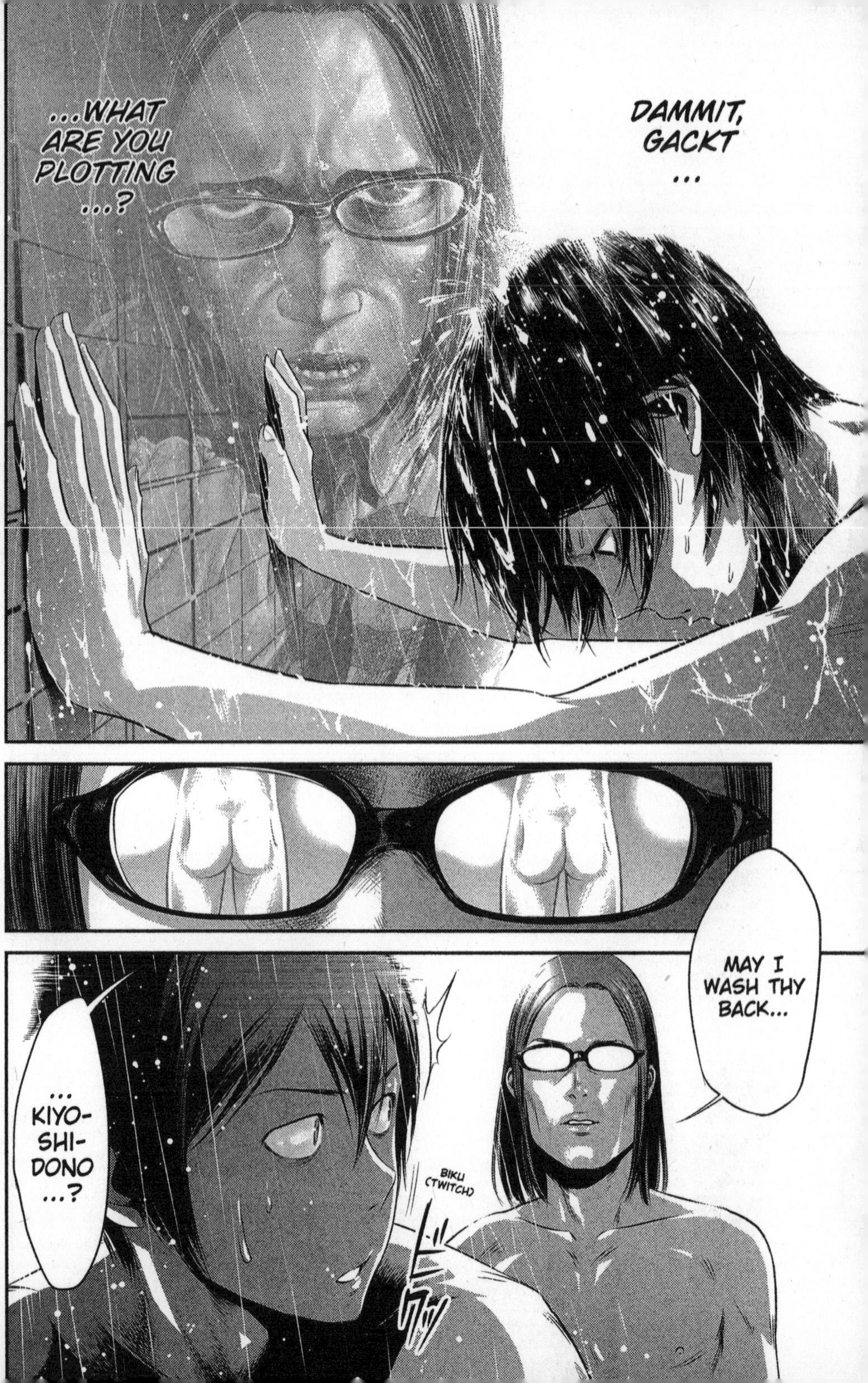

DAMMIT, GACKT ...
...WHAT ARE YOU PLOTTING ...?
MAY I WASH THY BACK...
BIKU (TWITCH)
... KIYO-SHI-DONO ...?

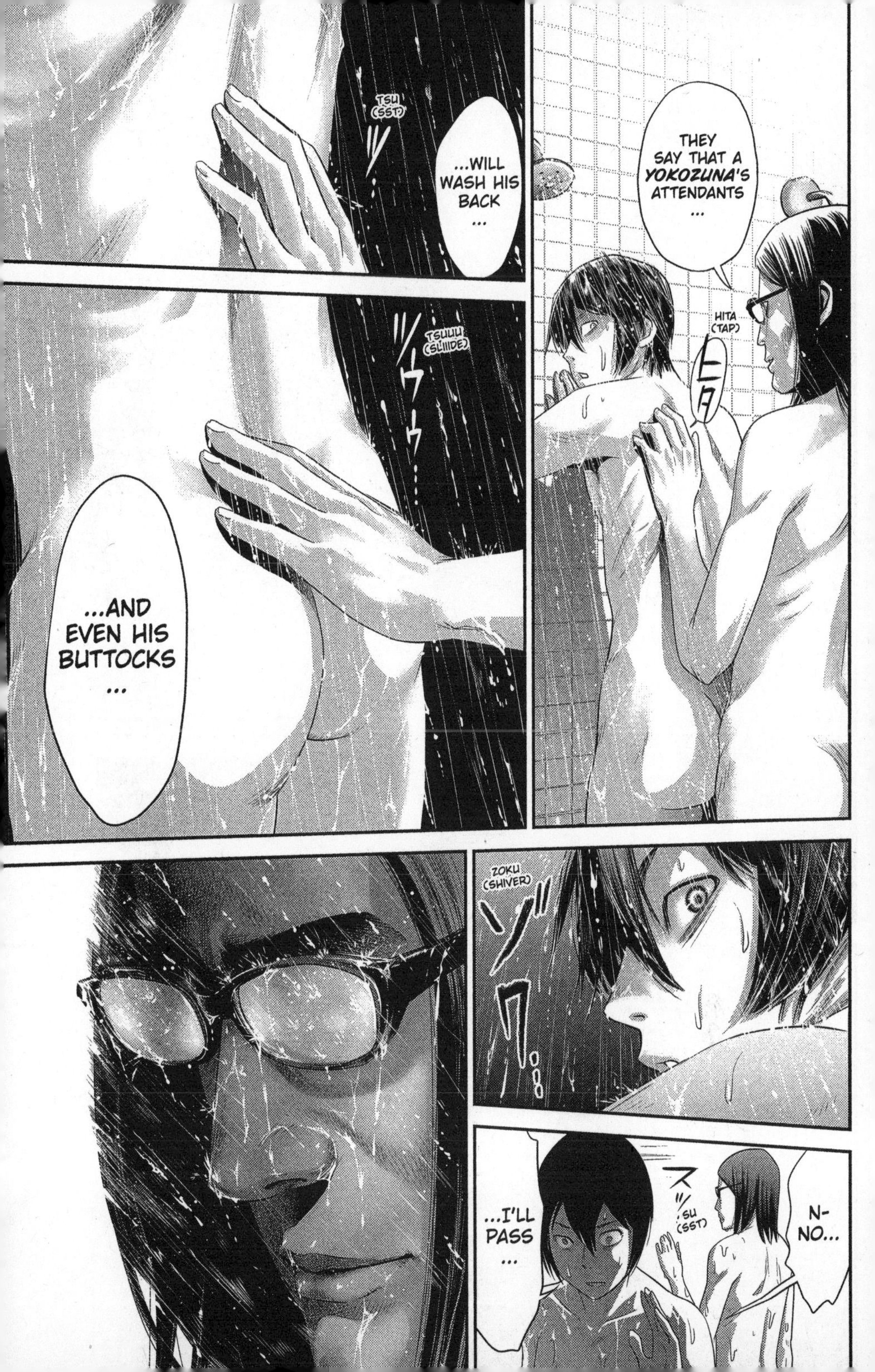
THEY SAY THAT A YOKOZUNA'S ATTENDANTS ...
HITA (TAP)
TSU (SST)
...WILL WASH HIS BACK ...
TSUUU (SLIIIDE)
...AND EVEN HIS BUTTOCKS ...
ZOKU (SHIVER)
N-NO...
SU (SST)
...I'LL PASS ...

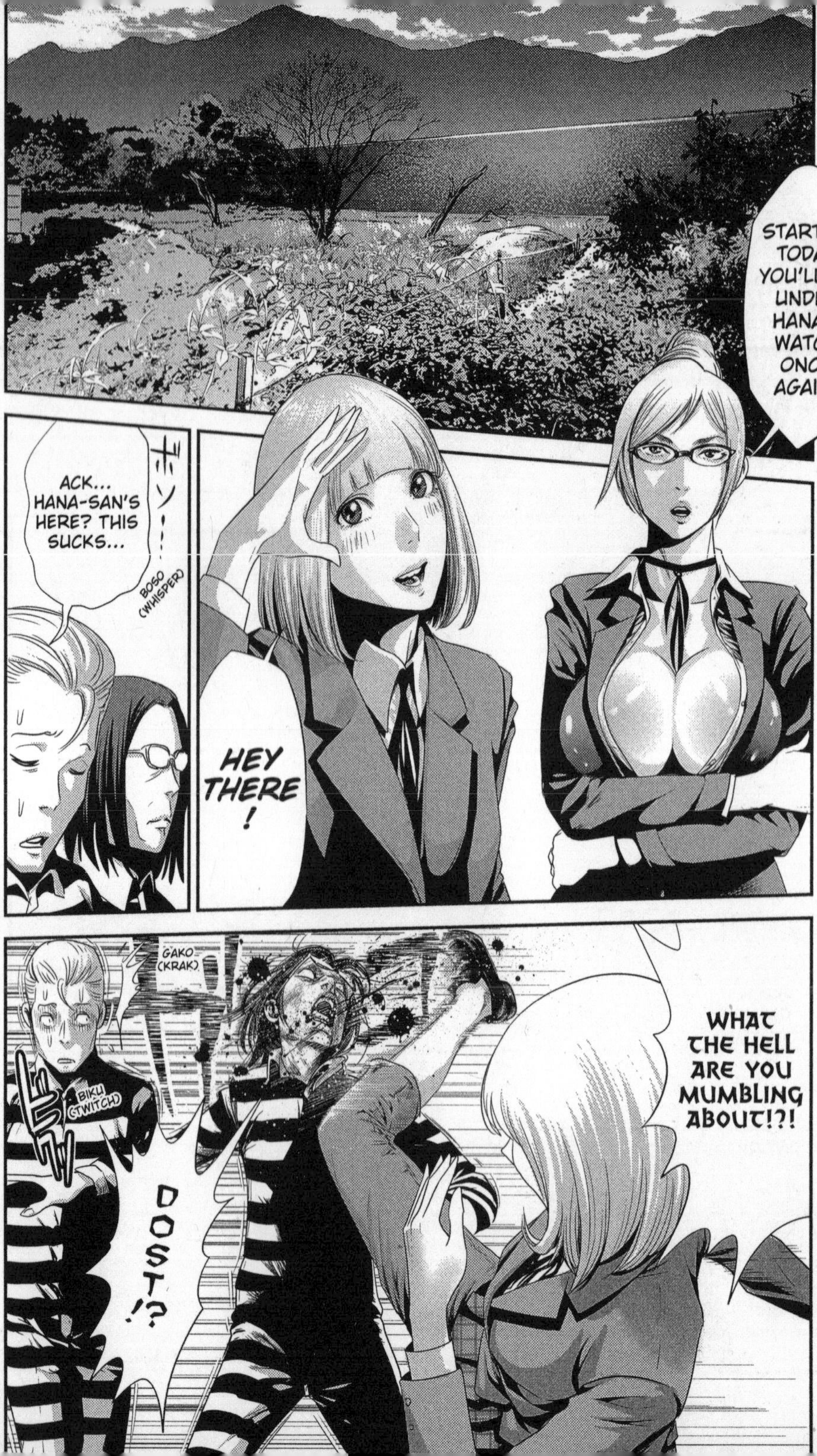
STARTING TODAY, YOU'LL BE UNDER HANA'S WATCH ONCE AGAIN.
HEY THERE!
ボソッ!!
BOSO (WHISPER)
ACK... HANA-SAN'S HERE? THIS SUCKS...
WHAT THE HELL ARE YOU MUMBLING ABOUT!?!
GAKO (KRAK)
DOST!?
BIKU (TWITCH)

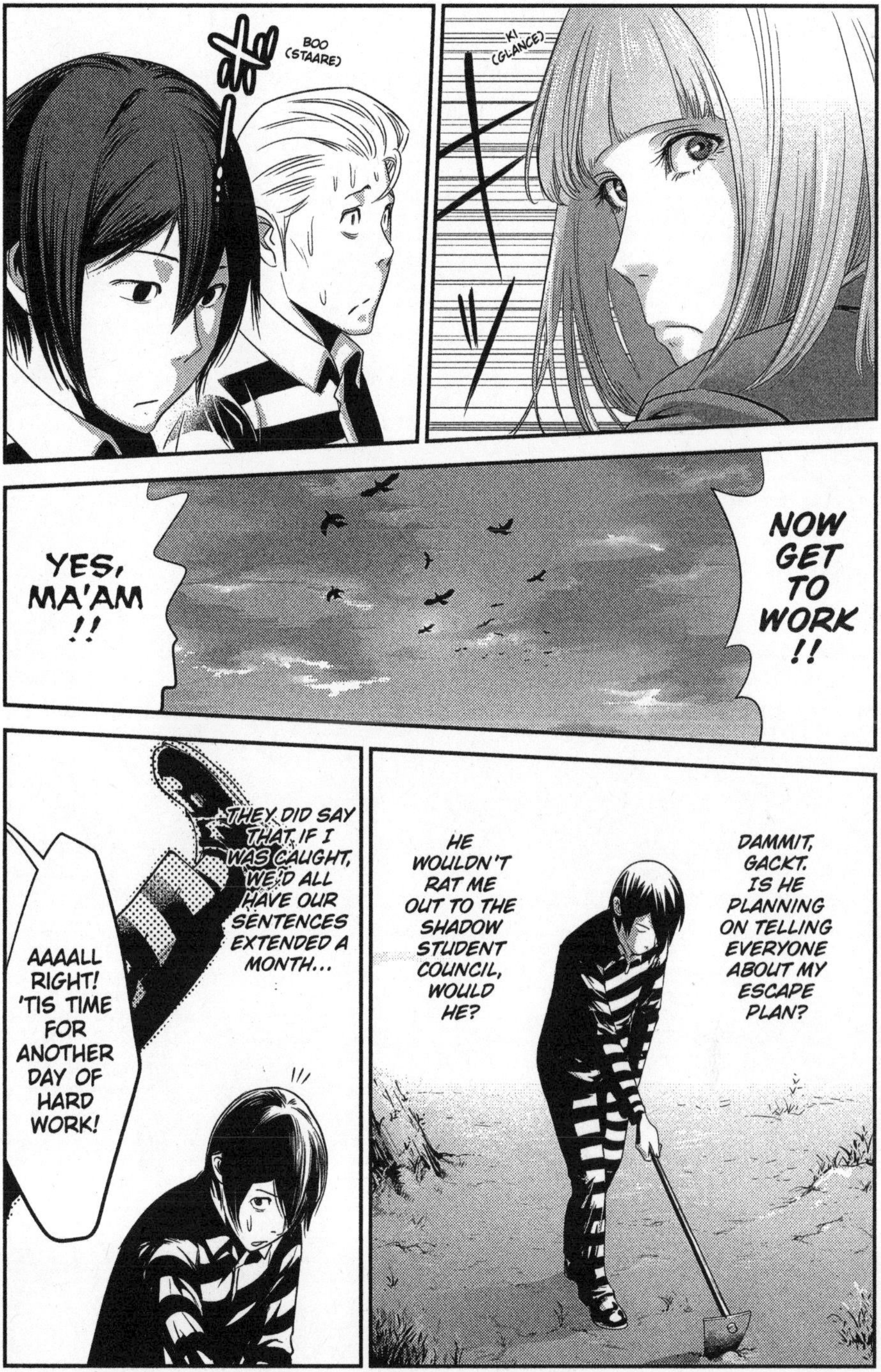
KI
(GLANCE)
BOO
(STAARE)
NOW GET TO WORK !!
YES, MA'AM !!
DAMMIT, GACKT. IS HE PLANNING ON TELLING EVERYONE ABOUT MY ESCAPE PLAN?
HE WOULDN'T RAT ME OUT TO THE SHADOW STUDENT COUNCIL, WOULD HE?
THEY DID SAY THAT IF I WAS CAUGHT, WE'D ALL HAVE OUR SENTENCES EXTENDED A MONTH...
AAAALL RIGHT! 'TIS TIME FOR ANOTHER DAY OF HARD WORK!

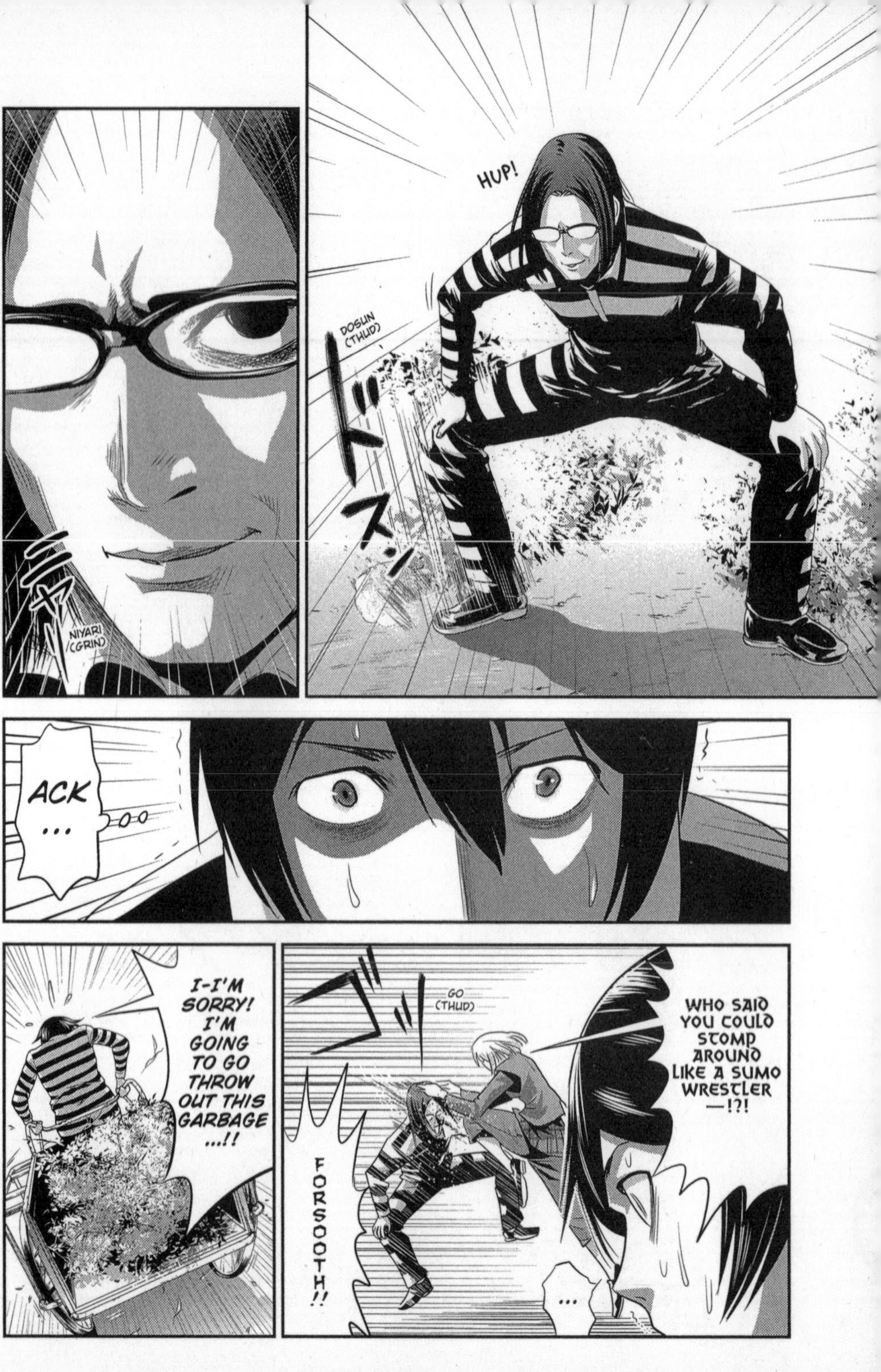
HUP!
DOSUN (THUD)
NIYARI (GRIN)
ACK ...
WHO SAID YOU COULD STOMP AROUND LIKE A SUMO WRESTLER—!?!
GO (THUD)
FORSOOTH!!
...
I-I'M SORRY! I'M GOING TO GO THROW OUT THIS GARBAGE ...!!

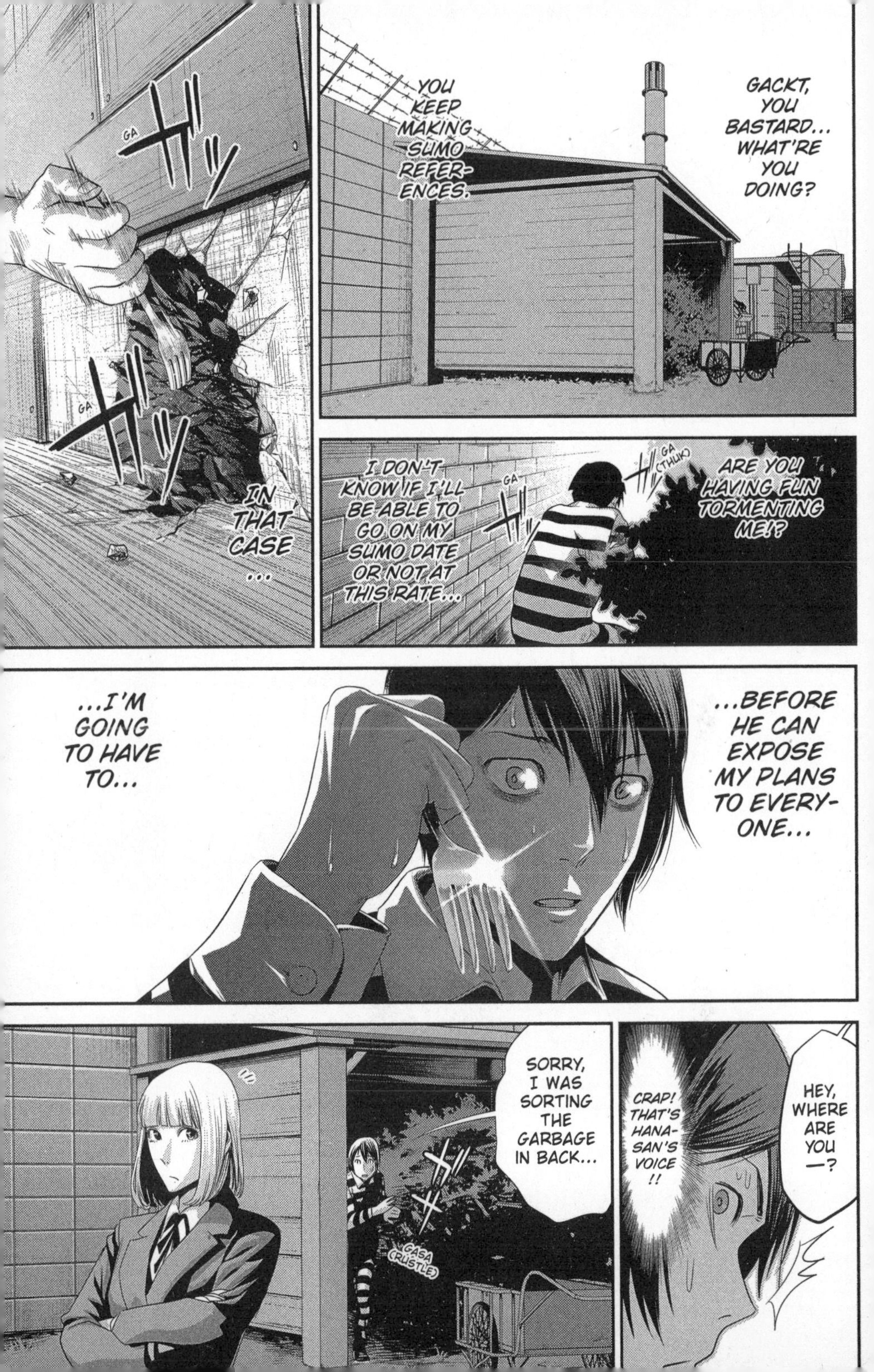
GACKT, YOU BASTARD... WHAT'RE YOU DOING?
YOU KEEP MAKING SUMO REFERENCES.
GA
GA
IN THAT CASE...
ARE YOU HAVING FUN TORMENTING ME!?
GA (THUK)
GA
I DON'T KNOW IF I'LL BE ABLE TO GO ON MY SUMO DATE OR NOT AT THIS RATE...
...BEFORE HE CAN EXPOSE MY PLANS TO EVERYONE...
...I'M GOING TO HAVE TO...
HEY, WHERE ARE YOU—?
CRAP! THAT'S HANA-SAN'S VOICE!!
SORRY, I WAS SORTING THE GARBAGE IN BACK...
GASA (RUSTLE)

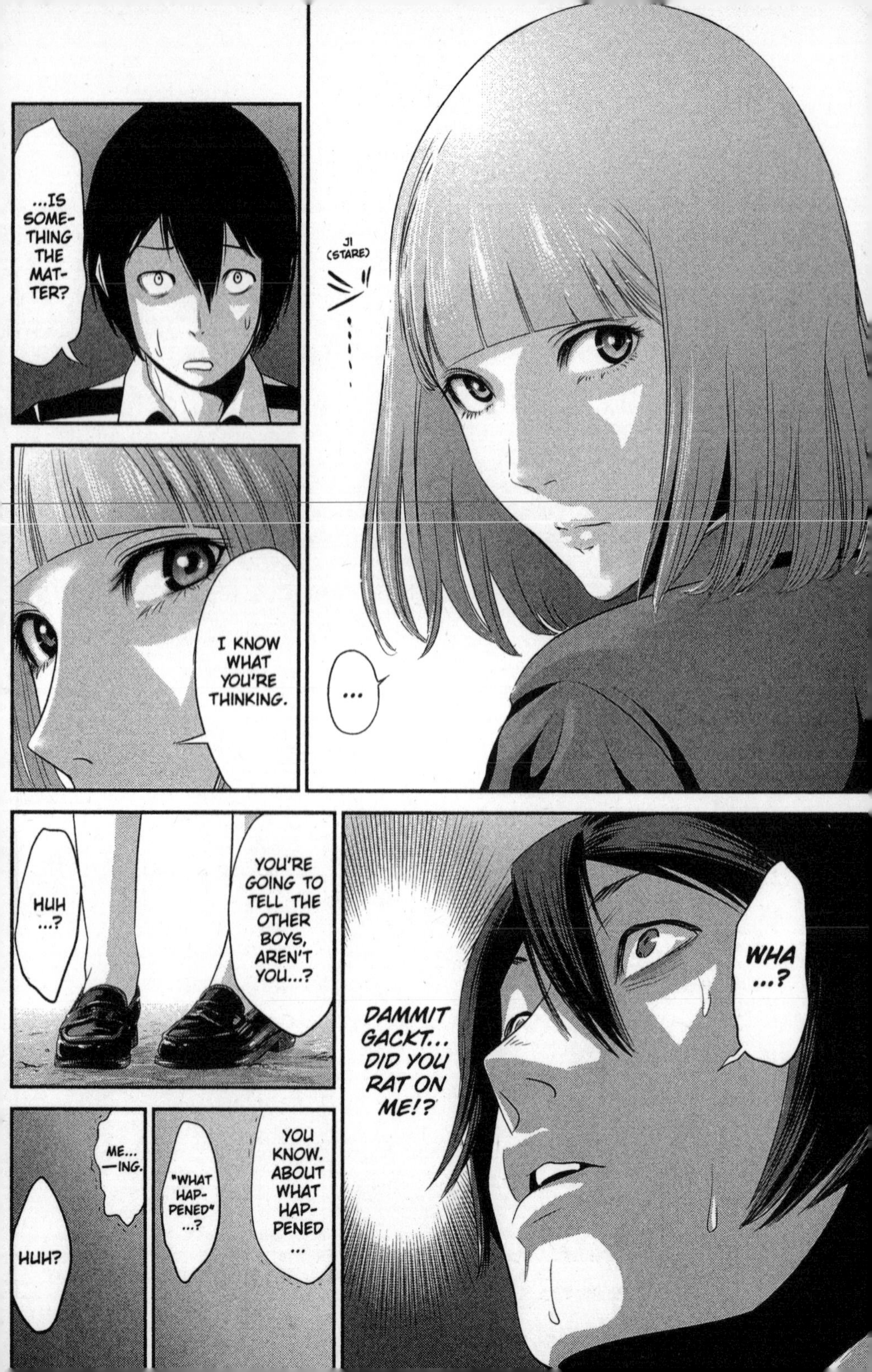
JI (STARE)
...
...IS SOMETHING THE MATTER?
I KNOW WHAT YOU'RE THINKING.
WHA ...?
DAMMIT GACKT... DID YOU RAT ON ME!?
YOU'RE GOING TO TELL THE OTHER BOYS, AREN'T YOU...?
HUH ...?
YOU KNOW. ABOUT WHAT HAPPENED ...
"WHAT HAPPENED" ...?
ME... —ING.
HUH?

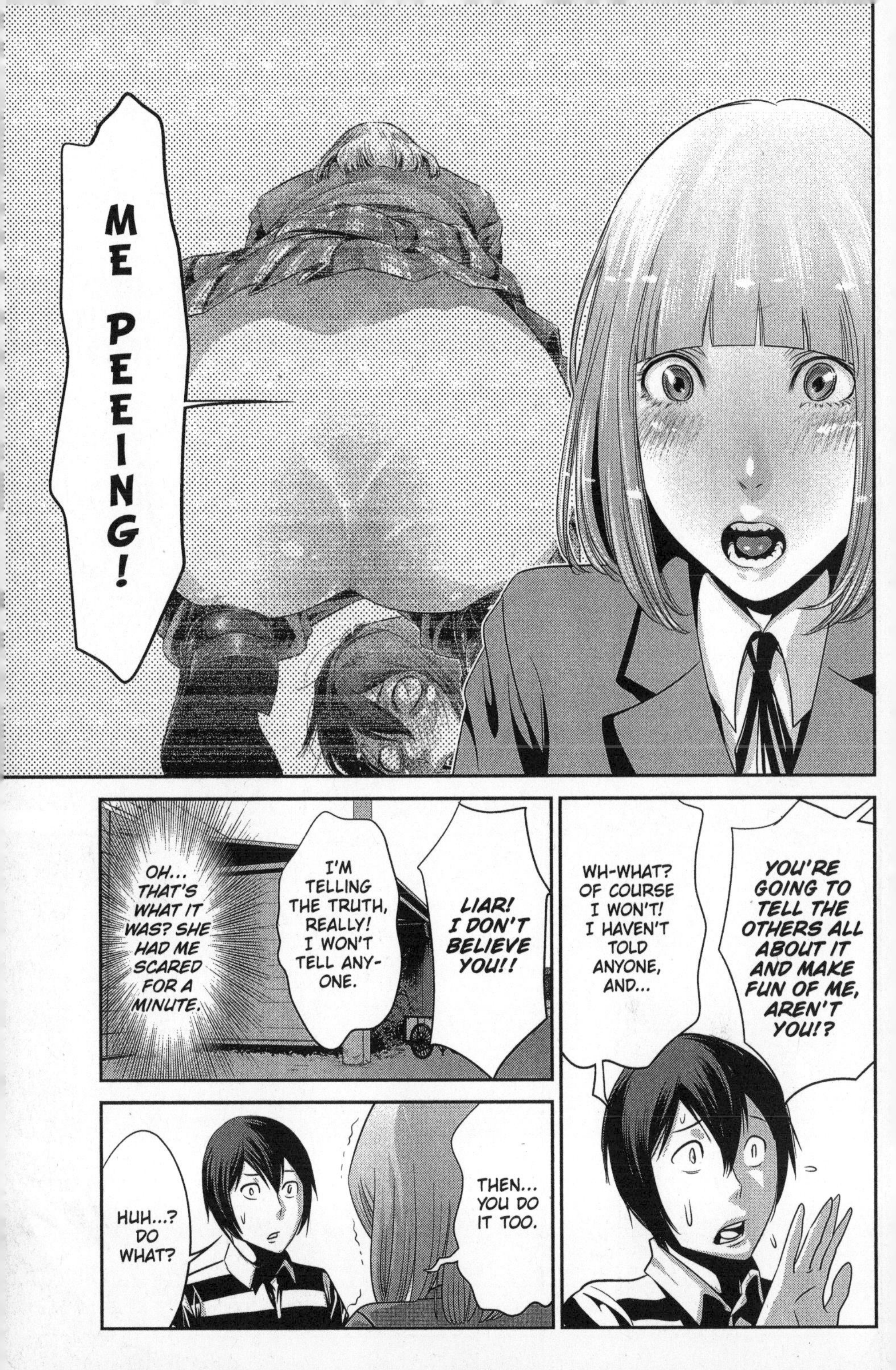

ME PEEING!
YOU'RE GOING TO TELL THE OTHERS ALL ABOUT IT AND MAKE FUN OF ME, AREN'T YOU!?
WH-WHAT? OF COURSE I WON'T! I HAVEN'T TOLD ANYONE, AND...
LIAR! I DON'T BELIEVE YOU!!
I'M TELLING THE TRUTH, REALLY! I WON'T TELL ANY-ONE.
OH... THAT'S WHAT IT WAS? SHE HAD ME SCARED FOR A MINUTE.
THEN... YOU DO IT TOO.
HUH...? DO WHAT?

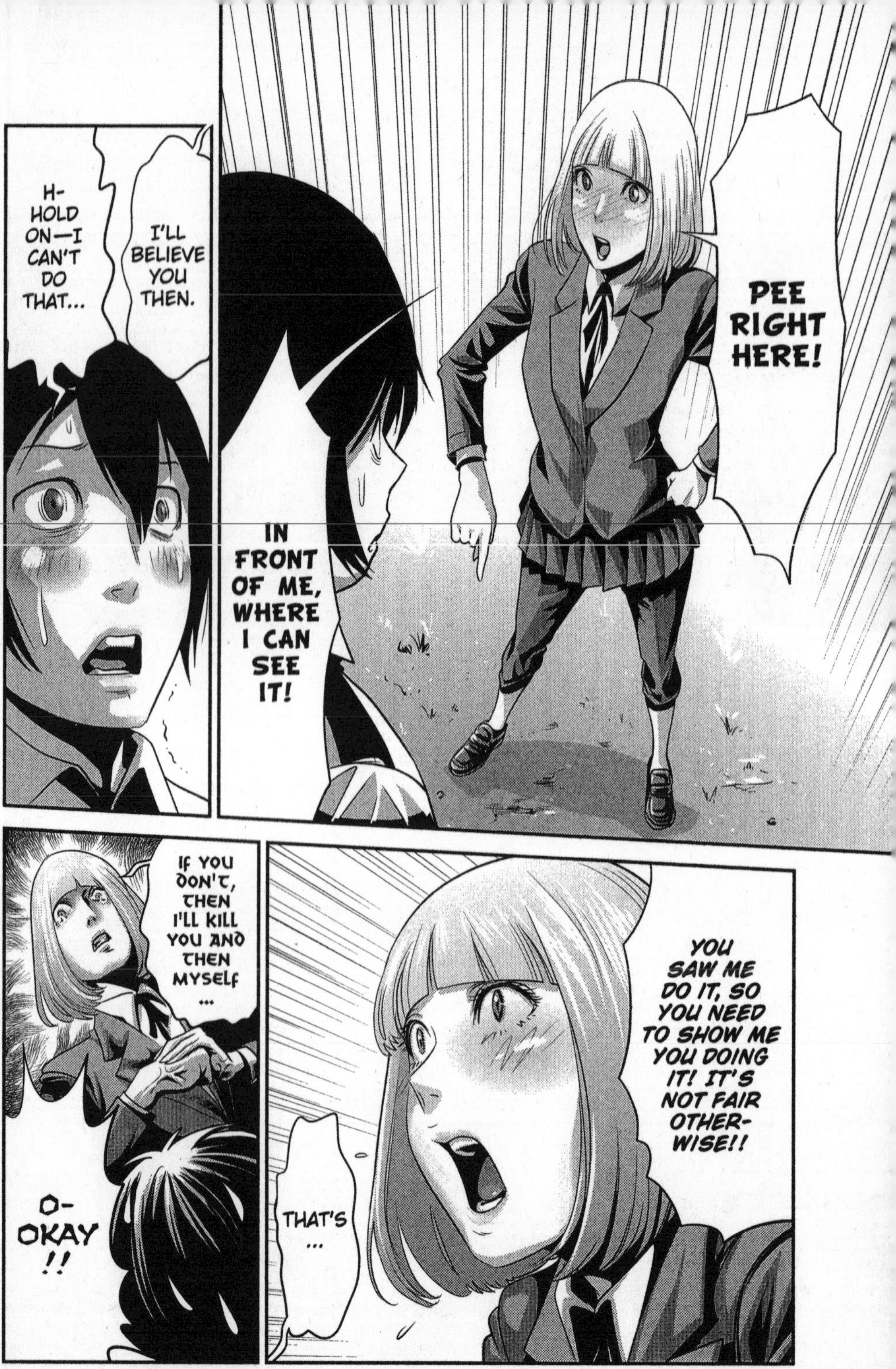
PEE RIGHT HERE!
IN FRONT OF ME, WHERE I CAN SEE IT!
I'LL BELIEVE YOU THEN.
H-HOLD ON—I CAN'T DO THAT...
YOU SAW ME DO IT, SO YOU NEED TO SHOW ME YOU DOING IT! IT'S NOT FAIR OTHER-WISE!!
THAT'S ...
IF YOU DON'T, THEN I'LL KILL YOU AND THEN MYSELF ...
O-OKAY !!

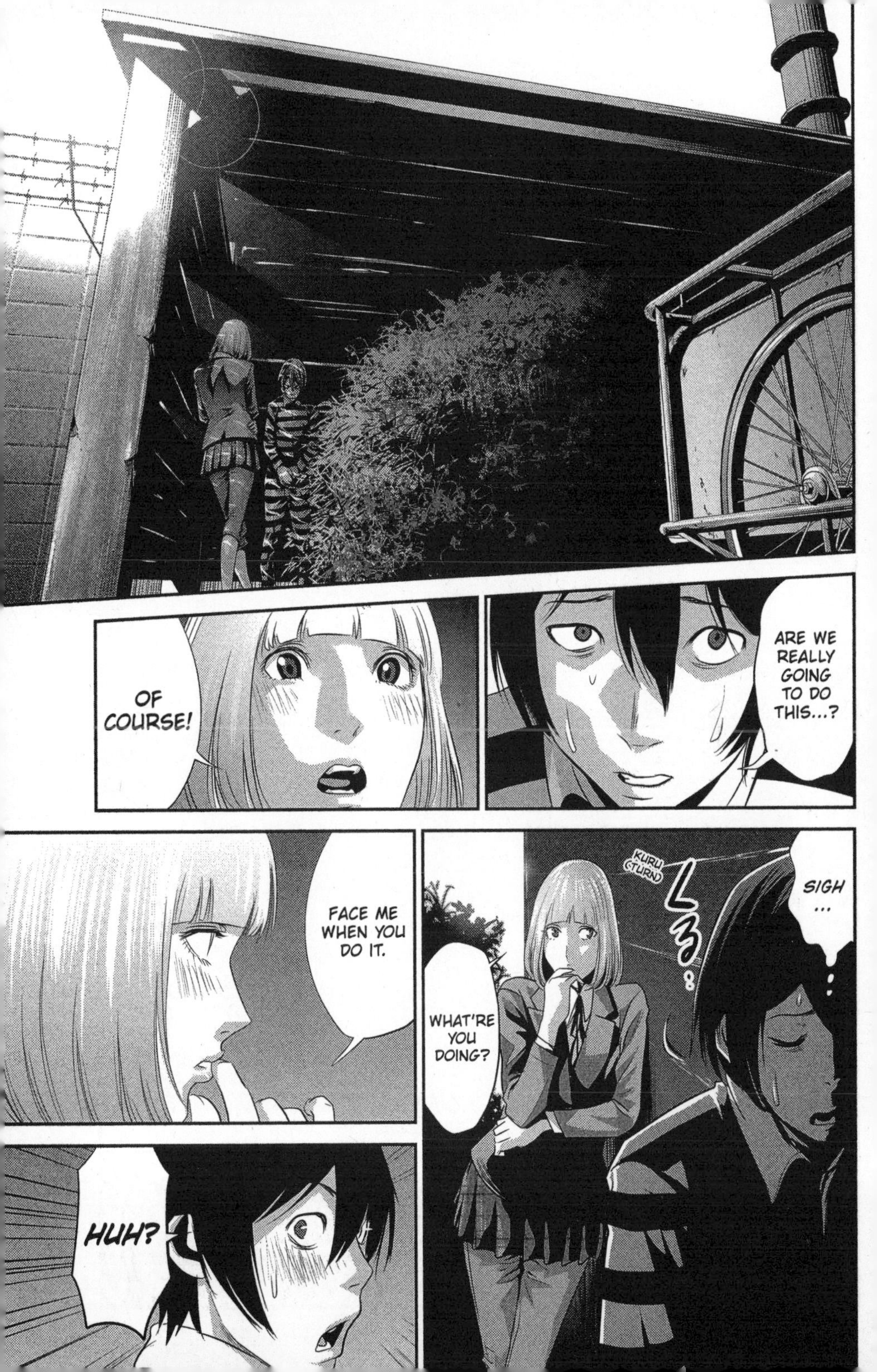
ARE WE REALLY GOING TO DO THIS...?
OF COURSE!
KURU (TURN)
SIGH...
WHAT'RE YOU DOING?
FACE ME WHEN YOU DO IT.
HUH?

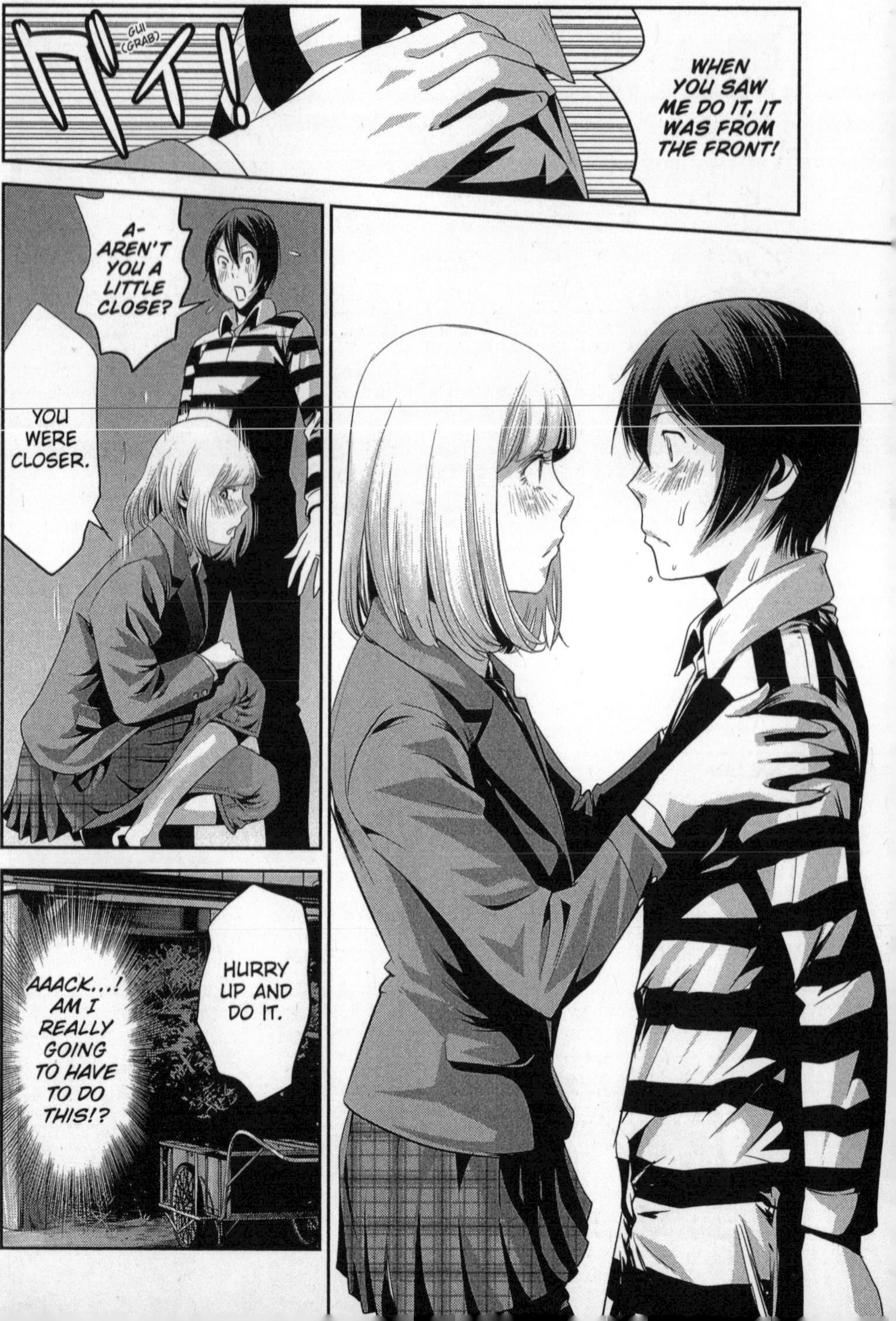
ガイ!
GUI (GRAB)
WHEN YOU SAW ME DO IT, IT WAS FROM THE FRONT!
A-AREN'T YOU A LITTLE CLOSE?
YOU WERE CLOSER.
HURRY UP AND DO IT.
AAACK...! AM I REALLY GOING TO HAVE TO DO THIS!?

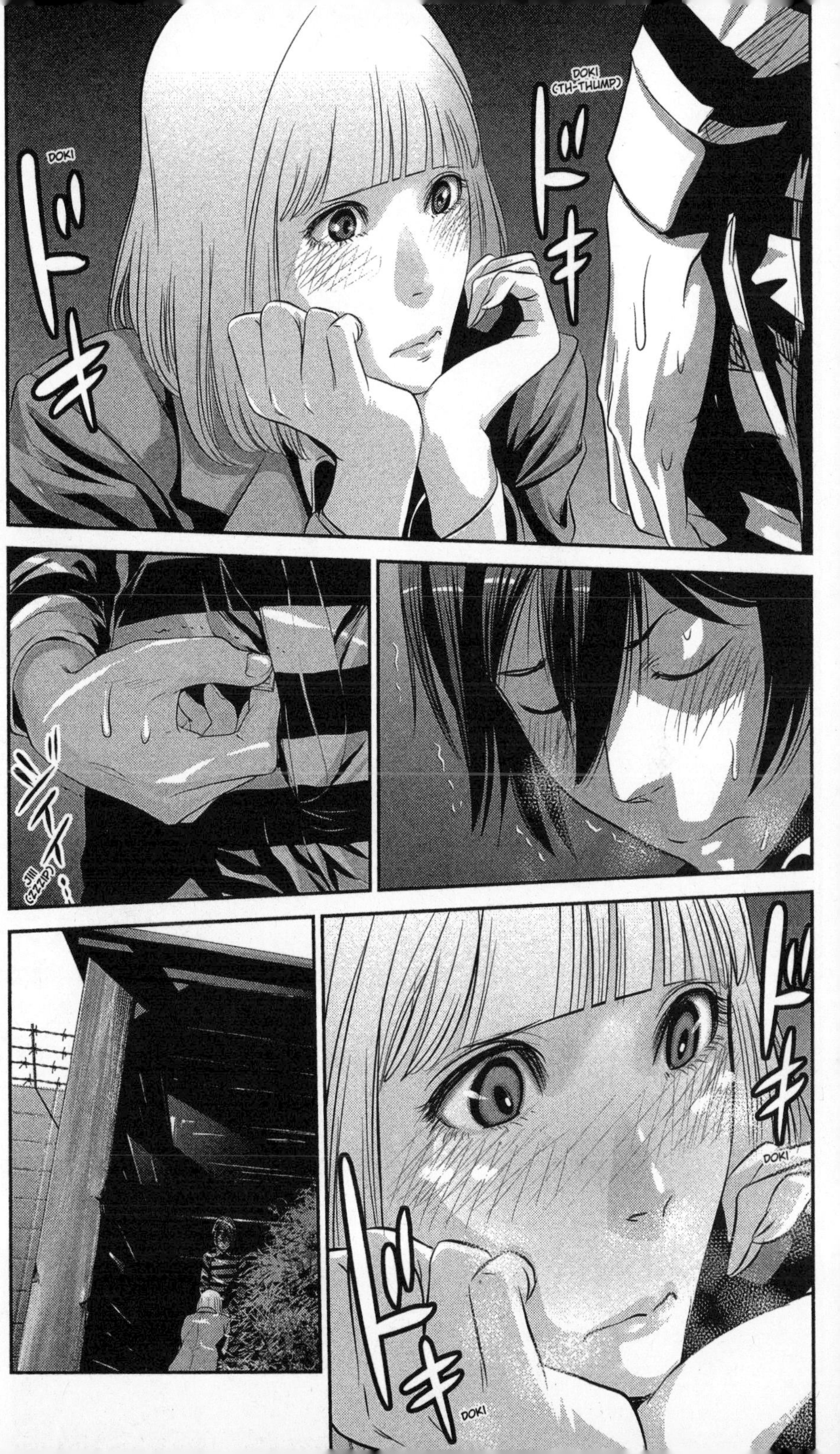

DOKI (TH-THUMP)
ドキ
DOKI
ドキ
ジィ〜
JIII (ZZZIP)
ドキ
DOKI
ドキ
DOKI

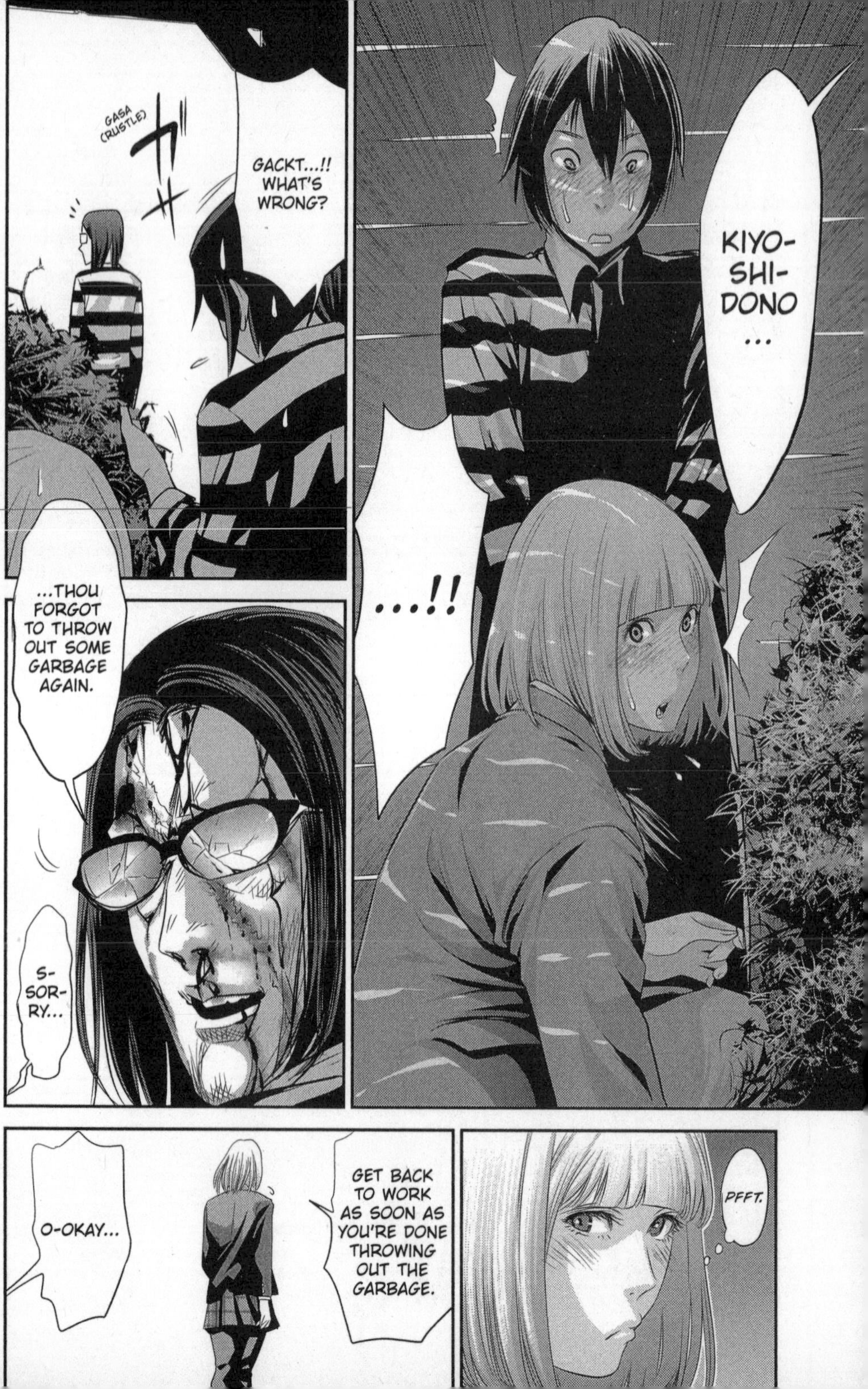
KIYO-SHI-DONO...
...!!
GASA (RUSTLE)
GACKT...!! WHAT'S WRONG?
...THOU FORGOT TO THROW OUT SOME GARBAGE AGAIN.
S-SORRY...
PFFT.
GET BACK TO WORK AS SOON AS YOU'RE DONE THROWING OUT THE GARBAGE.
O-OKAY...

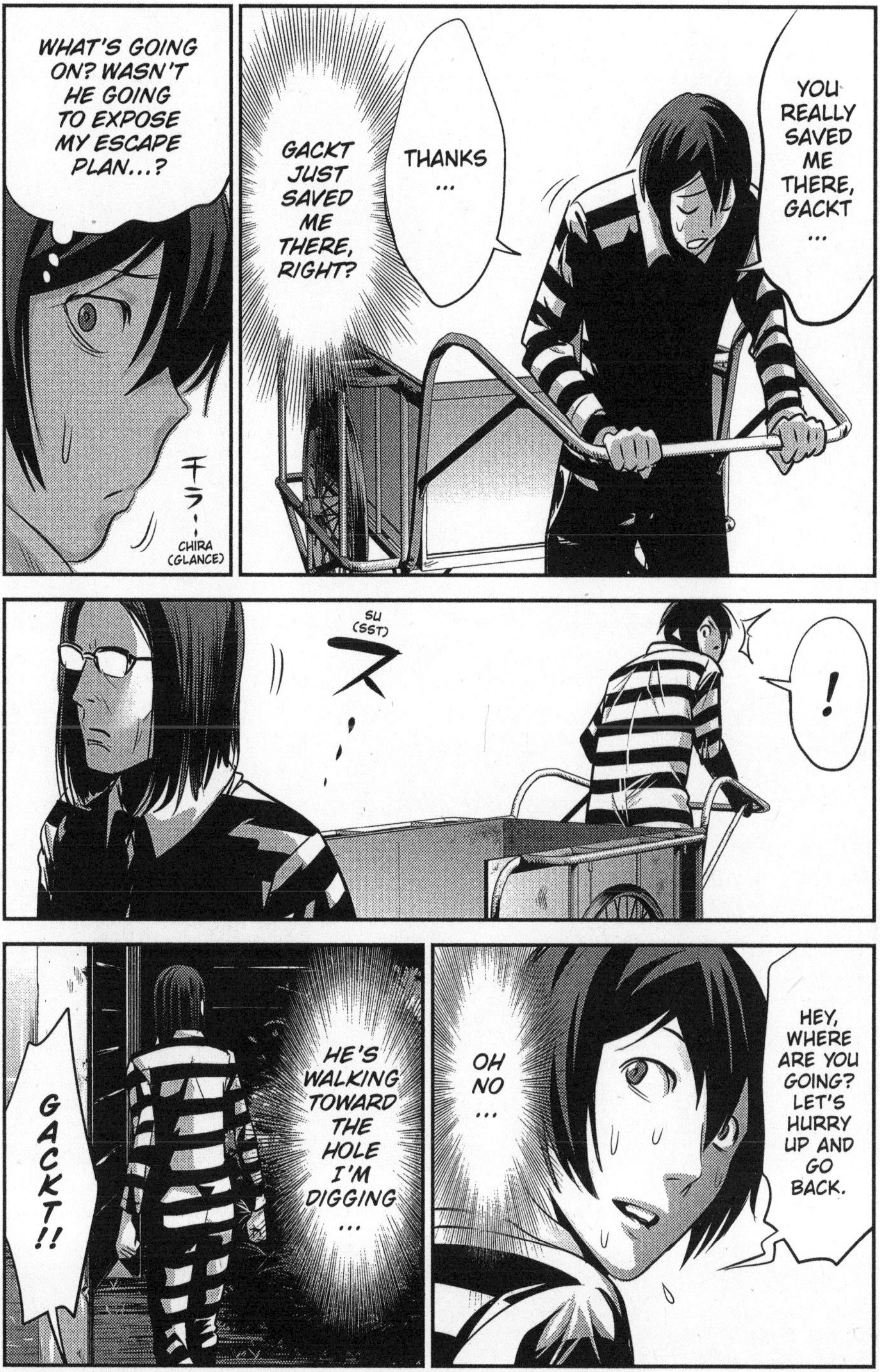
YOU REALLY SAVED ME THERE, GACKT ...
THANKS ...
GACKT JUST SAVED ME THERE, RIGHT?
WHAT'S GOING ON? WASN'T HE GOING TO EXPOSE MY ESCAPE PLAN...?
チラ・・
CHIRA (GLANCE)
!
ス
SU (SST)
HEY, WHERE ARE YOU GOING? LET'S HURRY UP AND GO BACK.
OH NO ...
HE'S WALKING TOWARD THE HOLE I'M DIGGING ...
GACKT!!

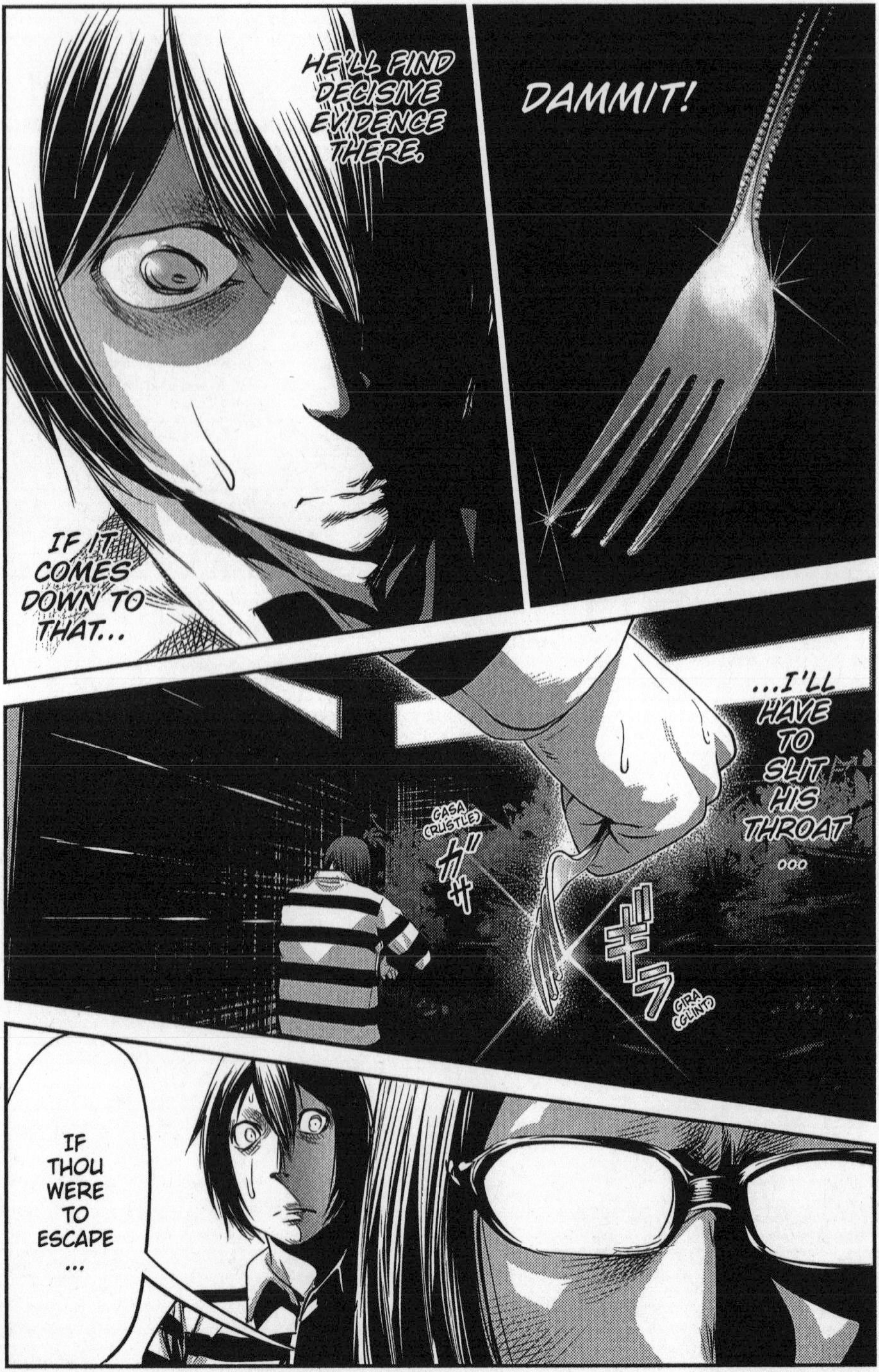
DAMMIT!
HE'LL FIND DECISIVE EVIDENCE THERE.
IF IT COMES DOWN TO THAT...
...I'LL HAVE TO SLIT HIS THROAT...
GASA (RUSTLE)
ガサ
ギラ
GIRA (GLINT)
IF THOU WERE TO ESCAPE...

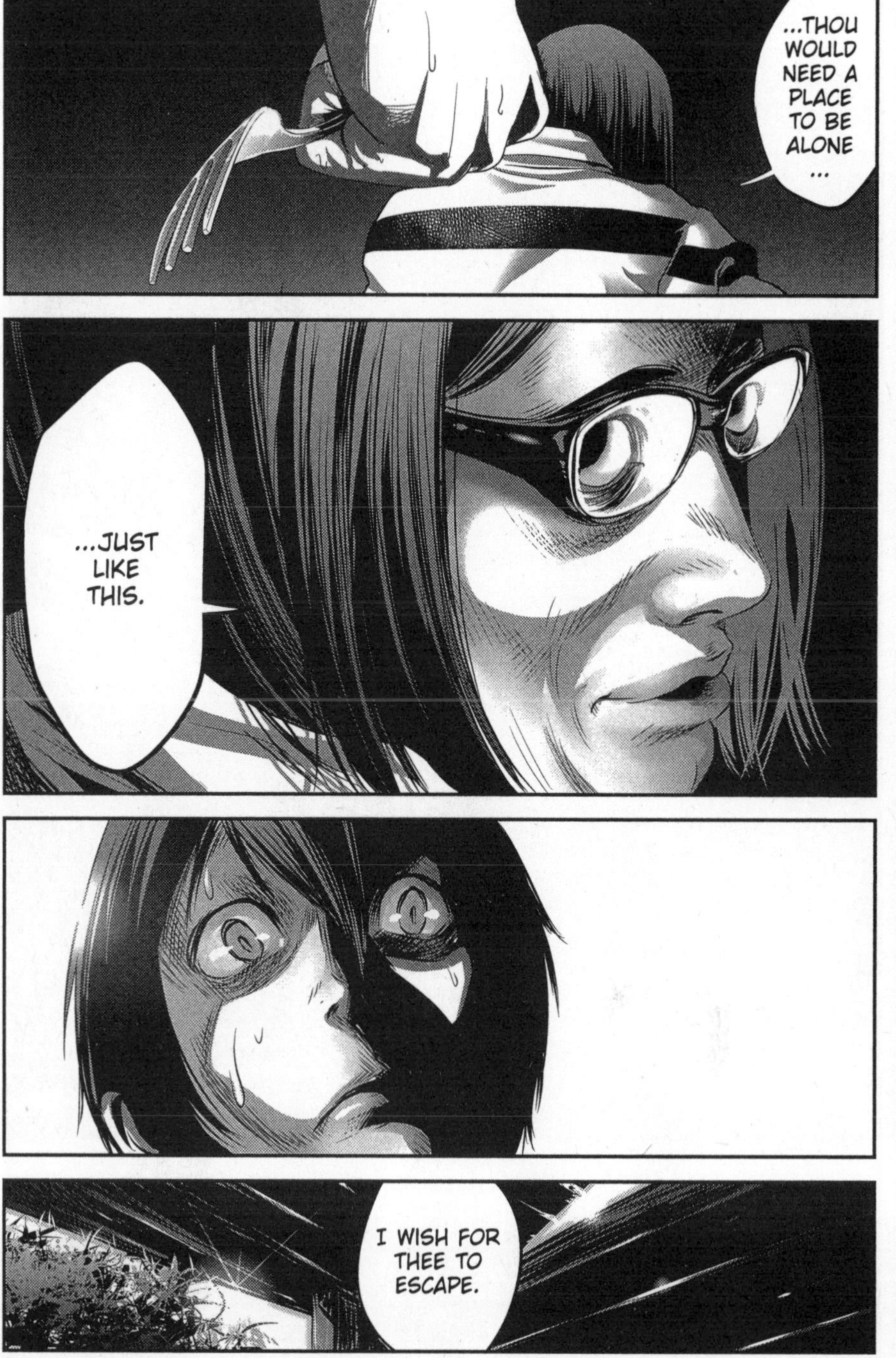
...THOU WOULD NEED A PLACE TO BE ALONE ...
...JUST LIKE THIS.
I WISH FOR THEE TO ESCAPE.

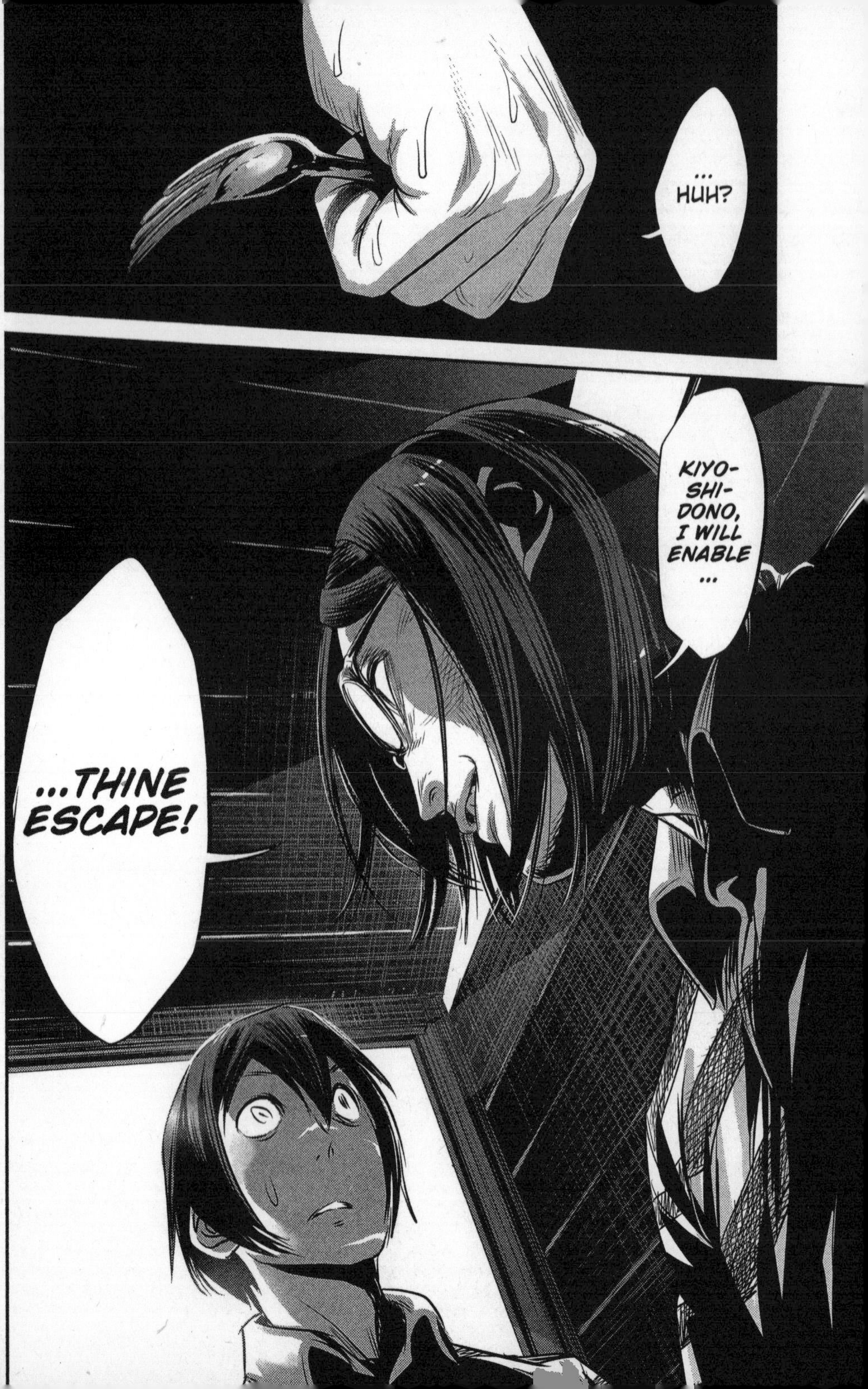
...HUH?
KIYO-SHI-DONO, I WILL ENABLE...
...THINE ESCAPE!

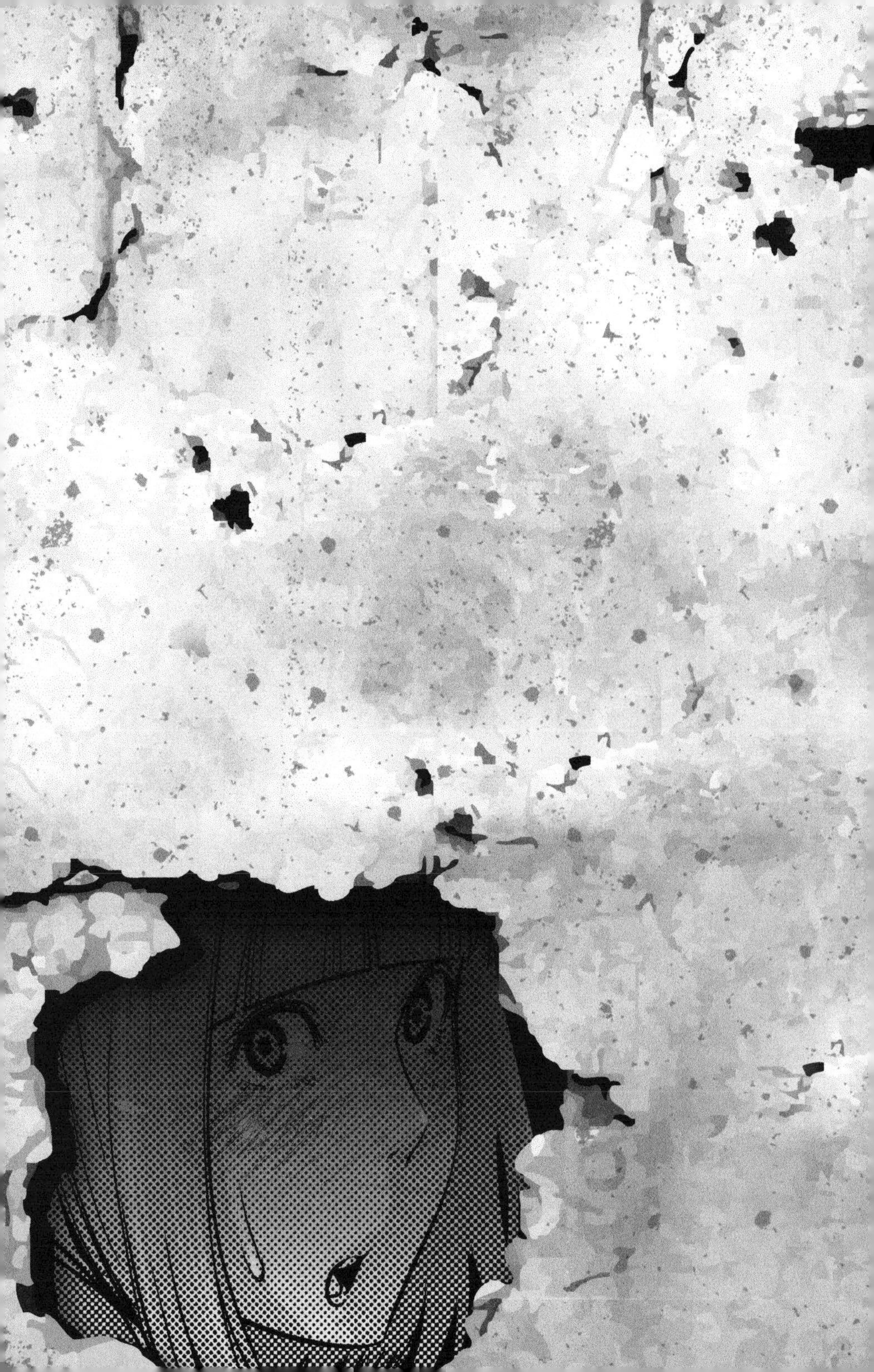

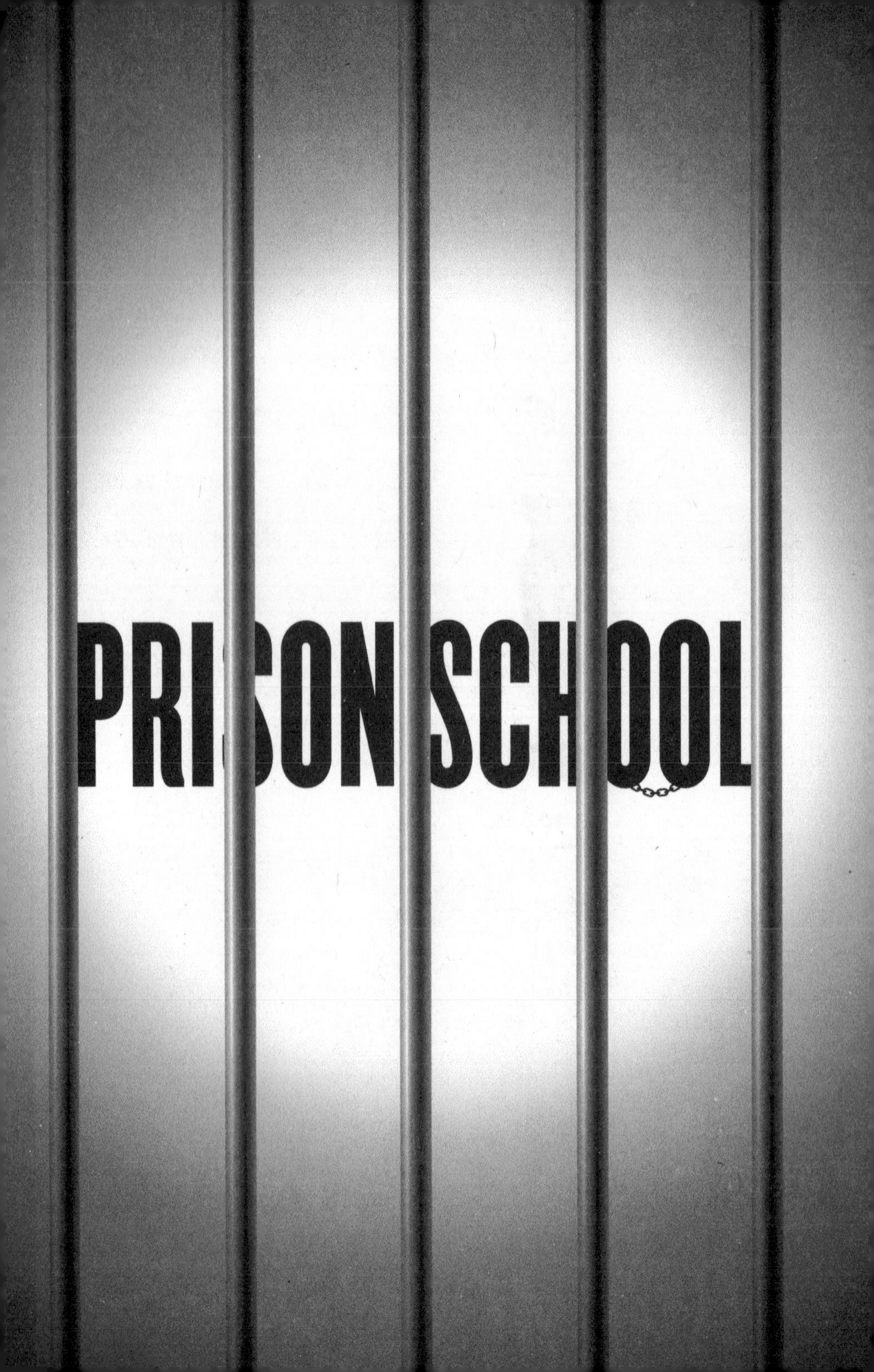
PRISON SCHOOL

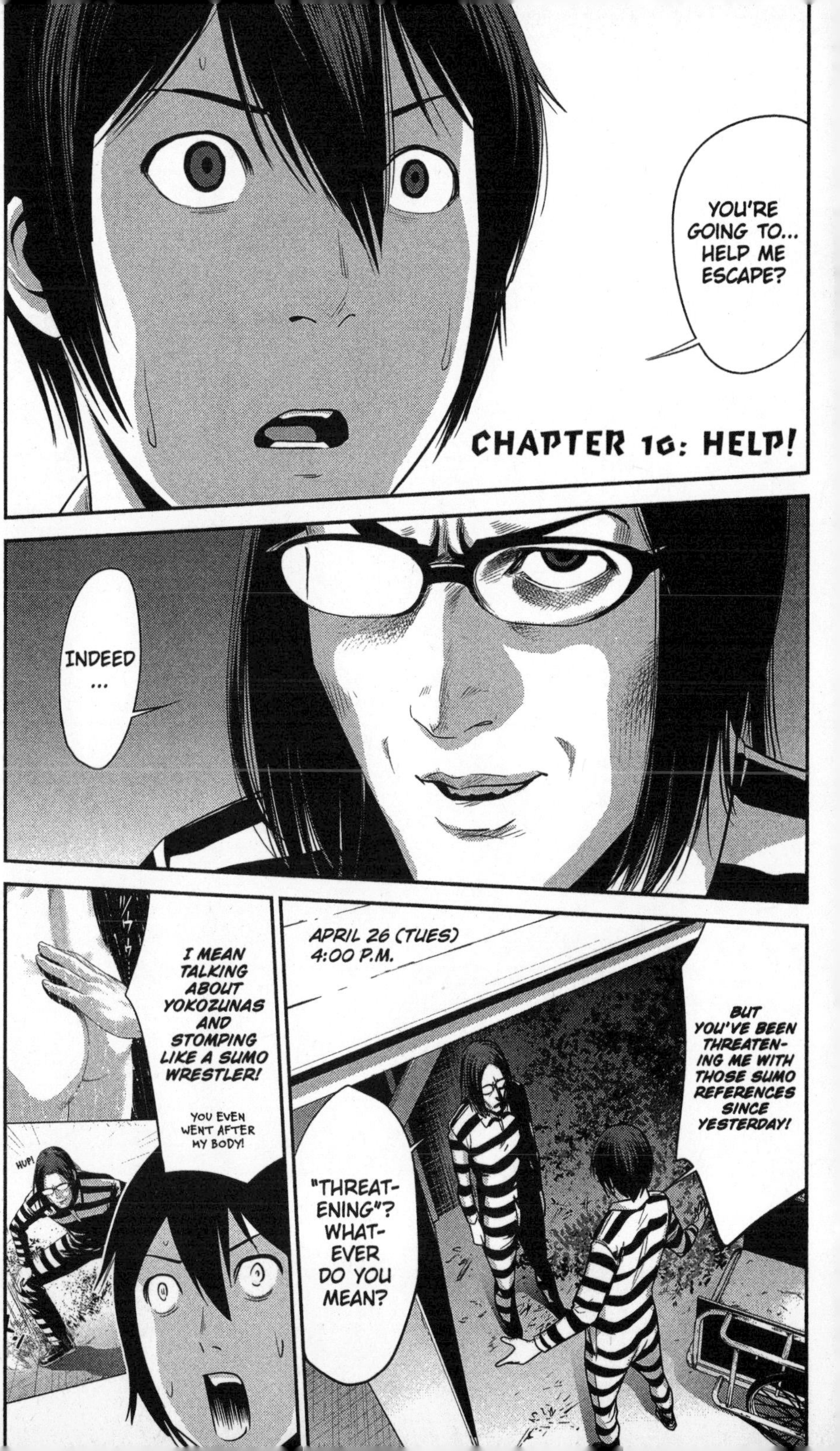
YOU'RE GOING TO... HELP ME ESCAPE?
CHAPTER 10: HELP!
INDEED ...
APRIL 26 (TUES) 4:00 P.M.
BUT YOU'VE BEEN THREATEN-ING ME WITH THOSE SUMO REFERENCES SINCE YESTERDAY!
"THREAT-ENING"? WHAT-EVER DO YOU MEAN?
I MEAN TALKING ABOUT YOKOZUNAS AND STOMPING LIKE A SUMO WRESTLER!
YOU EVEN WENT AFTER MY BODY!
HUP!

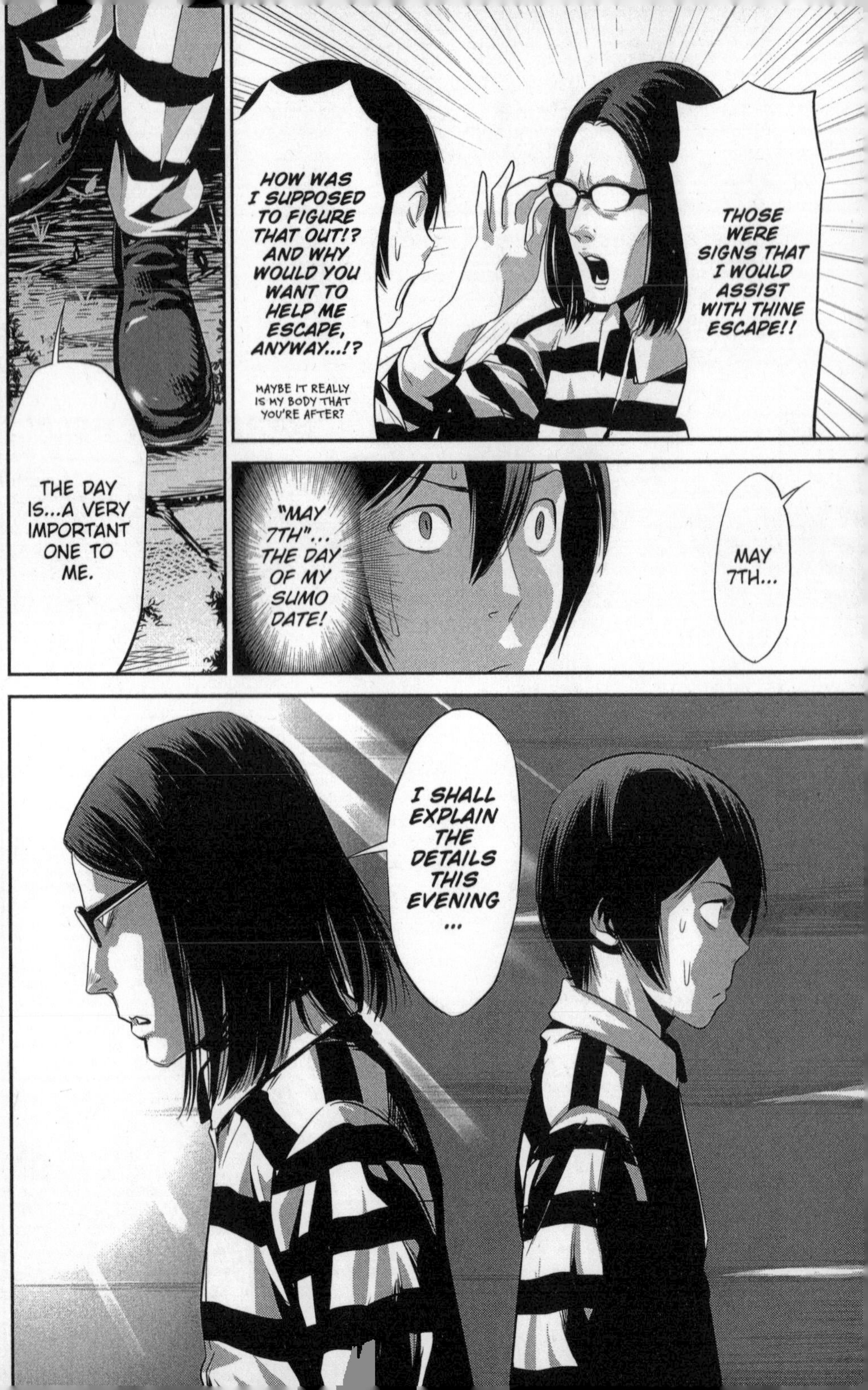
THOSE WERE SIGNS THAT I WOULD ASSIST WITH THINE ESCAPE!!
HOW WAS I SUPPOSED TO FIGURE THAT OUT!? AND WHY WOULD YOU WANT TO HELP ME ESCAPE, ANYWAY...!?
MAYBE IT REALLY IS MY BODY THAT YOU'RE AFTER?
MAY 7TH...
"MAY 7TH"... THE DAY OF MY SUMO DATE!
THE DAY IS...A VERY IMPORTANT ONE TO ME.
I SHALL EXPLAIN THE DETAILS THIS EVENING ...

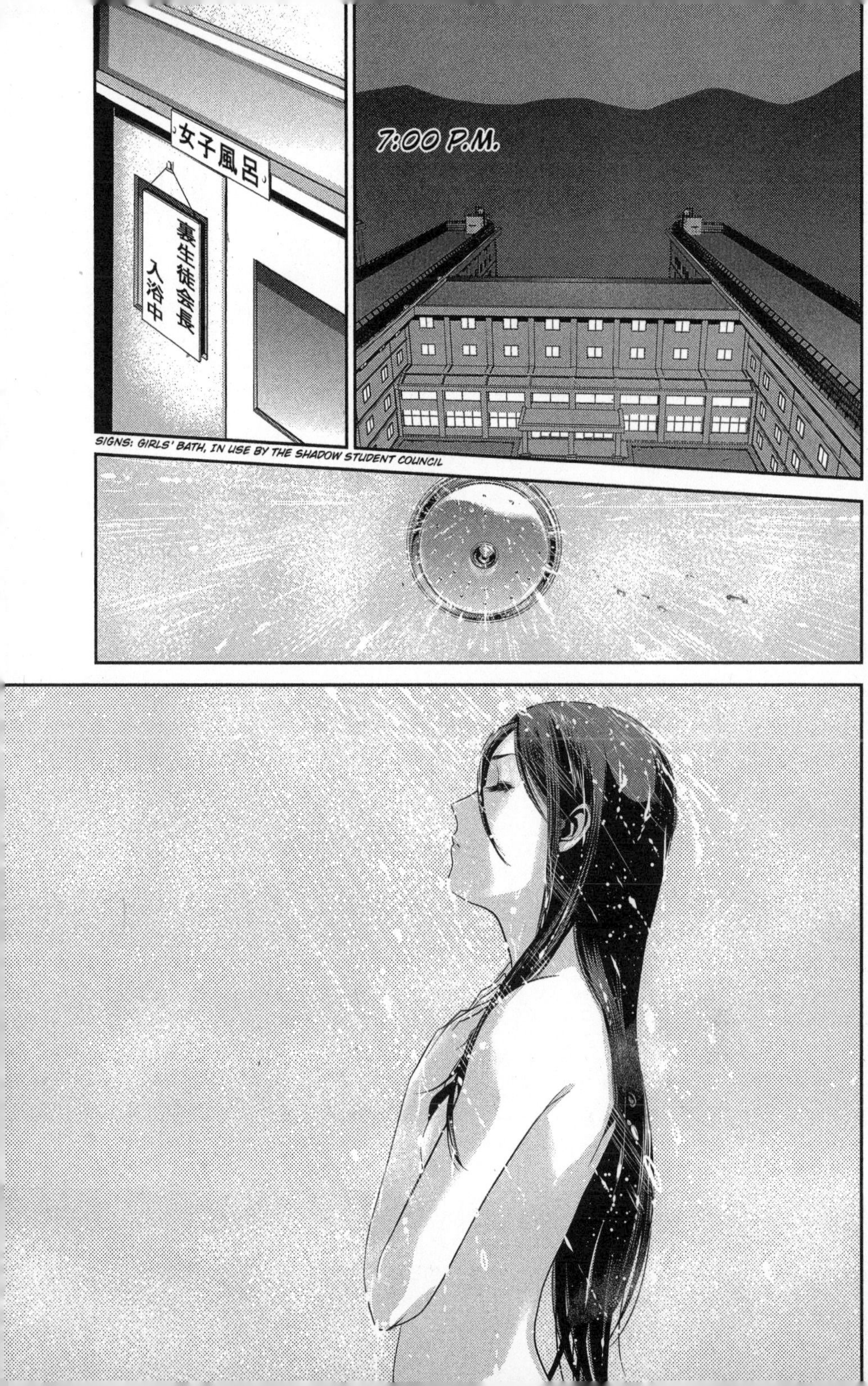
7:00 P.M.
女子風呂
裏生徒会長
入浴中
SIGNS: GIRLS' BATH, IN USE BY THE SHADOW STUDENT COUNCIL

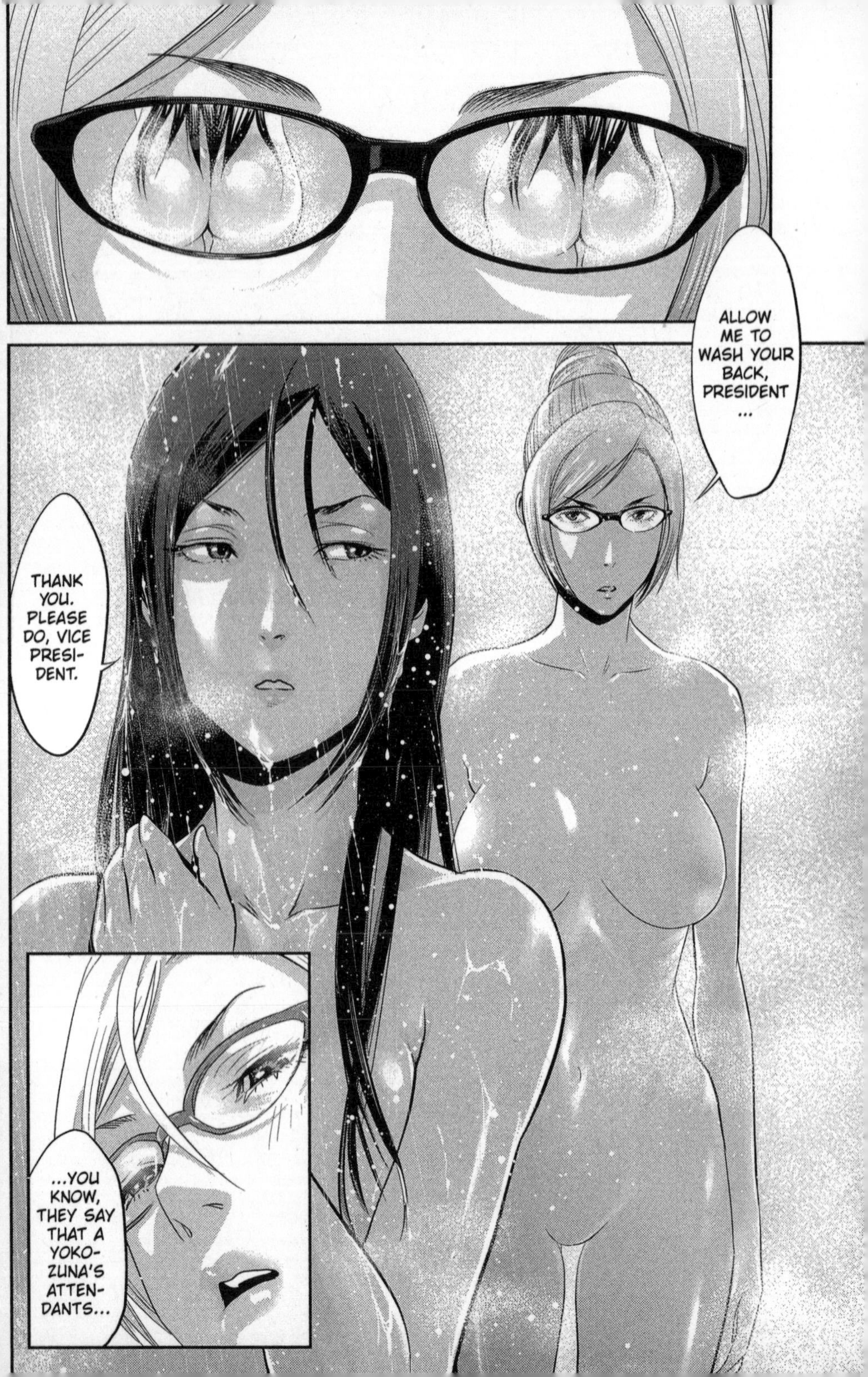
ALLOW ME TO WASH YOUR BACK, PRESIDENT ...
THANK YOU. PLEASE DO, VICE PRESI-DENT.
...YOU KNOW, THEY SAY THAT A YOKO-ZUNA'S ATTEN-DANTS...

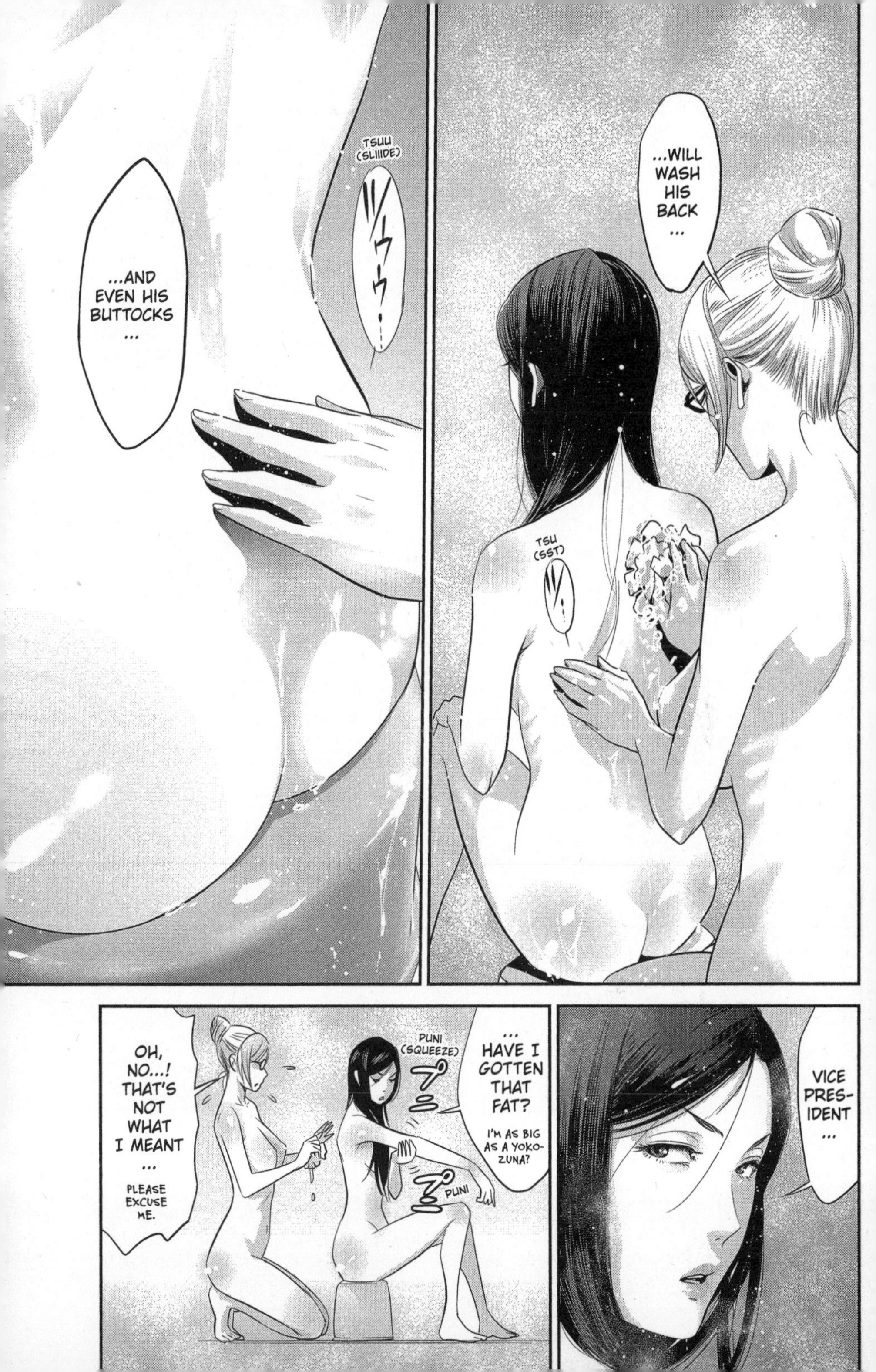
...WILL WASH HIS BACK ...
TSU (SST)
TSUU (SLIIIDE)
...AND EVEN HIS BUTTOCKS ...
VICE PRESIDENT ...
... HAVE I GOTTEN THAT FAT?
I'M AS BIG AS A YOKOZUNA?
PUNI (SQUEEZE)
PUNI
OH, NO...! THAT'S NOT WHAT I MEANT ...
PLEASE EXCUSE ME.

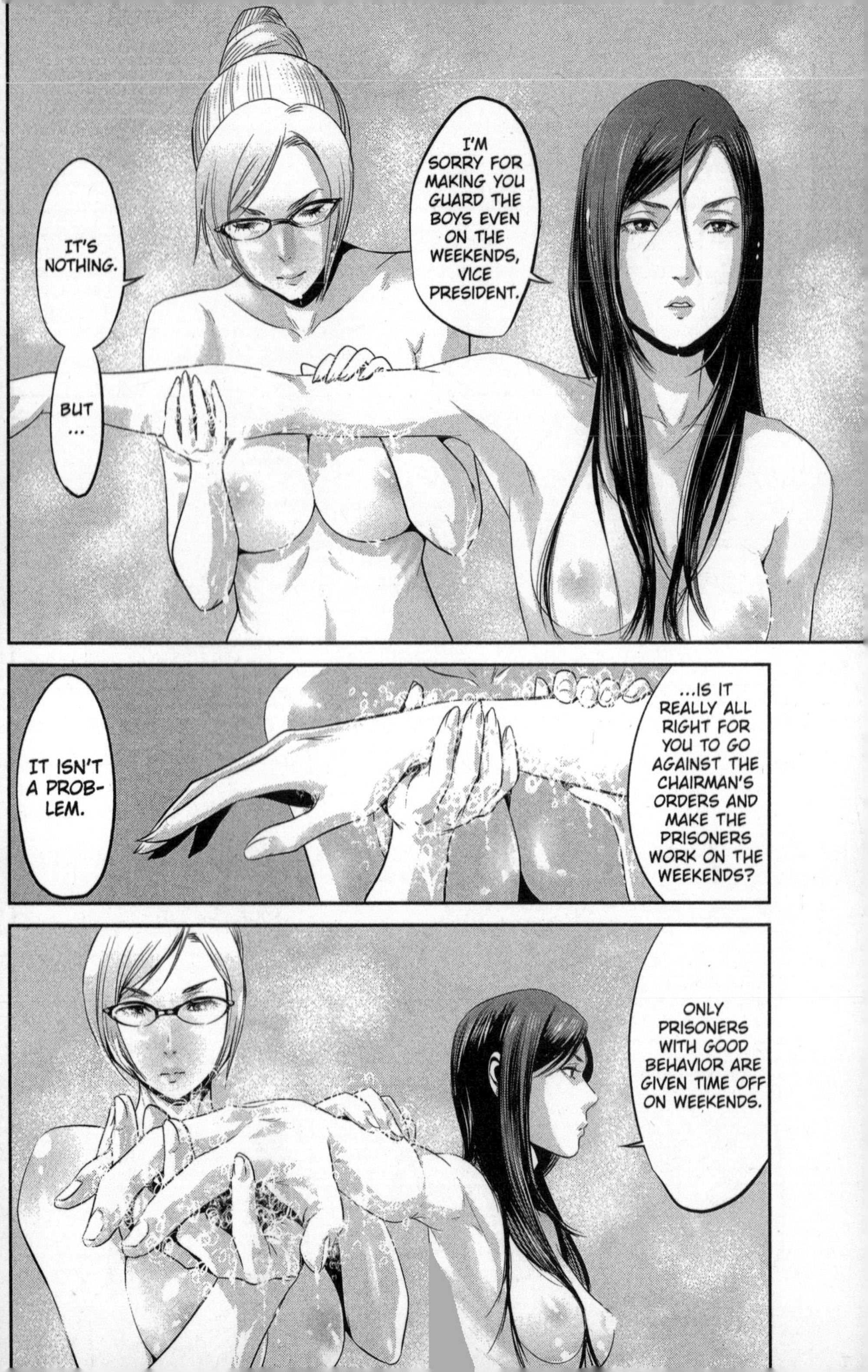
I'M SORRY FOR MAKING YOU GUARD THE BOYS EVEN ON THE WEEKENDS, VICE PRESIDENT.
IT'S NOTHING.
BUT ...
...IS IT REALLY ALL RIGHT FOR YOU TO GO AGAINST THE CHAIRMAN'S ORDERS AND MAKE THE PRISONERS WORK ON THE WEEKENDS?
IT ISN'T A PROB-LEM.
ONLY PRISONERS WITH GOOD BEHAVIOR ARE GIVEN TIME OFF ON WEEKENDS.

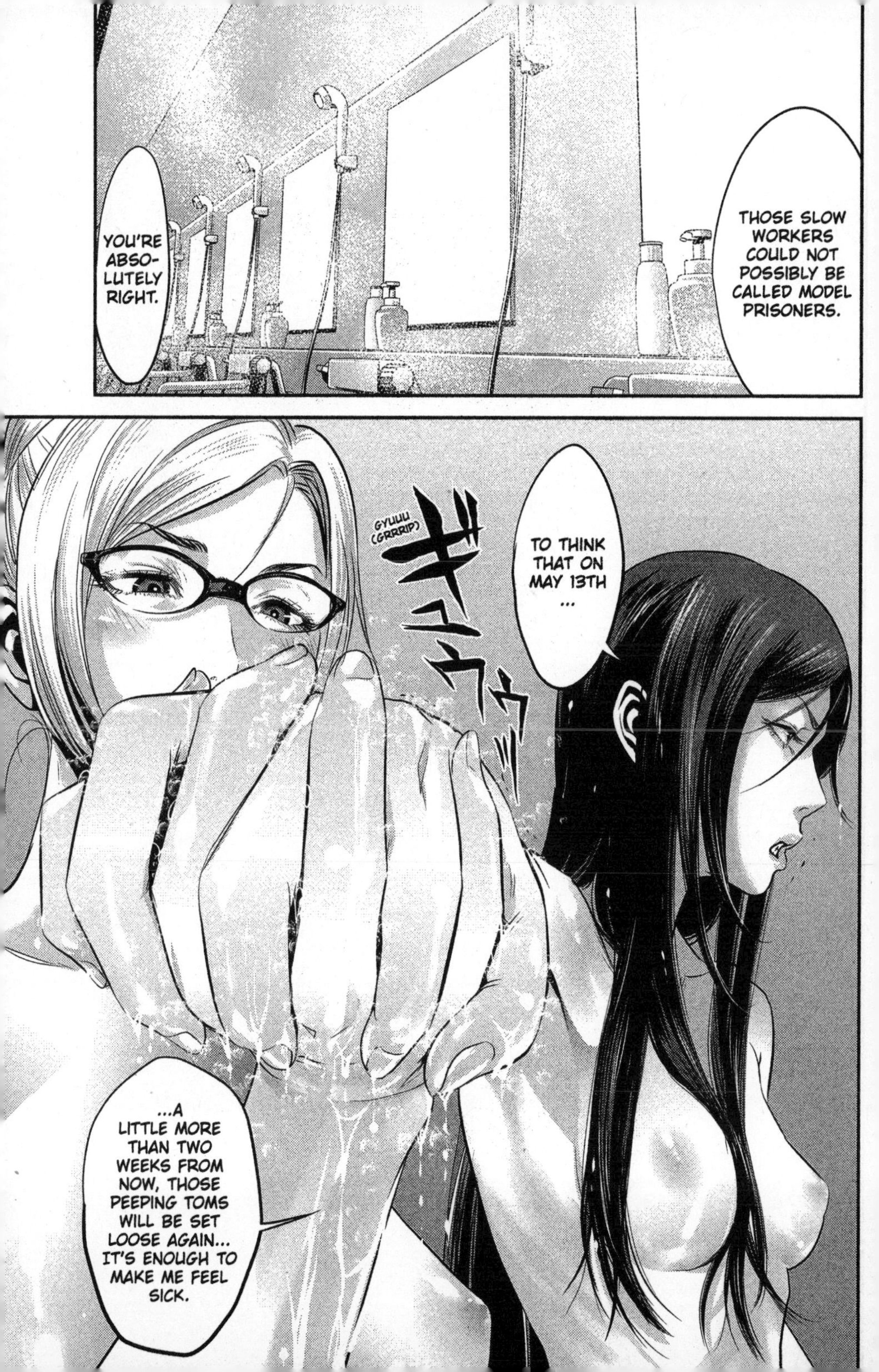
THOSE SLOW WORKERS COULD NOT POSSIBLY BE CALLED MODEL PRISONERS.
YOU'RE ABSO-LUTELY RIGHT.
TO THINK THAT ON MAY 13TH ...
GYUUU (GRRRIP)
...A LITTLE MORE THAN TWO WEEKS FROM NOW, THOSE PEEPING TOMS WILL BE SET LOOSE AGAIN... IT'S ENOUGH TO MAKE ME FEEL SICK.

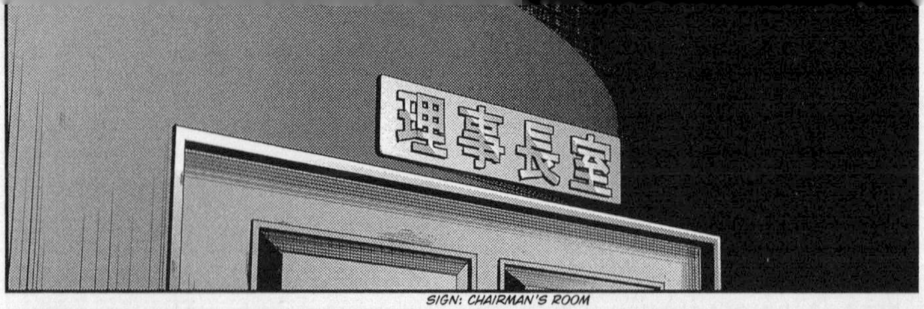
理事長室
SIGN: CHAIRMAN'S ROOM

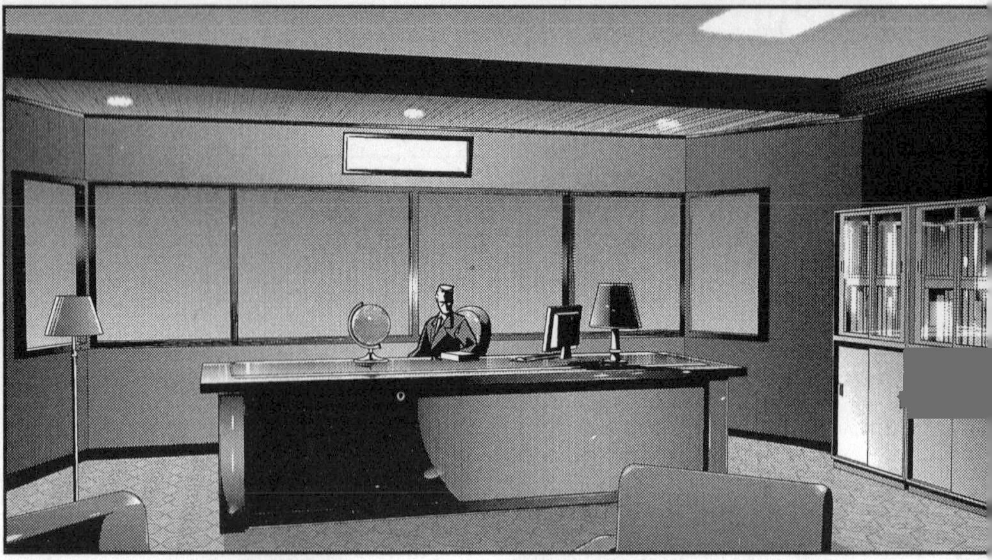

BOOK: OFFICIAL SHADOW STUDENT COUNCIL SHADOW GUIDEBOOK 2011 EDITION

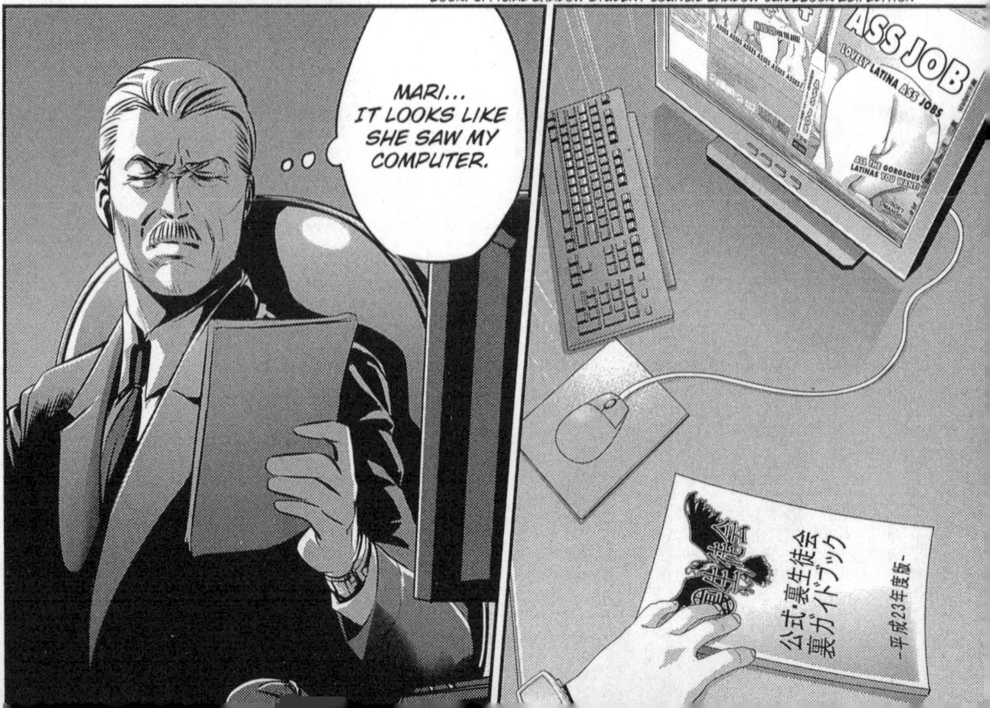
MARI... IT LOOKS LIKE SHE SAW MY COMPUTER.
ASS JOB
LOVELY LATINA ASS JOBS
ALL THE GORGEOUS LATINAS YOU WANT!
公式·裏生徒会裏ガイドブック
-平成23年度版-

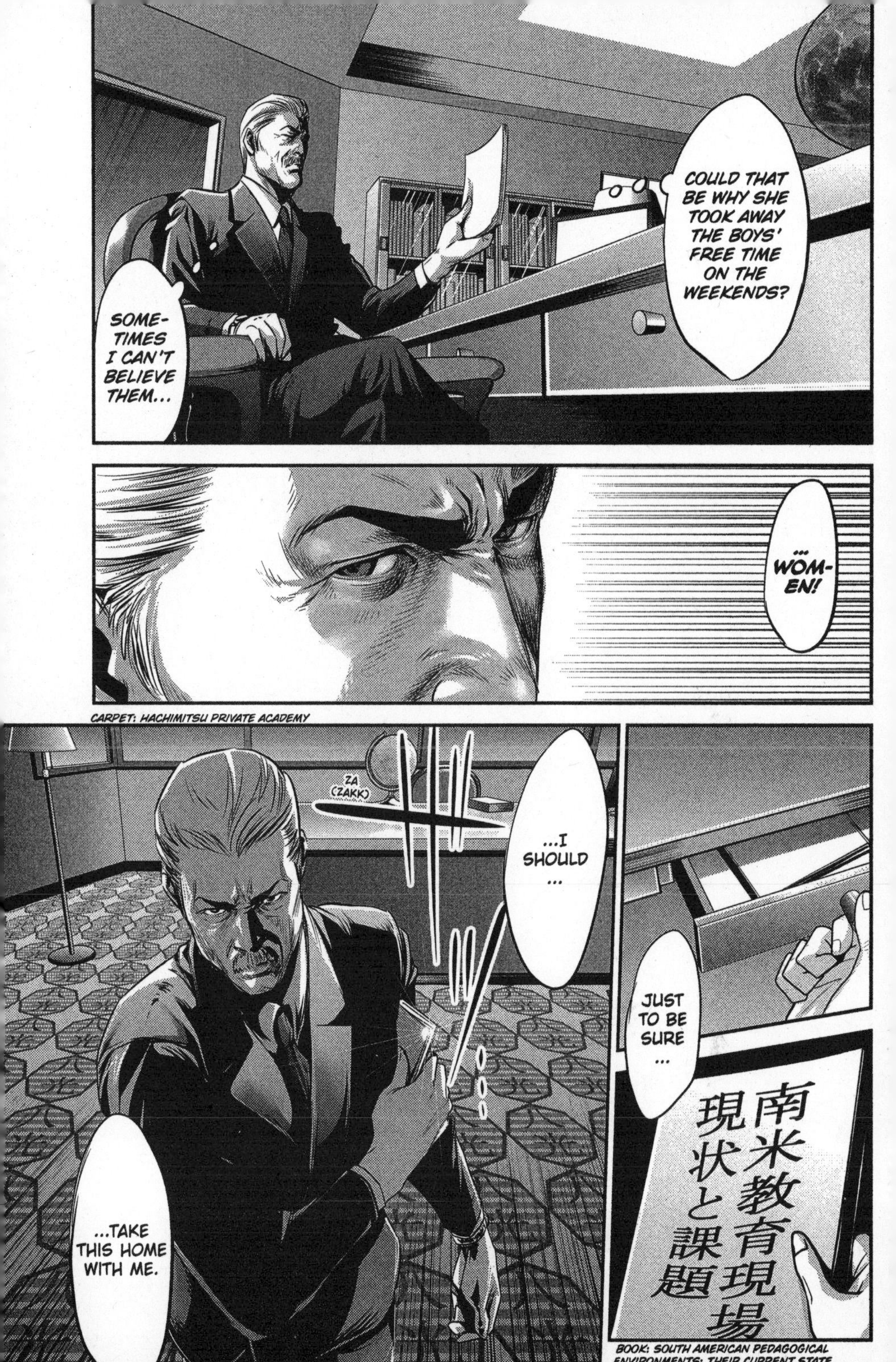
COULD THAT BE WHY SHE TOOK AWAY THE BOYS' FREE TIME ON THE WEEKENDS?
SOME-TIMES I CAN'T BELIEVE THEM...
...WOM-EN!
CARPET: HACHIMITSU PRIVATE ACADEMY
JUST TO BE SURE ...
南米教育現場
現状と課題
BOOK: SOUTH AMERICAN PEDAGOGICAL ENVIRONMENTS: THEIR CURRENT STATE AND FUTURE CHALLENGES
...I SHOULD ...
ZA (ZAKK)
...TAKE THIS HOME WITH ME.

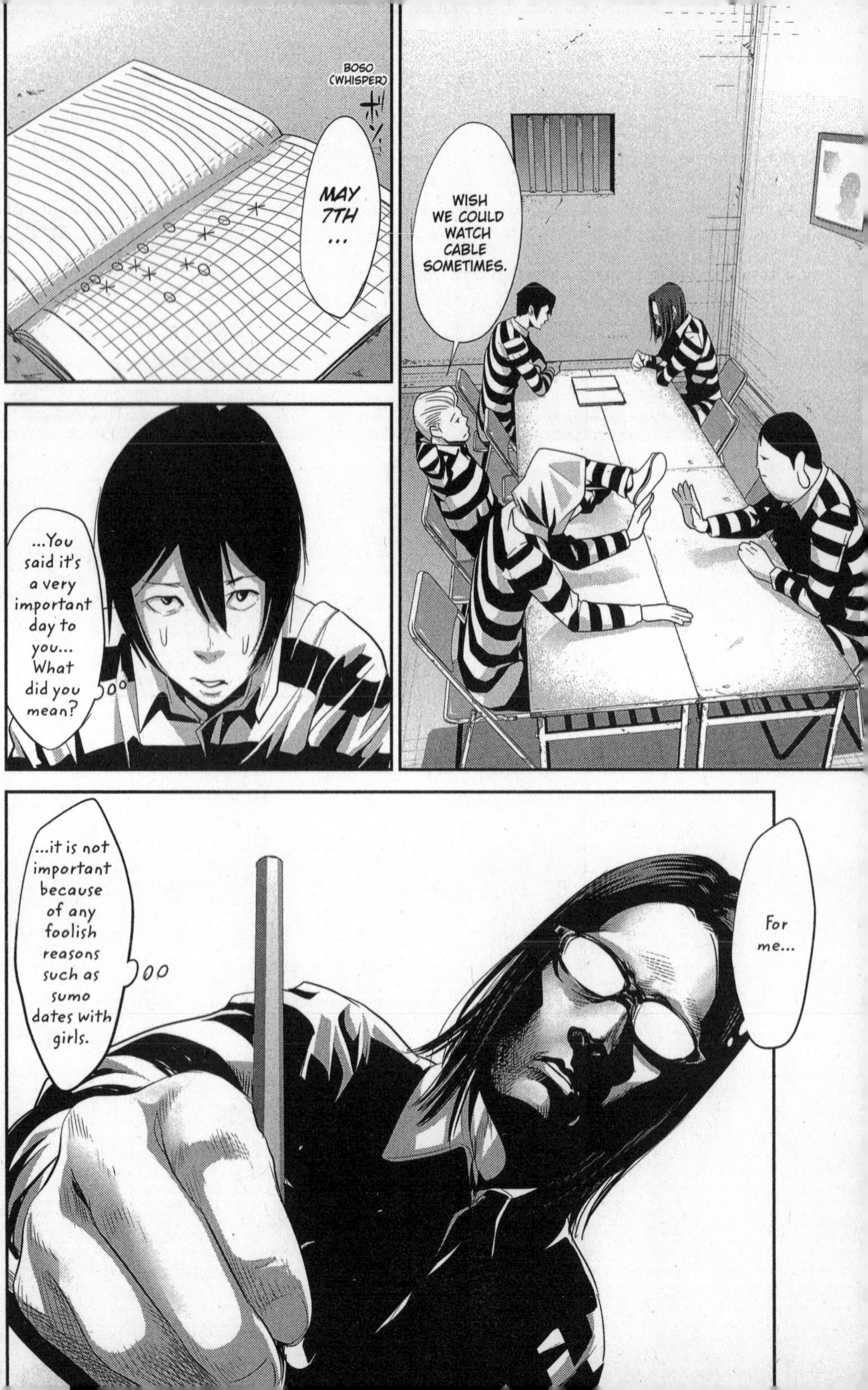
WISH WE COULD WATCH CABLE SOMETIMES.
BOSO (WHISPER)
MAY 7TH...
...You said it's a very important day to you... What did you mean?
For me...
...it is not important because of any foolish reasons such as sumo dates with girls.

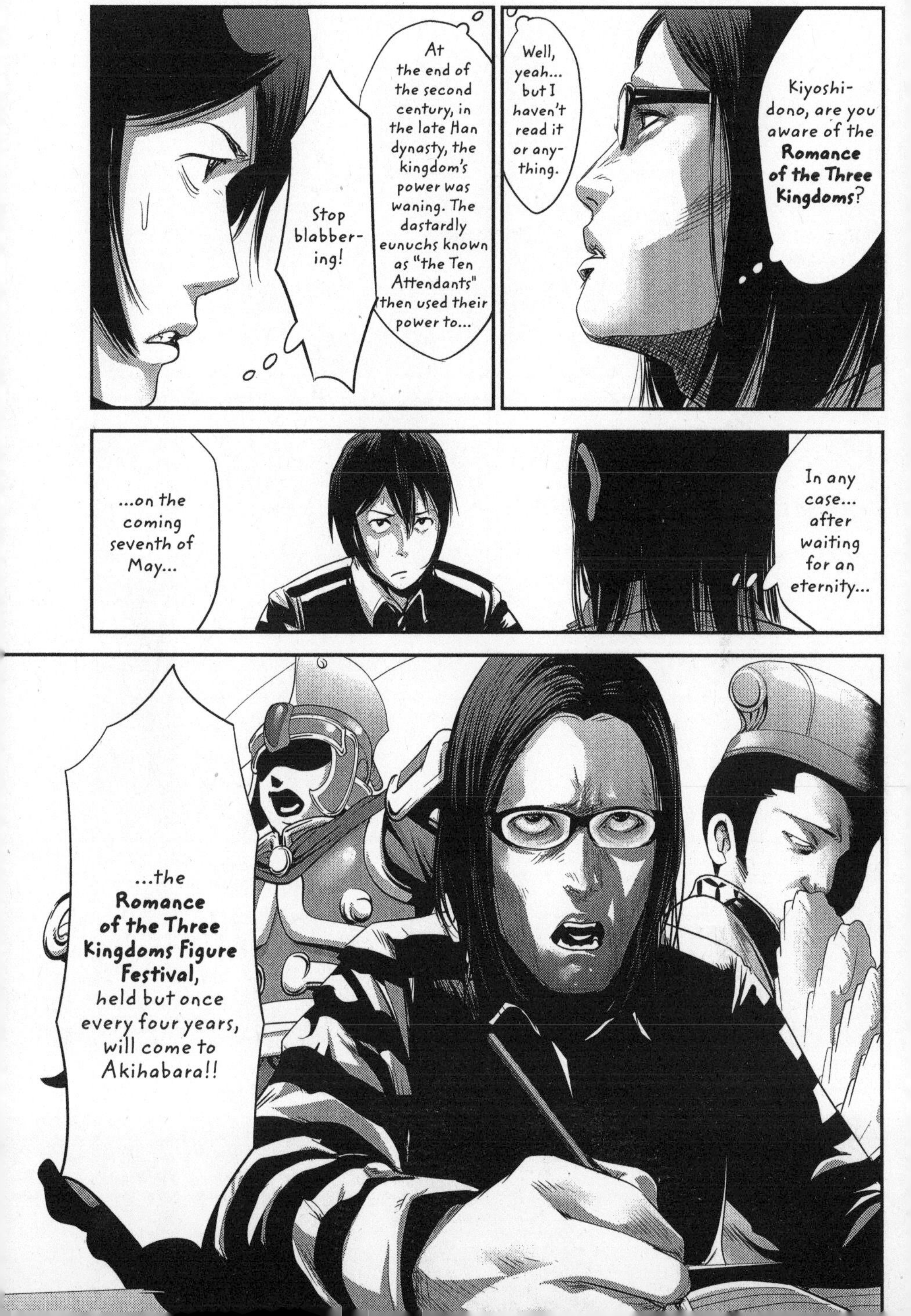
Kiyoshi-dono, are you aware of the **Romance of the Three Kingdoms**?
Well, yeah... but I haven't read it or anything.
At the end of the second century, in the late Han dynasty, the kingdom's power was waning. The dastardly eunuchs known as "the Ten Attendants" then used their power to...
Stop blabbering!
In any case... after waiting for an eternity...
...on the coming seventh of May...
...the **Romance of the Three Kingdoms Figure Festival**, held but once every four years, will come to Akihabara!!

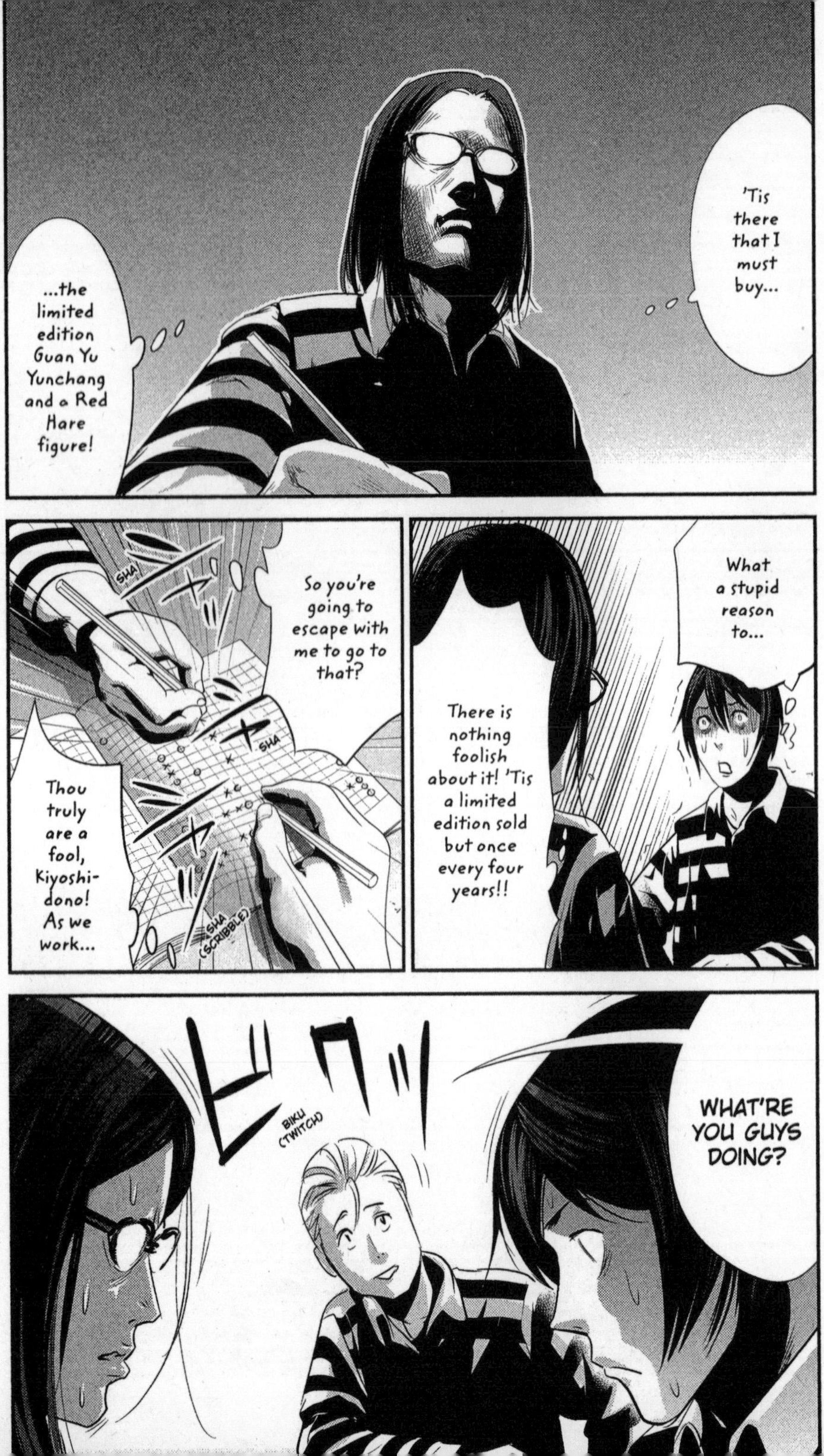
'Tis there that I must buy...
...the limited edition Guan Yu Yunchang and a Red Hare figure!
What a stupid reason to...
There is nothing foolish about it! 'Tis a limited edition sold but once every four years!!
So you're going to escape with me to go to that?
SHA
SHA
Thou truly are a fool, Kiyoshi-dono! As we work...
SHA (SCRIBBLE)
WHAT'RE YOU GUYS DOING?
BIKU (TWITCH)

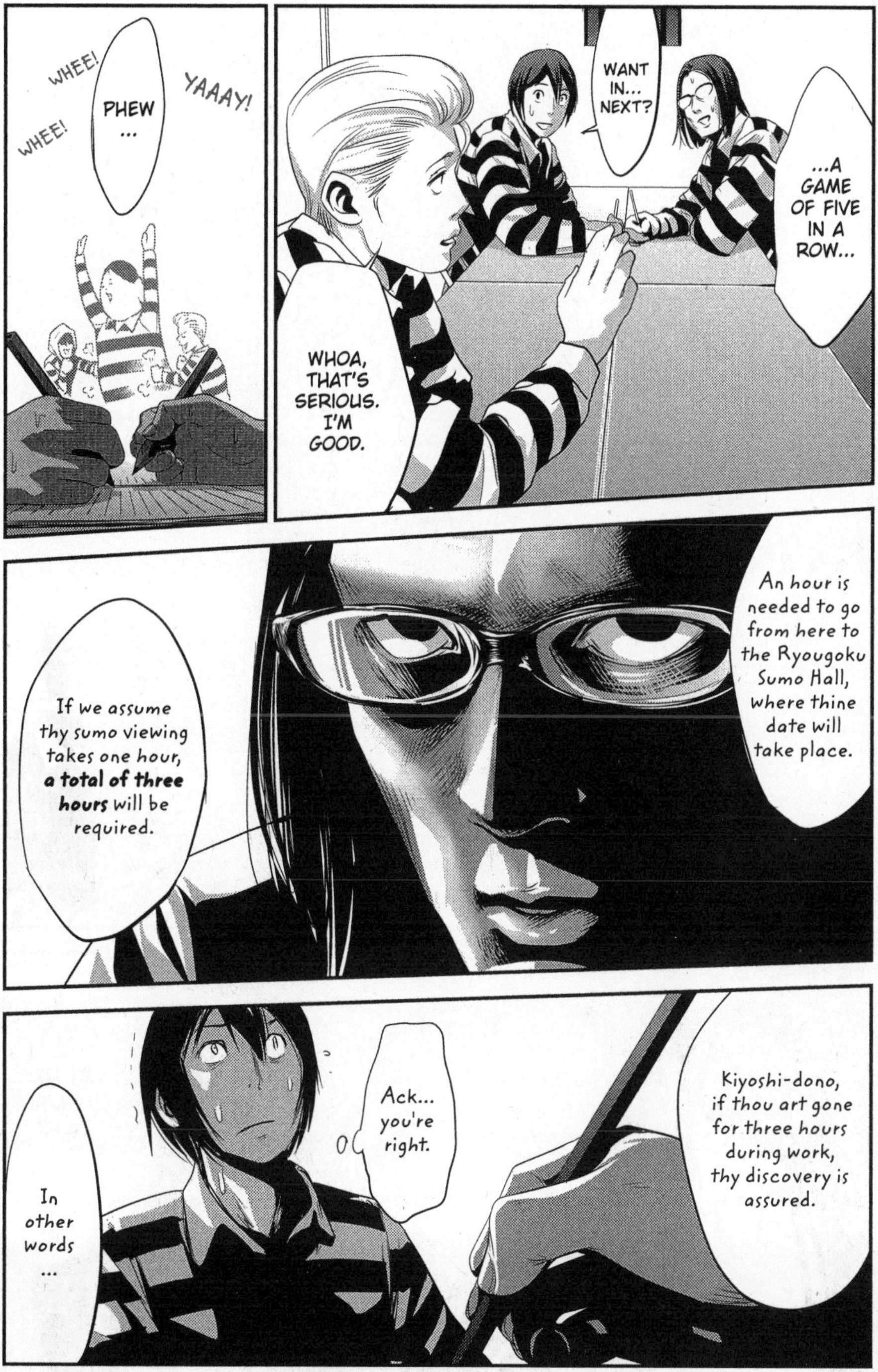
...A GAME OF FIVE IN A ROW...
WANT IN... NEXT?
WHOA, THAT'S SERIOUS. I'M GOOD.
YAAAY!
PHEW ...
WHEE!
WHEE!
An hour is needed to go from here to the Ryougoku Sumo Hall, where thine date will take place.
If we assume thy sumo viewing takes one hour, **a total of three hours** will be required.
Kiyoshi-dono, if thou art gone for three hours during work, thy discovery is assured.
Ack... you're right.
In other words ...

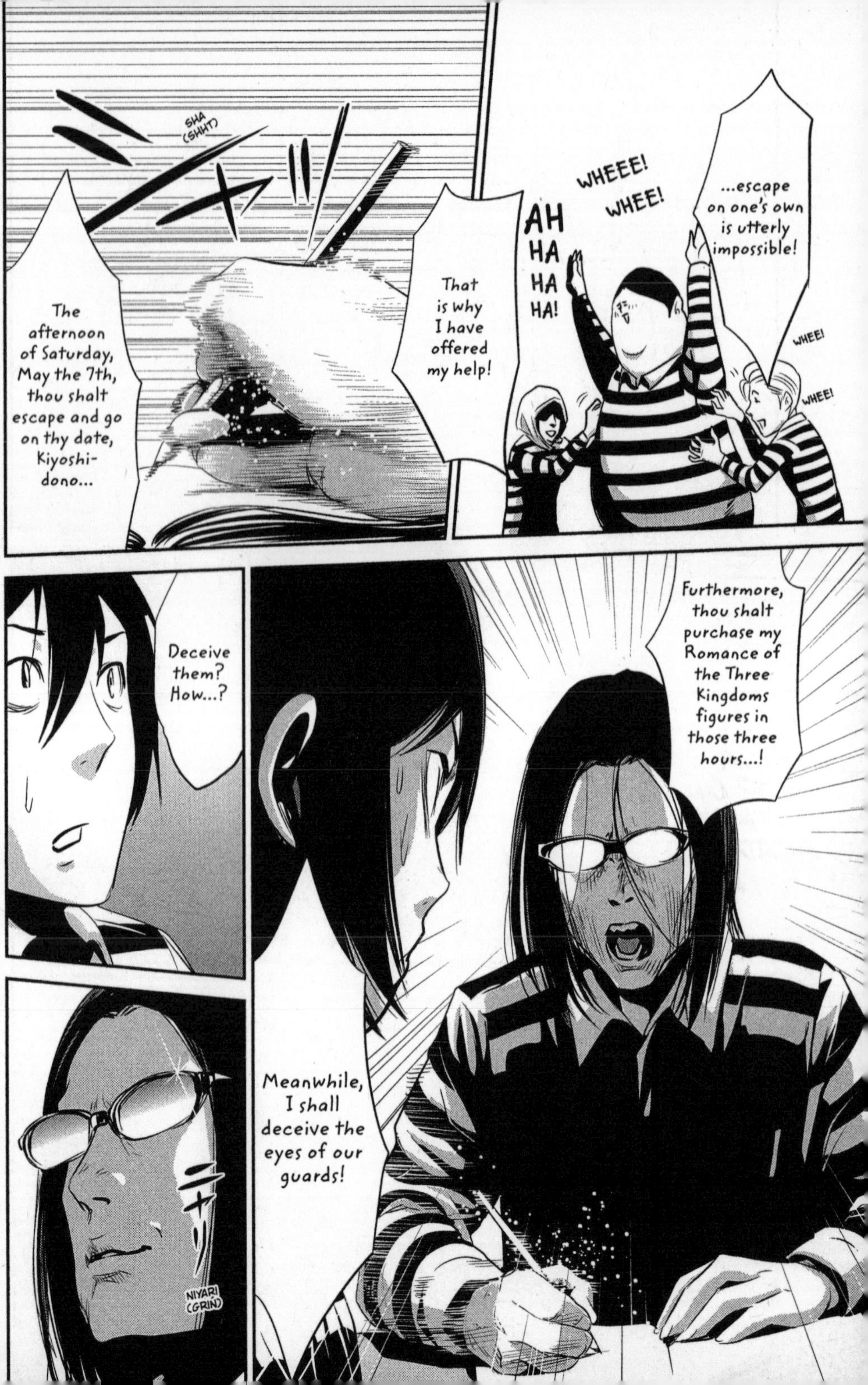
...escape on one's own is utterly impossible!
WHEEE! WHEE!
AH HA HA HA!
WHEE!
WHEE!
That is why I have offered my help!
SHA (SHHT)
The afternoon of Saturday, May the 7th, thou shalt escape and go on thy date, Kiyoshi-dono...
Furthermore, thou shalt purchase my Romance of the Three Kingdoms figures in those three hours...!
Deceive them? How...?
Meanwhile, I shall deceive the eyes of our guards!
NIYARI (GRIN)

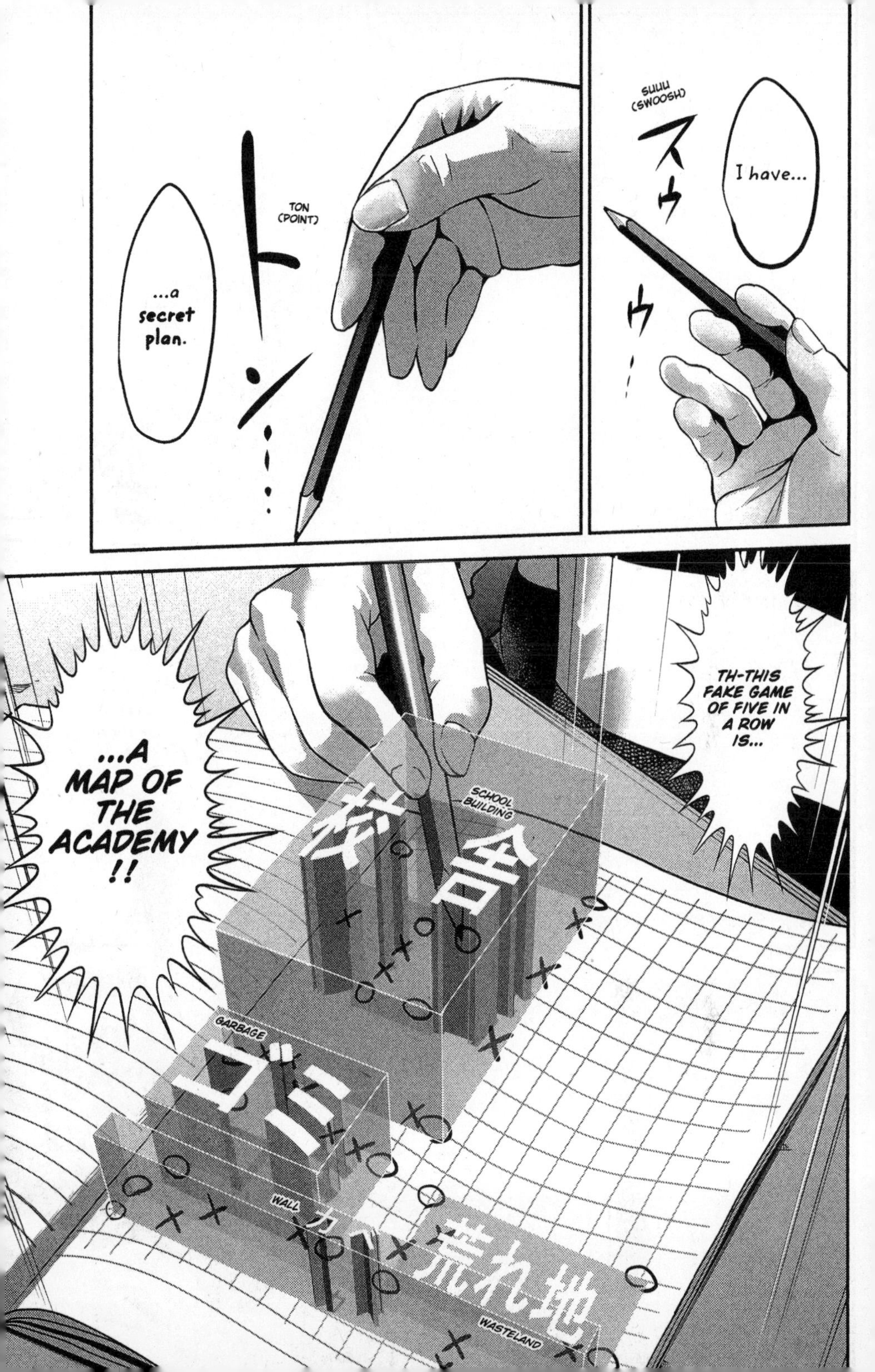
SUUU (SWOOSH)
I have...
TON (POINT)
...a secret plan.
TH-THIS FAKE GAME OF FIVE IN A ROW IS...
...A MAP OF THE ACADEMY!!
SCHOOL BUILDING
校舎
GARBAGE
ゴミ
WALL
カベ
WASTELAND
荒れ地

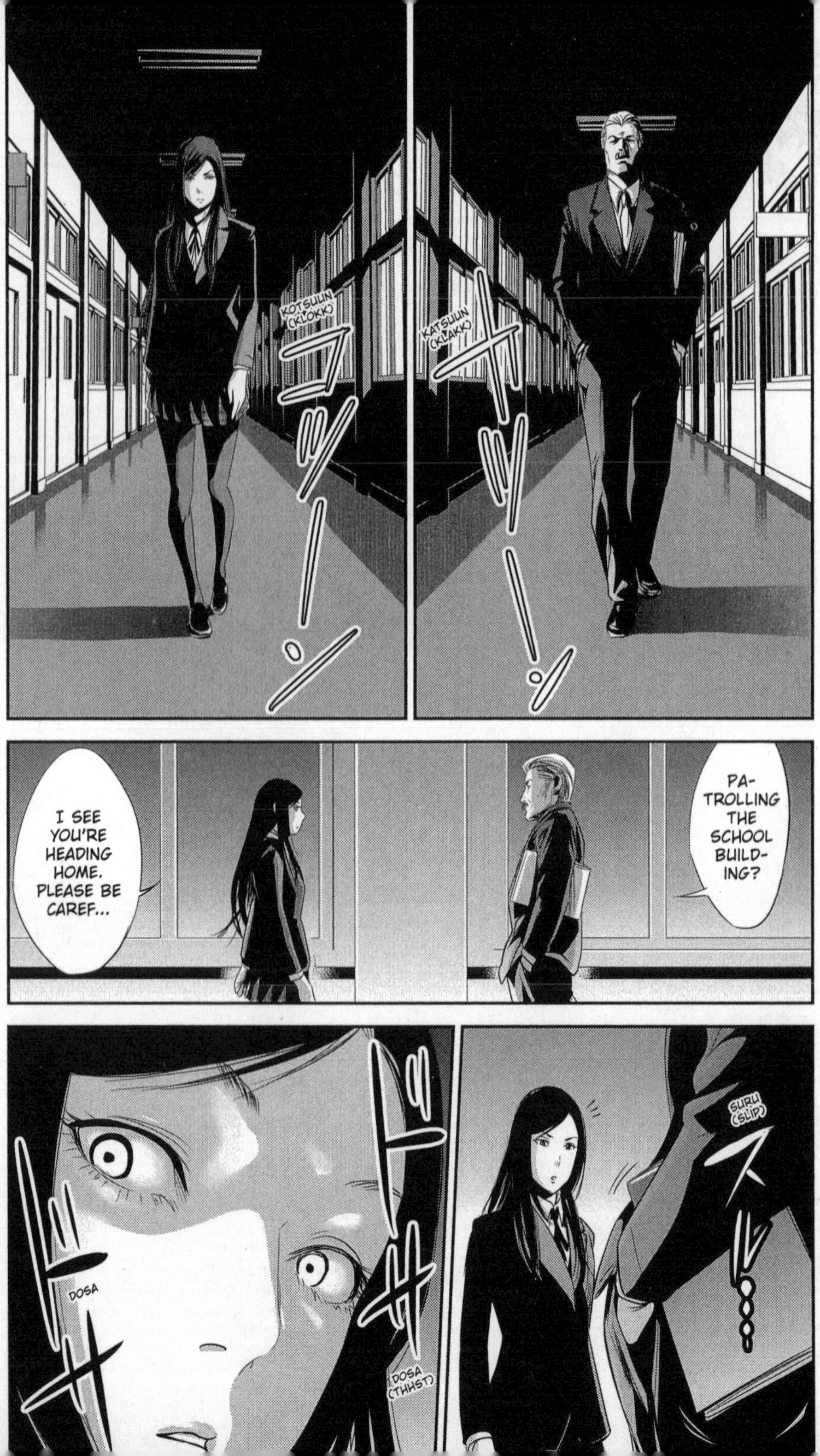

KATSUUN (KLAKK)
KOTSUUN (KLOKK)
PA-TROLLING THE SCHOOL BUILD-ING?
I SEE YOU'RE HEADING HOME. PLEASE BE CAREF...
SURU (SLIP)
DOSA (THHST)
DOSA

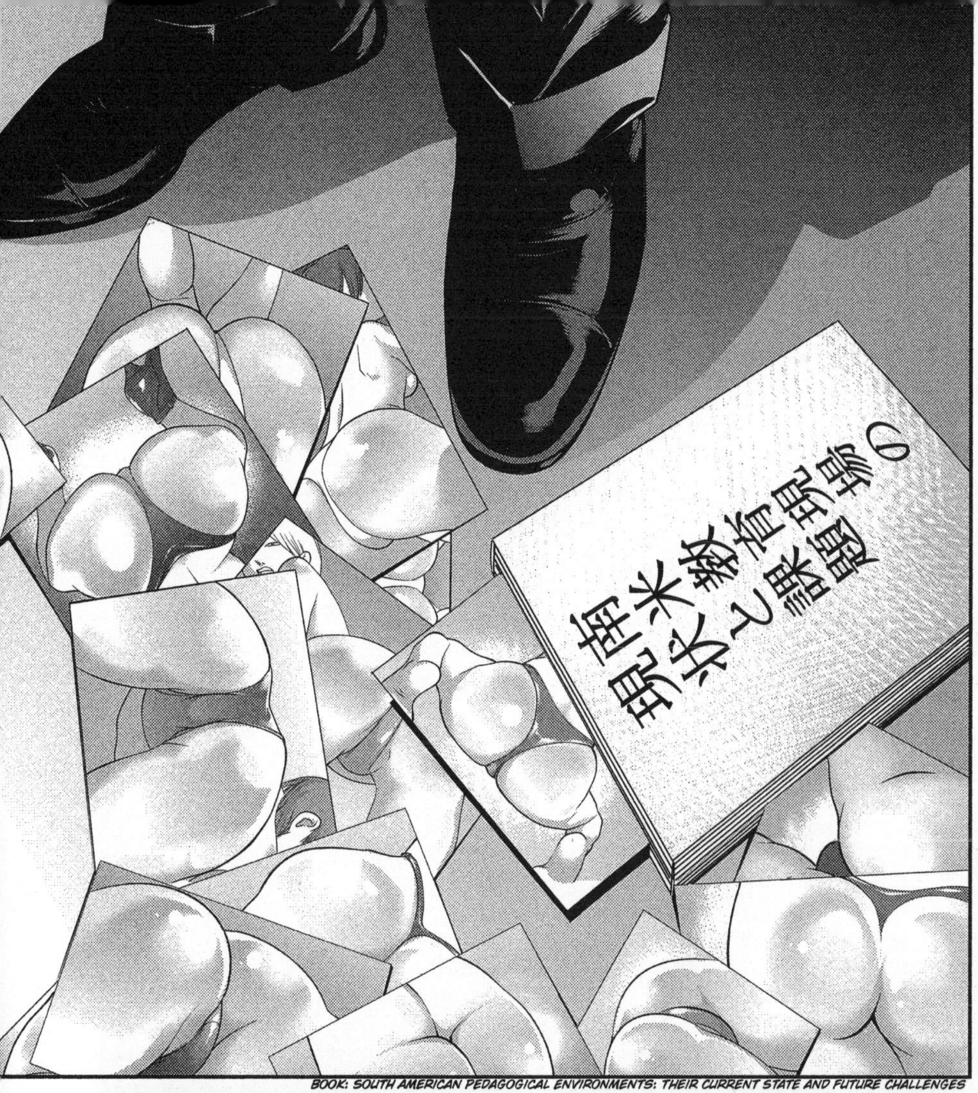
南米教育現場の現状と課題

BOOK: SOUTH AMERICAN PEDAGOGICAL ENVIRONMENTS: THEIR CURRENT STATE AND FUTURE CHALLENGES

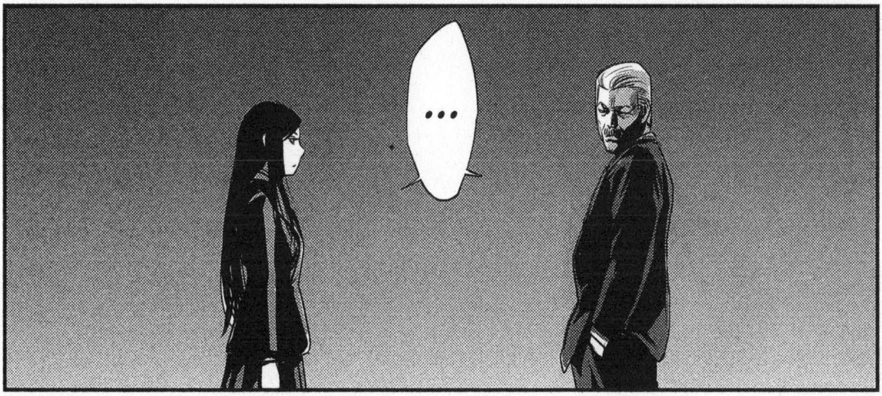
...

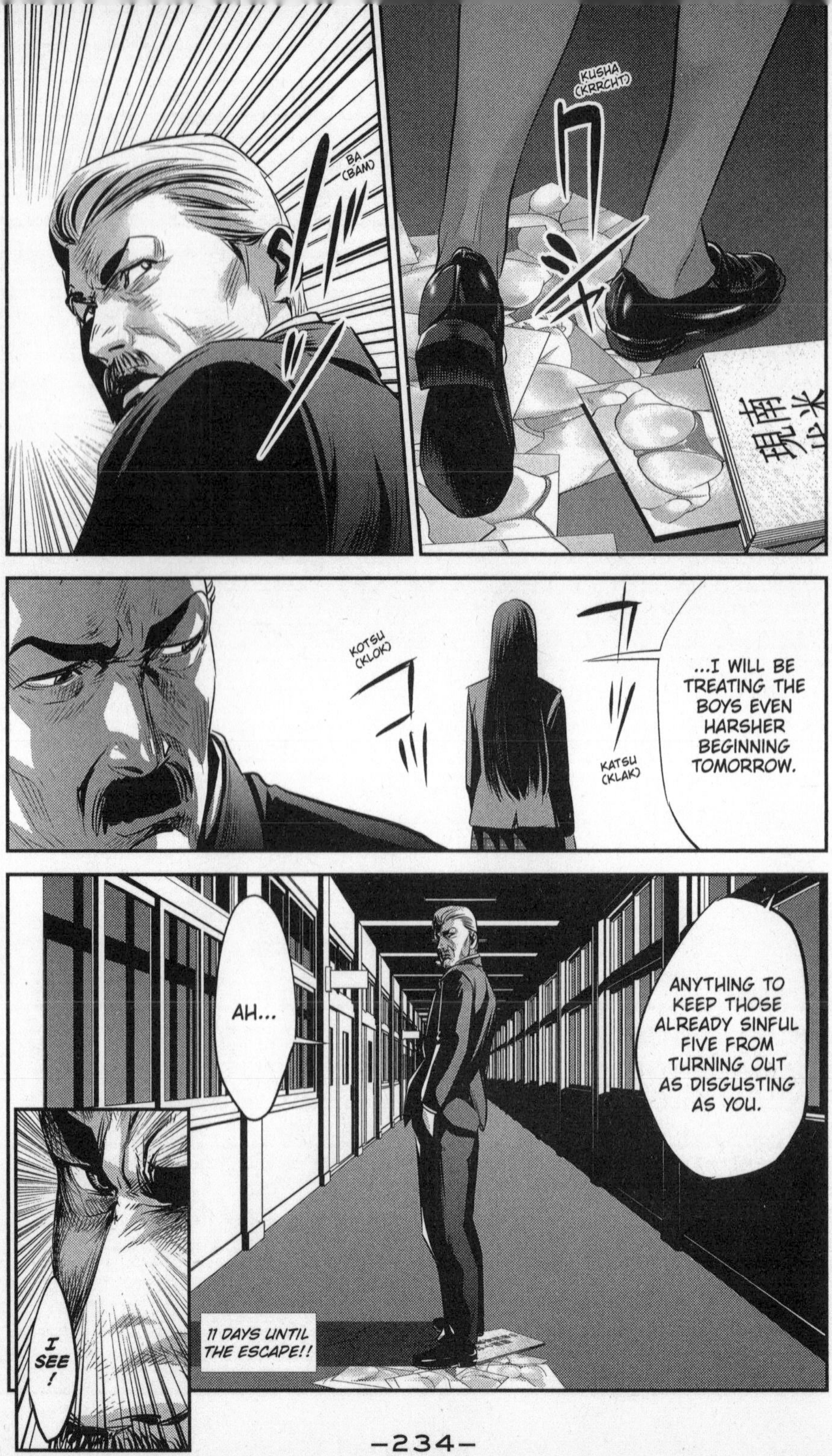
KUSHA (KRRCHT)
BA (BAM)
...I WILL BE TREATING THE BOYS EVEN HARSHER BEGINNING TOMORROW.
KATSU (KLAK)
KOTSU (KLOK)
ANYTHING TO KEEP THOSE ALREADY SINFUL FIVE FROM TURNING OUT AS DISGUSTING AS YOU.
AH...
11 DAYS UNTIL THE ESCAPE!!
I SEE!

CHAPTER 11: THE FIRST MISSION

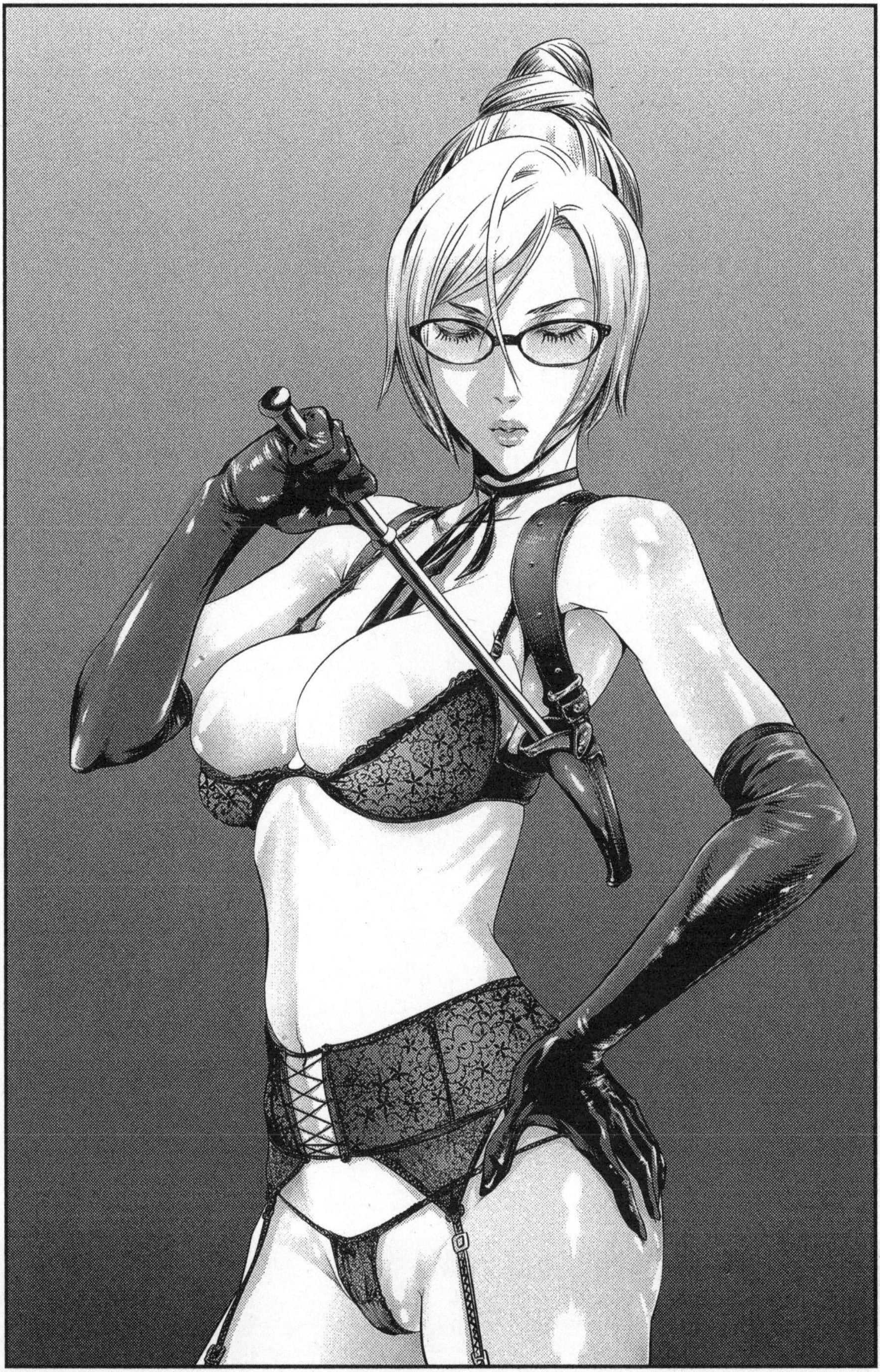

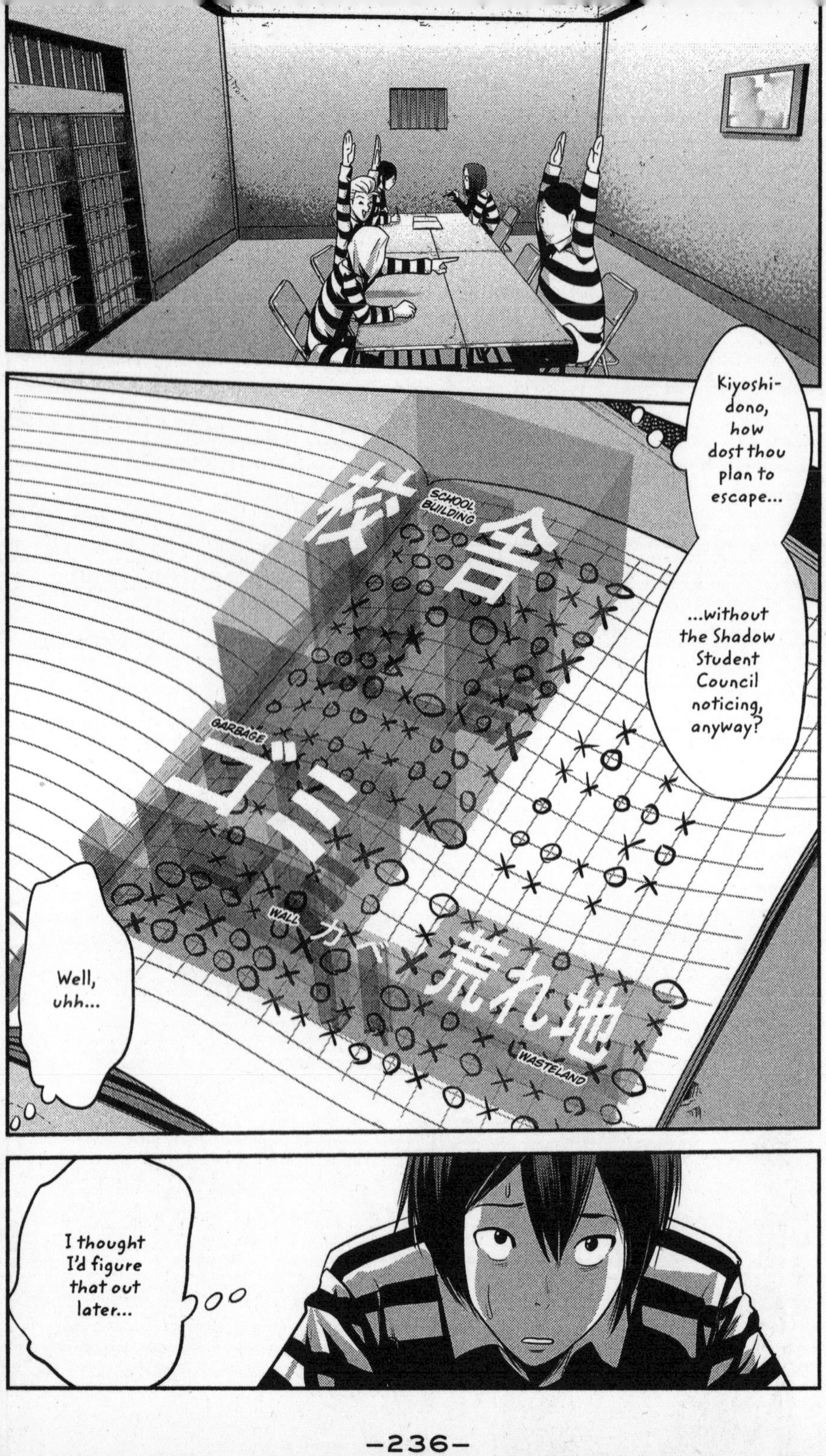

Kiyoshi-dono, how dost thou plan to escape...
...without the Shadow Student Council noticing, anyway?
校舎
SCHOOL BUILDING
ゴミ
GARBAGE
カベ
WALL
荒れ地
WASTELAND
Well, uhh...
I thought I'd figure that out later...

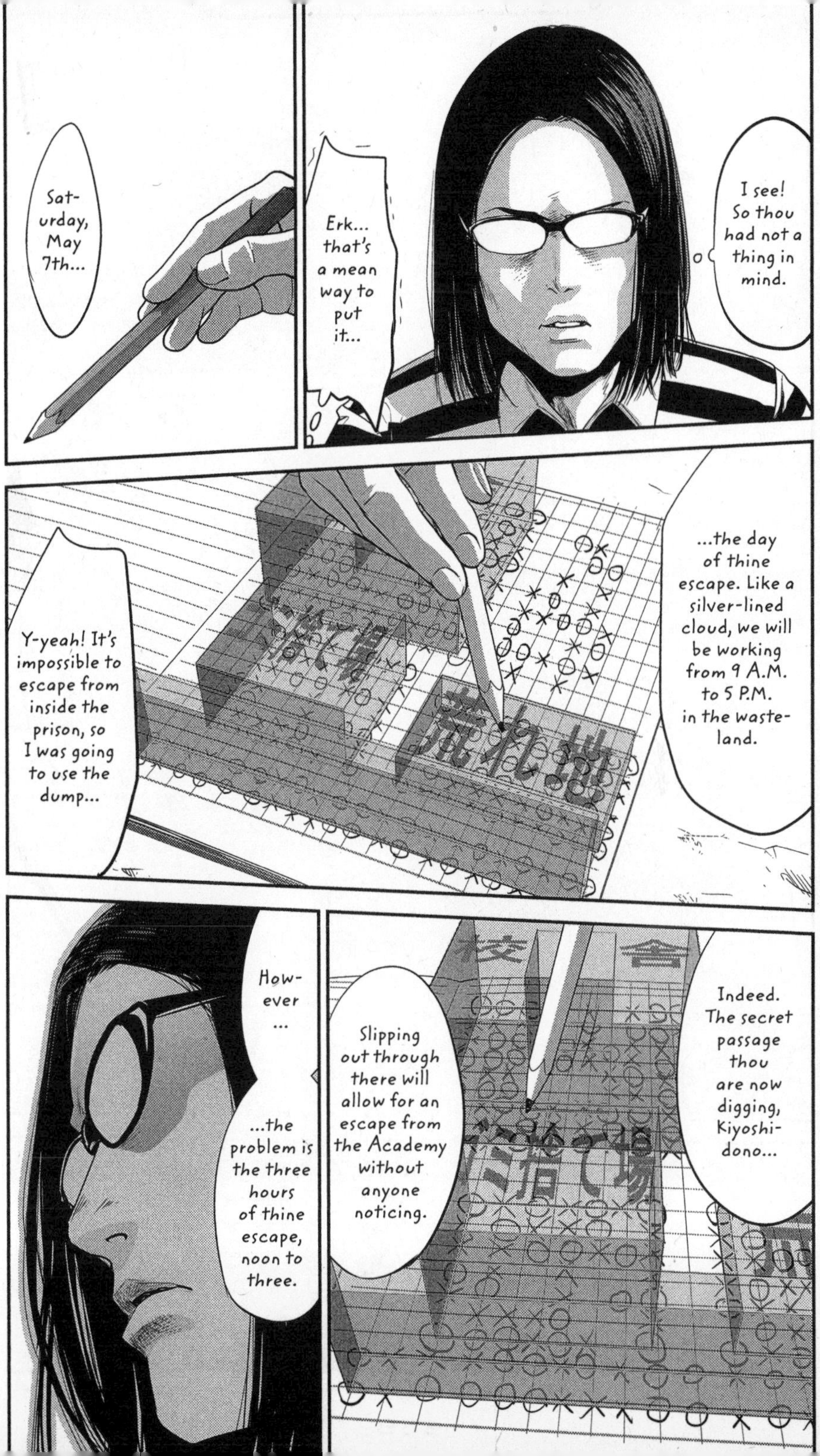
I see! So thou had not a thing in mind.
Erk... that's a mean way to put it...
Saturday, May 7th...
...the day of thine escape. Like a silver-lined cloud, we will be working from 9 A.M. to 5 P.M. in the wasteland.
Y-yeah! It's impossible to escape from inside the prison, so I was going to use the dump...
Indeed. The secret passage thou are now digging, Kiyoshi-dono...
Slipping out through there will allow for an escape from the Academy without anyone noticing.
However...
...the problem is the three hours of thine escape, noon to three.

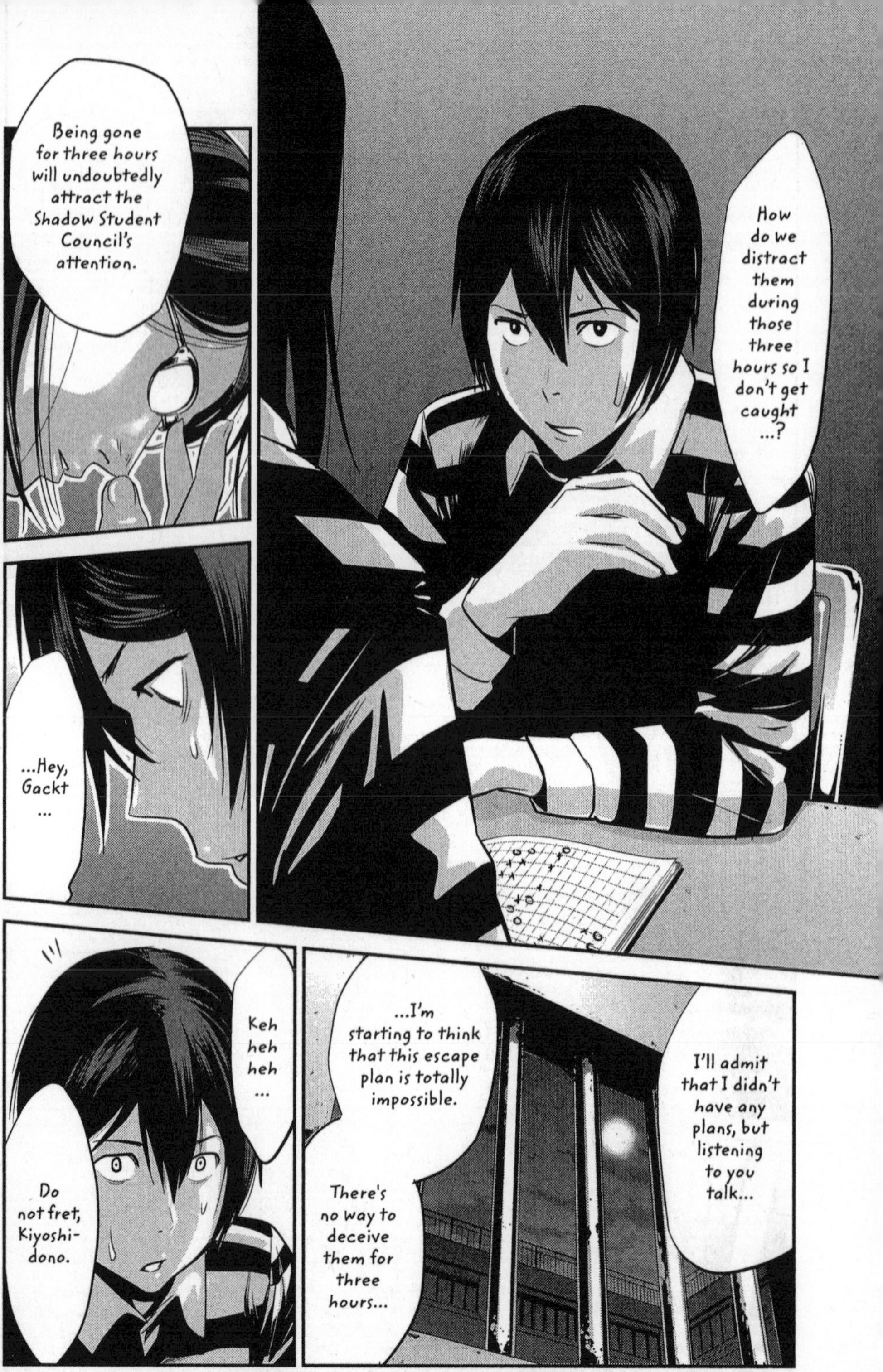
Being gone for three hours will undoubtedly attract the Shadow Student Council's attention.
How do we distract them during those three hours so I don't get caught ...?
...Hey, Gackt ...
I'll admit that I didn't have any plans, but listening to you talk...
...I'm starting to think that this escape plan is totally impossible.
There's no way to deceive them for three hours...
Keh heh heh ...
Do not fret, Kiyoshi-dono.

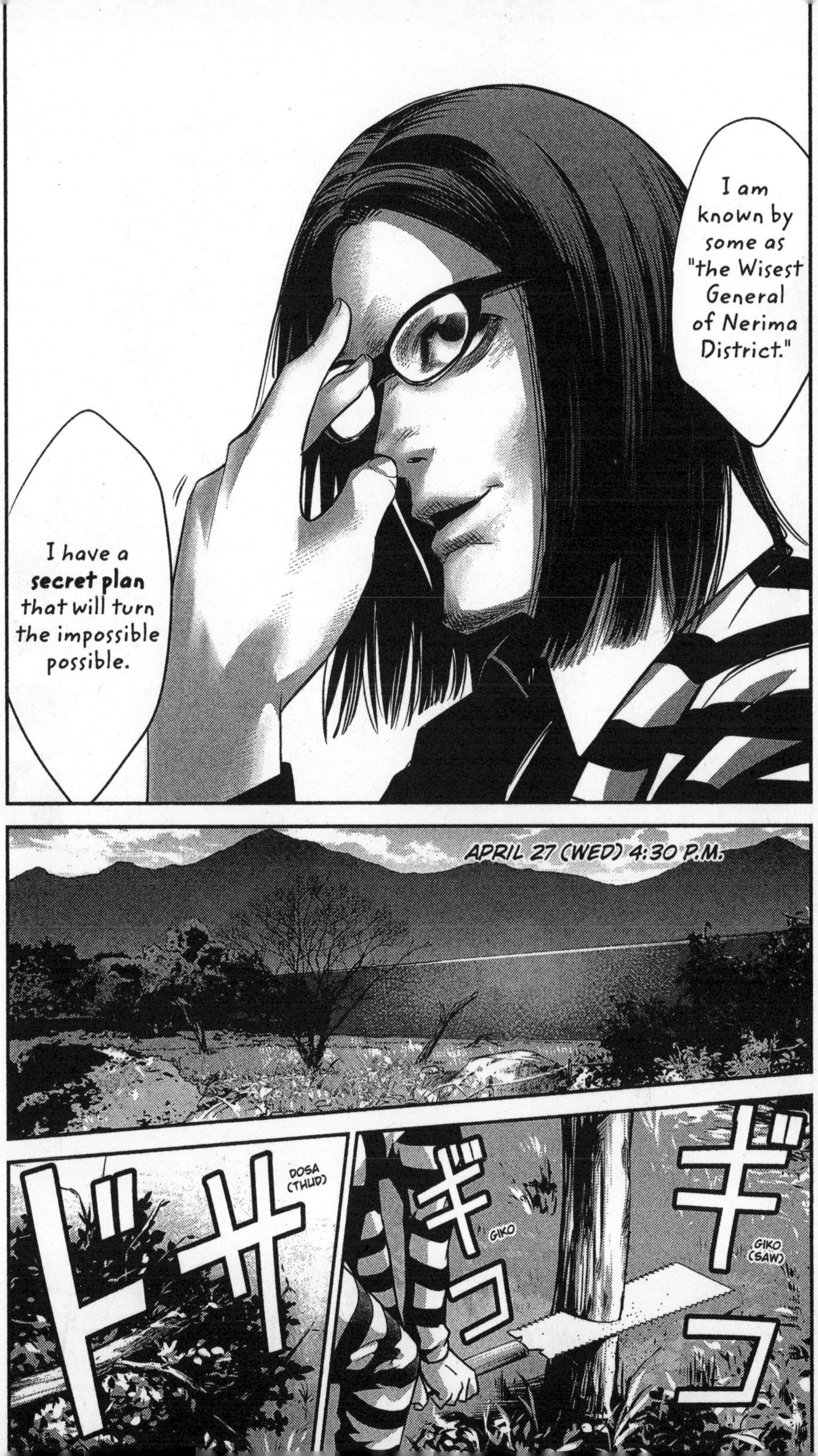
I am known by some as "the Wisest General of Nerima District."
I have a **secret plan** that will turn the impossible possible.
APRIL 27 (WED) 4:30 P.M.
ギコ
GIKO (SAW)
ギコッ
GIKO
ドサ
DOSA (THUD)

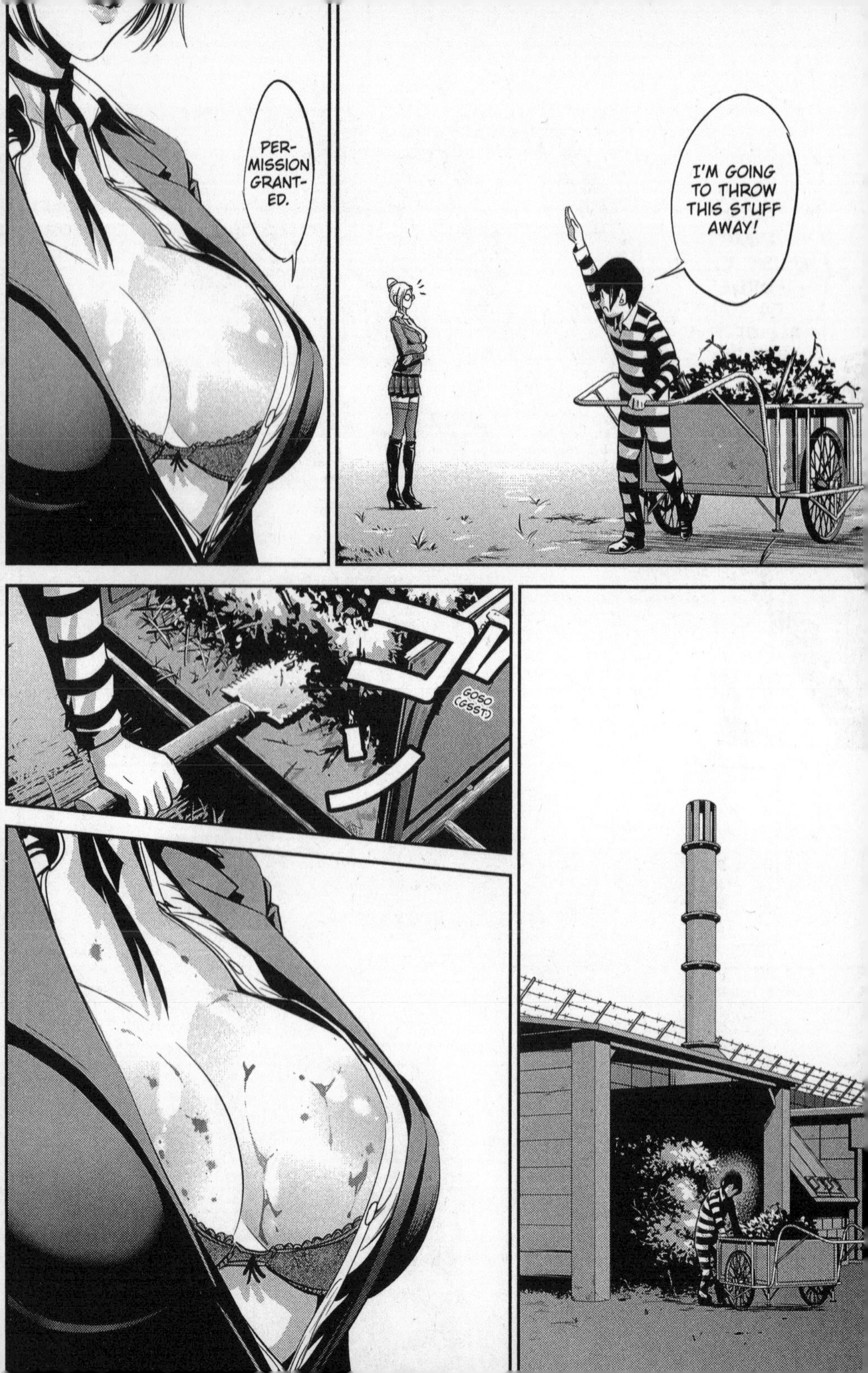
I'M GOING TO THROW THIS STUFF AWAY!
PER-MISSION GRANT-ED.
GOSO (GSST)

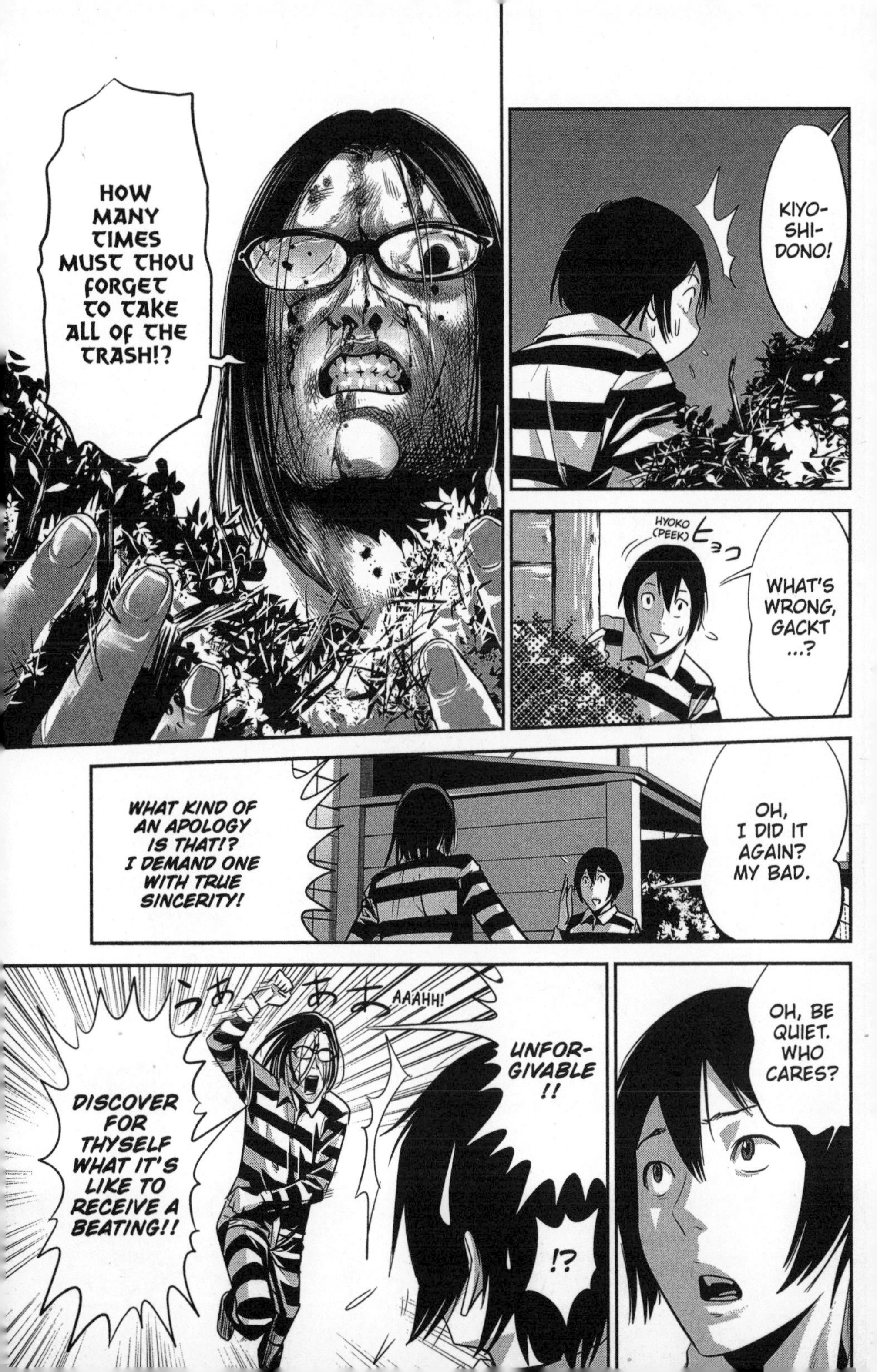
KIYO-SHI-DONO!
HYOKO (PEEK) ヒョコ
WHAT'S WRONG, GACKT ...?
HOW MANY TIMES MUST THOU FORGET TO TAKE ALL OF THE TRASH!?
OH, I DID IT AGAIN? MY BAD.
WHAT KIND OF AN APOLOGY IS THAT!? I DEMAND ONE WITH TRUE SINCERITY!
OH, BE QUIET. WHO CARES?
UNFORGIVABLE!!
!?
うああ AAAHH!
DISCOVER FOR THYSELF WHAT IT'S LIKE TO RECEIVE A BEATING!!

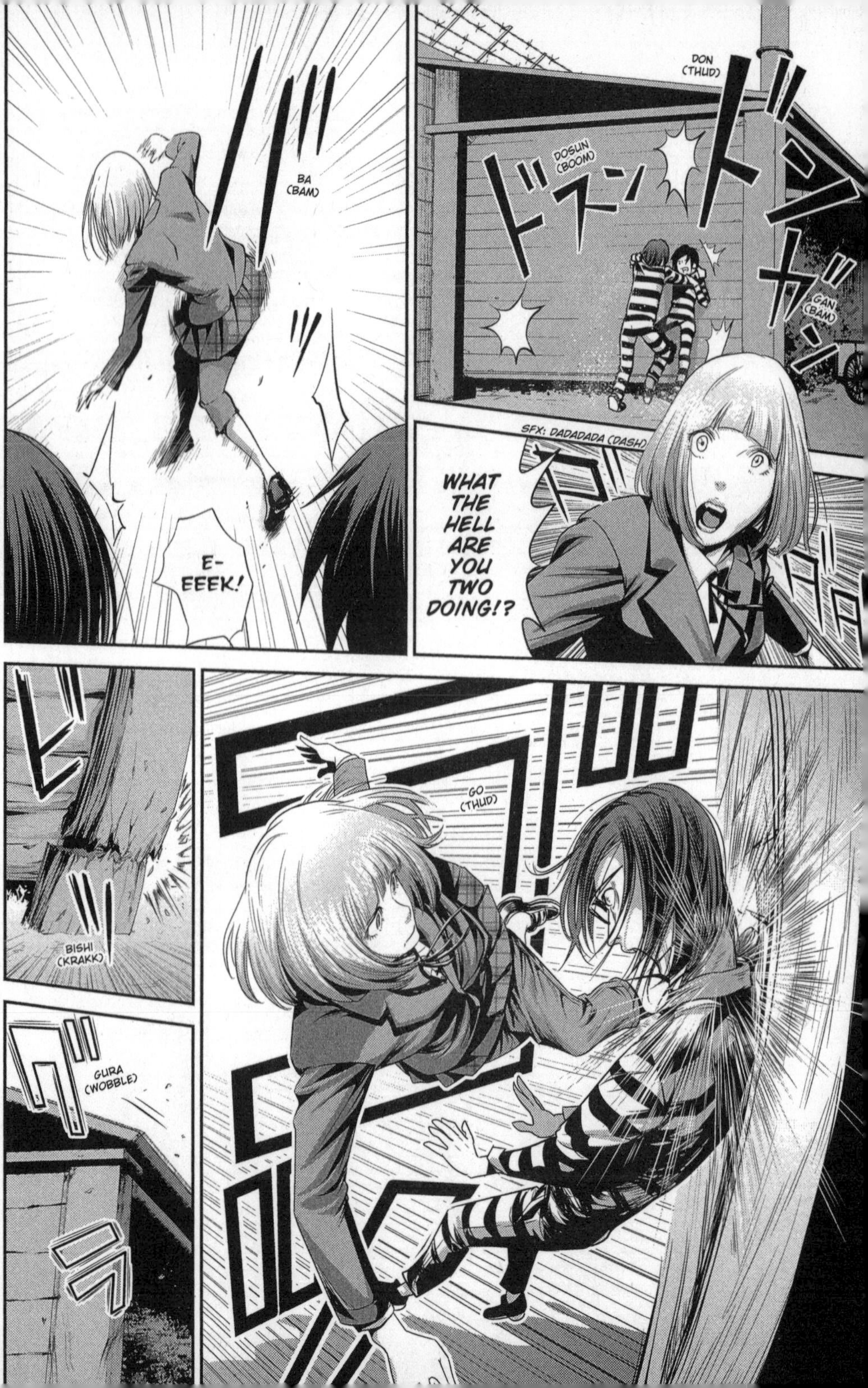
DON (THUD)
DOSUN (BOOM)
GAN (BAM)
SFX: DADADADA (DASH)
WHAT THE HELL ARE YOU TWO DOING!?
BA (BAM)
E-EEEK!
GO (THUD)
BISHI (KRAKK)
GURA (WOBBLE)

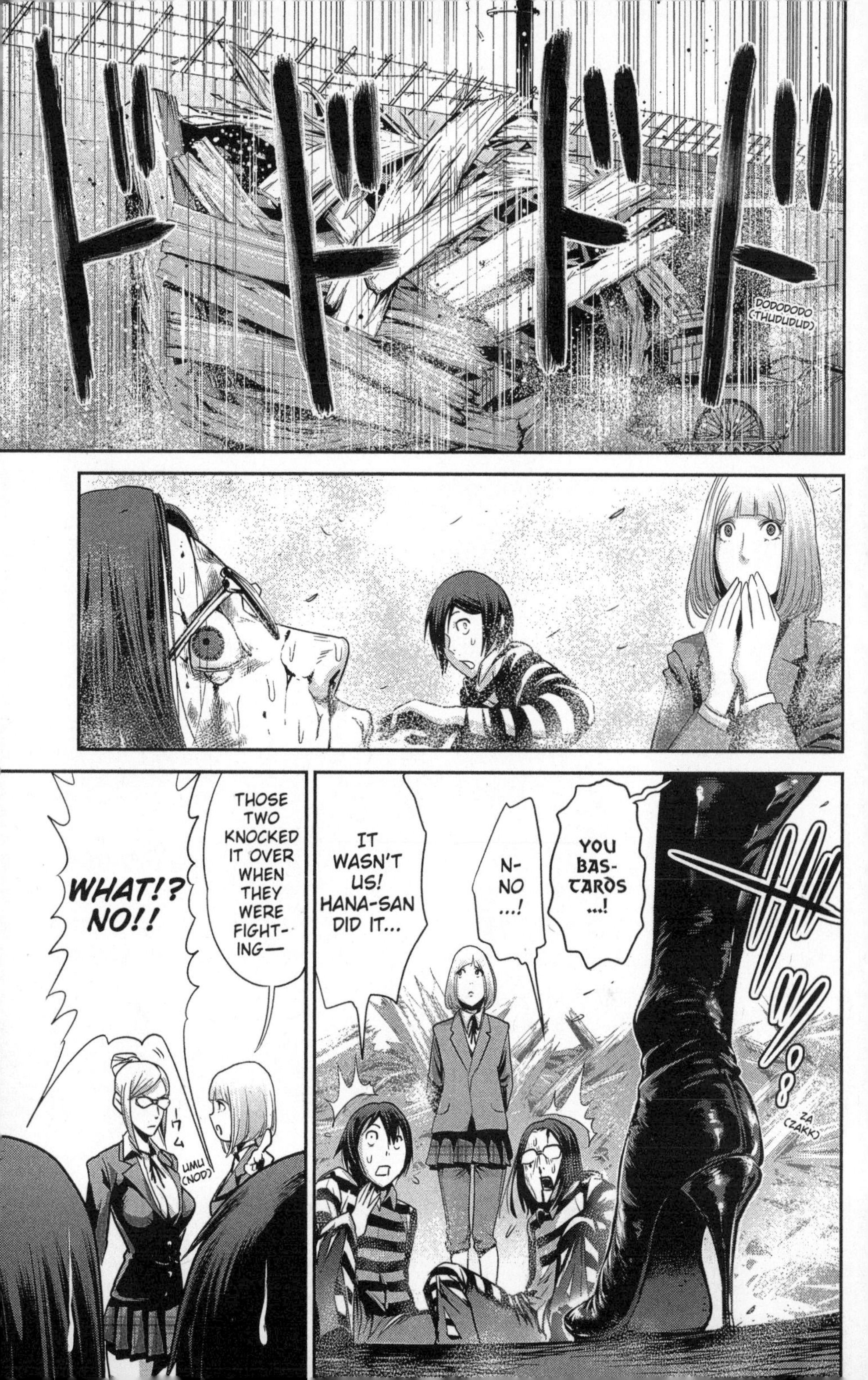
DODODODO
(THUDUDUD)
YOU BASTARDS ...!
N-NO ...!
IT WASN'T US! HANA-SAN DID IT...
THOSE TWO KNOCKED IT OVER WHEN THEY WERE FIGHTING—
WHAT!? NO!!
UMU
(NOD)
ZA
(ZAKK)

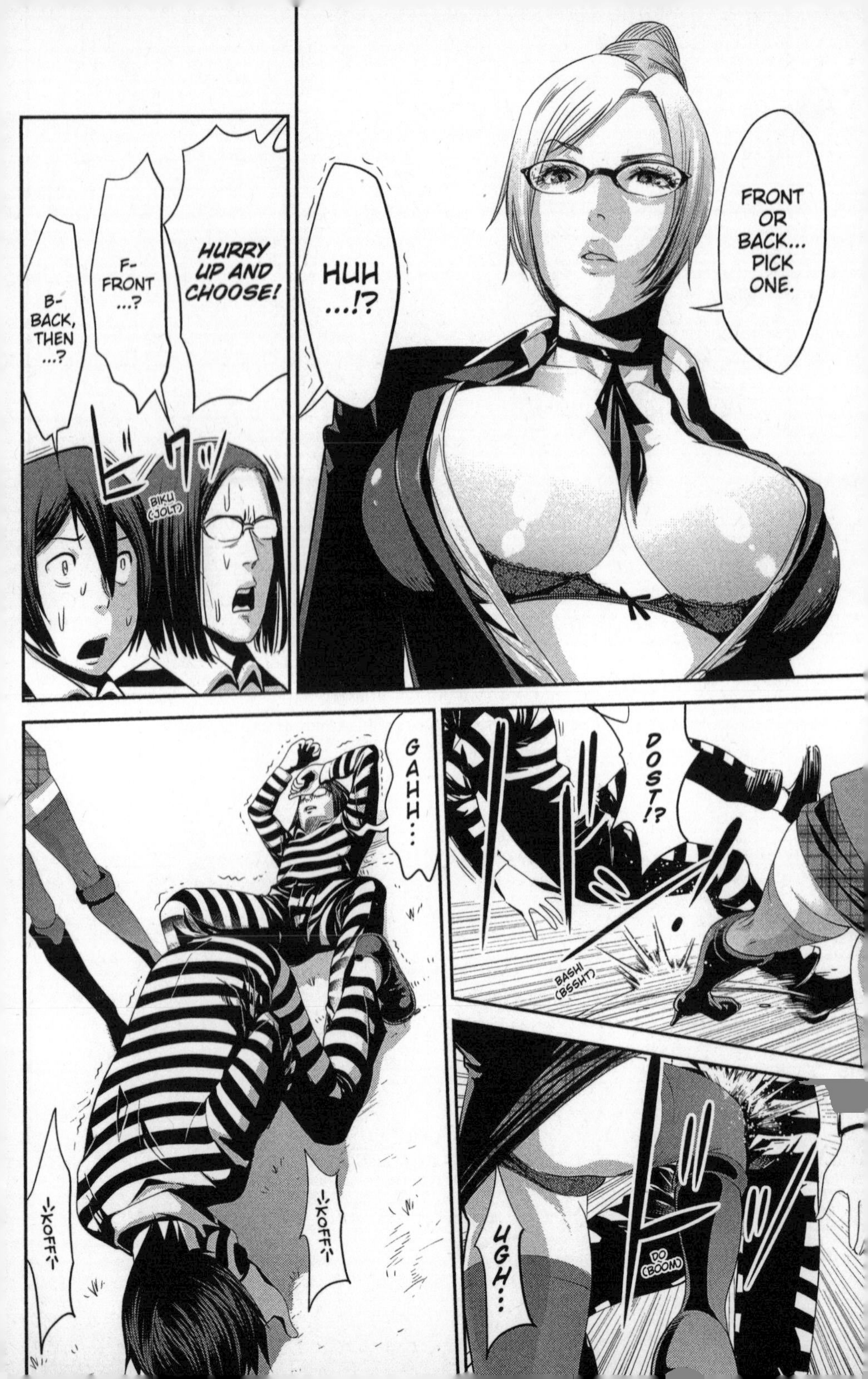
FRONT OR BACK... PICK ONE.
HUH ...!?
HURRY UP AND CHOOSE!
F-FRONT ...?
BIKU (JOLT)
B-BACK, THEN ...?
DOST!?
BASHI (BSSHT)
DO (BOOM)
UGH...
GAHH...
-KOFF-
-KOFF-

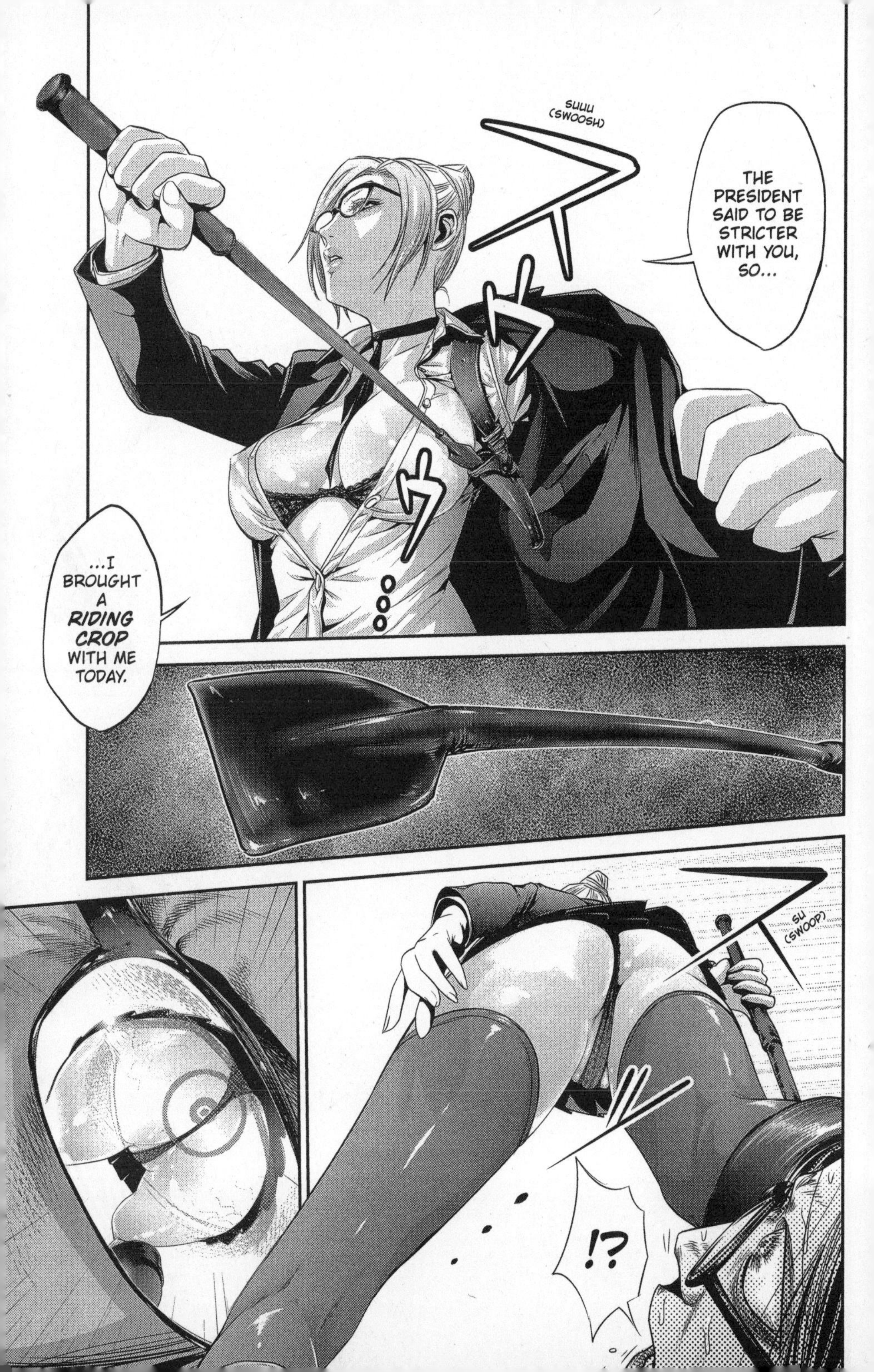
THE PRESIDENT SAID TO BE STRICTER WITH YOU, SO...
SUUU (SWOOSH)
...I BROUGHT A RIDING CROP WITH ME TODAY.
SU (SWOOP)
!?

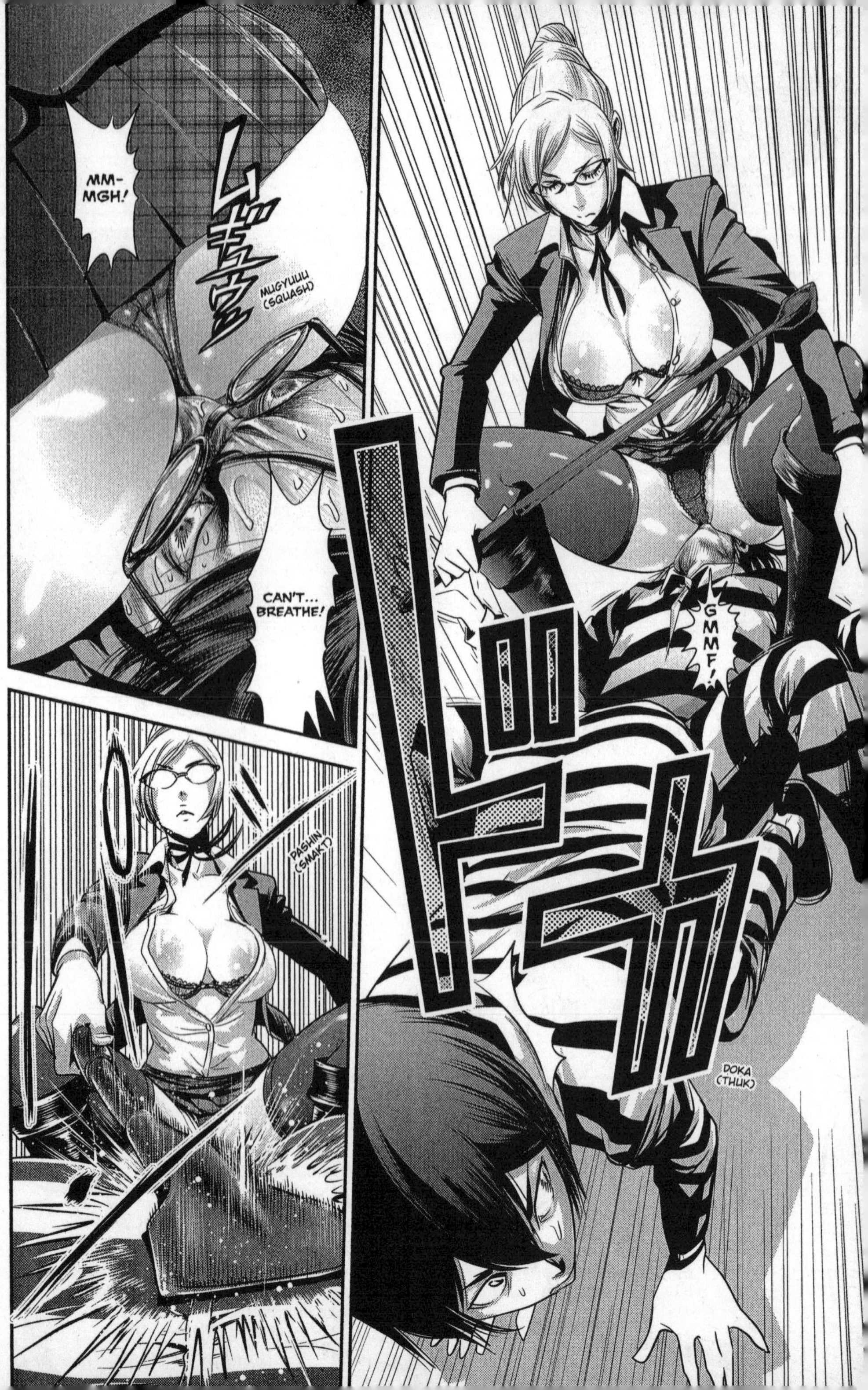
GMMF!
DOKA (THUK)
MM-MGH!
MUGYUUU (SQUASH)
CAN'T... BREATHE!
PASHIN (SMAKT)

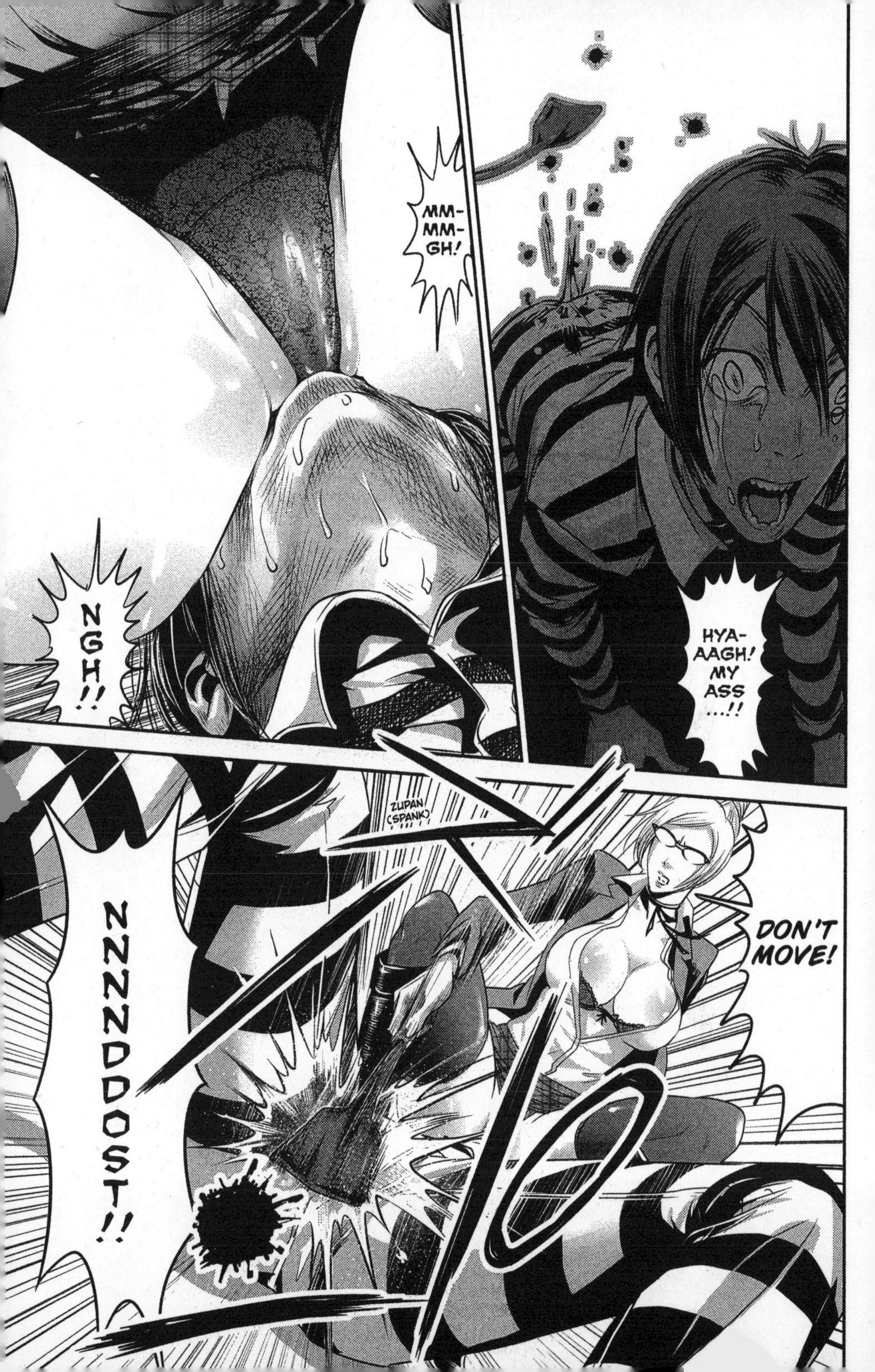
HYA-AAGH! MY ASS ...!!
MMM-MMGH!
NGH!!
DON'T MOVE!
ZUPAN (SPANK)
NNNNDDOOST!!

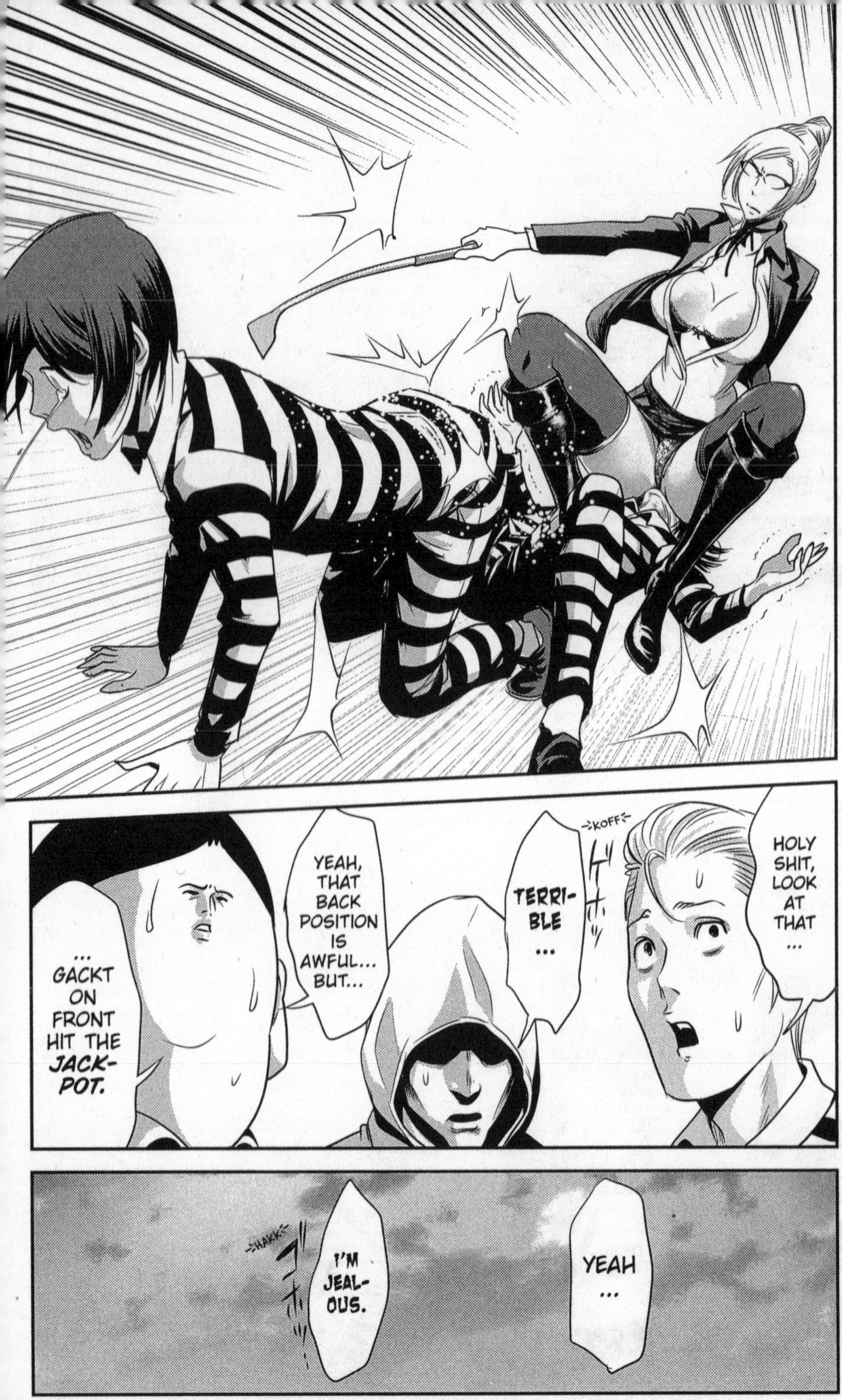
HOLY SHIT, LOOK AT THAT...
KOFF
TERRIBLE...
YEAH, THAT BACK POSITION IS AWFUL... BUT...
...GACKT ON FRONT HIT THE JACKPOT.
YEAH...
HAKK
I'M JEALOUS.

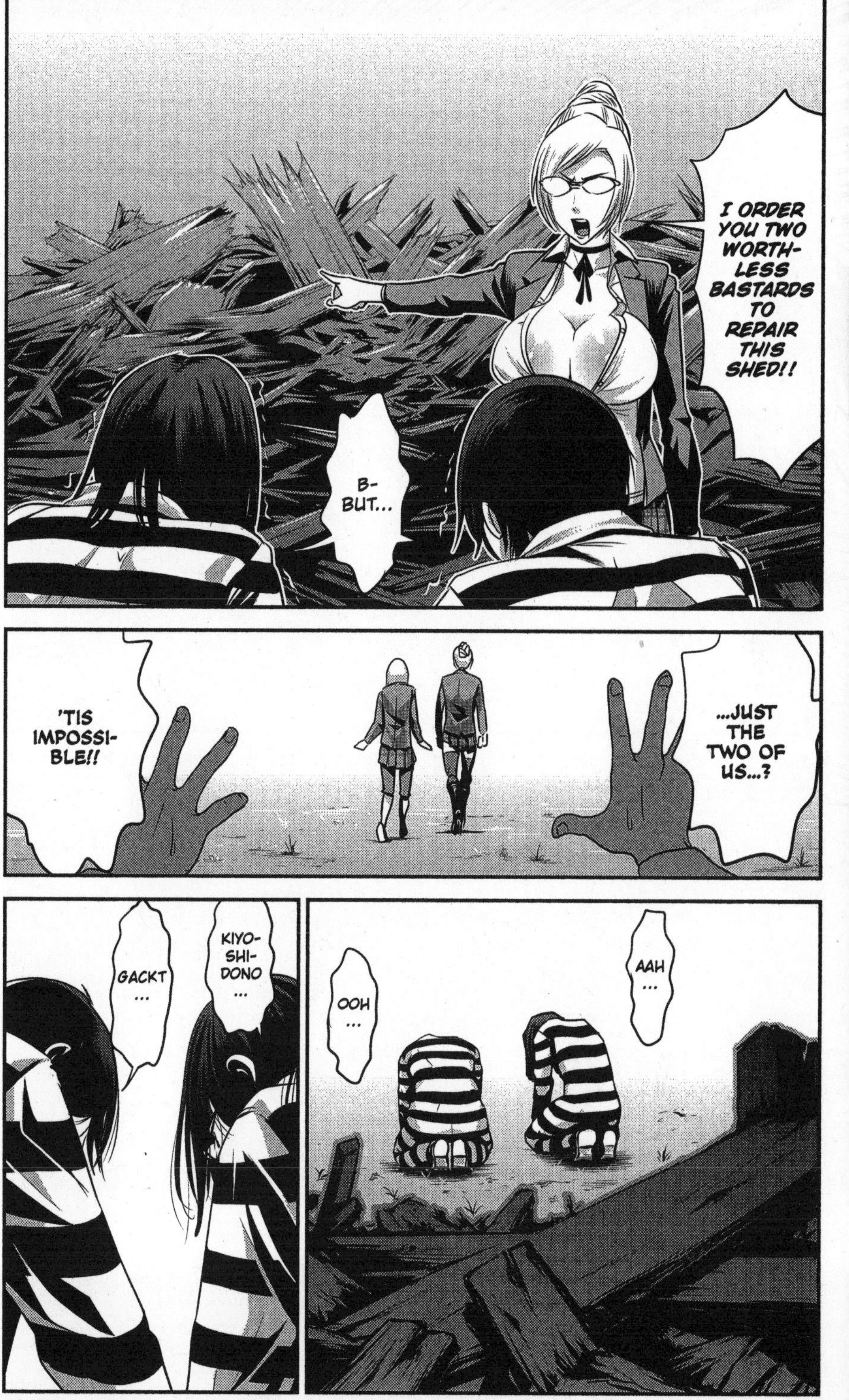
I ORDER YOU TWO WORTHLESS BASTARDS TO REPAIR THIS SHED!!
B-BUT...
...JUST THE TWO OF US...?
'TIS IMPOSSIBLE!!
KIYOSHI-DONO...
GACKT...
AAH...
OOH...

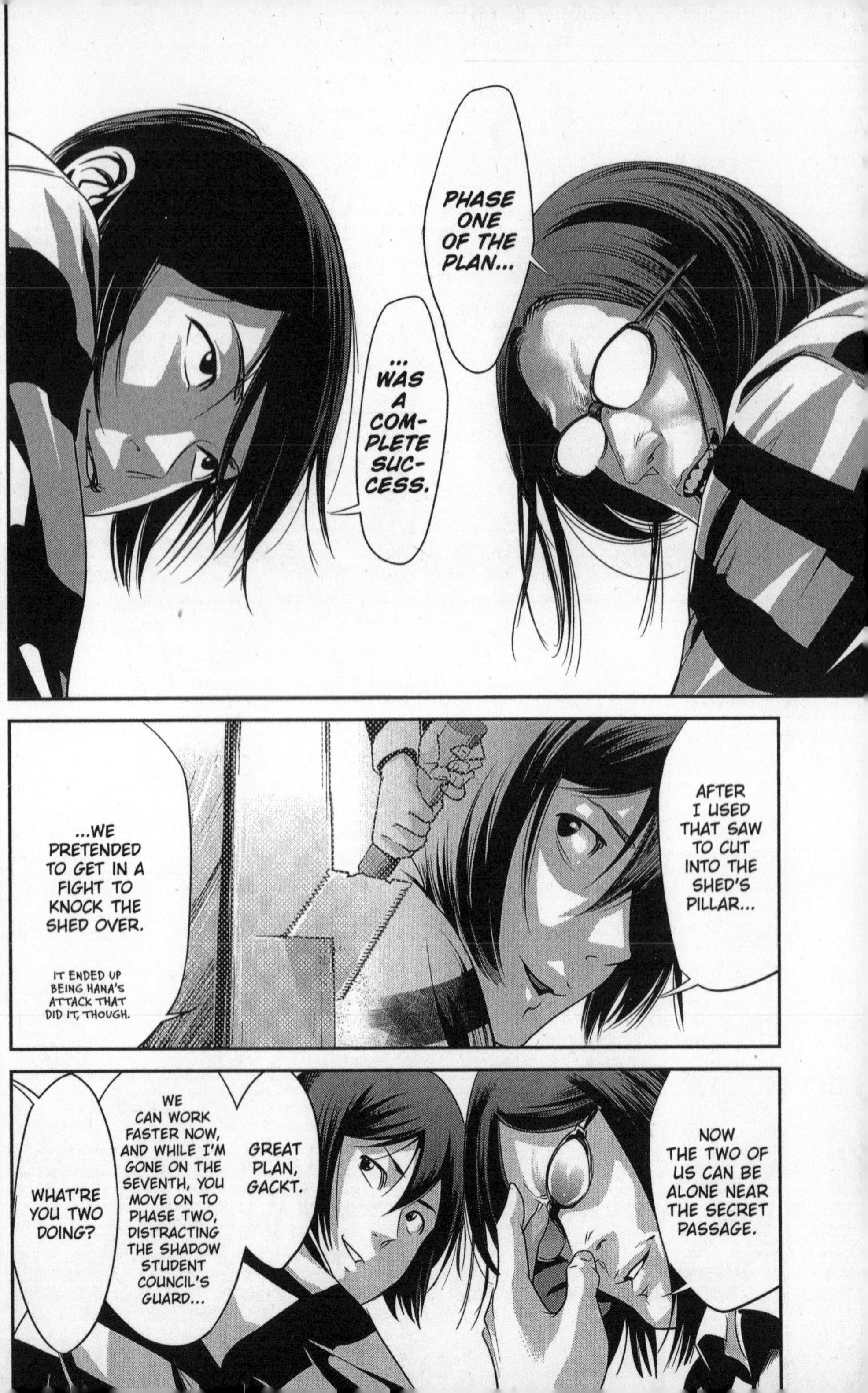
PHASE ONE OF THE PLAN...
...WAS A COMPLETE SUCCESS.
AFTER I USED THAT SAW TO CUT INTO THE SHED'S PILLAR...
...WE PRETENDED TO GET IN A FIGHT TO KNOCK THE SHED OVER.
IT ENDED UP BEING HANA'S ATTACK THAT DID IT, THOUGH.
NOW THE TWO OF US CAN BE ALONE NEAR THE SECRET PASSAGE.
GREAT PLAN, GACKT.
WE CAN WORK FASTER NOW, AND WHILE I'M GONE ON THE SEVENTH, YOU MOVE ON TO PHASE TWO, DISTRACTING THE SHADOW STUDENT COUNCIL'S GUARD...
WHAT'RE YOU TWO DOING?

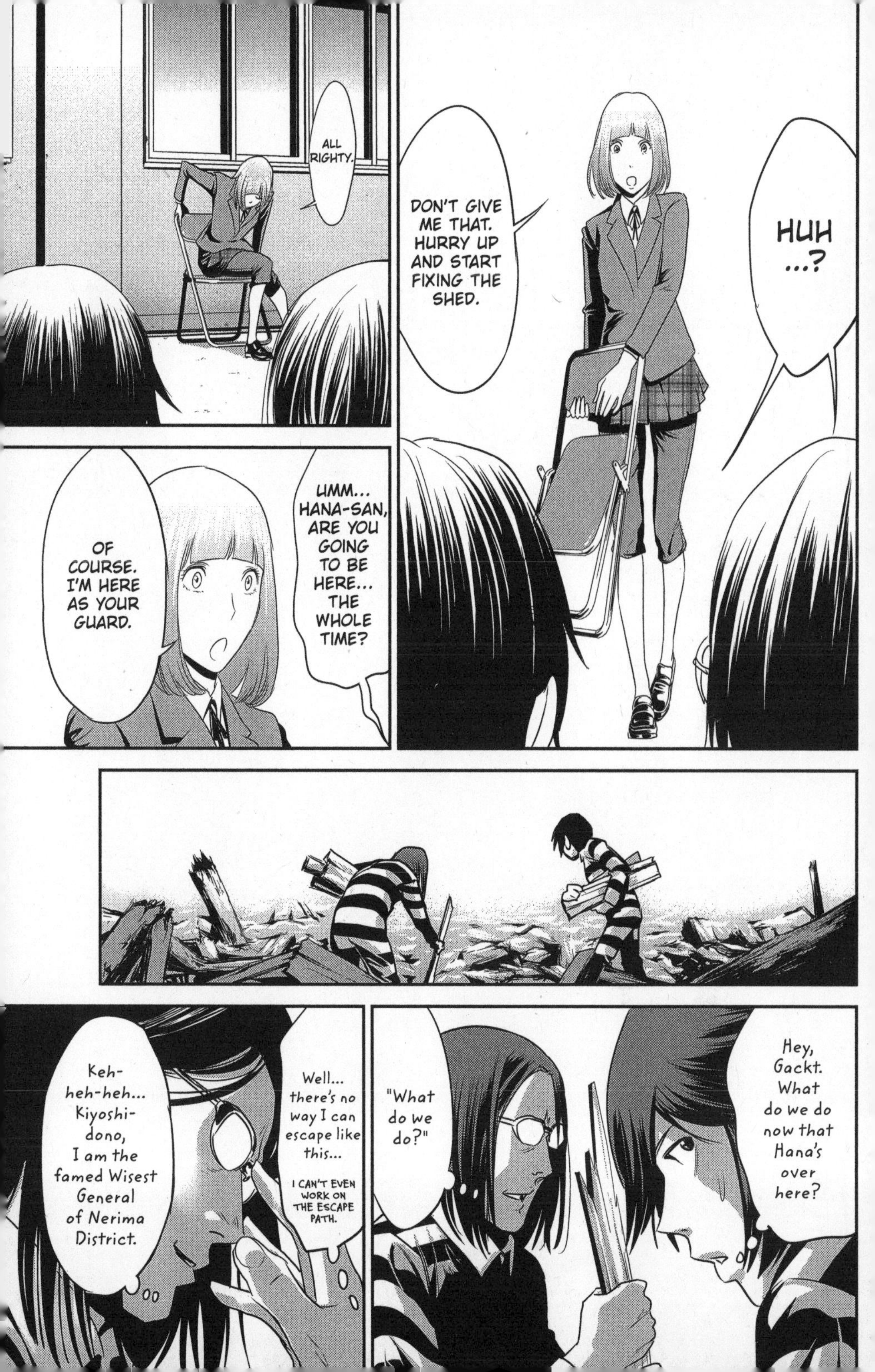
HUH ...?
DON'T GIVE ME THAT. HURRY UP AND START FIXING THE SHED.
ALL RIGHTY.
UMM... HANA-SAN, ARE YOU GOING TO BE HERE... THE WHOLE TIME?
OF COURSE. I'M HERE AS YOUR GUARD.
Hey, Gackt. What do we do now that Hana's over here?
"What do we do?"
Well... there's no way I can escape like this...
I CAN'T EVEN WORK ON THE ESCAPE PATH.
Keh-heh-heh... Kiyoshi-dono, I am the famed Wisest General of Nerima District.

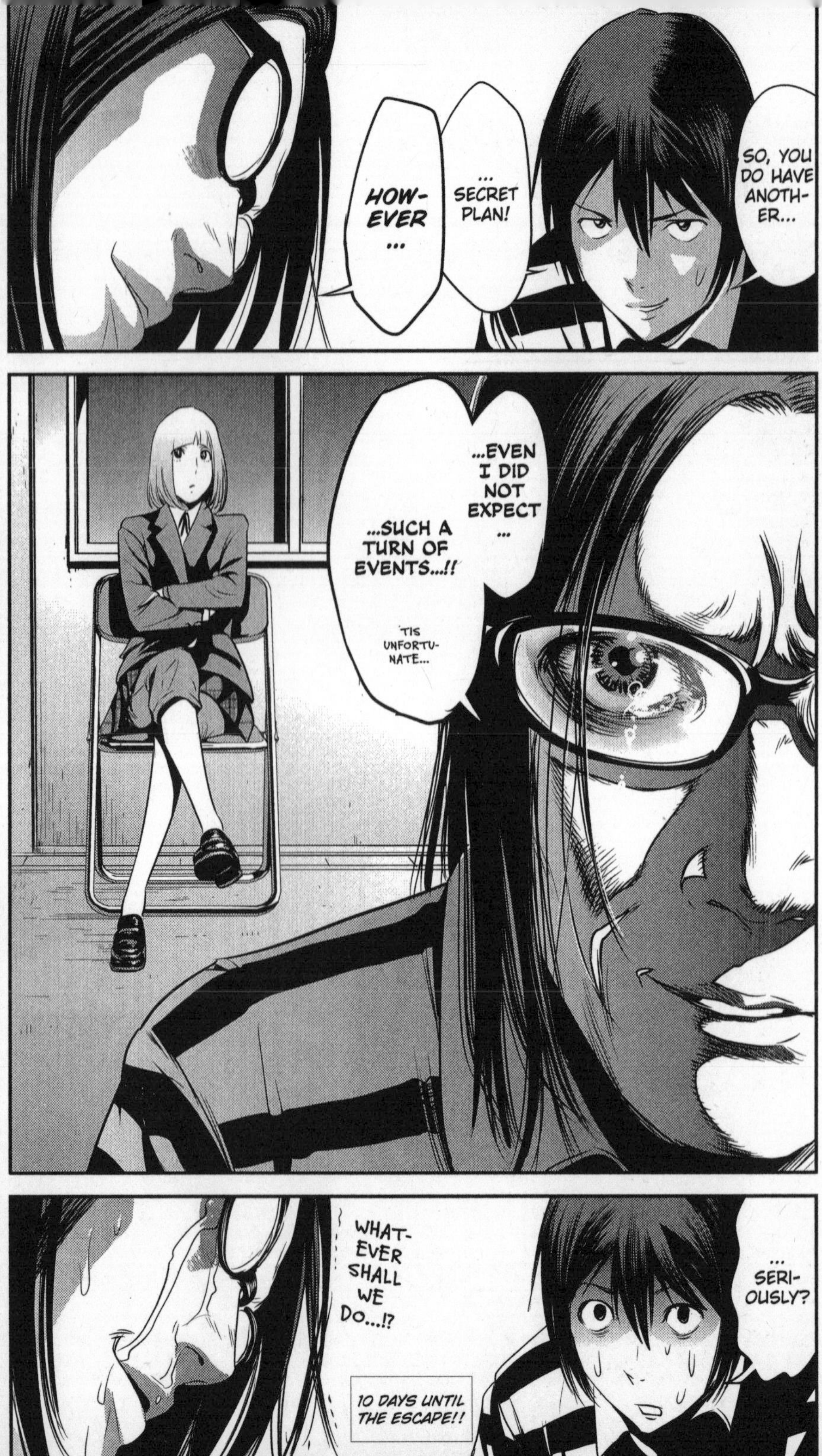
SO, YOU DO HAVE ANOTHER-ER...
... SECRET PLAN!
HOW-EVER ...
...EVEN I DID NOT EXPECT ...
...SUCH A TURN OF EVENTS...!!
TIS UNFORTU-NATE...
... SERI-OUSLY?
WHAT-EVER SHALL WE DO...!?
10 DAYS UNTIL THE ESCAPE!!

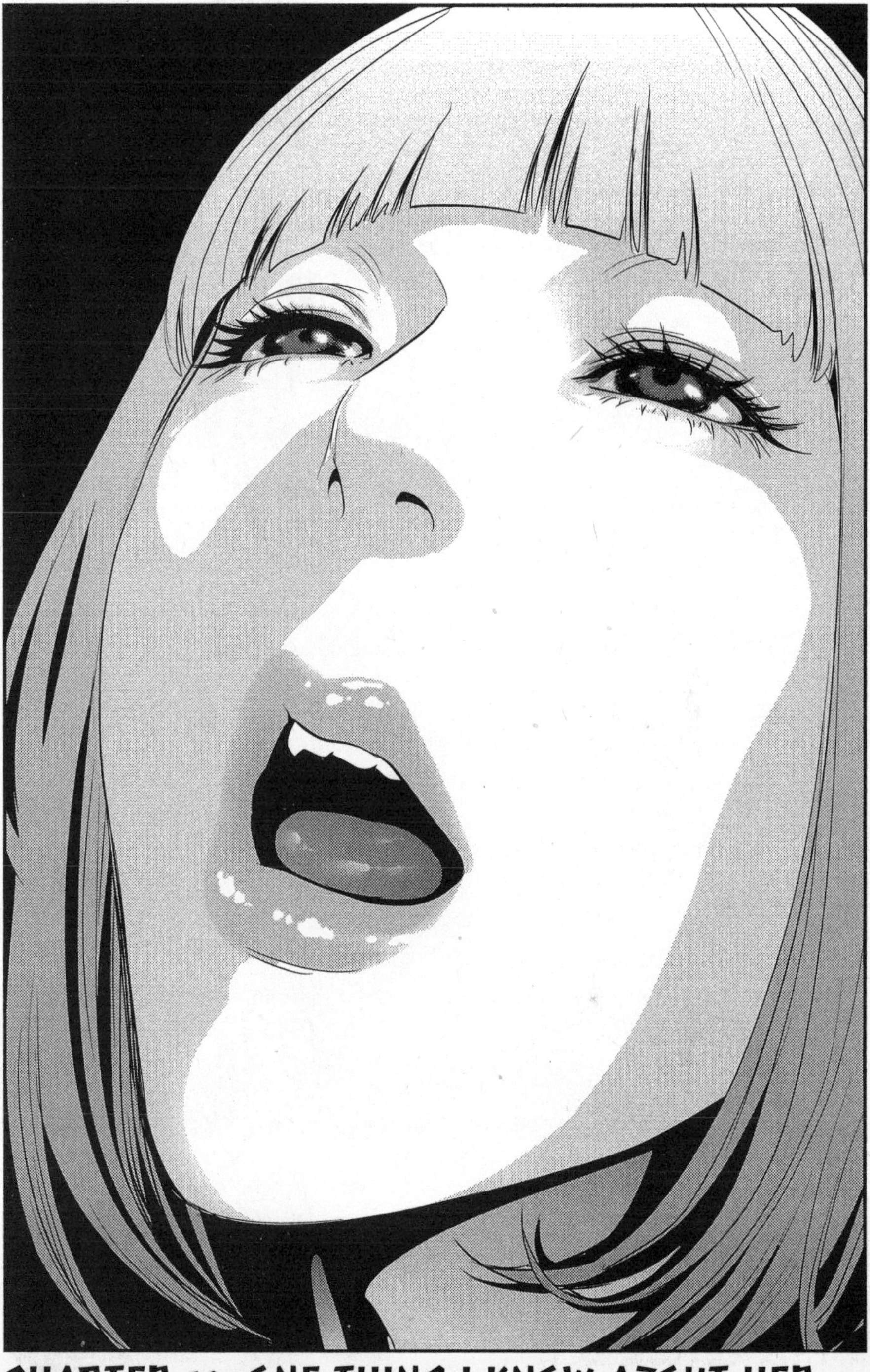

CHAPTER 12: ONE THING I KNOW ABOUT HER

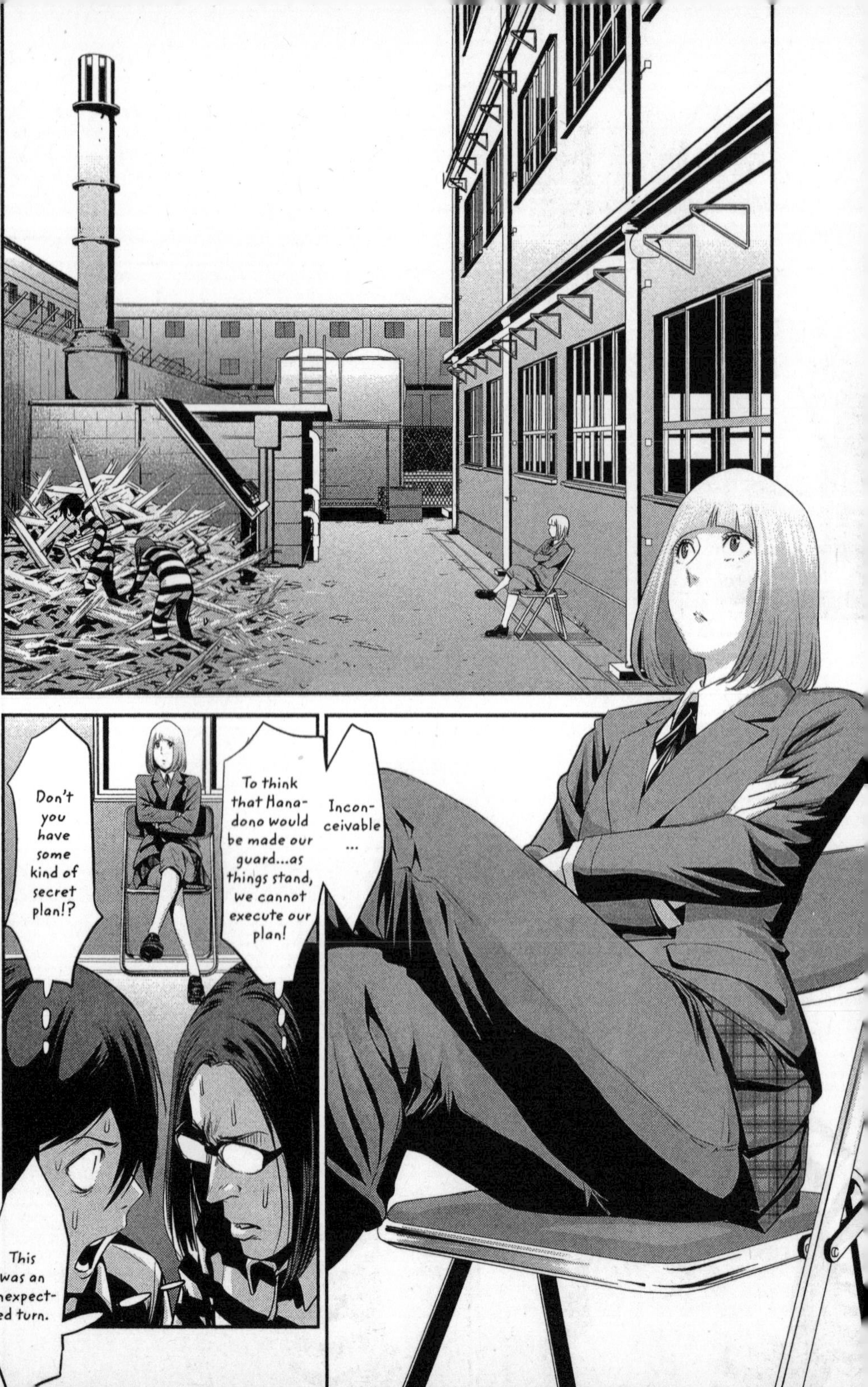

Inconceivable...
To think that Hana-dono would be made our guard...as things stand, we cannot execute our plan!
Don't you have some kind of secret plan!?
This was an unexpected turn.

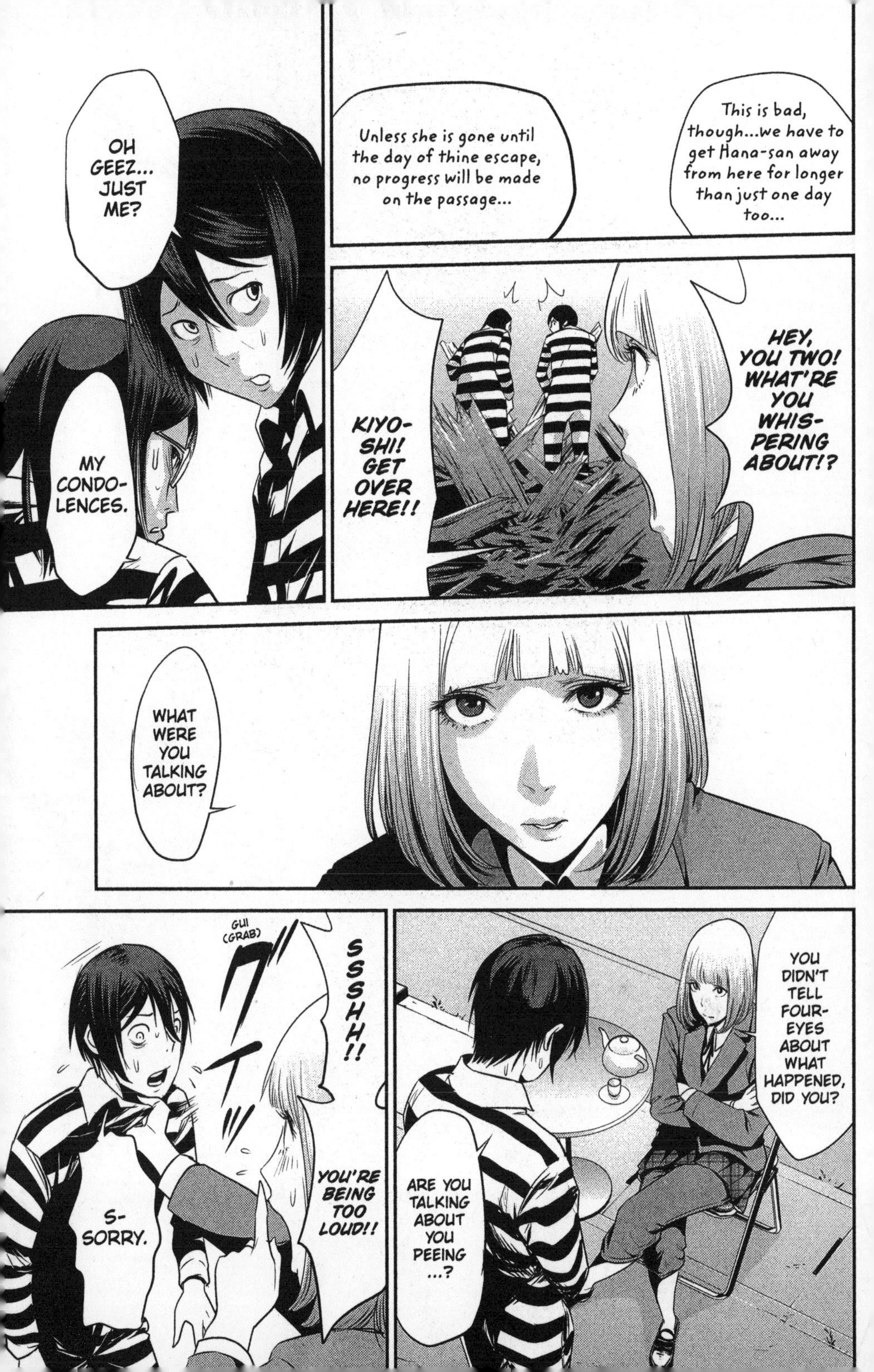
This is bad, though...we have to get Hana-san away from here for longer than just one day too...
Unless she is gone until the day of thine escape, no progress will be made on the passage...
OH GEEZ... JUST ME?
MY CONDOLENCES.
HEY, YOU TWO! WHAT'RE YOU WHIS-PERING ABOUT!?
KIYO-SHI! GET OVER HERE!!
WHAT WERE YOU TALKING ABOUT?
YOU DIDN'T TELL FOUR-EYES ABOUT WHAT HAPPENED, DID YOU?
ARE YOU TALKING ABOUT YOU PEEING ...?
SSSHH!!
GUI (GRAB)
YOU'RE BEING TOO LOUD!!
S-SORRY.

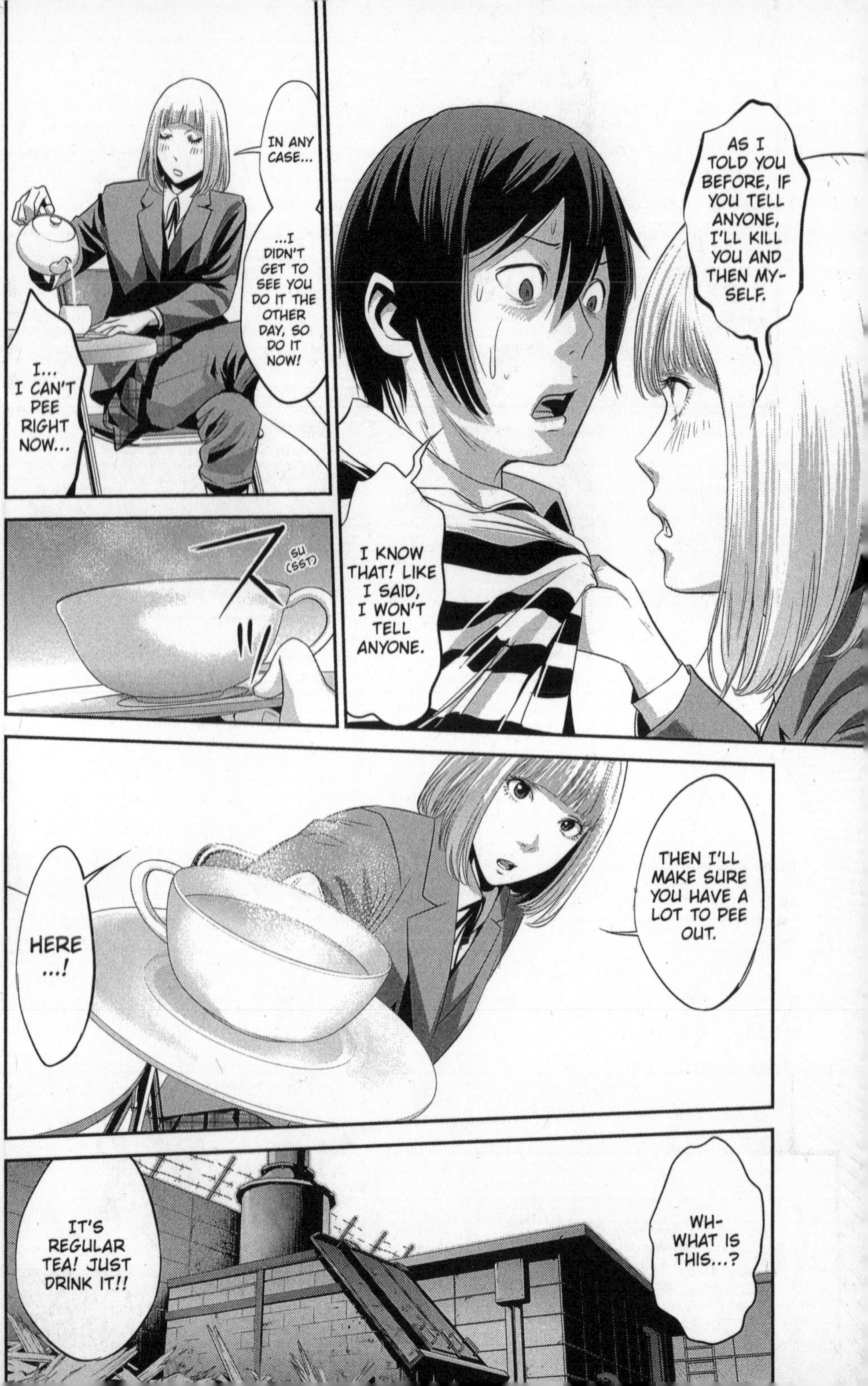
AS I TOLD YOU BEFORE, IF YOU TELL ANYONE, I'LL KILL YOU AND THEN MY-SELF.
I KNOW THAT! LIKE I SAID, I WON'T TELL ANYONE.
IN ANY CASE...
...I DIDN'T GET TO SEE YOU DO IT THE OTHER DAY, SO DO IT NOW!
I... I CAN'T PEE RIGHT NOW...
SU (SST)
THEN I'LL MAKE SURE YOU HAVE A LOT TO PEE OUT.
HERE ...!
WH-WHAT IS THIS...?
IT'S REGULAR TEA! JUST DRINK IT!!

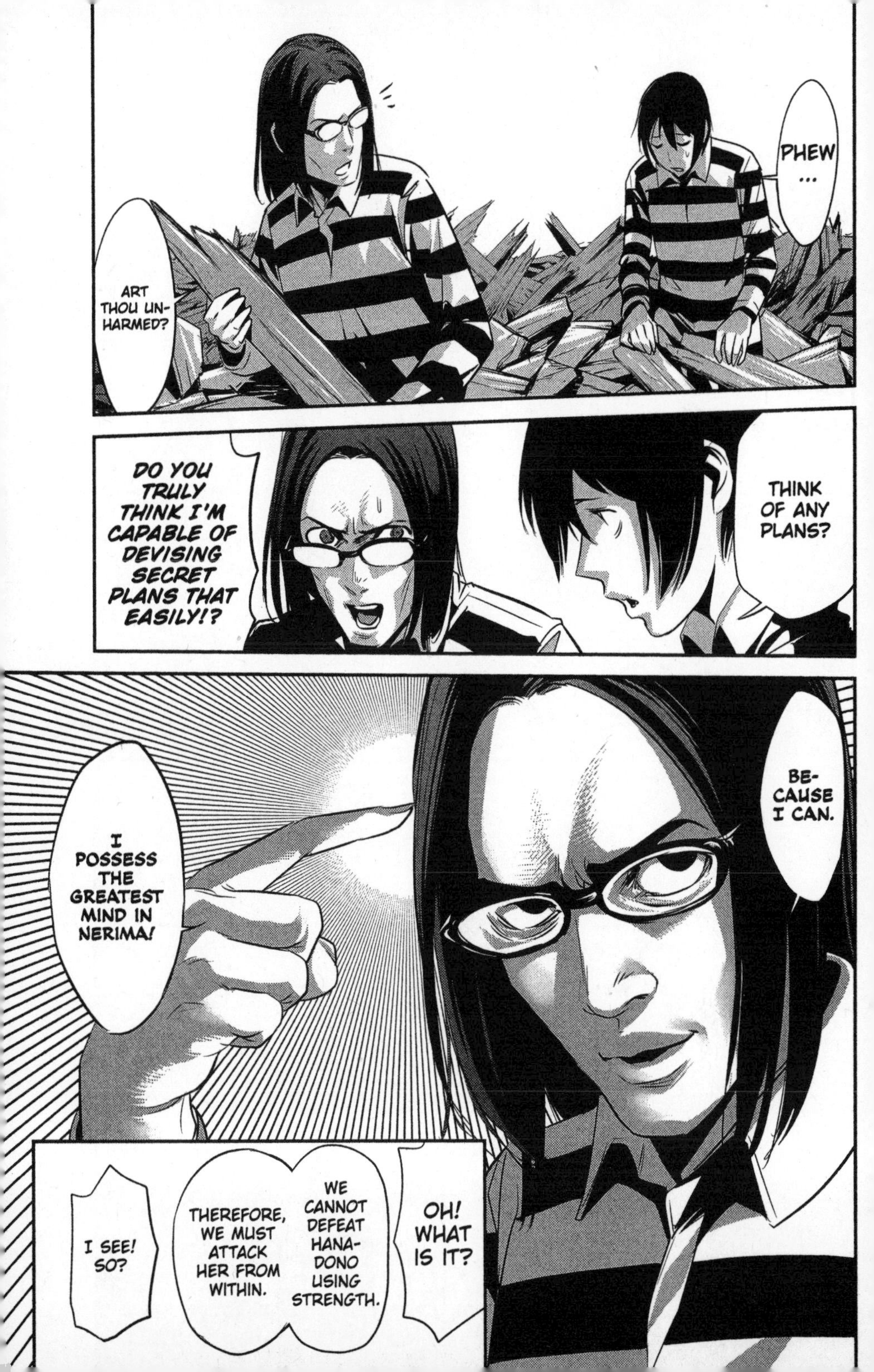
PHEW ...
ART THOU UN-HARMED?
THINK OF ANY PLANS?
DO YOU TRULY THINK I'M CAPABLE OF DEVISING SECRET PLANS THAT EASILY!?
BE-CAUSE I CAN.
I POSSESS THE GREATEST MIND IN NERIMA!
OH! WHAT IS IT?
WE CANNOT DEFEAT HANA-DONO USING STRENGTH.
THEREFORE, WE MUST ATTACK HER FROM WITHIN.
I SEE! SO?

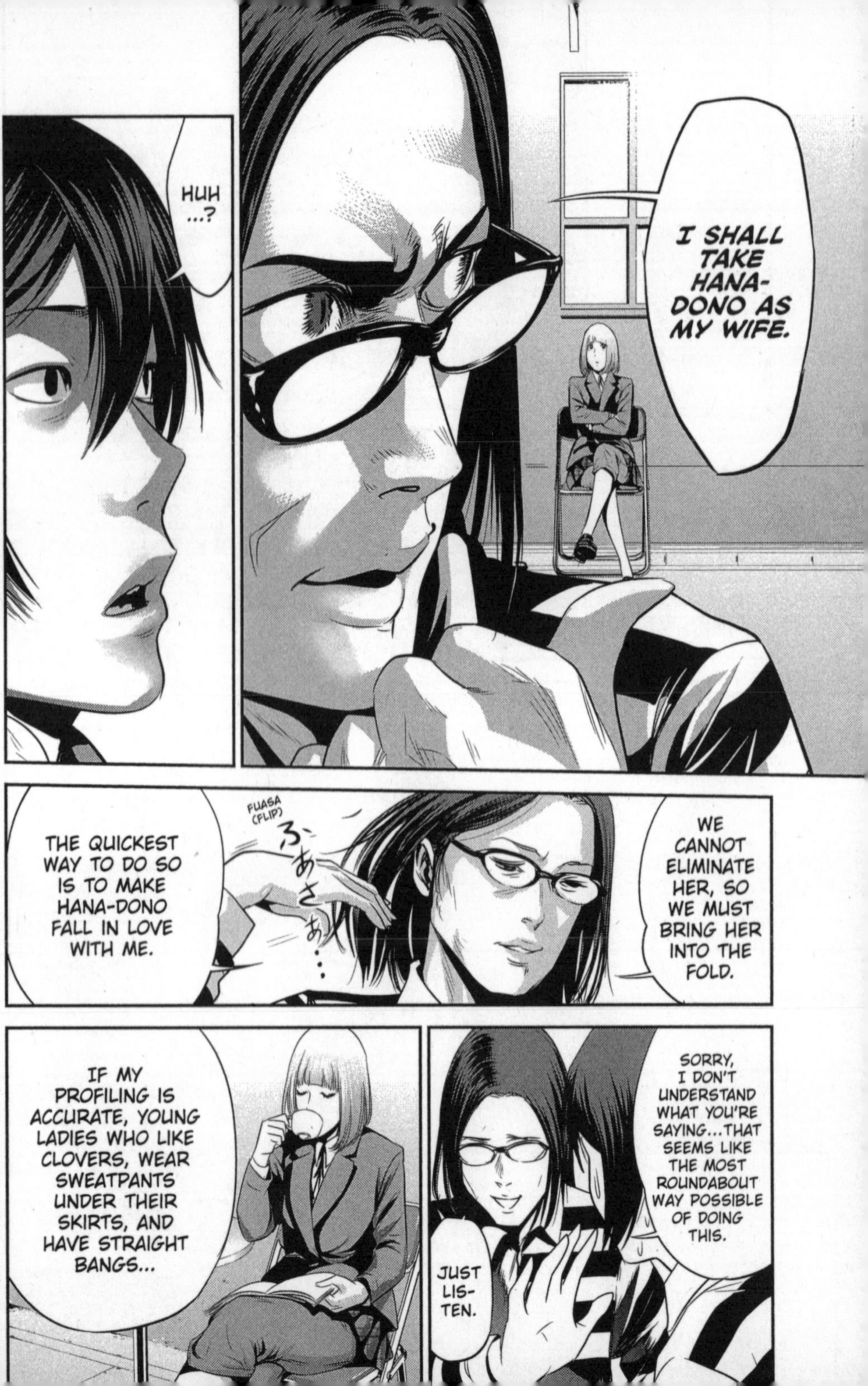
I SHALL TAKE HANA-DONO AS MY WIFE.
HUH ...?
WE CANNOT ELIMINATE HER, SO WE MUST BRING HER INTO THE FOLD.
FUASA (FLIP) ふあさあ…
THE QUICKEST WAY TO DO SO IS TO MAKE HANA-DONO FALL IN LOVE WITH ME.
SORRY, I DON'T UNDERSTAND WHAT YOU'RE SAYING...THAT SEEMS LIKE THE MOST ROUNDABOUT WAY POSSIBLE OF DOING THIS.
JUST LIS-TEN.
IF MY PROFILING IS ACCURATE, YOUNG LADIES WHO LIKE CLOVERS, WEAR SWEATPANTS UNDER THEIR SKIRTS, AND HAVE STRAIGHT BANGS...

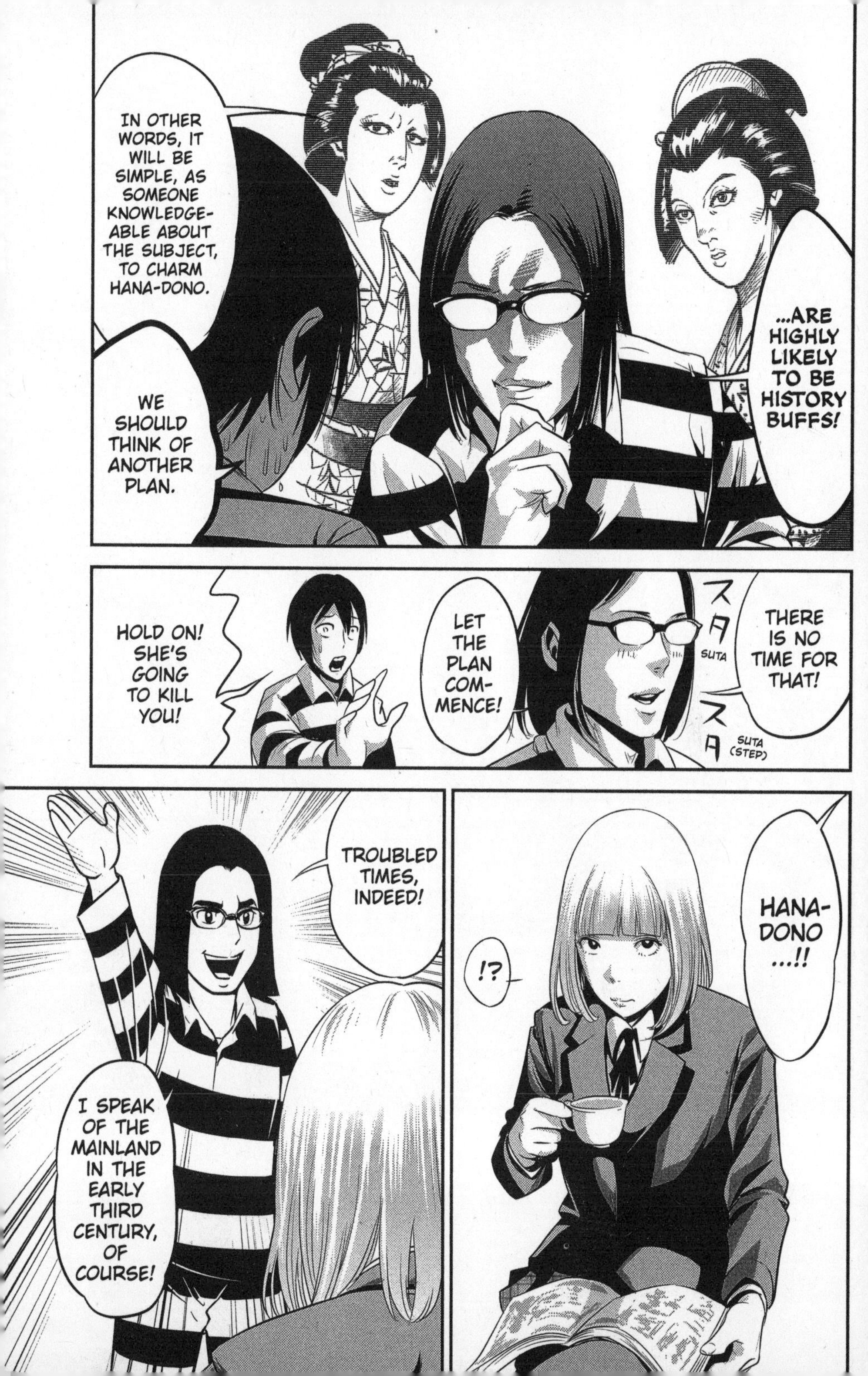
...ARE HIGHLY LIKELY TO BE HISTORY BUFFS!
IN OTHER WORDS, IT WILL BE SIMPLE, AS SOMEONE KNOWLEDGE-ABLE ABOUT THE SUBJECT, TO CHARM HANA-DONO.
WE SHOULD THINK OF ANOTHER PLAN.
THERE IS NO TIME FOR THAT!
スタ SUTA
スタ SUTA (STEP)
LET THE PLAN COM-MENCE!
HOLD ON! SHE'S GOING TO KILL YOU!
HANA-DONO ...!!
!?
TROUBLED TIMES, INDEED!
I SPEAK OF THE MAINLAND IN THE EARLY THIRD CENTURY, OF COURSE!

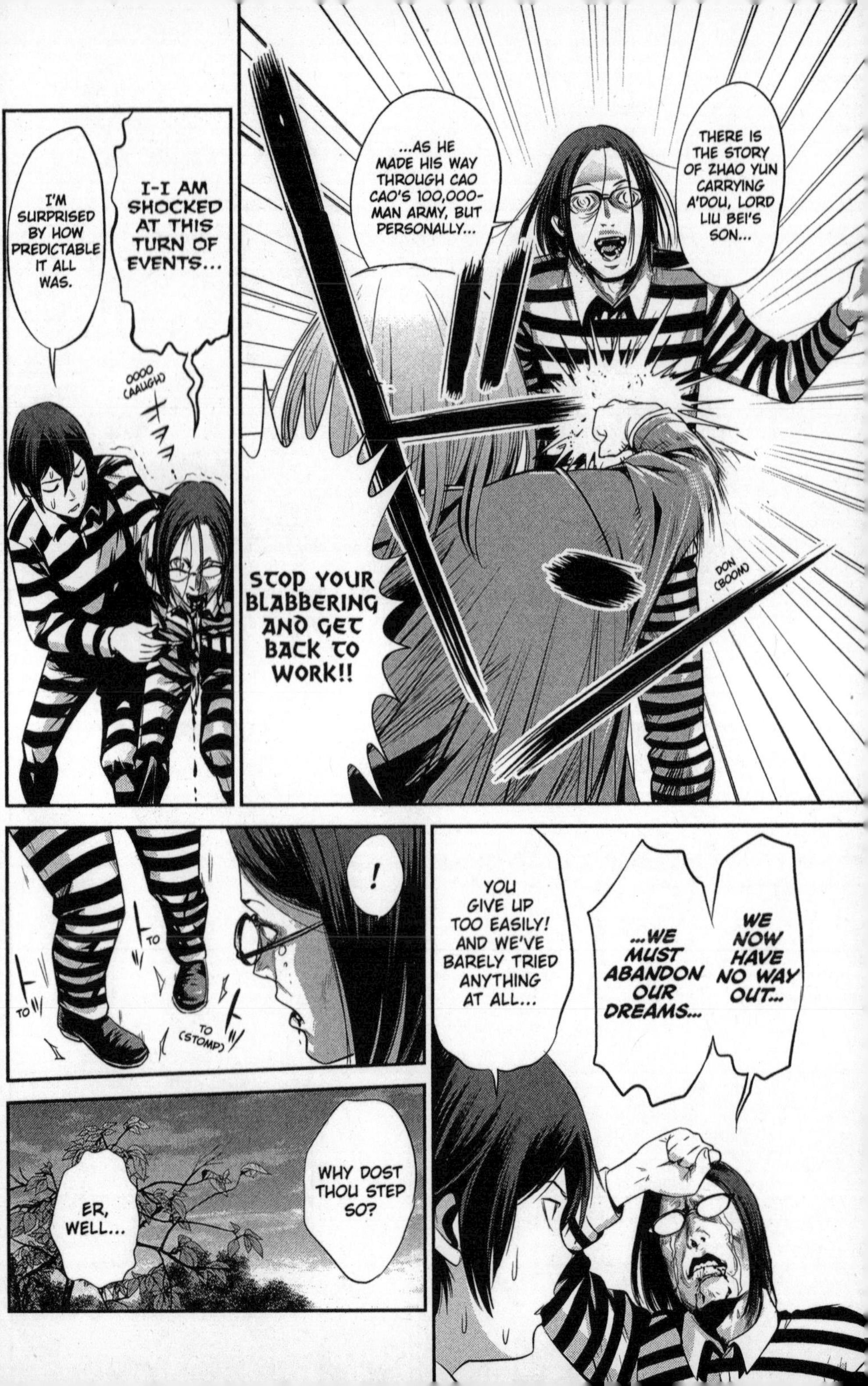
THERE IS THE STORY OF ZHAO YUN CARRYING A'DOU, LORD LIU BEI'S SON...
...AS HE MADE HIS WAY THROUGH CAO CAO'S 100,000-MAN ARMY, BUT PERSONALLY...
DON (BOOM)
STOP YOUR BLABBERING AND GET BACK TO WORK!!
I-I AM SHOCKED AT THIS TURN OF EVENTS...
I'M SURPRISED BY HOW PREDICTABLE IT ALL WAS.
OOOO (AAUGH)
WE NOW HAVE NO WAY OUT...
...WE MUST ABANDON OUR DREAMS...
YOU GIVE UP TOO EASILY! AND WE'VE BARELY TRIED ANYTHING AT ALL...
!
TO
TO
TO (STOMP)
WHY DOST THOU STEP SO?
ER, WELL...

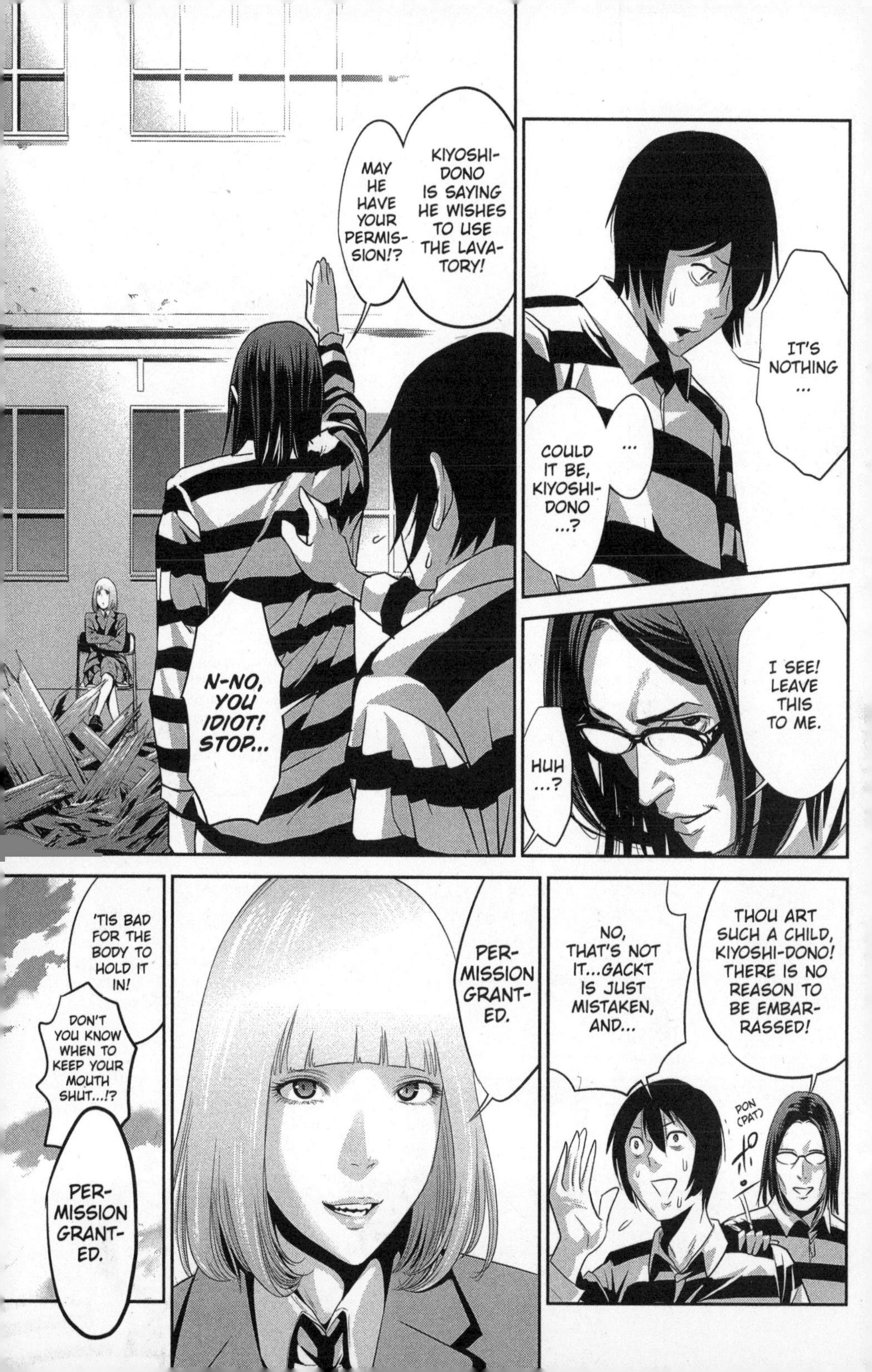

IT'S NOTHING...
...
COULD IT BE, KIYOSHI-DONO...?
I SEE! LEAVE THIS TO ME.
HUH...?
KIYOSHI-DONO IS SAYING HE WISHES TO USE THE LAVATORY!
MAY HE HAVE YOUR PERMISSION!?
N-NO, YOU IDIOT! STOP...
THOU ART SUCH A CHILD, KIYOSHI-DONO! THERE IS NO REASON TO BE EMBARRASSED!
PON (PAT)
NO, THAT'S NOT IT...GACKT IS JUST MISTAKEN, AND...
PERMISSION GRANTED.
'TIS BAD FOR THE BODY TO HOLD IT IN!
DON'T YOU KNOW WHEN TO KEEP YOUR MOUTH SHUT...!?
PERMISSION GRANTED.

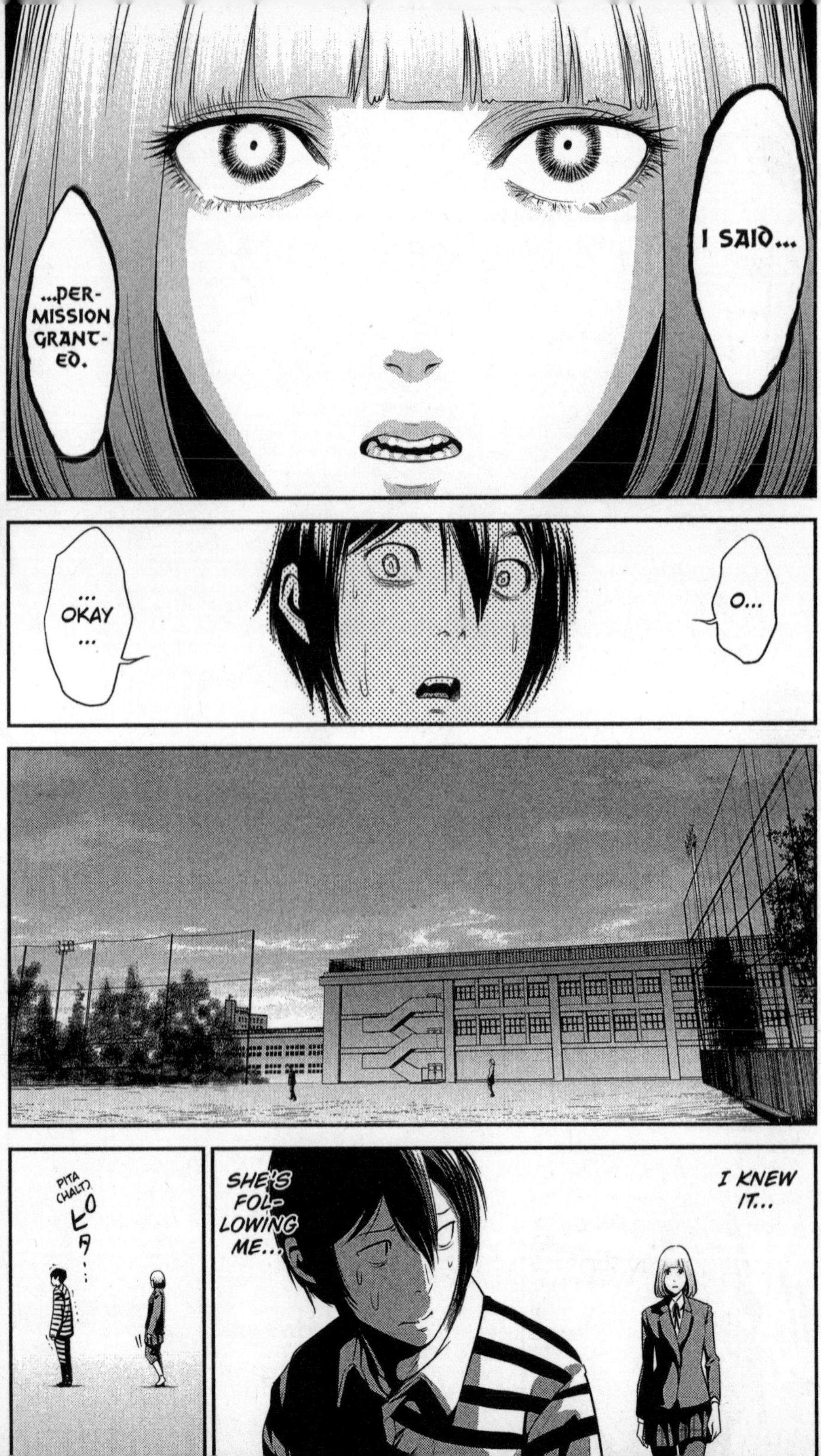
I SAID...
...PER-MISSION GRANT-ED.
O...
...OKAY...
I KNEW IT...
SHE'S FOL-LOWING ME...
PITA (HALT)
ピタ…

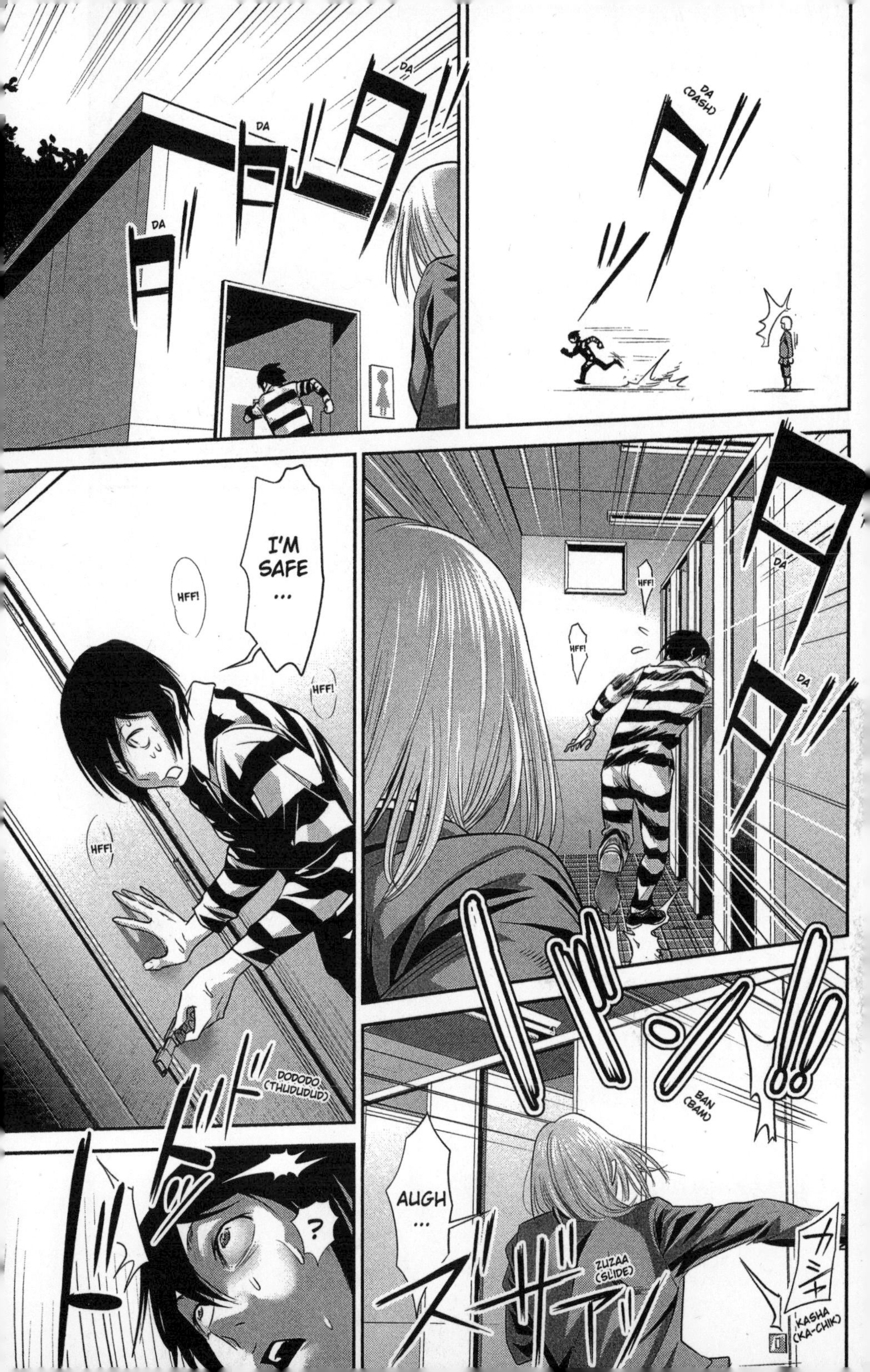

DA (DASH)
DA
DA
DA
DA
HFF!
HFF!
DA
I'M SAFE ...
HFF!
HFF!
HFF!
BAN (BAM)
DODODO (THUDUDUD)
?
AUGH ...
ZUZAA (SLIDE)
KASHA (KA-CHIK)

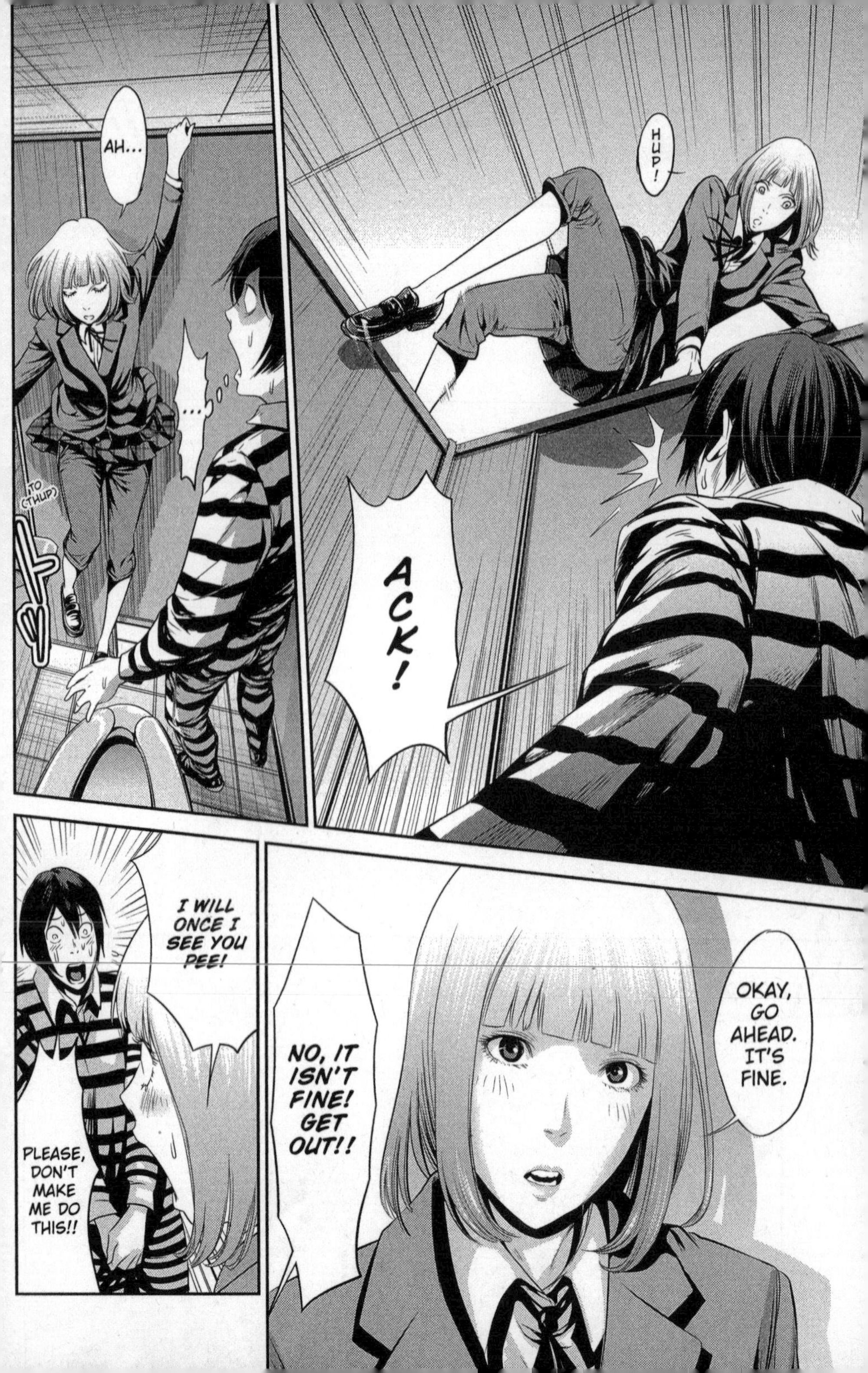
HUP!
ACK!
AH...
...
(THUP)
OKAY, GO AHEAD. IT'S FINE.
NO, IT ISN'T FINE! GET OUT!!
I WILL ONCE I SEE YOU PEE!
PLEASE, DON'T MAKE ME DO THIS!!

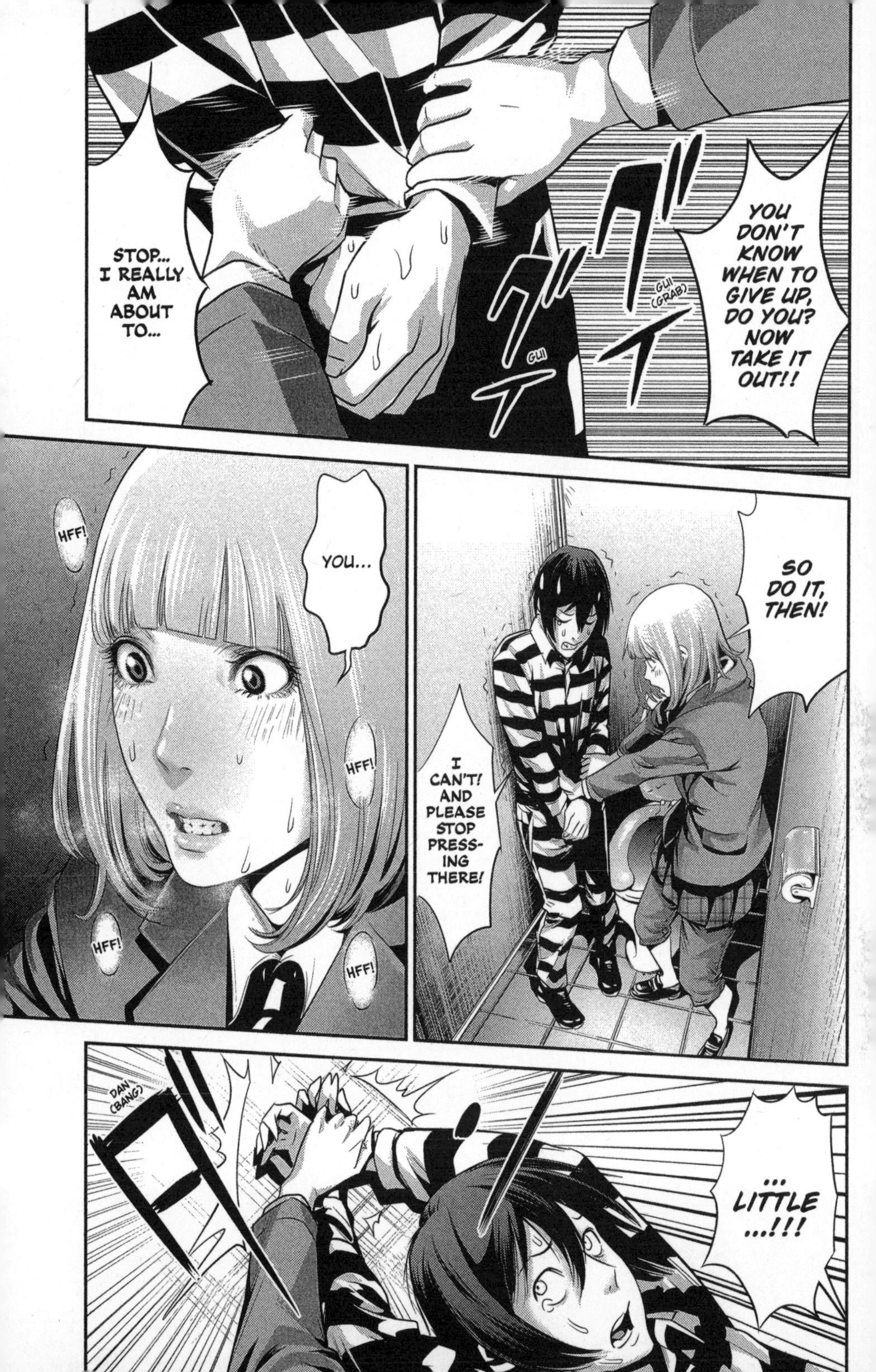
YOU DON'T KNOW WHEN TO GIVE UP, DO YOU? NOW TAKE IT OUT!!
GUI (GRAB)
GUI
STOP... I REALLY AM ABOUT TO...
SO DO IT, THEN!
I CAN'T! AND PLEASE STOP PRESS-ING THERE!
YOU...
HFF!
HFF!
HFF!
HFF!
... LITTLE ...!!!
DAN (BANG)

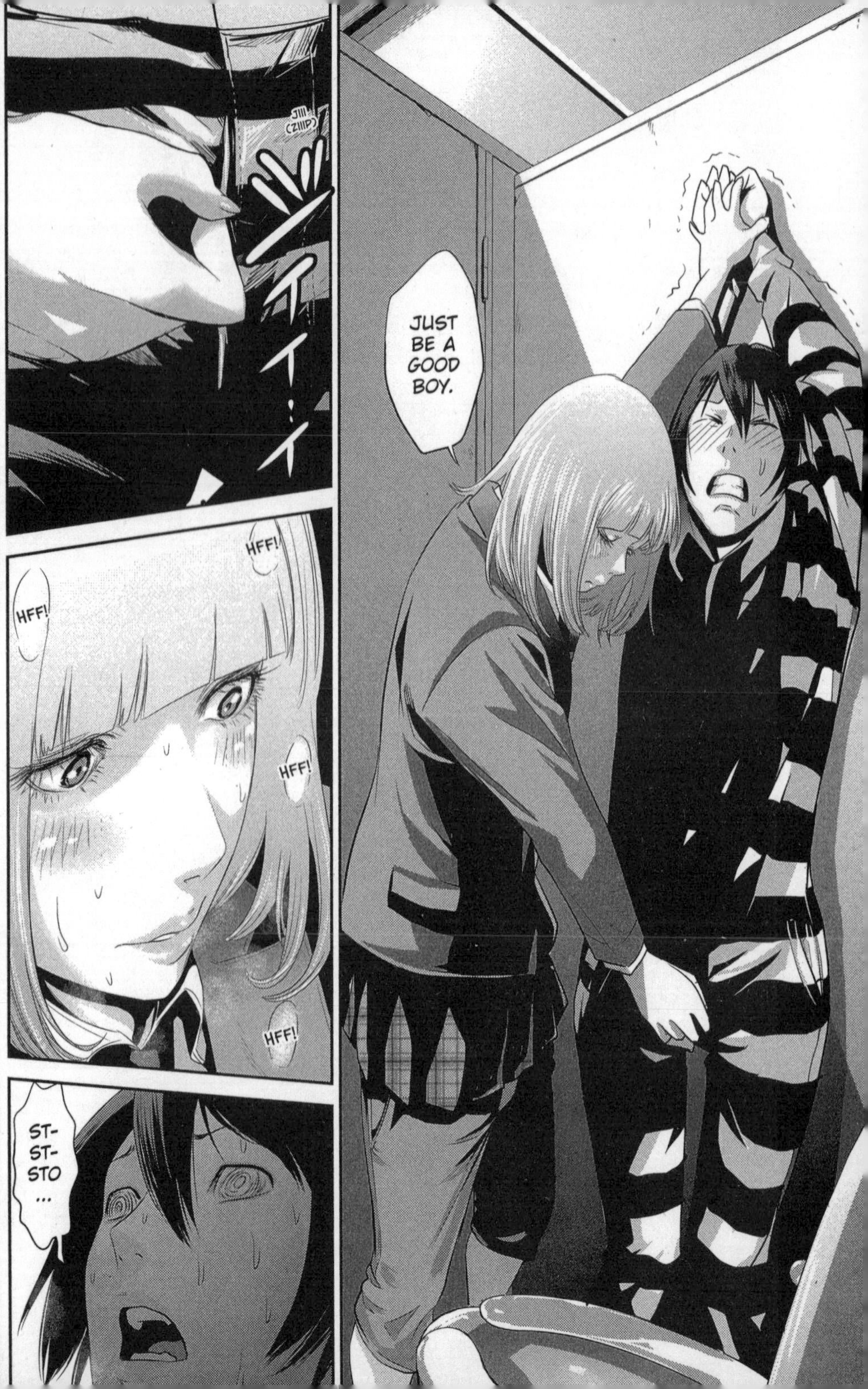

JUST BE A GOOD BOY.
JIII (ZIIIP)
HFF!
HFF!
HFF!
HFF!
ST- ST- STO ...

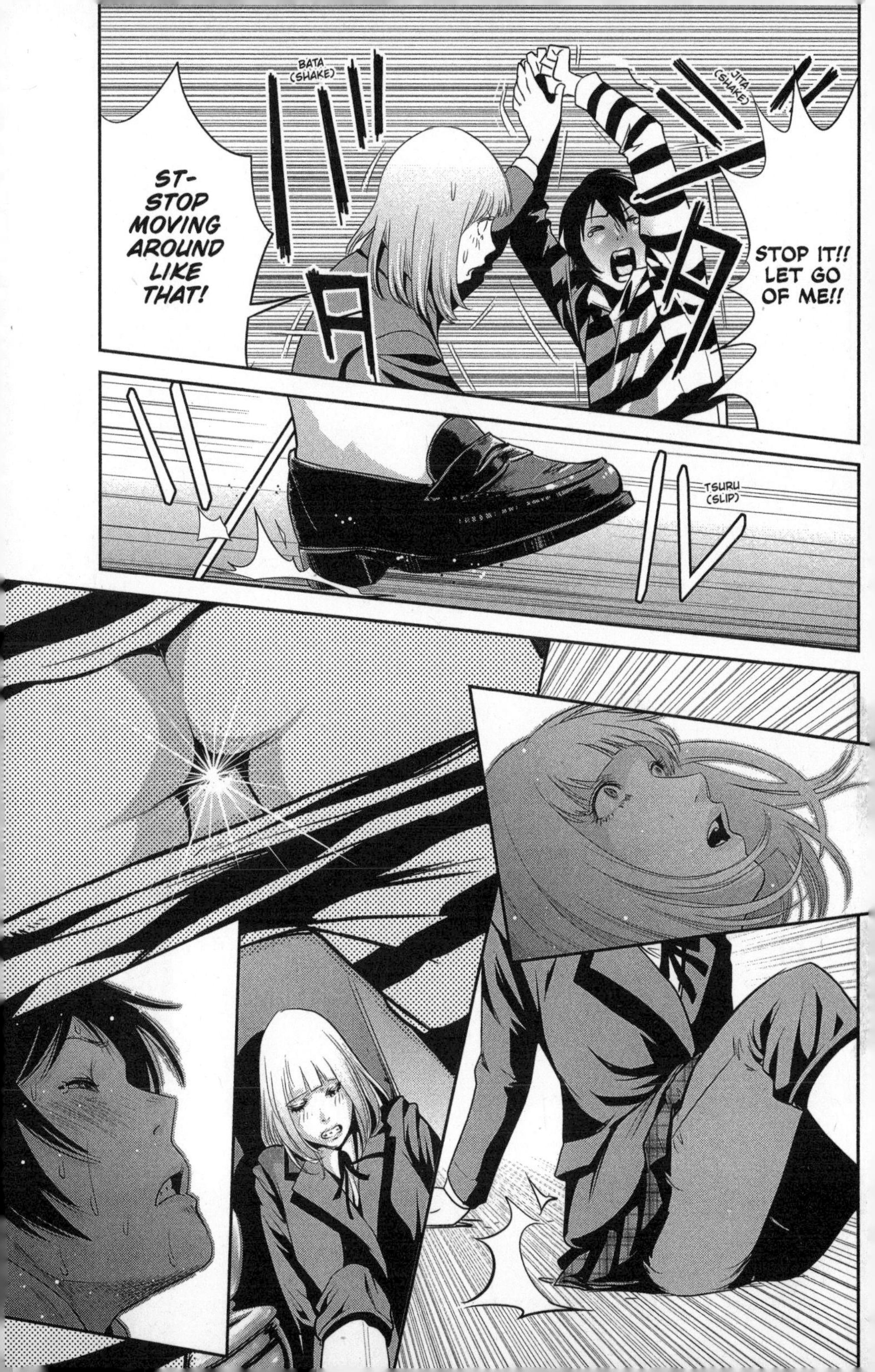
JITA (SHAKE)
BATA (SHAKE)
STOP IT!! LET GO OF ME!!
ST- STOP MOVING AROUND LIKE THAT!
TSURU (SLIP)

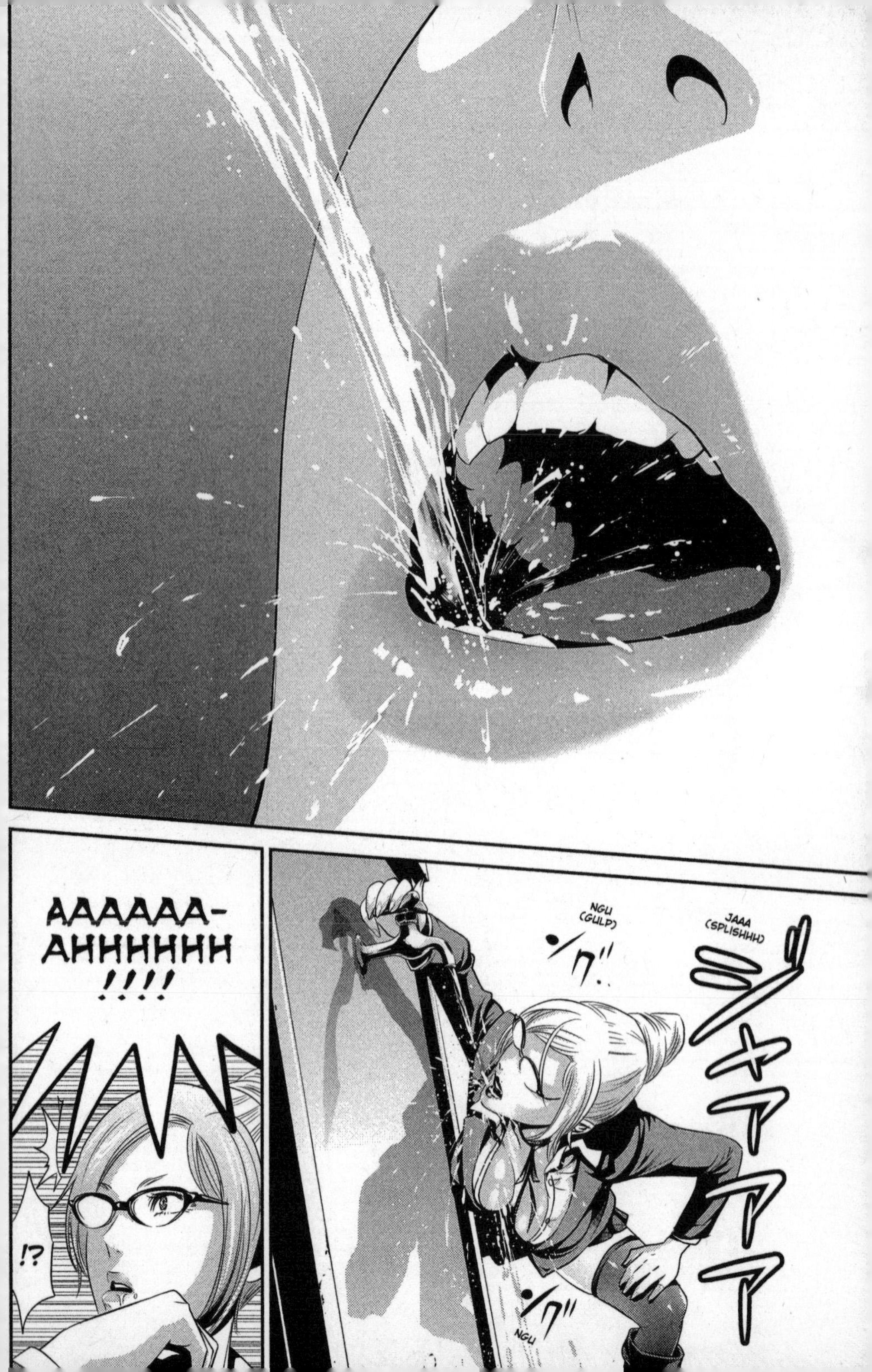

JAAA (SPLISHHH)
ジャアアア
NGU (GULP)
ング!!
NGU
ング
AAAAAA-AHHHHHH!!!!
!?

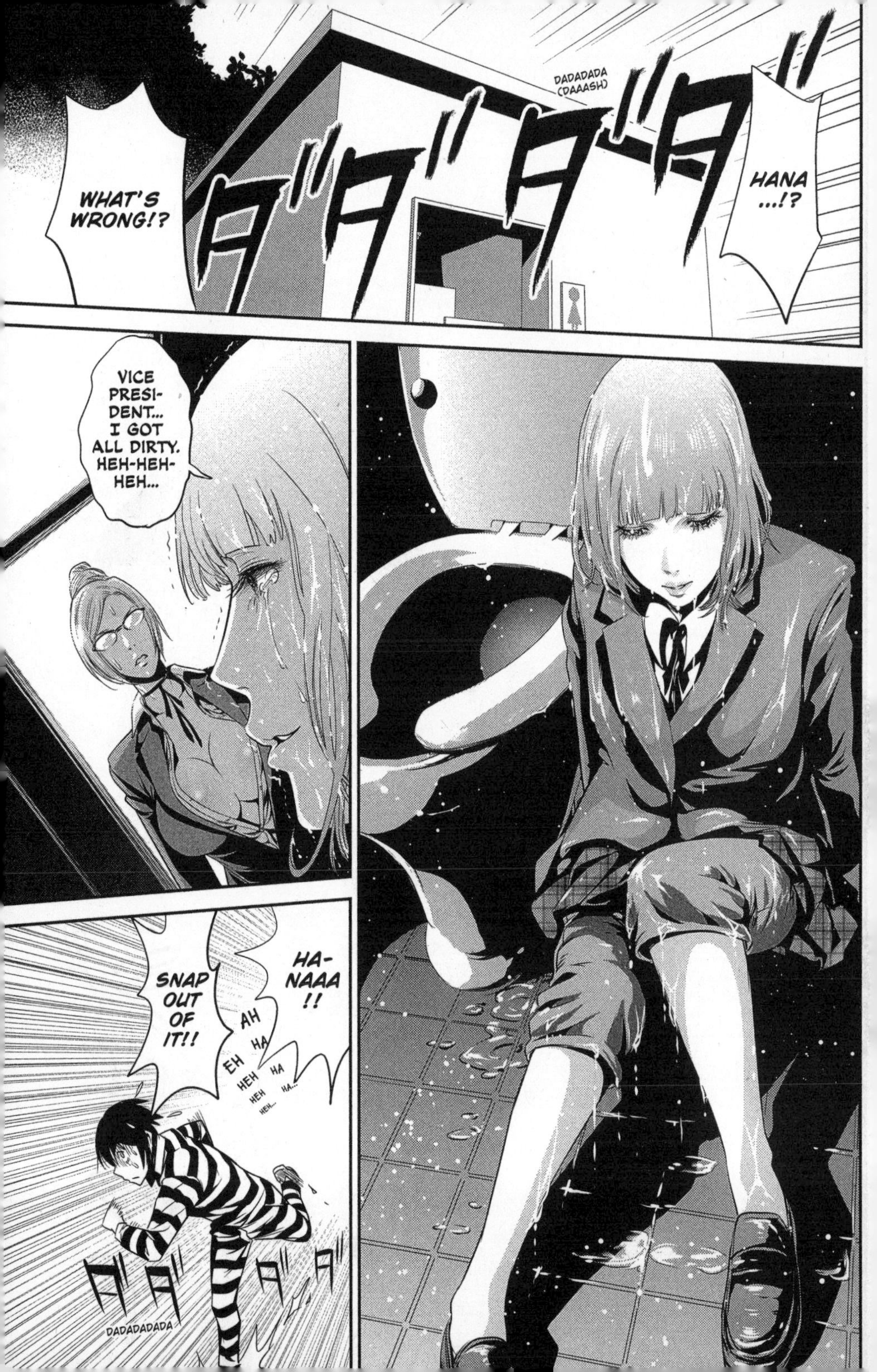
DADADADA (DAAASH)
HANA ...!?
WHAT'S WRONG!?
VICE PRESI-DENT... I GOT ALL DIRTY. HEH-HEH-HEH...
HA-NAAA!!
SNAP OUT OF IT!!
AH HA EH HA HEH HA HEH HA... HEH...
DADADADADA

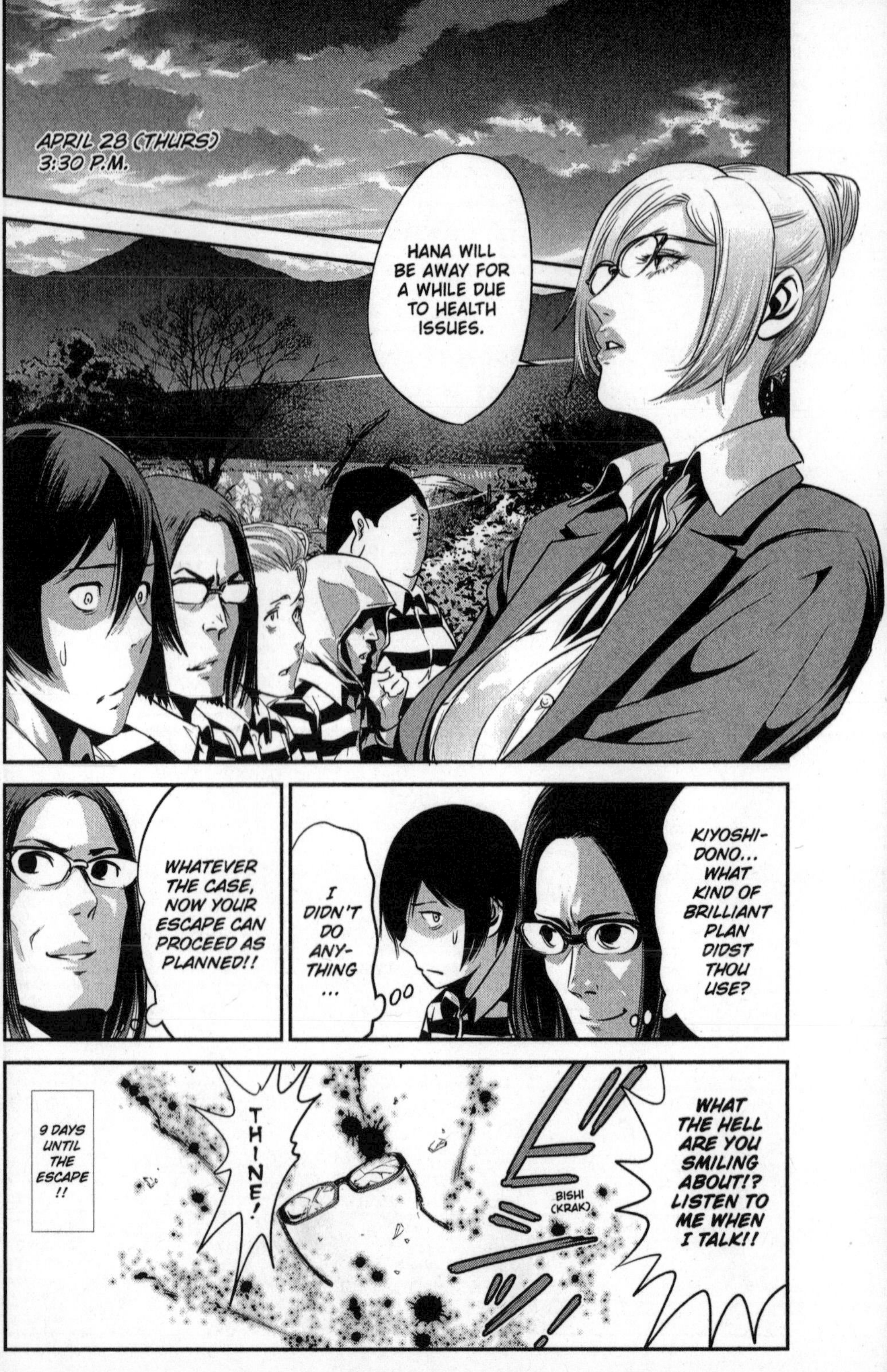
APRIL 28 (THURS) 3:30 P.M.
HANA WILL BE AWAY FOR A WHILE DUE TO HEALTH ISSUES.
KIYOSHI-DONO... WHAT KIND OF BRILLIANT PLAN DIDST THOU USE?
I DIDN'T DO ANYTHING...
WHATEVER THE CASE, NOW YOUR ESCAPE CAN PROCEED AS PLANNED!!
WHAT THE HELL ARE YOU SMILING ABOUT!? LISTEN TO ME WHEN I TALK!!
BISHI (KRAK)
THINE!
9 DAYS UNTIL THE ESCAPE !!

CHAPTER 13: TRAINING DAY

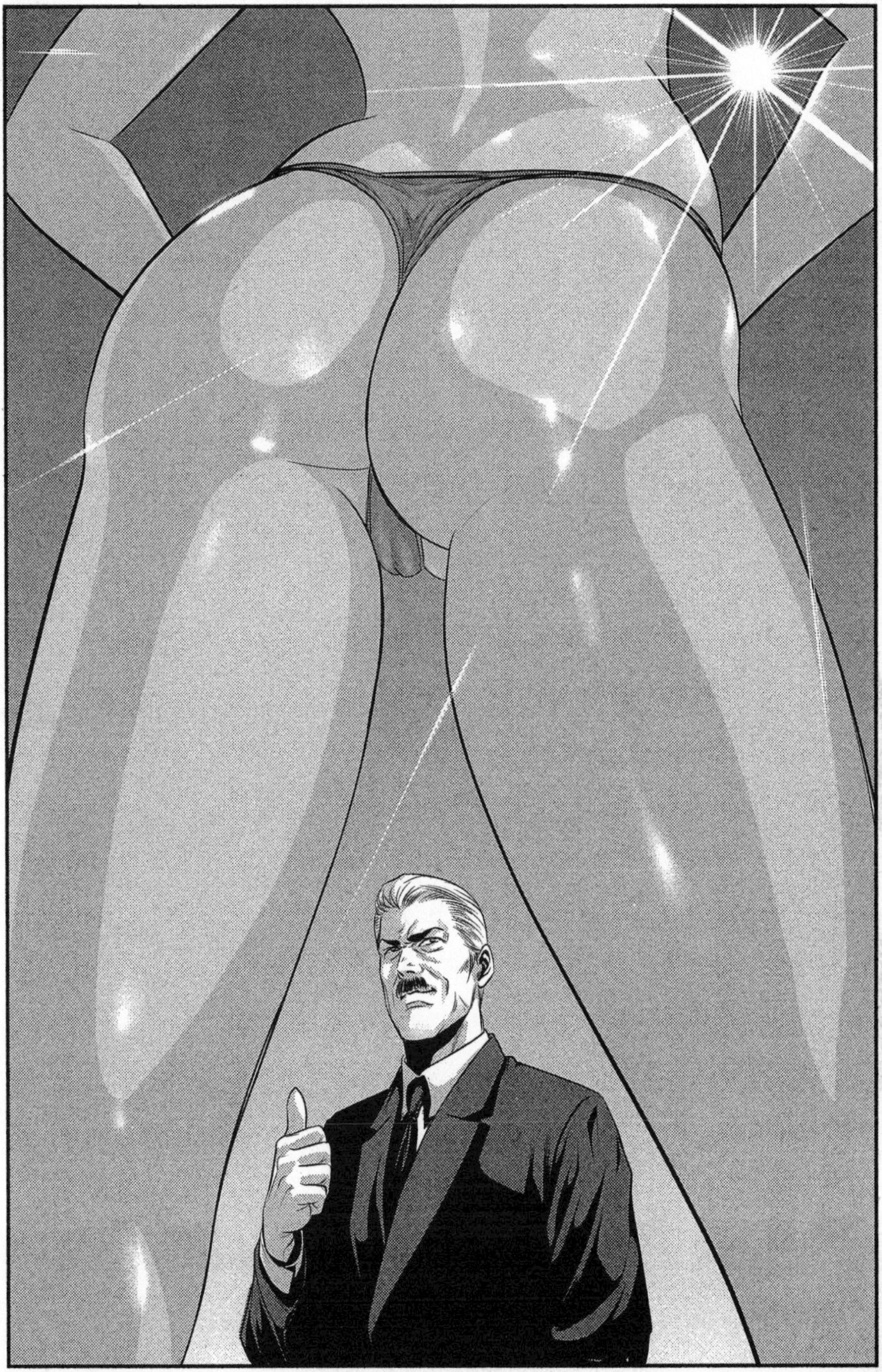

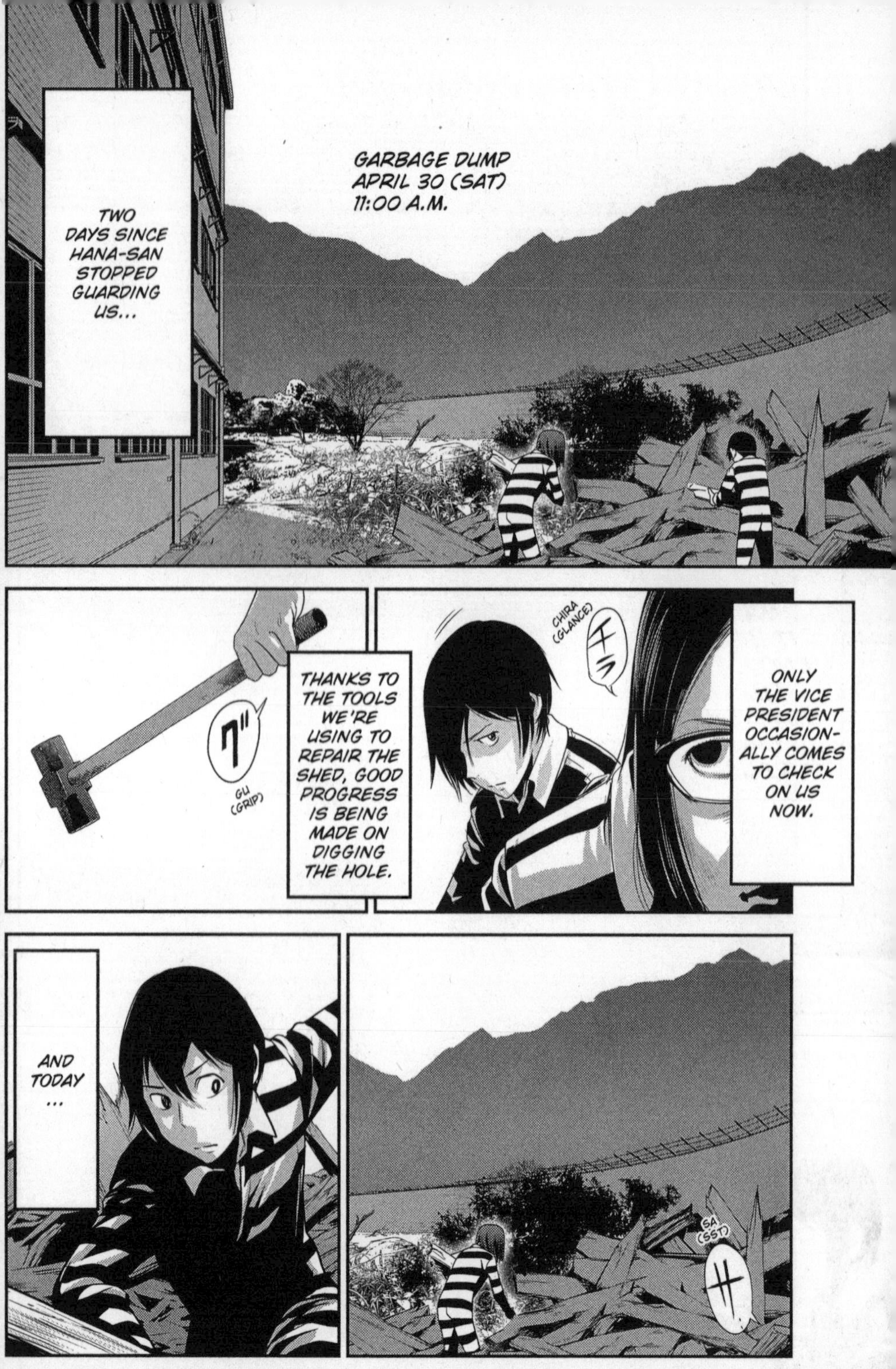
GARBAGE DUMP
APRIL 30 (SAT)
11:00 A.M.
TWO DAYS SINCE HANA-SAN STOPPED GUARDING US...
ONLY THE VICE PRESIDENT OCCASION-ALLY COMES TO CHECK ON US NOW.
チラ
CHIRA (GLANCE)
THANKS TO THE TOOLS WE'RE USING TO REPAIR THE SHED, GOOD PROGRESS IS BEING MADE ON DIGGING THE HOLE.
グ
GU (GRIP)
サ
SA (SST)
AND TODAY ...

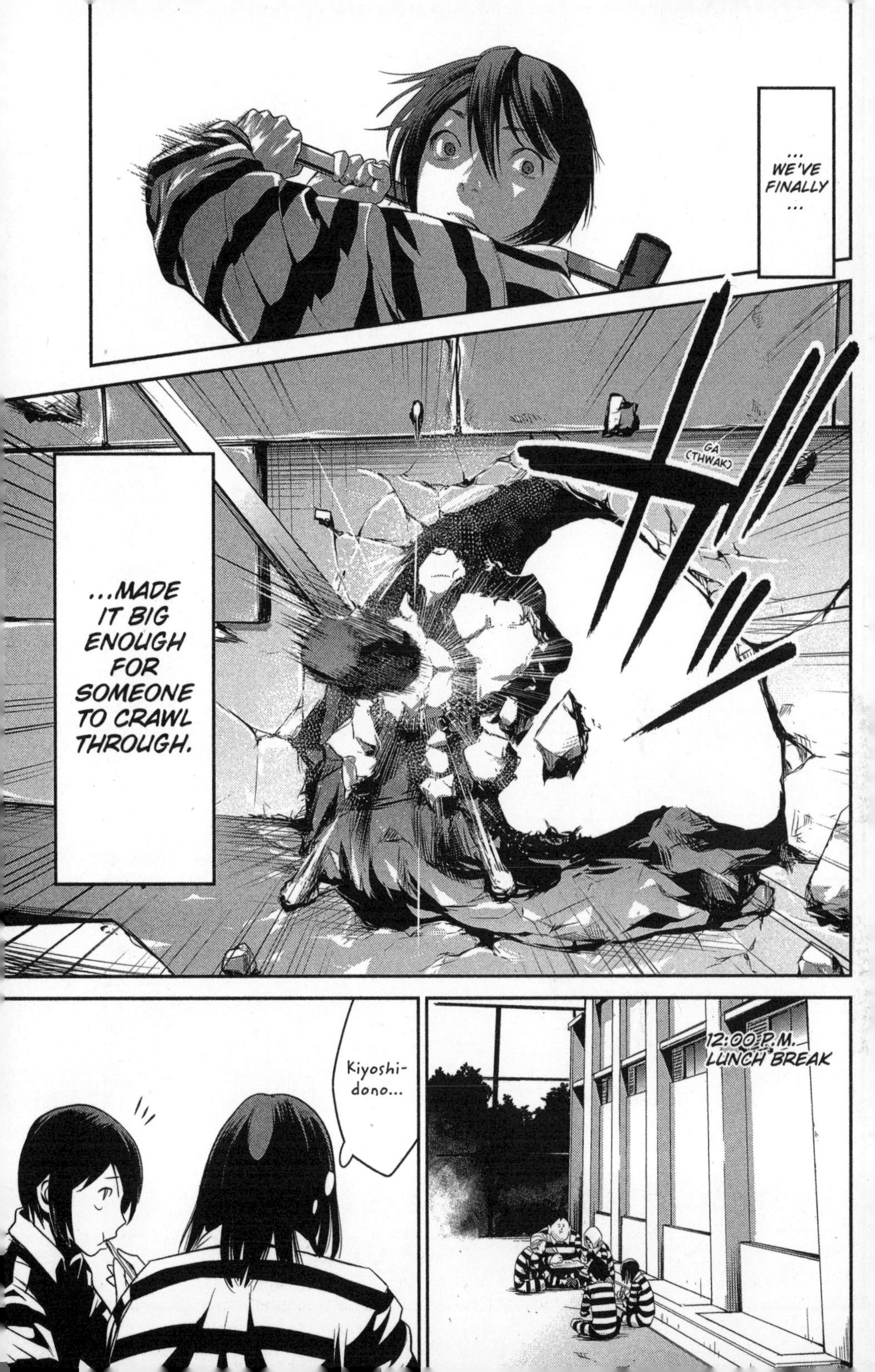
...WE'VE FINALLY...
GA (THWAK)
...MADE IT BIG ENOUGH FOR SOMEONE TO CRAWL THROUGH.
12:00 P.M. LUNCH BREAK
Kiyoshi-dono...

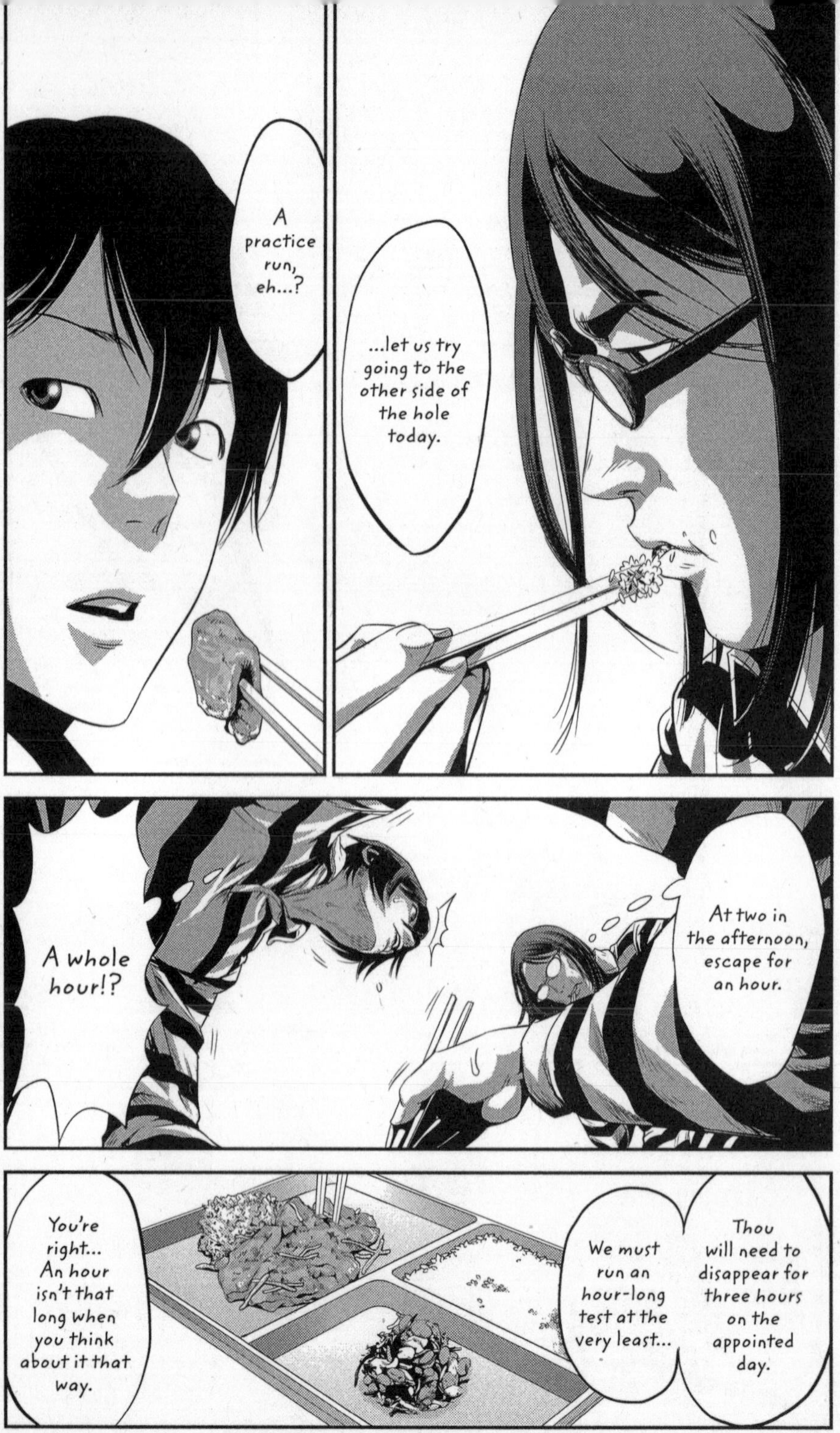
...let us try going to the other side of the hole today.
A practice run, eh...?
At two in the afternoon, escape for an hour.
A whole hour!?
Thou will need to disappear for three hours on the appointed day.
We must run an hour-long test at the very least...
You're right... An hour isn't that long when you think about it that way.

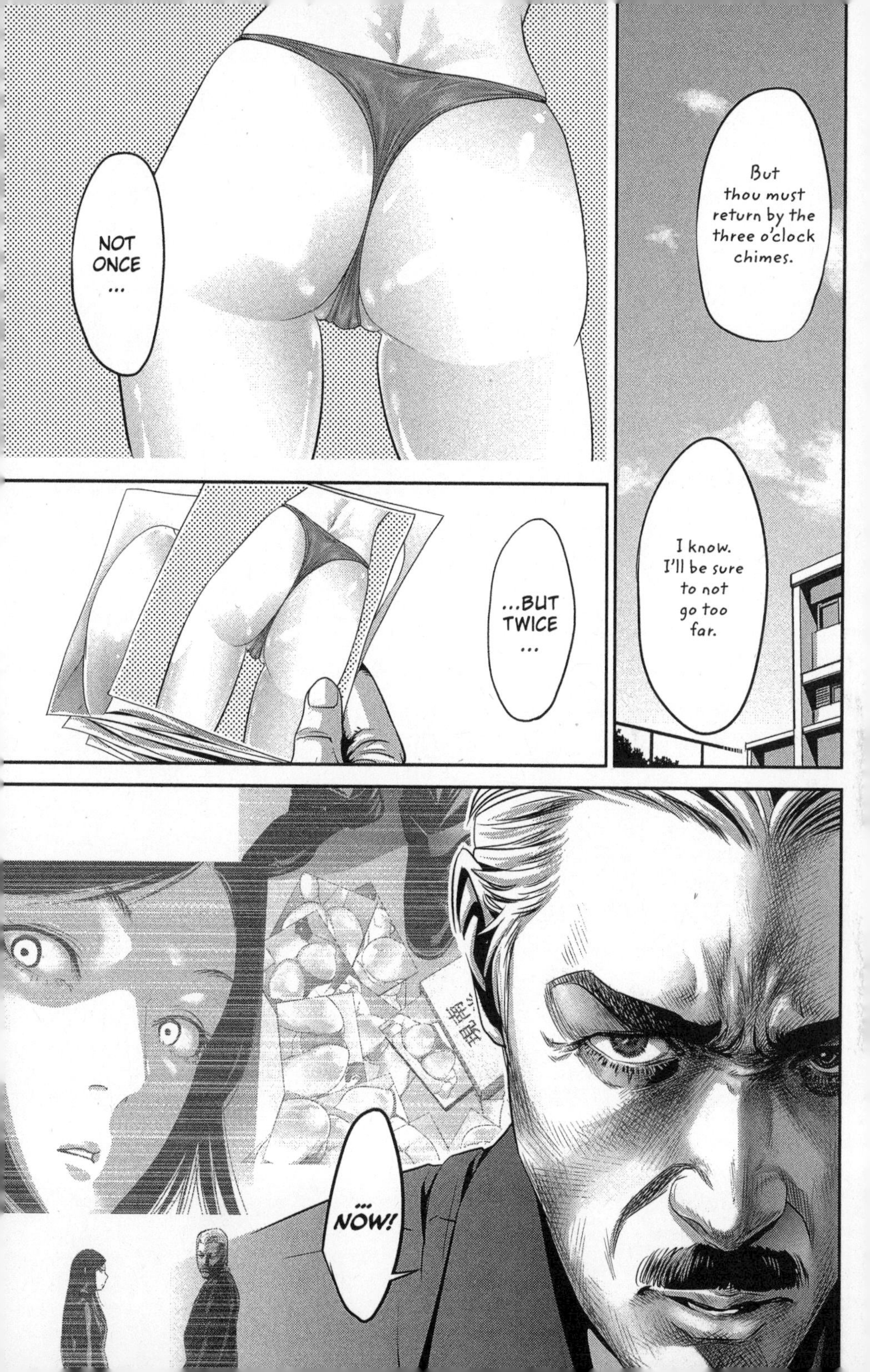
But thou must return by the three o'clock chimes.
I know. I'll be sure to not go too far.
NOT ONCE ...
...BUT TWICE ...
... NOW!

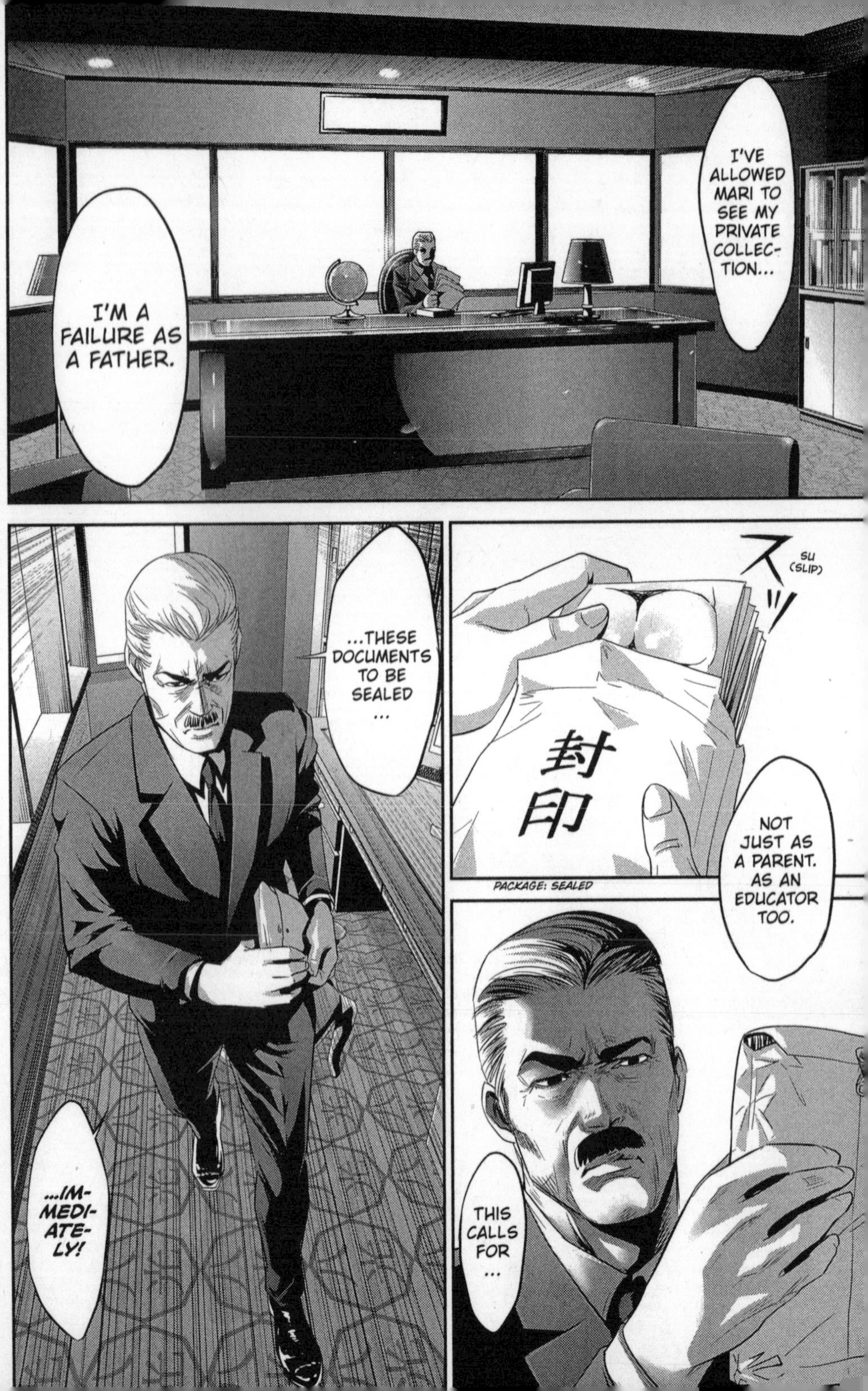
I'VE ALLOWED MARI TO SEE MY PRIVATE COLLEC-TION...
I'M A FAILURE AS A FATHER.
ス ッ
SU (SLIP)
封印
PACKAGE: SEALED
NOT JUST AS A PARENT. AS AN EDUCATOR TOO.
THIS CALLS FOR...
...THESE DOCUMENTS TO BE SEALED...
...IM-MEDI-ATE-LY!

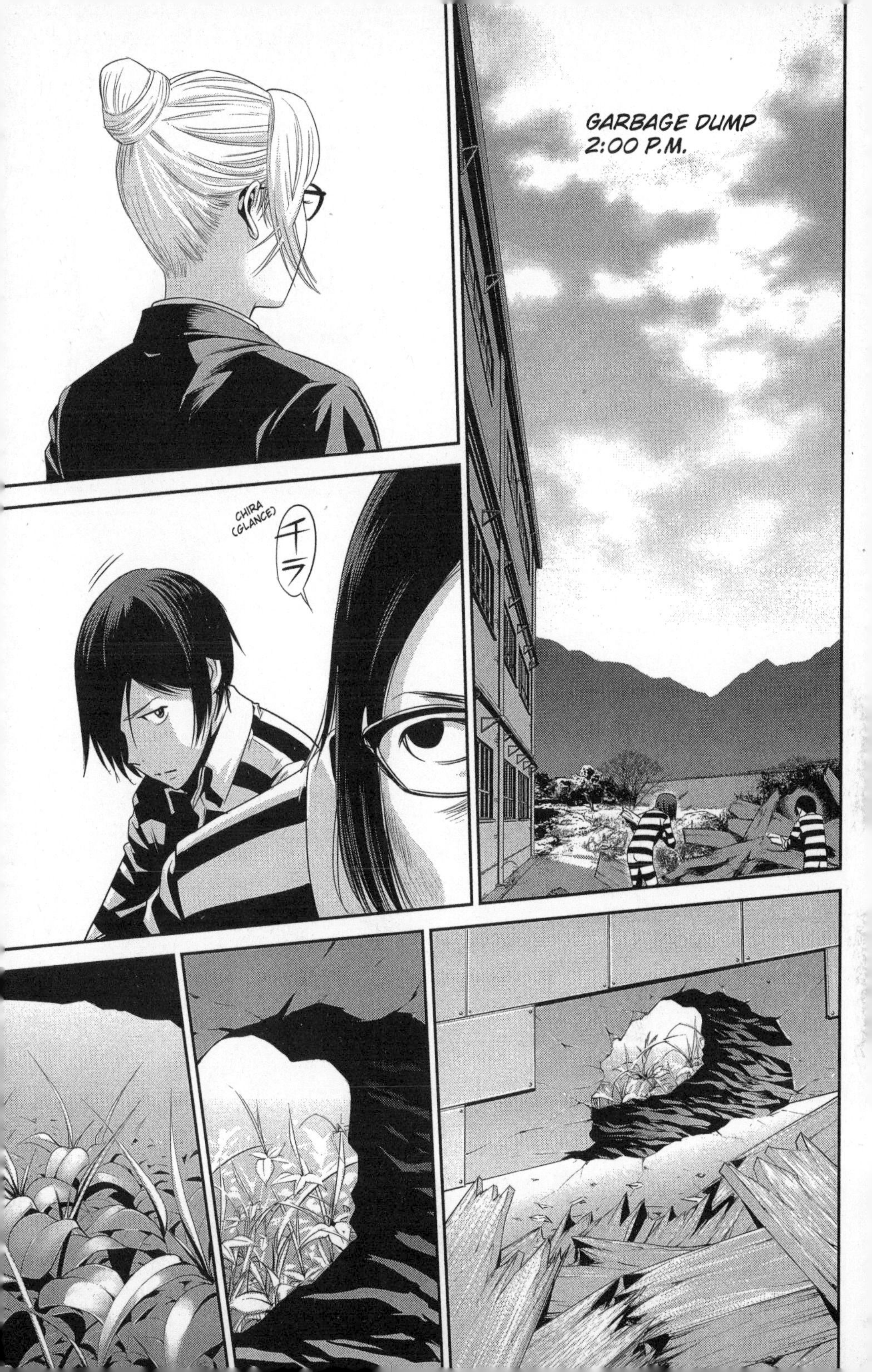
GARBAGE DUMP
2:00 P.M.
チラ
CHIRA (GLANCE)

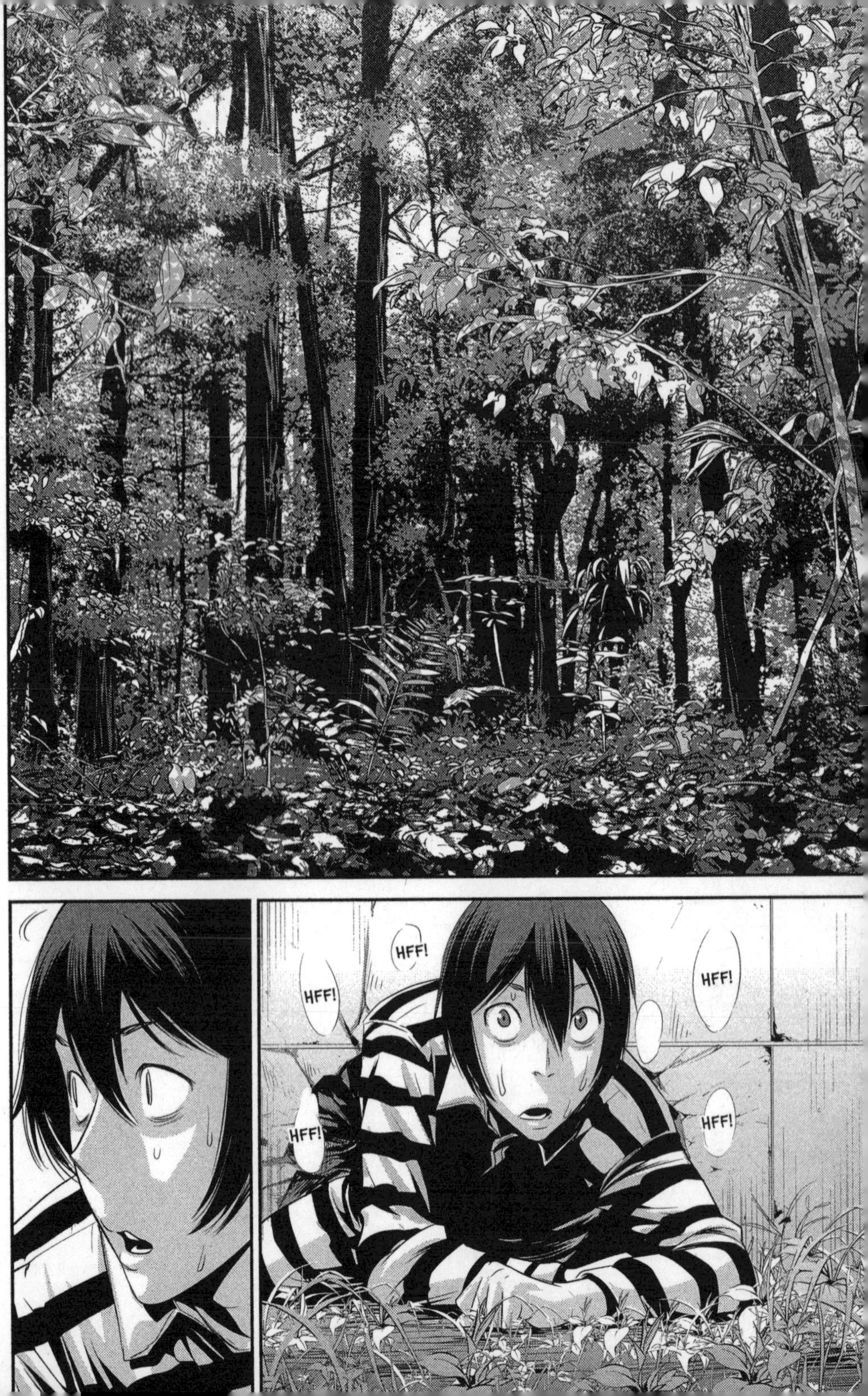
HFF!
HFF!
HFF!
HFF!
HFF!

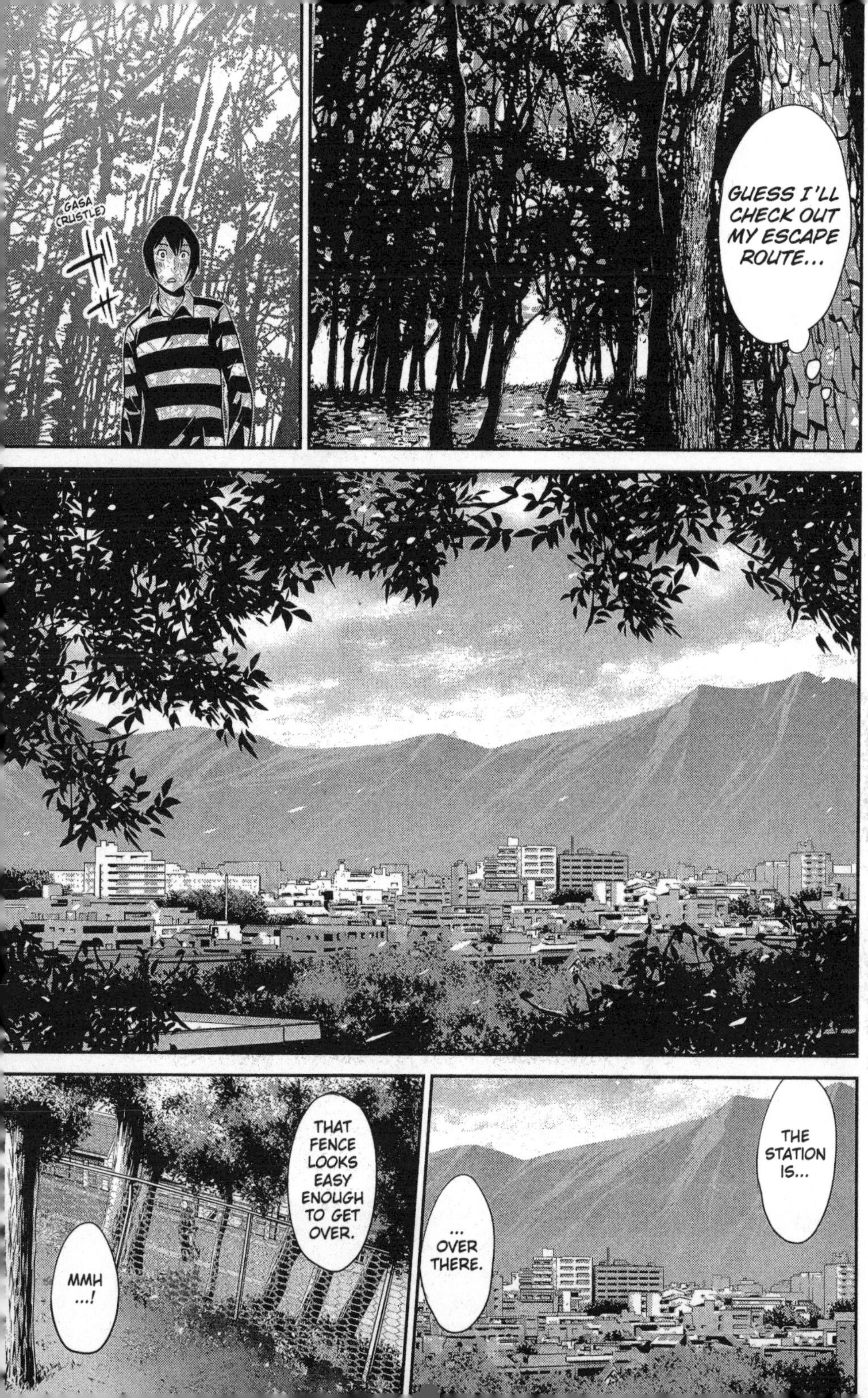
GUESS I'LL CHECK OUT MY ESCAPE ROUTE...
GASA (RUSTLE)
THE STATION IS...
... OVER THERE.
THAT FENCE LOOKS EASY ENOUGH TO GET OVER.
MMH ...!

UGH, GET A ROOM!

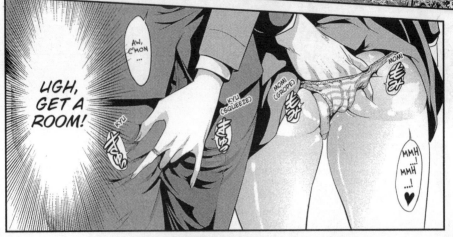

AW, C'MON ...

KYU (SQUEEZE)

MOMI (GROPE)

MOMI

KYU

MMH ...! MMH ...!

JUST YOU WATCH... NEXT WEEK, I'M GONNA BE WITH CHIYO-CHAN, AND I'M GONNA...

...FLIRT WITH HER, BUT NOT SO MUCH THAT SHE'LL HATE ME!!

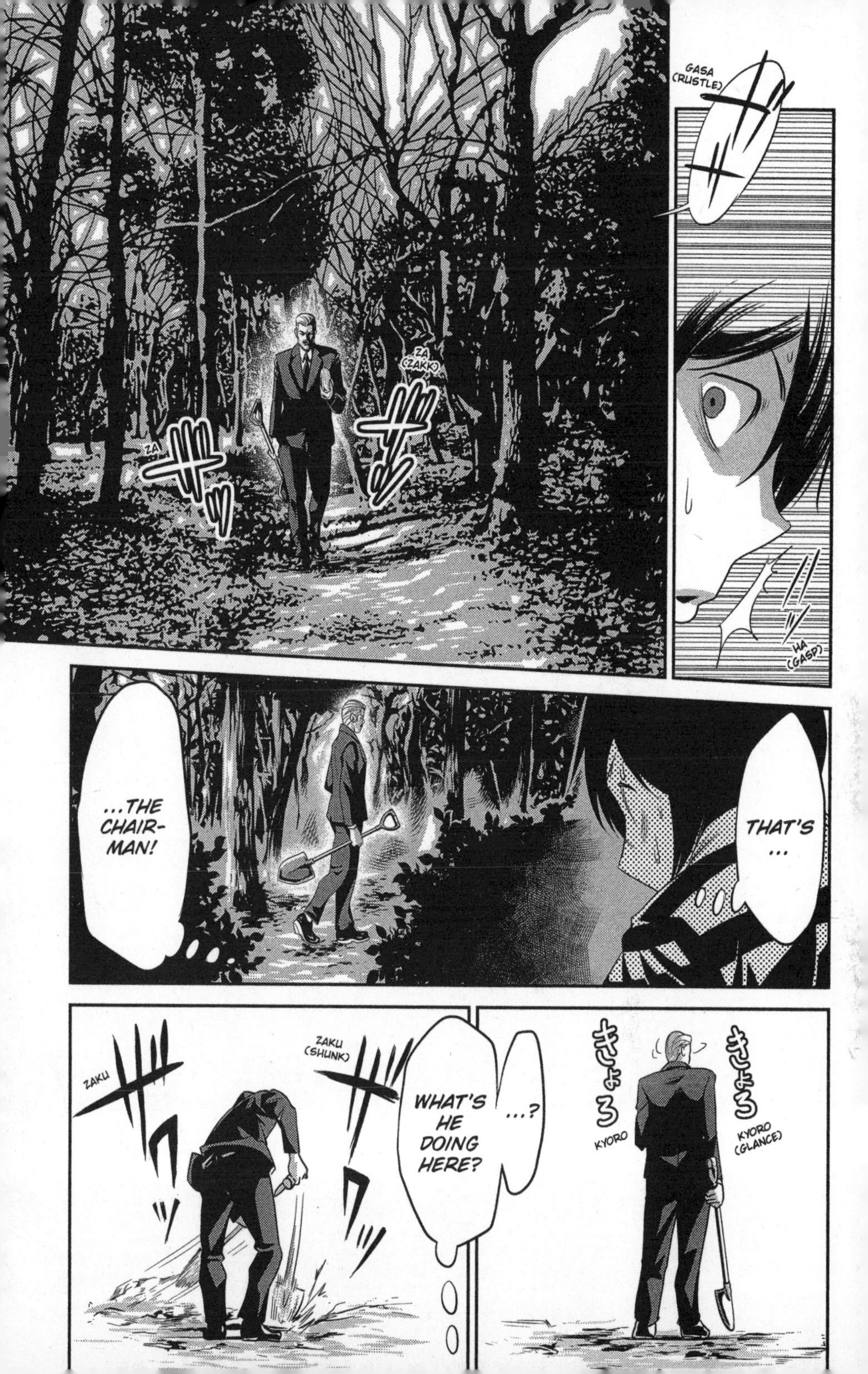
GASA (RUSTLE)
ZA (ZAKK)
ZA
HA (GASP)
THAT'S ...
...THE CHAIR-MAN!
KYORO (GLANCE)
KYORO
...?
WHAT'S HE DOING HERE?
ZAKU (SHUNK)
ZAKU

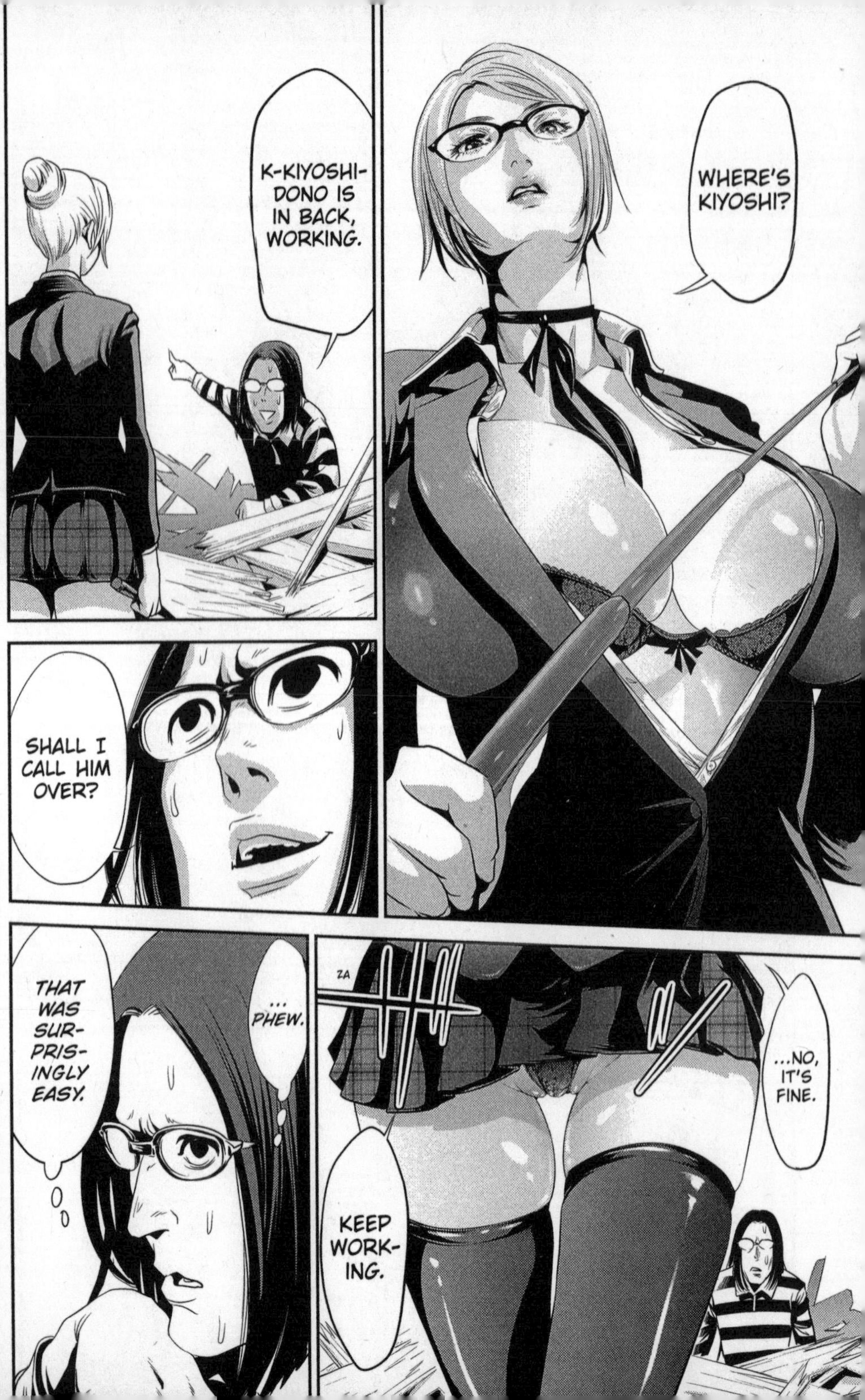
WHERE'S KIYOSHI?
K-KIYOSHI-DONO IS IN BACK, WORKING.
SHALL I CALL HIM OVER?
ZA
...NO, IT'S FINE.
KEEP WORK-ING.
...PHEW.
THAT WAS SUR-PRIS-INGLY EASY.

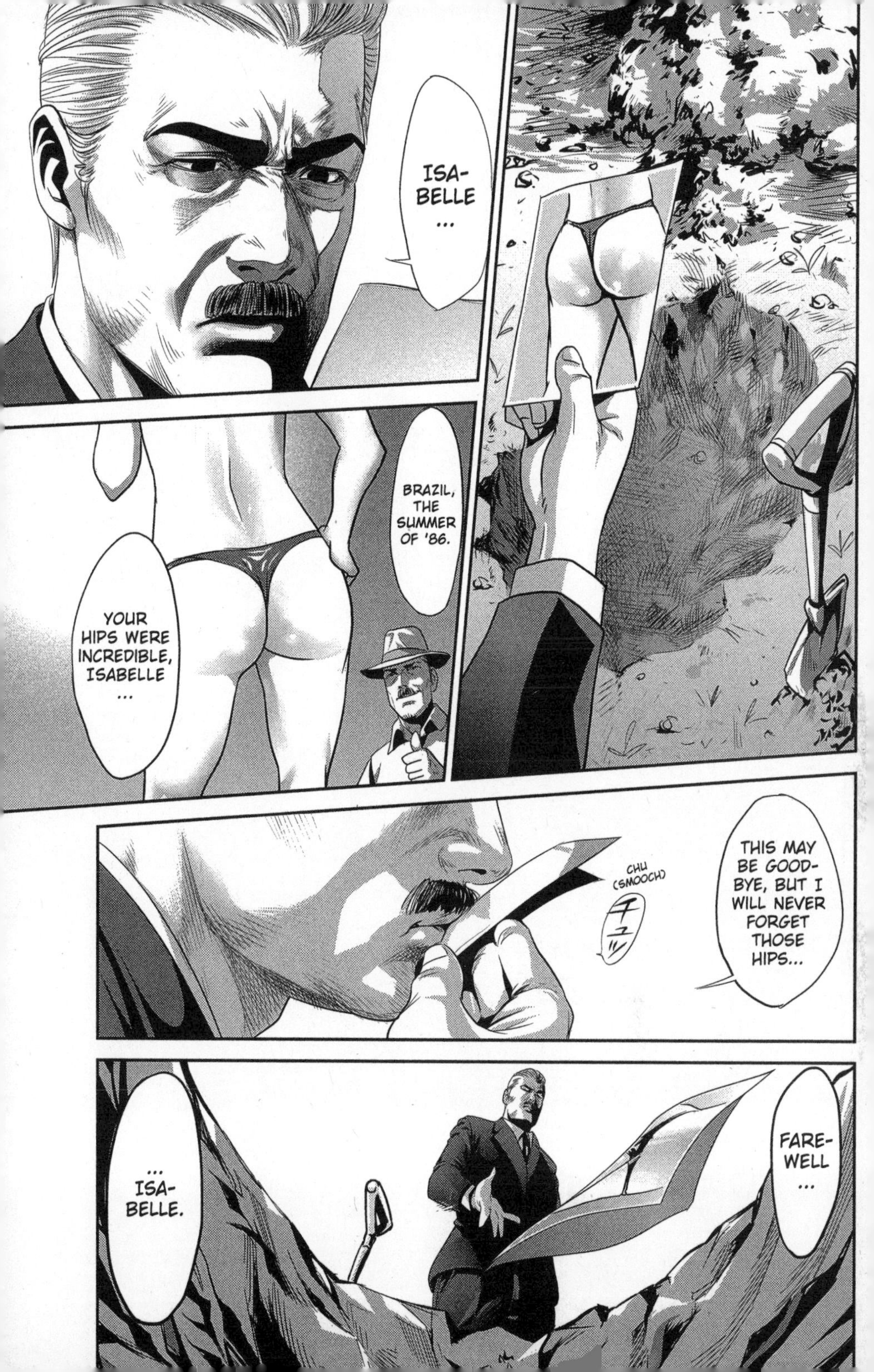
ISA-BELLE ...
BRAZIL, THE SUMMER OF '86.
YOUR HIPS WERE INCREDIBLE, ISABELLE ...
THIS MAY BE GOOD-BYE, BUT I WILL NEVER FORGET THOSE HIPS...
CHU (SMOOCH)
チュッ
FARE-WELL ...
... ISA-BELLE.

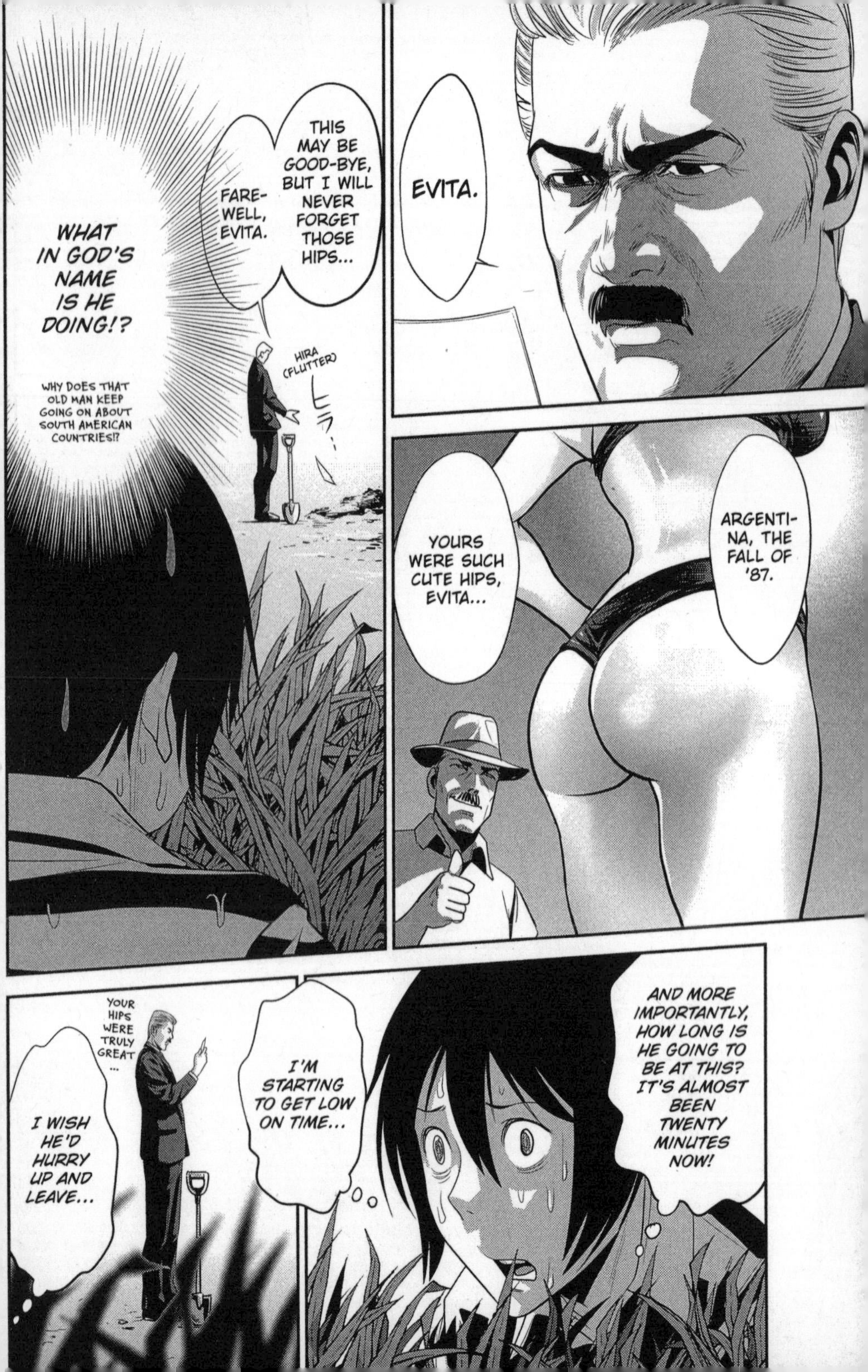
EVITA.
THIS MAY BE GOOD-BYE, BUT I WILL NEVER FORGET THOSE HIPS...
FARE-WELL, EVITA.
HIRA (FLUTTER)
WHAT IN GOD'S NAME IS HE DOING!?
WHY DOES THAT OLD MAN KEEP GOING ON ABOUT SOUTH AMERICAN COUNTRIES!?
ARGENTI-NA, THE FALL OF '87.
YOURS WERE SUCH CUTE HIPS, EVITA...
AND MORE IMPORTANTLY, HOW LONG IS HE GOING TO BE AT THIS? IT'S ALMOST BEEN TWENTY MINUTES NOW!
I'M STARTING TO GET LOW ON TIME...
YOUR HIPS WERE TRULY GREAT ...
I WISH HE'D HURRY UP AND LEAVE...

CHU
(SMOOCH)

KON
(CLANG)

KAN

KON

KIN
(CLANG)

OH NO...! THE THREE O'CLOCK CHIMES!

I NEED TO HURRY BACK, OR ELSE...

I-INDEED HE IS...

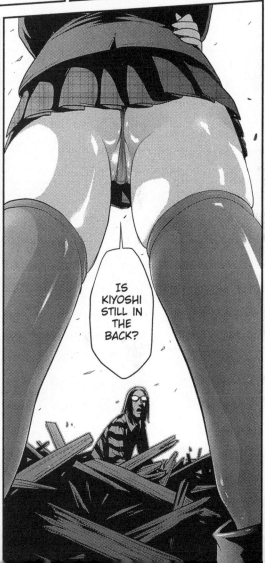

IS KIYOSHI STILL IN THE BACK?

HEY, KIYO-SHI!

GET OVER HERE.

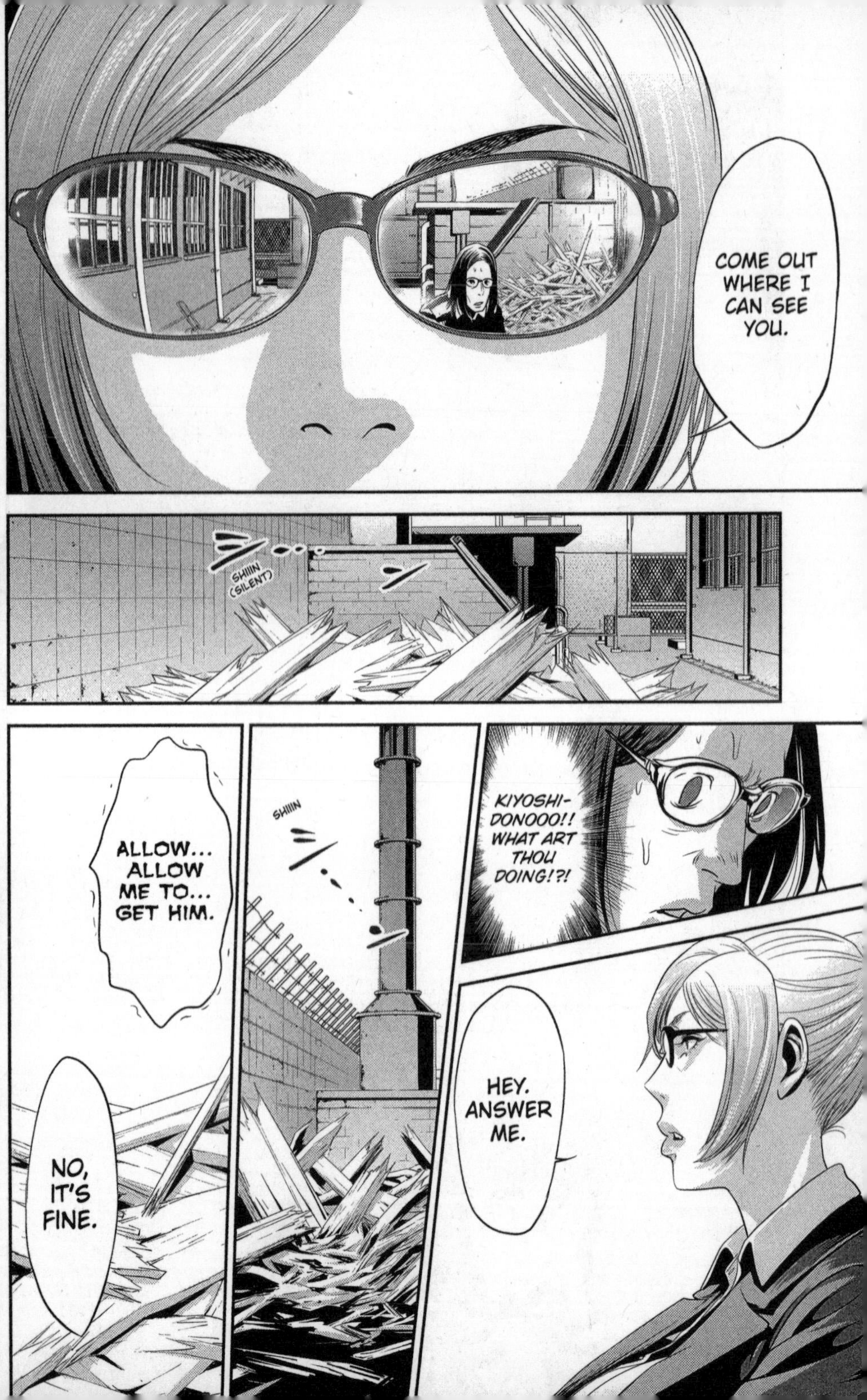
COME OUT WHERE I CAN SEE YOU.
SHIIIN (SILENT)
KIYOSHI-DONOOO!! WHAT ART THOU DOING!?!
SHIIIN
ALLOW... ALLOW ME TO... GET HIM.
HEY. ANSWER ME.
NO, IT'S FINE.

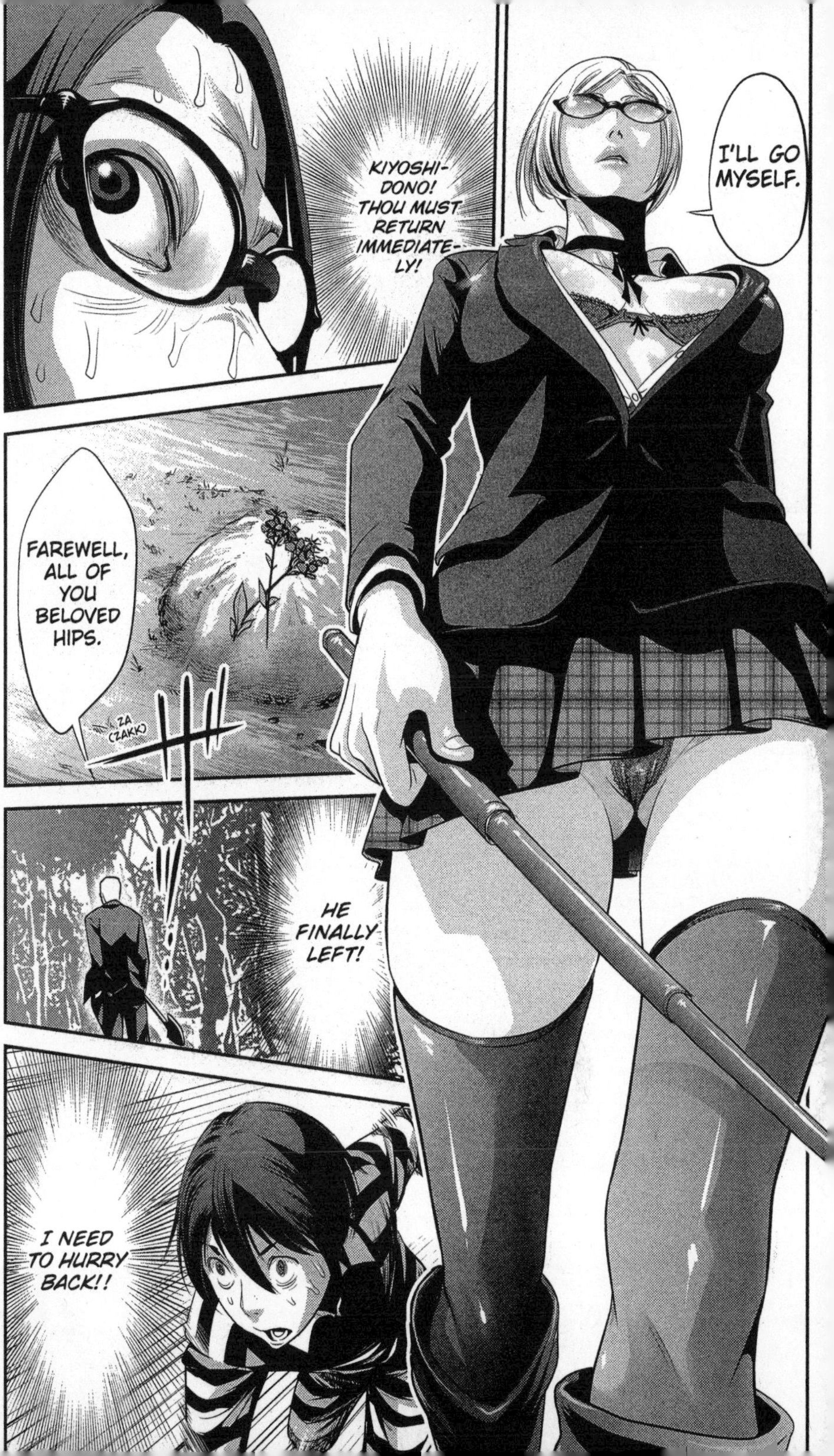
I'LL GO MYSELF.
KIYOSHI-DONO! THOU MUST RETURN IMMEDIATE-LY!
FAREWELL, ALL OF YOU BELOVED HIPS.
ZA (ZAKK)
HE FINALLY LEFT!
I NEED TO HURRY BACK!!

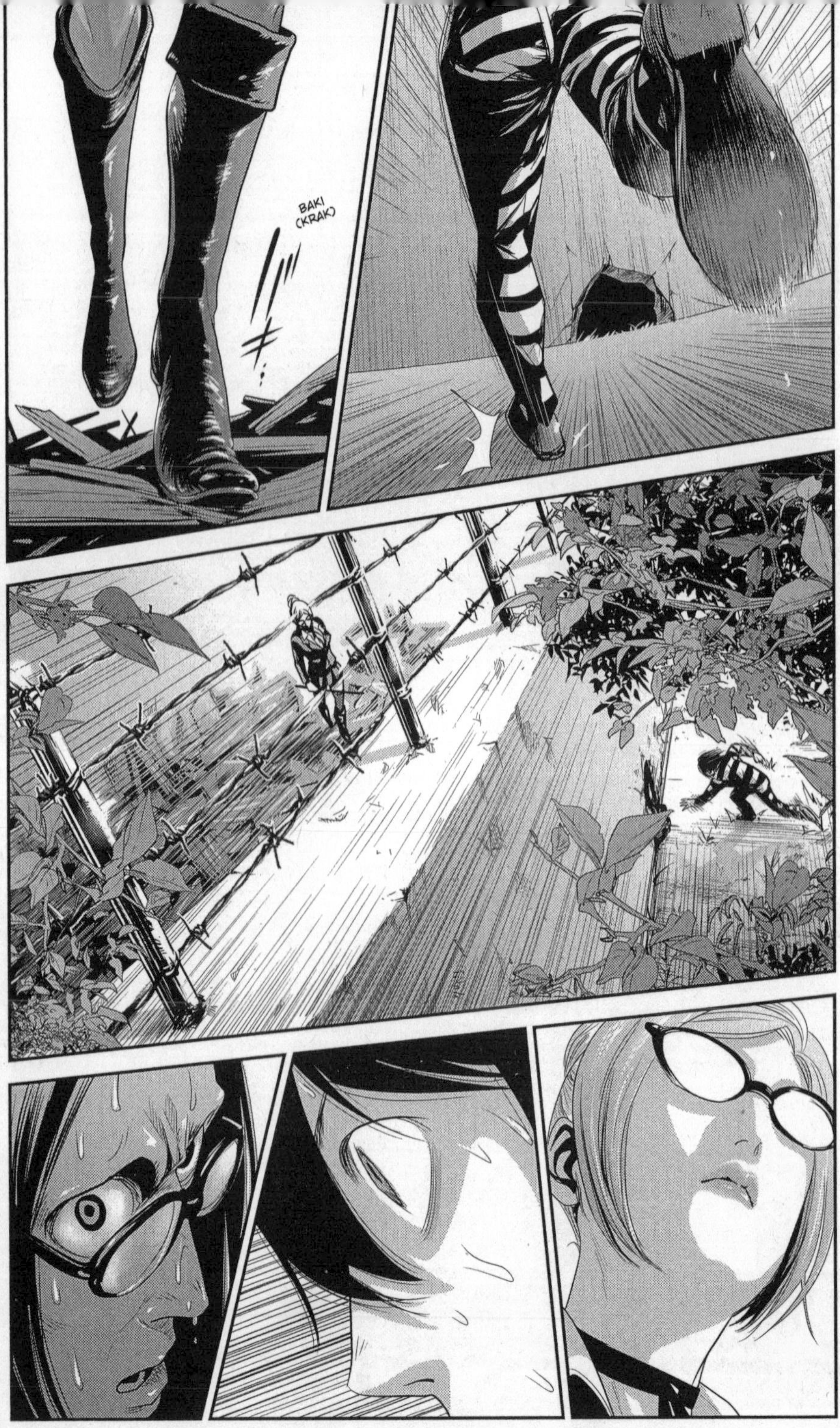
BAKI
(KRAK)

CHAPTER 14: KIYOSHI RETURNS

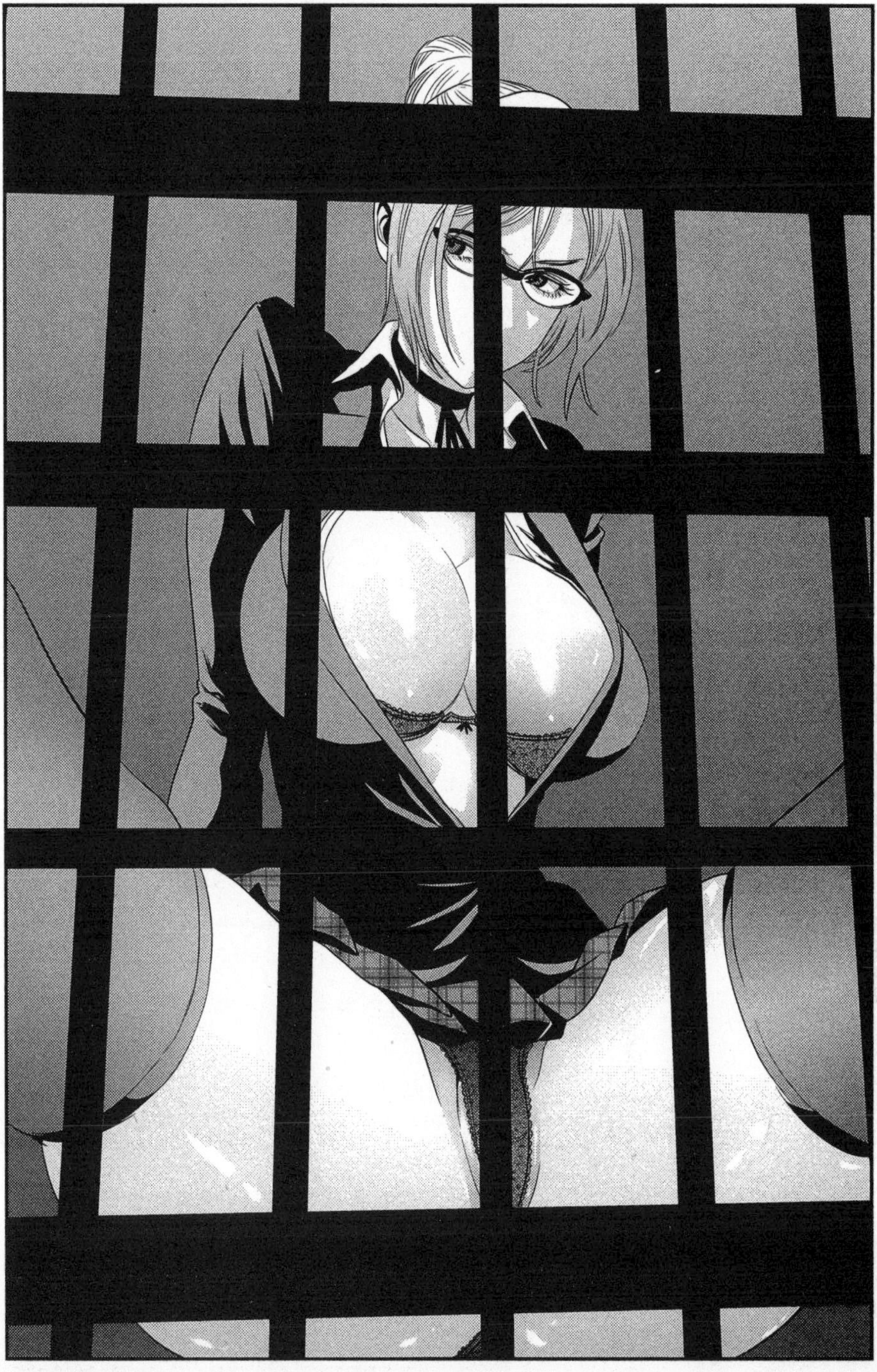

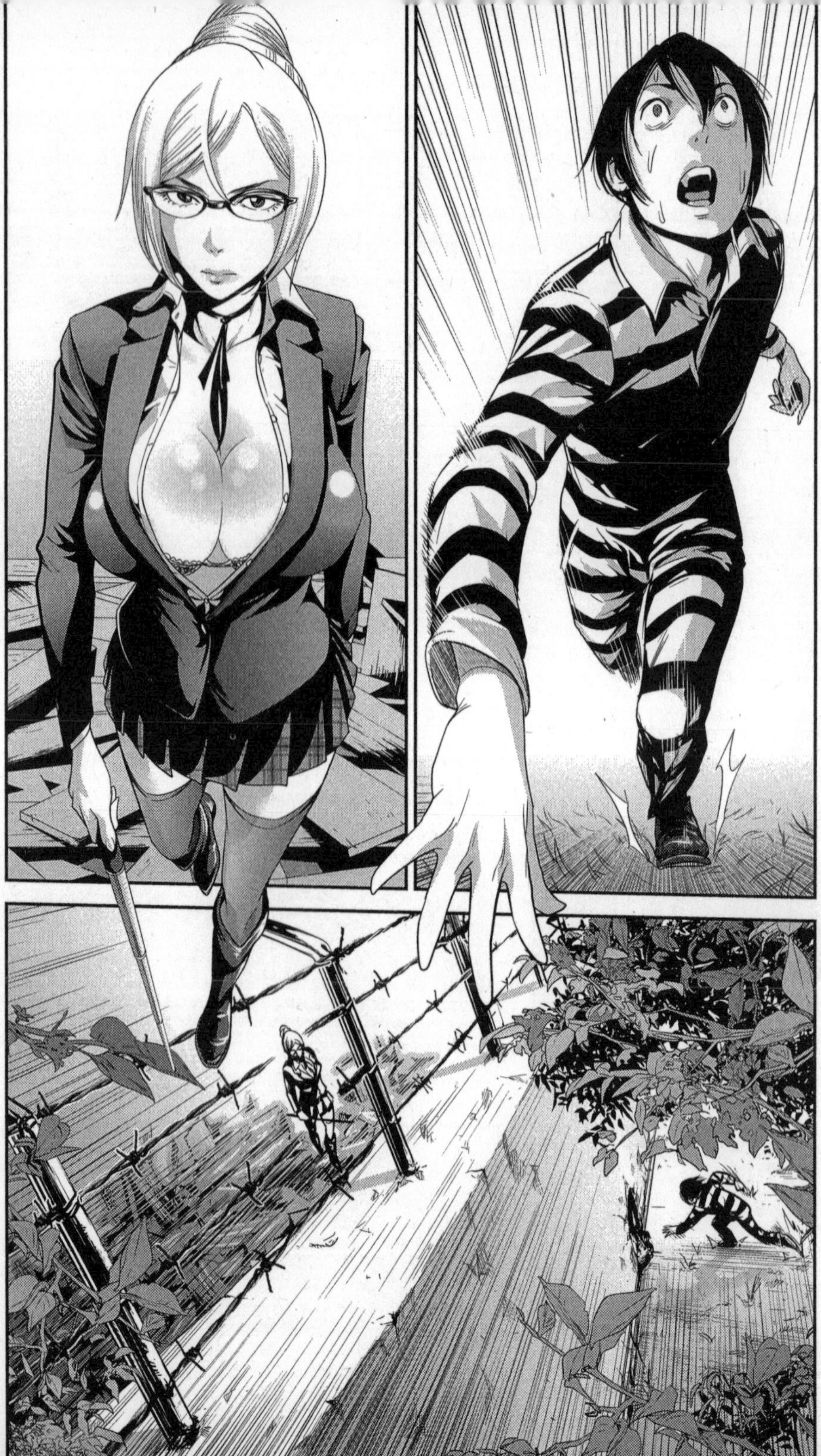

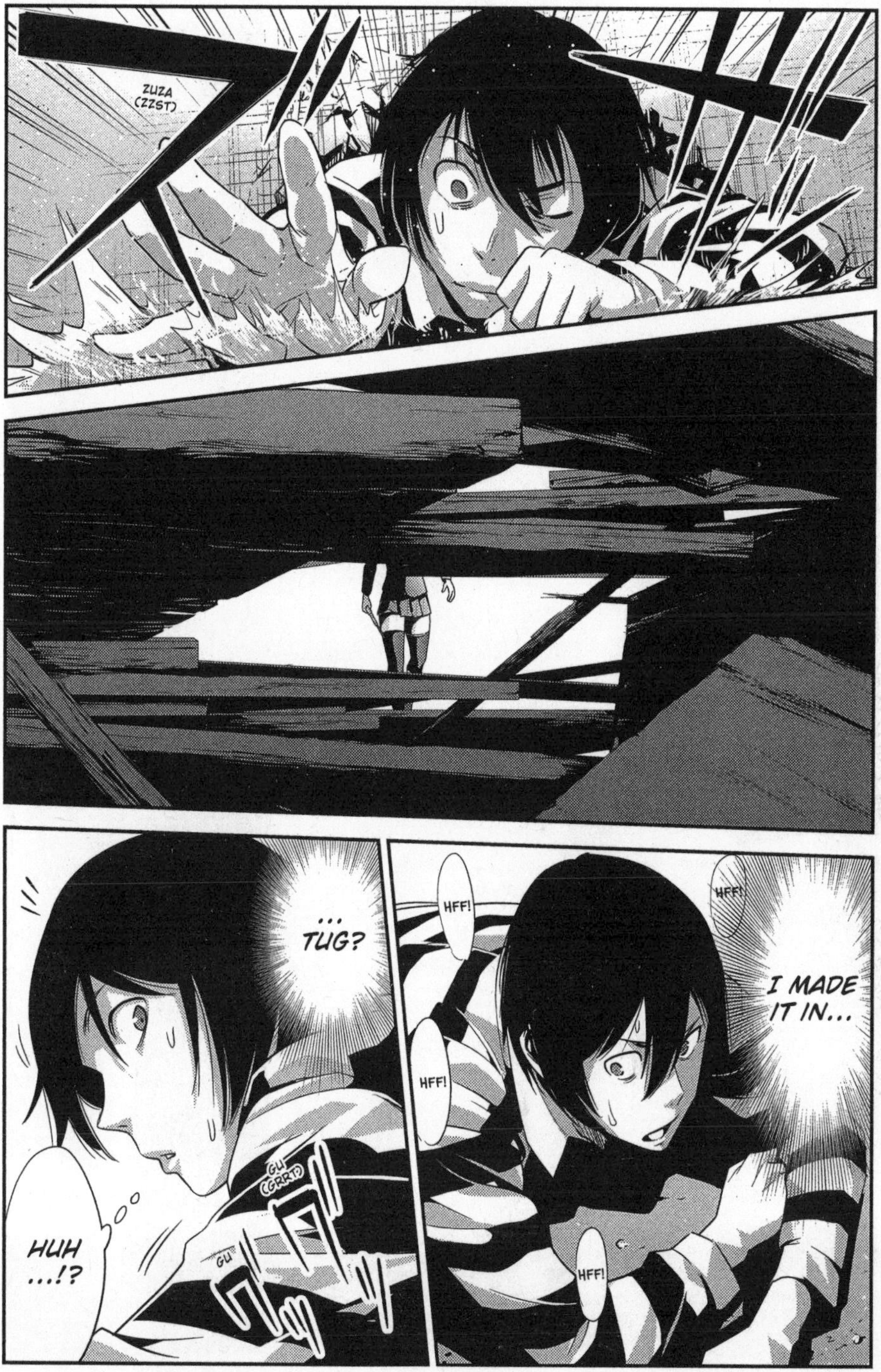
ZUZA
(ZZST)
HFF!
HFF!
I MADE IT IN...
HFF!
HFF!
... TUG?
GU
(GRRR)
GU
HUH ...!?

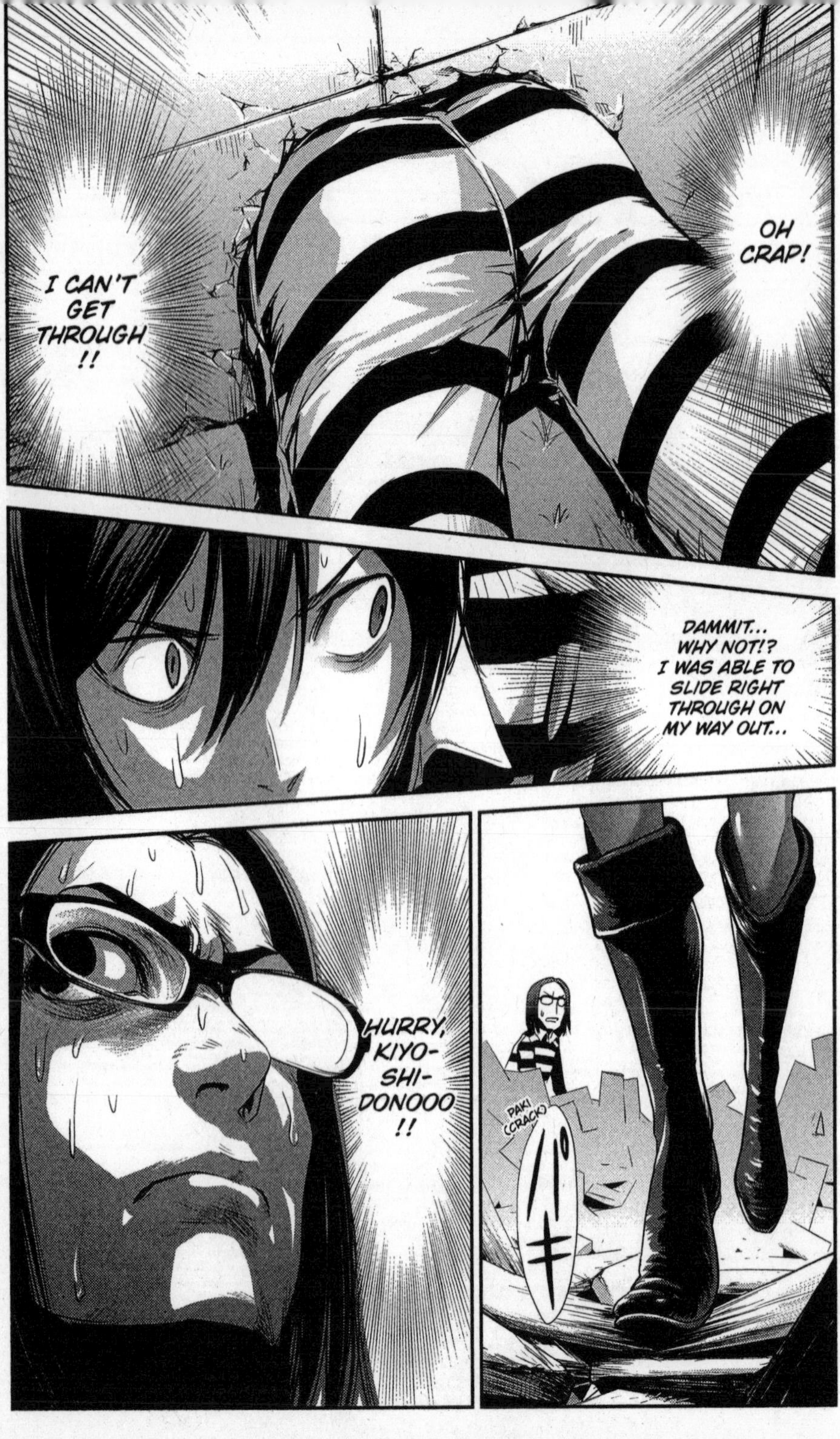
OH CRAP!
I CAN'T GET THROUGH !!
DAMMIT... WHY NOT!? I WAS ABLE TO SLIDE RIGHT THROUGH ON MY WAY OUT...
HURRY, KIYO-SHI-DONOOO !!
PAKI (CRACK)

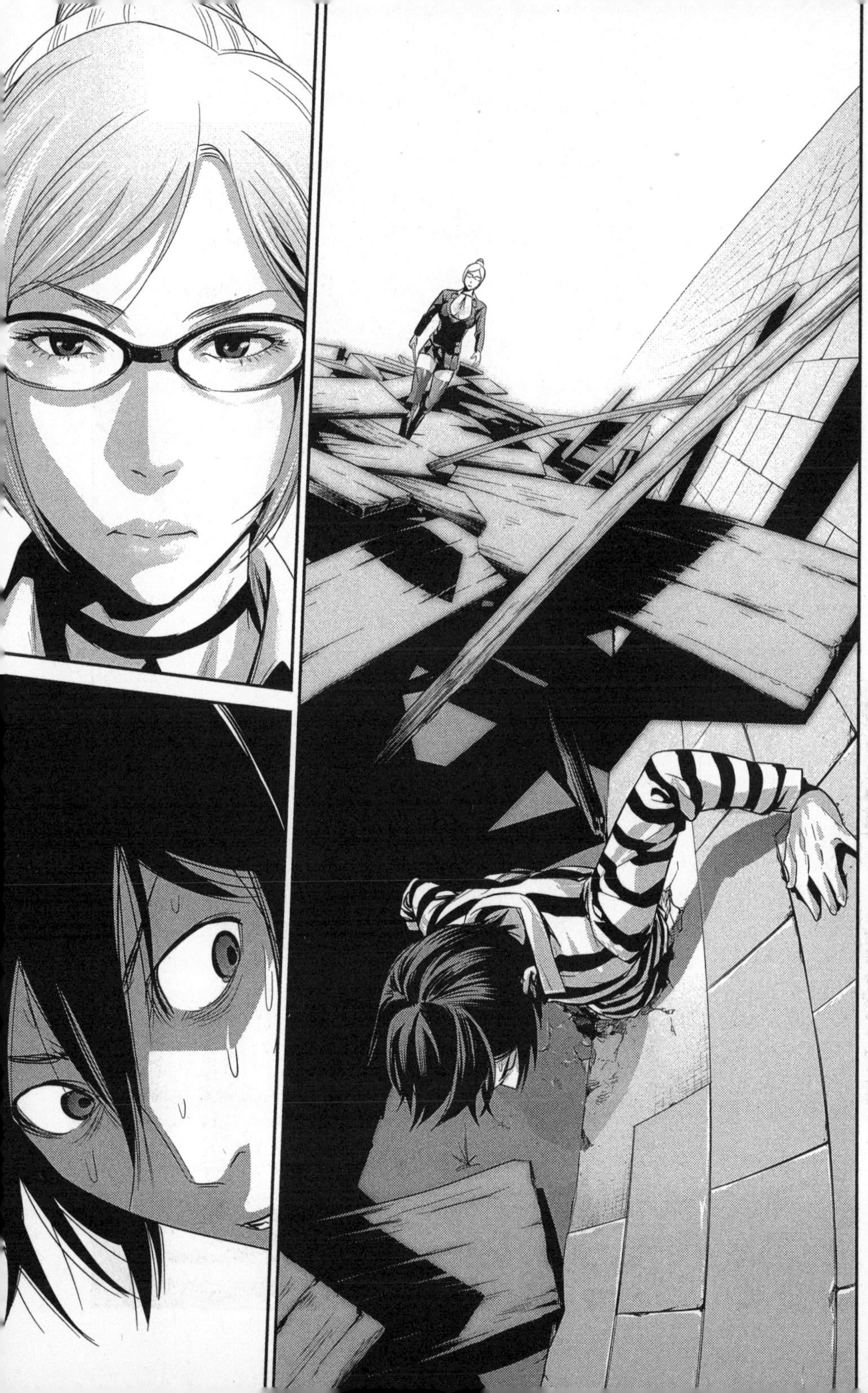

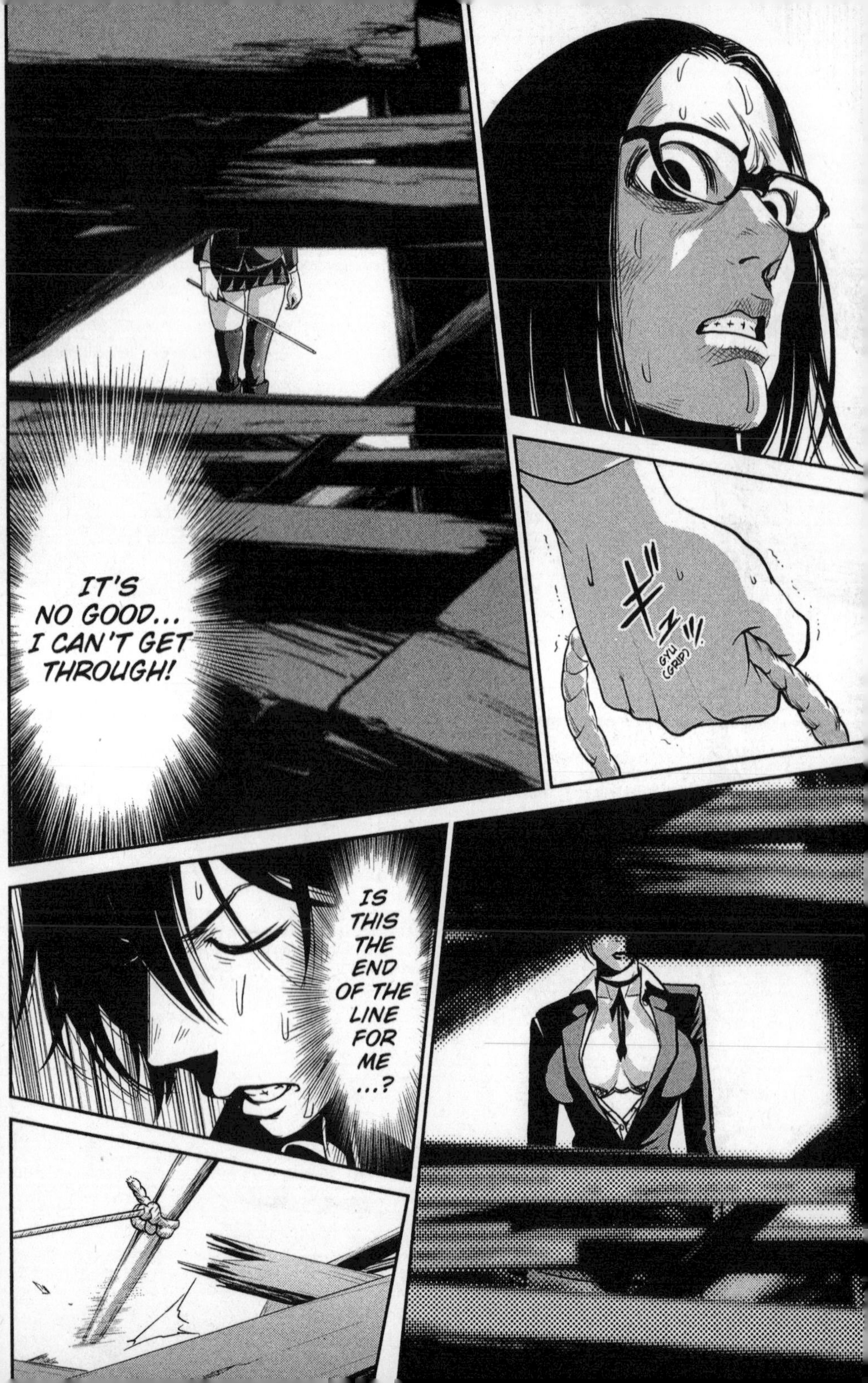

IT'S NO GOOD... I CAN'T GET THROUGH!
ギュ
GYU (GRIP)
IS THIS THE END OF THE LINE FOR ME ...?

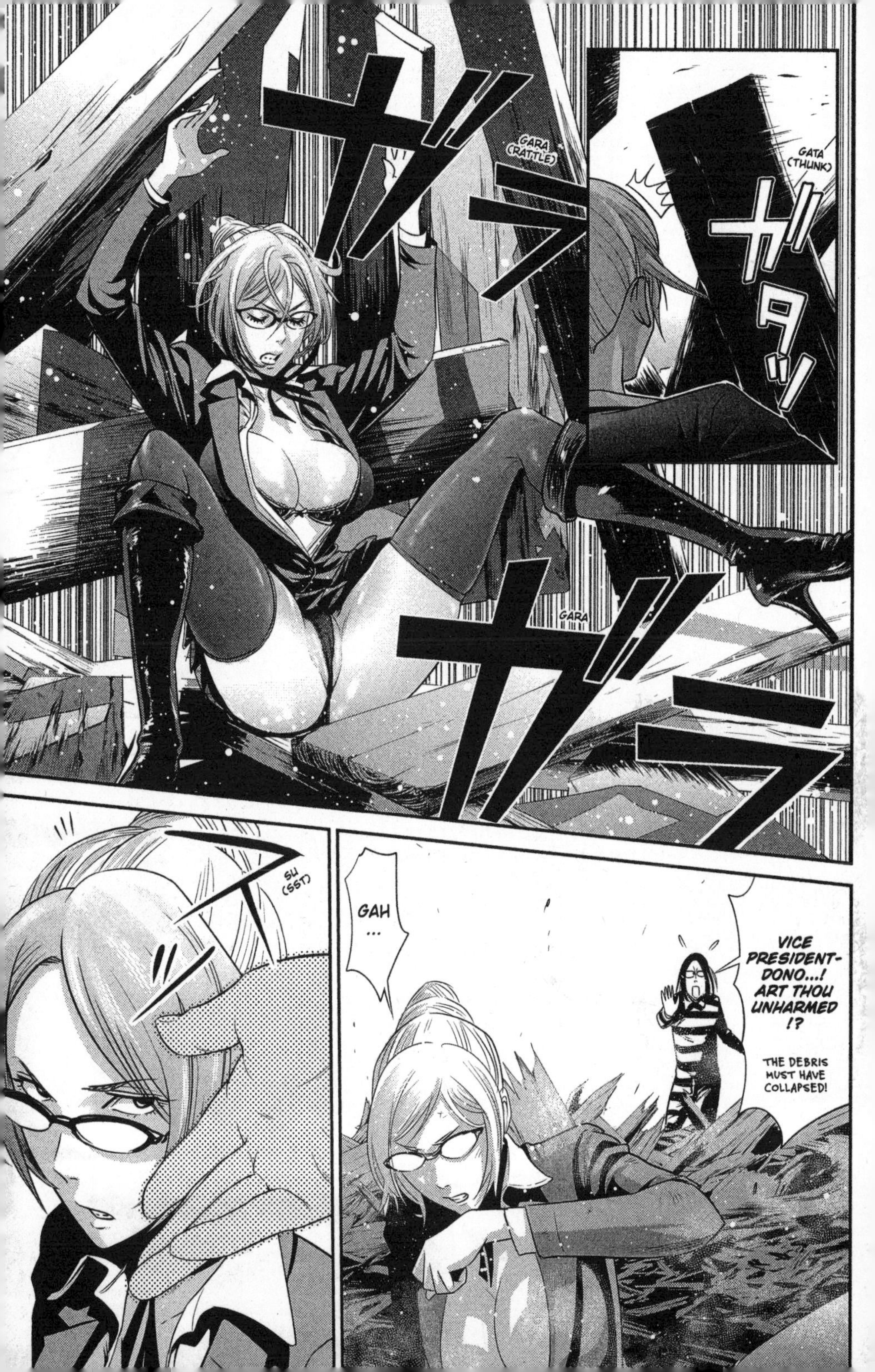
GATA (THUNK)
GARA (RATTLE)
GARA
SU (SST)
VICE PRESIDENT-DONO...! ART THOU UNHARMED !?
THE DEBRIS MUST HAVE COLLAPSED!
GAH ...

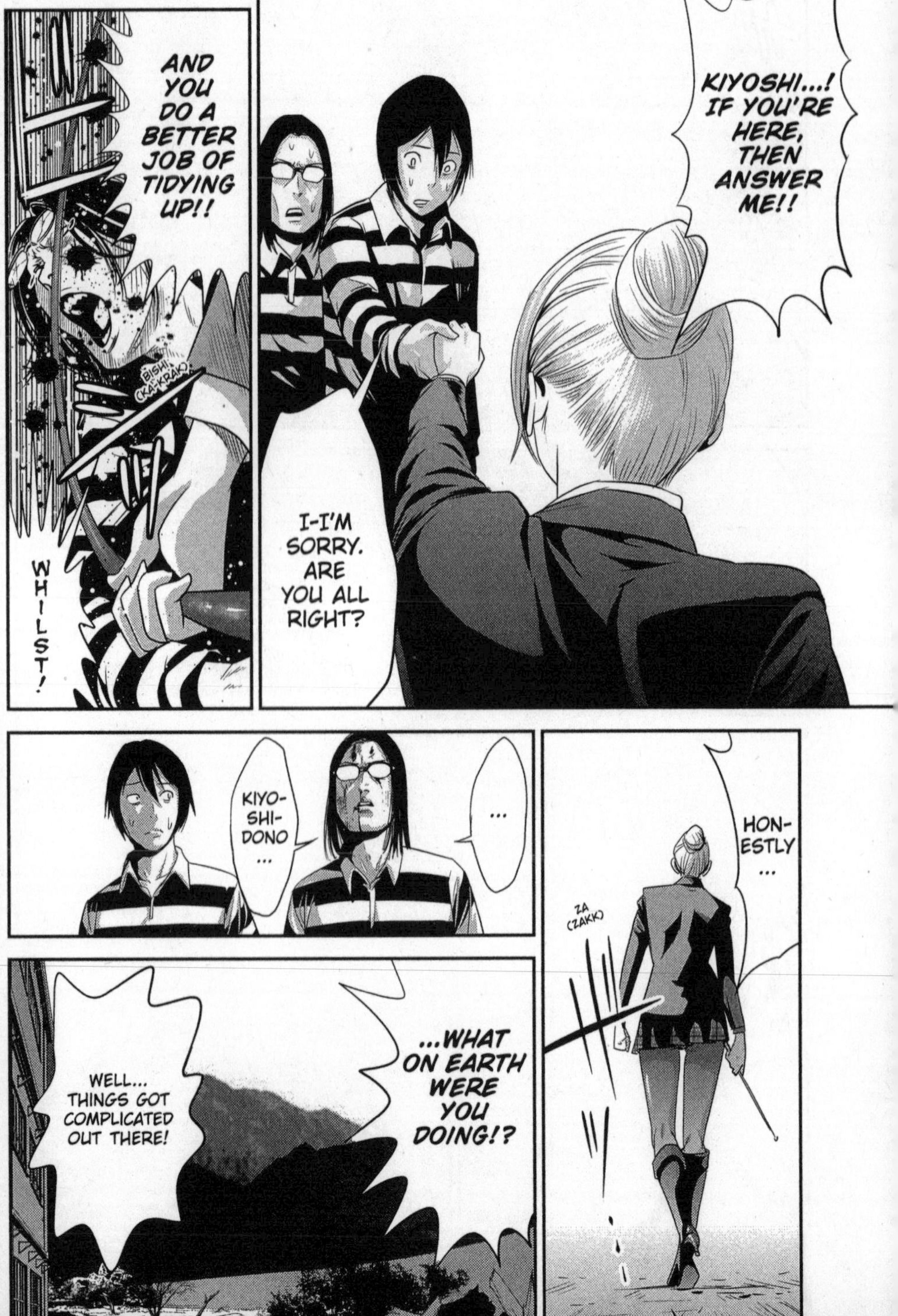
KIYOSHI...! IF YOU'RE HERE, THEN ANSWER ME!!
I-I'M SORRY. ARE YOU ALL RIGHT?
AND YOU DO A BETTER JOB OF TIDYING UP!!
BISHI (KA-KRAK)
WHILST!
HON-ESTLY ...
ZA (ZAKK)
...
KIYO-SHI-DONO ...
...WHAT ON EARTH WERE YOU DOING!?
WELL... THINGS GOT COMPLICATED OUT THERE!

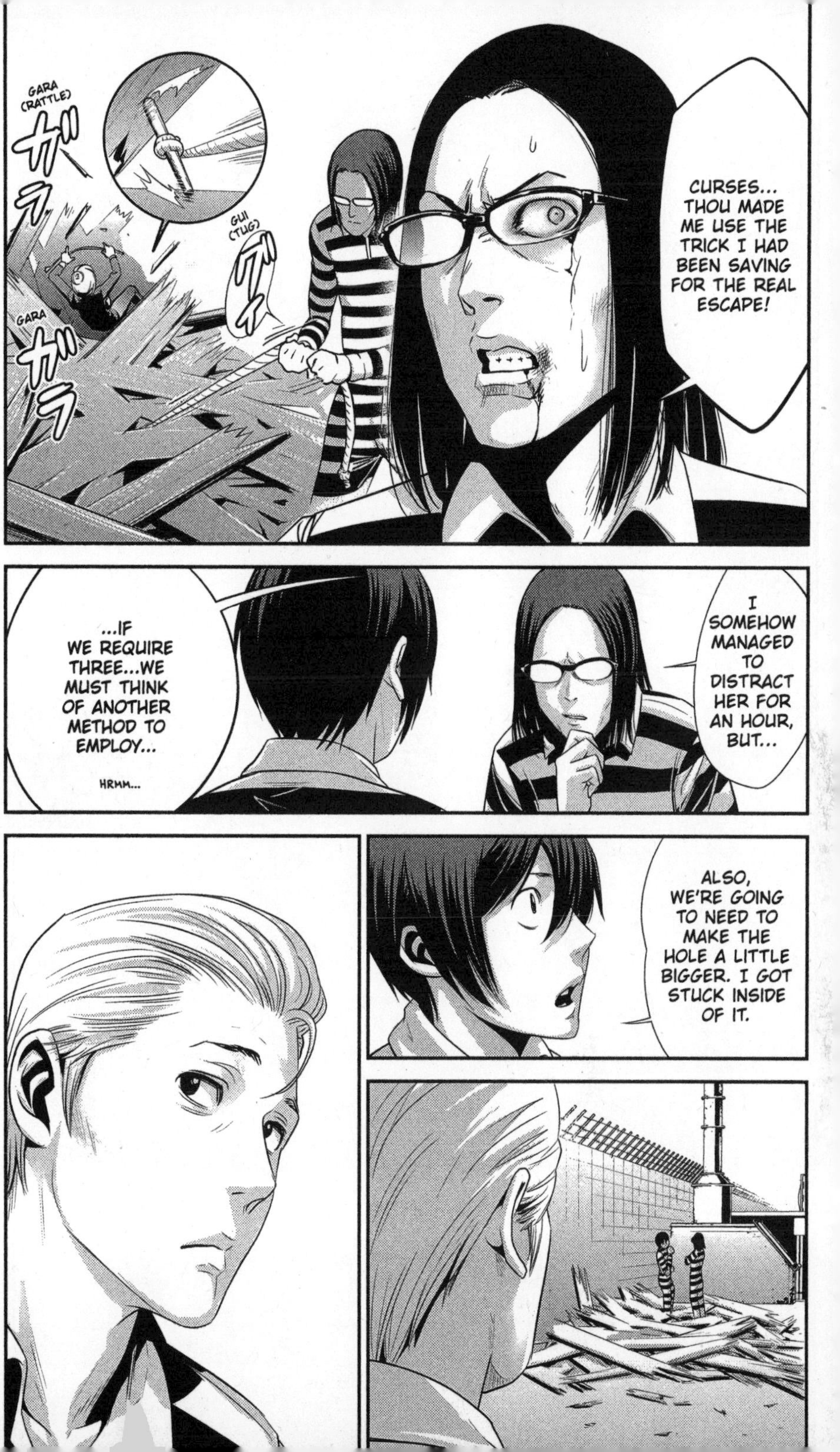
CURSES... THOU MADE ME USE THE TRICK I HAD BEEN SAVING FOR THE REAL ESCAPE!
GUI (TUG)
GARA (RATTLE)
GARA
I SOMEHOW MANAGED TO DISTRACT HER FOR AN HOUR, BUT...
...IF WE REQUIRE THREE...WE MUST THINK OF ANOTHER METHOD TO EMPLOY...
HRMM...
ALSO, WE'RE GOING TO NEED TO MAKE THE HOLE A LITTLE BIGGER. I GOT STUCK INSIDE OF IT.

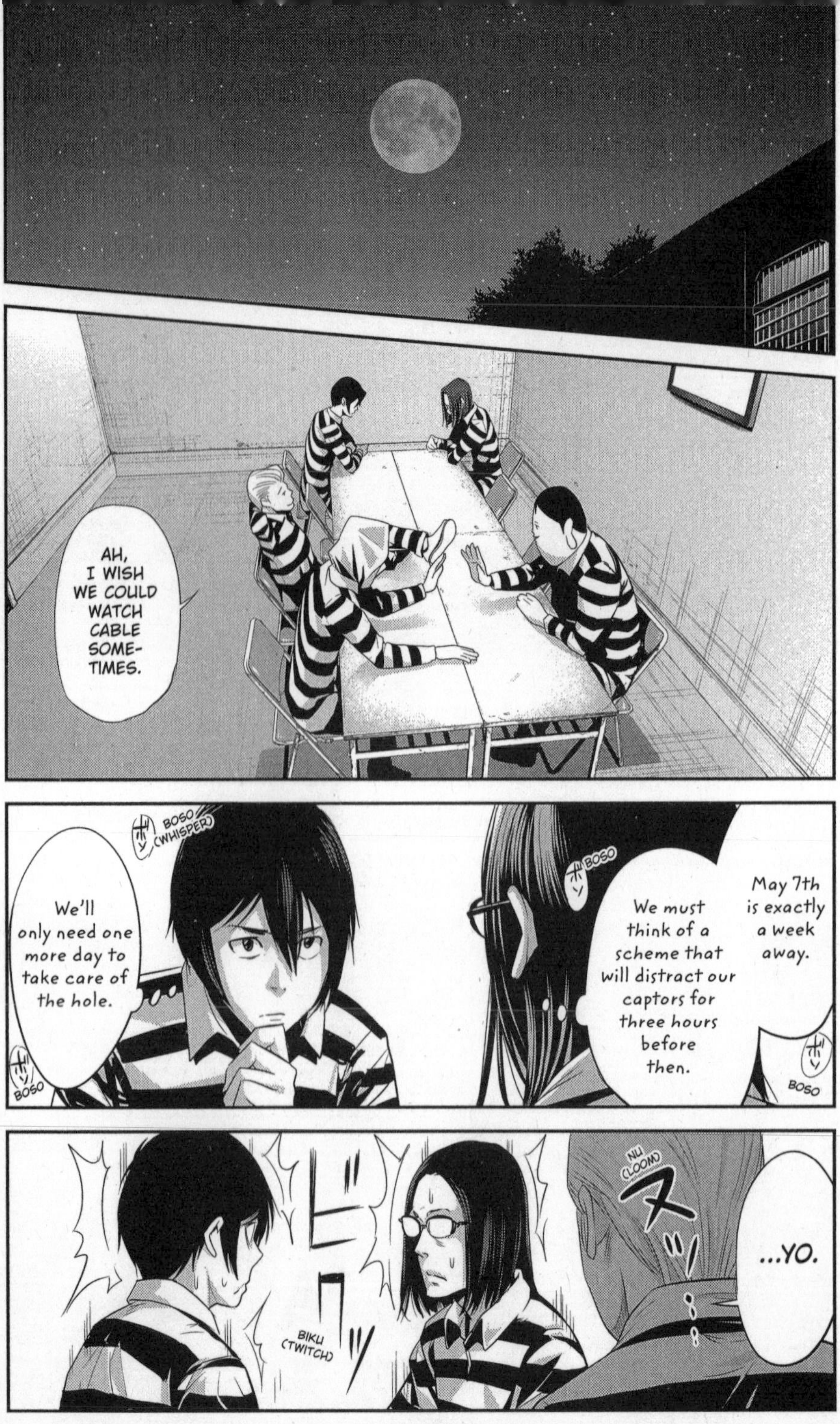
AH, I WISH WE COULD WATCH CABLE SOME-TIMES.
ボソ BOSO (WHISPER)
May 7th is exactly a week away.
ボソ BOSO
We must think of a scheme that will distract our captors for three hours before then.
ボソ BOSO
We'll only need one more day to take care of the hole.
ボソ BOSO
ヌッ NU (LOOM)
...YO.
ビクッ BIKU (TWITCH)

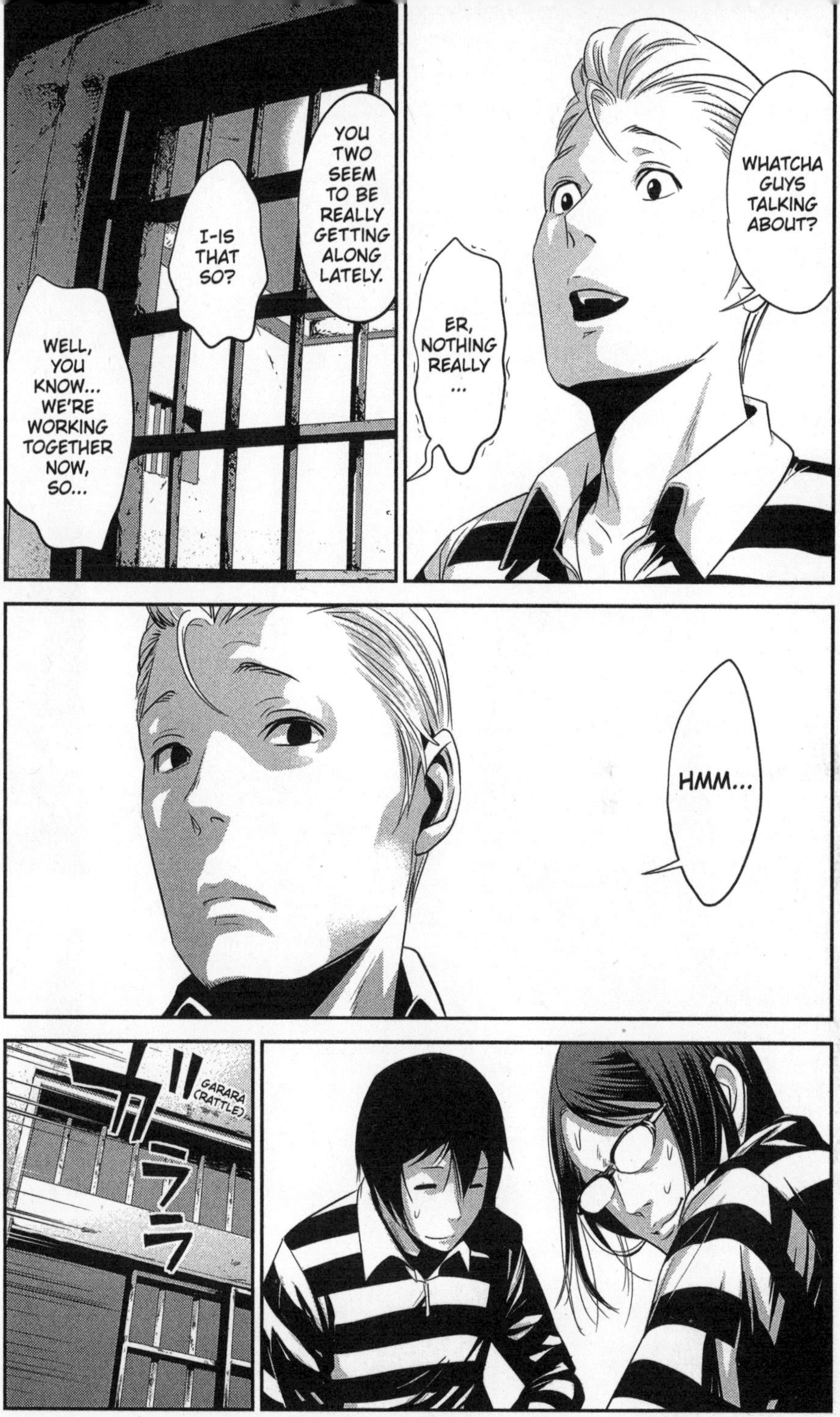
WHATCHA GUYS TALKING ABOUT?
ER, NOTHING REALLY ...
YOU TWO SEEM TO BE REALLY GETTING ALONG LATELY.
I-IS THAT SO?
WELL, YOU KNOW... WE'RE WORKING TOGETHER NOW, SO...
HMM...
GARARA (RATTLE)

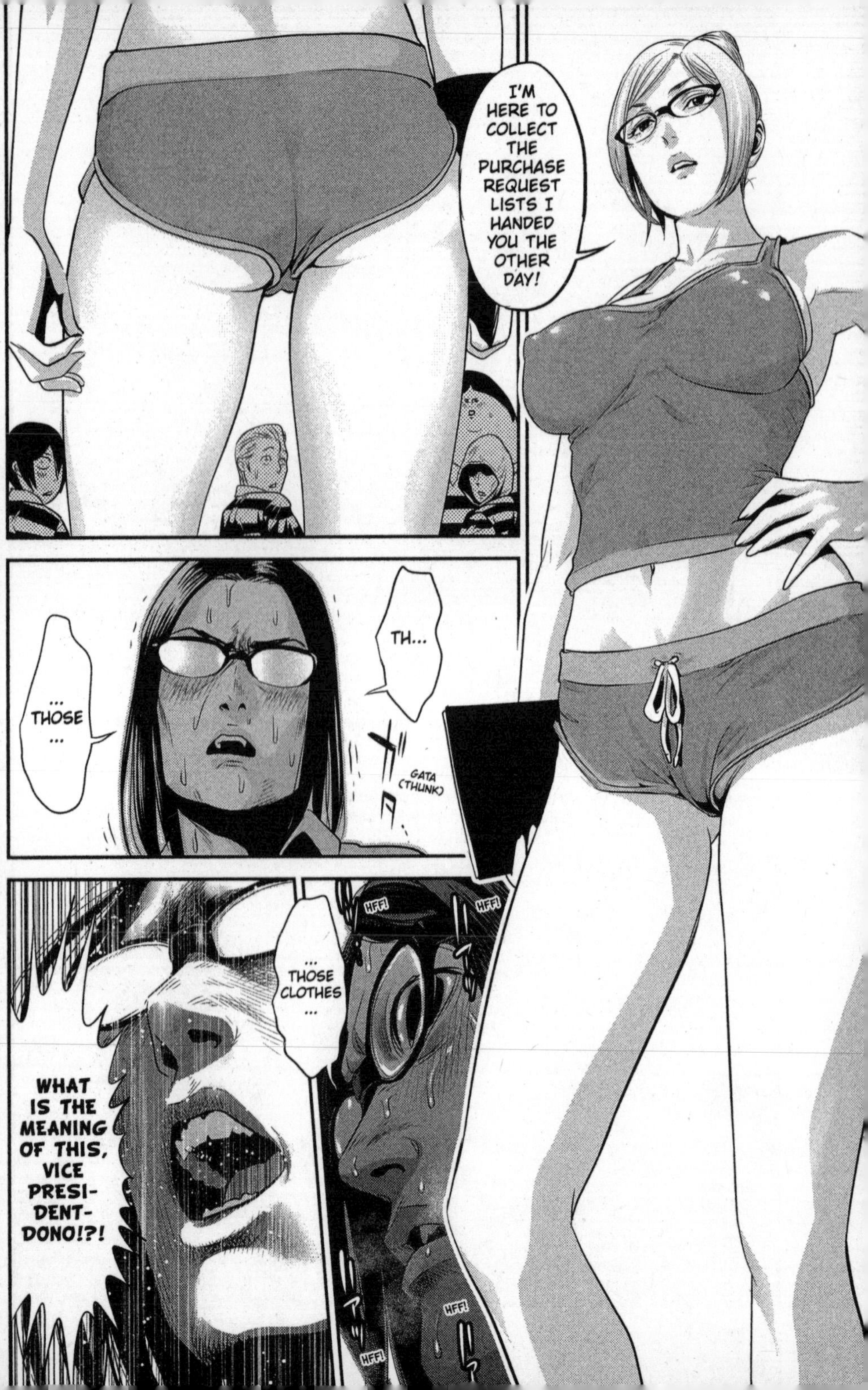
I'M HERE TO COLLECT THE PURCHASE REQUEST LISTS I HANDED YOU THE OTHER DAY!
TH...
GATA (THUNK)
... THOSE ...
HFF!
HFF!
... THOSE CLOTHES ...
WHAT IS THE MEANING OF THIS, VICE PRESI-DENT-DONO!?!
HFF!
HFF!

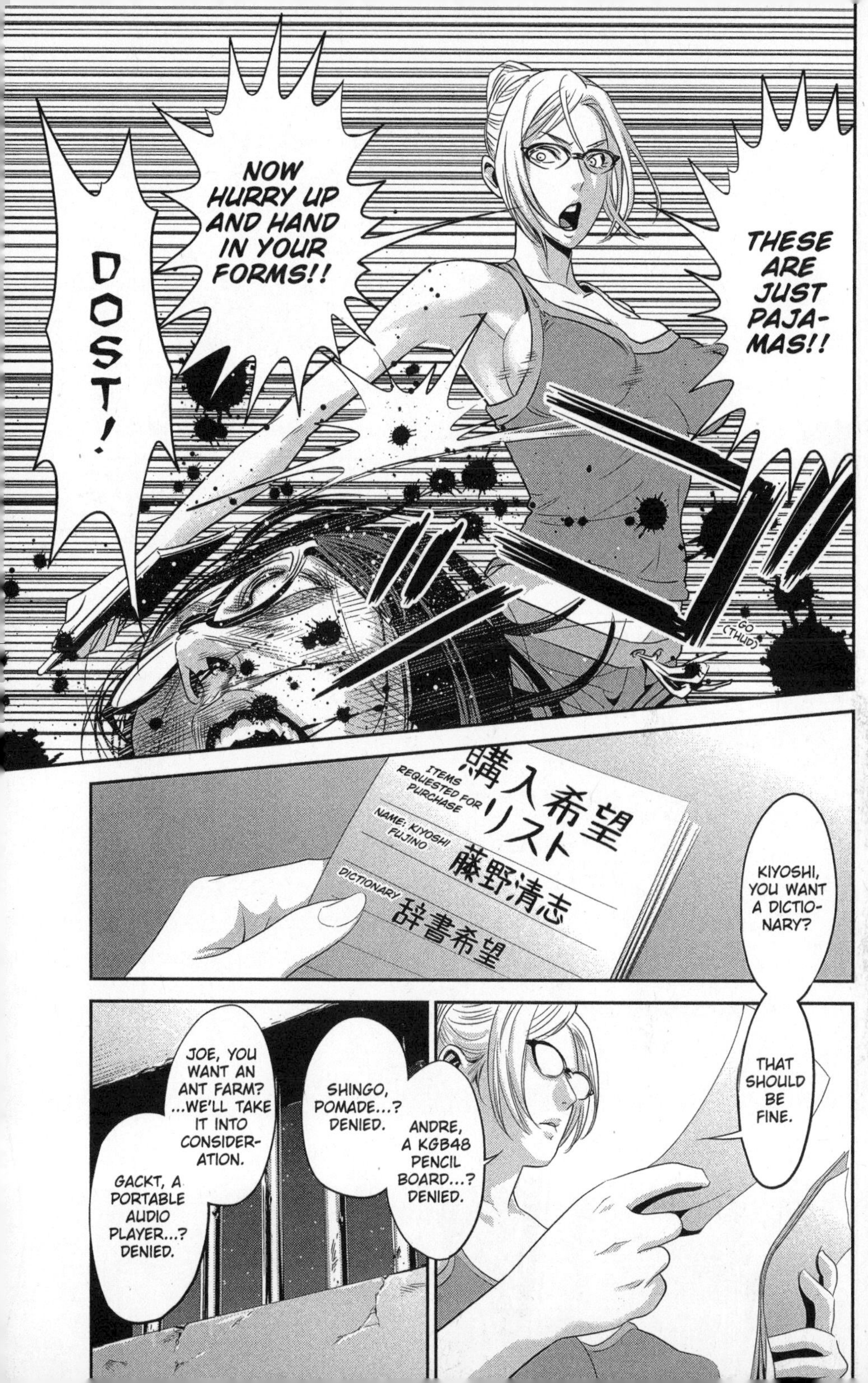
THESE ARE JUST PAJAMAS!!
NOW HURRY UP AND HAND IN YOUR FORMS!!
DOST!
GO (THUD)
購入希望リスト
ITEMS REQUESTED FOR PURCHASE
NAME: KIYOSHI FUJINO
藤野清志
DICTIONARY
辞書希望
KIYOSHI, YOU WANT A DICTIONARY?
THAT SHOULD BE FINE.
ANDRE, A KGB48 PENCIL BOARD...? DENIED.
SHINGO, POMADE...? DENIED.
JOE, YOU WANT AN ANT FARM? ...WE'LL TAKE IT INTO CONSIDERATION.
GACKT, A PORTABLE AUDIO PLAYER...? DENIED.

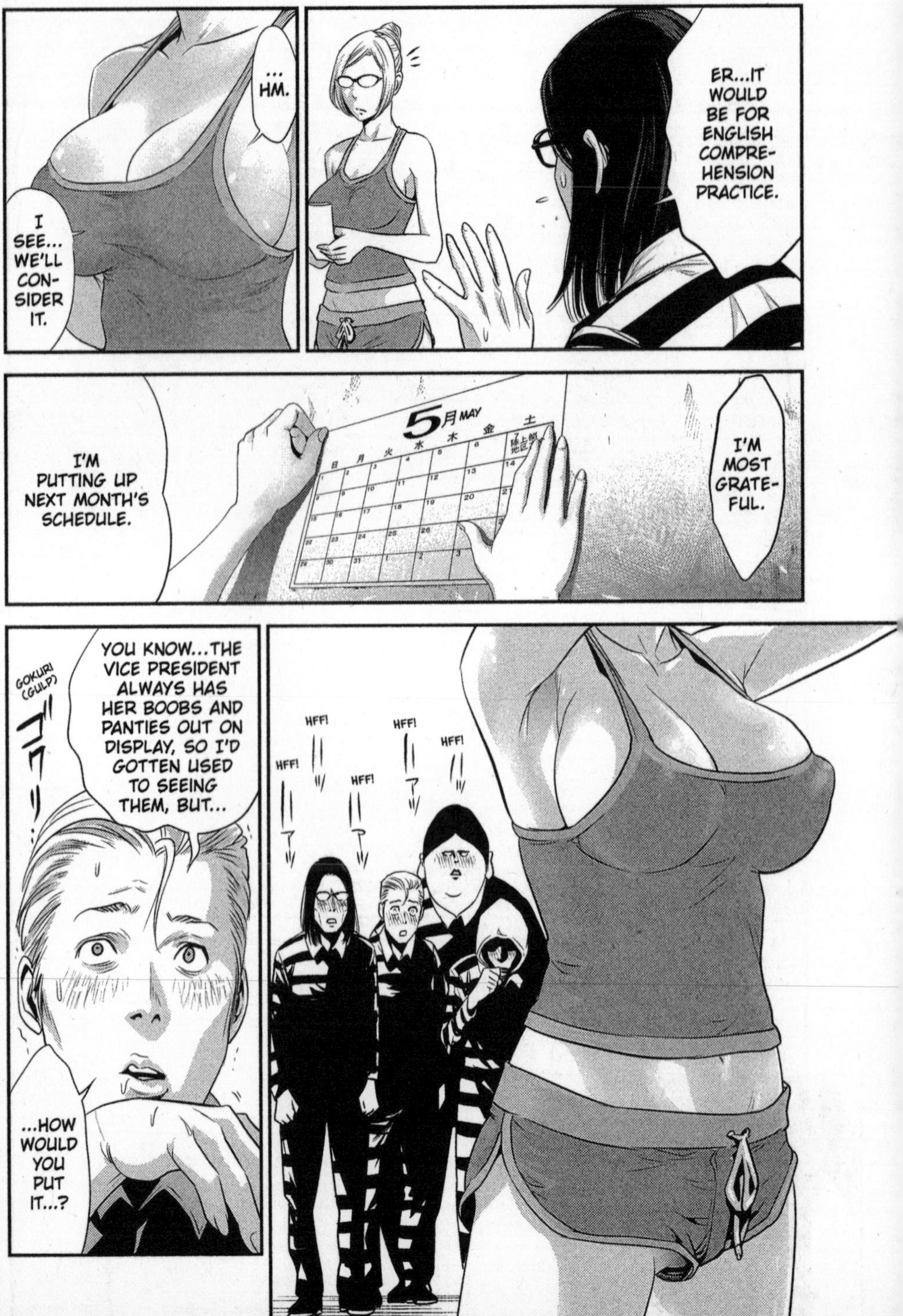
ER...IT WOULD BE FOR ENGLISH COMPRE-HENSION PRACTICE.
... HM.
I SEE... WE'LL CON-SIDER IT.
I'M MOST GRATE-FUL.
I'M PUTTING UP NEXT MONTH'S SCHEDULE.
5月 MAY
HFF!
HFF!
HFF!
HFF!
YOU KNOW...THE VICE PRESIDENT ALWAYS HAS HER BOOBS AND PANTIES OUT ON DISPLAY, SO I'D GOTTEN USED TO SEEING THEM, BUT...
GOKURI (GULP)
...HOW WOULD YOU PUT IT...?

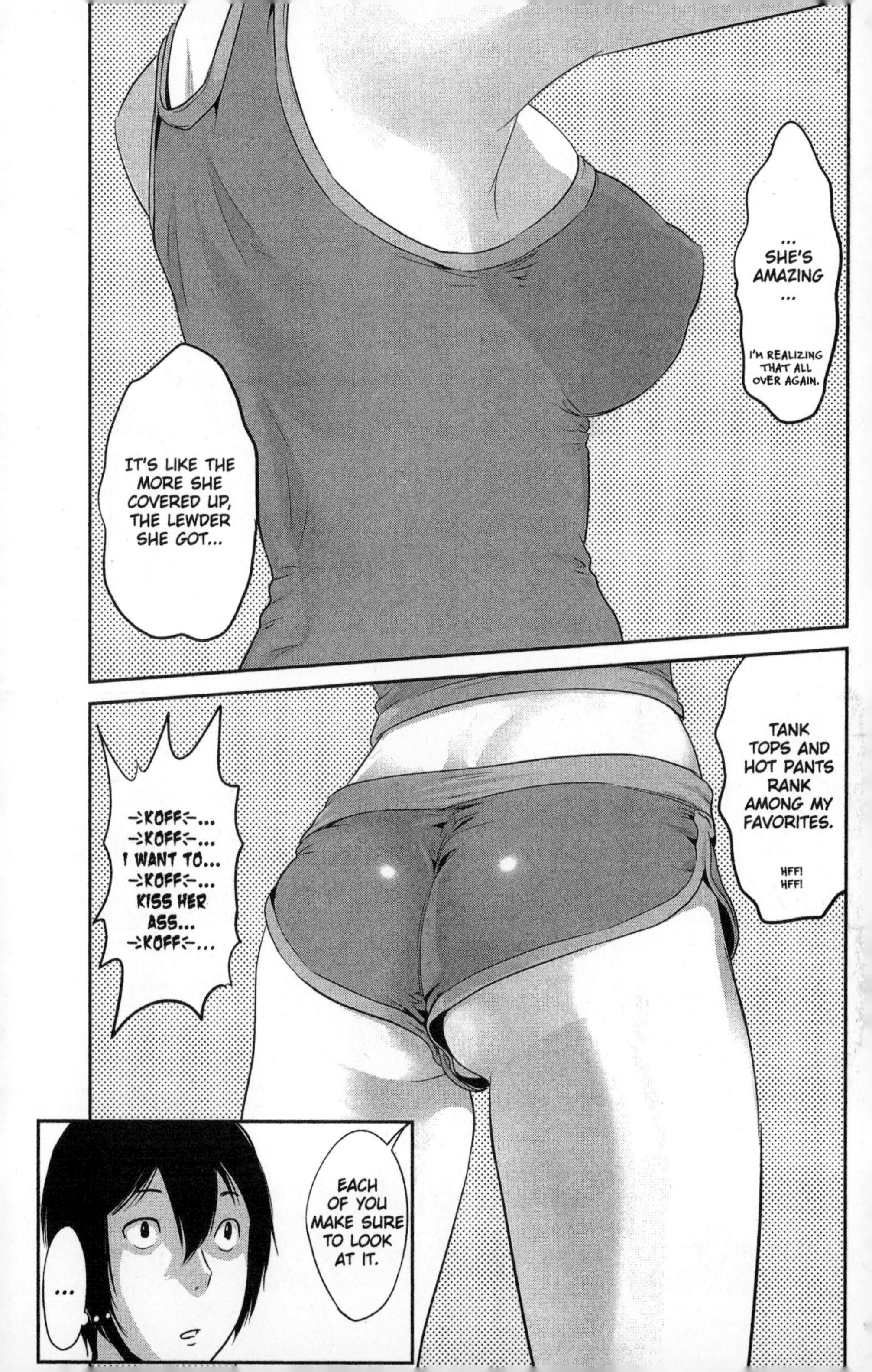
... SHE'S AMAZING ...
I'M REALIZING THAT ALL OVER AGAIN.
IT'S LIKE THE MORE SHE COVERED UP, THE LEWDER SHE GOT...
TANK TOPS AND HOT PANTS RANK AMONG MY FAVORITES.
HFF! HFF!
-KOFF-... -KOFF-... I WANT TO... -KOFF-... KISS HER ASS... -KOFF-...
EACH OF YOU MAKE SURE TO LOOK AT IT.
...

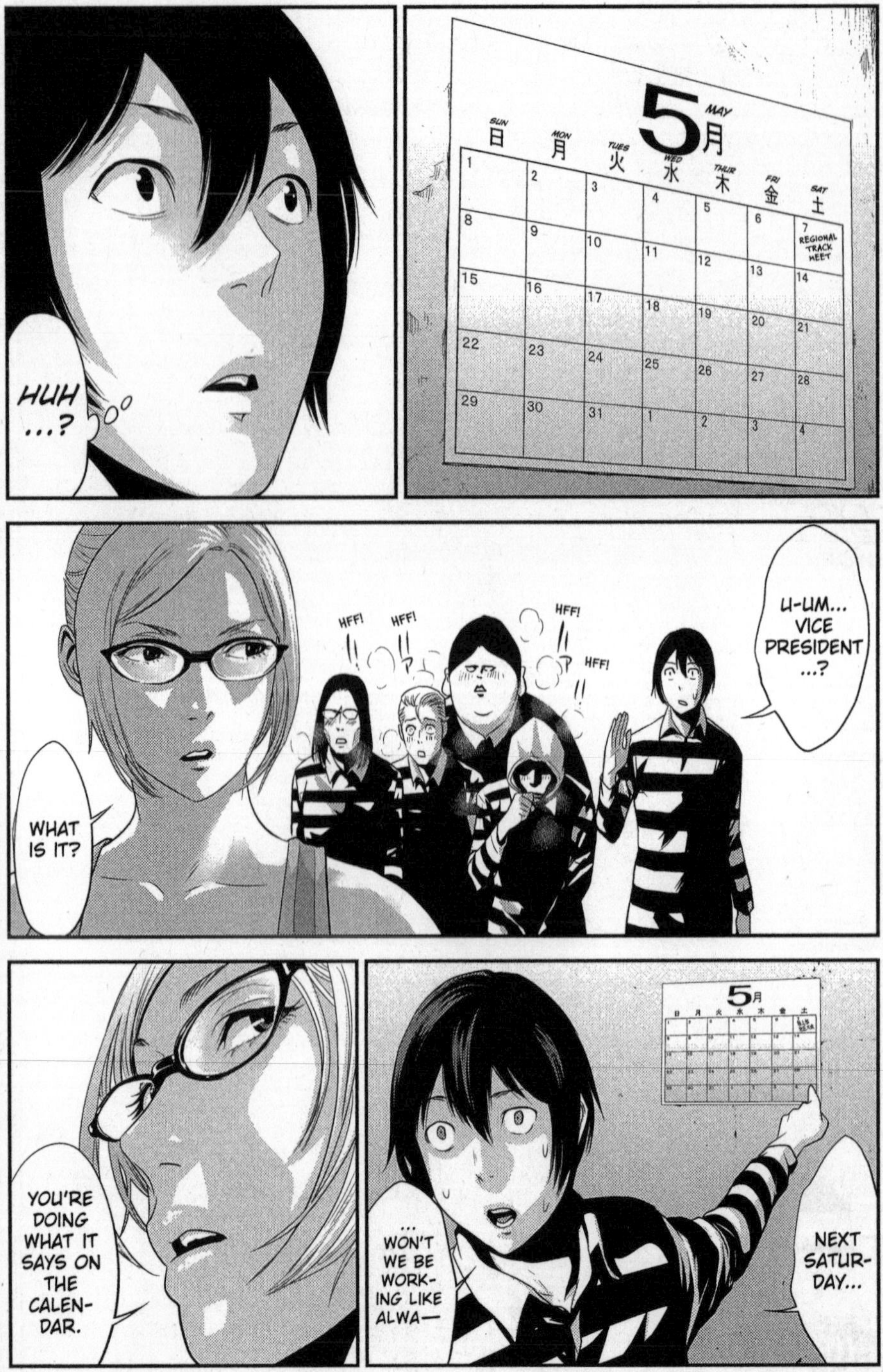
5月 MAY
SUN 日
MON 月
TUES 火
WED 水
THUR 木
FRI 金
SAT 土
REGIONAL TRACK MEET
HUH ...?
U-UM... VICE PRESIDENT ...?
HFF!
HFF!
HFF!
HFF!
WHAT IS IT?
NEXT SATUR-DAY...
... WON'T WE BE WORK-ING LIKE ALWA—
YOU'RE DOING WHAT IT SAYS ON THE CALEN-DAR.

5月

日 月 火 水 木 金 土

			4	5	6	7 REGIONAL TRACK MEET
			11	12	13	14
			18	19	20	21
		25	26	27	28
	2	3	4

A REGIONAL TRACK MEET WILL BE HELD AT THE ACADEMY ON MAY 7TH.

YOU'LL BE HELPING OUT THERE *INSTEAD OF YOUR REGULAR WORK.*

ANY OTHER QUES- TIONS?

N-NO, NOTHING ELSE.

THAT'S ALL, THEN.

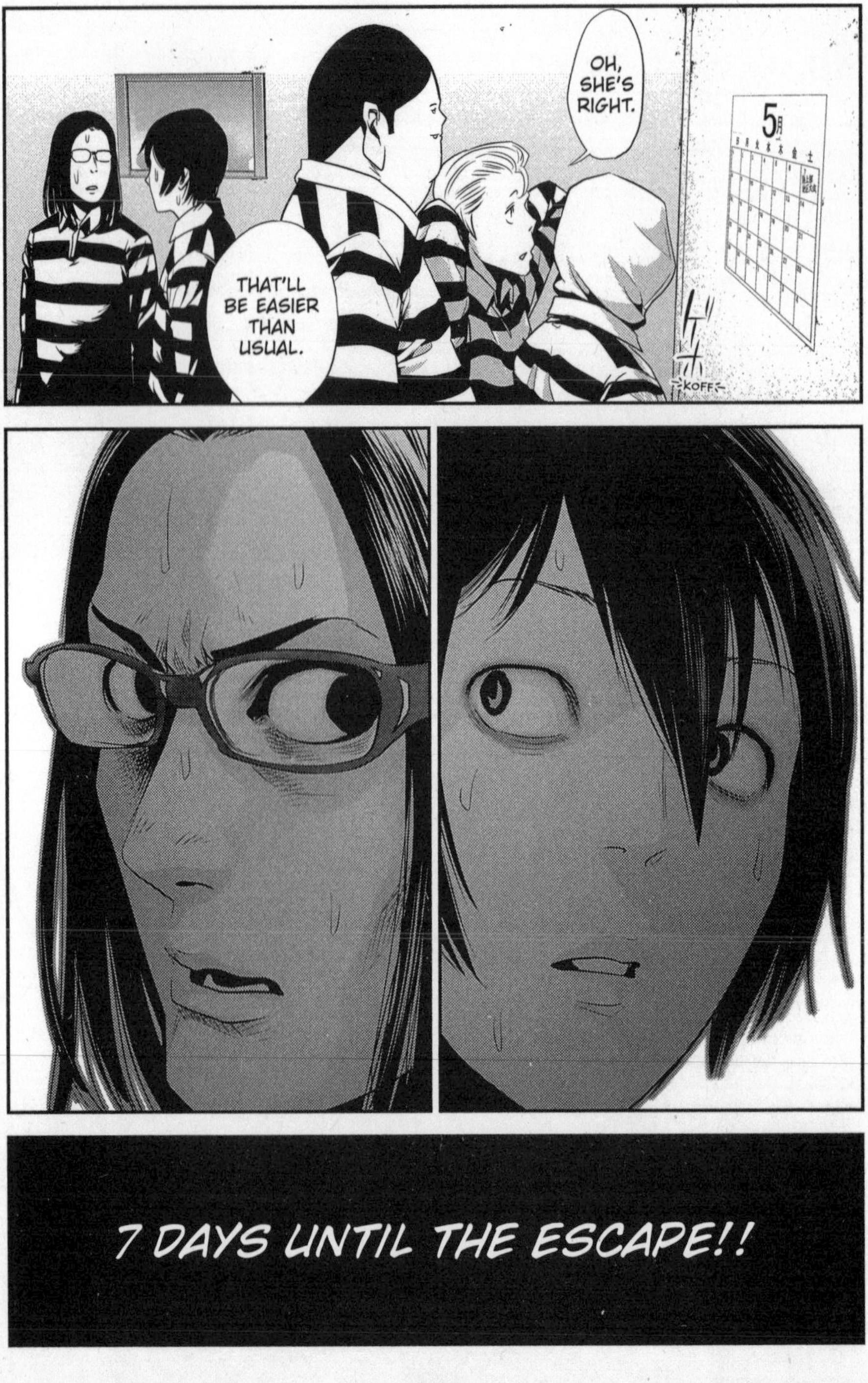
OH, SHE'S RIGHT.
THAT'LL BE EASIER THAN USUAL.
KOFF
7 DAYS UNTIL THE ESCAPE!!

CHAPTER 15: BROKEBACK PRISON

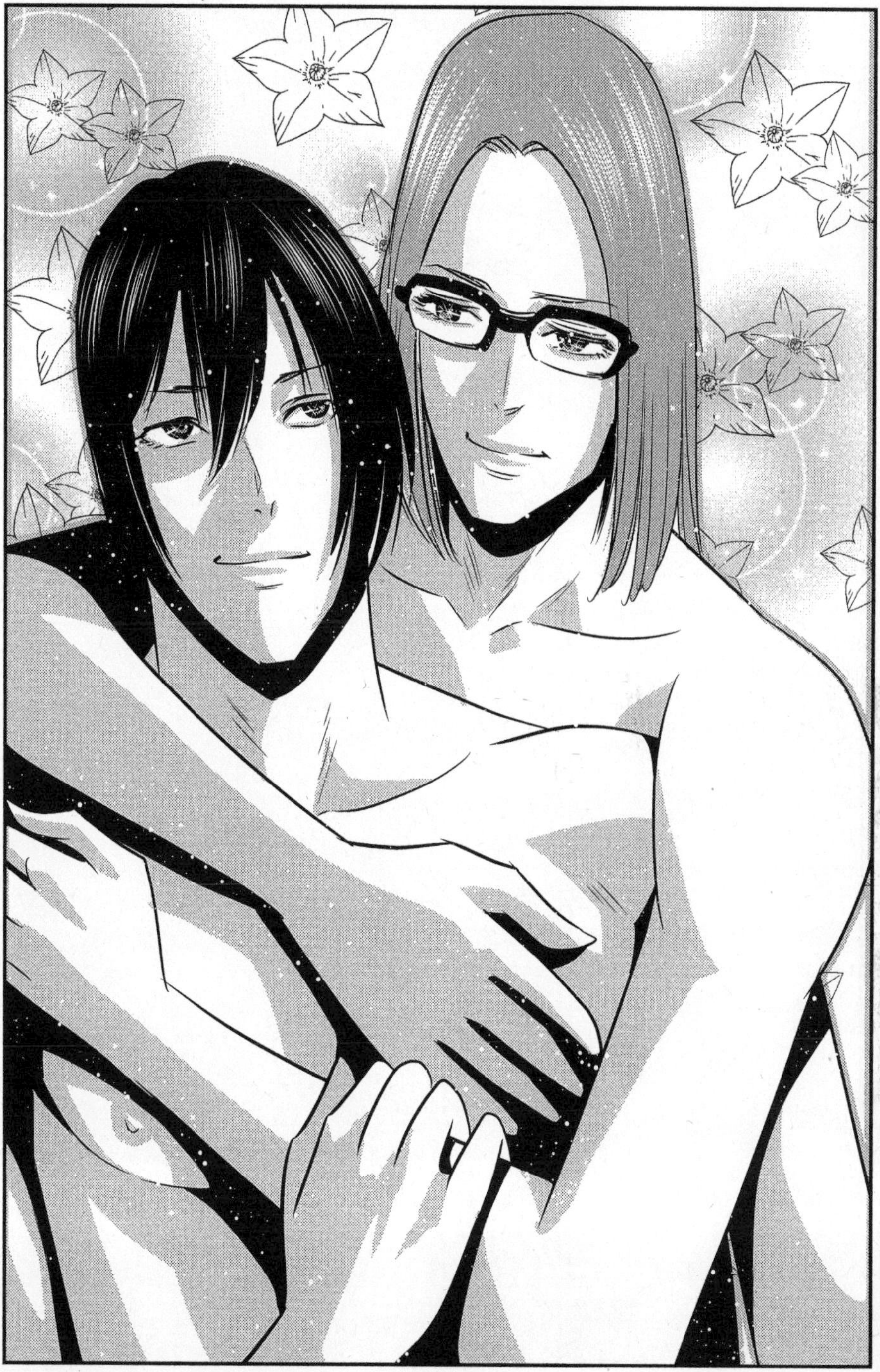

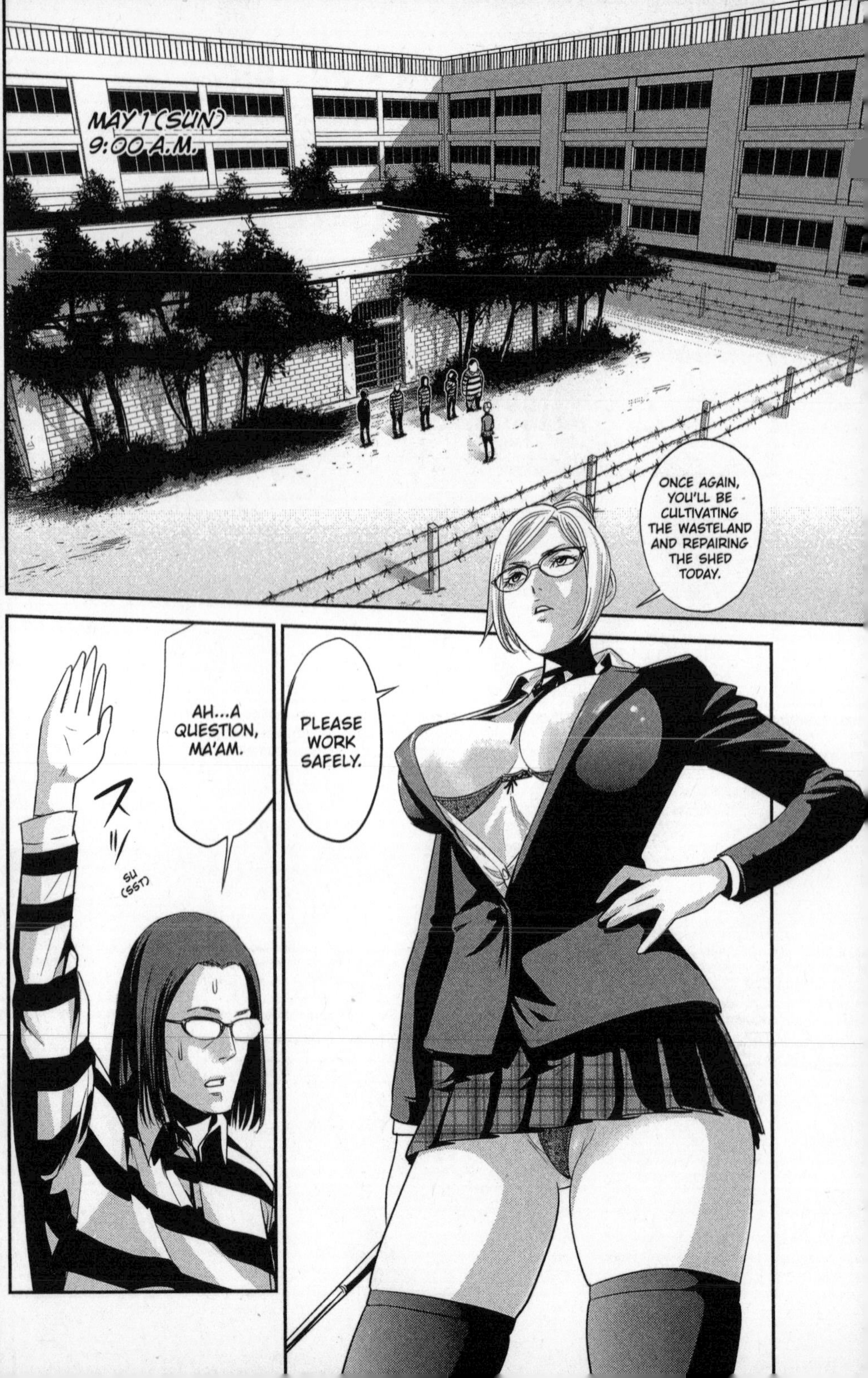
MAY 1 (SUN)
9:00 A.M.
ONCE AGAIN, YOU'LL BE CULTIVATING THE WASTELAND AND REPAIRING THE SHED TODAY.
PLEASE WORK SAFELY.
AH...A QUESTION, MA'AM.
ス
SU (SST)

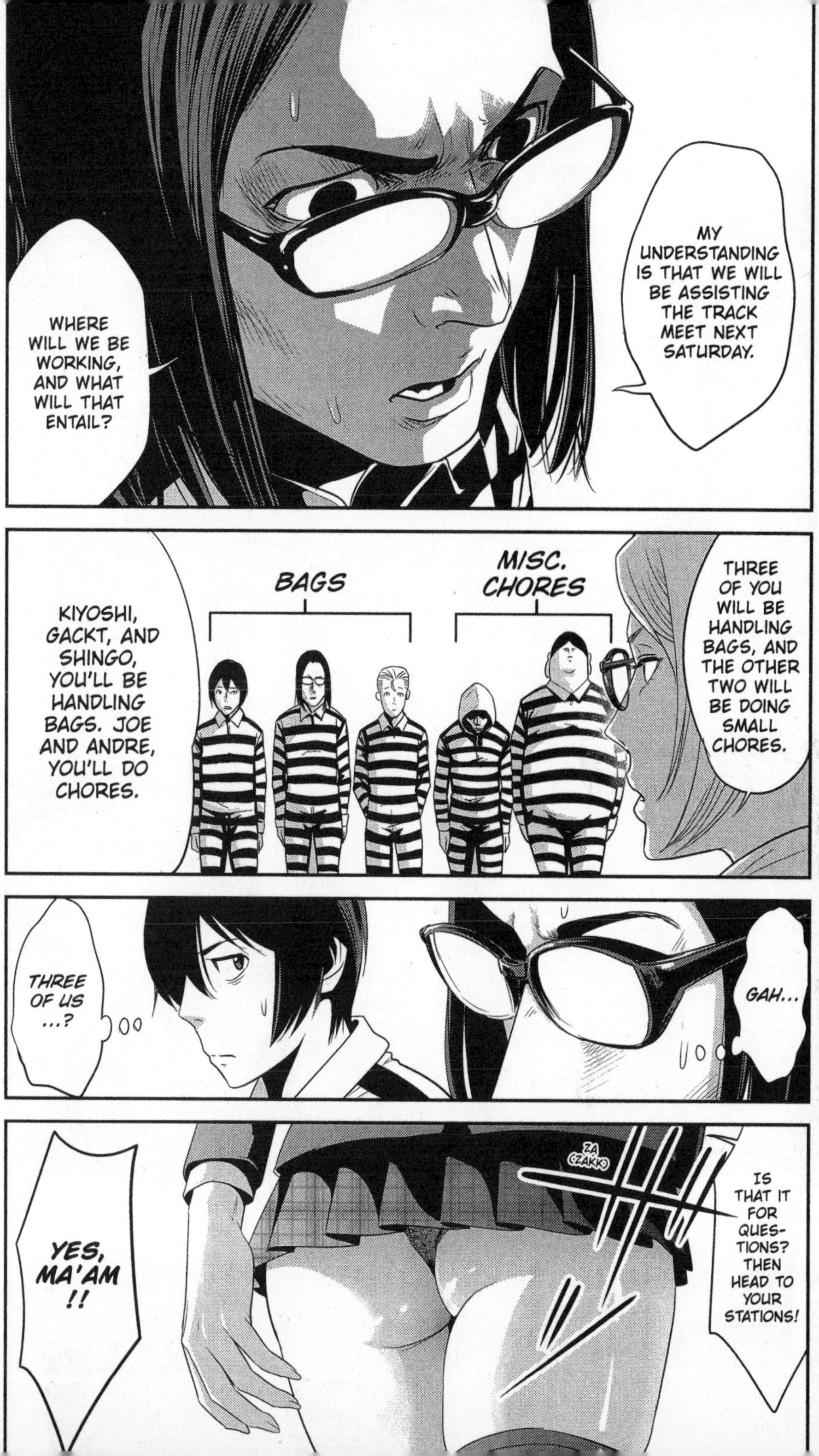
MY UNDERSTANDING IS THAT WE WILL BE ASSISTING THE TRACK MEET NEXT SATURDAY.
WHERE WILL WE BE WORKING, AND WHAT WILL THAT ENTAIL?
THREE OF YOU WILL BE HANDLING BAGS, AND THE OTHER TWO WILL BE DOING SMALL CHORES.
MISC. CHORES
BAGS
KIYOSHI, GACKT, AND SHINGO, YOU'LL BE HANDLING BAGS. JOE AND ANDRE, YOU'LL DO CHORES.
GAH...
THREE OF US ...?
ZA (ZAKK)
IS THAT IT FOR QUES-TIONS? THEN HEAD TO YOUR STATIONS!
YES, MA'AM !!

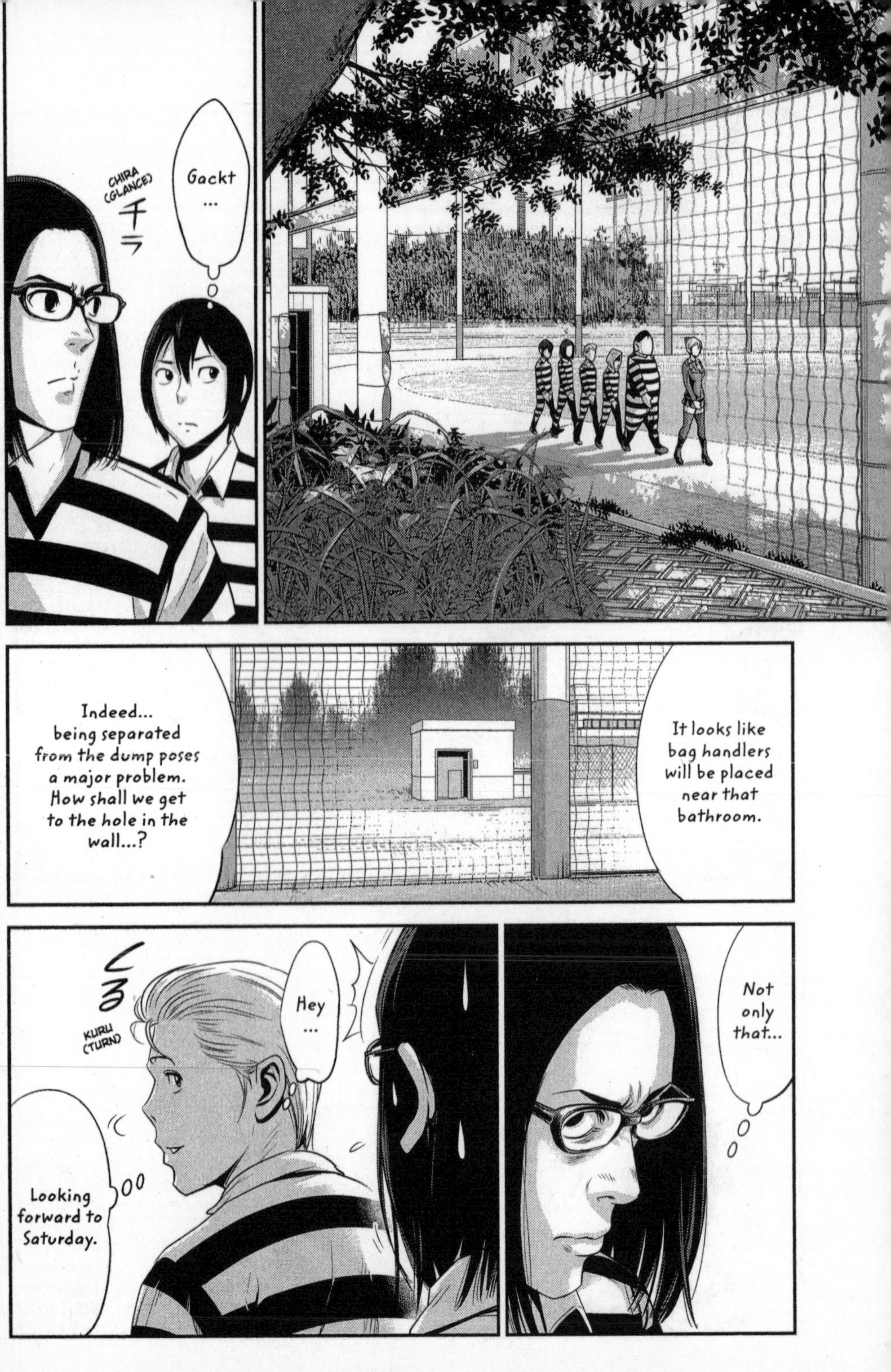
Gackt ...
CHIRA (GLANCE)
チラ
It looks like bag handlers will be placed near that bathroom.
Indeed... being separated from the dump poses a major problem. How shall we get to the hole in the wall...?
Not only that...
Hey ...
くる
KURU (TURN)
Looking forward to Saturday.

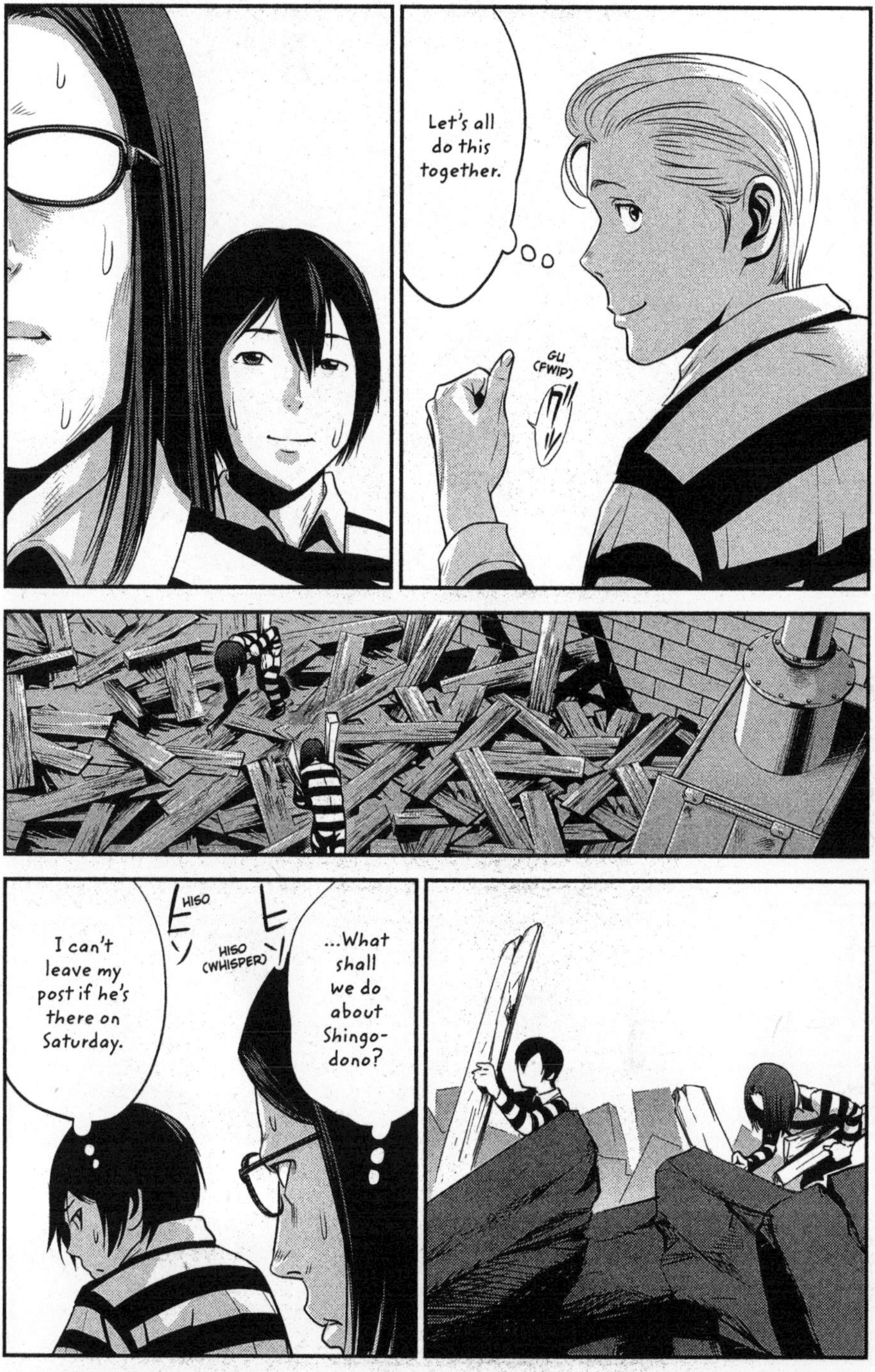
Let's all do this together.
GU (FWIP)
...What shall we do about Shingo-dono?
HISO (WHISPER)
HISO
I can't leave my post if he's there on Saturday.

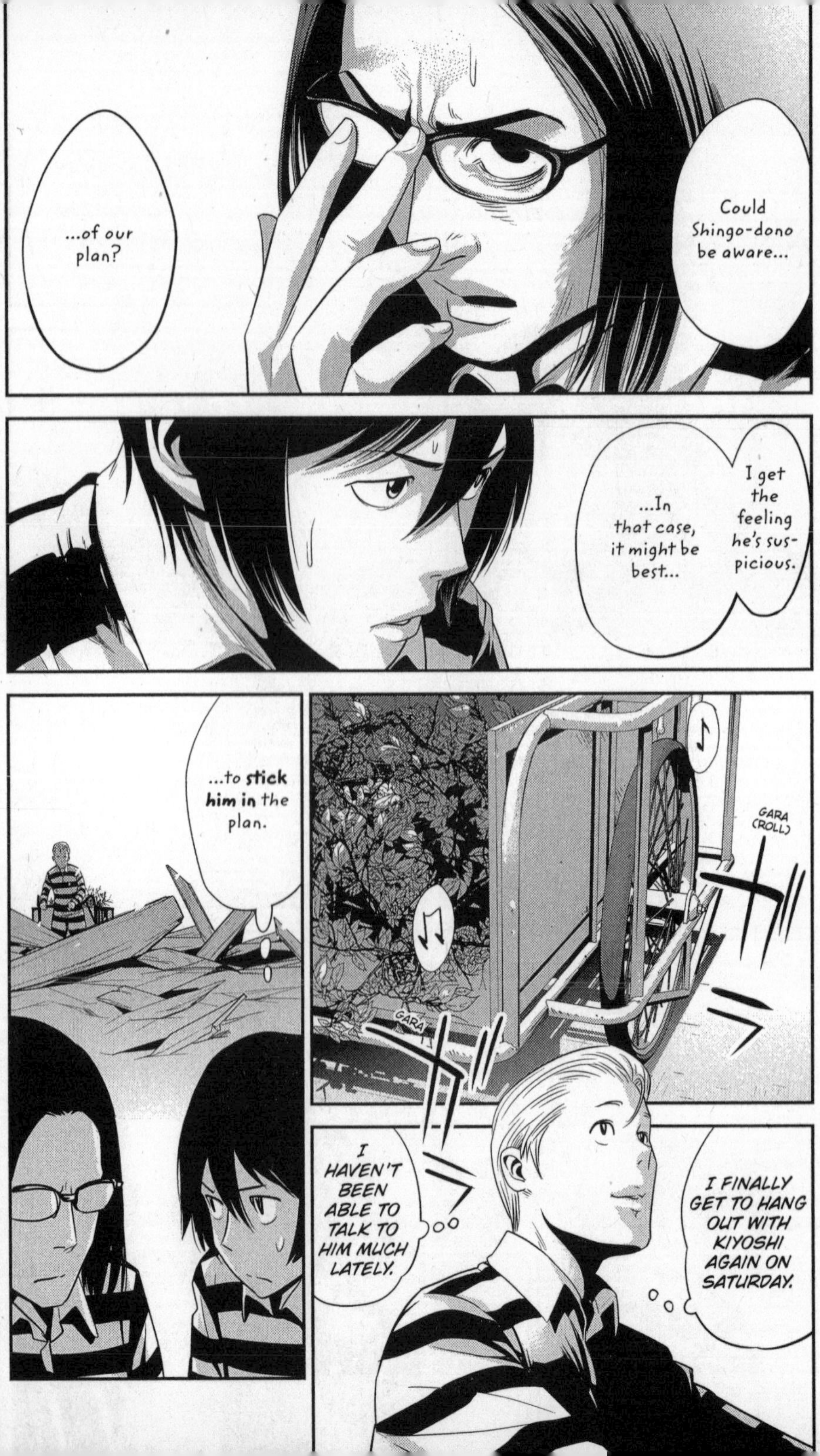
Could Shingo-dono be aware...
...of our plan?
I get the feeling he's suspicious.
...In that case, it might be best...
GARA (ROLL)
GARA
...to stick him in the plan.
I FINALLY GET TO HANG OUT WITH KIYOSHI AGAIN ON SATURDAY.
I HAVEN'T BEEN ABLE TO TALK TO HIM MUCH LATELY.

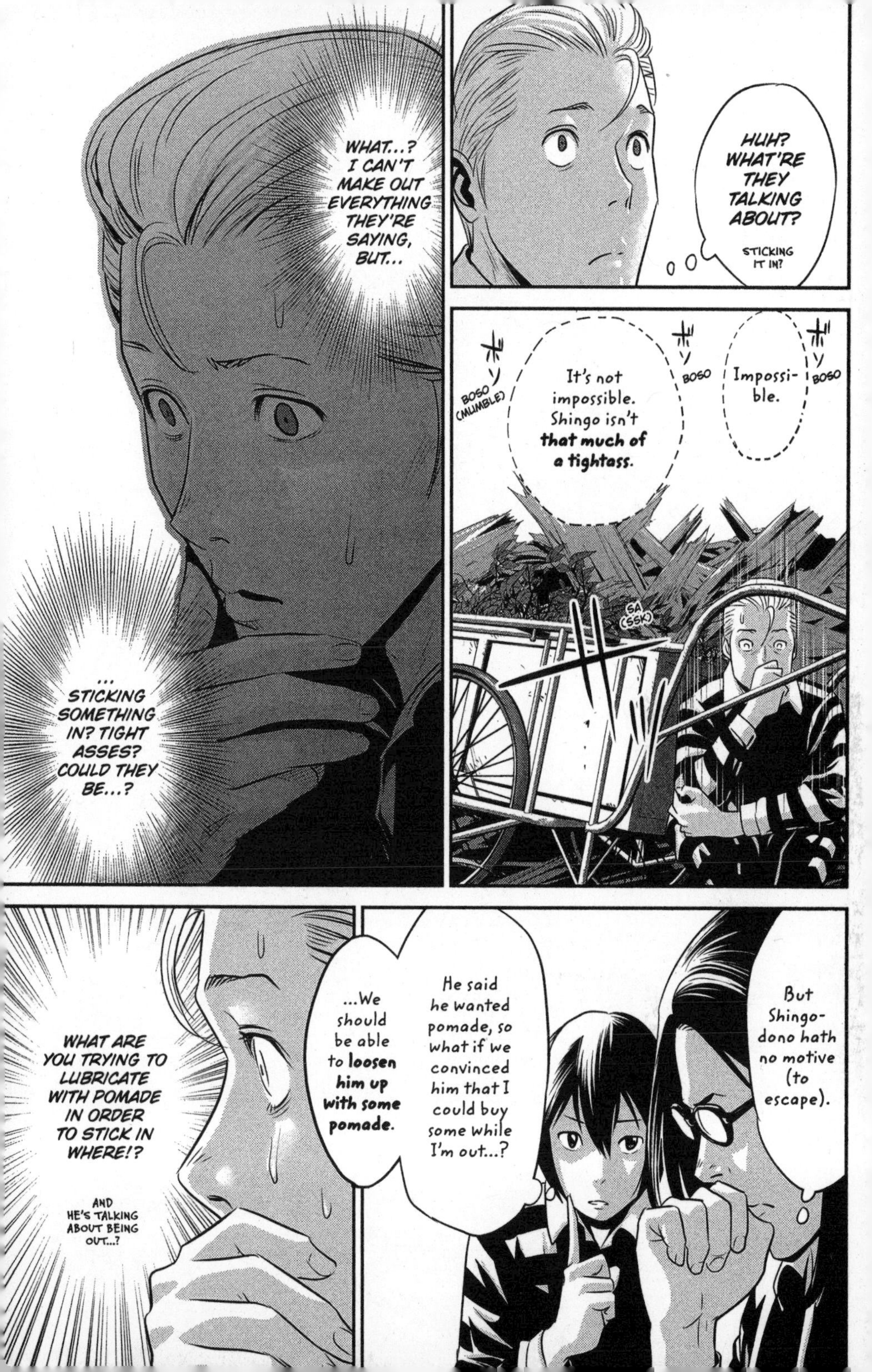
HUH? WHAT'RE THEY TALKING ABOUT?
STICKING IT IN?
BOSO
Impossible.
BOSO
It's not impossible. Shingo isn't **that much of a tightass.**
BOSO (MUMBLE)
SA (SSK)
WHAT...? I CAN'T MAKE OUT EVERYTHING THEY'RE SAYING, BUT...
... STICKING SOMETHING IN? TIGHT ASSES? COULD THEY BE...?
But Shingo-dono hath no motive (to escape).
He said he wanted pomade, so what if we convinced him that I could buy some while I'm out...?
...We should be able to **loosen him up with some pomade.**
WHAT ARE YOU TRYING TO LUBRICATE WITH POMADE IN ORDER TO STICK IN WHERE!?
AND HE'S TALKING ABOUT BEING OUT...?

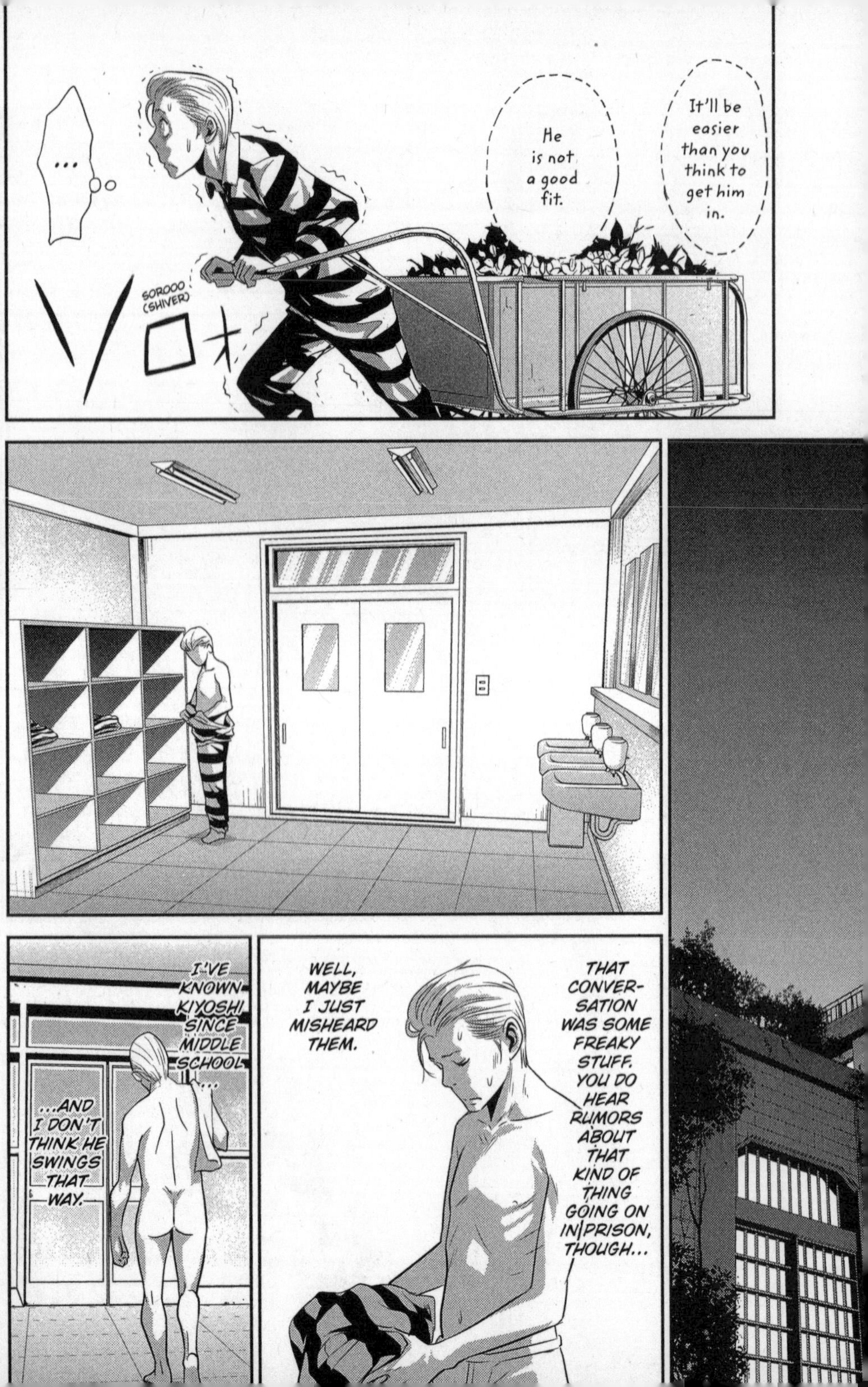
It'll be easier than you think to get him in.
He is not a good fit.
...
SOROOO (SHIVER)
THAT CONVER-SATION WAS SOME FREAKY STUFF. YOU DO HEAR RUMORS ABOUT THAT KIND OF THING GOING ON IN PRISON, THOUGH...
WELL, MAYBE I JUST MISHEARD THEM.
I'VE KNOWN KIYOSHI SINCE MIDDLE SCHOOL...
...AND I DON'T THINK HE SWINGS THAT WAY.

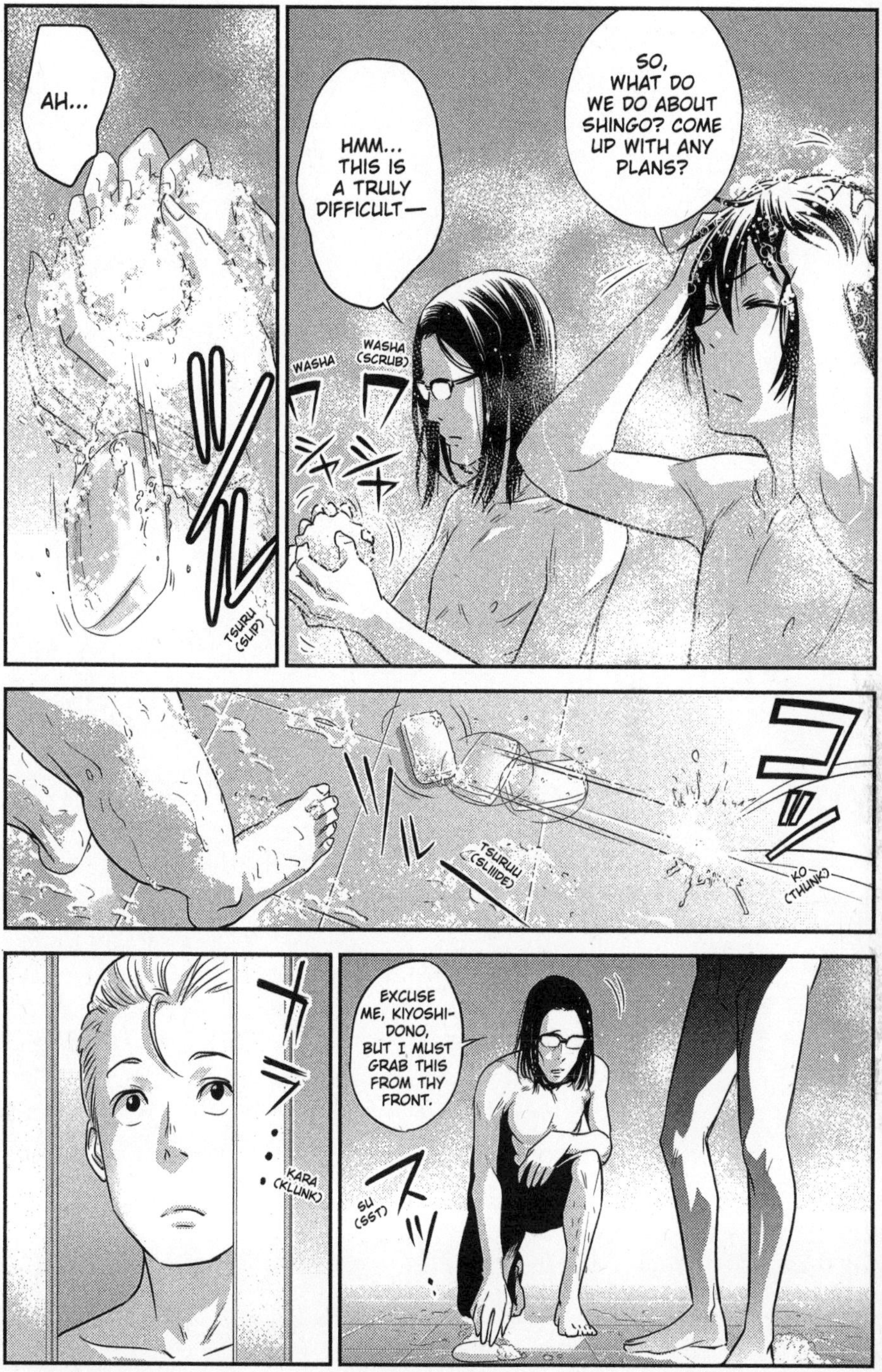
SO, WHAT DO WE DO ABOUT SHINGO? COME UP WITH ANY PLANS?
HMM... THIS IS A TRULY DIFFICULT—
WASHA (SCRUB)
WASHA
AH...
TSURU (SLIP)
KO (THUNK)
TSURUU (SLIIIDE)
EXCUSE ME, KIYOSHI-DONO, BUT I MUST GRAB THIS FROM THY FRONT.
SU (SST)
KARA (KLUNK)

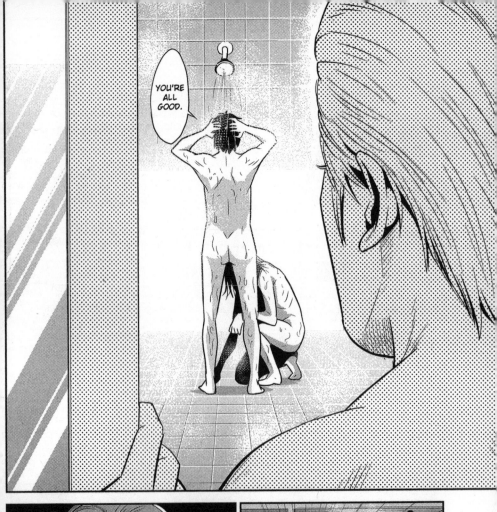

YOU'RE ALL GOOD.
BA (BAM)
...I THOUGHT THOSE TWO SEEMED UNUSU-ALLY FRIENDLY LATELY...
AND "YOU'RE ALL GOOD"? IS GACKT THAT SKILLED!?

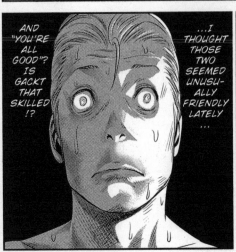

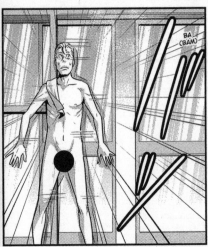

GAH!

TSURU
(SLIP)

THERE'S NO WAY...

NO, SHINGO. YOU'RE OVER-THINKING IT! YOU JUST MISCON-STRUED WHAT YOU SAW!

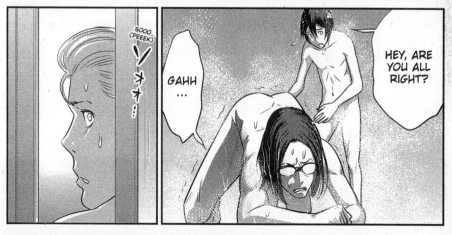

SOOO
(PEEEK)

GAHH...

HEY, ARE YOU ALL RIGHT?

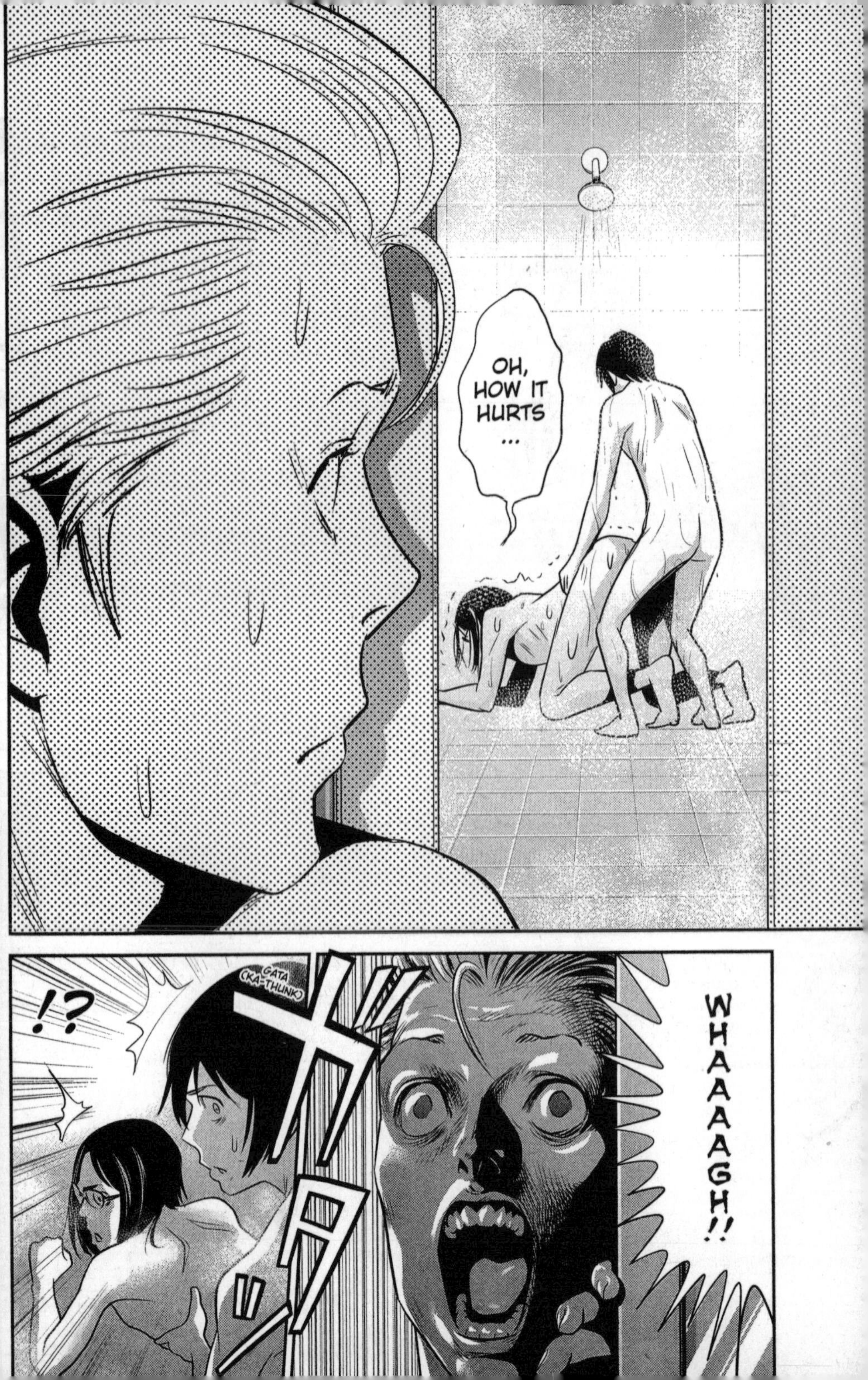
OH, HOW IT HURTS ...
GATA (KA-THUNK)
!?
WHAAAAAGH!!

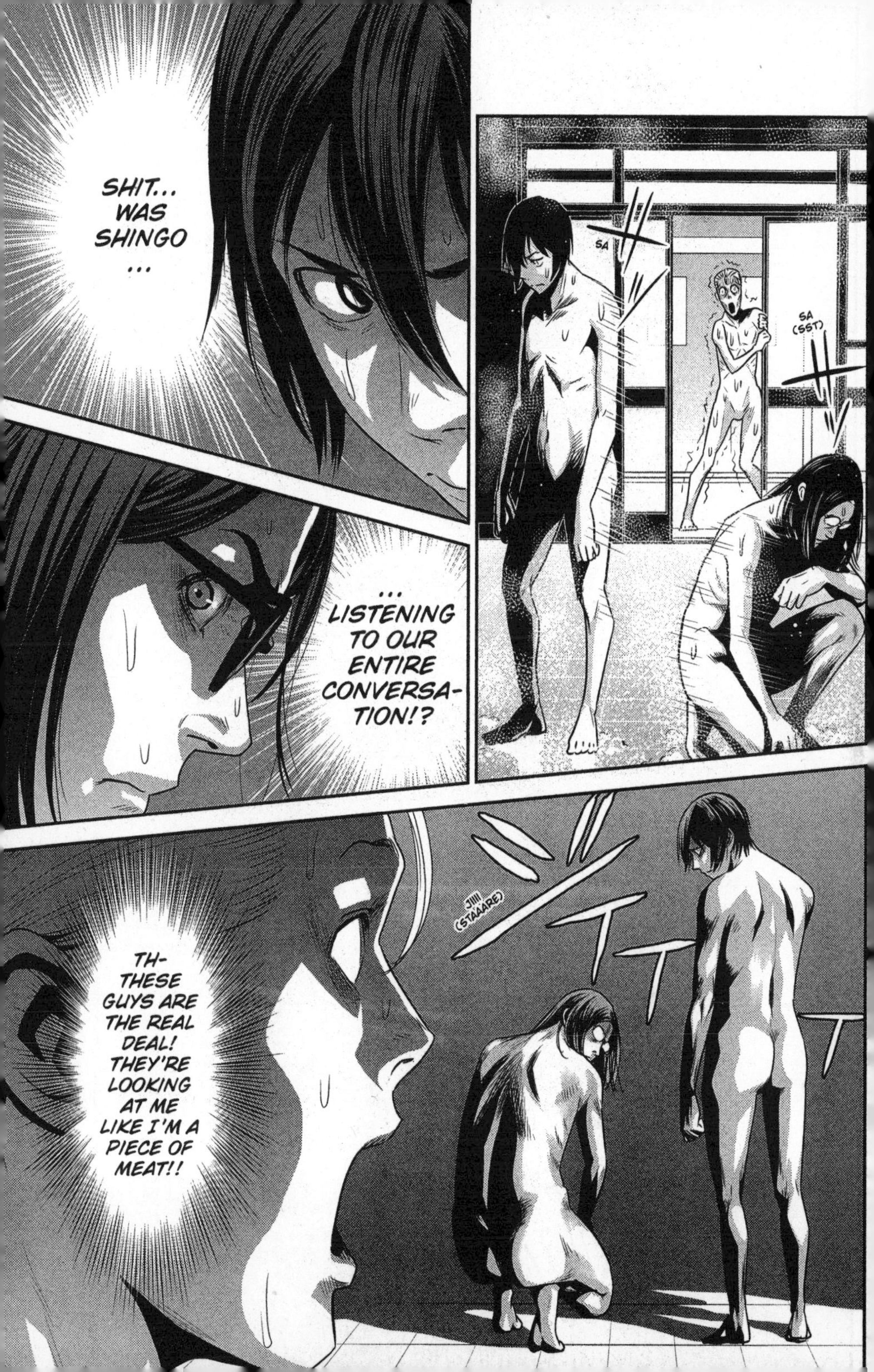

SA
SA (SST)
SHIT... WAS SHINGO ...
... LISTENING TO OUR ENTIRE CONVERSA-TION!?
JIIII (STAAARE)
TH-THESE GUYS ARE THE REAL DEAL! THEY'RE LOOKING AT ME LIKE I'M A PIECE OF MEAT!!

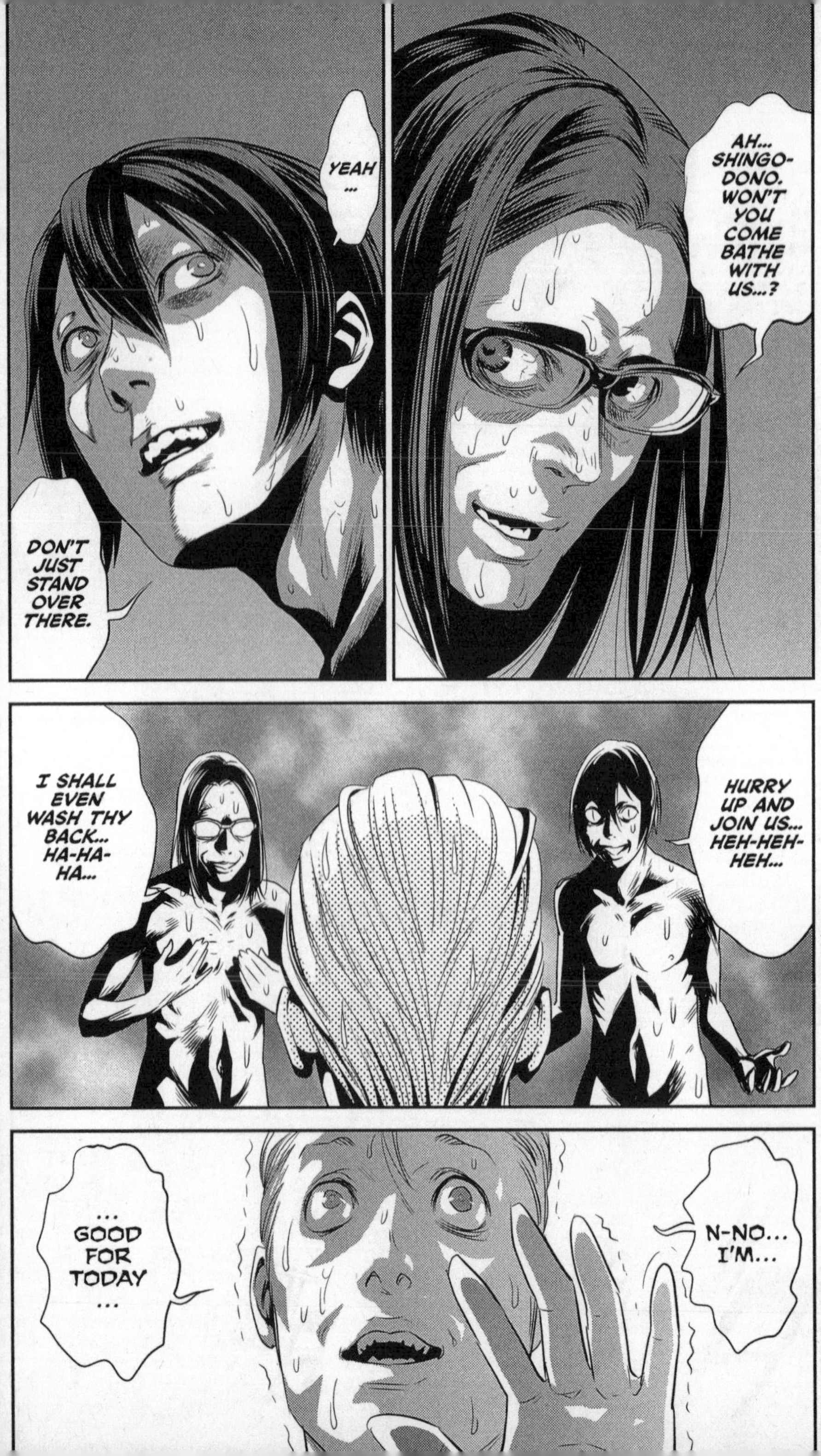
AH... SHINGO-DONO. WON'T YOU COME BATHE WITH US...?
YEAH...
DON'T JUST STAND OVER THERE.
HURRY UP AND JOIN US... HEH-HEH-HEH...
I SHALL EVEN WASH THY BACK... HA-HA-HA...
N-NO... I'M...
...GOOD FOR TODAY...

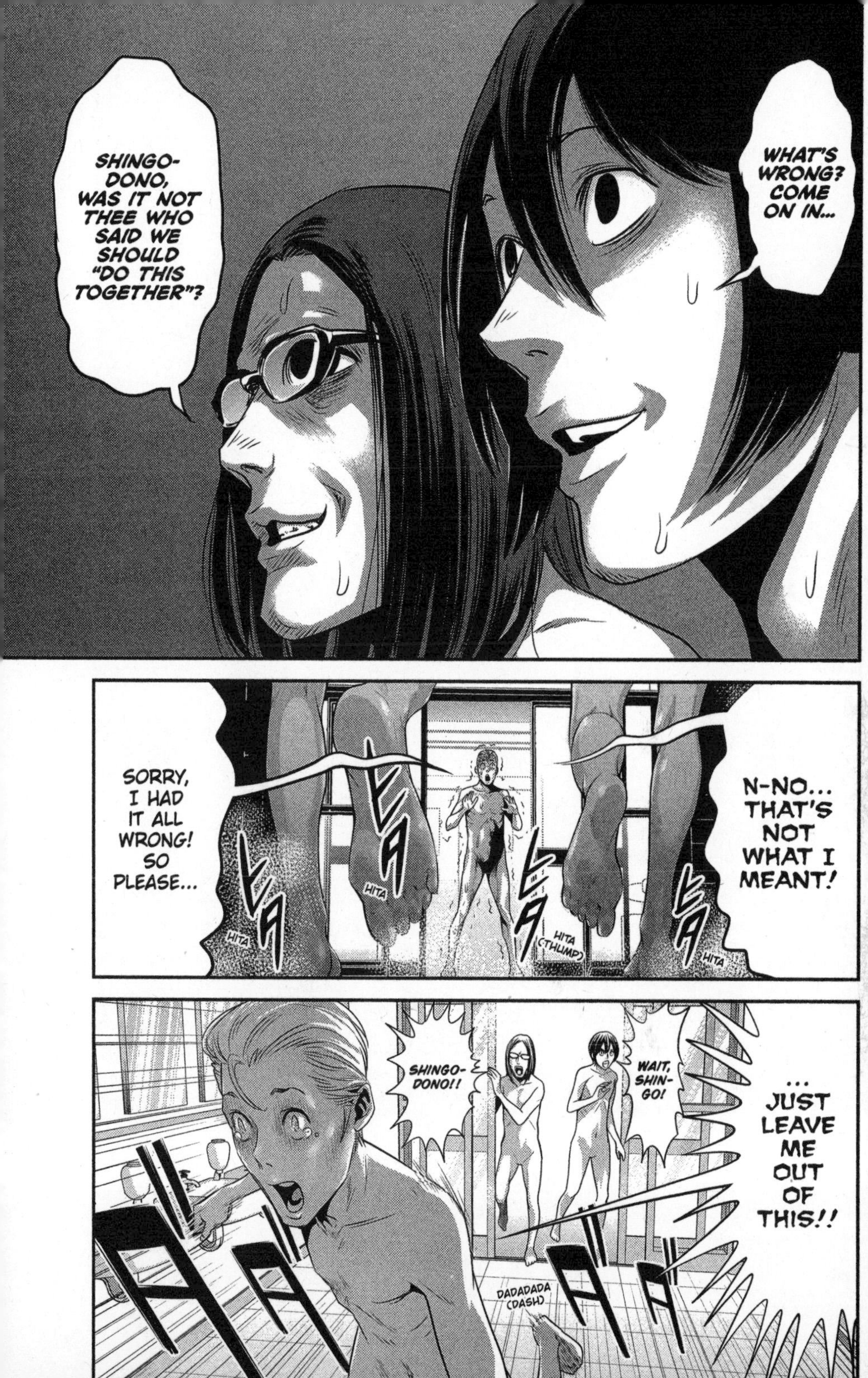
WHAT'S WRONG? COME ON IN...
SHINGO-DONO, WAS IT NOT THEE WHO SAID WE SHOULD "DO THIS TOGETHER"?
N-NO... THAT'S NOT WHAT I MEANT!
HITA
HITA (THUMP)
HITA
HITA
SORRY, I HAD IT ALL WRONG! SO PLEASE...
...JUST LEAVE ME OUT OF THIS!!
WAIT, SHINGO!
SHINGO-DONO!!
DADADADA (DASH)

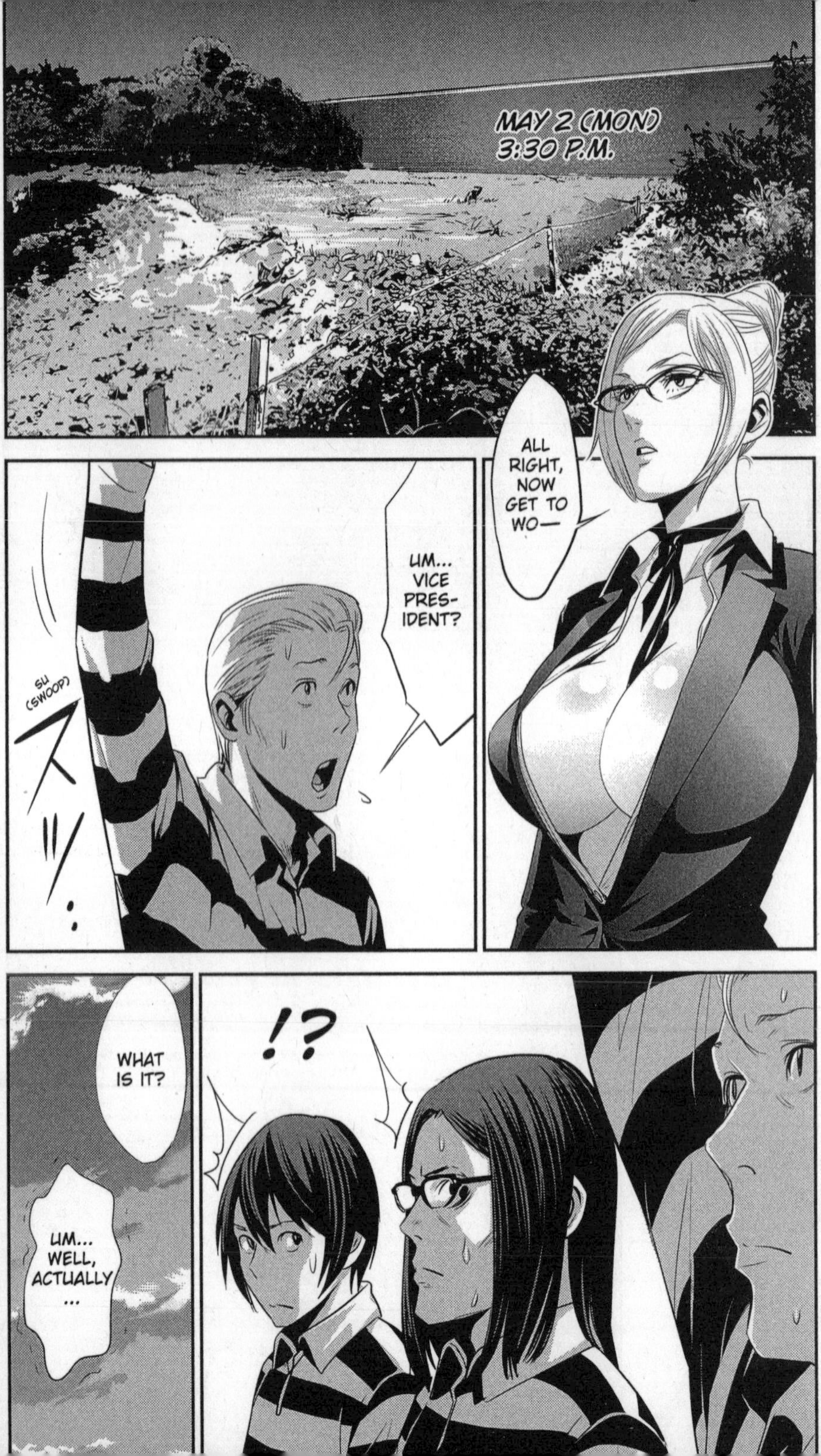
MAY 2 (MON)
3:30 P.M.
ALL RIGHT, NOW GET TO WO—
UM... VICE PRES-IDENT?
SU (SWOOP)
!?
WHAT IS IT?
UM... WELL, ACTUALLY ...

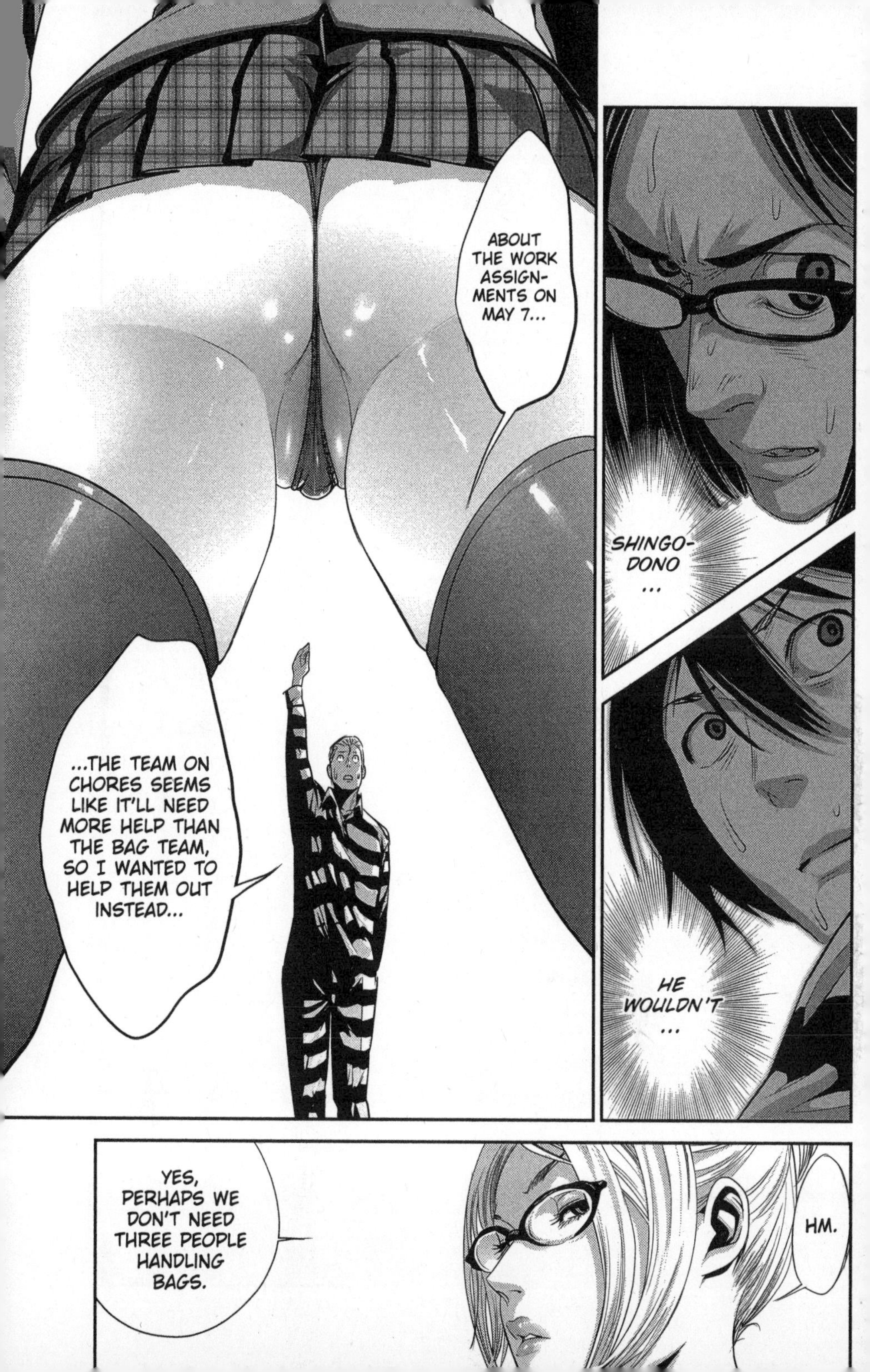
ABOUT THE WORK ASSIGN-MENTS ON MAY 7...
...THE TEAM ON CHORES SEEMS LIKE IT'LL NEED MORE HELP THAN THE BAG TEAM, SO I WANTED TO HELP THEM OUT INSTEAD...
SHINGO-DONO ...
HE WOULDN'T ...
HM.
YES, PERHAPS WE DON'T NEED THREE PEOPLE HANDLING BAGS.

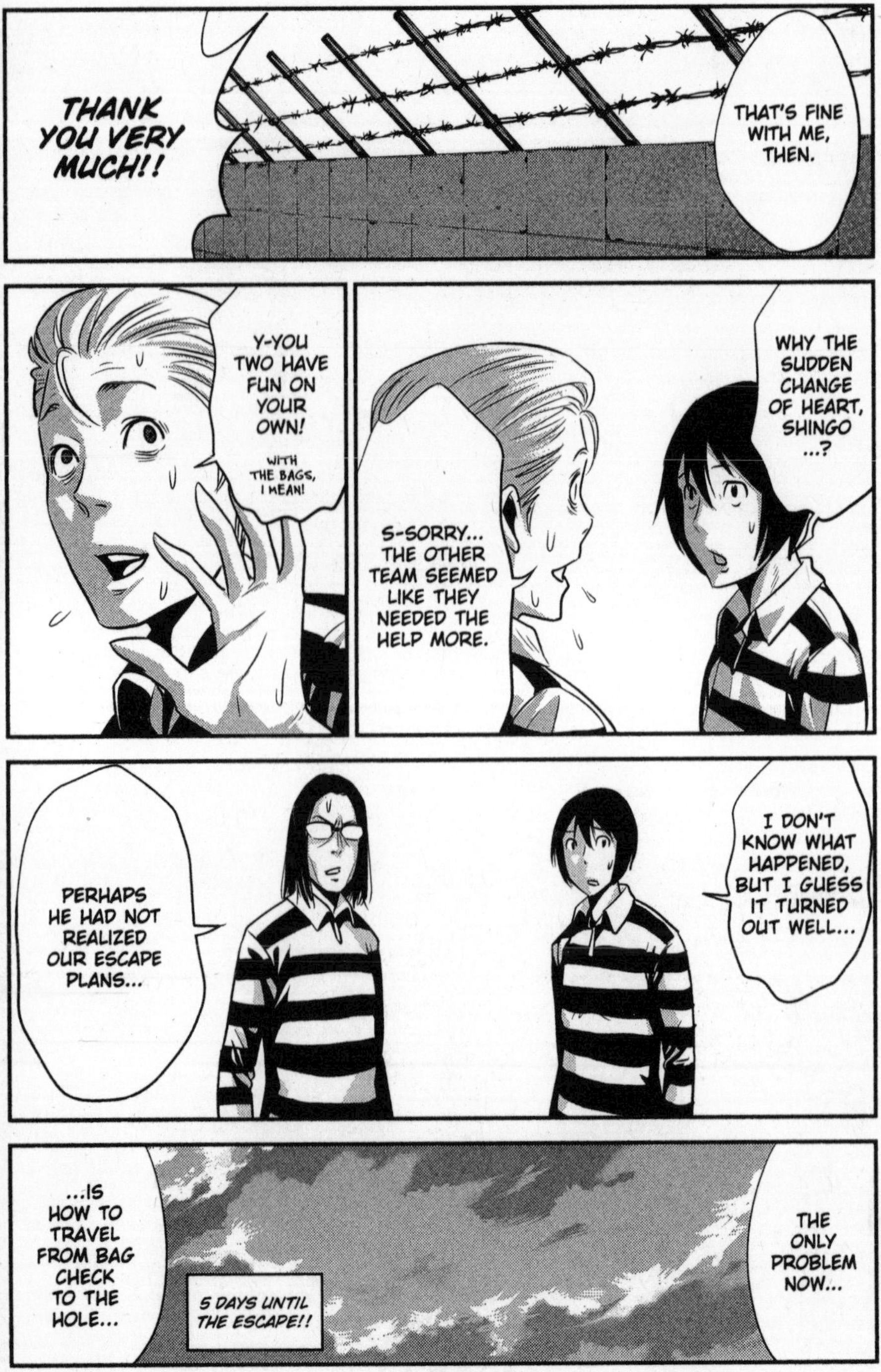
THAT'S FINE WITH ME, THEN.
THANK YOU VERY MUCH!!
WHY THE SUDDEN CHANGE OF HEART, SHINGO ...?
S-SORRY... THE OTHER TEAM SEEMED LIKE THEY NEEDED THE HELP MORE.
Y-YOU TWO HAVE FUN ON YOUR OWN!
WITH THE BAGS, I MEAN!
I DON'T KNOW WHAT HAPPENED, BUT I GUESS IT TURNED OUT WELL...
PERHAPS HE HAD NOT REALIZED OUR ESCAPE PLANS...
THE ONLY PROBLEM NOW...
...IS HOW TO TRAVEL FROM BAG CHECK TO THE HOLE...
5 DAYS UNTIL THE ESCAPE!!

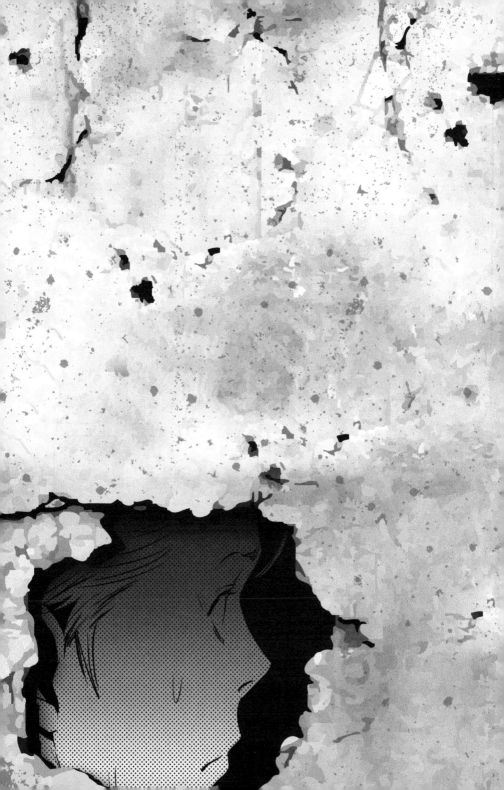

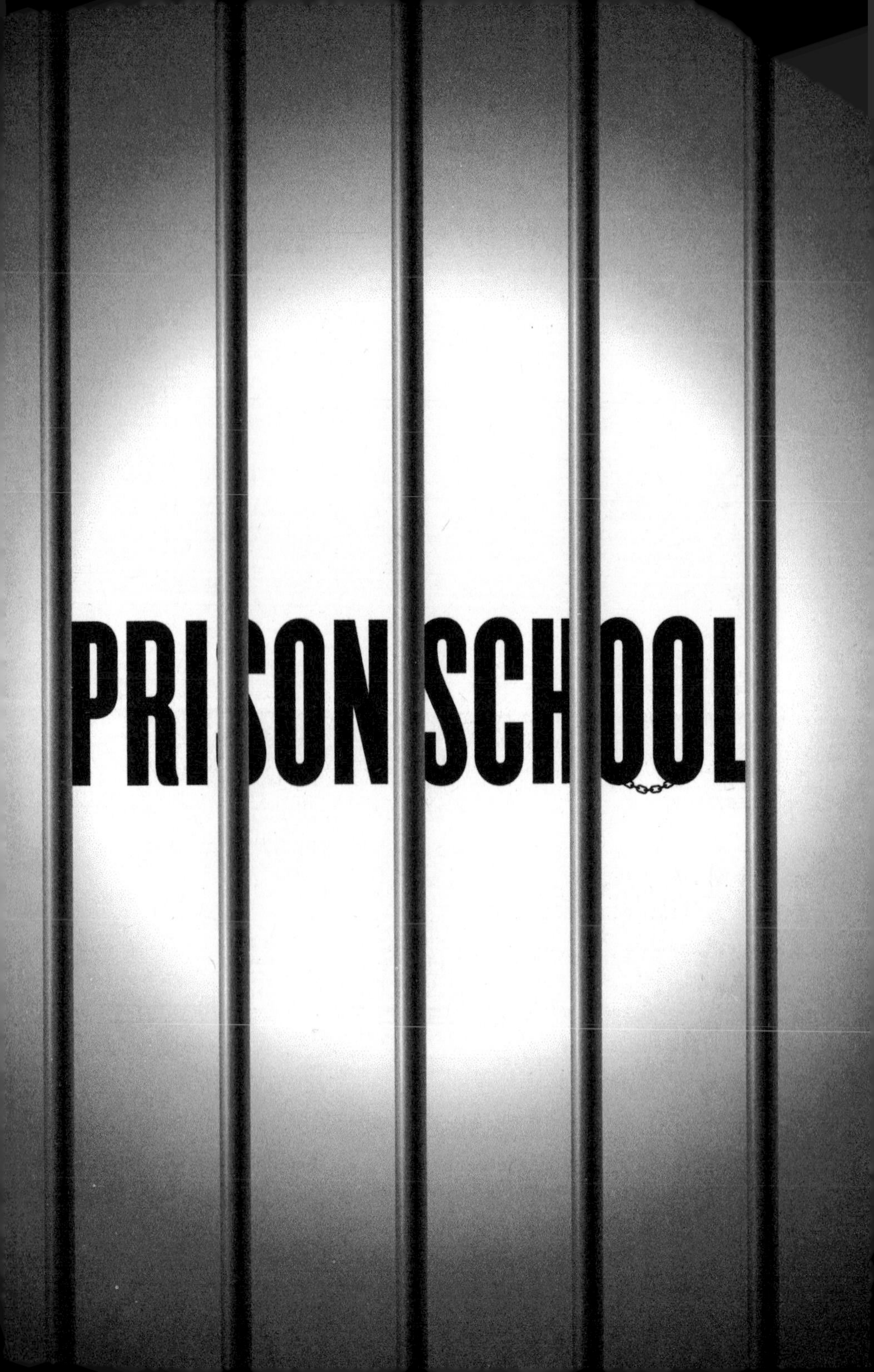
PRISON SCHOOL

CHAPTER 16: UNDERWORLD

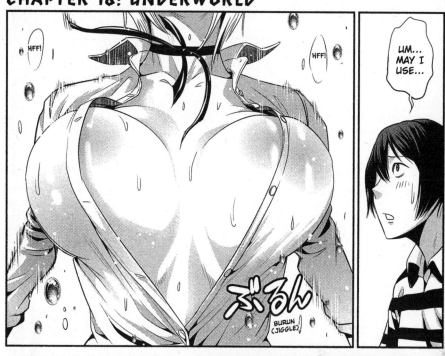

UM... MAY I USE...

HFF!

HFF!

ぶるん
BURUN
(JIGGLE)

UM...MAY I USE THE RESTROOM!?

HFF!

HFF!

BURURUN

ぶるるん

HFF!

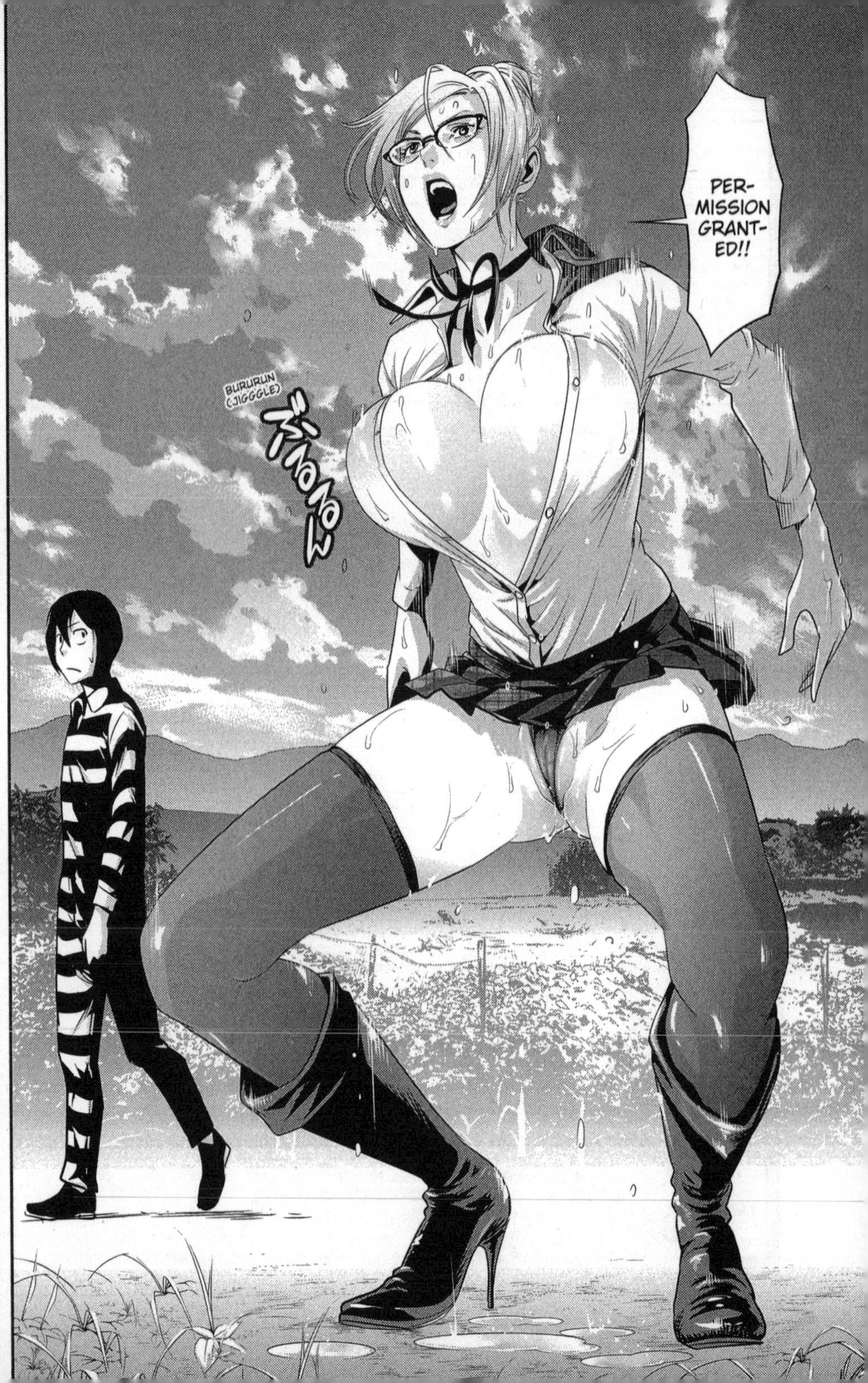
PER-MISSION GRANT-ED!!
BURURUN (JIGGGLE)

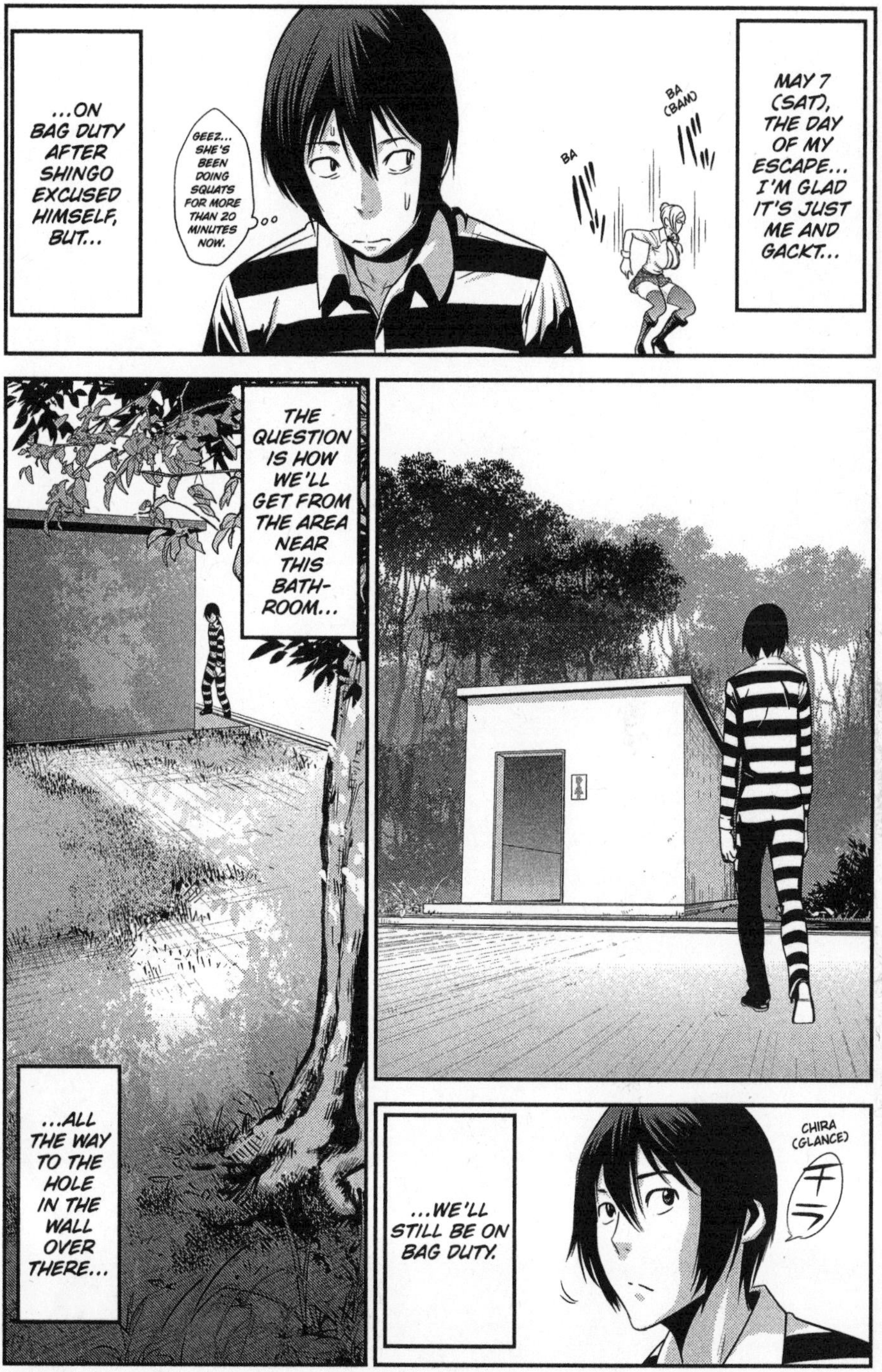
MAY 7 (SAT), THE DAY OF MY ESCAPE... I'M GLAD IT'S JUST ME AND GACKT...
BA (BAM)
BA
GEEZ... SHE'S BEEN DOING SQUATS FOR MORE THAN 20 MINUTES NOW.
...ON BAG DUTY AFTER SHINGO EXCUSED HIMSELF, BUT...
THE QUESTION IS HOW WE'LL GET FROM THE AREA NEAR THIS BATH-ROOM...
...ALL THE WAY TO THE HOLE IN THE WALL OVER THERE...
CHIRA (GLANCE)
チラ
...WE'LL STILL BE ON BAG DUTY.

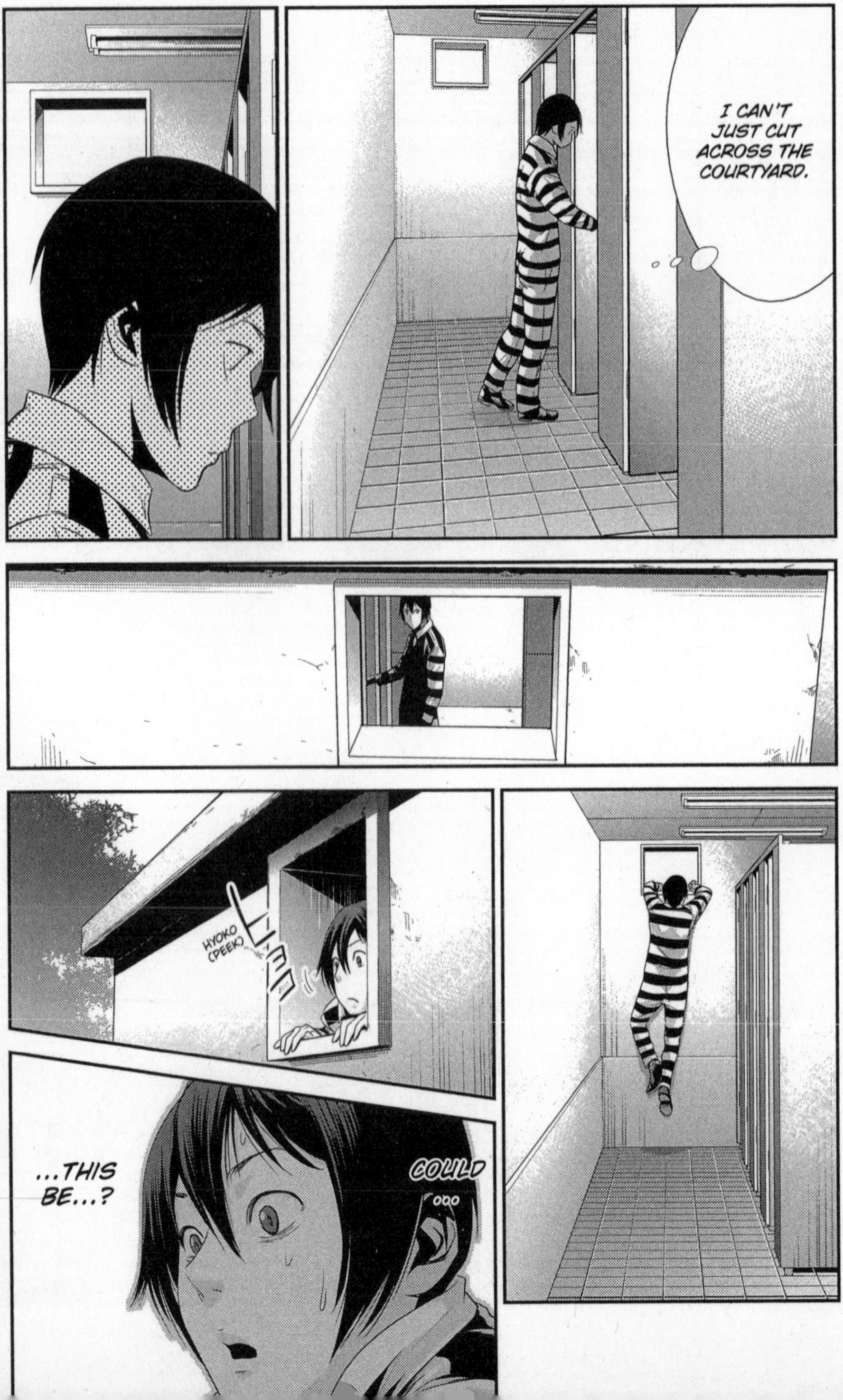
I CAN'T JUST CUT ACROSS THE COURTYARD.
HYOKO (PEEK)
COULD
...THIS BE...?

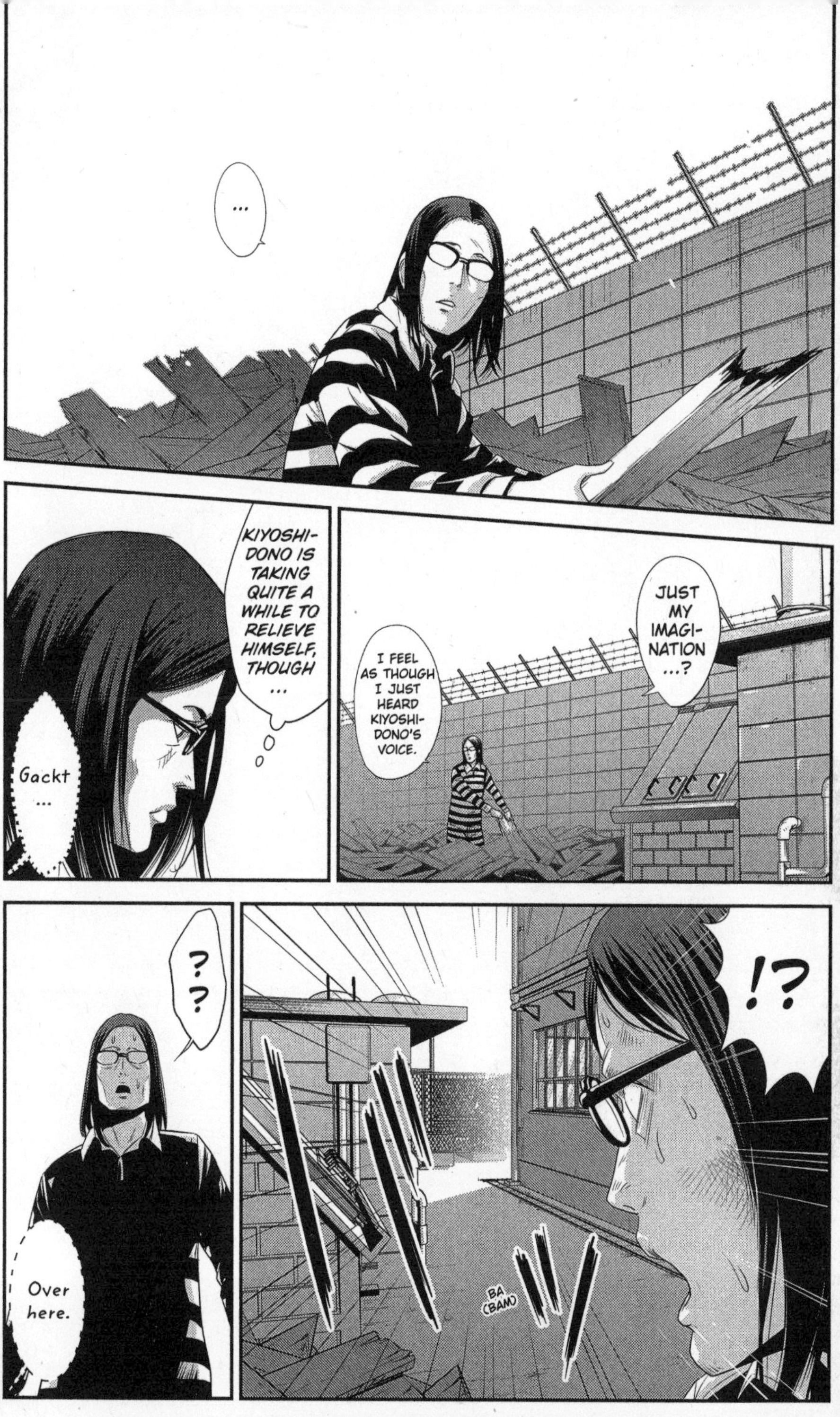
...
KIYOSHI-DONO IS TAKING QUITE A WHILE TO RELIEVE HIMSELF, THOUGH...
JUST MY IMAGINATION...?
I FEEL AS THOUGH I JUST HEARD KIYOSHI-DONO'S VOICE.
Gackt...
!?
BA (BAM)
??
Over here.

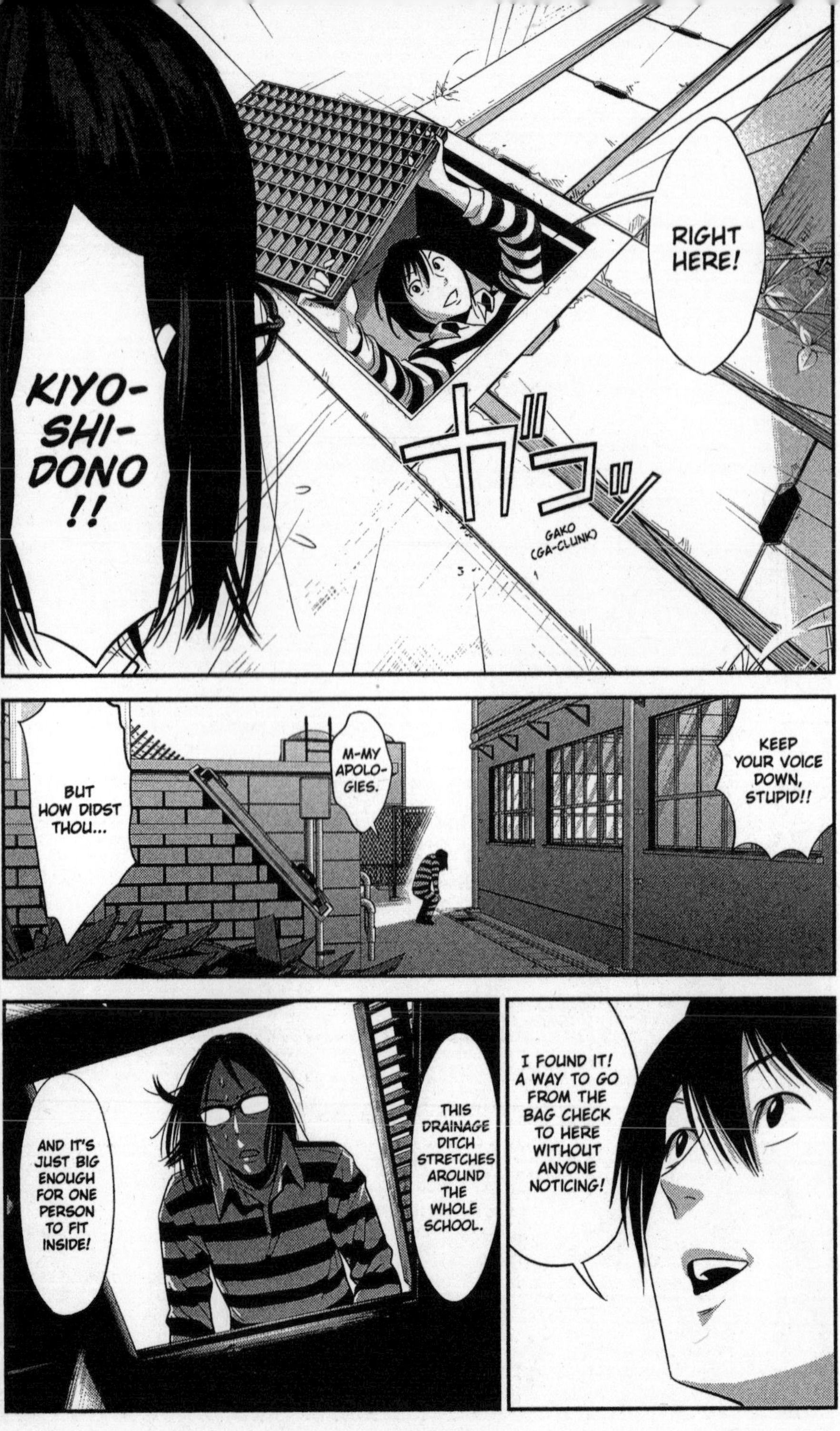
RIGHT HERE!
ガコッ
GAKO (GA-CLUNK)
KIYO-SHI-DONO!!
KEEP YOUR VOICE DOWN, STUPID!!
M-MY APOLOGIES.
BUT HOW DIDST THOU...
I FOUND IT! A WAY TO GO FROM THE BAG CHECK TO HERE WITHOUT ANYONE NOTICING!
THIS DRAINAGE DITCH STRETCHES AROUND THE WHOLE SCHOOL.
AND IT'S JUST BIG ENOUGH FOR ONE PERSON TO FIT INSIDE!

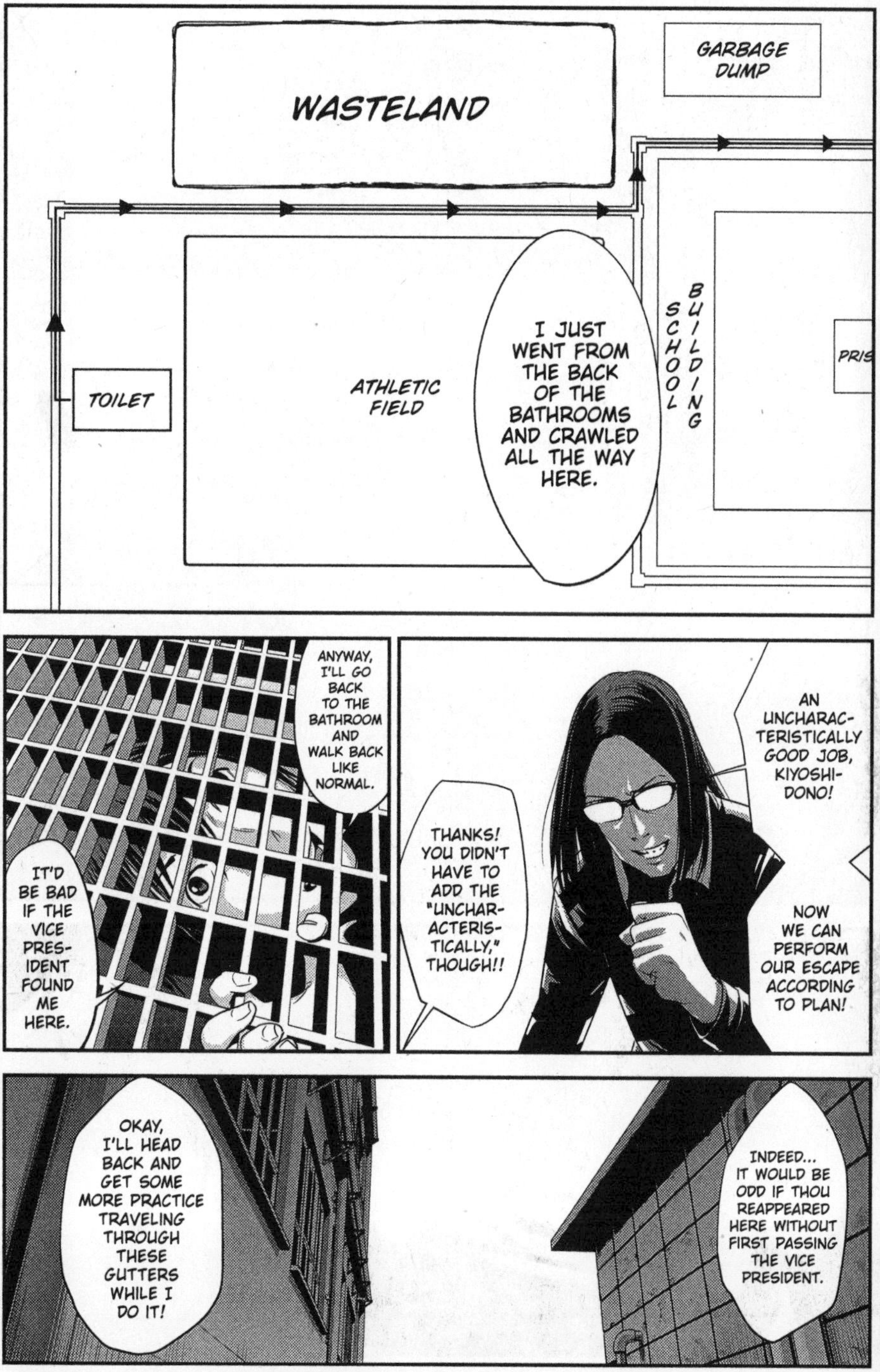
WASTELAND
GARBAGE DUMP
TOILET
ATHLETIC FIELD
SCHOOL BUILDING
PRIS
I JUST WENT FROM THE BACK OF THE BATHROOMS AND CRAWLED ALL THE WAY HERE.
AN UNCHARACTERISTICALLY GOOD JOB, KIYOSHI-DONO!
NOW WE CAN PERFORM OUR ESCAPE ACCORDING TO PLAN!
THANKS! YOU DIDN'T HAVE TO ADD THE "UNCHARACTERISTICALLY," THOUGH!!
ANYWAY, I'LL GO BACK TO THE BATHROOM AND WALK BACK LIKE NORMAL.
IT'D BE BAD IF THE VICE PRESIDENT FOUND ME HERE.
OKAY, I'LL HEAD BACK AND GET SOME MORE PRACTICE TRAVELING THROUGH THESE GUTTERS WHILE I DO IT!
INDEED... IT WOULD BE ODD IF THOU REAPPEARED HERE WITHOUT FIRST PASSING THE VICE PRESIDENT.

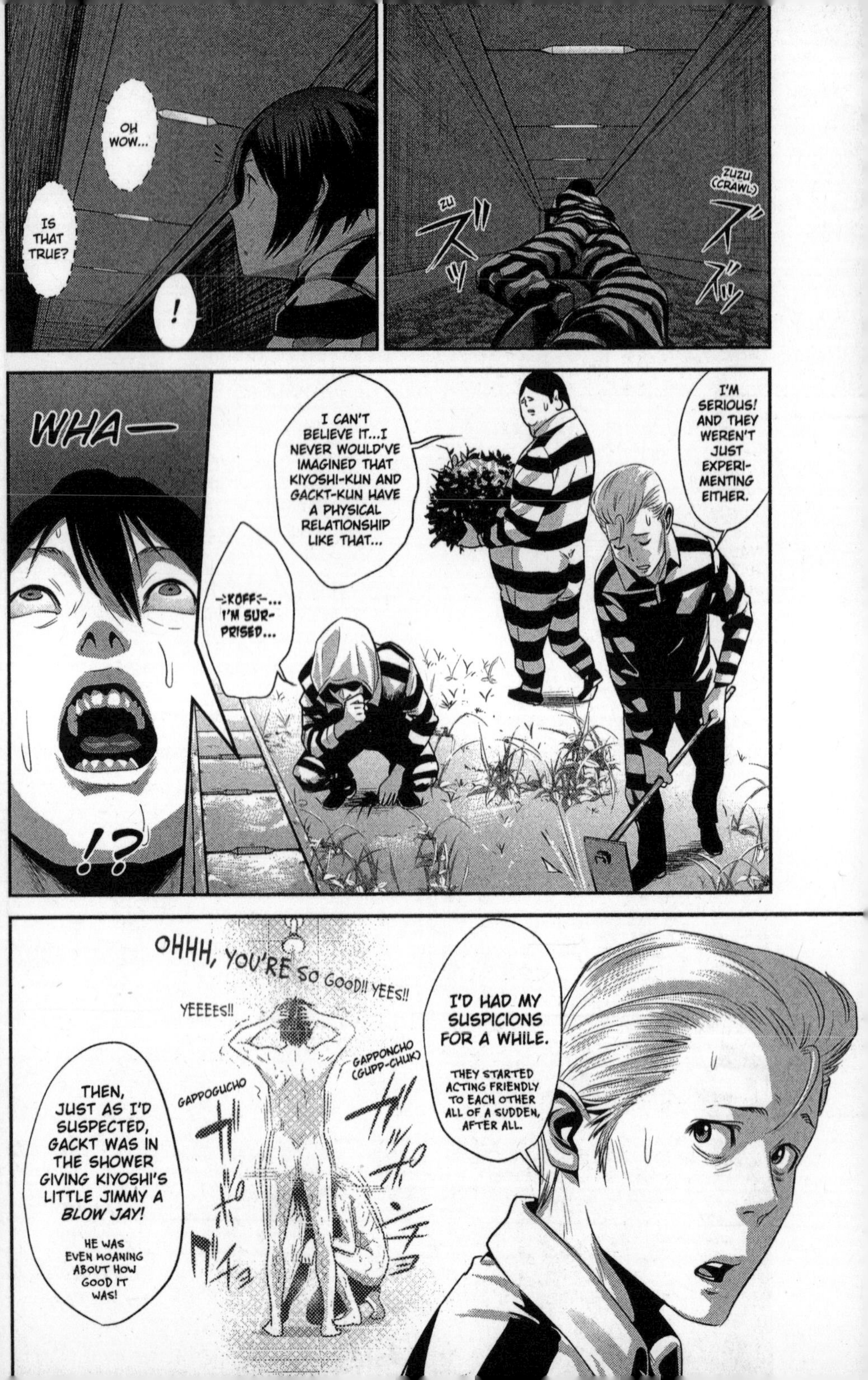
ZUZU (CRAWL)
ZU
OH WOW...
IS THAT TRUE?
!
I'M SERIOUS! AND THEY WEREN'T JUST EXPERIMENTING EITHER.
I CAN'T BELIEVE IT...I NEVER WOULD'VE IMAGINED THAT KIYOSHI-KUN AND GACKT-KUN HAVE A PHYSICAL RELATIONSHIP LIKE THAT...
-KOFF-... I'M SURPRISED...
WHA—
!?
I'D HAD MY SUSPICIONS FOR A WHILE.
THEY STARTED ACTING FRIENDLY TO EACH OTHER ALL OF A SUDDEN, AFTER ALL.
OHHH, YOU'RE SO GOOD!! YEES!!
YEEEEES!!
GAPPONCHO (GUPP-CHUK)
GAPPOGUCHO
THEN, JUST AS I'D SUSPECTED, GACKT WAS IN THE SHOWER GIVING KIYOSHI'S LITTLE JIMMY A *BLOW JAY!*
HE WAS EVEN MOANING ABOUT HOW GOOD IT WAS!

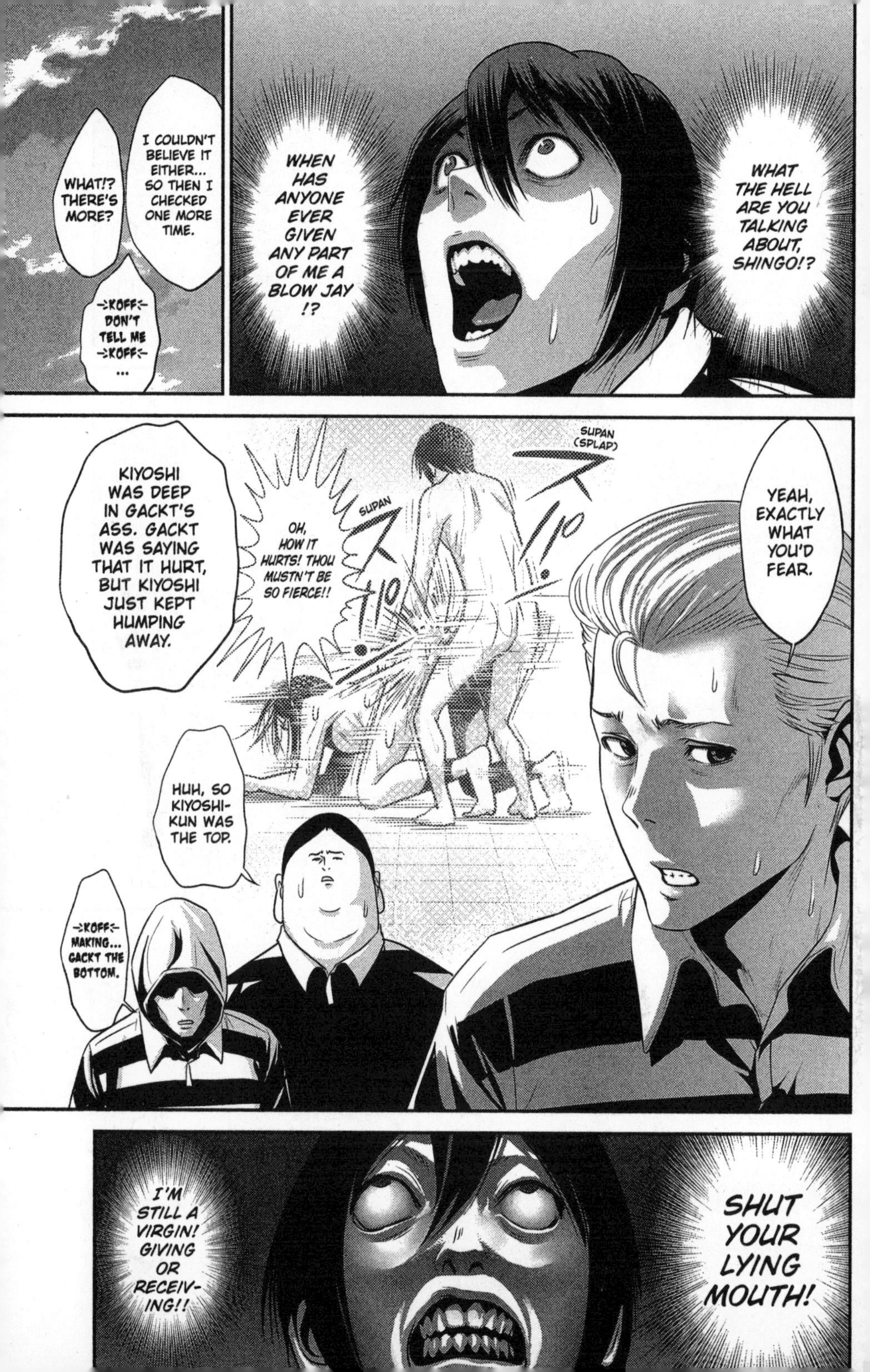
WHAT THE HELL ARE YOU TALKING ABOUT, SHINGO!?
WHEN HAS ANYONE EVER GIVEN ANY PART OF ME A BLOW JAY !?
I COULDN'T BELIEVE IT EITHER... SO THEN I CHECKED ONE MORE TIME.
WHAT!? THERE'S MORE?
-KOFF- DON'T TELL ME -KOFF- ...
SUPAN (SPLAP)
YEAH, EXACTLY WHAT YOU'D FEAR.
SUPAN
OH, HOW IT HURTS! THOU MUSTN'T BE SO FIERCE!!
KIYOSHI WAS DEEP IN GACKT'S ASS. GACKT WAS SAYING THAT IT HURT, BUT KIYOSHI JUST KEPT HUMPING AWAY.
HUH, SO KIYOSHI-KUN WAS THE TOP.
-KOFF- MAKING... GACKT THE BOTTOM.
SHUT YOUR LYING MOUTH!
I'M STILL A VIRGIN! GIVING OR RECEIV-ING!!

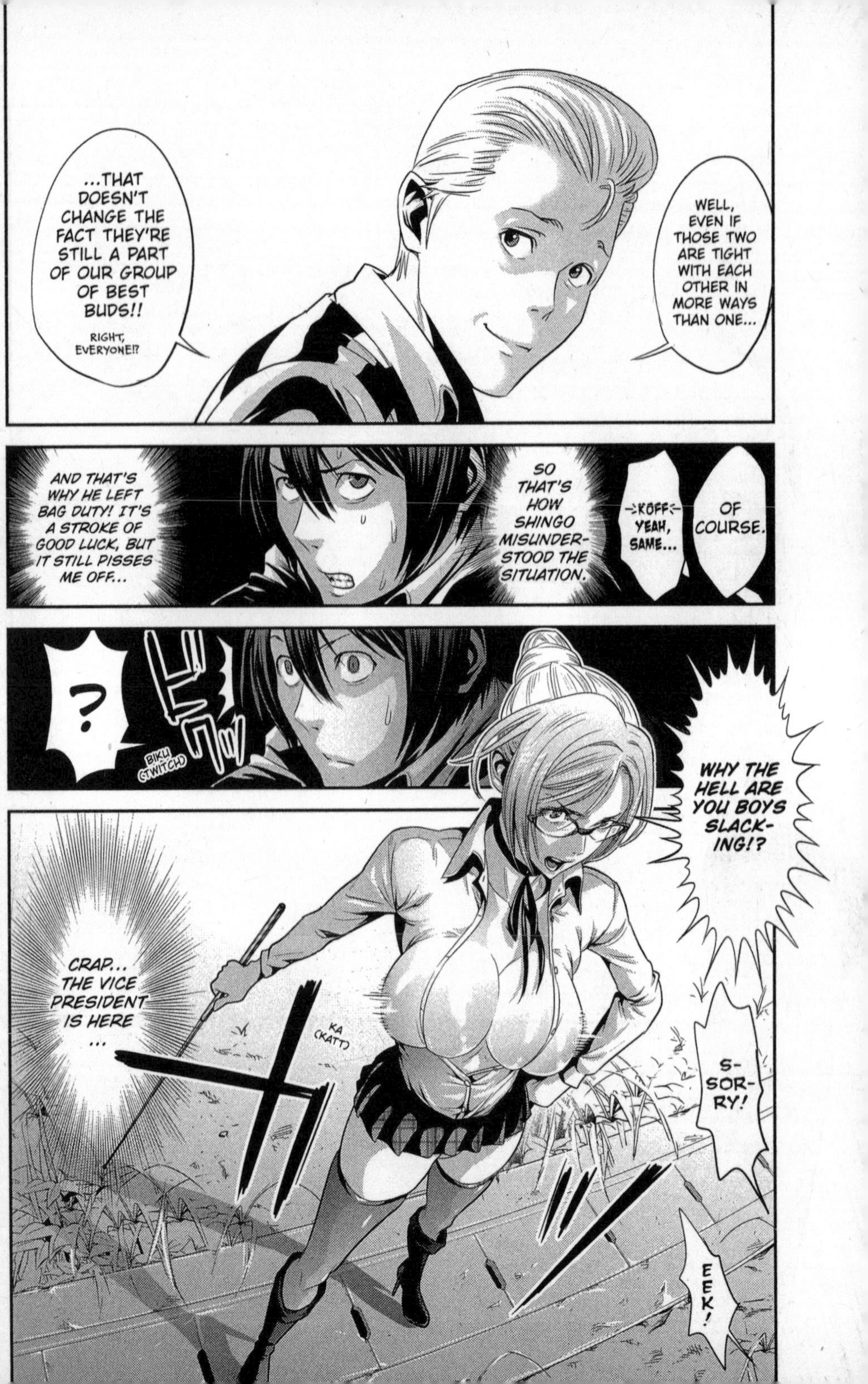
WELL, EVEN IF THOSE TWO ARE TIGHT WITH EACH OTHER IN MORE WAYS THAN ONE...
...THAT DOESN'T CHANGE THE FACT THEY'RE STILL A PART OF OUR GROUP OF BEST BUDS!!
RIGHT, EVERYONE!?
OF COURSE.
-KOFF- YEAH, SAME...
SO THAT'S HOW SHINGO MISUNDER-STOOD THE SITUATION.
AND THAT'S WHY HE LEFT BAG DUTY! IT'S A STROKE OF GOOD LUCK, BUT IT STILL PISSES ME OFF...
?
BIKU (TWITCH)
WHY THE HELL ARE YOU BOYS SLACK-ING!?
CRAP... THE VICE PRESIDENT IS HERE ...
KA (KATT)
S-SOR-RY!
EEK!

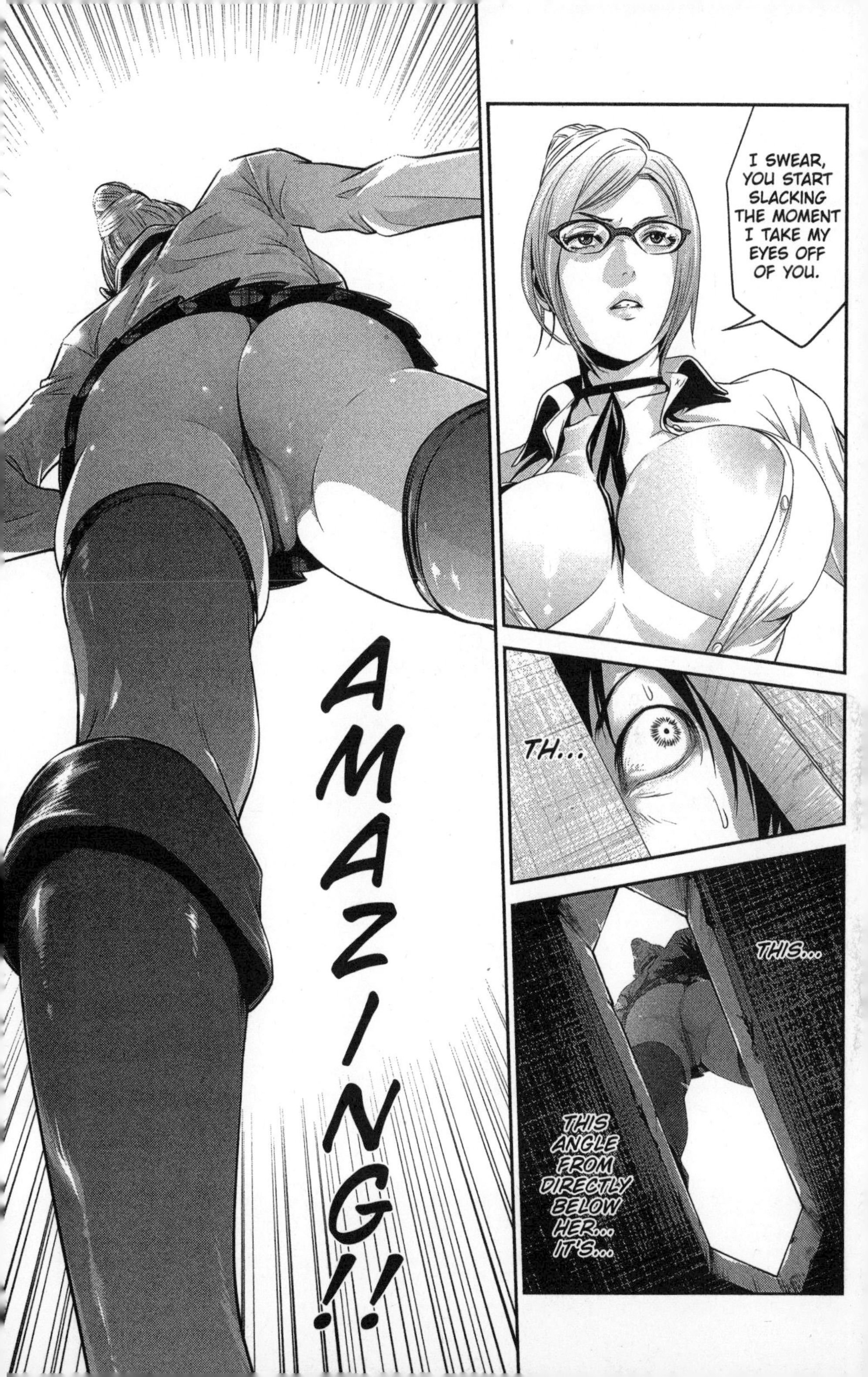
I SWEAR, YOU START SLACKING THE MOMENT I TAKE MY EYES OFF OF YOU.
TH...
THIS...
THIS ANGLE FROM DIRECTLY BELOW HER... IT'S...
AMAZING!!

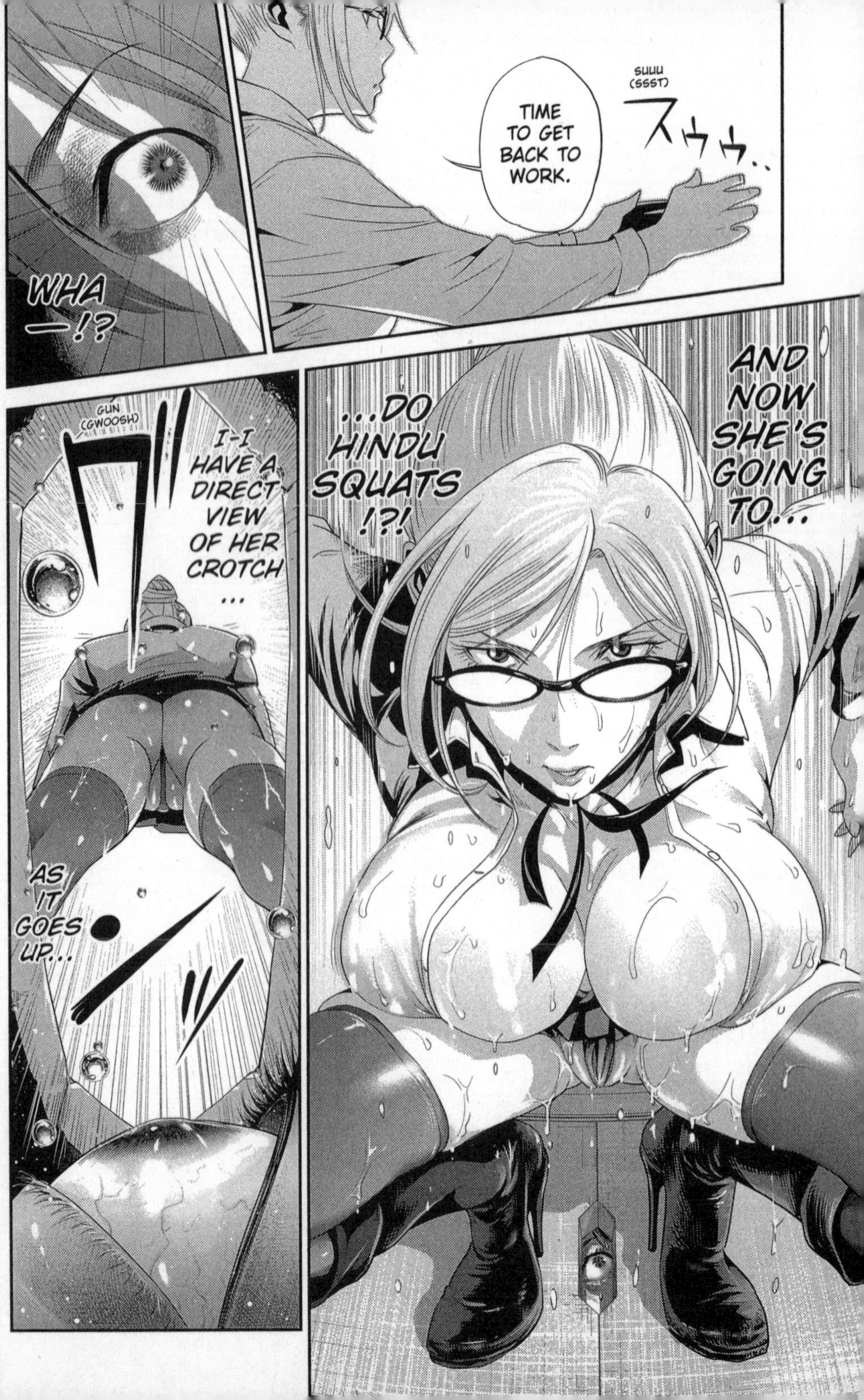
SUUU (SSST)
スゥゥ..
TIME TO GET BACK TO WORK.
WHA—!?
AND NOW SHE'S GOING TO...
...DO HINDU SQUATS!?!
GUN (GWOOSH)
I-I HAVE A DIRECT VIEW OF HER CROTCH...
AS IT GOES UP...

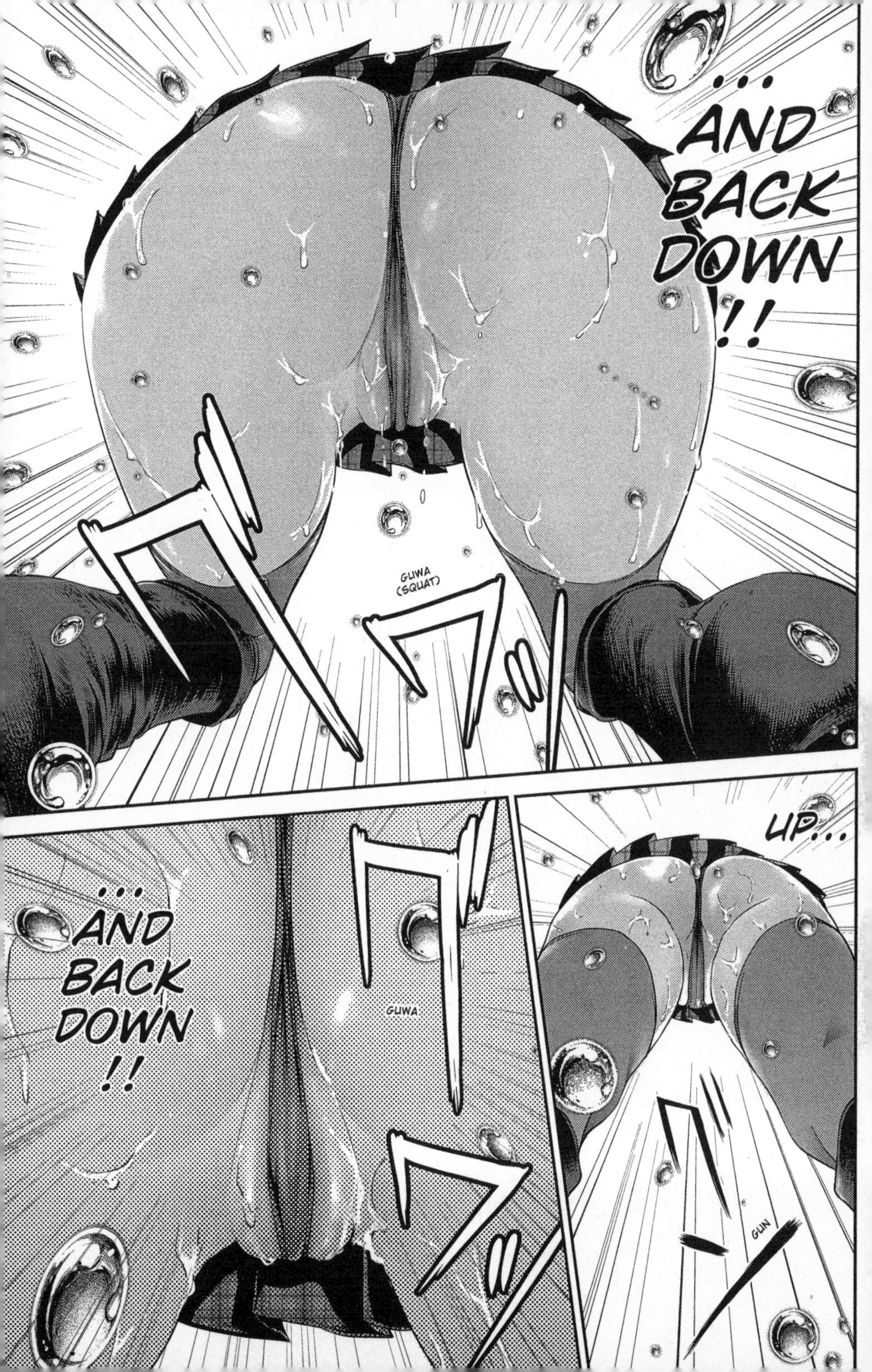

...AND BACK DOWN!!
GUWA (SQUAT)
UP...
GUN
...AND BACK DOWN!!
GUWA

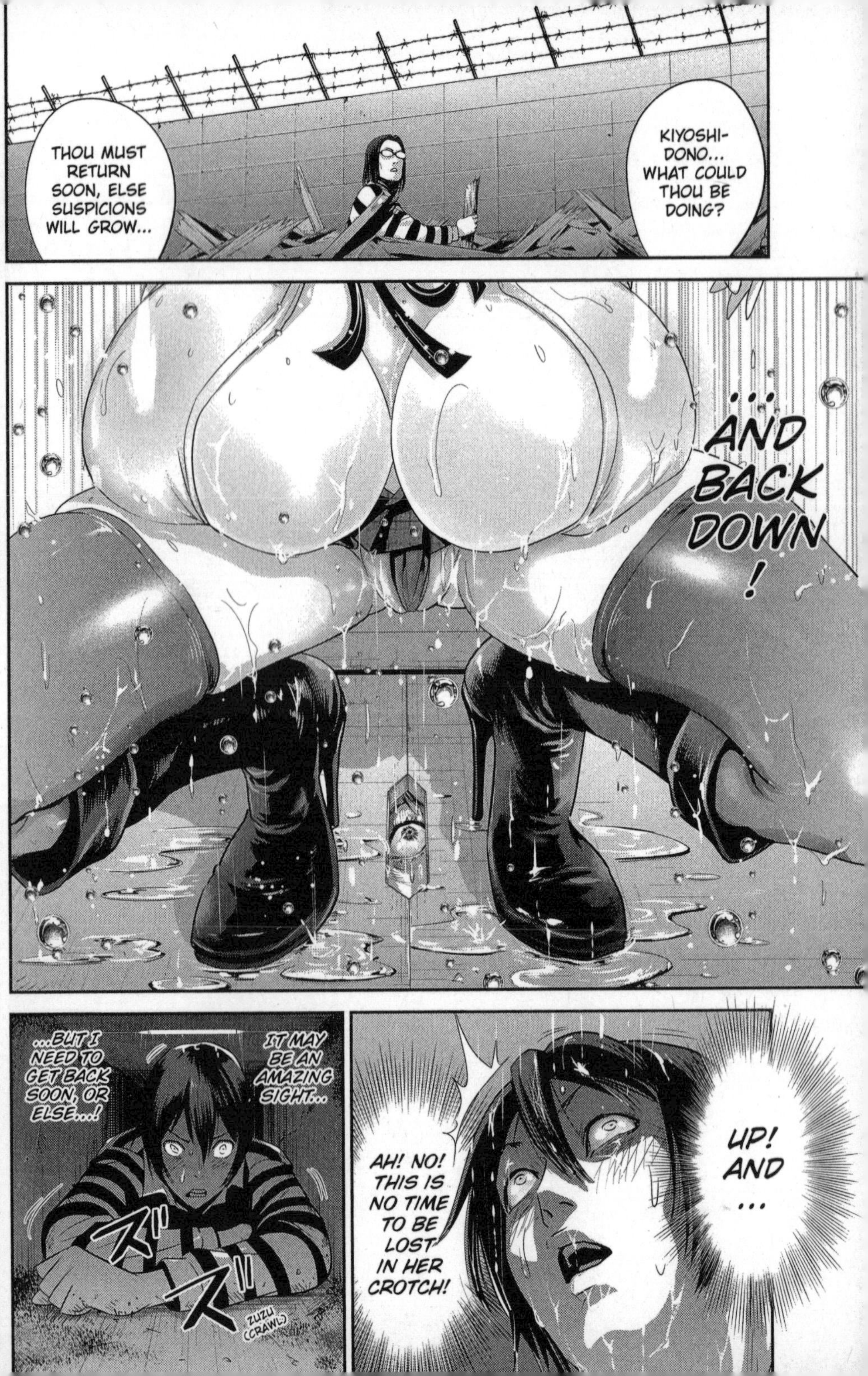
KIYOSHI-DONO... WHAT COULD THOU BE DOING?
THOU MUST RETURN SOON, ELSE SUSPICIONS WILL GROW...
...AND BACK DOWN!
UP! AND ...
AH! NO! THIS IS NO TIME TO BE LOST IN HER CROTCH!
IT MAY BE AN AMAZING SIGHT...
...BUT I NEED TO GET BACK SOON, OR ELSE...!
ZUZU (CRAWL)

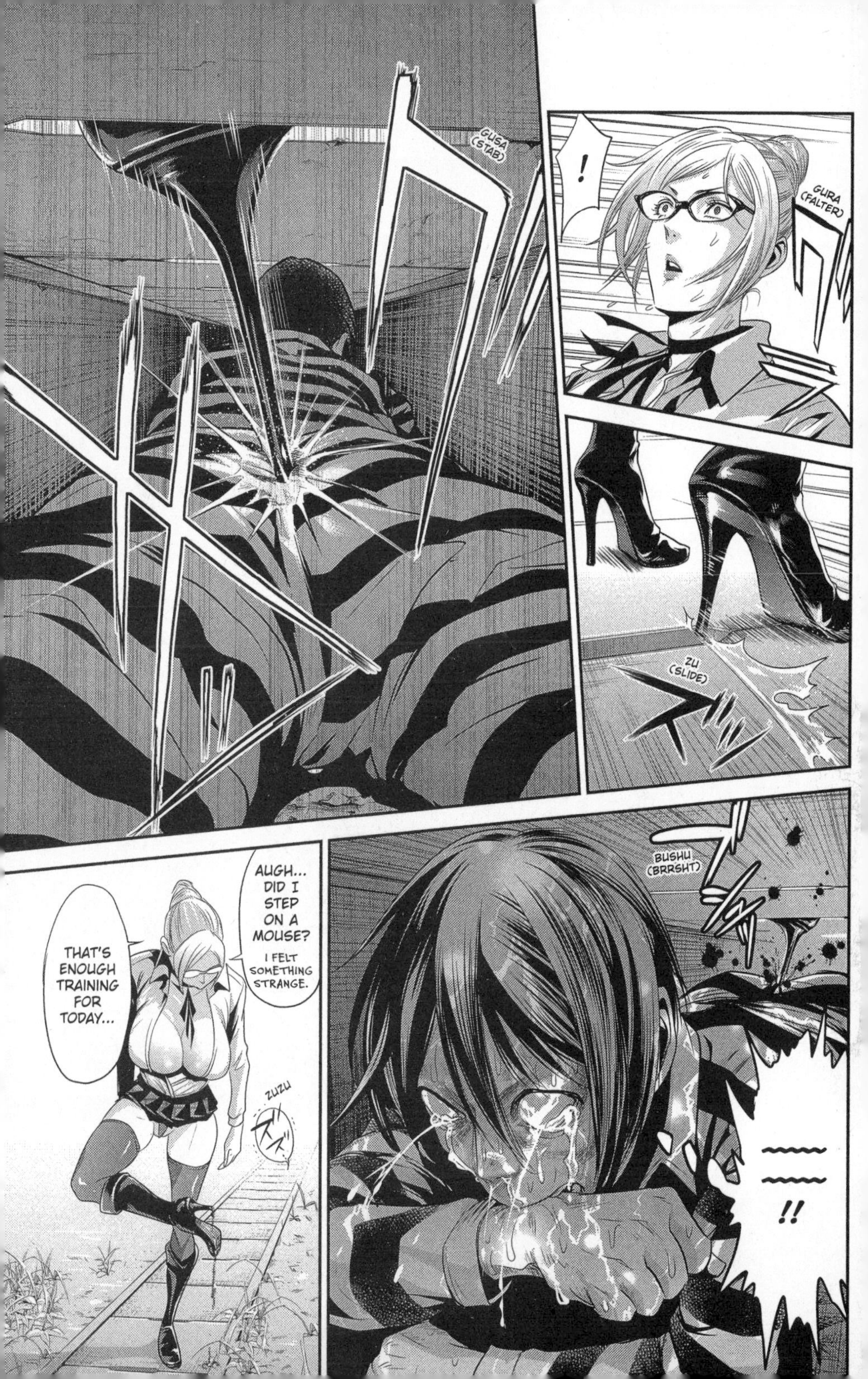

!
GURA (FALTER)
GUSA (STAB)
ZU (SLIDE)
BUSHU (BRRSHT)
~~~~ ~~~~ !!
AUGH... DID I STEP ON A MOUSE?
I FELT SOMETHING STRANGE.
THAT'S ENOUGH TRAINING FOR TODAY...
ZUZU
~~~~

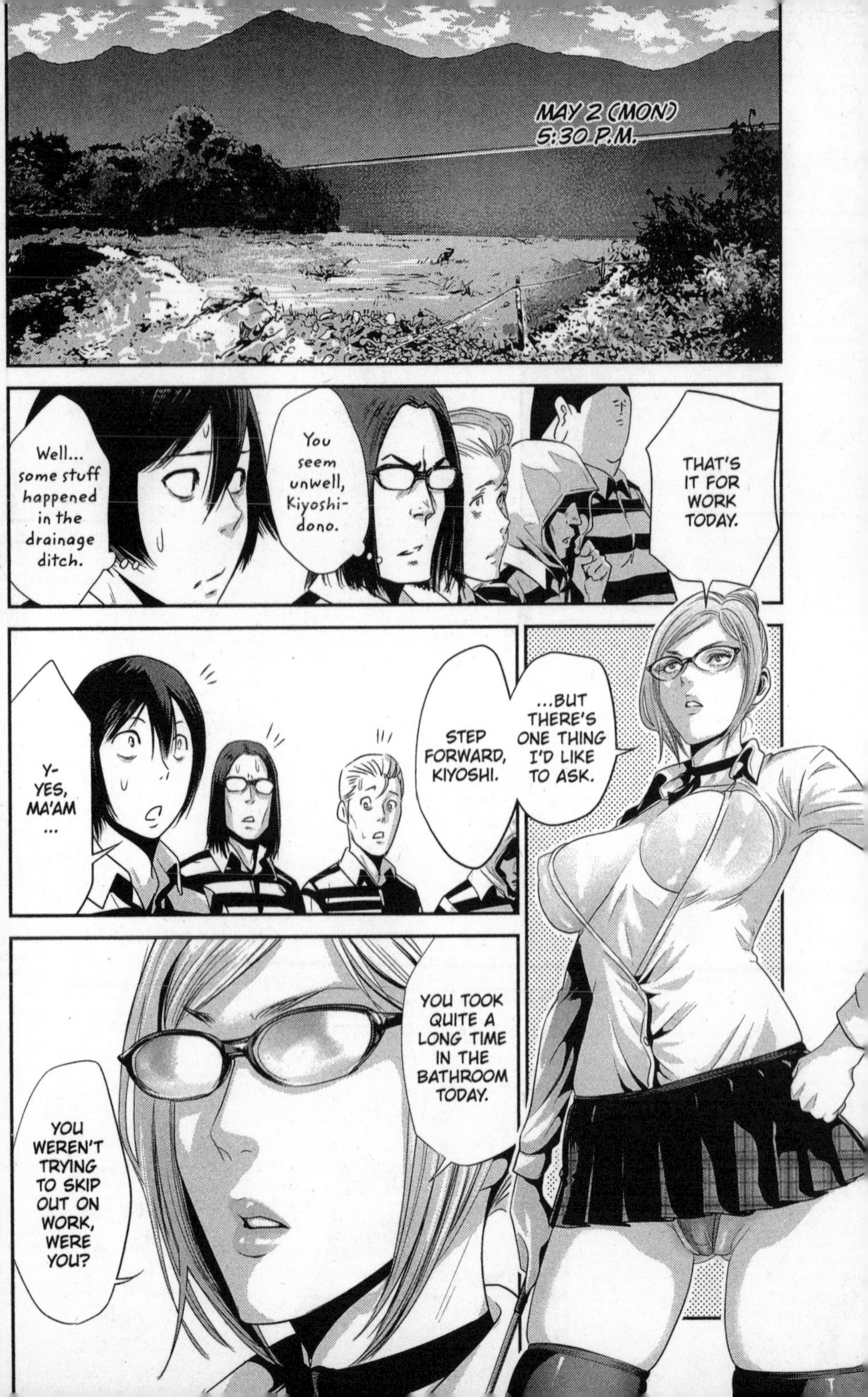
MAY 2 (MON) 5:30 P.M.
THAT'S IT FOR WORK TODAY.
You seem unwell, Kiyoshi-dono.
Well... some stuff happened in the drainage ditch.
...BUT THERE'S ONE THING I'D LIKE TO ASK.
STEP FORWARD, KIYOSHI.
Y-YES, MA'AM ...
YOU TOOK QUITE A LONG TIME IN THE BATHROOM TODAY.
YOU WEREN'T TRYING TO SKIP OUT ON WORK, WERE YOU?

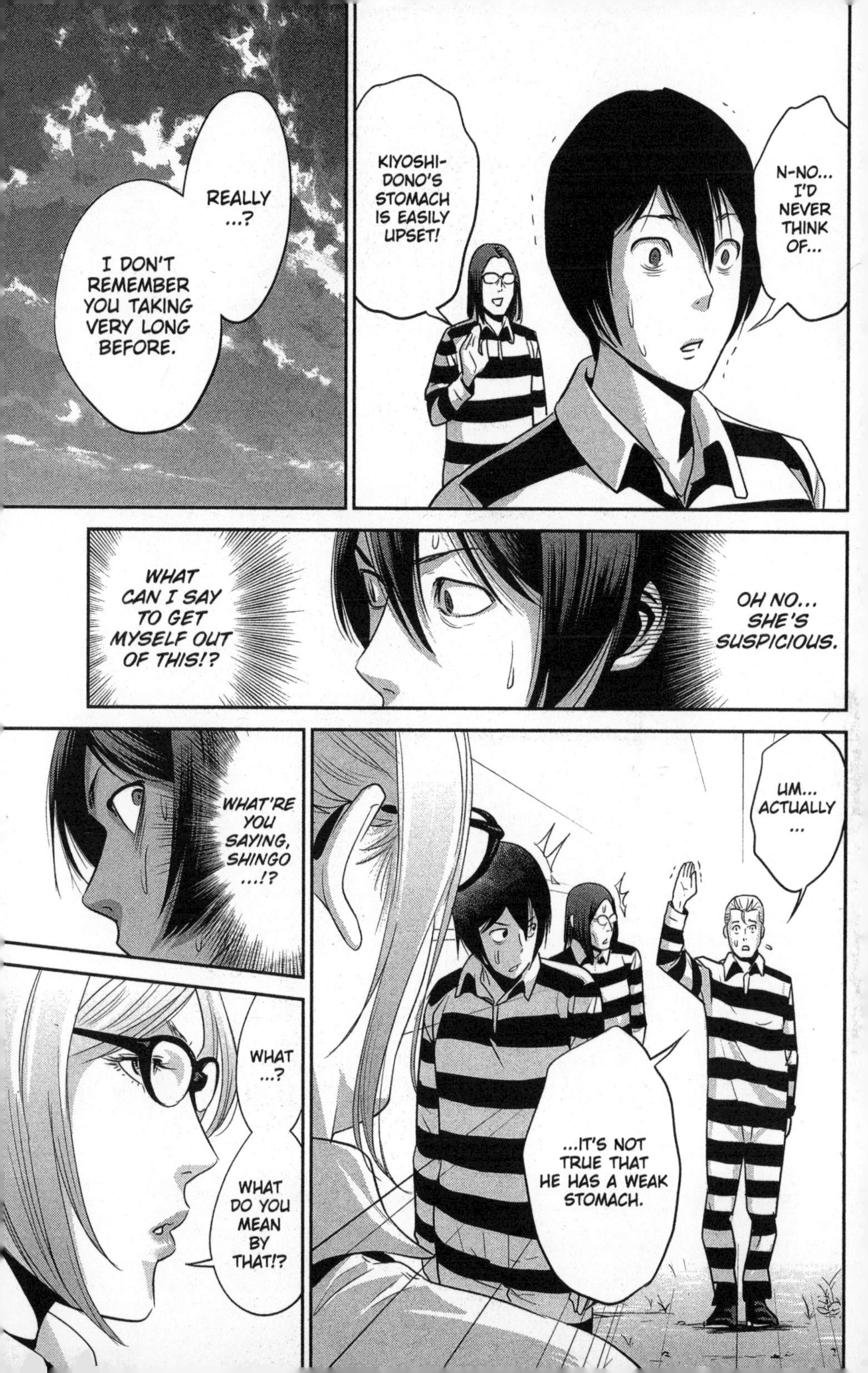
N-NO... I'D NEVER THINK OF...
KIYOSHI-DONO'S STOMACH IS EASILY UPSET!
REALLY ...?
I DON'T REMEMBER YOU TAKING VERY LONG BEFORE.
OH NO... SHE'S SUSPICIOUS.
WHAT CAN I SAY TO GET MYSELF OUT OF THIS!?
UM... ACTUALLY ...
...IT'S NOT TRUE THAT HE HAS A WEAK STOMACH.
WHAT'RE YOU SAYING, SHINGO ...!?
WHAT ...?
WHAT DO YOU MEAN BY THAT!?

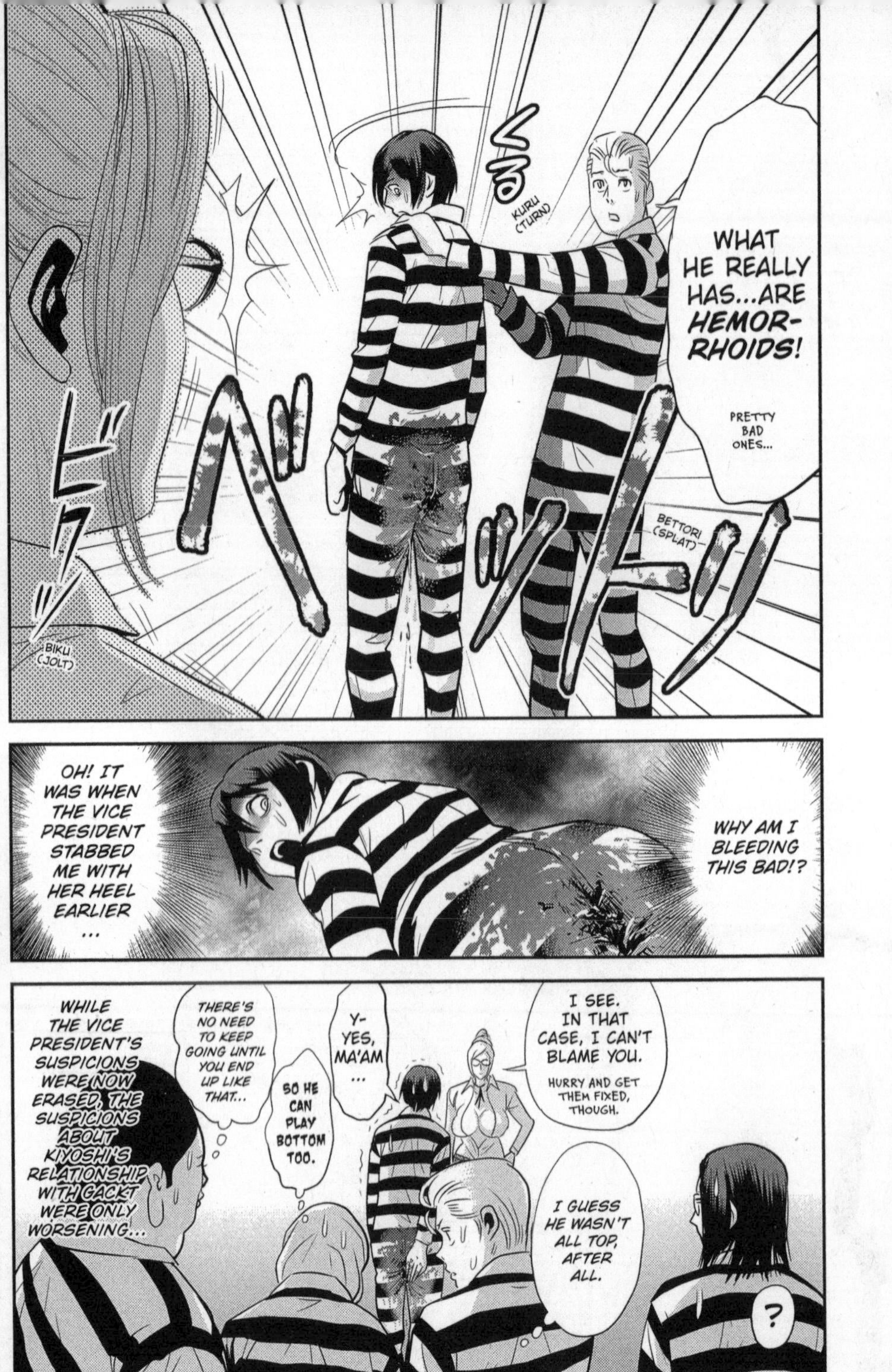
KURU (TURN)
WHAT HE REALLY HAS...ARE HEMORRHOIDS!
PRETTY BAD ONES...
BETTORI (SPLAT)
BIKU (JOLT)
WHY AM I BLEEDING THIS BAD!?
OH! IT WAS WHEN THE VICE PRESIDENT STABBED ME WITH HER HEEL EARLIER ...
I SEE. IN THAT CASE, I CAN'T BLAME YOU.
HURRY AND GET THEM FIXED, THOUGH.
Y-YES, MA'AM ...
THERE'S NO NEED TO KEEP GOING UNTIL YOU END UP LIKE THAT...
SO HE CAN PLAY BOTTOM TOO.
I GUESS HE WASN'T ALL TOP, AFTER ALL.
?
WHILE THE VICE PRESIDENT'S SUSPICIONS WERE NOW ERASED, THE SUSPICIONS ABOUT KIYOSHI'S RELATIONSHIP WITH GACKT WERE ONLY WORSENING...

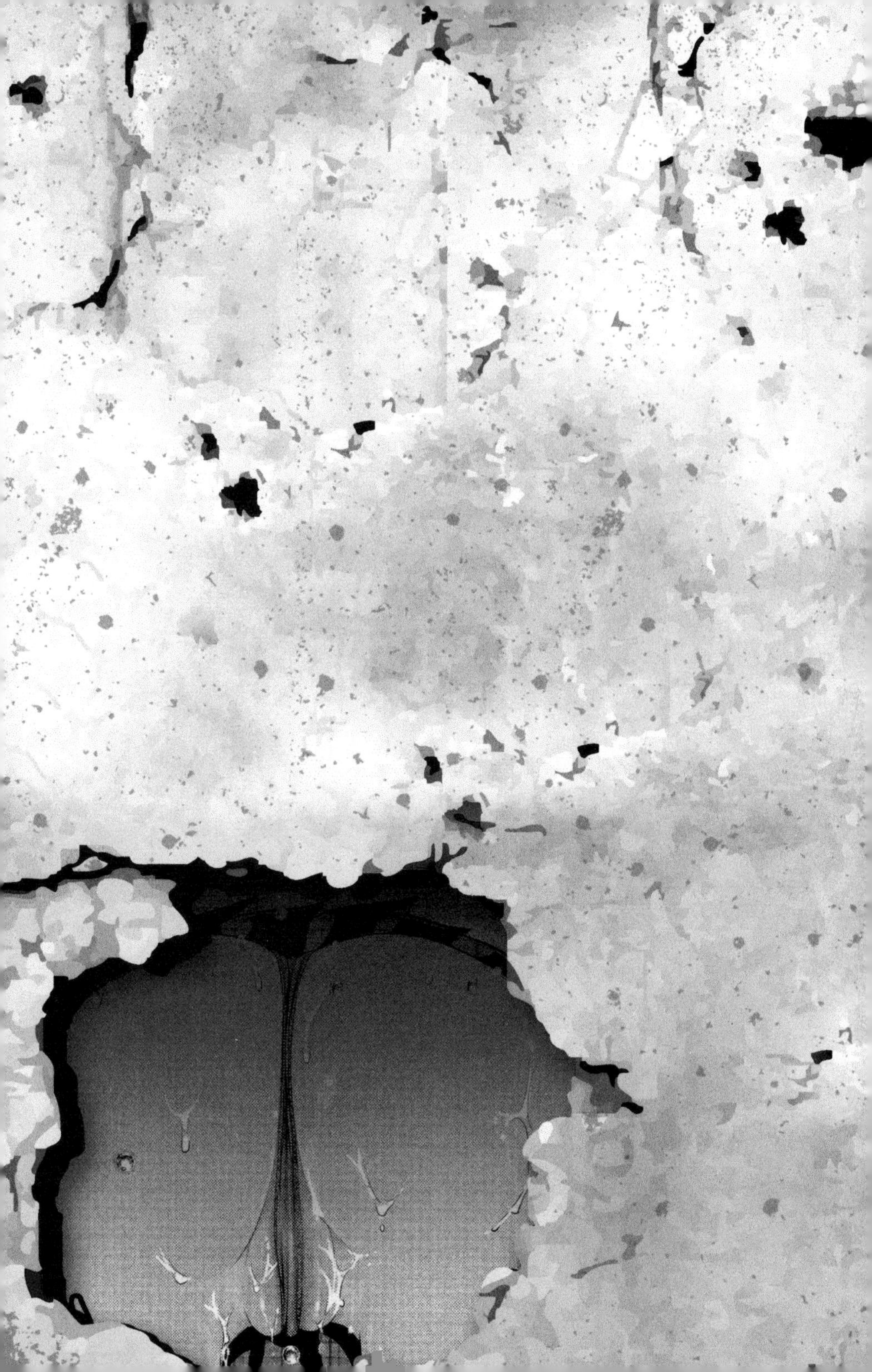

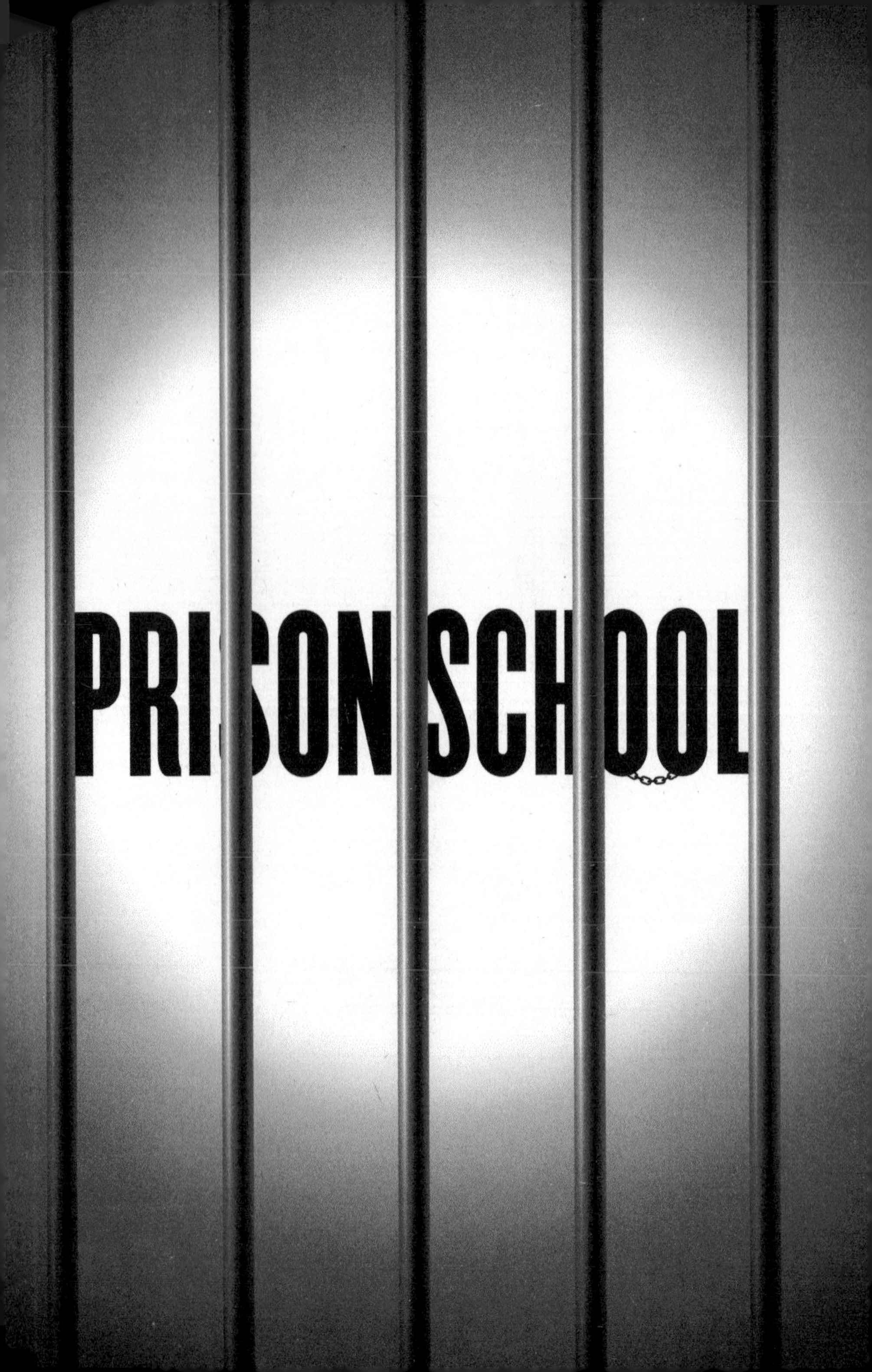
PRISON SCHOOL

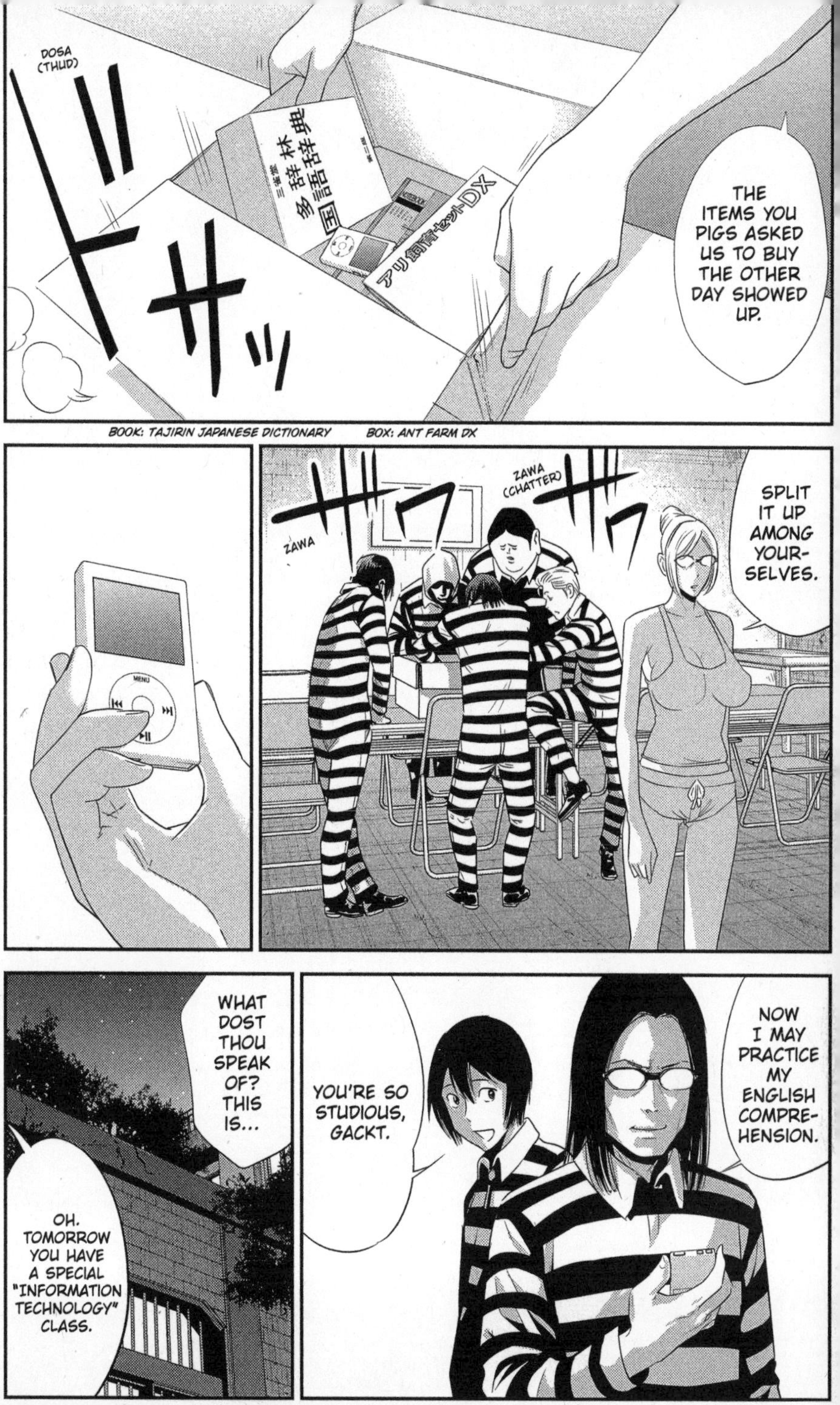
DOSA (THUD)
THE ITEMS YOU PIGS ASKED US TO BUY THE OTHER DAY SHOWED UP.
アリ飼育セットDX
BOOK: TAJIRIN JAPANESE DICTIONARY
BOX: ANT FARM DX
ZAWA (CHATTER)
ZAWA
SPLIT IT UP AMONG YOUR-SELVES.
MENU
NOW I MAY PRACTICE MY ENGLISH COMPRE-HENSION.
YOU'RE SO STUDIOUS, GACKT.
WHAT DOST THOU SPEAK OF? THIS IS...
OH. TOMORROW YOU HAVE A SPECIAL "INFORMATION TECHNOLOGY" CLASS.

CHAPTER 17: PANIC ROOM

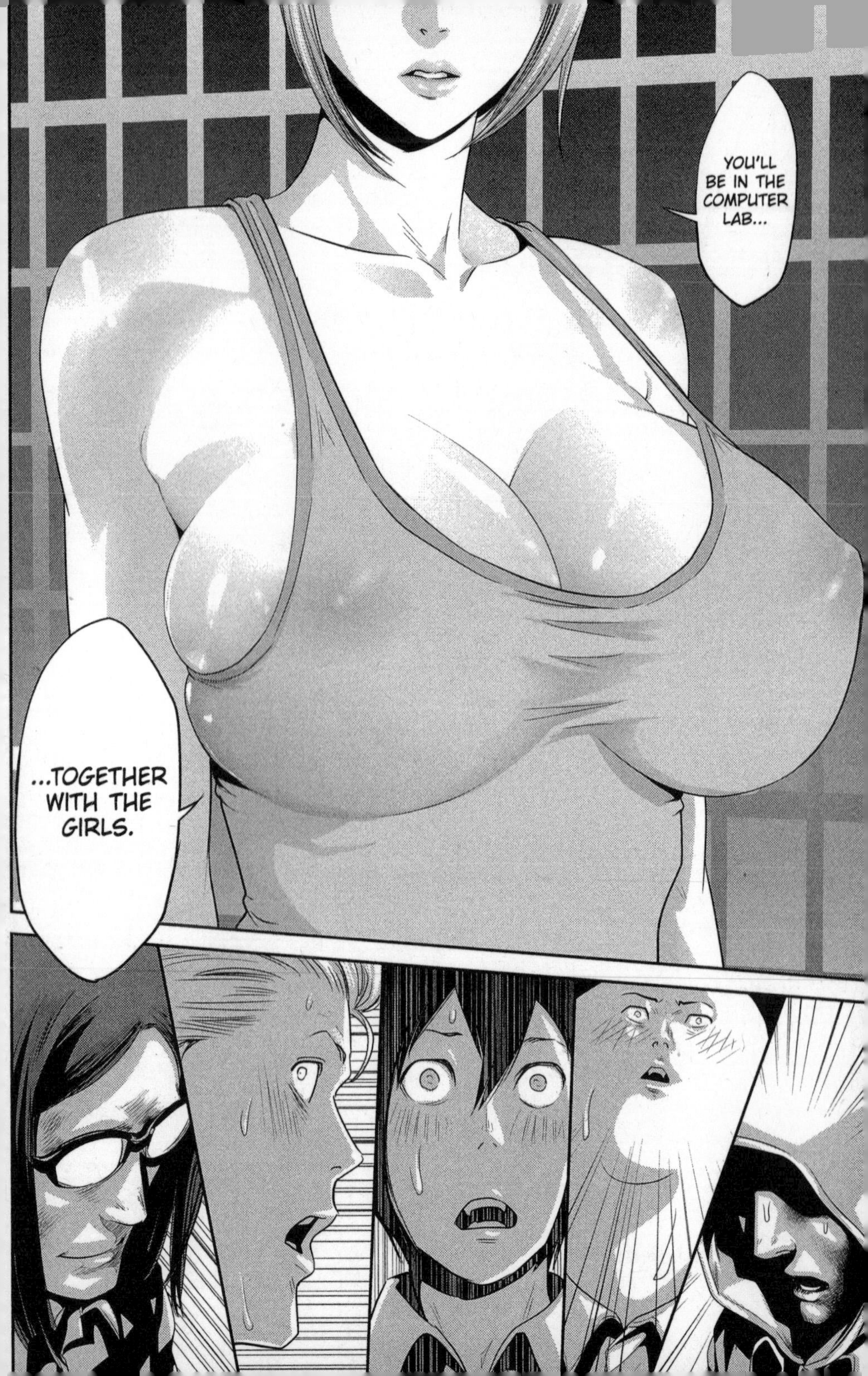
YOU'LL BE IN THE COMPUTER LAB...
...TOGETHER WITH THE GIRLS.

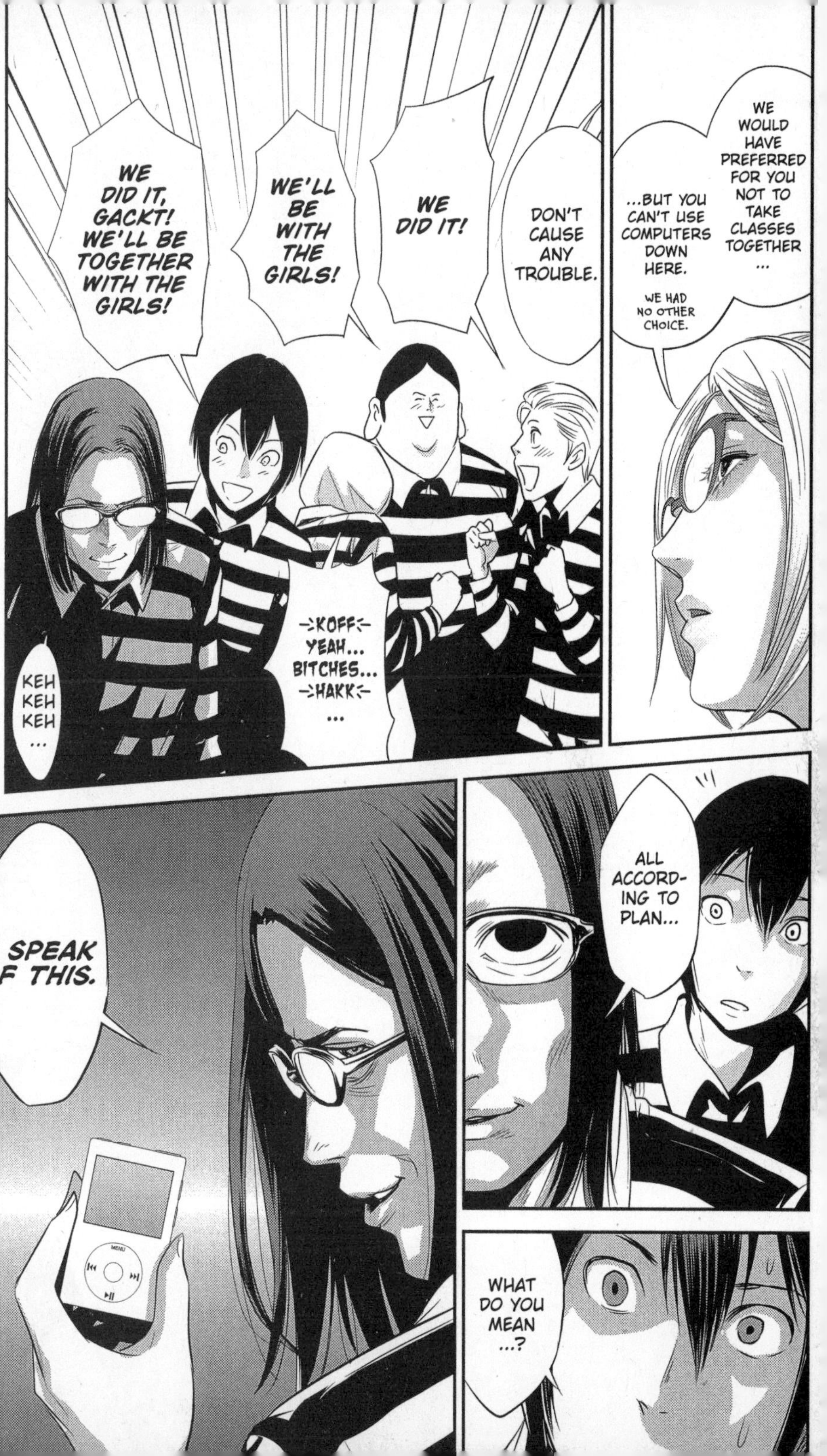

WE WOULD HAVE PREFERRED FOR YOU NOT TO TAKE CLASSES TOGETHER ...
...BUT YOU CAN'T USE COMPUTERS DOWN HERE.
WE HAD NO OTHER CHOICE.
DON'T CAUSE ANY TROUBLE.
WE DID IT!
WE'LL BE WITH THE GIRLS!
WE DID IT, GACKT! WE'LL BE TOGETHER WITH THE GIRLS!
-KOFF- YEAH... BITCHES... -HAKK- ...
KEH KEH KEH ...
ALL ACCORDING TO PLAN...
WHAT DO YOU MEAN ...?
I SPEAK OF THIS.

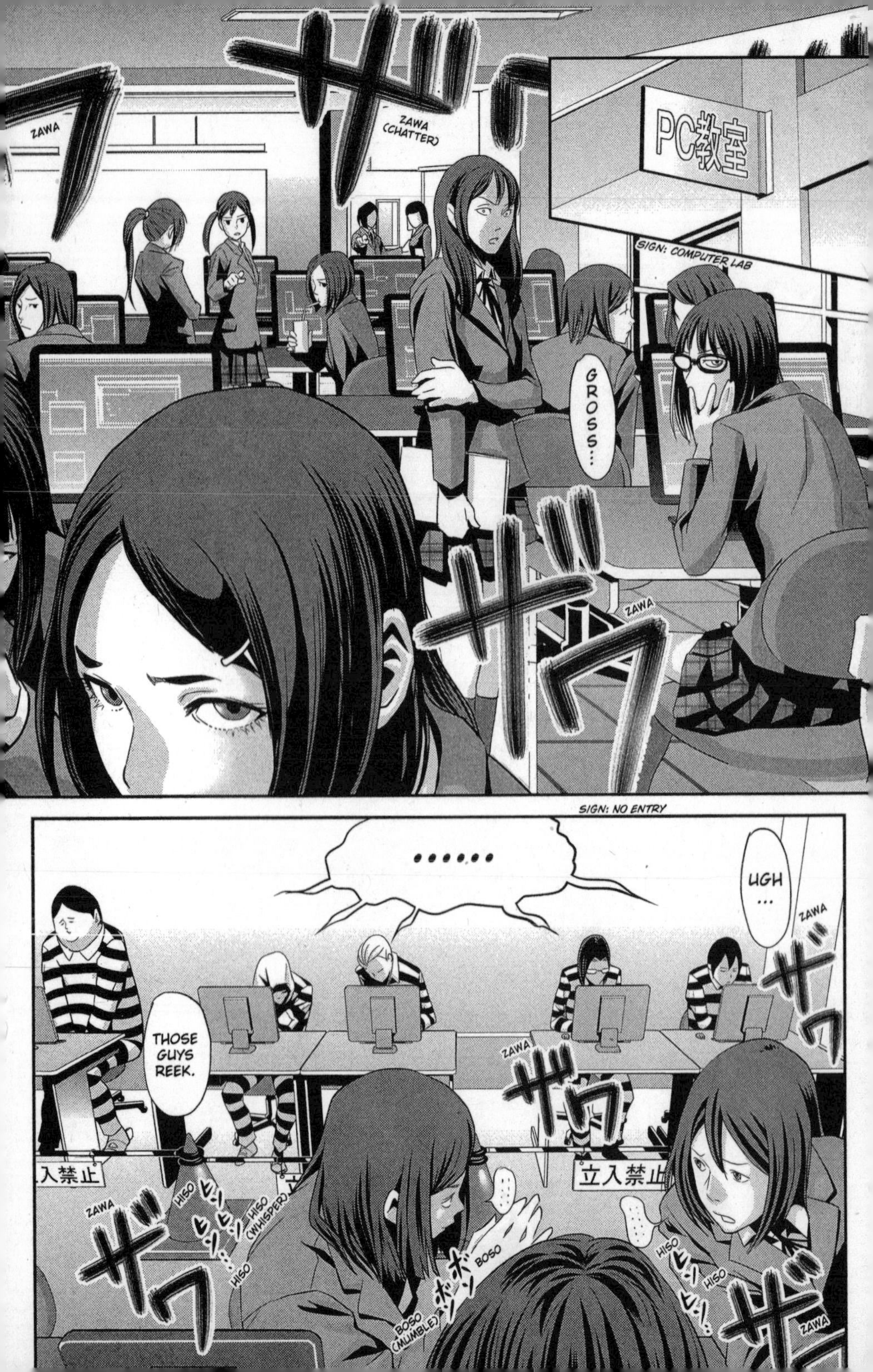

SIGN: COMPUTER LAB
PC教室
ZAWA (CHATTER)
ZAWA
GROSS...
ZAWA
SIGN: NO ENTRY
UGH...
......
ZAWA
ZAWA
THOSE GUYS REEK.
立入禁止
立入禁止
HISO (WHISPER)
HISO
HISO
ZAWA
BOSO
BOSO (MUMBLE)
HISO
HISO
ZAWA

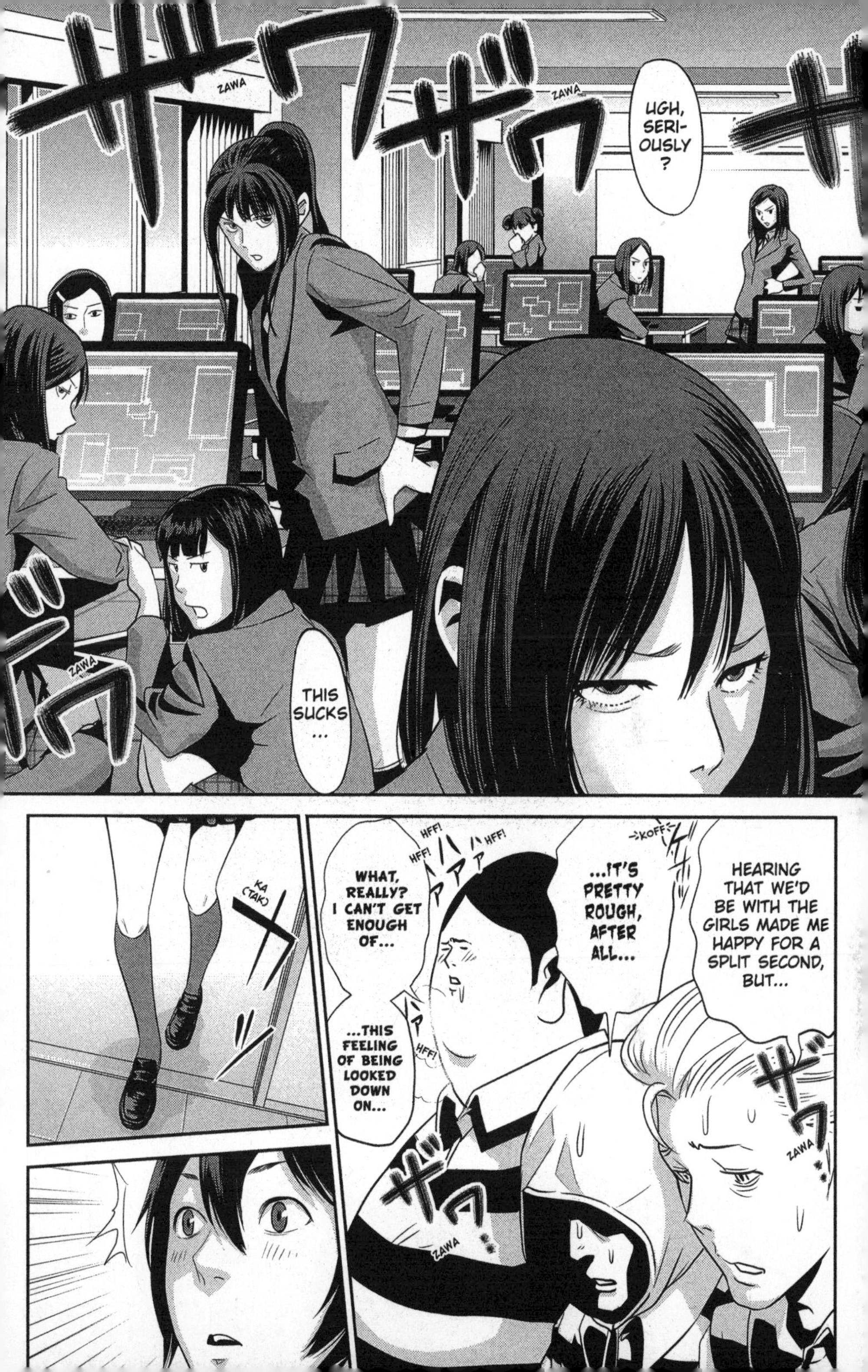
ZAWA
ZAWA
UGH, SERI-OUSLY?
THIS SUCKS...
ZAWA
HEARING THAT WE'D BE WITH THE GIRLS MADE ME HAPPY FOR A SPLIT SECOND, BUT...
KOFF
...IT'S PRETTY ROUGH, AFTER ALL...
HFF! HFF! HFF!
WHAT, REALLY? I CAN'T GET ENOUGH OF...
HFF!
...THIS FEELING OF BEING LOOKED DOWN ON...
KA (TAK)
ZAWA
ZAWA

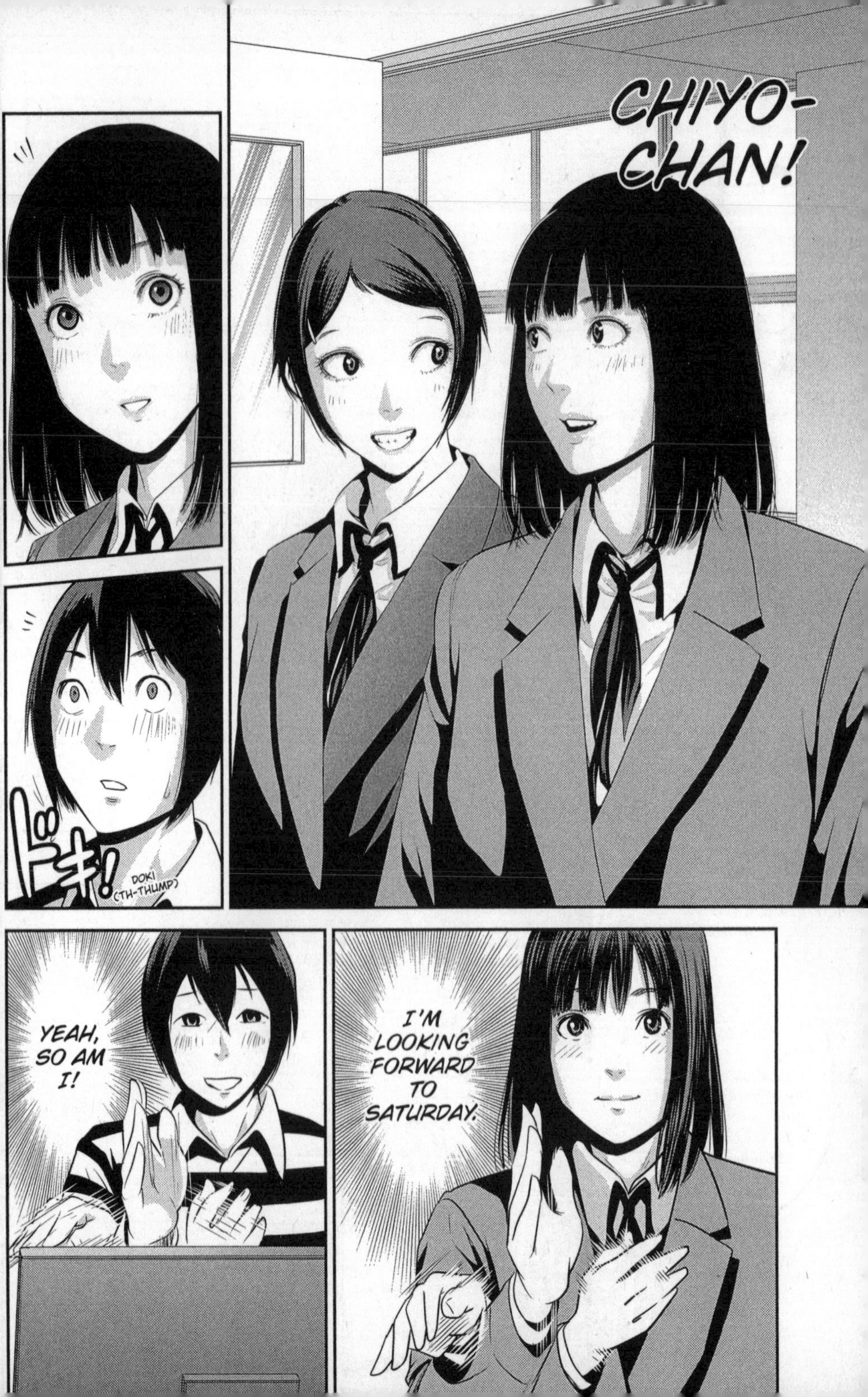
CHIYO-CHAN!
ドキ!
DOKI (TH-THUMP)
I'M LOOKING FORWARD TO SATURDAY.
YEAH, SO AM I!

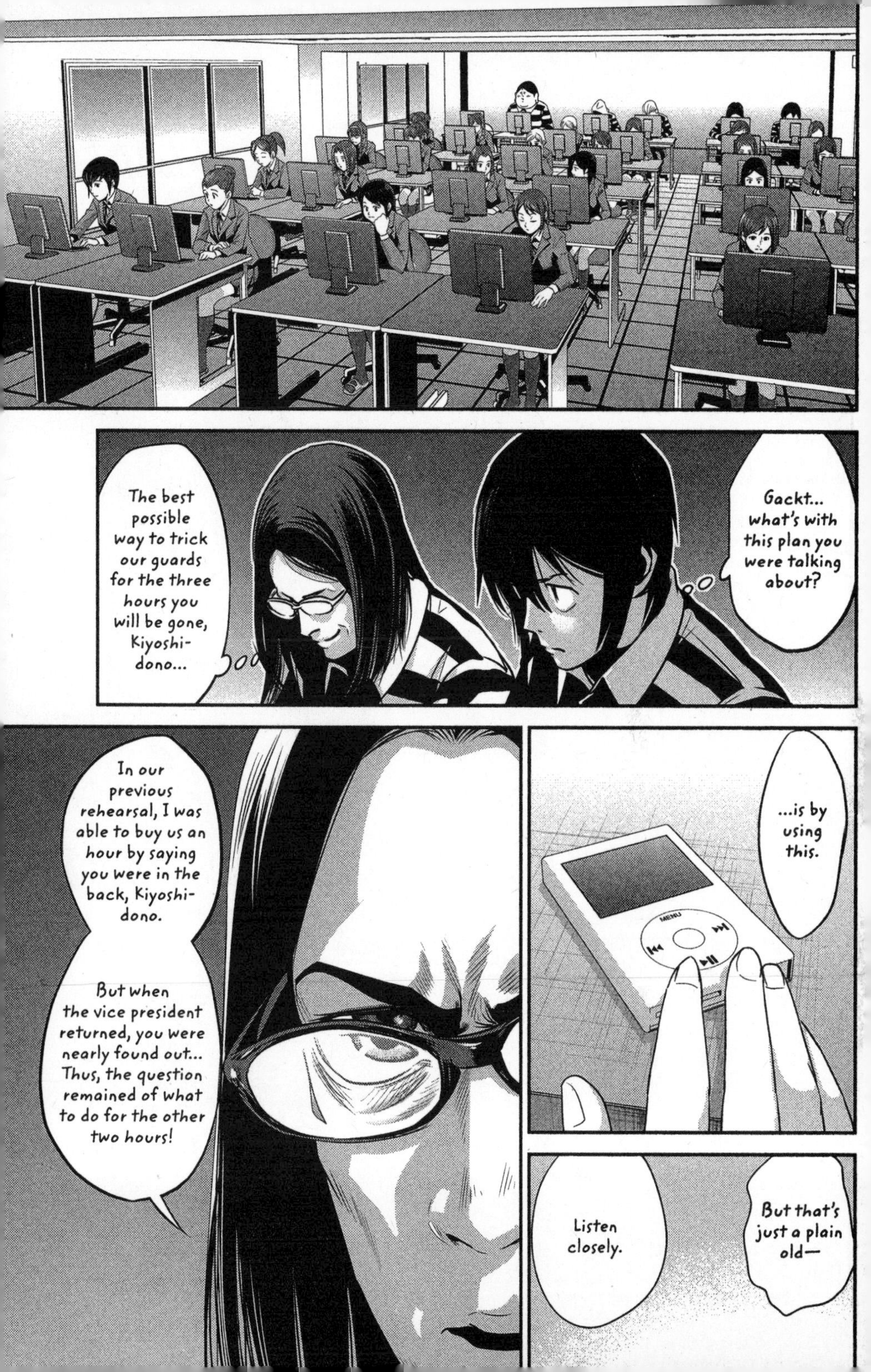
Gackt... what's with this plan you were talking about?
The best possible way to trick our guards for the three hours you will be gone, Kiyoshi-dono...
...is by using this.
MENU
But that's just a plain old—
Listen closely.
In our previous rehearsal, I was able to buy us an hour by saying you were in the back, Kiyoshi-dono.
But when the vice president returned, you were nearly found out... Thus, the question remained of what to do for the other two hours!

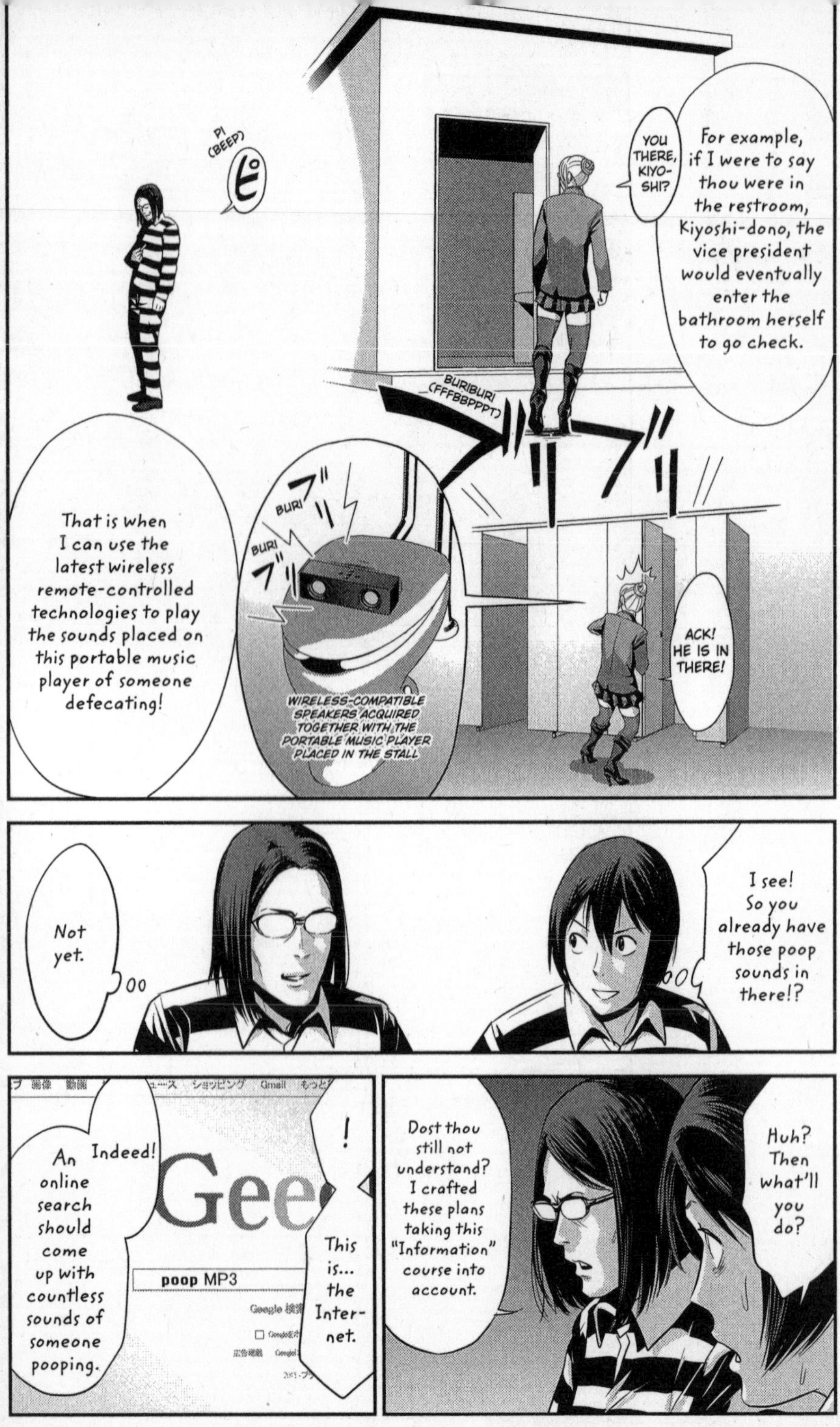
For example, if I were to say thou were in the restroom, Kiyoshi-dono, the vice president would eventually enter the bathroom herself to go check.
YOU THERE, KIYOSHI?
PI (BEEP)
BURIBURI (FFFBBPPPT)
ACK! HE IS IN THERE!
BURI
BURI
WIRELESS-COMPATIBLE SPEAKERS ACQUIRED TOGETHER WITH THE PORTABLE MUSIC PLAYER PLACED IN THE STALL
That is when I can use the latest wireless remote-controlled technologies to play the sounds placed on this portable music player of someone defecating!
I see! So you already have those poop sounds in there!?
Not yet.
Huh? Then what'll you do?
Dost thou still not understand? I crafted these plans taking this "Information" course into account.
!
This is... the Internet.
Indeed!
An online search should come up with countless sounds of someone pooping.
poop MP3

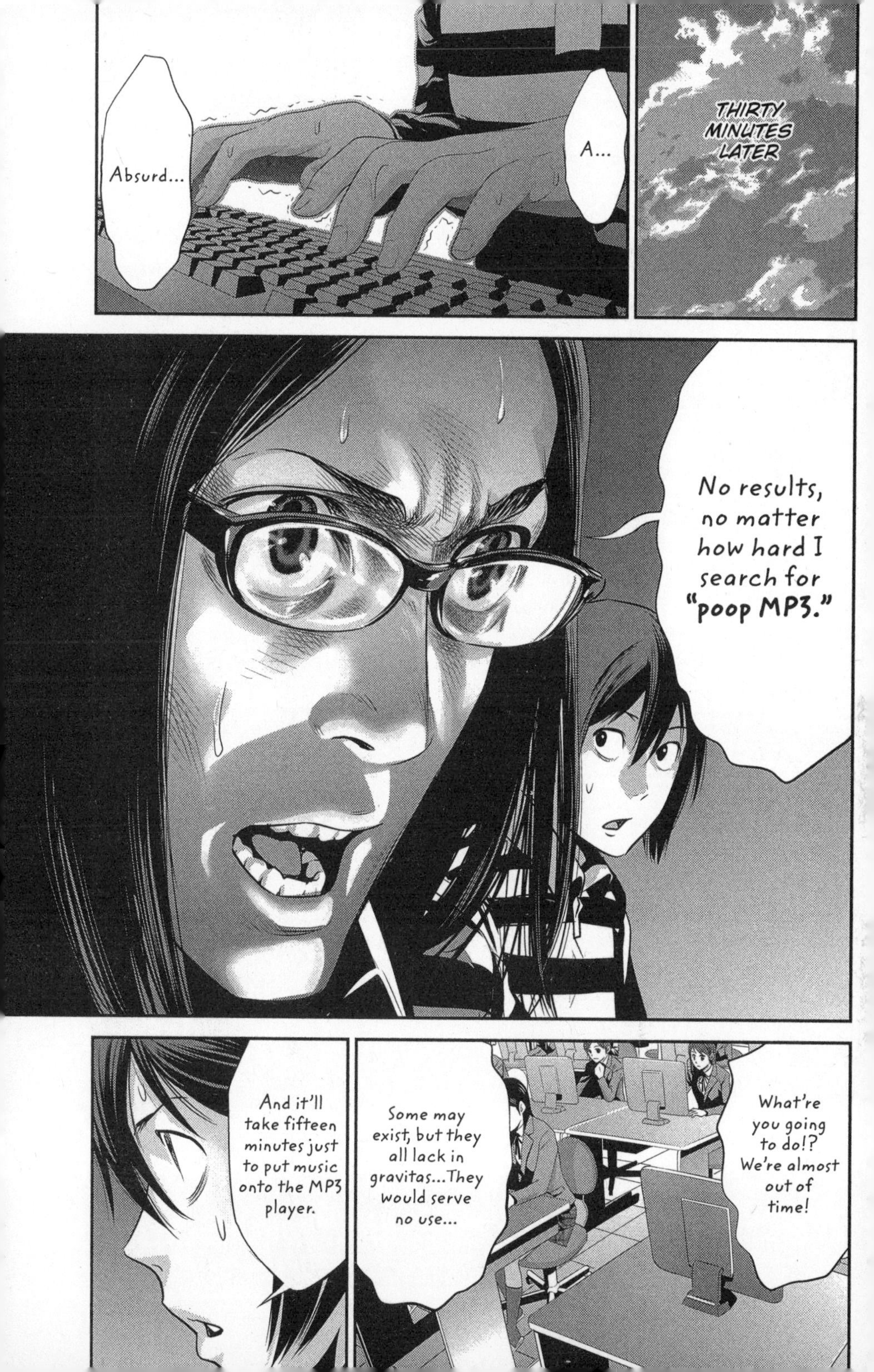
THIRTY MINUTES LATER
A...
Absurd...
No results, no matter how hard I search for "poop MP3."
What're you going to do!? We're almost out of time!
Some may exist, but they all lack in gravitas...They would serve no use...
And it'll take fifteen minutes just to put music onto the MP3 player.

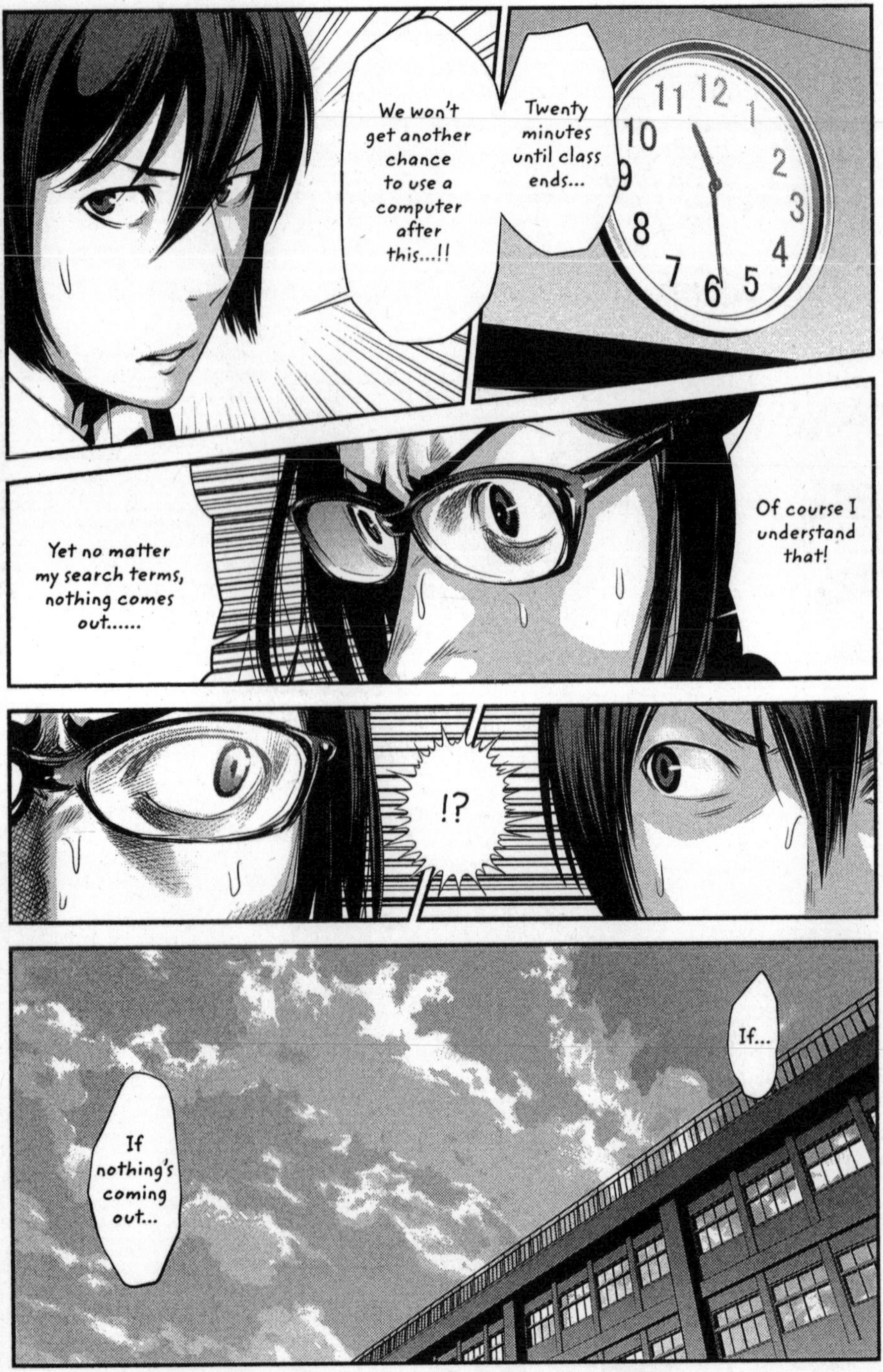
Twenty minutes until class ends...
We won't get another chance to use a computer after this...!!
Of course I understand that!
Yet no matter my search terms, nothing comes out......
!?
If...
If nothing's coming out...

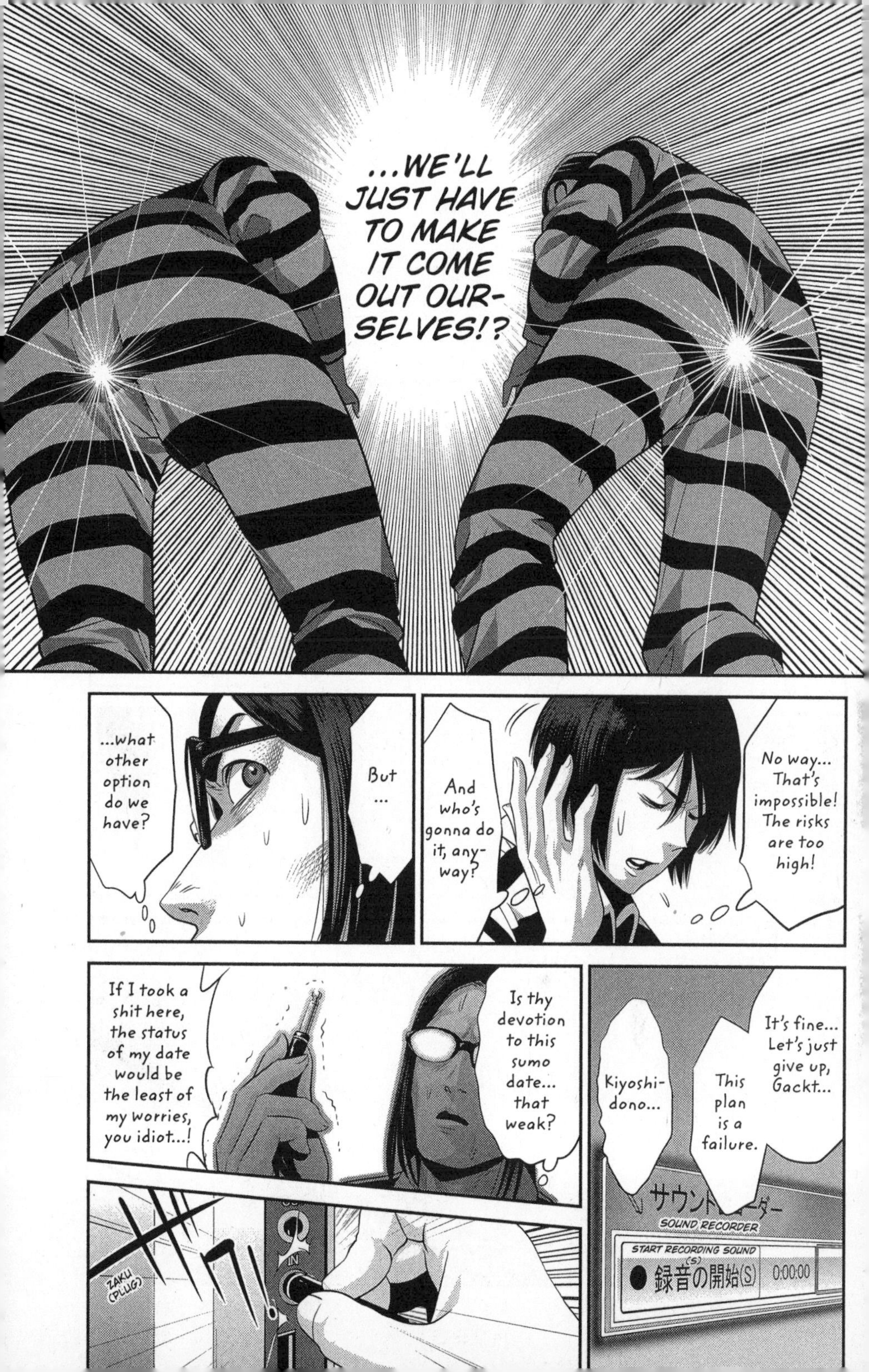
...WE'LL JUST HAVE TO MAKE IT COME OUT OUR-SELVES!?
No way... That's impossible! The risks are too high!
And who's gonna do it, any-way?
But ...
...what other option do we have?
It's fine... Let's just give up, Gackt...
This plan is a failure.
Kiyoshi-dono...
Is thy devotion to this sumo date... that weak?
If I took a shit here, the status of my date would be the least of my worries, you idiot...!
SOUND RECORDER
START RECORDING SOUND (S)
録音の開始(S)
0:00:00
ZAKU (PLUG)

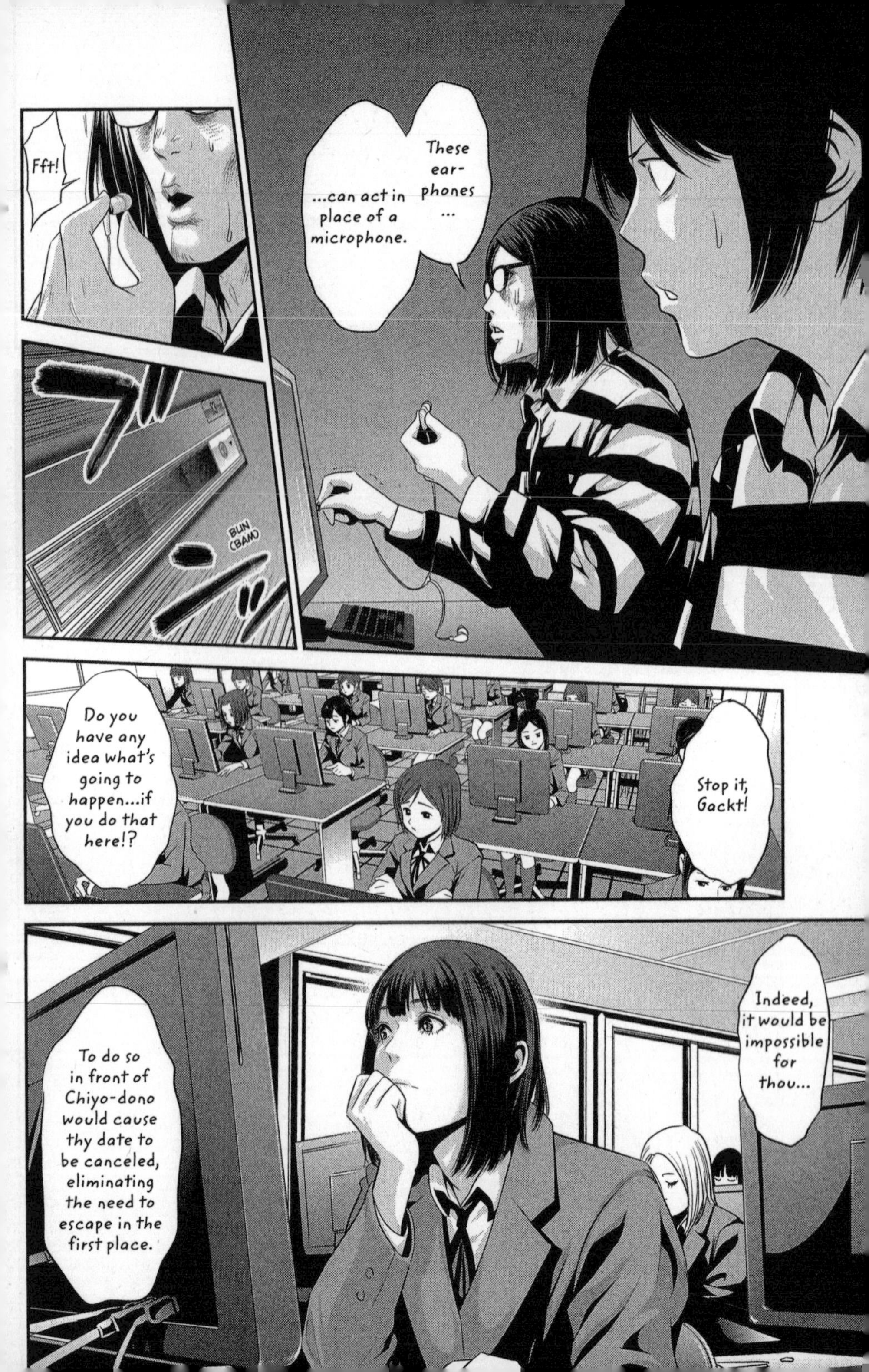
These earphones...
...can act in place of a microphone.
Fft!
BUN (BAM)
Stop it, Gackt!
Do you have any idea what's going to happen...if you do that here!?
Indeed, it would be impossible for thou...
To do so in front of Chiyo-dono would cause thy date to be canceled, eliminating the need to escape in the first place.

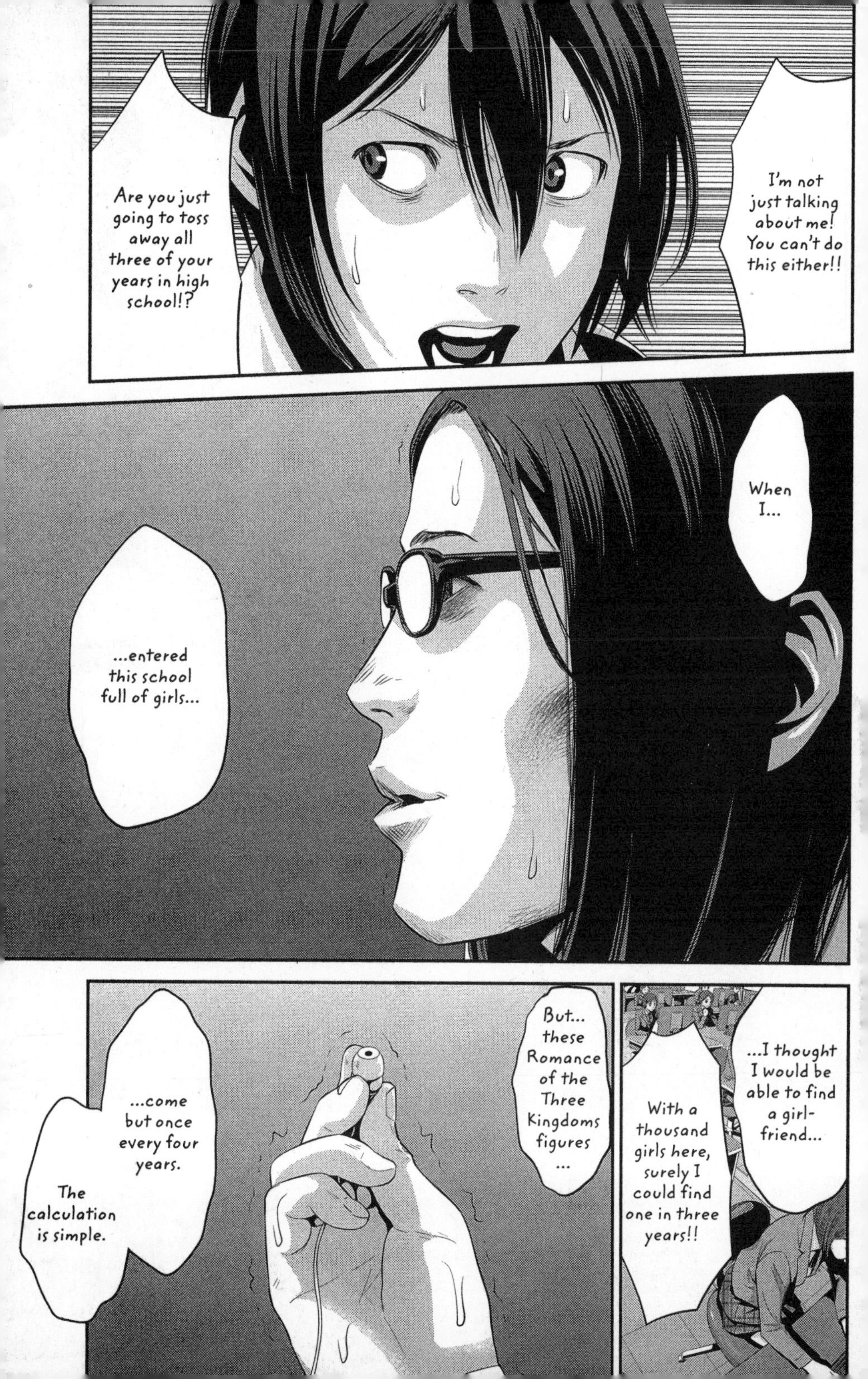
I'm not just talking about me! You can't do this either!!
Are you just going to toss away all three of your years in high school!?
When I...
...entered this school full of girls...
...I thought I would be able to find a girl-friend...
With a thousand girls here, surely I could find one in three years!!
But... these Romance of the Three Kingdoms figures ...
...come but once every four years.
The calculation is simple.

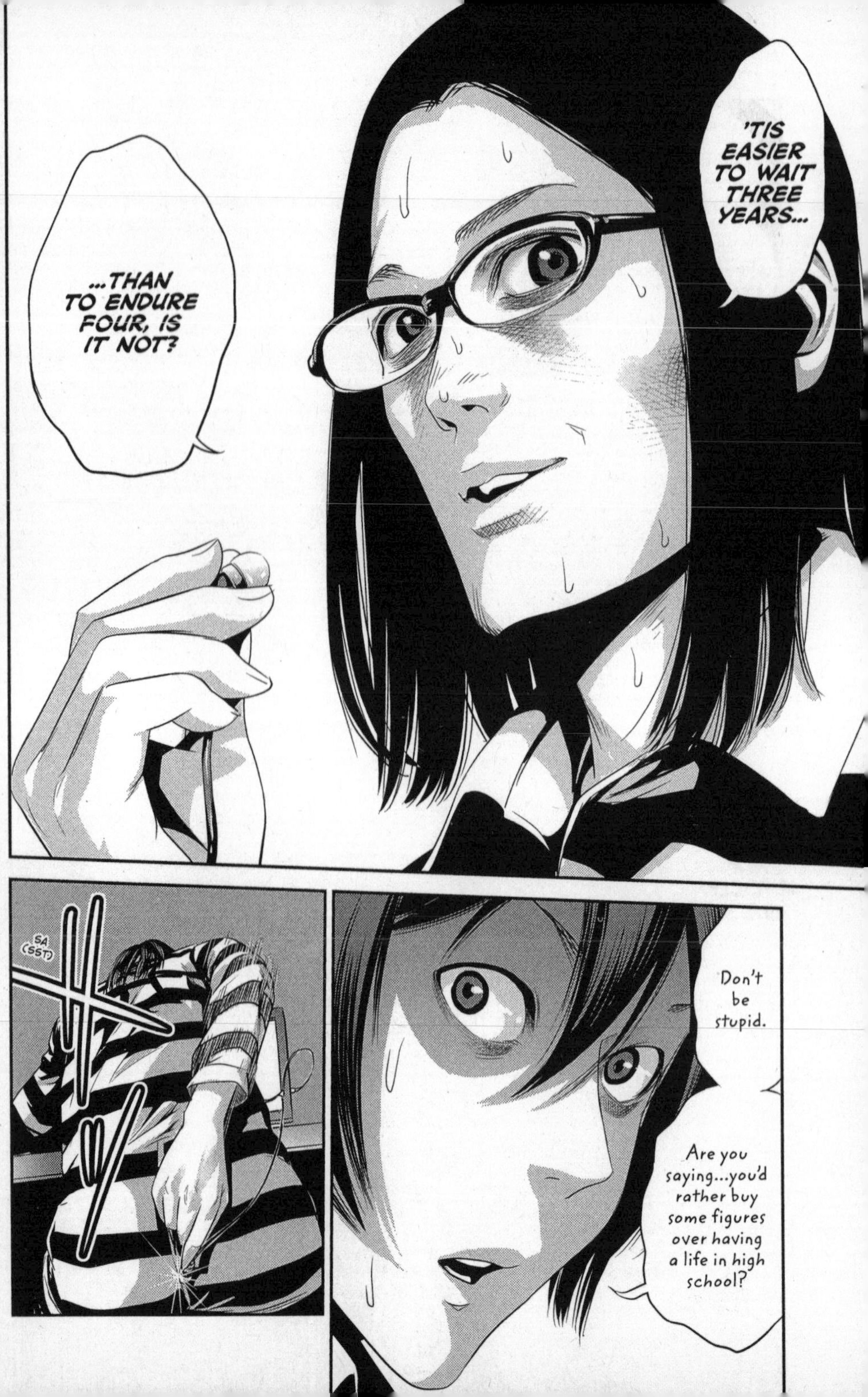
'TIS EASIER TO WAIT THREE YEARS...
...THAN TO ENDURE FOUR, IS IT NOT?
Don't be stupid.
Are you saying...you'd rather buy some figures over having a life in high school?
SA (SST)

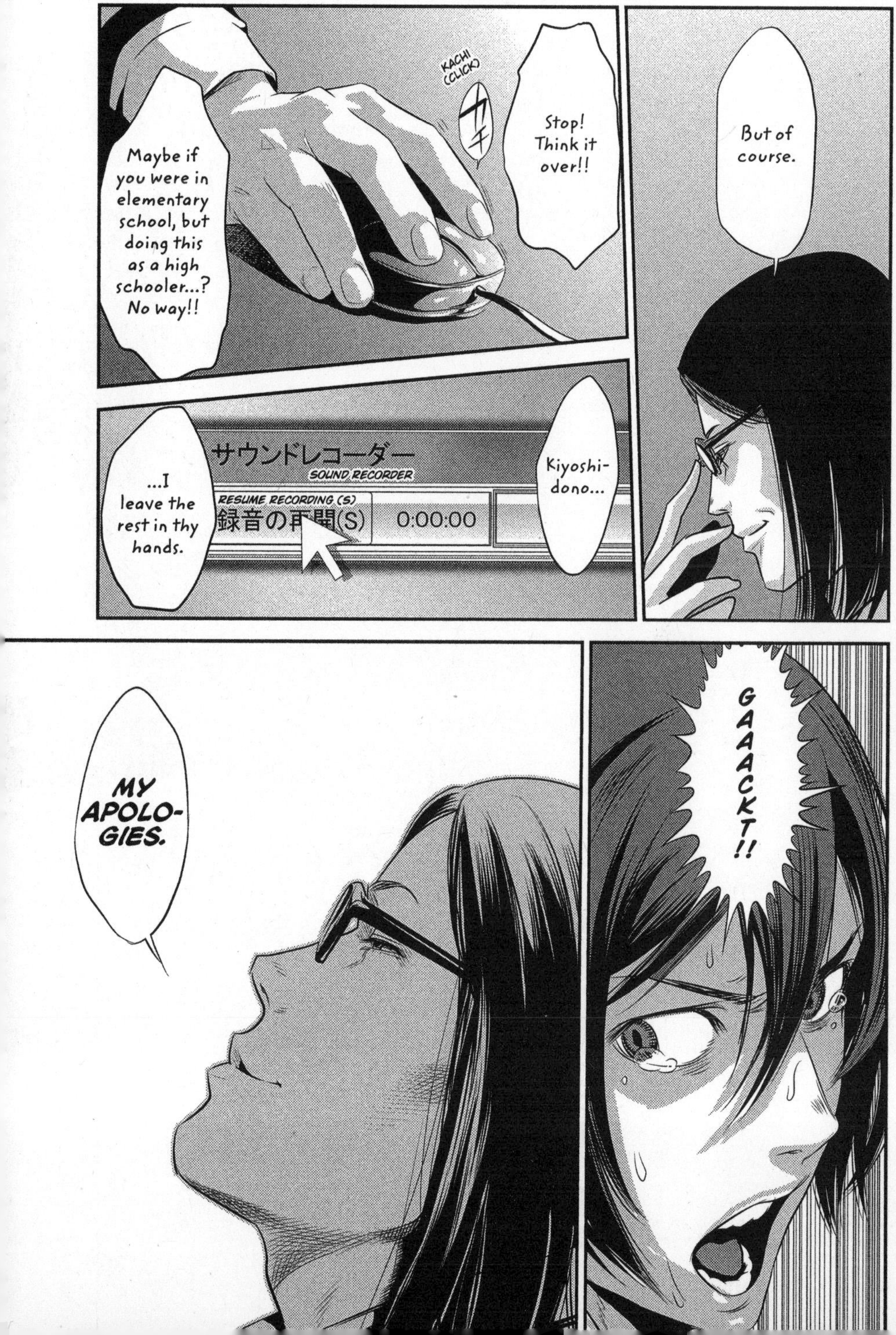
But of course.
Stop! Think it over!!
KACHI (CLICK)
カチ
Maybe if you were in elementary school, but doing this as a high schooler...? No way!!
Kiyoshi-dono...
サウンドレコーダー
SOUND RECORDER
RESUME RECORDING (S)
録音の再開(S)
0:00:00
...I leave the rest in thy hands.
GAAACKT!!
MY APOLOGIES.

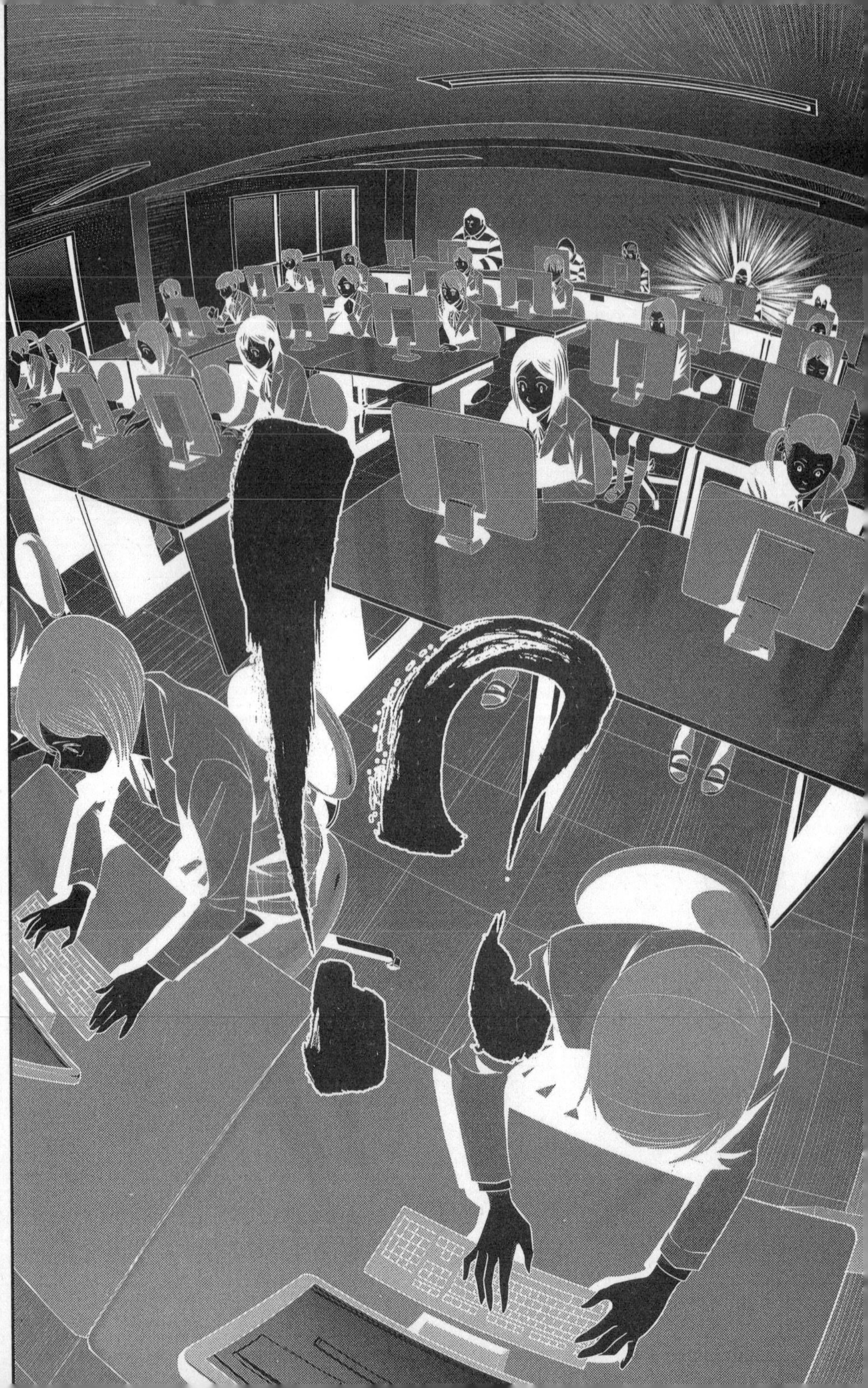

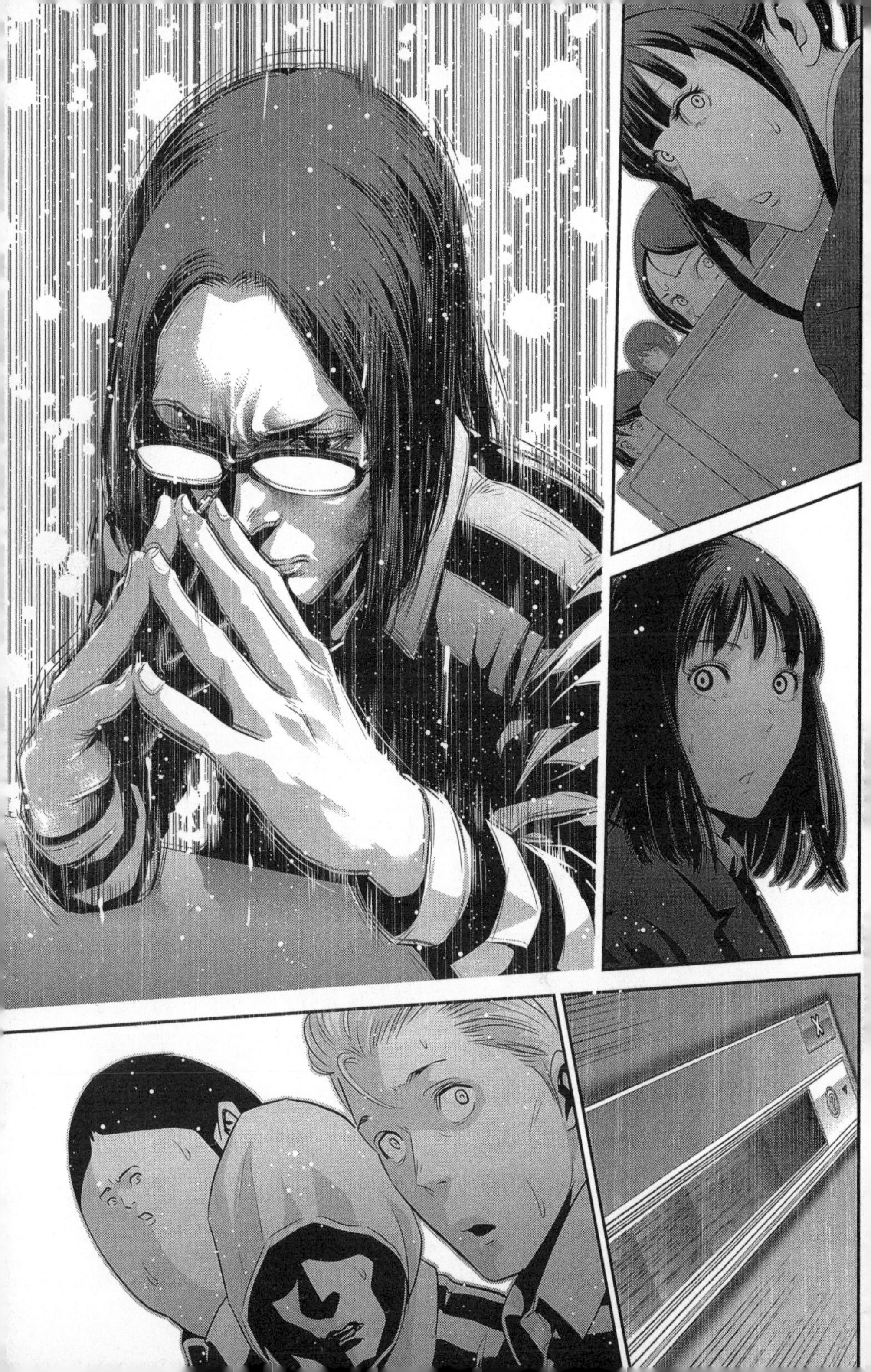
X

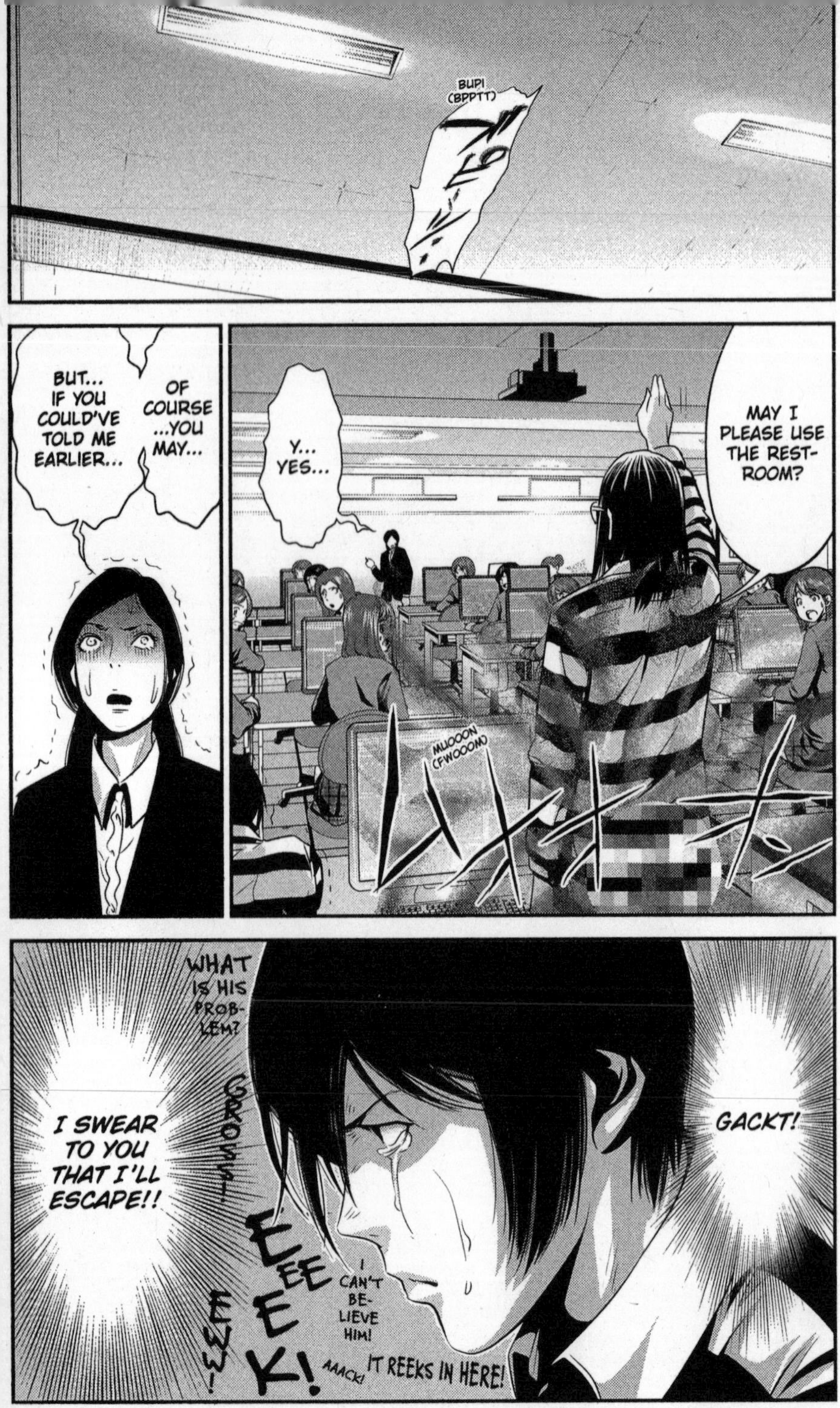
BUPI
(BPPTT)
MAY I PLEASE USE THE REST-ROOM?
Y... YES...
OF COURSE ...YOU MAY...
BUT... IF YOU COULD'VE TOLD ME EARLIER...
MUOOON
(FWOOOM)
GACKT!
I SWEAR TO YOU THAT I'LL ESCAPE!!
WHAT IS HIS PROB-LEM?
GROSS!
EEEEK!
EWW!
I CAN'T BE-LIEVE HIM!
AAACK!
IT REEKS IN HERE!

CHAPTER 18: THE FOUR HUNDRED BLOWS

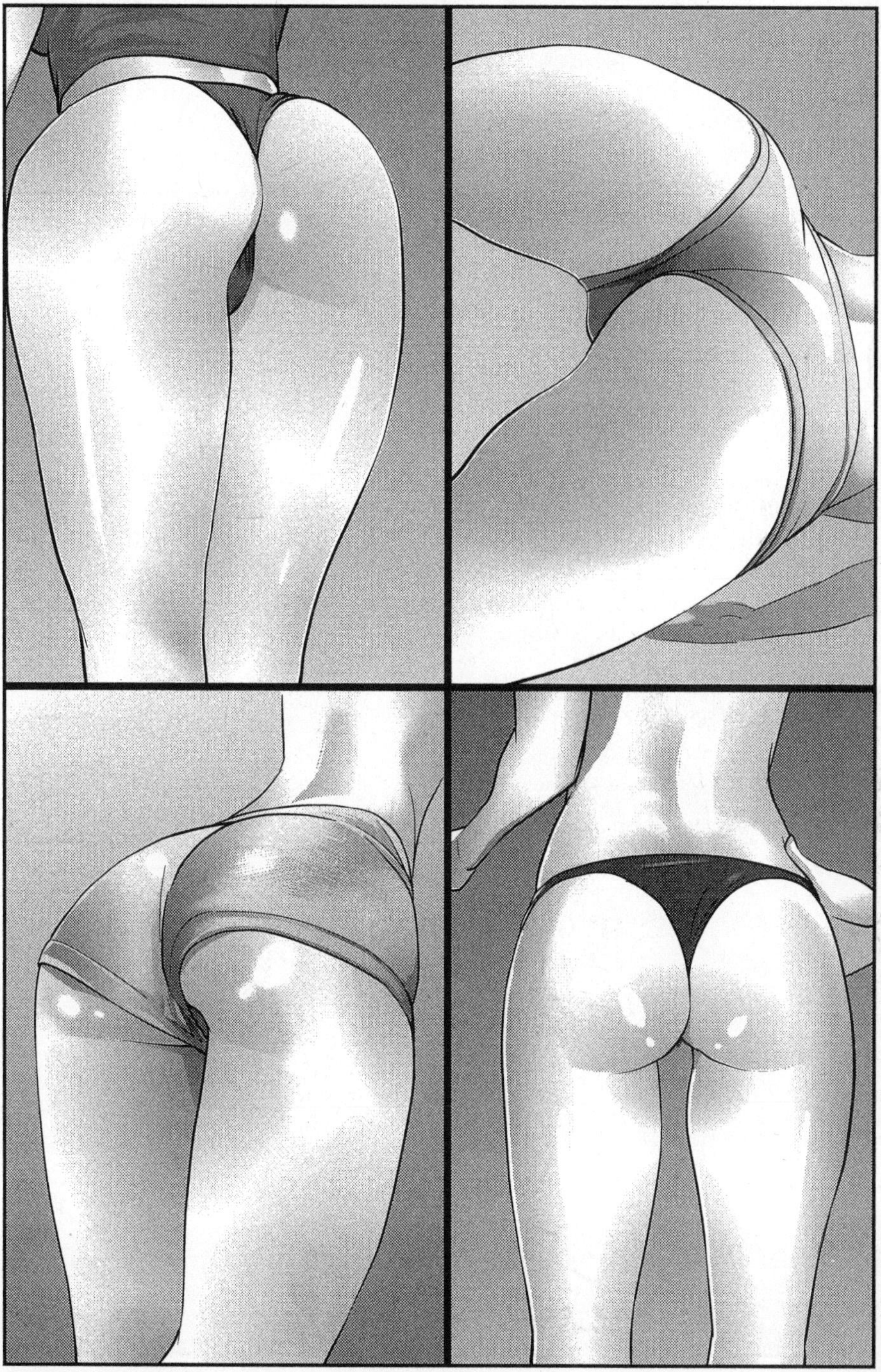

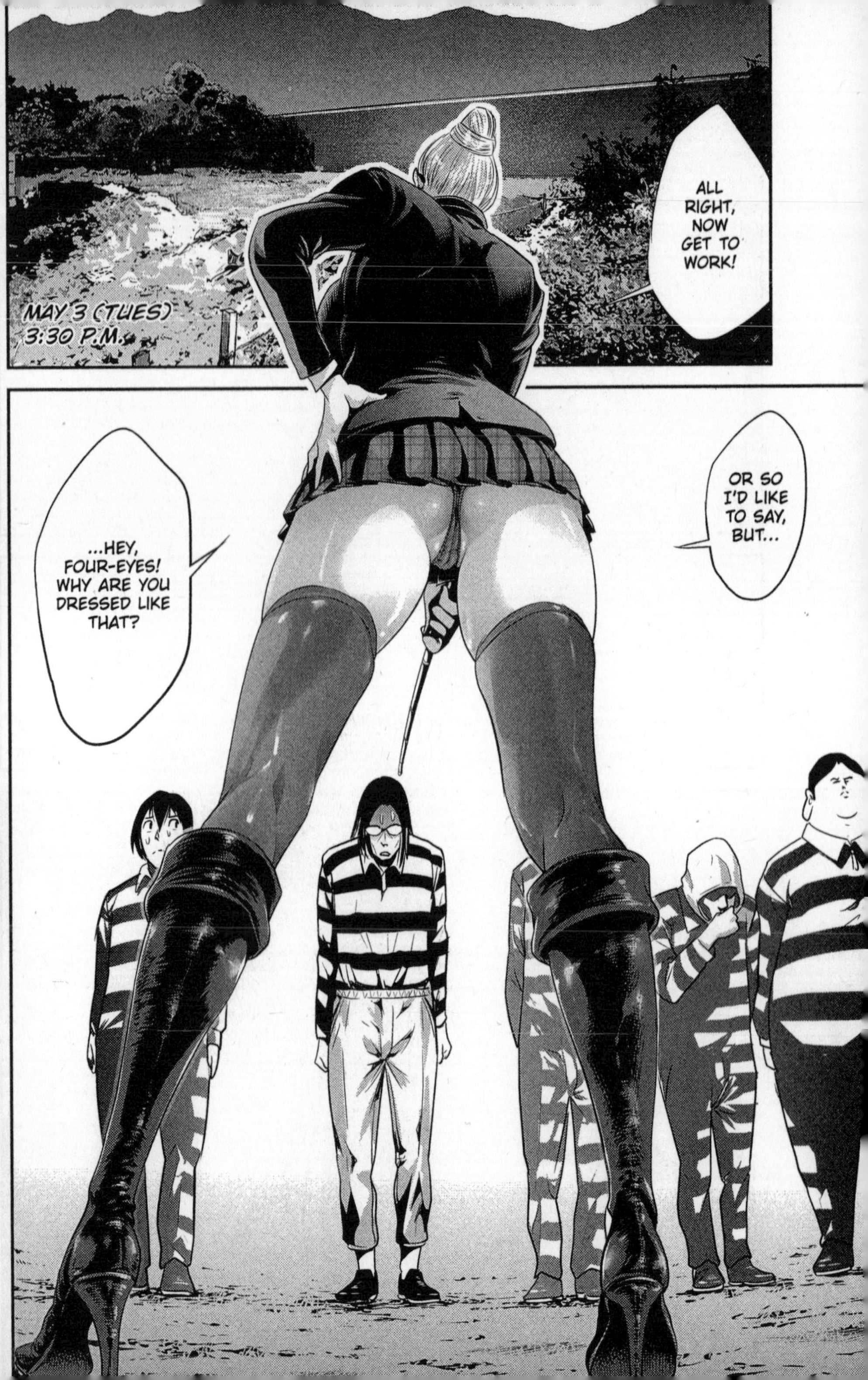
MAY 3 (TUES) 3:30 P.M.
ALL RIGHT, NOW GET TO WORK!
OR SO I'D LIKE TO SAY, BUT...
...HEY, FOUR-EYES! WHY ARE YOU DRESSED LIKE THAT?

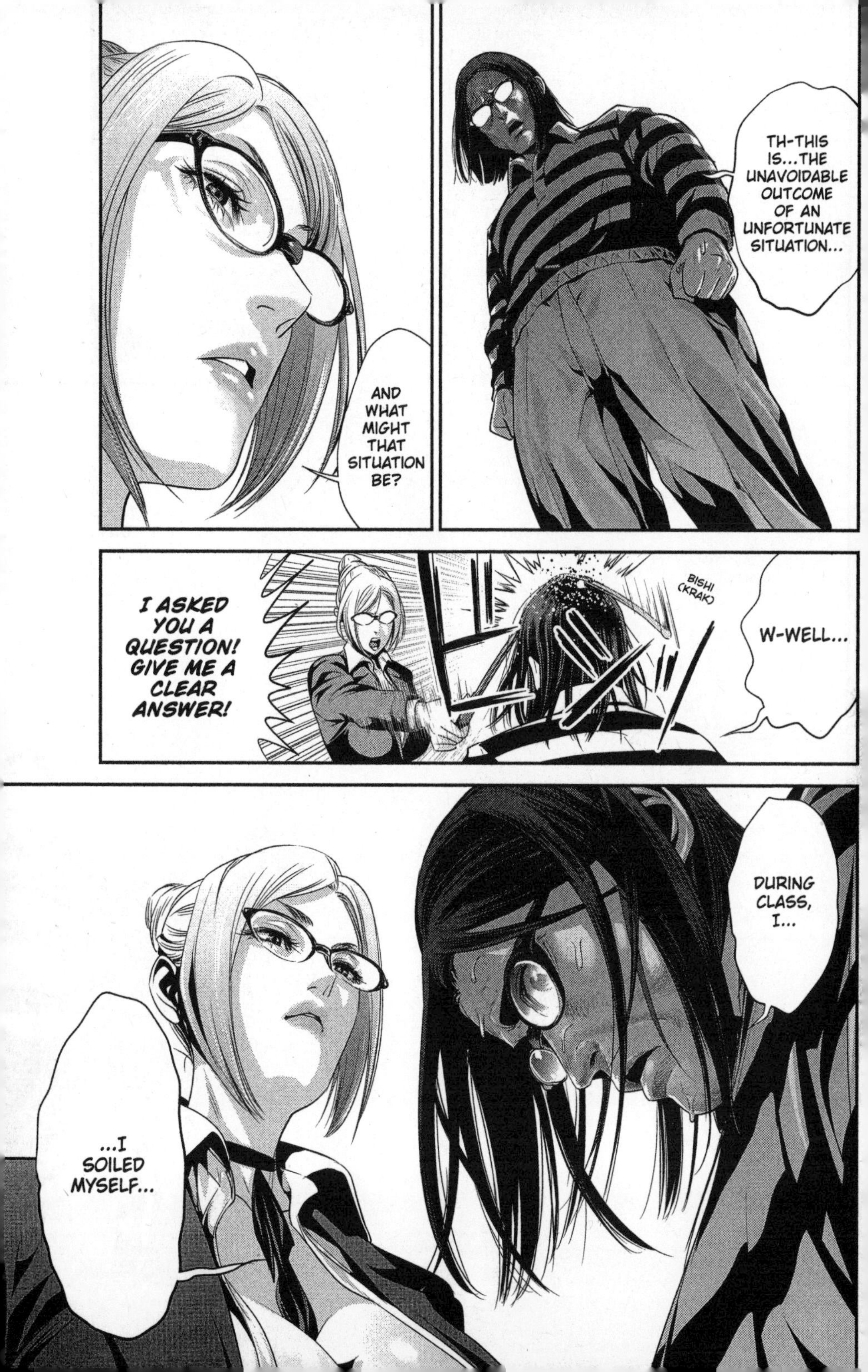
TH-THIS IS...THE UNAVOIDABLE OUTCOME OF AN UNFORTUNATE SITUATION...
AND WHAT MIGHT THAT SITUATION BE?
W-WELL...
BISHI (KRAK)
I ASKED YOU A QUESTION! GIVE ME A CLEAR ANSWER!
DURING CLASS, I...
...I SOILED MYSELF...

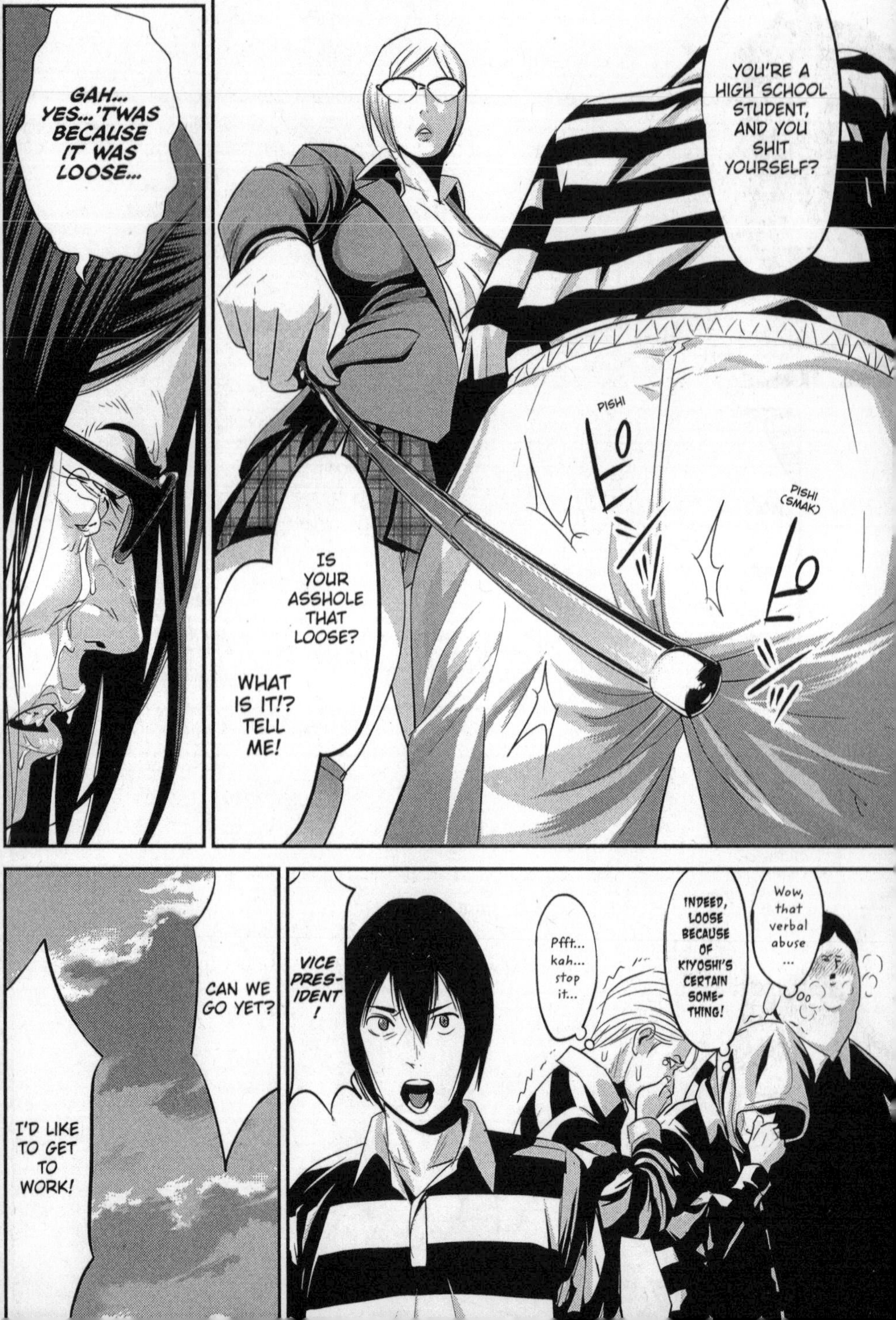
YOU'RE A HIGH SCHOOL STUDENT, AND YOU SHIT YOURSELF?
PISHI
PISHI (SMAK)
IS YOUR ASSHOLE THAT LOOSE?
WHAT IS IT!? TELL ME!
GAH... YES...'TWAS BECAUSE IT WAS LOOSE...
Wow, that verbal abuse ...
INDEED, LOOSE BECAUSE OF KIYOSHI'S CERTAIN SOME-THING!
Pfft... kah... stop it...
VICE PRES-IDENT!
CAN WE GO YET?
I'D LIKE TO GET TO WORK!

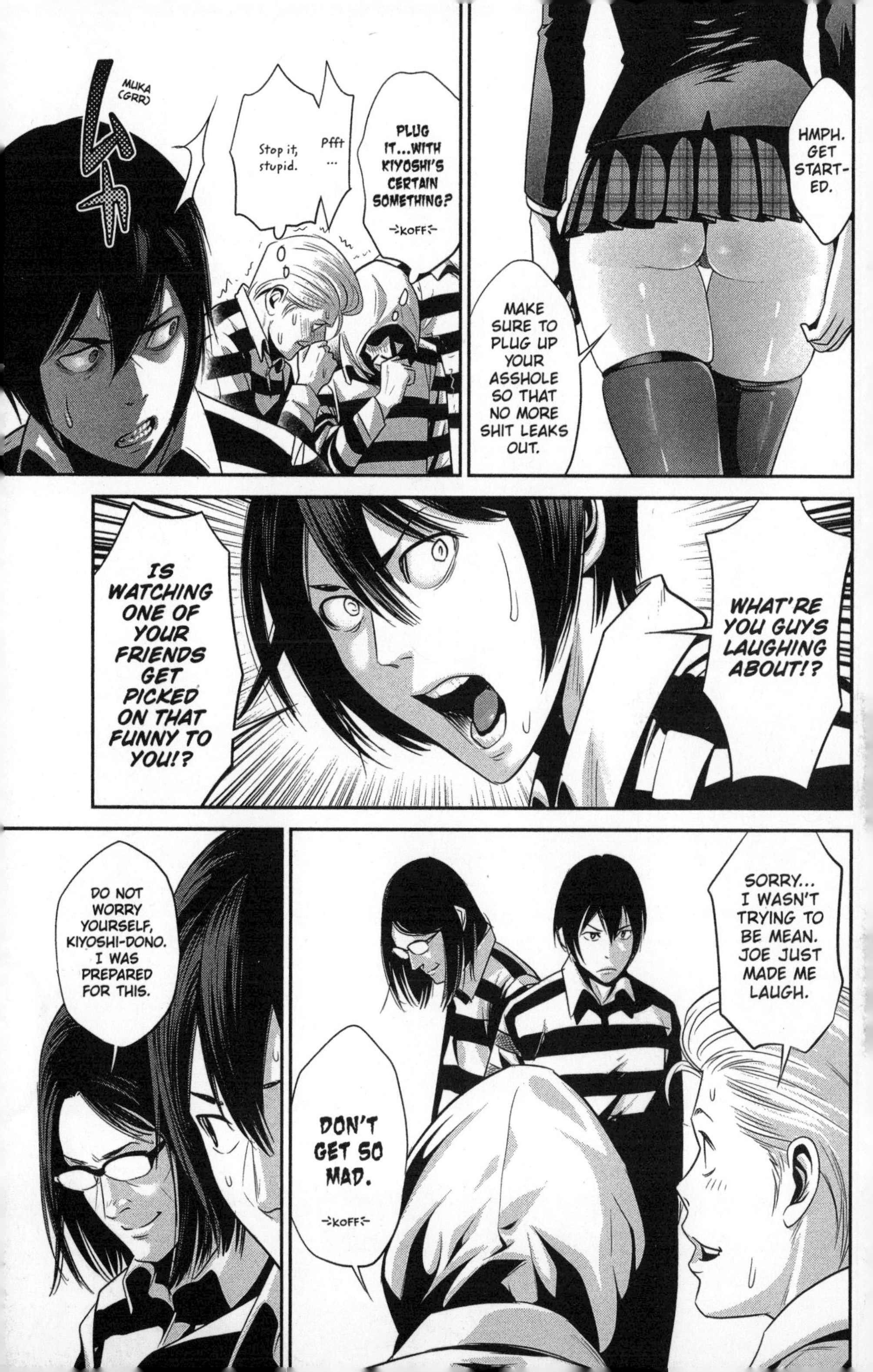
HMPH. GET START-ED.
MAKE SURE TO PLUG UP YOUR ASSHOLE SO THAT NO MORE SHIT LEAKS OUT.
PLUG IT...WITH KIYOSHI'S CERTAIN SOMETHING?
KOFF
Pfft ...
Stop it, stupid.
MUKA (GRR)
WHAT'RE YOU GUYS LAUGHING ABOUT!?
IS WATCHING ONE OF YOUR FRIENDS GET PICKED ON THAT FUNNY TO YOU!?
SORRY... I WASN'T TRYING TO BE MEAN. JOE JUST MADE ME LAUGH.
DON'T GET SO MAD.
KOFF
DO NOT WORRY YOURSELF, KIYOSHI-DONO. I WAS PREPARED FOR THIS.

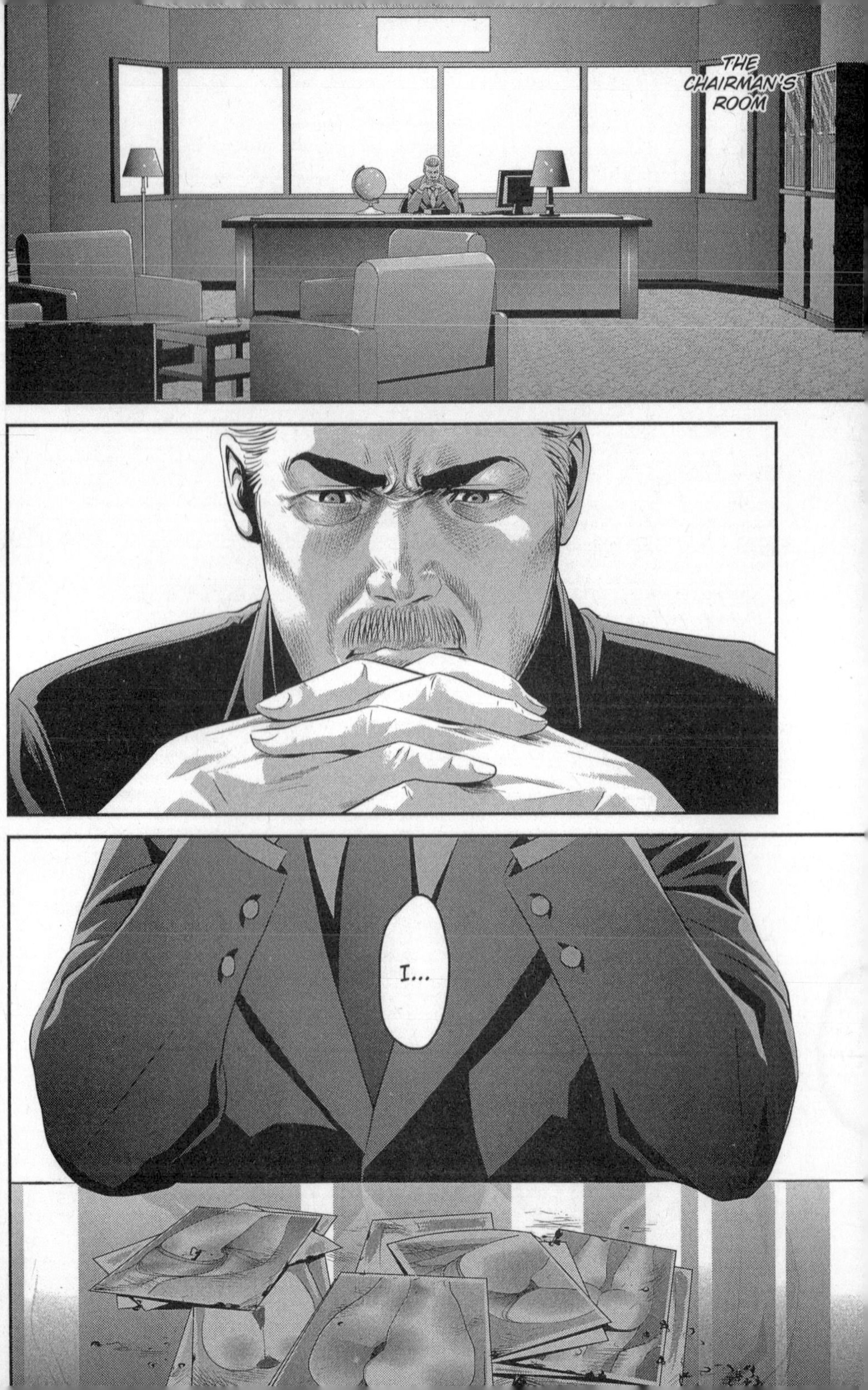
THE CHAIRMAN'S ROOM
I...

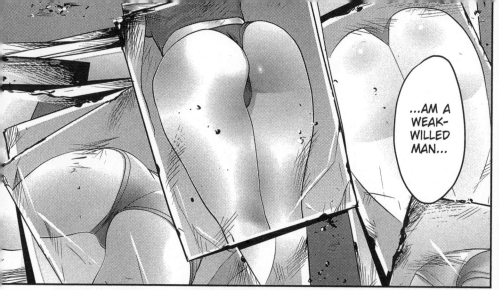

...AM A WEAK-WILLED MAN...

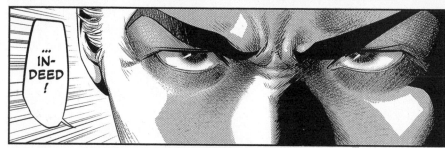

...IN-DEED!

GI (SQUEAK)

ZAKU (ZKKT)   ZAKU (ZKKT)

I HAD SAID MY FAREWELLS AND CUT OFF MY TIES, AND YET I DUG THESE LADIES BACK UP...

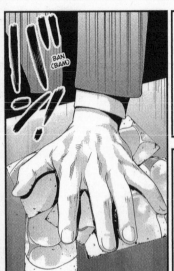

BAN
(BAM)

IT IS MY DUTY AS AN EDUCATOR...

YES, I MUST SEAL THESE IRREVERSIBLY.

...AS A FATHER... NO...AS A...

MÄN!

ZA
(ZAKK)

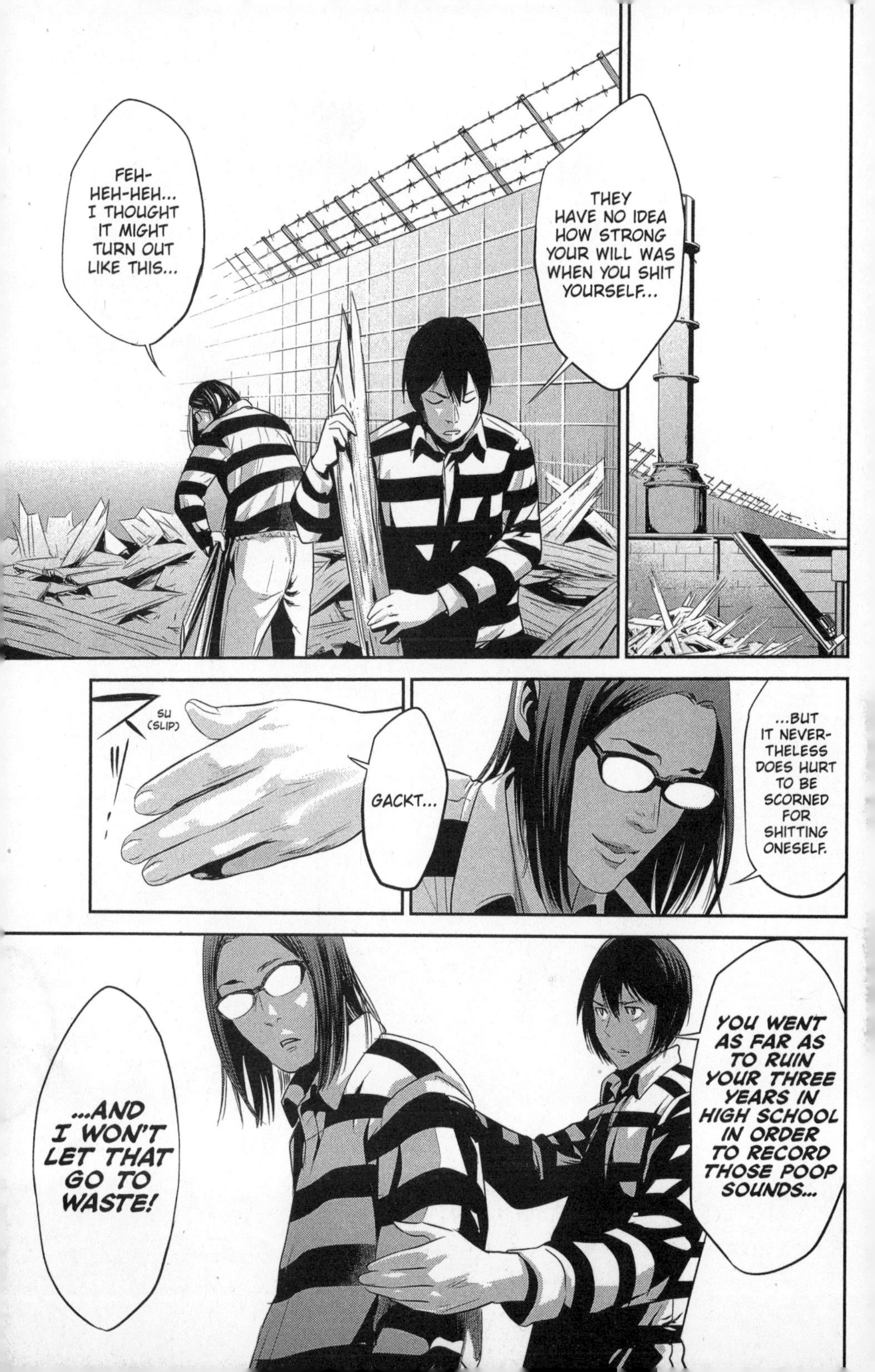
THEY HAVE NO IDEA HOW STRONG YOUR WILL WAS WHEN YOU SHIT YOURSELF...
FEH-HEH-HEH... I THOUGHT IT MIGHT TURN OUT LIKE THIS...
...BUT IT NEVER-THELESS DOES HURT TO BE SCORNED FOR SHITTING ONESELF.
GACKT...
SU (SLIP)
YOU WENT AS FAR AS TO RUIN YOUR THREE YEARS IN HIGH SCHOOL IN ORDER TO RECORD THOSE POOP SOUNDS...
...AND I WON'T LET THAT GO TO WASTE!

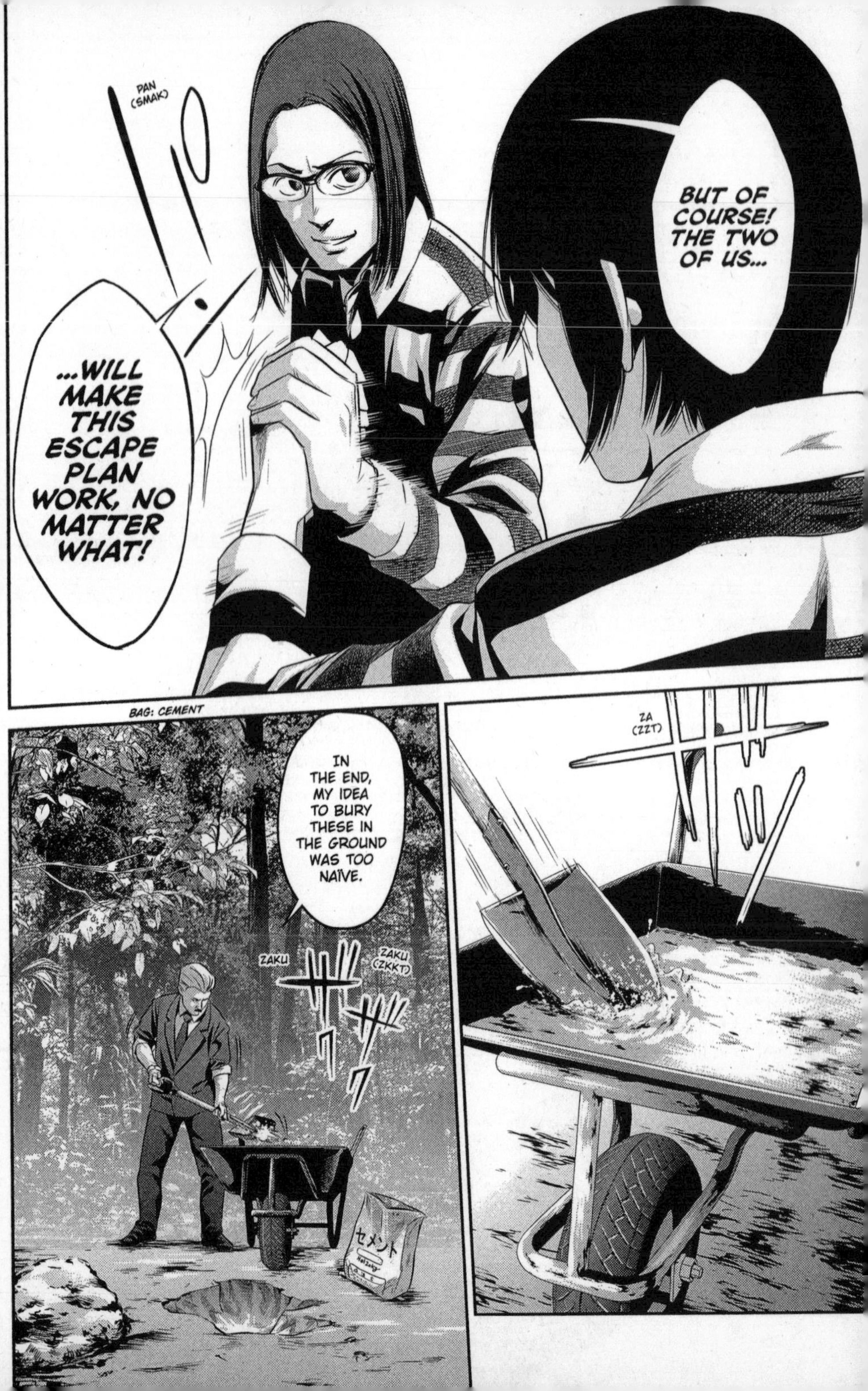
BUT OF COURSE! THE TWO OF US...
PAN (SMAK)
...WILL MAKE THIS ESCAPE PLAN WORK, NO MATTER WHAT!
ZA (ZZT)
BAG: CEMENT
IN THE END, MY IDEA TO BURY THESE IN THE GROUND WAS TOO NAÏVE.
ZAKU
ZAKU (ZKKT)
セメント

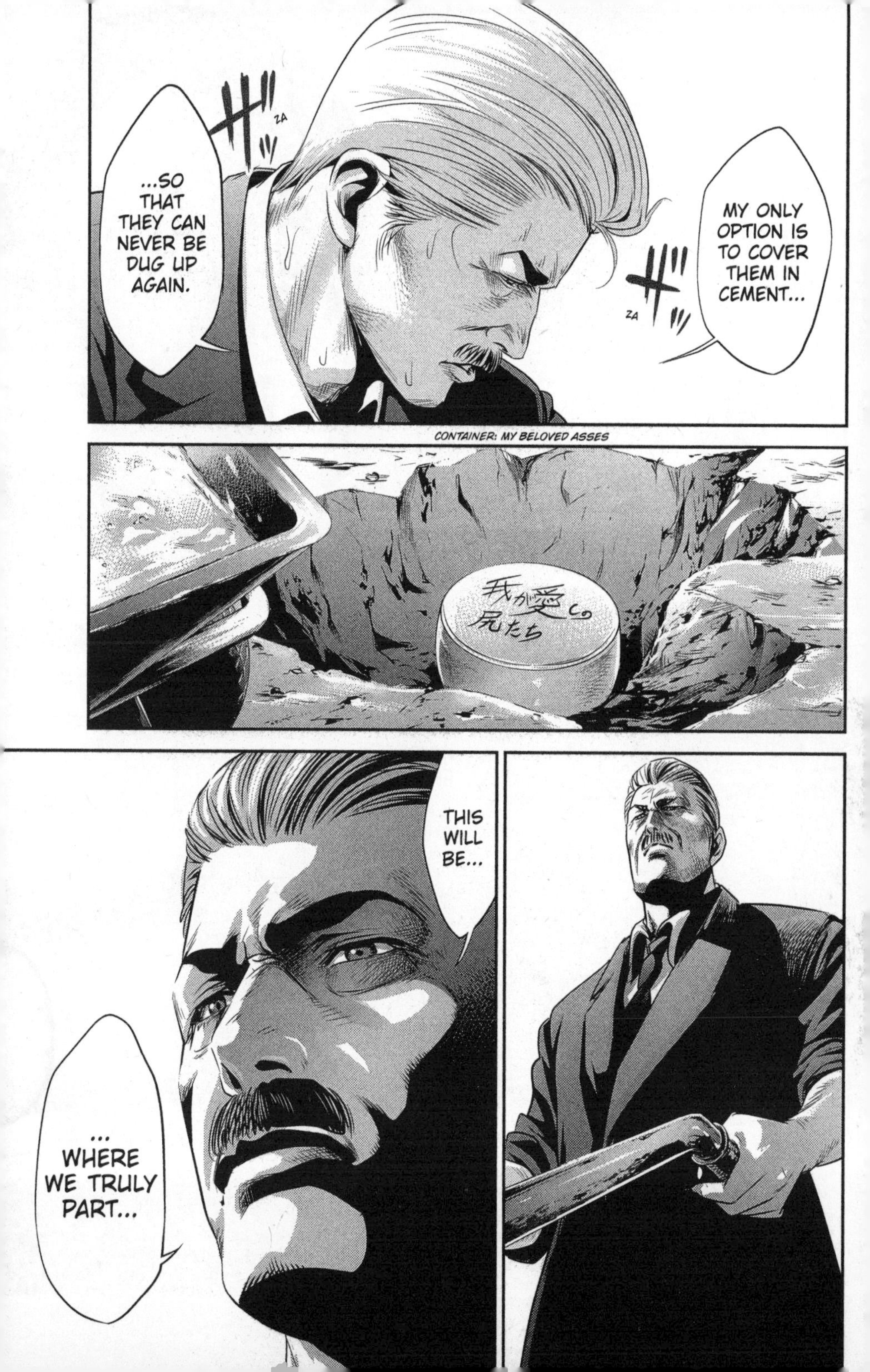
MY ONLY OPTION IS TO COVER THEM IN CEMENT...
ZA
...SO THAT THEY CAN NEVER BE DUG UP AGAIN.
ZA
CONTAINER: MY BELOVED ASSES
我が愛しの尻たち
THIS WILL BE...
... WHERE WE TRULY PART...

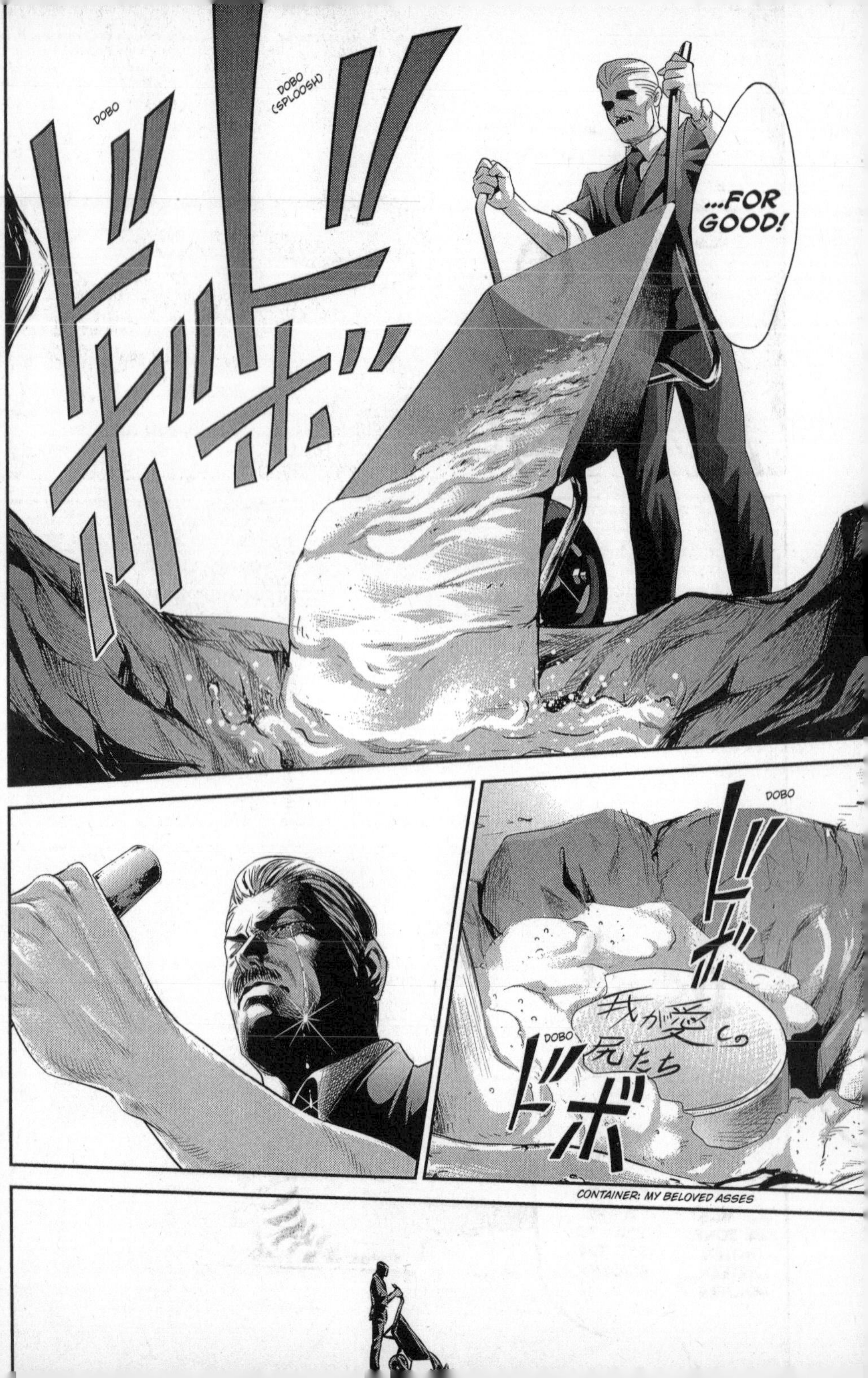
...FOR GOOD!
DOBO
DOBO (SPLOOSH)
DOBO
我が愛しの尻たち
DOBO
CONTAINER: MY BELOVED ASSES

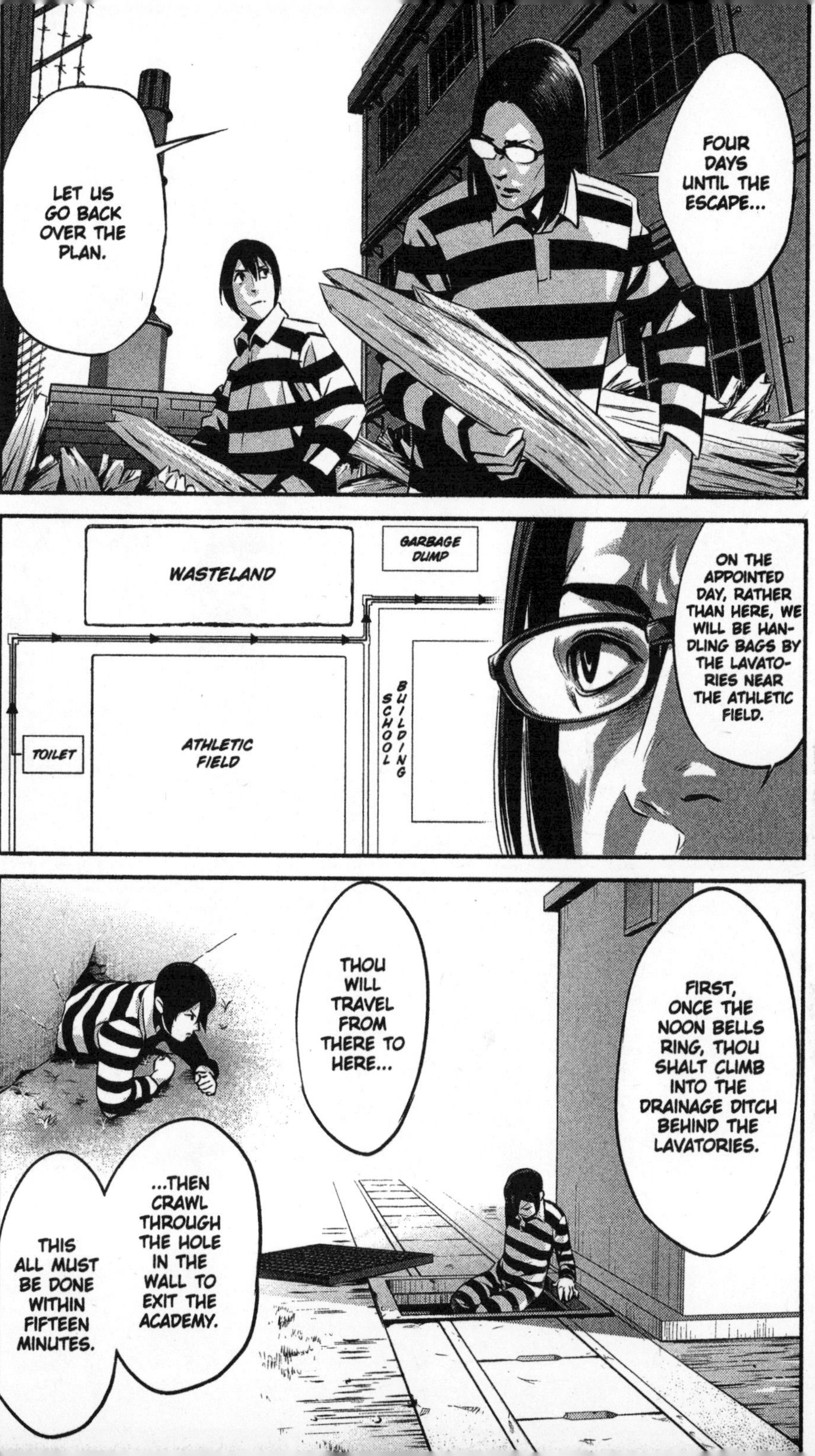
FOUR DAYS UNTIL THE ESCAPE...
LET US GO BACK OVER THE PLAN.
ON THE APPOINTED DAY, RATHER THAN HERE, WE WILL BE HANDLING BAGS BY THE LAVATORIES NEAR THE ATHLETIC FIELD.
GARBAGE DUMP
WASTELAND
SCHOOL BUILDING
TOILET
ATHLETIC FIELD
FIRST, ONCE THE NOON BELLS RING, THOU SHALT CLIMB INTO THE DRAINAGE DITCH BEHIND THE LAVATORIES.
THOU WILL TRAVEL FROM THERE TO HERE...
...THEN CRAWL THROUGH THE HOLE IN THE WALL TO EXIT THE ACADEMY.
THIS ALL MUST BE DONE WITHIN FIFTEEN MINUTES.

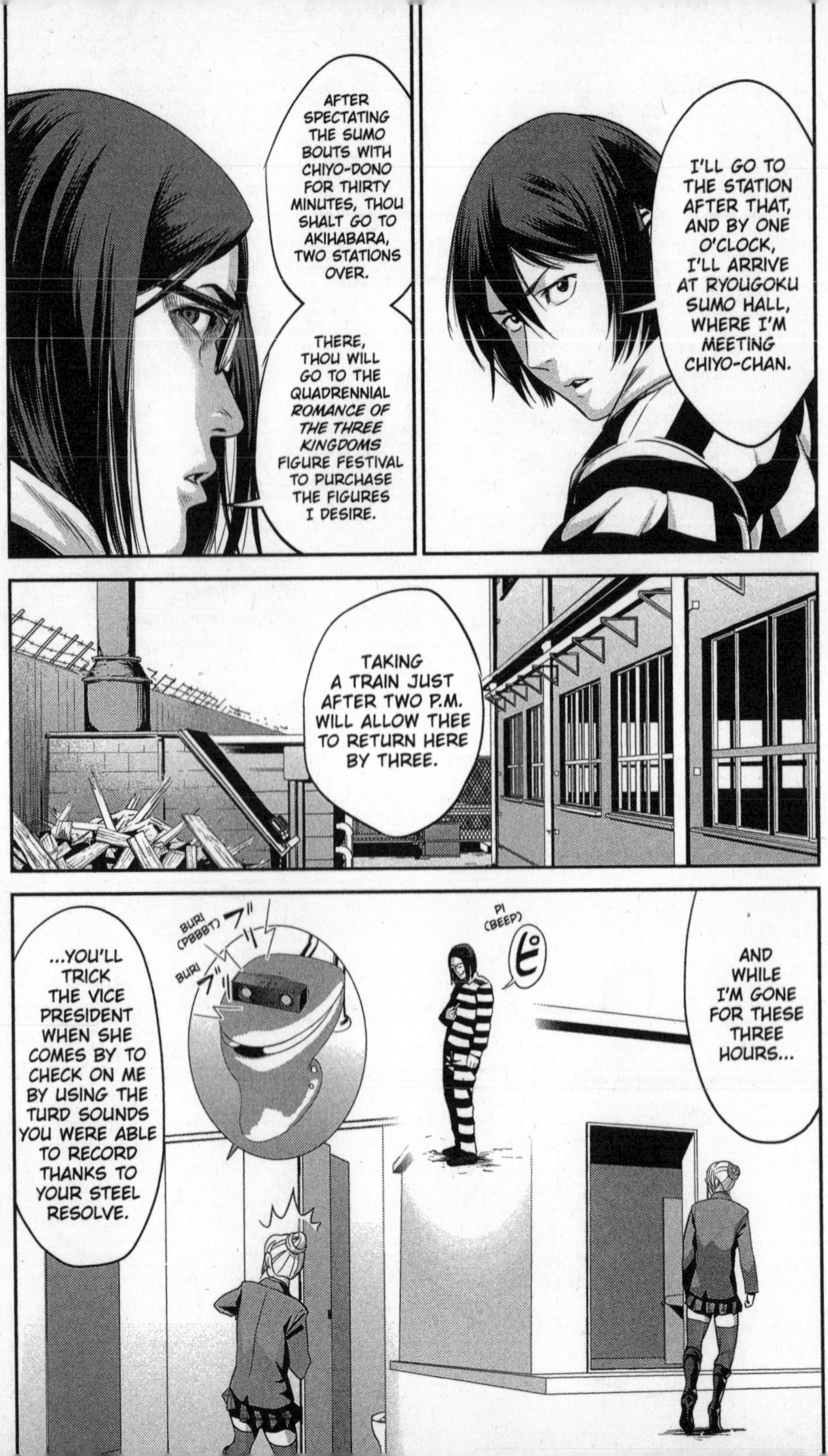
I'LL GO TO THE STATION AFTER THAT, AND BY ONE O'CLOCK, I'LL ARRIVE AT RYOUGOKU SUMO HALL, WHERE I'M MEETING CHIYO-CHAN.
AFTER SPECTATING THE SUMO BOUTS WITH CHIYO-DONO FOR THIRTY MINUTES, THOU SHALT GO TO AKIHABARA, TWO STATIONS OVER.
THERE, THOU WILL GO TO THE QUADRENNIAL *ROMANCE OF THE THREE KINGDOMS* FIGURE FESTIVAL TO PURCHASE THE FIGURES I DESIRE.
TAKING A TRAIN JUST AFTER TWO P.M. WILL ALLOW THEE TO RETURN HERE BY THREE.
AND WHILE I'M GONE FOR THESE THREE HOURS...
PI (BEEP) ピ
BURI (PBBBT) ブ
BURI ブ
...YOU'LL TRICK THE VICE PRESIDENT WHEN SHE COMES BY TO CHECK ON ME BY USING THE TURD SOUNDS YOU WERE ABLE TO RECORD THANKS TO YOUR STEEL RESOLVE.

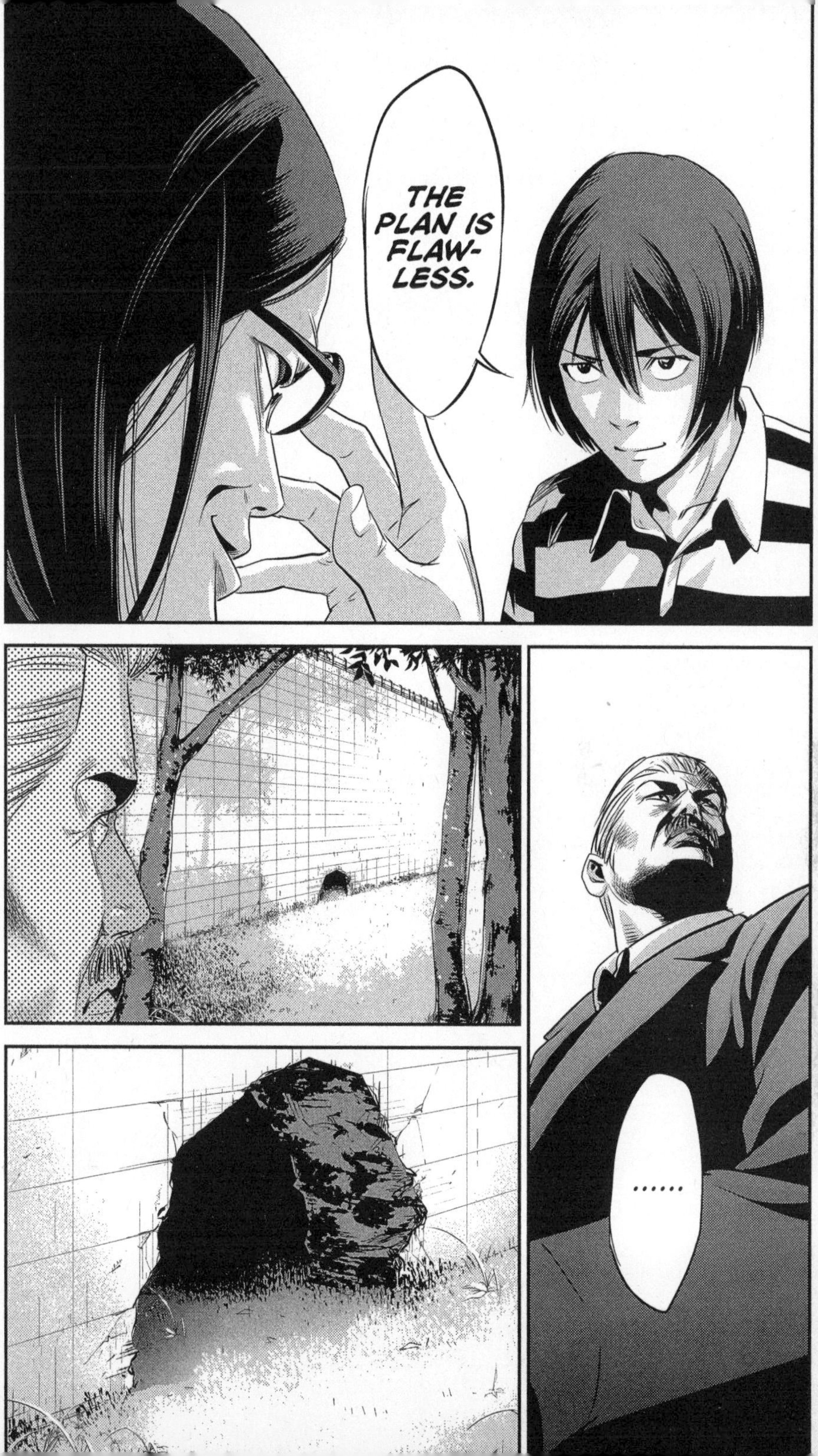
THE PLAN IS FLAWLESS.
......

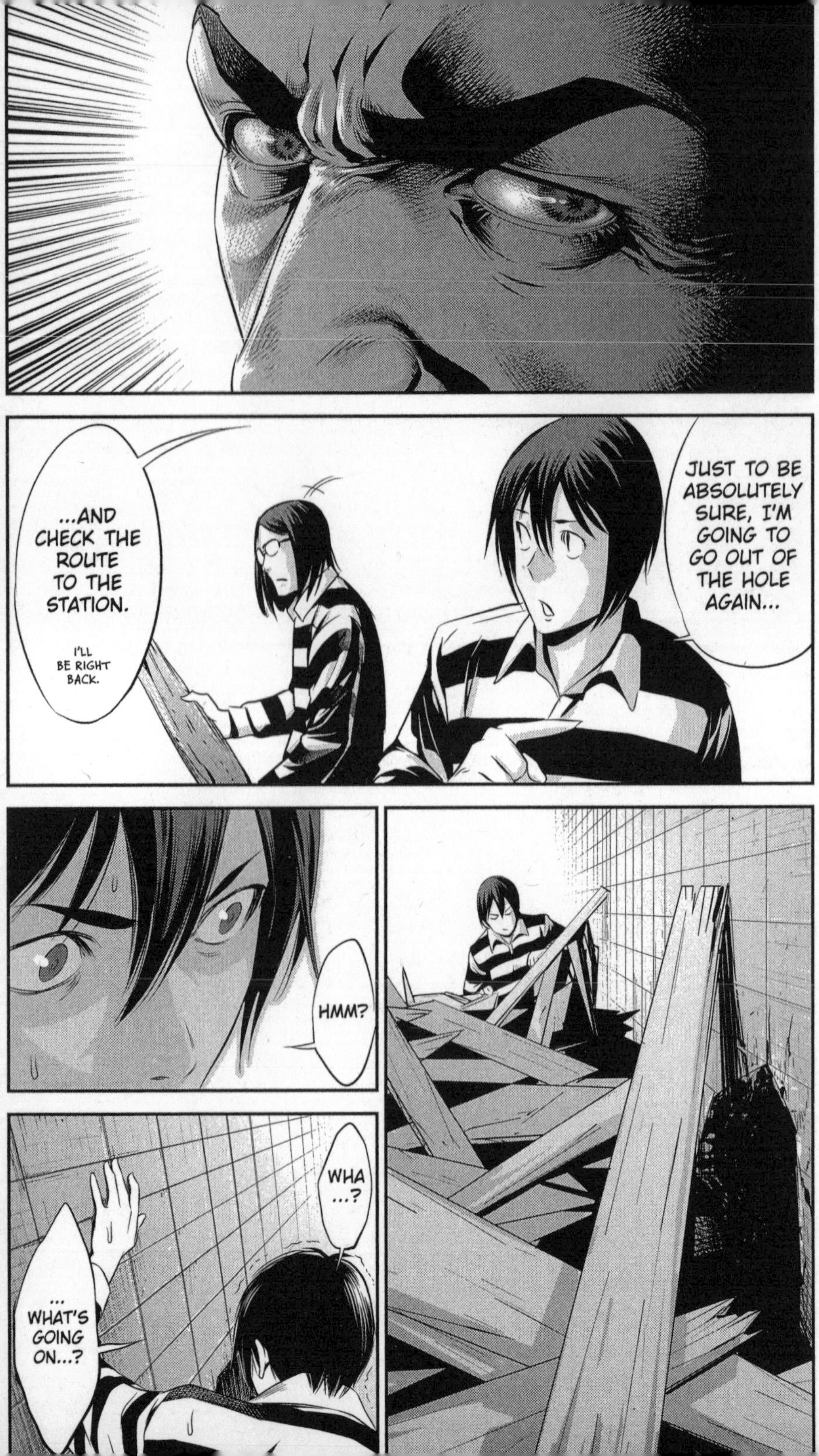
JUST TO BE ABSOLUTELY SURE, I'M GOING TO GO OUT OF THE HOLE AGAIN...
...AND CHECK THE ROUTE TO THE STATION.
I'LL BE RIGHT BACK.
HMM?
WHA ...?
... WHAT'S GOING ON...?

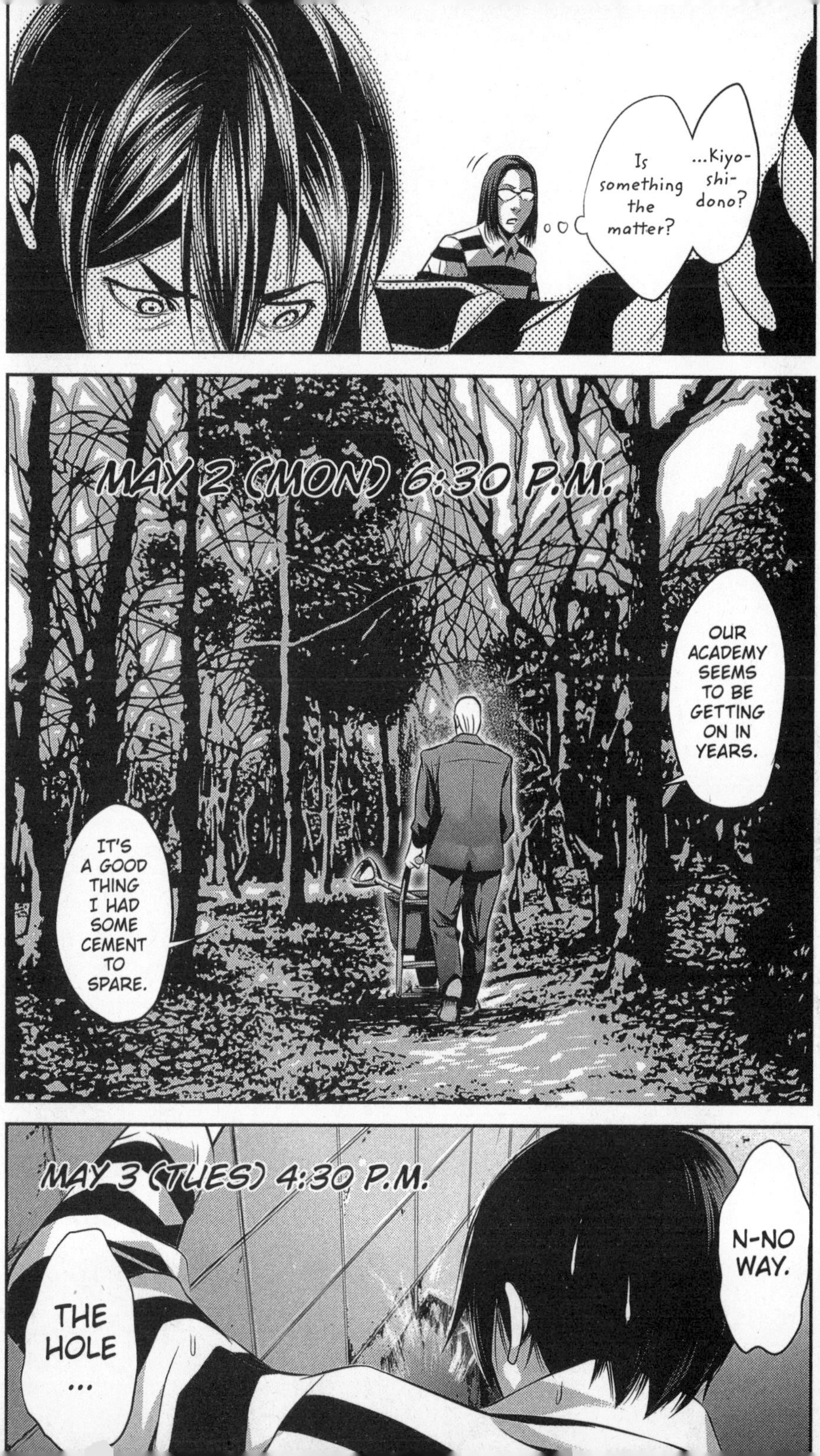
...Kiyo-shi-dono?
Is something the matter?
MAY 2 (MON) 6:30 P.M.
OUR ACADEMY SEEMS TO BE GETTING ON IN YEARS.
IT'S A GOOD THING I HAD SOME CEMENT TO SPARE.
MAY 3 (TUES) 4:30 P.M.
N-NO WAY.
THE HOLE ...

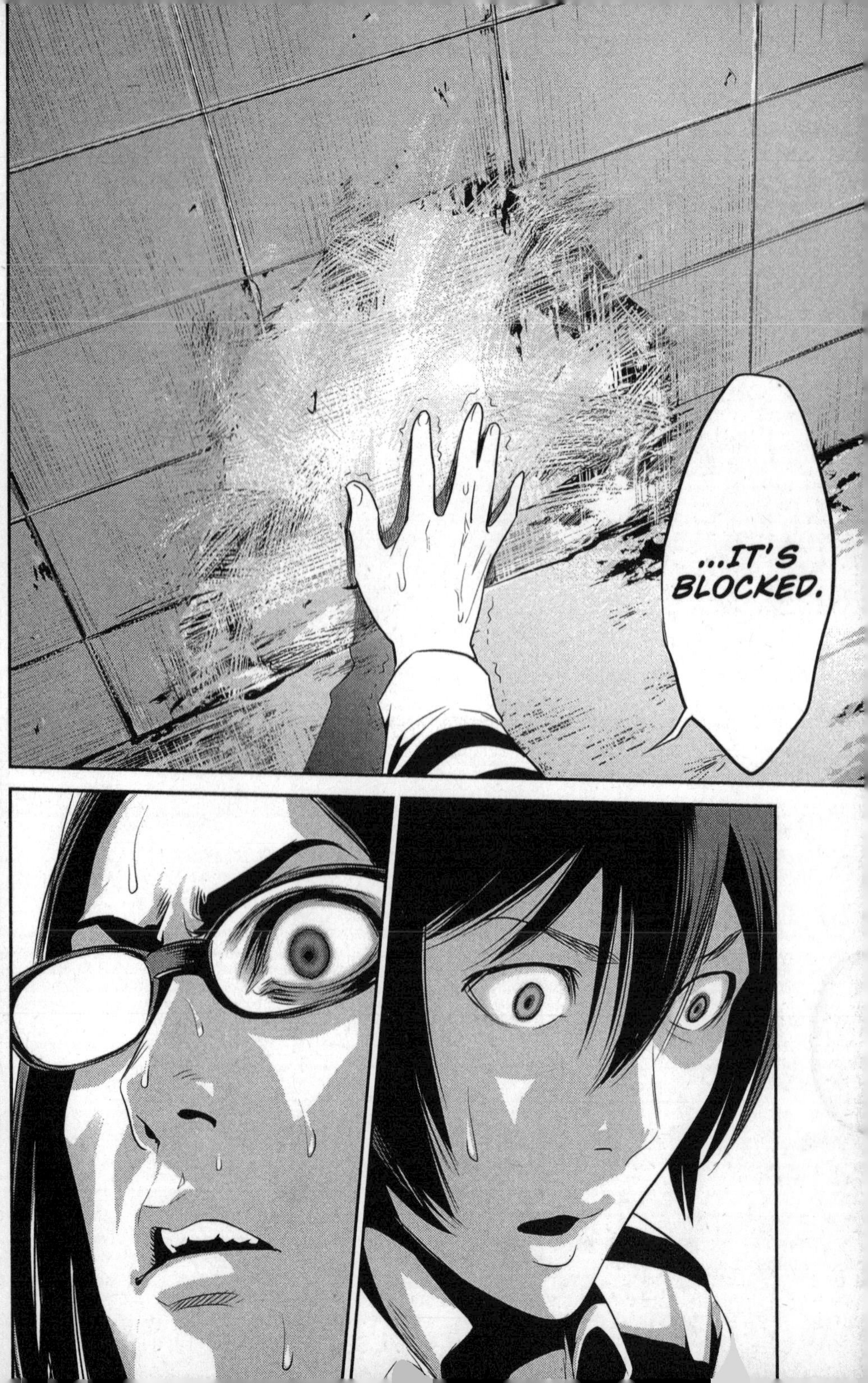
...IT'S BLOCKED.

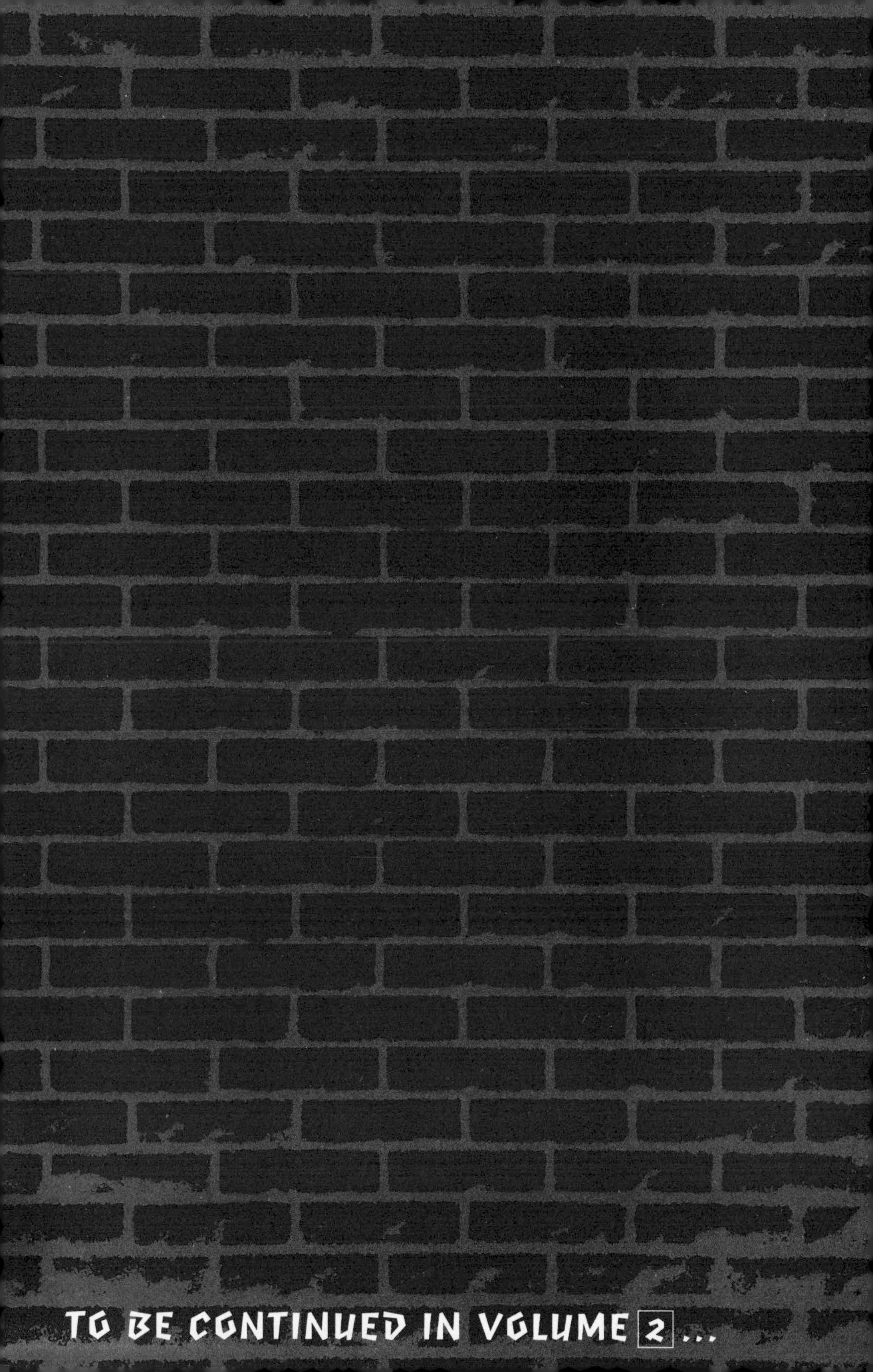
TO BE CONTINUED IN VOLUME 2 ...

TRANSLATION NOTES

Common Honorifics

no honorific: Indicates familiarity or closeness; if used without permission or reason, addressing someone in this manner would constitute an insult.

-san: The Japanese equivalent of Mr./Mrs./Miss. If a situation calls for politeness, this is the fail-safe honorific.

-dono: Conveys an indication of respect for the addressee.

-kun: Used most often when referring to boys, this indicates affection or familiarity. Occasionally used by older men among their peers, but it may also be used by anyone referring to a person of lower standing.

-chan: An affectionate honorific indicating familiarity used mostly in reference to girls; also used in reference to cute persons or animals of either gender.

-senpai: A suffix used to address upperclassmen or more experienced coworkers.

PAGE 24
Gottsuan desu! is a slang term used in sumo to say "thank you." The hand motion is also used to show thanks before receiving prize money after matches.

PAGE 49
Hara-kiri is an act of ritual suicide from disemboweling, prominently practiced by Japanese samurai.

PAGE 119
Four leaves &! is the English translation of the original Japanese title **Yotsuba&!** Have you noticed that each chapter name references titles of other media (books, movies, etc.)?

PAGE 127
Osu! is a traditional greeting in Japanese martial arts.

PAGE 164
The **Takarazuka performers** refers to Takarazuka Revue, which is an all-female musical theater troupe originating in Takarazuka, Japan.

PAGE 199
Yokozuna is the highest rank in Sumo that can be achieved in Japan.

PAGE 301
KGB48 seems to be a parody of AKB48 (Akihabara 48), a famous all-girls idol group best known for having forty-eight members.

PRISON SCHOOL

PRISON SCHOOL ❶

AKIRA HIRAMOTO

Translation: Ko Ransom

Lettering: Anthony Quintessenza

PRISON SCHOOL Vol. 1, 2
© 2011 Akira Hiramoto. All rights reserved.
First published in Japan in 2011 by Kodansha, Ltd. Tokyo.
Publication rights for this English edition arranged through Kodansha, Ltd. Tokyo.

Translation © 2015 by Hachette Book Group, Inc.

Yen Press
Hachette Book Group
1290 Avenue of the Americas
New York, NY 10104

www.hachettebookgroup.com
www.yenpress.com

Yen Press is an imprint of Hachette Book Group, Inc.
The Yen Press name and logo are trademarks of Hachette Book Group, Inc.

The publisher is not responsible for websites (or their content) that are not owned by the publisher.

First Yen Press Edition: July 2015

ISBN: 978-0-316-34365-7

10 9 8 7 6 5

BVG

Printed in the United States of America